THE "RACIAL" ECONOMY OF SCIENCE

RACE, GENDER, AND SCIENCE

Anne Fausto-Sterling, General Editor

THE "RACIAL" ECONOMY OF SCIENCE

TOWARD A DEMOCRATIC FUTURE

EDITED BY

SANDRA HARDING

INDIANA UNIVERSITY PRESS
Bloomington and Indianapolis

The paper used in this publication meets the minimum requirements
of American National Standard for Information Sciences—
Permanence of Paper for Printed Library Materials,
ANSI Z39.48-1984.

Manufactured in the United States of America

Library of Congress Cataloging-in-Publication Data
The "Racial" economy of science : toward a democratic future / edited
  by Sandra Harding.
        p.   cm. — (Race, gender, and science)
    Includes bibliographical references and index.
    ISBN 0-253-32693-1 (cloth : alk. paper). — ISBN 0-253-20810-6 (pbk. : alk. paper)
    1. Science—Social aspects.   2. Science—Political aspects.
  3. Science—History.   4. Minorities in science—History.   5. Women
  in science—History.   I. Harding, Sandra G.   II. Series.
  Q175.55.R3   1993
  306.4'5—dc20   92-31286

1 2 3 4 5 97 96 95 94 93

CONTENTS

IV. Science's Technologies and Applications

V. Objectivity, Method, and Nature: Value Neutral?

VI. THE FUTURE: TOWARD A DEMOCRATIC STRATEGY FOR WORLD SCIENCES

This collection brings together both classic and recent essays on the natural sciences by historians, anthropologists, linguists, biologists, engineers, policy analysts, sociologists, and community activists as well as statements by such institutions as the National Academy of Sciences, the Penang Conference on Science and Technology, and *The Black Scholar*. It is intended to show the richness and diversity of critical reflections on how Western sciences have been located in world history, to draw attention to the achievements and resources of scientific traditions in other cultures, and to stimulate thought about how to link scientific work more closely to democracy-advancing projects. All of these essays challenge the assumption that Western sciences have been entirely progressive forces in history as well as the assumption that it is individuals alone, or even primarily, who are responsible for the socially progressive or regressive consequences of science. Instead, all of the authors try to locate the broader social projects of Western cultures that have appropriated the resources of the sciences and to identify the features of Western sciences that have made them particularly attractive and susceptible to appropriation for racist and imperialist agendas.

Of course, many of the authors are themselves scientists or engineers; this collection is not "against scientists," who for the most part—like the rest of us—try to do the best they can in a world of confusing choices and of choices that appear much more limited than they should be. Nor are these authors engaged in "science bashing" or in "bashing" Western sciences. All of them value scientific knowledge and the resources it can provide when harnessed to projects of making and remaking democracy. They see sciences as containing both regressive and progressive tendencies and their task as to block the regressive and support the progressive. Moreover, readers will see author after author pointing out how better understandings of nature result when scientific projects are linked with and incorporate projects of advancing democracy; politically regressive societies are likely to produce partial and distorted accounts of the natural and social world. If these authors are right, then their essays make a contribution not only to the social studies of science but also to the natural sciences themselves: those who ignore the past are doomed to repeat it.

There are tensions and contradictions between the claims in these essays and between their images of science. Each author is writing from the perspective of some particular set of interactions with the sciences—their own or, often, other people's. They are analyzing the interactions with the sciences of would-be and actual scientists, of the victims of environmental disasters, or of the beneficiaries and victims of scientific descriptions of the races; they are reflecting on the changing goals institutions, practices, and personnel of the sciences in history and cross culturally. They are trying to figure out how to change one science or several. They are writing at different times in recent decades and at different stages in social studies of science scholarship. Different traditions of political philosophy shape their perceptions. Their perspectives on the sciences are diverse. Echoes of virtually every recent dispute about how to conceptualize race, racism, imperialism, colonialism, science, technology, the social studies, and philosophy of science and technology, and the relations between all or any of them can be found in these essays. These essays have been selected in part because the diversity and the tensions they exhibit raise new and provocative questions about the sciences and societies we have and those we could have.

In spite of the seriousness of the topics and the often horrendous practices and consequences of Western sciences and technologies reported by these authors, readers will find the collection energizing and even fun to read. The authors are excellent at drawing readers into their analyses. Many are superb stylists. Many are among the most distinguished and most widely known thinkers in their field. All of the essays are immediately accessible to a general audience.

There are two kinds of editorial introductions to the essays. The general introduction, Eurocentric Scientific Illiteracy—A Challenge for the World Community," sets the collection in the context of diverse current interests in the topic, provides an overview of the concerns of its six sections, and briefly previews several central themes in these writings to enable readers to follow the arguments in a more critical and informed way. There is also a brief introduction to each section that sets the section's essays in context and identifies a few of the questions that they raise for each other and for other sections of the collection. The epigraphs that open each of these section introductions add important perspectives on each section's themes.

Focusing on the "racial" economy of Western sciences is an action whose time is probably overdue. The introduction explains why in some detail, but I can note here that the declining authority of the West to determine how the rest of the world shall live requires a rethinking of the past, present, and future of Western sciences and their technologies no less than of other important Western institutions and practices.

Many people have contributed—directly or indirectly—to this collection. My motivation to bring these authors together inside one book slowly emerged as part of my growing realization that the issues centered in Western social studies of science (including the feminist science critiques in which I have worked) do not focus on a number of topics that are important to science analysts in other parts of the world and distort some of the issues they do discuss. Nor—in this sense—are Western sciences themselves universal (to understate the issue). The perspective of Westerners—even of some in the radical science movements—began to seem damagingly Eurocentric. This was particularly evident to me when I had the chance to lecture and consult in Costa Rica, Nicaragua, Honduras, and Guatemala in 1989 on a trip sponsored by the Women, Health and Development project of the Pan American Health Organization (a division of the World Health

Organization) and the University of Costa Rica, and in Puerto Rico on a trip sponsored by the Women and Science project of the Women's Studies Program at the University of Puerto Rico. Thus the most important source of inspiration has been the courageous and illuminating work of what turns out to be a long and relatively broad history of Western and Third World critics of racism and imperialism in Western sciences, though much of this work is not widely known in the West. I agree with these science observers that in whatever ways we can, Westerners must move as quickly (and wisely) as possible to harness Western sciences to democracy-advancing projects. Readers will see that there is great diversity of opinion about how that is to be done but none about the fact that it must be done.

A fellowship in the Institute for Advanced Studies at the University of Delaware in 1989–90 permitted me to do research on these issues. A visiting appointment in Women's Studies and Philosophy at the University of California at Los Angeles for two quarters in 1992 enabled me to discuss these materials with a number of scholars in relevant fields. Several students provided valuable discussions of some of these papers as well as of the issues of the book more generally; I thank especially Elena Heckathorne, Nadine Tanio, and Vandana Venkatesh. I also had the opportunity to discuss the project with seminar and lecture audiences in 1991 and 1992. I thank especially George Levine and the Rutgers University Center for the Study of Contemporary Culture, E. Ann Kaplan and the State University of New York at Stony Brook Humanities Center, the University of California at Los Angeles graduate anthropology seminar, Donna Haraway and the graduate seminar on science and technology in the History of Consciousness Program at the University of California at Santa Cruz, and the participants in the June 1992 History and Philosophy of Science in Science Education Conference at Kingston, Ontario.

Several friends have for years centered a critical examination of racism and Eurocentrism in their thinking and writings and thus provided me with ongoing inspiration and discussions. I am indebted especially to Margaret Andersen, Cynthia Enloe, Anne Fausto-Sterling, Donna Haraway, Ruth Hubbard, Bill Lawson, Joni Seager, and Sharon Traweek. Evelynn Hammonds's thoughtful review for Indiana University Press has left its traces in virtually every part of the editorial introductions. A number of individuals deserve thanks for their helpful advice on various parts of the project: Michael Adas, Anthony Appiah, Francesca Bray, Susantha Goonatilake, Frances Hanckel, Dorian Harding-Morick, Gary Nash, Robert Proctor, Karen Rosenberg, Karen Sacks, Londa Schiebinger, Anne Fausto-Sterling, and Sharon Traweek.

I did not always take the advice I received, and the errors that remain are entirely my own.

Grateful acknowledgment is made to the following sources for permission to reprint material in this anthology:

"Black Athena: Hostilities to Egypt in the Eighteenth Century," from *Black Athena*, vol. 1, by Martin Bernal. Copyright © 1987 by Rutgers, The State Uni-

THE "RACIAL" ECONOMY OF SCIENCE

INTRODUCTION

Eurocentric Scientific Illiteracy—A Challenge for the World Community

Sandra Harding

Scientific Illiteracy: Familiar and Unexpected

An unexpected form of scientific illiteracy has become more and more visible over the last few decades. Earlier criticisms focused on the scientific illiteracy of humanists or of the working classes; recent ones challenge the Eurocentrism or androcentrism of many scientists, policymakers, and other highly educated citizens that severely limits public understanding of science as a fully social process and thus, also, of the nature it studies. According to these latter-day criticisms, scientists and other members of dominant groups in the West also suffer from a kind of scientific illiteracy; they need a kind of scientific education that has not been available to them.

In particular, there are few aspects of the "best" science educations that enable anyone to grasp how nature-as-an-object-of-knowledge is always cultural: "In science, just as in art and in life, only that which is true to culture is true to nature."[1] These elite science educations rarely expose students to systematic analyses of the social origins, traditions, meanings, practices, institutions, technologies, uses, and consequences of the natural sciences that ensure the fully historical character of the results of scientific research. Consequently, most scientists are not in a position to evaluate in a maximally objective way important parts of the evidence that they use in arriving at their results of research; nor is the educated public provided with the information and skills it needs to detect such a problem. Thus public understanding is impoverished by the prevalence of partial and distorted pictures of nature and of the place of Western sciences in maximally objective accounts of world history.[2] For example, the failure of Westerners to link scientific thought about the green revolution, rain forest conservation, or toxic waste disposal to issues of social justice has generated only partial and distorted scientific accounts and policies that increase yet further the gap between the haves and the have-nots. We need "strong objectivity" instead of the only weak standards that have prevailed in the sciences—a topic to which I shall return.

One group that has particularly suffered from this second kind of scientific illiteracy is people constructed as racially or ethnically different or "other" from the dominant groups in the West. What we could refer to as overdeveloped elites in the West have underdeveloped the Third World and the people of Third World descent within the West, as a number of critics have put the point, and Western sciences appear to be deeply implicated in these processes.[3] My focus here will be on this "racial" economy of Western sciences and its accompanying Eurocentrism. By " 'racial' economy" I mean those institutions, assumptions, and practices that are responsible for disproportionately distributing along "racial" lines the benefits of Western sciences to the haves and the bad consequences to the have-nots, thereby enlarging the gap between them.[4] By "Eurocentrism" I mean the assumption that Europe functions autonomously from other parts of the world; that Europe is its own origin, final end, and agent; and that Europe and people of European descent in the Americas and elsewhere owe nothing to the rest of the world.[5]

These are strong charges—but they are the ones that emerge from a broad array of scientific, historical, and philosophic studies such as the ones included in this collection. To repeat a point made in the preface, these are not charges made by critics hostile to science; many of the critics are scientists who are calling for better science. After all, the sciences build in modes of self-correction; making such criticisms and thoughtfully responding to them is exactly how the growth of knowledge is supposed to occur and how it has often advanced in the past. Nor are these critics engaged in bashing specifically Western sciences. The problem is not Western sciences per se but certain configurations within them, such as Eurocentrism, that need to be cut out of our institutions, assumptions, and practices. The solution to these problems for people living in the West is not to end or devalue Western traditions wholesale or to seek escape from them in mythologized sciences of the past or of non-Western societies. Our solution cannot be escape to "elsewhere." Instead, we must learn to take responsibility for the sciences we have now and have had in the past, to acknowledge their limitations and flaws as we also value their indubitable strengths and achievements. But to do so requires a more realistic and objective grasp of their origins and effects "elsewhere" as well as in the West.

Of course, the earlier problems of scientific illiteracy have not disappeared. The earlier concern was that far too many people were ignorant of or indifferent to scientific learning. Some critics, such as C. P. Snow, focused on the "two cultures" problem: humanists and scientists were not interested in understanding each other's concerns and ways of thinking. Consequently the two groups were unable to discuss with each other important public policy issues. Writing in the late 1950s, Snow saw the scientific illiteracy of humanists in the West as an obstacle to the scientific, technological, and economic development of the have-not nations.[6]

Others have focused on a different "two cultures" problems: the low level of science education achieved by the vast majority of U.S. citizens who drop out of school early or take every opportunity to avoid science and math courses. One concern here is to "keep U.S. science strong" by recruiting more women and racial minorities into science careers as fewer and fewer white males enter the sciences. Another concern is the failure of the sciences to provide an adequate level of general science education to racial and ethnic minorities, women, and the working class. How can these groups make intelligent decisions about their own lives and the public policies that affect their lives—about their health, occupational safety, and environment, for example—when they lack scientific information and the ability to evaluate it (commodities that are all too difficult even for members of the privileged groups to obtain)? How can they participate fully in national and international decisions about such issues without scientific skills? An effective pursuit of democracy requires that those who bear the consequences of decisions have a proportionate share in making them.[7] The failure of the United States to distribute science educations democratically compromises its commitments to and competence at democracy.

These earlier concerns have by no means disappeared or become less important. But discussions of the new scientific illiteracy provide an enlarged perspective on them. Western sciences clearly have been and continue to be complicit with racist, colonial, and imperial projects. Not surprisingly, Westerners fail to situate their understandings of both nature and the sciences within maximally realistic and objective world histories. Full acknowledgment and analysis of these Eurocentric tendencies leads to the recognition that racially marginalized groups, at least, may have good reasons for avoiding sciences that have had undoubted good effects for those in positions to benefit from them but, nevertheless, in other respects appear to be effectively committed to increasing consumerism and profit, maintaining social control, and legitimating the authority of elites.[8] So the emerging understanding of the scientific illiteracy of the most highly educated groups contributes to a better understanding of the causes of one form of the earlier scientific illiteracy in the West. It must be noted also that in the Third World, science is often a means for individuals to escape marginalization and to join an international elite. The glamour and power of science co-opt as well as coerce.[9] Privileged classes in the Third World, too, are often concerned only to benefit themselves.

Fortunately, valuable resources have begun to appear from a number of diverse sources that can help to produce a more objective understanding of the nature and consequences of Western sciences in world communities—past, present, and future.

New Resources for Understanding the "Racial" Economy of Science

Anti-Eurocentric Movements

Around the world as well as in the West, new social movements have challenged the authority of the West to impose its values and standards on peoples with histories and present concerns that are opposed to those of privileged groups in the West. All of the world's peoples bear the consequences of policies made in the West, but they do not get a fair share in making decisions that will have such powerful effects on their lives.

Scientific and technological issues often arise in these analyses. How and why are Western sciences implicated by these critiques? What would sciences and technologies look like that were designed *for* the majority of the world's peoples instead of only for already overadvantaged Westerners and Third World elites? Should there be many different but equal culturally specific sciences, or only one "world science"? Insightful responses to such questions are provided in many of the essays in this collection.

The New Social Studies of Science and Technology

Recent work in the social studies of science and technology also provides new resources. Of course scientist-historians such as J. D. Bernal and Joseph Needham as well as the radical science movement had long shown that the cognitive content of natural science claims has been coherent with the distinctive concerns of the cultures within which they have developed, not just with science traditions that have been imagined to be autonomous from their surrounding cultures.[10] Moreover, such influences on science have played important roles in the growth of scientific knowledge, not just in its retardation, as the conventional view claimed. Our best beliefs as well as our worst ones have social causes. Historians, sociologists, and anthropologists of science have pursued such arguments in greater detail more recently.[11]

The new gender-focused studies of science have provided especially insightful analyses of how social interests and values get into the cognitive content of the sciences, as a number of the authors in this collection point out. Even the least likely fields and aspects of science have turned out to bear the fingerprints of androcentric projects. Physics and logic, the prioritizing of mathematics and abstract thought, standards of objectivity, good method, rationality—all of these have been thought immune to social influences. And yet feminist critiques have revealed androcentric fingerprints even here—for example, in the mechanistic models of early modern astronomy and physics and in the coding of reason as part of ideal masculinity.[12] The feminist arguments help to clear the ground for asking similarly pointed questions about the racial and Eurocentric traces in such abstract areas of the sciences, and they provide valuable resources for such projects. Moreover, racism and Eurocentrism often appear in gender-specific forms. Furthermore, Third World cultures have their own legacies of androcentrism and sexism, as a number of Third World authors point out in these essays.

Diversity Concerns in Educational Institutions

There are now new audiences and resources for addressing these topics in every level of U.S. educational institutions. Elementary and high schools are increasingly concerned to provide more realistic and inclusive pictures of the world and of their students' lives. For one thing, the world is still shrinking; changes in the world community appear on television every day; increasing numbers of people in the United States have gotten to know people from other countries—either there or here. For another, the demographic "coloring" of America makes the shortcomings of Eurocentric educations even more obvious.

Many university administrators, faculty, and students are actively concerned to decrease the Eurocentrism that has marred their curricula, courses, research, and scholarship. No doubt some of this concern by administrators and faculty is self-serving. They want to create courses, curricula, and intellectual environments that will attract minority students in the United States who must become a larger proportion of the professionals of tomorrow, given the aging of the white population. They want to attract tuition monies from foreign students, since the pool of traditional U.S. students is shrinking. Moreover, in such fields as business, engineering, and international relations, there is a perceived need to train Western managers and administrators who are capable of interacting more effectively in international markets as they manage U.S. business and domestic and foreign relations in ways that will "keep America strong." Furthermore, these fields are happy to train foreign managers in U.S. ways of doing business.

These realities, however, should not distract us from appreciating the growing strength of the yearnings many Western people have not to be on the "wrong side" of history morally, politically, or scientifically. Many people want to act fairly and responsibly and to understand how nature and social relations really work in order to advance democracy. No one wants to have to confront the perception by others that he or she is irresponsibly ignorant or greedy. Most people do not want to find out that Eurocentric biases blocked their critical thinking and made them unintentionally responsible for increasing their own ignorance and for worsening conditions for the already worst off. The diversity concerns on campuses offer new resources for thinking about Western sciences and new audiences for such thoughts.

Reflexive Science Tendencies

The natural sciences themselves provide new resources and audiences for these topics. Of course, many natural scientists—of "first world" as well as Third World descent—have been the most persistent and illuminating critics of the "racial" economy of the sciences. Their numbers are increasing, and here as in other fields scientists express the same yearnings to learn how to locate themselves and their projects in more objective, more realistic, less chauvinistic understandings of local and international politics. There is an increasing recognition among scientists themselves that the economics and politics of science shape the results of research in the best as well as the worst moments in the sciences, that sciences tend toward their uses, that the sciences need to expand and transform their goals and methods of research if they are seriously to confront the fact that "only that which is true to culture is true to nature." Even a National Academy of Sciences document now argues that the notion of scientific methods should be enlarged beyond its familiar meanings of "double-blind trials, randomization of experimental subjects, and the proper use of controls" and its obvious use of observational and intellectual tools.

> The term "methods" can be interpreted more broadly. Methods include the judgments scientists make about interpretation or reliability of data. They also include the decisions scientists make about which problems to pursue or when to conclude an investigation. Methods involve the ways scientists work with each other and exchange information.[13]

As this document goes on to point out, the way for scientists to avoid allowing social biases to distort their work is "by trying to identify their own values and the effects those values have on their science. One of the best ways to do this is by studying the history, philosophy and sociology of science. Human values change very slowly, and the lessons of the past remain of great relevance today."[14] Especially noteworthy here is the implication that the values most troublesome to identify are those shared by cultural communities—the ones that "change very slowly." Clearly many scientists are coming to understand that Western sciences have produced less than the maximally objective understandings of nature's regularities and their underlying causal tendencies and that it is possible and necessary to develop stronger standards of objectivity.

Science Education

Educators in the United States are now concerned to improve science education at every level in order to attract into the sciences and to retain more women and racial minorities. The older scientific illiteracy problem led to the improved design of many general science courses in order to educate humanists in the "mysteries of nature." And it led to various projects to recruit and retain in the sciences members of underrepresented groups. But neither project has made much effort to include the new histories and social studies of the sciences inside science courses and curricula. Being able to explain the regularities of nature and their underlying causal tendencies is inseparable from providing the same kinds of explanations of the social relations of science. Science education has suffered from its lack of attention to such phenomena as the "racial" economy of science, perhaps fearing that any but the most minimal admission of error in the past—such as the many cases discussed in this collection—would generate the accurate perception that not enough has been done to block such antidemocratic and ignorance-producing tendencies today. This "ostrich strategy," however, has lost its effectiveness. It is harder and harder to maintain the public fiction that U.S. science and technology policy at home and abroad is always—or even usually—right. This is an opportune moment to examine what changes should be made in science education if a greater diversity of U.S. students are reasonably to perceive that U.S. sciences are for them and not primarily for militarism, consumerism, profit, and social control, and if all U.S. citizens more generally are to have good reasons to be proud of our sciences.

The Changing World Community

Last but not least is the timeliness of these issues for current attempts to figure out desirable social relations for the world community. It is scary to contemplate how the power that Western sciences and technologies make available is likely to result in increased destruction to humans and our environments—and especially to economically and politically marginalized humans and environments—unless this power can be harnessed quickly to work on agendas for more democratic world communities. What scientific and technological knowledge do the victims of Eurocentrism need in order to articulate and to achieve their best course within communities that resist democratization? What knowledge do well-intentioned members of dominant groups in the West need in order to understand the contemporary and historical locations from which their sciences have emerged, what they can and cannot do to decrease the partiality and distortion of their accounts of nature and social relations, and how to link the sciences more effectively to social justice agendas? These issues are too important to be left to scholars and scientists alone; increasingly they are recognized as issues for every citizen of the world.

Sciences in (and before) Eurocentric History; Eurocentric History in Sciences

Six topics have been selected as particularly useful for thinking further about these interests and needs.

Early Non-Western Scientific Traditions

With few exceptions, at least until recent decades, Westerners have sacrificed empirical and theoretical adequacy in order to promote the claims that the exemplary processes and achievements of "their" science prove that it is different in kind from those of any other cultures' knowledge seeking and that Western sciences and their technologies are the most important measures of human progress. These chauvinists insist that the development of modern sciences shows how progressive, rational, and civilized is the modern West in contrast to the backward, irrational, and primitive "rest."

It is clear, however, that the high cultures of China and Islam produced experimental sciences, mathematics, and technologies that were earlier and often equal or, in some cases, superior to those of at least the early modern period in Europe. Moreover, Africa and the Americas were by no means left in "the primitive"; they too generated important scientific and technological advances that were earlier and superior to European achievements. For example, carbon steel was produced in what is now Tanzania some 1,500 years ago by methods of such sophistication that they were not matched in Europe until the nineteenth century.[15] Experimental agriculture apparently was developed in the Andes before the Columbian encounter. Its knowledge was appropriated by the European conquerors and recycled through European science, without acknowledgment of its origins. In other cases, non-Westerners have been kept ignorant of their culture's own achievements. As Michael Adas points out, British colonial administrators did not allow Indians to be taught their own contributions to mathematics.[16]

Moreover, as one scholar after another has noted, European sciences progressed primarily because of the military, economic and political power of European cultures, not because of the purported greater rationality of Westerners or the purported commitment of their sciences to the pursuit of disinterested truths.[17] If the success of these sciences required the military and political defeat of non-European peoples, we are entitled to skepticism about claims that the history of these sciences is unmitigatedly the history of *human* progress; progress for some has been at the expense of disempowerment, impoverishment, and sometimes genocide for many others. Finally, the world still can learn from these non-Western traditions; without nourishing the illusion that we can or should escape from the West into "elsewhere," we can recognize that the pool of valuable scientific ideas is not restricted to what has been produced by dominant groups in the West. In short, early non-Western science traditions need to be evaluated in more objective ways, and the Western traditions need to be more objectively situated in world history.

Science Constructs "Race"

A second useful focus is on how the sciences have actively participated in the construction of the category of "race." It has now been forty years since some biologists and physical anthropologists began to point out that the concept of race is incompatible with evolutionary theory. They have shown why population genetics should replace the concept of a fixed and discrete cluster of biological attributes as the empirically and theoretically adequate way to explain human variation. Moreover, it turns out that there is greater genetic variation within every "racial" group than there is between any two of them.

Yet scientists in such fields as biology, medicine, and public health still use this apparently anachronistic concept of race. Some still demand accounts of the biological basis for racial distinctions. In other cases, racially marked groups appeal to race differences on their own behalf—for example, when Native Americans demand treatment for their high rates of diabetes. Of course these high rates of diabetes should be eliminated. However, even though biologists know that it is population genetics that explains variations in the distribution of diabetes, the rhetorical use of racial categories codes race as fixed, and thus this dynamic ends up supporting the older notion of "the races."[18]

Another way to put this point is that race is socially constructed yet also "lived in";[19] it is manufactured yet also "material," as many essays in this collection demonstrate. Moreover, peoples of color appeal to their racial identities and their shared locations in material race relations in order to describe the conditions of their lives, and also to draw together and energize the victims of racism and Eurocentrism for emancipatory struggles. "Whites" can engage in similarly liberatory practices if they insist on the importance of speaking critically of racism and Eurocentrism from their objective location "as whites" in the social order. We live "as whites" in ways structured by real economic, political, and social relations; the fact that racial difference is socially constructed does not prevent it from having real, structural effects in society.

The histories of scientific constructions of race are especially revealing. For one thing, what now clearly appears as racist research often was conducted by the most distinguished scientists of the day. Moreover, these scientists were not all political regressives; some were in other respects among the most progressive white thinkers of their day on race issues. Clearly, racist and Eurocentric beliefs and practices cannot be attributed solely to "crackpots," to intentional racism, or to prejudices—bad attitudes and false beliefs—as the dominant liberal social theory would have it.

These histories also reveal various strategies that targets of scientific racism used to fight back. Especially important has been the use of socially legitimated discourses about nature that were alternative to those of the sciences—for example, religion.[20] Such lessons from the past draw attention to the radical potential of the emerging discourses on nature and on the sciences in the new social movements, in literary and cultural studies, and in other sites of reflection and debate that are outside the sciences themselves.

Who Gets to Do Science? Who Gets to Direct Science?

It should appear paradoxical that the natural sciences, with methods admired supposedly because they maximize the identification and elimination of social biases that researchers might bring into science, nevertheless have severely restricted the chance to direct science to elites or those with aspirations to join elites. Is it scientific method or restricting researchers primarily to white men that is supposed to be responsible for the (purported) value neutrality and universal validity of Western scientific claims?

Does the claim that science is more democratic than the social structure of the larger society get used as a tactic to exclude minorities from science, to placate those privileged few let into the top ranks of the sciences, and to keep the direction of the sciences firmly in the control of the overadvantaged groups in the West? Various proposals have appeared for increasing the numbers of minorities in the sciences and for their more democratic participation in the direction of scientific research. Do these succeed in recognizing the full array of obstacles to achieving these goals? How should they be strengthened?

Science's Technologies and Applications

Are the sciences innocent when they or their technologies are used in racist and Eurocentric ways? Yes, according to the conventional view. And yet it has become increasingly clear in the last few decades that no sharp line can be drawn between "pure sciences" and their technologies and applications. Examining case studies of technologies and applications that have gone wrong reveals what is also wrong with the problematics, background assumptions, metaphors, research designs, interpretations of evidence, social environment, functions and purposes of the sciences that generated these applications and technologies.

Metatheory and Philosophy of Science

The widespread existence of racist and Eurocentric results of scientific research leads to questions about the adequacy of the metatheories and philosophies of science that have directed scientific practices, the social studies of the sciences, and popular beliefs about science. Should we go beyond the criticisms of specific bad consequences of the sciences to develop stronger standards of good method and of how to maximize objectivity than the only weak and ineffectual ones we have had? To the extent that culturewide beliefs are not critically identified, it is cultures, not individuals, who are the subjects of scientific knowledge. Do the sciences need a more adequate account of the subject or agent of knowledge?

Since science must use metaphors to extend and revise its theories, what should we think about the political regressiveness of some of the most widely used such metaphors—the Garden of Eden metaphors for "wild nature," for instance, or the rape metaphors for scientific method, and the feminine metaphors for racial "others"? If it is true that nature-as-an-object-of-knowledge is irretrievably social, as many argue, are the natural sciences usefully conceptualized as *social* sciences? Can we develop this idea without losing the ability to insist on the distinction between "natural facts" and people's perceptions of them? Clearly the metatheories and philosophies of the sciences need an even more thorough overhauling than the new social studies of science have imagined.

Visions and Strategies for the Future

Which sciences should we develop for a democratic world community? The answers to this question have tended to be either naïve or insufficiently ambitious. For example, they have assumed that it is possible to isolate and practice pure sciences and that there is no need to make changes in the Eurocentric and racist societies in which the pursuit of "value-neutral science" has been an integral part. Or they have focused on strategies for recruiting more racial minorities into the sciences and retaining them there without questioning the racism and Eurocentrism of the kinds of projects for which science is funded and on which racial minorities are supposed to want to work. Sometimes they have called for "sciences of our own"—alternative sciences that are *for* racial minorities and people in developing countries—without producing strategies for dealing with the ways in which access to scientific training and to the resources for research are firmly controlled by Western elites who clearly will try to block the development of, or to coopt, alternative sciences. Moreover, conceptualizing the project here as creating "alternative" sciences leaves Western sciences setting the standard for "real science."

Sometimes they have adopted a "forward to the past" posture, seeking to ground knowledge seeking for today in premodern world views and practices rather than in a critical winnowing of past and present practices. Frequently they have assumed that racist assumptions can be eliminated without also addressing androcentric and misogynous ones, although it is clear that "race" and gender, racism and sexism, construct and maintain each other, as they also do class oppression and heterosexism. Sciences free of racist and Eurocentric assumptions cannot be achieved apart from the elimination of the other social hierarchies into which they are firmly locked; sciences will be no more emancipatory than are the larger social agendas that nourish and guide knowledge seeking. But if we follow the important popular slogan "Think globally; act locally," what are the best ways to begin to transform the sciences? Which present practices and programs—in the West and "elsewhere"—should be supported and further developed?

Conceptual Challenges

Conceptual challenges arise in any attempt to identify and analyze the structure of Western science's involvement with projects of racism and Eurocentrism. Here are four that have already been mentioned and that have wide-reaching consequences for reflecting on the essays in this collection.

1. *"Race," class, and gender form a matrix of privilege.* Class and gender policies have constructed and maintained racial hierarchies just as race policies have done for class and gender hierarchies. Consequently, to understand race policies and projects, one must also understand how they both make use of and regenerate class and gender projects. Let us pursue this challenge in more detail.

First, it is important to keep in mind that the concept of race is constructed in at least three forms—individual, structural, and symbolic. It appears as a characteristic of individuals, of course. But it also appears as a characteristic of the structure of societies—some are more organized by racial hierarchies than are others. Thus South Africa, Nazi Germany, and the American South during and after slavery, with their elaborate structures of racial classification and restrictions on which races can do which activities, simply *have* more race than do other less rigidly and comprehensively racially stratified societies. Moreover, race also appears as a symbolic system in which "black," "brown," "yellow," "red," and "dark" signify evil, ignorance, danger, and pollution and "white" and "light" signify good, knowledge, safety, and purity. Apparently this symbolic system was already in place in Europe in the Middle Ages.[21]

Moreover, these three aspects of race are sometimes in conflict with each other. Invocations of racial symbolism and stereotypes frequently increase just when race as a structural system is changing or is perceived to be weakening—for example, after the abolition of slavery in the United States and after the successes of the civil rights movement in the 1960s. It has been in these periods that projects of scientific racism accelerate their attempts to provide biological justifications for racist social structures and for meanings (symbols) of racial difference.

Gender and class hierarchies are interlocked with racial hierarchies in each of these three forms: individual, structural, and symbolic. Gender and class policies and projects construct different racial identities for women and men, rich and poor; different positions within a racial structure; and different meanings of race. In other words, in societies where "race" has been constructed, we each occupy a determinate race, class, and gender location in our society's matrix of social hierarchies, and each such location gives us an individual race, class, and gender, assigns us to different activities, and gives symbolic meanings to those identities and activities.[22] (Ethnicity, religion, and sexuality can provide additional significant dimensions to our social location.)

A number of good consequences can follow from recognizing that race functions as a part of a social matrix that is structured also by gender and class. It draws attention to the way whites, too, have a specific location in such a matrix and are perceived and even required to act in certain ways regardless of individual desires and intentions. I will always be treated as "white" (in a bank, at a philosophy conference, in a classroom, in a convenience store at midnight, walking on the street) and expected to make the kinds of assumptions characteristic of the dominant race (e.g., to accept "white" privileges, such as assuming that I will be regarded by any and every audience as qualified to speak about "women [race unspecified] and science").[23]Moreover, it draws attention to the way racial differences are always constructed by, and themselves construct, class and gender differences. My privileges as a "white" person are specific to my gender and class; for example, men of my race and class have different privileges than do I; "white" women of other classes are subject to different conditions and expectations. Much social theory mystifies the social order by assuming that race, gender, and class are parallel but fundamentally separate social systems. Matrix theory shows the importance of centering and problematizing their mutually constructing and interactive processes. It shifts attention from efforts to explain race, gender, and class as autonomous "things" to efforts to explain the flexible and dynamic relations between them.

To focus on race and science thus presents several challenges. First, when class, gender, and whatever other forms of stratification and social meaning in a particular society are not also clearly in focus, such an account can provide only a partial and, perhaps in some ways, distorted understanding of race, science, and their intersection. It is easy to forget this, since much of the otherwise most interesting literature in this field does not recognize the importance of focusing on gender or, sometimes, class dimensions of racial histories (as alert readers will notice in some of the essays in this collection). Furthermore, this argument about a "matrix of oppression" is itself controversial. Some thinkers believe that it is class agendas alone that have produced and that maintain today the forms of racism and sexism that we see in the world around us. For them, it will seem distorting and inappropriately limiting to center attention on "race and Western science" when, in their view, both are entirely products of attempts by Western economies to increase their profit and social control. Such objections should not be lightly dismissed, since these Marxist traditions have contributed comprehensive and illuminating descriptions and explanations of just how Western economies have contributed to scientific racism and imperialism—from biological determinism to ecological destruction and genocide. They continue to provide important analyses today.

In spite of these possible objections, there are good reasons to frame a project specifically about Eurocentrism, race, and science. For one thing, class and gender projects often appear in Eurocentric and racial forms and thus can usefully be examined in those terms. Since gender, race, and class construct each other, we can learn a great deal by centering racial concepts, histories, and contemporary agendas so as to discover where and how they are shaped by, and in turn shape, class, gender, and other social structures and meanings. Moreover, many thinkers hold that whatever their origins, racial phenomena exist today at least partially independent of agendas of class exploitation. They have come to have a life at least partially of their own.

Others have claimed a "post-Marxist position," noting that Marxist insights are now part of the intellectual inheritance of the contemporary West, whether or not this is recognized or used by all. From this perspective, the new social movements that result in science projects, such as contemporary feminist and antiracist ones, simply are post-Marxisms, not merely in the sense that they come after orthodox Marxism or reject its fundamental insights but also in the sense that they adapt and use Marxist understandings to describe and explain both different phenomena and later ones than orthodox Marxism was designed to illuminate.[24] From this perspective, the alternatives to post-Marxism are either anachronistic pre-Marxism or anachronistic antique Marxism.

The fact of the matter is that many peoples in the world choose to identify themselves not as raceless economic men but as members of racially exploited and marginalized groups or, for a small but increasing number, of Eurocentric and racially overadvantaged groups. Peoples of color have themselves asserted their own "racial" identities as a way to mobilize resistance to Western racism, and they have explored the alternative cultural identities and histories that were rejected by Westerners, identities that have been developed as survival strategies and forms of resistance to racism and Eurocentrism. Moreover, many "whites" are making a project of learning to think and act out of their own particular "racial" historical social locations rather than assuming that their thoughts and actions are not at all shaped by these conditions from which they issue. They are trying to learn how to take responsibility for their racial position in history.

For these reasons, analyses focused on the Eurocentric and racist agendas that have directed Western sciences can provide resources for advancing both the sciences themselves and the social studies of science as well as more general democratic projects.

2. *Science is a contested zone.* In one sense, it is obvious that we cannot turn to today's sciences—the supposed models of Western objectivity and rationality—to resolve questions about the racism or imperialism of Western science, for it is exactly those sciences and beliefs about them that are on trial; it appears absurd to expect the "fox" to help us understand or judge the way he has "guarded the chicken coop." Their complicity with Eurocentric and racist projects is a regressive aspect of the sciences and popular belief.

But in another sense, it is exactly scientific procedures that have proved so effective in identifying racist and imperialist tendencies in the sciences, and it is in the name of greater objectivity and scientific rationality (as well as social justice) that alternative accounts are proposed. We want less partial and distorted descriptions and causal explanations—more scientific ones—of why and how Eurocentric assumptions and projects have shaped Western sciences, and of how to link scientific projects more firmly to democratic ones—the concerns of all of the authors in this collection. Moreover, scientists themselves have been in the forefront generation after generation in producing these criticisms and alternative accounts. The sciences also have a progressive history of opposition to Eurocentric and racist projects.

In short, science is a contested zone here, as it has been in other contexts and should be at its very best. Science is a terrain on which inherited social beliefs may be rigorously challenged and visions for the future debated. The Western scientific ethos as well as the history of scientific institutions and practices contains both progressive and regressive tendencies, and the societies that produce science have fought over who will control these resources. Antiracist and anti-Eurocentric projects intend to advance the progressive tendencies and block the regressive ones. What we should fear is not such discussions but their silencing. As Robert Proctor points out about Nazi medicine in his essay reprinted here, the depoliticization of science is always at least as dangerous as its inappropriate politicization.[25] So the goal of critics of racism and Eurocentrism is to make more democratic the political discussions of the sciences. That is, it is not to "politicize" the sciences but to prevent their dangerous depoliticization.

3. *"Pure science"? "Pure nature"?* Over fifty years of massive external funding of scientific research and development plus thirty years of the new social studies of science have made it virtually impossible to locate thoughtful observers of science who will even try to defend the view that there is such a thing as "pure

science" that can usefully be distinguished from its social origins, meanings, institutions, practices, technologies, and uses. With the collapse of this distinction, it is no longer possible to provide plausible arguments that there is any part of the scientific process that is in principle immune from responsibility for the bad consequences of Western sciences.

Too many science teachers and researchers in universities evidently have thought that they could point to their own ignorance of the origins and (predictable) consequences of their work as evidence of the purity of their work and the enterprise to which they recruit students. This planned ignorance of researchers and teachers has been encouraged partially through dividing between different groups of workers the tasks of selecting scientific problems, of producing information about nature, and of funding the sciences and generating applications and technologies from this information. This division of labor has helped to maintain the illusion that what is done in "pure research"—often located in university science departments—has nothing to do with the science policy constructed in governments and industries or with what goes on at the other end of science in engineering and medical research departments, industry, "development" projects, or military establishments. These days this illusion is virtually impossible to maintain as the "pure science" departments more and more come to depend on federal funding. Ignorance of the predictable uses of the results of scientific research is not evidence for science's purity.

There are a number of ways in which the purported autonomy of the cognitive content of the sciences is breached. For one thing, social and political problems are frequently redefined as technological or scientific ones. In other words, the origin of technological and scientific problems is always to be found partially in social and political problems.[26] Thus which scientific questions get asked depends largely upon who—which historically located social group—gets to do the asking. Should "the problem" be conceptualized as how to limit the reproduction of people of Third World descent or how to create a more egalitarian distribution at international as well as local levels of food, health resources, labor power, and other natural and social resources? Which scientific picture of this part of nature and social relations will be created depends on who gets to decide which question is to be answered.

Second, modern science is constituted at its very core as use oriented. Scientific experimentation privileges intervention in nature as the way to obtain reliable information. The usefulness of science for applications and technologies is not extrinsic to obtaining scientific information; instead it is the ethic directing the modern scientific enterprise and often claimed to distinguish it from earlier sciences.[27] Relatedly, science uses technologies to conduct research, and these technologies themselves carry social and political values. Galileo's telescope moved authority about the heavens from the church to anyone who looked through it. Today, sophisticated instruments require a more highly educated scientific work force, and decisions about who will gain access to such education, beginning in kindergarten and even in infancy, are political ones. As long as the United States tolerates such a low level of the general education upon which scientific educations depend, people of Third World descent in the United States are unlikely to gain access to the sciences and their technologies. These sciences and technologies thereby become means of limiting democracy.

Furthermore, scientific projects have social and political meanings to the people who do them, to the societies that support them, and to those around the world who bear the consequences of these projects. Some would say that sciences simply *are* their meanings and uses. For example, they would point out that both the referents and the meanings of race-difference research will tend toward the uses of such research.

These are the kinds of arguments that make it difficult to defend the view that there is such a thing as "pure science." Of course this is not to deny that "pure curiosity" leads children into science educations and scientists into the forefronts of knowledge. But individual intentions do not determine the social functions of individual or institutional actions nor the uses that others have in mind for the results of their curiosity. It is structural and historical explanations of science that are needed, not explanations of individuals' motives.

If there is no such thing as "pure science," should we still believe in "pure nature," unsullied by human meanings and interventions? On one hand, of course, nature existed before the evolution of hominids to humans, and it sets constraints on the beliefs societies and individuals can hold and still manage to survive—humans will not be the last phenomenon to exit from the world. On the other hand, it doesn't set all that many constraints on human belief, as the anthropological and historical records demonstrate. It is obvious that even our best theories are always underdetermined by their evidence; they can never be "proved true" but are always only "not yet proved false." This line of argument does deny that what scientists observe, describe, or explain is "pure nature."

Scientists, like the rest of us, *can* observe only nature-as-an-object-of-knowledge. These objects of knowledge in significant respects are similar to the subject of knowledge—those who do the observing. The same kinds of social influences that shape knowers and their scientific projects also shape nature-as-an-object-of-knowledge. Most people would be willing to admit this similarity for the subjects and objects of social science research but would think it absurd to make such a claim for the natural sciences. After all, trees, rocks, planetary orbits, and electrons do not constitute themselves as historical actors. They existed before there were any human societies and no doubt will exist after them. What they are does not depend on what they think they are; they do not think or carry on any of the other activities that distinguish human communities from other constituents of the world around us. But this distinction turns out to be irrelevant to the point here, since scientists never can observe the trees, rocks, planetary orbits, or electrons in a state in which they are untouched by human activities or meanings. Instead, they are destined to observe something different but, hopefully, systematically related to nature apart from human perceptions: nature-as-an-object-of-knowledge.

Trees, rocks, planetary orbits, and electrons always appear to natural scientists only as they are already socially constituted in exactly some of the ways that humans and their communities are already constituted for the social scientist. Such objects are already in effect removed from "pure nature" into social life—they are social objects—by, first of all, the contemporary general cultural meanings that these objects have for everyone, including the entire scientific community.[28] They also become socially constituted through the shapes and meanings these objects gain for scientists because of earlier generations of scientific discussion about them. Scientists never observe nature apart from such traditions; even when they criticize some aspects of them they must assume others in order to carry on the criticism. They could not do science if they did not both borrow from and criticize these traditions. Their assumptions about what they see are always shaped by "conversations" they carry on with scientists of the past.

Additionally, scientists' own interactions with such objects also culturally constitute them: to treat a piece of nature with respect, violence, degradation, curiosity, or indifference is to participate in culturally constituting such an object of knowledge. In these respects, nature-as-an-object-of-knowledge simulates social life, and the processes of science themselves are a significant contributor to this phenomenon.

Last, critics point out that there is no "pure" residue separable from these meanings and uses once we note that the intended or claimed purity of scientific research itself is fully pregnant with diverse meanings and uses to scientists, science policymakers, and the rest of us who are—intentionally or not—science consumers. In physics, often held up as the paradigm of "pure science" in spite of its consistent history of service to militarism and industry, virtually no research is now funded which cannot be predicted to generate technologically and politically useful information, even though (or precisely because) the ignorance of the scientists who generate this information about its probable usefulness is carefully planned and cultivated.[29]

4. *The need for "strong method" and "strong objectivity."* In light of the disappearance of "pure science" and "pure nature," is scientific method, as conventionally conceptualized, strong enough to identify and eliminate distorting social interests and values from the results of research? Are the existing standards of objectivity strong enough to guide the development of scientific methods that are effective at achieving such goals?

It is scientific method that is supposed to maximize objectivity by guarding against the intrusion of obscuring and distorting social values into the results of research. But it is now widely recognized that scientific method has been "operationalized" both too narrowly and too broadly to achieve this goal. It has been operationalized too narrowly insofar as only the context of justification—the part of science where hypotheses are tested and evidence gathered for or against them—is guided by systematic methods of research. But if the selection of problems to pursue in the first place—the questions asked—shapes the picture of the world the sciences produce, then the "context of discovery," where hypotheses are selected and refined, must also be subject to systematic critical methodological controls. Many critics of the natural sciences argue that racist and Eurocentric political concerns shaped the questions the sciences have asked and that this is why the results of such research have been racist and Eurocentric.[30] The sciences need a "logic of discovery" to deal with this problem; they need a systematic method for identifying assumptions that shape the selection of problems as "scientific" in the first place.

But method has also been operationalized too broadly, for it is clear that not all social interests and values deteriorate the objectivity of the results of research. Democratic values, ones that prioritize seeking out criticisms of dominant belief from the perspective of the lives of the least advantaged groups, tend to increase the objectivity of the results of research.[31] After all, conventional understandings of scientific method are relatively effective at identifying the social values and interests that differ between the members of a scientific community. That is exactly the goal of the directive that observations and experiments should be repeated by different groups of scientists. But values and interests shared by all or virtually all members of a scientific community are not easily detected by such methods. If a scientific community is restricted primarily to people of one race (or gender, class, ethnicity, or sexuality), or if its members share certain Eurocentric values regardless of their racial or geographic origins, it will be hard to detect racist or Eurocentric values. Thus the systematic activation of democracy-increasing interests and values—especially in representing diverse interests in the sciences when socially contentious issues are the object of concern—in general contributes to the objectivity of science; it is wrong to imagine that scientific method requires the elimination of all social values from scientific processes.[32] So scientific method has been operationalized too narrowly and too broadly, in different respects, to achieve the elimination of objectivity-damaging social values and interests.

As noted earlier, the dominant conception of objectivity is implicated in these damaging limits of scientific method. A stronger, more adequate notion of objectivity would require methods for systematically examining all of the social values shaping a particular research process, not just those that happen to differ between the members of a scientific community.[33] Social communities, not either individuals or "no one at all," should be conceptualized as the "knowers" of scientific knowledge claims. Culturewide beliefs that are not critically examined within scientific processes end up functioning as evidence for or against hypotheses.

Modern Western sciences have been constituted from their very beginnings by both democracy-enhancing and democracy-retarding values. In spite of its obvious hierarchical structure, the scientific community today is often still conceptualized as a community of equals where any member is supposedly entitled and encouraged to criticize others' claims. The results of research are claimed to be public property, available for anyone's scrutiny. Moreover, early modern science refused to separate the social good of science from its social projects, as later scientific communities did and as positivism insisted.[34] Obviously, these ideals today bear little relationship to the actual structure and practices of many parts of contemporary sciences.

My point is a different one, however; modern science also incorporates certain authoritarian elements left over from its origins in struggles with religion. It insists on the monologic voice characteristic of totalitarian rulers or of God. It adopts a religious attitude, both toward the "pure nature" it observes and toward its own activities, that rewards fanaticism and the idea of "true believers" who have a pipeline to the one true story about the world. It frequently exhibits a paranoia about the possibility of "outsiders" influencing science, conceptualizing them as "crackpots" and megalomaniacs all too manipulative in their appeal to the ignorant masses, who are imagined as all too ready to swarm up and overwhelm fragile reason.[35] And it conceptualizes scientists (and the mathematicians and philosophers who support their projects regard themselves similarly) as chosen people, as elites, as persons morally superior to the "average man"—and, it goes without saying, to women and to "barbarians and savages."

The criticisms of racism and Eurocentrism in the sciences reveal the need for stronger standards of objectivity and more effective—stronger—methods of research. "Strong objectivity" requires that scientists give the same kind of critical descriptions and explanations of the subject of scientific knowledge—the scientific community in the enlarged sense of those who generate scientific problems—that social scientists at their best give to the objects of their research. "Nativist" accounts of the sciences (or of nature) are not enough; "outsider" perspectives are required to achieve causal accounts.

Many additional challenges remain for thinkers embarking on the project of gaining a more objective understanding of Western sciences and their place in world histories. Only when Westerners recognize and accept the unattractive underside of science will the sciences no longer provide a haven for those who find that psychic dynamic useful to them as individuals who are members of dominant races, classes, or genders.

Meanwhile we can note that while "the truth" will not enable us to end oppressive social relations, less false beliefs are definitely the better kind to have when engaged in such a project. An examination of Western science's complicity with racist, imperialist, and Eurocentric projects enables us to gain a more critical, more scientific perspective on an important part of that Western "unconscious" and thus on the history some groups in the West and "elsewhere" have been busy making, and continue to attempt to make even as we read.

N O T E S

1. Ludwik Fleck, *Genesis and Development of a Scientific Fact* (Chicago: University of Chicago Press, 1979 [1935]), 35; quoted by Ruth Hubbard in *The Politics of Women's Biology* (New Brunswick, N.J.: Rutgers University Press, 1990).

2. Since "Western science" has important origins in the scientific traditions of diverse cultures back through history and around the world (as many authors in this collection

point out), since it is now pursued in virtually every country around the world, and since referring to it as "Western" reinstates the West-East contrast that so many authors in this book are trying to undermine, I should refer to it in some other way—perhaps as "international science." Doing so, however, loses an important focus on the Eurocentrism entrenched in "Western sciences," and it also introduces a term that evidently no other author in the book has found useful. Consequently, I shall stick with this problematic term. Readers should understand it as always in "scare" quotation marks—"Western" science—that is, as a social construct of Eurocentrism.

3. Walter Rodney, *How Europe Underdeveloped Africa* (Washington, D.C.: Howard University Press, 1982); Manning Marable, *How Capitalism Underdeveloped Black America* (Boston: South End Press, 1983).

4. There is no uncontroversial shorthand to use in referring to the complicity of Western sciences in projects of racism/ethnocentrism/Eurocentrism/colonialism/imperialism. Moreover, one cannot separate these issues from those of class and gender in the sciences any more than in any other area of social life. Note that when the term *race* is used here, it is always to be understood as a social construction—as "race."

5. Conversations with Donna Haraway lead me to put the issue this way.

6. C. P. Snow, *The Two Cultures: And A Second Look* (Cambridge: Cambridge University Press, 1964; part 1 first published in 1959).

7. John Dewey puts the point this way in *Democracy and Education* (New York: Macmillan, 1961).

8. As for the humanists, are they repelled among other reasons, by the hostility to the projects of the humanities, the simplistic conception of representing reality and the refusal of a critical reflexivity that are endemic in the sciences and so much of the social studies of science?

9. I thank Francesca Bray for pointing this out.

10. J. D. Bernal, *Science in History* (Cambridge, Mass.: MIT Press, 1971); Joseph Needham, *The Grand Titration: Science and Society in East and West* (Toronto: University of Toronto Press, 1969) (see excerpt in this volume); and Joseph Needham, with the collaboration of Wang Ling (Wang Ching-Ning), Lu Gwei-Djen, Ho Ping-Yu, Kenneth Robinson, Tshao Thien-Chhin, and others, *Science and Civilization in China* (seven volumes in twelve parts), Cambridge: Cambridge University Press, 1954). Two journals that give a good sense of the diversity in the radical science movement are *Science for the People* (now, unfortunately, no longer publishing) and the more recent *Science as Culture* (26 Freegrove Rd., London N7 9RQ, England).

11. For example, see Barry Barnes, *Interests and the Growth of Knowledge* (Boston: Routledge & Kegan Paul, 1977); David Bloor, *Knowledge and Social Imagery* (London: Routledge & Kegan Paul, 1977); Donna Haraway, *Primate Visions: Gender, Race, and Nature in the World of Modern Science* (New York: Routledge, 1989); Evelyn Keller, *Reflections on Gender and Science* (New Haven, Conn.: Yale University Press, 1984); Bruno Latour and Steve Woolgar, *Laboratory Life: The Social Construction of Scientific Facts* (Beverly Hills, Calif.: Sage, 1979); Carolyn Merchant, *The Death of Nature: Women, Ecology, and the Scientific Revolution* (New York: Harper & Row, 1980); and Andrew Pickering, ed., *Science as Practice and Culture* (Chicago: University of Chicago Press, 1992). There have been many more important works in these veins. Jerome Ravetz's *Scientific Knowledge and Its Social Problems* (New York: Oxford University Press, 1971) and Thomas Kuhn's *Structure of Scientific Revolutions* (2d ed.) (Chicago: University of Chicago Press, 1970) were important in generating the more recent studies.

12. E.g., see the works by Haraway, Keller, and Merchant (n. 11); Susan Bordo, *The Flight to Objectivity* (Albany: State University of New York Press, 1987); Sandra Harding and Merrill Hintikka, eds., *Discovering Reality: Feminist Perspectives on Epistemology, Metaphysics, Methodology and Philosophy of Science* (Dordrecht: Reidel, 1983); Alison Jaggar, "The Role of the Emotions in Knowledge," in *Gender/Body Knowledge,* ed. Alison Jaggar and Susan Bordo (New Brunswick, N.J.: Rutgers University Press, 1989); Elizabeth

Lloyd, *The Man of Reason: Male and Female in Western Philosophy* (Minneapolis: University of Minnesota Press, 1984); Andrea Nye, *Words of Power: A Feminist Reading in the History of Logic* (Boulder, Colo.: Westview Press, 1989); Londa Schiebinger, *The Mind Has No Sex: Women in the Origins of Modern Science* (Cambridge, Mass.: Harvard University Press, 1989).

13. National Academy of Sciences, *On Being a Scientist* (Washington, D.C.: National Academy of Sciences Press, 1989), 5–6.

14. Ibid., 8.

15. Debra Shore, "Steel Making in Ancient Africa," in Ivan Van Sertima, ed., *Blacks in Science: Ancient and Modern* (New Brunswick, N.J.: Transaction Books, 1986).

16. Jack Weatherford, *Indian Givers: What the Native Americans Gave to the World* (New York: Crown, 1988). Michael Adas, *Machines as the Measure of Men: Science, Technology and Ideologies of Western Dominance* (Ithaca, N.Y.: Cornell University Press, 1989). I thank Evelynn Hammonds for drawing this example to my attention.

17. See, e.g., Margaret Jacob, *The Cultural Meanings of the Scientific Revolution* (New York: Knopf, 1988), 251; Paul Forman, "Behind Quantum Electronics: National Security as Bases for Physical Research in the U.S., 1940–1960," *Historical Studies in Physical and Biological Sciences* 18 (1987), and many of the essays in Ziauddin Sardar, ed., *The Revenge of Athena: Science, Exploitation and the Third World* (London: Mansell, 1988).

18. I thank Anne Fausto-Sterling for this example.

19. I thank Donna Haraway for putting the point this way. See also Michael Omi and Howard Winant, *Racial Formation in the United States* (New York: Routledge and Kegan Paul, 1986).

20. Nancy Leys Stepan and Sander L. Gilman, "Appropriating the Idioms of Science: The Rejection of Scientific Racism," in Dominick La Capra, *The Bounds of Race: Perspectives on Hegemony and Resistance* (Ithaca, N.Y.: Cornell University Press, 1991), reprinted in this collection. See also Cynthia Eagle Russett, *Sexual Science: The Victorian Construction of Womanhood* (Cambridge, Mass.: Harvard University Press, 1989).

21. Winthrop Jordan, *White over Black: American Attitudes toward the Negro: 1550–1812* (Baltimore: Penguin, 1969).

22. See, e.g., Gisela Boch, "Racism and Sexism in Nazi Germany: Motherhood, Compulsory Sterilization, and the State," *Signs* 8, no. 3 (1983); Patricia Hill Collins, *Black Feminist Thought: Knowledge, Consciousness and the Politics of Empowerment* (Boston: Routledge, 1991); Bonnie Thornton Dill, "Race, Class, and Gender: Prospects for an All-Inclusive Sisterhood," *Feminist Studies* 9 (1983); Bell Hooks, *Feminist Theory: From Margin to Center* (Boston: South End Press, 1983); Elizabeth Spelman, *Inessential Woman: Problems of Exclusion in Feminist Thought* (Boston: Beacon Press, 1988); Maxine Baca Zinn et al., "The Costs of Exclusionary Practices in Women's Studies," *Signs* 11, no. 2 (1986).

23. See Peggy McIntosh, "White Privilege and Male Privilege: A Personal Account of Coming to See Correspondences through Work in Women's Studies," in *Race, Class, and Gender: An Anthology*, ed. Margaret L. Andersen and Patricia Hill Collins (Belmont, Calif.: Wadsworth, 1992).

24. E.g., see Ernesto Laclau and Chantal Mouffe, *Hegemony and Socialist Strategy: Towards a Radical Democratic Politics* (London: Verso, 1985).

25. Robert Proctor, "The Politics of Knowledge," chap. 10 of *Racial Hygiene: Medicine under the Nazis* (Cambridge, Mass.: Harvard University Press, 1988).

26. "Partially," because scientific traditions (themselves fully social and political) also contribute to identifying which problems will get defined as scientific ones.

27. Hilary Rose and Steven Rose, "The Incorporation of Science," in *Ideology of/in the Natural Sciences,* ed. Hilary and Steven Rose (Cambridge, Mass.: Schenkman, 1979).

28. See Merchant's discussion (cited in n. 11) of the meanings of organicism and mechanism in the early modern period in Europe; Donna Haraway's discussion (in this collection) of differences in the ways Anglo-American and Japanese primatology communities conceptualize nature; Lezek Kolakowski's description of the political and social values

carried by Copernican and Galilean astronomy in *The Alienation of Reason: A History of Positivist Thought,* trans. N. Guterman (Garden City, N.Y.: Anchor Books, 1969); and Linnaeus's classification of minerals with living matter in his *Systema Natura* (I thank Anne Fausto-Sterling for this last example).

29. See Forman (cited in n. 17).

30. As we saw, the National Academy of Sciences proposes that scientific method should be construed far more broadly than popularly imagined. It should be noted that its agenda is not mine; it is concerned to protect scientific property from devaluation due to reports of experimental fraud, plagiarism, patent stealing, and the like.

31. This is the argument of standpoint theories of knowledge that trace their intellectual history back to Hegel's reflection on how much more comprehensive and less distorted is the understanding of the master-slave relation from the perspective of the slave's activities than from the master's. For example, from the perspective of the slave's activities, one can see that the slave is a human agent, trying to escape the lash, dissembling and forcing a smile on her face to hide her bitterness and anger, and so forth. From the perspective of the master's activities, everything the slave does appears to flow from the slave's "nature" or the master's will. See Nancy Hartsock, "The Feminist Standpoint: Developing the Ground for a Specifically Feminist Historical Materialism," in Harding and Hintikka, *Discovering Reality,* (cited in n. 12); Dorothy Smith, *The Everyday World as Problematic: A Sociology for Women* (Boston: Northeastern University Press, 1987); and chap. 5 of my *Whose Science? Whose Knowledge? Thinking from Women's Lives* (Ithaca, N.Y.: Cornell University Press, 1991) for a discussion of this alternative epistemology.

32. Of course, the term *democracy* is itself a contested zone, with different groups struggling to restrict or expand its meanings and uses according to their own purposes. Dominant groups frequently like to insist on only a kind of caricature definition of democracy: science policy committees consisting of one scientist from each state, as one person sarcastically proposed to me. A stronger statement of democratic procedures would be the one mentioned earlier: that those who bear the consequences of decisions should have a proportionate share in making them. Also, the argument here is not that democratic decision making should substitute for sound scientific decisions but rather that in many respects the latter will improve by attempts to institute the former.

33. I have proposed a notion of "strong objectivity" and of "strong method" in *Whose Science? Whose Knowledge?* and in other essays. See also my *Science Question in Feminism* (Ithaca, N.Y.: Cornell University Press, 1986).

34. Cf. W. Van den Daele, "The Social Construction of Science," in *The Social Production of Scientific Knowledge,* ed. E. Mendelsohn, P. Weingart, and R. Whitley (Dordrecht: Reidel, 1977).

35. These dangerous outsiders are frequently gender coded feminine; the scientific "knower" is conceptualized as the model of the rational, power-indifferent, individual, male hero struggling to establish and maintain order against the unruly hordes driven by irrational passions and desires for power. See the discussions in Bordo, Jaggar, Keller, Lloyd and Merchant cited earlier (nn. 11 and 12).

PART ONE

Early Non-Western
Scientific Traditions

The discovery of primitiveness was an ambiguous invention of a history incapable of facing its own double.

> V. Y. Mudimbe, *The Invention of Africa*

It is true that in modern Western culture, the theoretical models propounded by the professional scientists do, to some extent, become the intellectual furnishings of a very large sector of the population. . . . But the layman's ground for accepting the models propounded by the scientists is often no different from the young African villager's ground for accepting the models propounded by one of his elders. In both cases the propounders are deferred to as the accredited agents of tradition. . . . For all the apparent up-to-dateness of the content of his world-view, the modern Western layman is rarely more "open" or scientific in his outlook than is the traditional African villager.

> Robin Horton, "African Traditional Thought and Western Science"

Resistance to the critique of Eurocentrism is always extreme, for we are here entering the realm of the taboo. The calling into question of the Eurocentric dimension of the dominant ideology is more difficult to accept even than a critical challenge to its economic dimension. For the critique of Eurocentrism directly calls into question the position of the comfortable classes of this world.

> Samir Amin, *Eurocentrism*

Columbus's attitude with regard to the Indians is based on his perception of them. We can distinguish here two component parts, which we shall find again in the following century and, in practice, down to our own day in every colonist in his relations to the colonized. . . . Either he conceives the Indians (though without using these words) as human beings altogether, having the same rights as himself; but then he sees them not only as equals but also as identical, and this behavior leads to assimilationism, the projection of his own values on the others. Or else he starts from the difference, but the latter is immediately translated into terms of superiority and inferiority (in his case, obviously, it is the Indians who are inferior). What is denied is the existence of a human substance truly other, something capable of being not merely an imperfect state of oneself. These two elementary figures of the experience of alterity are both grounded in egocentrism, in the identification of our own values with values in general, of our *I* with the universe—in the conviction that the world is one.

Tzvetan Todorov, *The Conquest of America*

Western histories of science conventionally have told the story of human scientific and technological achievements as one only about the modern West. They sometimes acknowledge that other peoples have produced technological achievements, such as the Egyptian pyramids, and that medieval Arabic mathematics was highly advanced. Little more needs to be said about non-Western scientific traditions, they assume. The roots of modern science are to be found in ancient Greece, they say, and modern science is uniquely an accomplishment of the modern West. In fact, according to its enthusiasts, it is *the* most distinguished of the West's many distinguished contributions to human progress: "who could deny that Newton's achievement is evidence that pure science exemplifies the creative accomplishment of the human spirit at its pinnacle?"[1] This kind of Western chauvinism has been used by generations of Western observers of non-Western peoples to claim that it is the ability to produce scientific thought that distinguishes the modern West from what they see as these barbarian, primitive, or underdeveloped cultures.

Without diminishing the brilliance or importance of modern Western science, a reevaluation has been emerging recently of the causes of its development, of its parallels and contrasts with independently valuable scientific traditions of other societies, of its debts to them, and of the adequacy of the common assumption that this Western science contributed only to "human progress" and not also at least equally to the de-development, the regress, of the Third World as well as of certain groups in the West. The three selections included in this section focus not only on the scientific traditions of three non-Western cultures but also on three Eurocentric strategies for devaluing them: deny that these achievements are really science; rewrite the history of the origins of European "civilization" to make it self-generating; and, through conquest, appropriate others' knowledge, recycle it as Western, and suppress knowledge of its origins.

In the 1950s Joseph Needham, a British scientist, began to publish accounts of the sciences and technologies of the Chinese high cultures and of the importance to the development of European sciences of the discoveries and inventions that Europeans borrowed from China but rarely acknowledged. In the essay here, he contrasts the "poverties and triumphs" of Chinese science with Western sciences and shows what's wrong with leading Western histories of science that are obsessed with establishing the uniqueness of Western sciences at the expense of the empirical and theoretical adequacy of their accounts.

The second selection is from Martin Bernal's *Black Athena: The Afroasiatic*

Roots of Classical Civilization. In the first of a projected three-volume study, Bernal focuses on what he calls the fabrication of ancient Greece between 1785 and 1985. He argues in the chapters reprinted here that it is no accident that "the Aryan model" of the origins of Greek civilization—the model "which most of us have been brought up to believe"—was developed to replace "the ancient model" in the early nineteenth century. Counter to the views held in the ancient world itself and on up until the late eighteenth century, the Aryan model introduced the idea that Africans and Semites had nothing to do with the creation of the classical Greek civilization, which modern European science claimed as its origin.[2] "For eighteenth- and nineteenth-century Romantics and racists," Bernal writes, "it was simply intolerable for Greece, which was seen not merely as the epitome of Europe but also as its pure childhood, to have been the result of the mixture of native Europeans and colonizing Africans and Semites. Therefore the Ancient Model had to be overthrown and replaced by something more acceptable." Moreover, the selection notes that for complex reasons Newton and Boyle were involved in creating and disseminating this revisionist history of the origins of modern European civilization. Thus the spread of Newtonian science also disseminated the Aryan model.

The discourse Bernal sets out to undermine had been contested by African and African American writers since the nineteenth century. This earlier and ongoing resistance to the Aryan model has largely been ignored by white Western scholars. Moreover, it is important to note that it is only through the work of Muslim scholars from Spain, the Middle East, and North Africa in the Middle Ages that the classical Greek tradition was transmitted to modern Europe. Finally, we need to question the notion of "civilization," with its insistent division of cultures into advanced and backward ones, that still is the focus of this important analysis. If we problematize that notion, we can gain a more balanced understanding of the outstanding accomplishments of simpler societies and a more objective grasp of the limitations of complex ones.[3]

Anthropologist Jack Weatherford reports on the immense improvement of the nutrition of Europe and many other parts of the world made possible by the agricultural experiments of the ancient Peruvians, and especially by their development of over three thousand varieties of potatoes that would grow under different ecological conditions. Eurocentric historians fail to describe the process that Weatherford reveals by which European conquests of the Americas appropriated the scientific and technological knowledge of the indigenous peoples and recycled it back through European and U.S. sciences, suppressing awareness of its sources in the Americas.

These and other histories have made it perfectly clear that the peoples responsible for modern science have come from many parts of the world; "the West" has always been a multicultural creation. So-called European sciences have incorporated and learned from many of these earlier traditions. As historian Eric R. Wolf observes, "the world of humankind constitutes a manifold, a totality of interconnected processes, and inquiries that disassemble this totality into bits and then fail to reassemble it falsify reality."[4] Furthermore, those scientific traditions that never left their traces in modern Western science are nevertheless interesting and important parts of the history of world sciences. As Tzvetan Todorov points out in the epigraph opening this section, it is time for Westerners to give up the egocentrism that propels us to obliterate the human other.

Moreover, the advance of European sciences and, in many cases, the decline of Third World scientific traditions have been caused in large part by European military, economic, and political conquests.[5] In Eurocentric histories these events are presented as the highest achievements of Europe's "civilizing" mission. In this scheme, the sciences and technologies of non-Western societies must be conceptualized as primitive in order to demonstrate the progress and success of the West. The authors in this section challenge this story.

Is Western science the only modern science possible and desirable? Do not modern Westerners define science—"real science"—too narrowly, as Needham argues, thereby devaluing forms of scientific thought and activity simply because they were or are not the forms favored in the sciences most useful to dominant groups in the modern West? What contributions do these older scientific traditions promise for the contemporary world? As some of the essays in section VI argue, perhaps we should think of these other sciences as providing diversity in the pool of scientific thought from which innovative, adaptable, and sturdy sciences can be developed for less war-loving and greedy societies of the future.

N O T E S

1. I. B. Cohen, *The Birth of a New Physics* (New York: Doubleday, 1960), 189–90.

2. Afroasiatic elements were introduced a second time into early modern European science when Bruno and others drew on ancient Egyptian concepts and themes. In a later chapter Bernal goes on to point out that the peoples living in what is now Egypt looked far more "African" and less Semitic in the past than they do today.

3. E. Frances White makes these points in her review of Bernal's book, "Civilization Denied: Questions on *Black Athena*," in *Radical America*, vol. 21, no. 5 (1987), 38–40. For important discussions by scholars of African descent of the origins of Greek culture, see Cheikh Anta Diop, *The African Origin of Civilization: Myth or Reality?*, trans. M. Cook (Westport, Conn.: L. Hill, 1974); George G. M. James, *Stolen Legacy* (New York: Philosophical Library, 1954); and Yosef Ben Jochannan, *Black Man of the Nile, Africa, Africa the Mother of Civilization* (New York: Alkebu Lan Books, 1971). For guides to Islamic scientific achievements, see, e.g., I. A. Sabra, "The Scientific Enterprise," in B. Lewis, ed. *The World of Islam* (London: 1976); George Sarton, *Introduction to the History of Science*, 3 vols. (Baltimore: Johns Hopkins University Press, 1927–48); the *MAAS Journal of Islamic Science*; and the *Journal of Arabic Science and Philosophy*. Reports of early African scientific and technological achievements can be found in *The Journal of African Civilizations*. See Lacinay Keita, "African Philosophical Systems: A Rational Reconstruction," *Philosophical Forum 9*, nos. 2–3 (1977–78), for an account of the intellectual interactions between Asia, Africa, and Europe from the classical Greek thinkers through the European Renaissance that have made what peoples of European descent think of as Western thought in fact truly multicultural. In "Blaspheming Like Brute Beasts: Multiculturalism in Historical Per-

spective," *Contention*, vol. 1, no. 3 (Spring 1992), A. E. Barnes provides an illuminating account of the importance and long history of multiculturalism in Europe.

4. Eric R. Wolf, *Europe and the People without History* (Berkeley: University of California Press, 1982), 3. Evelynn Hammonds's comments greatly improved my thinking in this introduction.

5. See the papers in Patrick Pettijean, Catherine Jami, and Anne Marie Moulin, eds., *Science and Empires: Historical Studies about Scientific Development and European Expansion* (Dordrecht: Kluwer, 1992) in addition to many of the sources cited in the editor's introduction.

POVERTIES AND TRIUMPHS OF THE CHINESE SCIENTIFIC TRADITION

Joseph Needham

The historical civilization of China is, with the Indian and the European-Semitic, one of the three greatest in the world, yet only in recent years has any enquiry been begun into its contributions to science and technology. Apart from the great ideas and systems of the Greeks, between the first and the fifteenth centuries the Chinese, who experienced no "dark ages," were generally much in advance of Europe; and not until the scientific revolution of the late Renaissance did Europe draw rapidly ahead. Before that time, however, the West had been profoundly affected not only in its technical processes but in its very social structures and changes by discoveries and inventions emanating from China and East Asia. Not only the three which Lord Bacon listed (printing, gunpowder and the magnetic compass) but a hundred others—mechanical clockwork, the casting of iron, stirrups and efficient horse-harness, the Cardan suspension and the Pascal triangle, segmental-arch bridges and pound-locks on canals, the stern-post rudder, fore-and-aft sailing, quantitative cartography—all had their effects, sometimes earth-shaking effects, upon a Europe more socially unstable.

Why, then, did modern science, as opposed to ancient and medieval science (with all that modern science implied in terms of political dominance), develop only in the Western world? Nothing but a careful analysis, a veritable titration, of the cultures of East and West will eventually answer this question. Doubtless many factors of an intellectual and philosophical character played their part, but there were certainly also important social and economic causes which demand investigation.

· · ·

In what follows an attempt will be made to describe some of the elements of strength and weakness in the growth and development of the indigenous Chinese tradition of science and invention, in contrast with that of Europe.

· · ·

Both East and West had strengths and weaknesses now well discernible as we look back along the course which man's knowledge of nature and control of nature took in the diverse regions of the Old World.

• • •

First of all it is essential to define the differences between ancient and medieval science on the one hand, and modern science on the other. I make an important distinction between the two. When we say that modern science developed only in Western Europe at the time of Galileo in the late Renaissance, we mean surely that there and then alone there developed the fundamental bases of the structure of the natural sciences as we have them today, namely the application of mathematical hypotheses to Nature, the full understanding and use of the experimental method, the distinction between primary and secondary qualities, the geometrisation of space, and the acceptance of the mechanical model of reality. Hypotheses of primitive or medieval type distinguish themselves quite clearly from those of modern type. Their intrinsic and essential vagueness always made them incapable of proof or disproof, and they were prone to combine in fanciful systems of gnostic correlation. In so far as numerical figures entered into them, numbers were manipulated in forms of "numerology" or number-mysticism constructed *a priori*, not employed as the stuff of quantitative measurements compared *a postiori*. We know the primitive and medieval Western scientific theories, the four Aristotelian elements, the four Galenical humours, the doctrines of pneumatic physiology and pathology, the sympathies and antipathies of Alexandrian proto-chemistry, the *tria prima* of the alchemists, and the natural philosophies of the Kabbala. We tend to know less well the corresponding theories of other civilizations, for instance the Chinese theory of the two fundamental forces Yin and Yang, or that of the five elements, or the elaborate system of the symbolic correlations. In the West Leonardo da Vinci, with all his brilliant inventive genius, still inhabited this world; Galileo broke through its walls. This is why it has been said that Chinese science and technology remained until late times essentially Vincian, and that the Galilean break-through occurred only in the West. That is the first of our starting-points.

Until it had been universalized by its fusion with mathematics, natural science could not be the common property of all mankind. The sciences of the medieval world were tied closely to the ethnic environments in which they had arisen, and it was very difficult, if not impossible, for the people of those different cultures to find any common basis of discourse. That did not mean that inventions of profound sociological importance could not diffuse freely from one civilization to another—mostly in fact from east to west. But the mutual incomprehensibility of the ethnically-bound concept systems did severely restrict possible contacts and transmissions in the realm of scientific ideas. This is why technological elements spread widely through the length and breadth of the Old World, while scientific elements for the most part failed to do so.

Nevertheless the different civilizations did have scientific interchanges of great importance. It is surely quite clear by now that in the history of science and technology the Old World must be thought of as a whole. Even Africa may have been within its circuit. But when this oecumenical view is taken, a great paradox presents itself. Why did modern science, the mathematization of hypotheses about Nature, with all its implications for advanced technology, take its meteoric rise *only* in the West at the time of Galileo? This is the most obvious question which many have asked but few have answered. Yet there is another which is of quite equal importance. Why was it that between the second century B.C. and the sixteenth century A.D. East Asian culture was much *more* efficient than the European West in applying human knowledge of Nature to useful purposes? Only an analysis of the social and economic structures of Eastern and Western cultures, not forgetting the great role of systems of ideas, will in the end suggest an explanation of both these things.

The Face of Science and Technology in Traditional China

Before the river of Chinese science flowed, like all other such rivers, into this sea of modern science, there had been remarkable achievements in mathematics. Decimal place-value and a blank space for the zero had begun in the land of the Yellow River earlier than anywhere else, and decimal metrology had gone along with it. By the first century B.C. Chinese artisans were checking their work with sliding calipers decimally graduated. Chinese mathematical thought was always profoundly algebraic, not geometrical, and in the Sung and the Yuan (twelfth to fourteenth centuries A.D.) the Chinese school led the world in the solution of equations, so that the triangle called by Pascal's name was already old in China in A.D. 1300. We often find examples of this sort; the system of linked and pivoted rings which we know as the Cardan suspension was commonly used in China a thousand years before Cardan's time. As for astronomy, I need only say that the Chinese were the most persistent and accurate observers of celestial phenomena anywhere before the Renaissance. Although geometrical planetary theory did not develop among them they conceived an enlightened cosmology, mapped the heavens using our modern co-ordinates, and kept records of eclipses, comets, novae and meteors still useful, for example to the radio-astronomers, today. A brilliant development of astronomical instruments also occurred, including the invention of the equatorial mounting and the clock-drive; and this development was in close dependence upon the contemporary capabilities of the Chinese engineers. Their skill affected also other sciences such as seismology, for it was a Chinese man of science, Chang Hêng, who built the first practical seismograph about A.D. 130.

Three branches of physics were particularly well developed in ancient and medieval China—optics, acoustics and magnetism. This was in striking contrast with the West where mechanics and dynamics were relatively advanced but magnetic phenomena almost unknown. Yet China and Europe differed most profoundly perhaps in the great debate between continuity and discontinuity, for just as Chinese mathematics was always algebraic rather than geometrical, so

Chinese physics was faithful to a prototypic wave theory and perennially averse to atoms. One can even trace such contrasts in preferences in the field of engineering, for whenever an engineer in classical China could mount a wheel horizontally he would do so, while our forefathers preferred vertical mountings— water-mills and wind-mills are typical examples.

A pattern which we very often find in comparing China's achievements with those of Europe is that while the Chinese of the Chou, Chhin and Han, contemporary with the Greeks, did not rise to such heights as they, nevertheless in later centuries there was nothing in China which corresponded to the period of the Dark Ages in Europe. This shows itself rather markedly in the sciences of geography and cartography. Although the Chinese knew of discoidal cosmographic world-maps, they were never dominated by them. Quantitative cartography began in China with Chang Hêng and Phei Hsiu about the time when Ptolemy's work was falling into oblivion, indeed soon after his death, but it continued steadily with a consistent use of the rectangular grid right down to the coming of the Jesuits in the seventeenth century A.D. The Chinese were also very early in the field with advanced survey methods and the making of relief maps. In the geological sciences and in meteorology the same pattern presents itself.

Mechanical engineering and indeed engineering in general was a field in which classical Chinese culture scored special triumphs. Both the forms of efficient harness for equine animals—a problem of linkwork—originated in the Chinese culture-area, and there also water-power was first used for industry about the same time as in the West (first century A.D.); not, however, so much for grinding cereals as for the operation of metallurgical bellows. The development of iron and steel technology in China constitutes a veritable epic, with the mastery of iron-casting some fifteen centuries before its achievement in Europe. Contrary to the usual ideas, mechanical clockwork began not in early Renaissance Europe but in Thang China, in spite of the highly agrarian character of East Asian civilization. Civil engineering also shows many extraordinary achievements, notably iron-chain suspension bridges and the first of all segmental arch structures, the magnificent bridge built by Li Chhun in A.D. 610. Hydraulic engineering was always prominent in China on account of the necessity of control of waterways for river conservation (defence against flood and drought), irrigation, and tax-grain transport.

In martial technology the Chinese also showed notable inventiveness. The first appearance of gunpowder occurs among them in the ninth century A.D., and from A.D. 1000 onwards there was a vigorous development of explosive weapons some three centuries before they appeared in Europe. Probably the key invention was that of the fire-lance at the beginning of the twelfth century A.D., in which a rocket composition enclosed in a bamboo tube was used as a close-combat weapon. From this derived, I have little doubt, all subsequent barrel guns and cannon of whatever material constructed. Other aspects of technology also have their importance, especially that of silk in which the Chinese excelled so early. Here the mastery of a textile fibre of extremely long staple appears to have led to the first development of technical devices so important as the driving-belt and the chain-drive. It is also possible to show that the first appearance of the standard method of converting rotary to longitudinal motion is found in connexion with later forms of the metallurgical blowing-engine referred to above. I must pass over other well-known inventions such as the development of paper, block-printing and movable-type printing, or the astonishing story of porcelain.

There was no backwardness in the biological fields, either, and here we find many agricultural inventions arising from an early time. As in other subjects, we have texts which parallel those of the Romans such as Varro and Columella from a similar period. If space permitted, one could take examples from plant protection which would include the earliest known use of the biological control of insect pests. Medicine is a field which aroused the interests of the Chinese in all ages, and which was developed by their special genius along lines perhaps more different from those of Europe than in any other case. I think that I can do no more here than refer simply to one remarkable fact, namely that the Chinese were free from the prejudice against mineral remedies which was so striking in the West; they needed no Paracelsus to awaken them from their Galenical slumbers for in these they had never participated. They were also the greatest pioneers of the techniques of inoculation.

Contrasts between China and the West

Let us come now to the further examination of some of the great contrasts to which I have already referred. In the first place it can be shown in great detail that the *philosophia perennis* of China was an organic materialism. This can be illustrated from the pronouncements of philosophers and scientific thinkers of every epoch. The mechanical view of the world simply did not develop in Chinese thought, and the organicist view in which every phenomenon was connected with every other according to hierarchical order was universal among Chinese thinkers. Nevertheless this did not prevent the appearance of great scientific inventions such as the seismograph, to which we have already referred. In some respects this philosophy of Nature may even have helped. It was not so strange or surprising that the lodestone should point to the pole if one was already convinced that there was an organic pattern in the cosmos. If, as is truly the case, the Chinese were worrying about the magnetic declination before Europeans even knew of the polarity, that was perhaps because they were untroubled by the idea that for action to occur it was necessary for one discrete object to have an impact upon another; in other words, they were inclined *a priori* to field theories, and this predilection may very well also account for the fact that they arrived so early at a correct conception of the cause of sea tides. One may find remarkable statements, as early as the San Kuo period, of action at a distance taking place without any physical contact across vast distances of space.

Again, as we have said, Chinese mathematical thought and practice was invariably algebraic, not geometrical. No Euclidean geometry spontaneously developed among them, and this was doubtless inhibitory for the advances they were able to make in optics, where however, incidentally, they were never handicapped by the rather absurd Greek idea that rays were sent forth by the eye. Euclidean geometry was probably brought to China in the Yuan (Mongol) period but did not take root until the arrival of the Jesuits. Nevertheless all this did not prevent the successful realization of great engineering inventions—we have mentioned two already, the most useful method of interconversion of rotary and rectilinear motion by means of eccentric, connecting-rod and piston-rod; and the successful achievement of the oldest form of mechanical clock. What this involved was the invention of an escapement, namely a mechanical means of slowing down the revolution of a set of wheels so that it would keep time with humanity's primary clock, the apparent diurnal revolution of the heavens. In this connexion it is interesting to find that Chinese practice was not, as might at first sight be supposed, purely empirical. The successful erection of the great clock-tower of Su Sung at Khaifêng in A.D. 1088 was preceded by the elaboration of a special theoretical treatise by his assistant Han Kung-Lien, which worked out the trains of gears and general mechanism from first principles. Something of the same kind had been done on the occasion of the first invention of this kind of clock by I-Hsing and Liang Ling-Tsan early in the eighth century A.D., six centuries before the first European mechanical clocks with their verge-and-foliot escapements. Moreover, though China had no Euclid, that did not prevent the Chinese from developing and consistently employing the astronomical coordinates which have completely conquered modern astronomy and are universally used today, nor did it prevent their consequent elaboration of the equatorial mounting, although there was nothing but a sighting-tube, and as yet no telescope, to put in it.

Thirdly, there is the wave-particle antithesis. The prototypic wave theory with which the Chinese concerned themselves from the Chhin and Han onwards was connected with the eternal rise and fall of the two basic natural principles, the Yang and Yin. From the second century A.D. onwards atomistic theories were introduced to China time after time, especially by means of the Buddhist contacts with India, but they never took any root in Chinese scientific culture. All the same this lack of particulate theory did not prevent the Chinese from curious achievements such as the recognition of the hexagonal system of snowflake crystals many centuries before this was noticed in the West. Nor did it hinder them from helping to lay the foundation of knowledge of chemical affinity, as was done in some of the alchemical tractates of the Thang, Sung and Yuan. There the absence of particulate conceptions was probably less inhibitory than it otherwise might have been, because it was only after all in the post-Renaissance period in Europe that these theories became so fundamental for the rise of modern chemistry.

I should not want to disagree altogether with the idea that the Chinese were a fundamentally practical people, inclined to distrust all theories. One must beware, however, of carrying this too far, because the Neo-Confucian school in the eleventh, twelfth and thirteenth centuries A.D. achieved a wonderful philosophical synthesis strangely parallel in time with the scholastic synthesis of Europe. One might also say that the disinclination of the Chinese to engage in theory, especially geometrical theory, brought advantages with it. For example, Chinese astronomers did not reason about the heavens like Eudoxus or Ptolemy but they did avoid the conception of crystalline celestial spheres which dominated medieval Europe. By a strange paradox, when Matteo Ricci came to China at the end of the sixteenth century A.D. he mentioned in one of his letters a number of the foolish ideas entertained by the Chinese, among which prominently figured the fact that "they do not believe in crystalline celestial spheres"; it was not long before the Europeans did not either. Moreover, this fundamental practicality did not imply an easily satisfied mind. Very careful experimentation was practised in classical Chinese culture. For example the discovery of magnetic declination would not have occurred unless the geomancers had been attending most carefully to the positions of their needles, and the triumphs of the ceramics industry could never have been achieved without fairly accurate temperature measurement and the means of repetition at will of oxidizing or reducing conditions within the kilns. The fact that relatively little written material concerning these technical details has come down to us springs from social factors which prevented the publication of the records which the higher artisans certainly kept. Enough remains, either by title, like the *Mu Ching* (Timberwork Manual) which we shall speak of again, or in MS. form, like the Fukien shipwrights' manual, to show that this literature existed.

The Old World Origins of the New Science

Now I should like to return to the question raised at the beginning, and go a little further into the distinction between modern science on the one hand, and ancient and medieval science on the other. I shall thus have to deal somewhat more fully with certain points that have already been touched upon. As the contributions of the Asian civilizations are progressively uncovered by research, an opposing tendency seeks to preserve European uniqueness by exalting unduly the role of the Greeks and claiming that not only modern science, but science as such, was characteristic of Europe, and of Europe only, from the very beginning. For these thinkers the application of Euclidean deductive geometry to the explanation of planetary motion in the Ptolemaic system constituted already the marrow of science, which the Renaissance did no more than propagate. The counterpart of this is a determined effort to show that all scientific developments in non-European civilizations were really nothing but technology.

For example, our most learned medievalist has recently written:

> Impressive as are the technological achievements of ancient Babylonia, Assyria, and Egypt, of ancient China and India, as scholars have presented them to us they lack the essential elements of science, the generalized conceptions of sci-

entific explanation and of mathematical proof. It seems to me that it was the Greeks who invented natural science as we know it, by their assumption of a permanent, uniform, abstract order and laws by means of which the regular changes observed in the world could be explained by deduction, and by their brilliant idea of the generalized use of scientific theory tailored according to the principles of non-contradiction and the empirical test. It is this essential Greek idea of scientific explanation, "Euclidean" in logical form, that has introduced the main problems of scientific method and philosophy of science with which the Western scientific tradition has been concerned.[1]

Again in a recent interesting and stimulating survey entitled *Science since Babylon* we read:

> What is the origin of the peculiarly scientific basis of our own high civilization? . . . Of all limited areas, by far the most highly developed, most recognizably modern, yet most continuous province of scientific learning, was mathematical astronomy. This is the mainstream that leads through the work of Galileo and Kepler, through the gravitation theory of Newton, directly to the labours of Einstein and all mathematical physicists past and present. In comparison, all other parts of modern science appear derivative or subsequent; either they drew their inspiration directly from the successful sufficiency of mathematical and logical explanation for astronomy, or they developed later, probably as a result of such inspiration in adjacent subjects. . . . Our civilization has produced not merely a high intellectual grasp of science but also a high scientific technology. By this is meant something distinct from the background noise of the low technology that all civilizations and societies have evolved as part of their daily life. The various crafts of the primitive industrial chemists, of the metallurgists, of the medical men, of the agriculturists—all these might become highly developed without presaging a scientific or industrial revolution such as we have experienced in the past three or four centuries.[2]

Even the distinguished and enlightened author of *Science in History* writes (in correspondence):

> The chief weakness of Chinese science lay precisely in the field which most interested them, namely astronomy, because they never developed the Greek geometry, and perhaps even more important, the Greek geometrical way of seeing things which provided the Renaissance with its main intellectual weapon for the breakthrough. Instead they had only the extremely precise recurrence methods deriving from Babylonian astronomy, and these, on account of their exactitude, gave them a fictitious feeling of understanding astronomical phenomena.[3]

Finally the author of a noted book, *The Edge of Objectivity*, says:

> Albert Einstein once remarked that there is no difficulty in understanding why China or India did not create science. The problem is rather why Europe did, for science is a most arduous and unlikely undertaking. The answer lies in

Greece. Ultimately science derives from the legacy of Greek philosophy. The Egyptians, it is true, developed surveying techniques and conducted certain surgical operations with notable finesse. The Babylonians disposed of numerical devices of great ingenuity for predicting the patterns of the planets. But no Oriental civilization graduated beyond technique or thaumaturgy to curiosity about things in general. Of all the triumphs of the speculative genius of Greece, the most unexpected, the most truly novel, was precisely its rational conception of the cosmos as an orderly whole working by laws discoverable in thought. . . . [4]

The statement of Einstein here referred to is contained in a now famous letter which he sent to J. E. Switzer of San Mateo, California, in 1953. It runs:

> Dear Sir,
>   The development of Western science has been based on two great achievements, the invention of the formal logical system (in Euclidean geometry) by the Greek philosophers, and the discovery of the possibility of finding out causal relationships by systematic experiment (at the Renaissance). In my opinion one need not be astonished that the Chinese sages did not make these steps. The astonishing thing is that these discoveries were made at all.
>
> Sincerely yours,
Albert Einstein.

It is very regrettable that this Shavian epistle with all its lightness of touch is now being pressed into service to belittle the scientific achievements of the non-European civilizations. Einstein himself would have been the first to admit that he knew almost nothing concrete about the development of the sciences in the Chinese, Sanskrit and Arabic cultures except that *modern* science did not develop in them, and his great reputation should not be brought forward as a witness in this court. I find myself in complete disagreement with all these valuations and it is necessary to explain briefly why.

First, these definitions of mathematics are far too narrow. It would of course be impossible to deny that one of the most fundamental elements in Galileo's thinking was the geometrical study of kinematic problems. Again and again he praises the power of geometry as opposed to "logic." And geometry remained the primary tool for studying the problems of physical motion down to the early nineteenth century. But vast though the significance of deductive geometry was, its proofs never exhausted the power of the mathematical art. Although we speak of the Hindu-Arabic numerals, the Chinese were in fact the first, as early as the fourteenth century B.C., to be able to express any desired number, however large, with no more than nine signs. Chinese mathematics, developing the earlier Babylonian tradition, was always, as I have already said, overwhelmingly arithmetical and algebraical, generating such concepts and devices as those of decimal place-value, decimal fractions and decimal metrology, negative numbers, indeterminate analysis, the method of finite differences, and the solution of higher numerical equations. Very accurate values of π were early computed. The Han mathematicians anticipated Horner's method for obtaining the roots of higher powers. The triangle of binomial coefficients, as we have seen, was already considered old in the *Ssu Yuan Yü Chien* of A.D. 1303. Indeed in the thirteenth and fourteenth centuries A.D. the Chinese algebraists were in the forefront of advance as their Arabic counterparts had been in previous centuries, and so also the Indian mathematicians when they originated trigonometry (as we know it) nearly a thousand years earlier. To say that whatever algebra was needed by Vieta and by Newton they could easily have invented themselves may be uncritical genius-worship, but it is worse, it is unhistorical, for the influence of Asian ways of computation on European mathematicians of the later Middle Ages and the Renaissance is well established. And when the transmissions are examined the balance shows that between 250 B.C. and A.D. 1250, in spite of all China's isolations and inhibitions, a great deal more mathematical influence came out of that culture than went in.

Moreover the astronomical application of Euclidean geometry in the Ptolemaic system was not all pure gain. Apart from the fact (which some of these writers unaccountably seem to forget) that the resulting synthesis was in fact objectively wrong, it ushered the Western medieval world into the prison of the solid crystalline celestial spheres—a cosmology incomparably more naïve and *borné* than the infinite empty spaces of the Chinese *hun-thien* school or the relativistic Buddhist philosophers. It is in fact important to realize that Chinese thought on the world and its history was over and over again more boldly imaginative than that of Europe. The basic principles of Huttonian geology were stated by Shen Kua in the late eleventh century A.D., but this was only a counterpart of a Plutonian theme recurring since the fourth century A.D., that of the *sang thien* or mountains which had once been at the bottom of the sea. Indeed the idea of an evolutionary process, involving social as well as biological change, was commonly entertained by Chinese philosophers and scientifically interested scholars, even though sometimes thought of in terms of a succession of world renewals following the catastrophes and dissolutions assumed in the recurrent *mahākalpas* of Indian speculation. One can see a striking echo of this open-mindedness in the calculations made by I-Hsing about A.D. 724 concerning the date of the last general conjunction. He made it come out to 96,961,740 years before—rather a different scale from "4004 B.C. at six o'clock in the evening."

Thirdly, the implied definitions of science are also much too narrow. It is true that mechanics was the pioneer among the modern sciences, the "mechanistic" paradigm which all the other sciences sought to imitate, and emphasis on Greek deductive geometry as its base is so far justifiable. But that is not the same thing as saying that geometrical kinematics is all that science is. Modern science itself has not remained within these Cartesian bounds, for field theory in physics and organic conceptions in biology have deeply modified the earlier mechanistic world-picture. Here knowledge of magnetic phenomena was all-important, and this was a typically Chinese gift to Europe. Although we do not know the way-stations through which it came, its priority of time is such as to place the burden of proof on those who would wish to believe in an independent discovery. The fact is that science has many aspects other than geometrical theorizing. To begin with, it is nonsense to say that the assumption of a permanent, uniform, abstract order and laws by means of which the regular changes in the world could be explained, was a purely Greek invention. The order of Nature was for the ancient Chinese the *Tao*, and as a *chhang Tao* it was an "unvarying Way." "Every natural phenomenon," says the fourth-century B.C. *Chi Ni Tzu* book, "the product of Yin and Yang, has its fixed compositions and motions with regard to other things in the network of Nature's relationships." "Look at things," wrote Shao Yung in the eleventh century A.D., "from the point of view of things, and you will see their true nature; look at things from your own point of view, and you will see only your own feelings; for nature is neutral and clear, while feelings are prejudiced and dark." The organic pattern in Nature was for the medieval Chinese the *Li*, and it was mirrored in every subordinate whole as one or another *wu li* of particular things and processes. Since the thought of the Chinese was in all ages profoundly organic and impersonal they did not envisage laws of a celestial law-giver—but nor did the Greeks, for it is easily possible to show that the full conception of Laws of Nature attained definitive status only at the Renaissance.

What the Chinese did do was to classify natural phenomena, to develop scientific instruments of great refinement for their respective ages, to observe and record with a persistence hardly paralleled elsewhere, and if they failed (like all medieval men, Europeans included) to apply hypotheses of modern type, they experimented century after century obtaining results which they could repeat at will. When one recites this list of the forms of scientific activity it becomes difficult to see how anyone could deny them their status as essential components of fully developed world science, biological and chemical as well as astronomical and physical, if it was not in the interest of some instinctive *parti pris*.

Elaborating, *kho hsüeh*, the traditional and current Chinese term for science, means "classification knowledge." The first star catalogues, probably pre-Hipparchan, open its story in China. It is then exemplified in the long series of rational pharmacopœias which begins with the second-century B.C. *Shen Nung Pên Tshao*. It helped to lay the basis of our knowledge of chemical affinity in the theories of polarities (*i*) and categories (*lei*) found in treatises such as the fifth-century A.D. *Tshan Thung Chhi Wu Hsiang Lei Pi Yao*. If systematic classifications of parhelic phenomena in the heavens (*Chin Shu*), and of the diseases of men and animals on earth (*Chu Shih Ping Yuan*), were worked out a full thousand years before Scheiner and Sydenham, this was only the expression of the firm hold which the Chinese had on this basic form of scientific activity. Perhaps the view of science which I am criticizing rests partially on too great a preoccupation with astronomy, and too little with biology, mineralogy and chemistry.

Then as to apparatus. That the Hellenistic Greeks were capable of producing highly complicated scientific instruments is shown by the anti-Kythera computing machine, but this is a very rare, indeed a unique example. It would be fairer to admit that throughout the first fifteen centuries of our era Chinese instrument-making was generally ahead, and (as in such instances as the seismograph and the mechanical clock) often much ahead, of anything that Europe could show.

Actually the invention of clockwork was directly connected with the very absence of planetary models in Chinese thinking, for while on ecliptic co-ordinates no real body ever moves, declination circles are tracks of true motion, and the equatorial-polar system was a direct invitation to construct planetaria mechanically rotated. So, too, modern positional astronomy employs not the ecliptic co-ordinates of the Greeks but the equatorial ones of the Chinese. Nor need we confine ourselves to the astronomical sciences here, for a wealth of advanced techniques is to be found in those alchemical treatises of which the *Tao Tsang* is full.

Surely, again, observation, accurate and untiring, is one of the foundation-stones of science. What records from an antique culture are of vital interest to radio-astronomers today? Nothing from Greece, only the nova, comet and meteor lists of China's star-clerks. They it was who first established (by the seventh century A.D. at least) the constant rule (*chhang tsê*) that the tails of comets point away from the sun. Renaissance astronomers who quarrelled so much among themselves about the priority of the study of sun-spots might have been somewhat abashed if they had known that these had been observed since the first century B.C. in China, and not only observed but recorded in documents reliably handed down. When Kepler penned his New Year letter on the hexagonal form of snowflake crystals in A.D. 1611 he did not know that his contemporary Hsieh Tsai-Hang was puzzling over just the same thing, not, however, as a new idea but as a fact which had been known and discussed since the original discovery reported by Han Ying in the second century B.C. When we look for the original root of the cloud-seeding process in the comparison of snow-flake crystals with those of various salts and minerals, we find it not in the eighteenth-century A.D. experiments of Wilcke but in the acute observation of Chu Hsi in the twelfth century A.D. Thus it will surely be apparent that if God could geometrize so could the Tao, and the Europeans were not the only men who could trace its operations in forms both living and non-living. Finally if an example is needed from the biological sciences, let us remember the brilliant empirical discovery of deficiency diseases clearly stated by the physician Hu Ssu-Hui in the fourteenth century A.D.

Degree of accuracy in observation is also relevant. Indeed it is a vital feature, for it springs from that preoccupation with quantitative measurement which is one of the most essential hallmarks of true science. The old astronomical lists gave stellar positions in measured degrees, of course, the hydraulic engineers were recording precisely the silt-content of rivers in the first century B.C., and the pharmacists early developed their systems of dosages, but another example, less known, is more striking. Of the dial-and-pointer readings which make up so much of modern science, a search throughout the medieval world between the eighth and the fourteenth centuries A.D. would reveal instruments capable of giving them only in China. I refer to the needles of the magnetic compasses used first by geomancers, then (at least a century before Europe) by the sea-captains. Now it is a remarkable fact (as we have seen) that the Chinese were worrying about the cause of magnetic declination for a considerable time before Europeans knew even of magnetic directivity. Indeed the geomantic compass in its final form embodies two additional rings of points, one staggered 7½° east and the other 7½° west—these represent the remains of observations of declination, eastwards before about A.D. 1000 and westwards thereafter. We have reason to believe that this disturbing discovery was first made some time in the ninth or tenth centuries A.D., and it could never have been made if the observers had not been marking with extraordinary accuracy—and honesty—the "true path" of the needle. It is even legitimate to compare this feat in principle with the discovery of the inert or noble gases so long afterwards by Rayleigh and Ramsay, residual bubbles which others had put down to experimental error or simply neglected. The honesty deserves emphasis also, for it was not shown so clearly when Europeans came up against the same phenomenon four or five centuries later. Or one might say that they had a greater tolerance of error, being content with "there or thereabouts." The history of magnetic declination in the West has been obscured by the fact that the compass-makers "fiddled" the instrument by fixing a card askew to make it read right, and little or nothing was written about the matter till the sixteenth century A.D. Similarly, Robert Norman used to "fiddle" his compasses to make the needles lie horizontally, until one day he lost his temper and really looked into the trouble, so rediscovering "dip" or inclination.

Perhaps the greatest objection to the attempt of the Hellenizers to save European superiority is the fact that the Greeks were not really experimenters. Controlled experimentation is surely the greatest methodological discovery of the scientific revolution of the Renaissance, and it has never been convincingly shown that any earlier group of Westerners fully understood it. I do not propose to claim this honour for the medieval Chinese either, but they came just as near it theoretically, and in practice often went beyond European achievements. Although the ceramics technologists of China undoubtedly paid great attention to their temperatures and to the oxidizing-reducing atmospheres of their kilns, I shall not return to this here, for the Hellenizers would no doubt include the immortal products of the Sung potters in that "background noise of low technology" which was all that non-European cultures could attain. I prefer, then, to take other examples: Tu Wan's labelling of fossil brachiopods ("stone swallows") to demonstrate that if they ever flew through the air it was only to drop down by process of weathering, or the long succession of pharmaceutical experiments on animals carried out by the alchemists from Ko Hung to Chhen Chih-Hsü, or the many trials made by the acoustics experts on the resonance phenomena of bells and strings, or the systematic strength-of-material tests which internal evidence shows must have been undertaken before the long beam bridges across the Fukienese estuaries could have been constructed. Is it possible to believe that apparatus so complex as that of the water-wheel linkwork escapement clocks, or indeed much of the textile machinery, could ever have been devised without long periods of workshop experimentation? The fact that written records of it have not come down to us is only what we should expect in a medieval literary culture. The fact that none of it was carried out on isolated and simplified objects, such as balls rolling down inclined planes, is again only what was characteristic of pre-Renaissance practice everywhere.

I do not say that the Greek *praeparatio evangelica* was not an essential part of the background of modern science. What I do want to say is that modern exact and natural science is something much greater and wider than Euclidean geometry and Ptolemaic mathematical astronomy; more rivers than those have emptied into its sea. For anyone who is a mathematician and a physicist, perhaps a Cartesian, this may not be welcome; but I myself am professionally a biologist and a chemist, more than half a Baconian, and I therefore do *not* think that what constituted the spearhead of the Galilean break-through constitutes the whole of science. What happened to crystallize the mathematization of experimental hypotheses when the social conditions were favourable does not exhaust the essence. If mechanics was the primary science, it was *primus inter pares*. If physics celestial and terrestrial has the battle-honours of the Renaissance, it is not to be confused with the whole army of science, which has many brave regiments besides.

"The spearhead, but not the whole, of science." In pondering over a better way of representing the situation, it occurred to me that we ought perhaps to make a clearer distinction between factors which were concerned in the direct historical genesis of modern science, and factors which fell into place later after the Galilean break-through. We shall also have to distinguish more clearly between science and technology. Suppose we erect a classification of four pigeon-holes, science vertically on the left and technology vertically on the right, and let the upper boxes represent direct historical genesis while the lower ones represent subsequent reinforcement. Then taking the upper left-hand compartment first, the contribution of the Greeks will have the greatest share, for Euclidean deductive geometry and Ptolemaic astronomy, with all that they imply, were undoubtedly the largest factor in the birth of the "new, or experimental, science"—in so far as any antecedents played a part at all, for we must not undervalue its basic originality. In spite of Ptolemy and Archimedes, the occidental ancients did not, as a whole, experiment. But Asian contributions will not be absent from this compartment, for not only must we leave a place for algebra and the basic numerational and computational techniques, we must not forget the significance of magnetism, and knowledge of this realm of phenomena had been built up exclusively in the Chinese culture-area, which thus powerfully influenced Europe through Gilbert and Kepler. Here one remembers also the adoption of the Chinese equatorial co-ordinates by Tycho. But the Greeks predominate. In the upper right-hand compartment the situation is entirely different, for in technology Asian influences in and before the Renaissance (especially Chinese) were legion—I need mention only the efficient horse-harnesses, the technology of iron and steel, the inventions of gunpowder and paper, the escapement of the mechanical clock, and basic engineering devices such as the driving-belt, the chain-drive, and the standard method of converting rotary to rectilinear motion, together with nautical techniques such as the leeboard and the stern-post rudder. Alexandria also ran.

The lower compartments will now be available to take achievements of the Asian cultures which, though not genetically connected with the first rise of modern science yet deserve all praise; they may or may not be directly genetically related to their corresponding developments in post-Renaissance modern science. A case of direct influence could be found in the Chinese doctrine of infinite empty space instead of solid crystalline celestial spheres, but it did not operate until after Galileo's time. Cases of later incorporation would be the development of undulatory theory in eighteenth-century A.D. physics, which immensely elaborated characteristically Chinese ideas without directly building on them, or the use of ancient and medieval Chinese records by radio-astronomers. So also, if atomism, not mathematics, proved to be the soul of chemistry, which found itself so much later than physics, this elaborated Indian and Arabic ideas of great subtlety without knowingly basing itself thereon. A good case of the absence of any influence would be the seismograph as used in China from the second to the seventh centuries A.D.; though an outstanding achievement, it was almost certainly unknown to any of the scientific men who developed seismographs in post-Renaissance Europe. Chinese biological and pathological classification systems occupy the same position; they were clearly unknown to Linnaeus and Sydenham, but none the less worthy of study, for only by drawing up the balance-sheet in full shall we ever ascertain what each civilization contributed to human advancement. It is not legitimate to require of every scientific or technological activity that it should have contributed to the advancement of the European culture-area. What happened in other civilizations is entirely worth studying for its own sake. Must the history of science be written solely in terms of one continuous thread of linked influences? Is there not an ideal history of human thought and knowledge of nature, in which every effort can find its place, irrespective of what influences it received or handed on? Modern universal science and the history and philosophy of universal science will embrace all in the end.

It only remains to consider the contents of the right-hand lower compartment. Here we have to think of technical inventions which only became incorporated, whether or not by re-invention, into the corpus of modern technology after the Renaissance period. A case in point might be the paddle-wheel boat, but it is uncertain, for we do not know whether the first European successes were based on a Byzantine idea never executed, or on a vast fund of practical Chinese achievement during the preceding millennium. A better case would be the differential gear, for though present in the south-pointing carriage of ancient China, it must almost certainly have arisen again independently in Europe. So also the Chinese methods of steel-making by the co-fusion process and by the direct oxygenation of cast iron, though of great seniority to the siderurgy of Europe, were not able to exert any influence upon it, if indeed they did, which is still uncertain, until long after the Renaissance. Similarly it might be unwise to connect too closely the crucible steel of Huntsman with that of the age-old Indian wootz process.

In all this I have tried to offer an *opinio conciliatrix* in friendly fashion to those who may have been shocked by the objective attitude which I always seek to adopt in weighing European claims. If we think out the matter as I suggest, we may feel greater need for recognizing several kinds of values; the value of that which helped directly to effect the Galilean break-through, the value of that which became incorporated in modern science later on, and last but not least, the value of that residue which yet renders other civilizations no less worthy of study and admiration than Europe.

The erroneous perspective which I am criticizing can be seen particularly well in the use of the possessive plural personal pronoun. Some Western historians of science constantly speak of "*our* modern culture" and "*our* high civilization" (I italicize). *The Edge of Objectivity* reveals even more clearly the mood in which they approach the comparative study of men's efforts to understand and control the natural world.

> Anxious though our moments are, today is not the final test of wisdom among statesmen or virtue among peoples. The hard trial will begin when the instruments of power created by the West come fully into the hands of men not of the West, formed in cultures and religions which leave them quite devoid of the Western sense of some ultimate responsibility to man in history. The secular legacy of Christianity still restrains our world in some slight measure, however self-righteous it may have become on one side and however vestigial on the other. Men of other traditions can and do appropriate *our* science and technology, but not our history or values. And what will the day hold when China wields the bomb? And Egypt? Will Aurora light a rosy-fingered dawn out of the East? Or Nemesis?

This is certainly very near the edge. It would induce in the reader a lamentable and unworthy attitude of mind in which fear would jostle its counterpart, possessiveness. Surely it would be better to admit that men of the Asian cultures also helped to lay the foundations of mathematics and all the sciences in their medieval forms, and hence to set the stage for the decisive break-through which came about in the favourable social and economic milieu of the Renaissance. Surely it would be better to give more attention to the history and values of these non-European civilizations, in actual fact no less exalted and inspiring than our own. Then let us give up that intellectual pride which boasts that "we are the people, and wisdom was born with us." Let us take pride enough in the undeniable historical fact that *modern* science was born in Europe and only in Europe, but let us not claim thereby a perpetual patent thereon. For what was born in the time of Galileo was a universal palladium, the salutary enlightenment of all men without distinction of race, colour, faith or homeland, wherein all can qualify and all participate. Modern universal science, yes; Western science, no!

N O T E S

1. A. C. Crombie, "The Significance of Medieval Discussions of Scientific Method for the Scientific Revolution," in *Critical Problems in the History of Science,* ed. Marshall Claggett (Madison, Wis., 1959), 79.

2. D. J. de Solla Price, *Science since Babylon* (New Haven, Conn., 1961).

3. J. D. Bernal.

4. C. C. Gillispie, *The Edge of Objectivity: An Essay in the History of Scientific Ideas* (Princeton, N.J., 1960).

BLACK ATHENA

Hostilities to Egypt in the Eighteenth Century

Martin Bernal

Almost always the men who achieve these fundamental inventions of a new paradigm have either been very young or very new to the field
whose paradigm they change.

> Thomas Kuhn, *The Structure of Scientific
> Revolutions*

My use of this quotation from Thomas Kuhn is an attempt to justify my presump-
tion, as someone trained in Chinese history, to write on subjects so far removed
from my original field. For I shall be arguing that although the changes of view
that I am proposing are not paradigmatic in the strict sense of the word, they are
none the less fundamental.

These volumes are concerned with two models of Greek history: one viewing
Greece as essentially European or Aryan, and the other seeing it as Levantine, on
the periphery of the Egyptian and Semitic cultural area. I call them the "Aryan"
and the "Ancient" models. The "Ancient Model" was the conventional view
among Greeks in the Classical and Hellenistic ages. According to it, Greek culture had arisen as the result of colonization, around 1500 B.C., by Egyptians and
Phoenicians who had civilized the native inhabitants. Furthermore, Greeks had
continued to borrow heavily from Near Eastern cultures.

Most people are surprised to learn that the Aryan Model, which most of us
have been brought up to believe, developed only during the first half of the
nineteenth century. In its earlier or "Broad" form, the new model denied the
truth of the Egyptian settlements and questioned those of the Phoenicians. What
I call the "Extreme" Aryan model, which flourished during the twin peaks of
anti-Semitism in the 1890s and again in the 1920s and '30s, denied even the
Phoenician cultural influence. According to the Aryan Model, there had been an
invasion from the north—unreported in ancient tradition—which had overwhelmed the local "Aegean" or "Pre-Hellenic" culture. Greek civilization is seen
as the result of the mixture of the Indo-European-speaking Hellenes and their

indigenous subjects. It is from the construction of this Aryan Model that I call this volume *The Fabrication of Ancient Greece 1785–1985.*

I believe that we should return to the Ancient Model, but with some revisions; hence I call what I advocate in Volume 2 of *Black Athena* the "Revised Ancient Model." This accepts that there is a real basis to the stories of Egyptian and Phoenician colonization of Greece set out in the Ancient model. However, it sees them as beginning somewhat earlier, in the first half of the second millennium B.C. It also agrees with the latter that Greek civilization is the result of the cultural mixtures created by these colonizations and later borrowings from across the East Mediterranean. On the other hand, it tentatively accepts the Aryan Model's hypothesis of invasions—or infiltrations—from the north by Indo-European speakers sometime during the fourth or third millennium B.C. However, the revised Ancient model maintains that the earlier population was speaking a related Indo-Hittite language which left little trace in Greek. In any event, it cannot be used to explain the many non-European elements in the later language.

If I am right in urging the overthrow of the Aryan Model and its replacement by the Revised Ancient one, it will be necessary not only to rethink the fundamental bases of "Western Civilization" but also to recognize the penetration of racism and "continental chauvinism" into all our historiography, or philosophy of writing history. The Ancient Model had no major "internal" deficiencies, or weaknesses in explanatory power. It was overthrown for external reasons. For eighteenth- and nineteenth-century Romantics and racists it was simply intolerable for Greece, which was seen not merely as the epitome of Europe but also as its pure childhood, to have been the result of the mixture of native Europeans and colonizing Africans and Semites. Therefore the Ancient Model had to be overthrown and replaced by something more acceptable.

• • •

The nineteenth and twentieth centuries have been dominated by the paradigms of progress and science. Within learning there has been the belief that most disciplines made a quantum leap into "modernity" or 'true science" followed by steady, cumulative, scholarly progress. In the historiography of the Ancient East Mediterranean these "leaps" are perceived to have taken place in the nineteenth century, and since then scholars have tended to believe that their work has been qualitatively better than any that has gone before. The palpable successes of natural science during this period have confirmed the truth of this belief in that area. Its extension to historiography is less securely based. Nevertheless, the destroyers of the Ancient Model and the builders of the Aryan believed themselves to be "scientific." To these German and British scholars, the stories of Egyptian colonization and civilizing of Greece violated "racial science" as monstrously as the legends of sirens and centaurs broke the canons of natural science. Thus all were equally discredited and discarded.

For the past hundred and fifty years, historians have claimed to possess a "method" analogous to those used in natural science. In fact, ways in which the modern historians differ from the 'prescientific" ones are much less certain. The best of the earlier writers were self-conscious, used the test of plausibility and tried to be internally consistent. Furthermore, they cited and evaluated their sources. By comparison, the "scientific" historians of the nineteenth and twenti- eth centuries have been unable to give formal demonstrations of "proof" or es- tablish firm historical laws. Today, moreover, the charge of "unsound methodology" is used to condemn not merely incompetent but also unwelcome work. The charge is unfair, because it falsely implies the existence of other meth- odologically sound studies with which to contrast it.

Considerations of this kind lead to the question of positivism and its require- ment of "proof." Proof or certainty is difficult enough to achieve, even in the experimental sciences or documented history. In the fields with which this work is concerned it is out of the question: all one can hope to find is more or less plausibility. To put it another way, it is misleading to see an analogy between scholarly debate and criminal law. In criminal law, since conviction of an inno- cent person is so much worse than acquittal of a guilty one, the courts rightly demand proof "beyond reasonable doubt" before a conviction can be made. But neither conventional wisdom nor the academic *status quo* has the moral rights of an accused person. Thus debates in these areas should not be judged on the basis of *proof,* but merely on *competitive plausibility.* In these volumes I cannot, and therefore do not attempt to, *prove* that the Aryan Model is "wrong." All I am trying to do is to show that it is less plausible than the Revised Ancient Model and that the latter provides a more fruitful framework for future research.

Twentieth-century prehistory has been bedevilled by a particular form of this search for proof, which I shall call "archaeological positivism." It is the fallacy that dealing with "objects" makes one "objective"; the belief that interpretations of archaeological evidence are as solid as the archaeological finds themselves. This faith elevates hypotheses based on archaeology to a "scientific" status and demotes information about the past from other sources—legends, place names, religious cults, language and the distribution of linguistic and script dialects. In these volumes it is maintained that all these sources must be treated with great caution, but that evidence from them is not categorically less valid than that from archaeology.

The favourite tool of the archaeological positivists is the "argument from silence": the belief that if something has not been found, it cannot have existed in significant quantities. This would appear to be useful in the very few cases where archaeologists have failed to find something predicted by the dominant model, in a restricted but well-dug area. For instance, for the past fifty years it has been believed that the great eruption on Thera took place during the ceramic period Late Minoan IB, yet despite extensive digging on this small island, no sherd of this ware has appeared below the volcanic debris. This suggests that it would be useful to look again at the theory. Even here, however, some pots of this type could still turn up, and there are always questions about the definition of ceramic styles. In nearly all archaeology—as in the natural sciences—it is virtually im- possible to *prove* absence.

It will probably be argued that these attacks are against straw men, or at least dead men. "Modern archaeologists are much too sophisticated to be so positivist," and "no serious scholar today believes in the existence, let alone the importance, of 'race.' " Both statements may be true, but what is claimed here is that modern archaeologists and ancient historians of this region are still working with models set up by men who were crudely positivist and racist. Thus it is extremely implausible to suppose that the models were not influenced by these ideas. This does not in itself falsify the models, but—given what would now be seen as the dubious circumstances of their creation—they should be very carefully scrutinized, and the possibility that there may be equally good or better alternatives should be seriously taken into account. In particular, if it can be shown that the Ancient Model was overthrown for externalist reasons, its supersession by the Aryan Model can no longer be attributed to any explanatory superiority of the latter; therefore it is legitimate to place the two models in competition or to try to reconcile them.

• • •

We are now approaching the nub of this volume and the origins of the forces that eventually overthrew the Ancient Model, leading to the replacement of Egypt by Greece as the fount of European civilization. I concentrate on four of these forces: Christian reaction, the rise of the concept of "progress," the growth of racism, and Romantic Hellenism. All are related; to the extent that Europe can be identified with Christendom, "Christian reaction" is concerned with the growth of European hostility to Asia and Africa and the increase of tension between Egyptian religion and Christianity.

On the question of "progress," I argue that its rise as a dominant paradigm damaged Egypt for two reasons. The country's great antiquity put it *behind* later civilizations; while its long and stable history, which had been a source of admiration, now became reason to despise it as static and sterile. In the long run we can see that Egypt was also harmed by the rise of racism and the need to disparage every African culture; during the eighteenth century, however, the ambiguity of Egypt's "racial" position allowed its supporters to claim that it was essentially and originally "white." Greece, by contrast, benefited from racism, immediately and in every way; and it was rapidly seen as the "childhood" of the "dynamic" "European race."

Racism and "progress" could thus come together in the condemnation of Egyptian/African stagnation and praise of Greek/European dynamism and change. Such assessments fitted perfectly with the new Romanticism, which not only emphasized the importance of geographical and national characteristics and the categorical differences between peoples but saw dynamism as the highest value. Moreover, Greek states were small and often quite poor and their national poet was Homer, whose heroic epics fitted splendidly with the eighteenth-century Romantic passion for Northern ballads, most of which were extremely gory, like the *Iliad*. Here, as with language, a special relationship was seen between Greece and Northern Europe which was marred only by Greece's geographical position in the South-Eastern Mediterranean and the Ancient Model, which emphasized her close association with the Middle East. All in all, while Egypt, along with China and Rome, were the models of the Enlightenment, Greece became allied to the lesser, but growing eighteenth-century intellectual and emotional current of Romanticism.

Christian Reaction

Here it should be emphasized that for most of the almost 2,000 years with which we are concerned, the tension or "contradiction" between Christianity and the Egyptian "twofold" philosophy was not—in the Leninist or Maoist sense—an "antagonistic" one. As movements confined to the elite, Hermeticism and Masonry did not fundamentally threaten the social, political or even the religious *status quo*. However, the exclusive claims of Judaeo-Christian-Islamic monotheisms make any kind of unconformity difficult to tolerate, and there have been periods of bitter rivalry between the two traditions.

The ruthless and bloody destruction of Gnosticism and Neo-Platonism by the early Church was mentioned in Chapter II. In the fifteenth and sixteenth centuries, however, the Church generally tolerated or even encouraged Platonism and Hermeticism. The execution of Bruno was not surprising, given his blatant attacks on the Judaeo-Christian tradition and his call for a return to Egyptian religion. Moreover, the burning was followed not by a ban on the study of Egypt but by the encouragement and massive funding of what Frances Yates calls Athanasius Kircher's "reactionary Hermeticism" or, to put it more charitably, a Church-sanctioned "Egyptology" which included Kircher's establishment of Coptic studies.[1] Although Hermeticism and Rosicrucianism were often influential in Northern European intellectual circles, they did not loom large in the violence of the Thirty Years War in Germany, the Fronde revolts in France and the antimonarchical struggles in England and Holland. The religious struggles between Catholic and Protestant or High and Low Church had little or nothing to do with Hermeticism.

Neo-Platonism and Hermeticism, as I have said, were often philosophies espoused by moderates as attempts to transcend the raging political and religious battles of the time. Similarly, the atomist atheism associated with Thomas Hobbes grew up in an atmosphere of despair at competing brands of religion. Thus in England in the 1660s and 1670s moderate men like Ralph Cudworth, who were concerned with two main foes, Catholic superstition and Puritan Enthusiasm, saw Platonism as an antidote to both.[2] Apart from its transcendence over sectarian squabbles, its doctrine that there was a light or life immanent in the world weakened the Enthusiasts'—or inspired believers'—claims to have a monopoly of holy spirit. Furthermore, Cudworth believed that the danger of atheism from the Egypto-Platonic identification of spirit with matter, or the Creator with the Creation, was less acute than that from Hobbesian mechanical, atomist atheism.[3]

Newton was intellectually formed in this atmosphere and it is in this context that his early admiration for the Egyptians, referred to in the last chapter, must be seen. However, his attitude towards Egypt changed drastically in the 1690s and the last years of his life were spent on chronological works, of which the most important was *The Chronology of Ancient Kingdoms Amended*. Here, as mentioned on p. 168, Newton *proved*, on the basis of the Bible and astronomy, that the claims for antiquity made by the Egyptians and other peoples had been grossly exaggerated, and that the Israelites had existed long before all the others.

Newton's most recent biographer, Professor Westfall, describes this as "a work of colossal tedium" and believes that in it Newton had "produced a book with no evident point and no evident form." The only explanation Westfall can give for it is that it had a concealed deist message.[4] But the same could be said for most of Newton's works, and I do not think it provides a sufficient motive for the immense labour he put into his *Chronology*. Indeed, it could be argued that it was the most orthodox work Newton ever wrote: William Whiston, who can be described as Newton's deist conscience, fiercely attacked *The Chronology*, as did the French atheist Fréret.[5] Furthermore, as Westfall points out, Newton had effectively been co-opted by the Establishment by the end of his life. Thus I think it more useful to see *The Chronology* as the result of what the modern intellectual historian Professor Pocock describes as "a complete reversal in Cudworth's attempt to demonstrate that ancient thinking was naturally in accord with Christian theology."

Pocock attributes this partly to the "impact of Spinoza," an attribution that has problems because, as the historian Professor Colie has shown, Cudworth was fully aware of Spinoza's thinking by the 1670s, and his great work *The True Intellectual System of the Universe* contained an attack on Spinoza's position.[6] This is not to deny that Spinoza's pantheism continued to weaken the possibility of a Christian Platonism after the publication of Cudworth's work in 1679. However, the new factors after the "Glorious Revolution" of 1689 were Toland and the Radical Enlightenment. All in all, I think Newton's later work and his lowering of the antiquity of the Egyptians and other ancient peoples should generally be seen as a "respectable" deist and Christian defence against the Radical Enlightenment and the latter's use of the antiquity of Egypt and the Orient. As with Bruno in the sixteenth century, the peaceful coexistence between Christianity and esoteric Egyptian religion and philosophy, which had lasted through most of the Renaissance, broke down in the 1690s and the Christians struck back.

The "Triangle": Christianity and Greece against Egypt

The defence of Newtonianism brought Greek studies into alliance with Christianity, and this brings us to a central concern of this volume, which is less with the binary conflict between Egypt and the Bible than with the triangular relations between Christianity, Egypt and Greece. During the first centuries of the Christian era the main struggle was between Christians and pagans. As the dominant culture of the East Mediterranean during this period was Hellenic with a religion based on Egypt, both Christians and pagans—of whom the most influential were the Neo-Platonists—saw the distinctions between Egypt, the Orient and Greece as relatively unimportant. Jews like Josephus and Church Fathers like Clement of Alexandria and Tatian, on the other hand, scored points against the Greeks by pointing out the lateness and shallowness of Greek civilization in comparison with those of the Egyptians, Phoenicians, Chaldaeans, Persians and so on and, of course, the Israelites. They also stressed Greece's heavy cultural borrowings from the more ancient peoples.[7]

The possibility of pitting Greeks against the Egyptians, Chaldaeans and others, in the defence of Christianity, did not occur until the Renaissance. I have already pointed out that Erasmus' hostility to Hermeticism in the early sixteenth century was essentially linked to his defence of Christianity and religion against magic. Erasmus, however, was also a champion of pure Latinity and the study of Greek.

During these same decades, Germans were becoming aware of striking similarities between their language and Greek. The nouns of both had four cases rather than the five of Latin. Both Greek and German used the definite article and made massive use of particles and of prepositions with verbs. After the Reformation, and the break away from *Roman* Catholicism, the relationship became much stronger, with the new image of Greek and German as the two languages of Protestantism. Luther fought the church of Rome with the Greek Testament. Greek was a sacred Christian tongue which Protestants could plausibly claim was more authentically Christian than Latin. With the spread of the Reformation to England, Scotland and Scandinavia, a feeling developed that the Teutonic-speaking peoples were "better" and more "manly" than the Romance-speaking nations of France, Spain and Italy and that their languages as a whole were superior to Latin and on a par with Greek. As a seventeenth-century English writer put it:

> Our language was a dialect of the Teutonick, and although then but in her infancie, yet not so rude as hopefull, being most fruitfull and copious in significant and well-founding rootes and Primitives and withall capable and apt for diffusion from those her rootes into such a Greek-like ramosity [sic] of derivations and compositions, beyond the power of Latine and her off-spring dialects . . . [8]

Greek studies flourished in Protestant schools and universities throughout the sixteenth and seventeenth centuries. It is striking, for instance, how many of the major French Hellenists of the seventeenth century—including Isaac Casaubon and Mme Dacier, who will be discussed when I come to the cult of Homer—were brought up as Huguenots.[9] From using Greek to attack Roman Catholic superstition, it was not such a long step to employing it against Egyptian magic. Nevertheless, Casaubon's criticism of the antiquity of the Hermetic Texts was not juxtaposing a rational Greece to a magical and superstitious Egypt. It was using critical methods of approach to Greek texts to discredit the age, and hence the value, of Egyptian wisdom.

A similar approach was used seventy years later by Richard Bentley. Known in his lifetime as the hated and tyrannical Master of Trinity College Cambridge, Bentley is, however, a hero in the history of Classics as the discoverer of the *digamma*, or rather of the fact that the w sound represented as *F* in some Greek alphabets had existed in Homeric and other Greek dialects, in which it was not written. This Bentley did with extreme ingenuity by observing that in certain cases words beginning with vowels did not elide or come together with the preceding syllables. He is even more respected for his rigorous critical scholarship which, though not particularly appreciated in his own day, has given him the later reputation as the greatest English Classicist of all time.[10]

Richard Bentley was also the first man to popularize Newtonian physics and to spell out its theological and political implications: that, as matter could not move itself, a god—of generally regular habits—was needed to create and maintain the universe, just as a king was necessary to a Whig constitutional monarchy. Bentley put this scheme forward in 1692, when he preached the first series of sermons or lectures set up by the famous Anglo-Irish chemist Sir Robert Boyle against "notorious infidels, namely, Atheists, Theists, Pagans, Jews and Mahometans."[11] Bentley hardly mentioned the last two. His concern was clearly with the first three, and most of all with the Radical Enlightenment. He seems to have been especially concerned with the radical thinker and pioneer of Freemasonry John Toland's use of Bruno's Egyptian notion of animate matter, which the radical had used to attack Newtonian physics. Bentley and his circle also seem to have known about Toland's republicanism. Toland was fully aware of the interconnections between his physics and his politics.[12] Bentley used his own formidable intelligence and Classical scholarship not only to expound the Newtonian system and its implications, but also to cast doubt on the reliability and age of the Greek sources referring to Egyptian and Oriental wisdom and astronomy.[13] Thus he tried to deprive Toland and the radicals of one of their most powerful sources of legitimacy.

What most concerns us here, however, is the alliance between Newton and Bentley and the combination of the new science and critical Classical scholarship to defend the *status quo*. It is ironic that these two men, who were always on, if not over, the brink of Arianism or deism became two of the most effective defenders of the Christian Establishment.[14]

"Progress"

It is frequently said that the clearest eighteenth-century statement of the idea of "progress" was that of Condorcet's *Sketch of a historical table of the progress of the human spirit*, written in 1793. However, most of the ideas Condorcet propounded there had been set out earlier in a speech *On the Successive Progress of the Human Spirit*, given in 1750 by the nineteen-year-old Anne Robert Turgot. Turgot, who later became a finance minister of Louis XVI, was close to the leading Physiocrats and was a promoter of Chinese economic ideas. He was subsequently described as the founder of political economy. From the speech and unfinished draft histories, his ideas on "progress" are quite clear.[15]

These ideas are important in themselves and because of their bearing on the views held by Turgot and his contemporaries on the Egyptians, Phoenicians and Greeks. According to the new paradigm, these civilizations had to be seen in ascending order as the human spirit "progressed." But, as in all schemes of historical evolution—notably the Hegelian and the Marxist—each stage was seen as having started out beneficially "progressive" but as having later slipped into decadence and opposition to the new forces. Thus Turgot saw Egypt and China as initially pioneering: "they advanced with great strides towards perfection."[16]

The Egyptians and Chinese were perceived as having been mathematicians, philosophers and metaphysicians. Unfortunately, in both civilizations these "sciences" had been sapped by superstition and priestly dogmatism. Just as Bishop Warburton had tried to exculpate the priests on this issue out of "clerical solidarity," so intellectuals like Turgot and Condorcet were delighted to have yet another stick with which to beat them, for here, as in the modern world, priests could largely be blamed for the decadence.[17] However, Turgot differed from the Physiocrats, who admired contemporary China, by condemning the country to the past; and this part of the "progressive" scheme brought him—or kept him—very close to the old, regressive picture of the Egyptians as having been in possession—probably from the Israelites—of a pure and true religion, but as having lost it.

Turgot also saw the decadence as the result of the despotism of Egyptian and Chinese government. Like Montesquieu, however, who had attributed it to the morally improving effects of irrigation, Turgot maintained that Egyptian and Chinese governments were not as bad as their hot climates would seem to determine, or as the Mahometan forms actually were.[18] Like Brucker and most eighteenth-century thinkers, Turgot included the Pythagoreans, Neo-Platonists and, by implication, Plato himself among the decadent Asiatic metaphysicians.[19] For him, the higher stages of the progress of the human spirit began with Aristotle's logic and continued directly to Bacon, Galileo, Kepler, Descartes, Newton and Leibniz.[20] As far as Greece was concerned Turgot, although encouraged by the country's disunity and liberty, believed that "it was only after many centuries that one saw the appearance of philosophers in Greece."[21]

For Turgot the real Hellenic glory was in poetry, which derived directly from the richness of the Greek language. This richness had come about because

> the Phoenicians, inhabiting an arid coast, made themselves the agents of exchange between peoples. Their vessels spread throughout the Mediterranean. They began to reveal nation to nation, astronomy, navigation and geography perfected each other. The coasts of Greece and Asia Minor were filled with colonies. . . . From the mixtures of these independent colonies with the an-

cient peoples of Greece and with the remains of successive barbarian invasions the Greek nation was formed . . . by these multiple mixtures this rich language was formed, expressive and sonorous, the language for all the arts.[22]

The liberal denial of the Egyptians in favour of the Phoenicians was an indication of future attitudes on their relative importance. Otherwise, Turgot's statement reflects the contemporary linguistic research already mentioned in connection with Barthélemy, and Turgot's scheme also seems to reflect the origin of French from a mixture of Celtic, Latin and Germanic languages. This does not, however, affect its competitive plausibility against the equally subjective image of Greek as a language that was somehow "pure," like the idealized German. The picture of purity is extremely improbable, not only on geographical and historical grounds but also, as Turgot pointed out, on linguistic ones too.

While Turgot and his contemporaries proclaimed and articulated the new vision of "progress," they retained respect for the Egyptians and Phoenicians and never questioned the legends of their having colonized and civilized Greece.[23] Nevertheless, the introduction of the "progressive" paradigm was ultimately fatal to the reputation of the Egyptians. Their antiquity—which had previously been one of their major assets—now became a liability.

The obverse to the fall of the Egyptians was a rise in the status of the Greeks. Before coming to this, however, we must consider the two forces that aided Christian reaction and the "progressive" paradigm in the overthrow of the Ancient Model: racism and Romanticism.

Racism

All cultures have some degree of prejudice for, or more often against, people whose appearance is unusual. However, the intensity and pervasiveness of Northern European, American and other colonial racism since the seventeenth century have been so much greater than the norm that they need some special explanation.

It is difficult to say whether or not racism was unusually strong before the sixteenth century, the first in which Northern Europeans came into frequent contact with peoples from other continents. In the early anti-Semitic ballads about the alleged murder of Little Sir Hugh, the evil Jews do not appear to have been seen as particularly dark.[24] It is even possible that with the influx of French and Italians after the Norman Conquest, dark colouring had high status, and early ballads do sometimes contrast the poor fair girl with the rich brown one. On the other hand, there is no doubt that the "fair maid" is seen as morally superior and the ballads of two sisters, which appear to have very old Norse antecedents, lay emphasis on the wicked dark sister as opposed to the good fair one.[25]

By the fifteenth century, too, there is no doubt that clear links were seen between dark skin colour and evil and inferiority, when the newly arrived Gypsies were feared and hated for both their darkness and their alleged sexual prowess.[26] Whether or not this concern with and dislike of the dark "other" was exceptionally intense in medieval Northern Europe, it is generally accepted that a more clear-cut racism grew up after 1650 and that this was greatly intensified by the increased colonization of North America, with its twin policies of extermination of the Native Americans and enslavement of Africans. Both these presented moral problems to Protestant societies, in which equality of all men before God, and personal liberty, were central values which could be eased only by strong racism.

The Classical writer most often appealed to to justify slavery was Aristotle, who argued at length in its favour. The appeal was linked to the fact that his work was shot through with the belief that Greeks were inherently superior to other peoples:

> The races that live in cold regions and those of Europe are full of courage and passion but somewhat lacking in skill and brainpower; for this reason, while remaining generally independent, they lack political cohesion and the ability to rule others. On the other hand, the Asiatic races have both brains and skill but are lacking in courage and willpower; so they have remained both enslaved and subject. The Hellenic race, occupying a mid position geographically, has a measure of both. Hence it has continued to be free, to have the best political institutions and to be capable of ruling others given a single constitution.[27]

In this way Aristotle linked "racial superiority" to the right to enslave other peoples, especially those of a "slavish disposition."

Similar perceptions of "racial" differences appear to have been central to the thought of John Locke, the philosopher of the late-seventeenth-century Whigs. There is no doubt that Locke, who was personally involved with slave-owning American colonies, was what we should now call a racist, as was the great eighteenth-century philosopher David Hume. Whether or not these attitudes affected their philosophies is more debatable, but Harry Bracken and Noam Chomsky's arguments for this connection seem very plausible.[28]

Locke's consistent disparagement of Native Americans was essential to his politics, because the land the indigenous population inhabited was needed to provide a wilderness available for English and other settlers. The possibility of such colonization was necessary to the argument that men had a choice as to whether or not they joined the Social Contract, with all its manifest inequalities.[29] Locke refused to justify the enslavement of people of the same nationality, and called what might appear to be slavery of this kind mere "drudgery." For him, as for most thinkers of the time, slavery was justified only when it was the result of capture as an alternative to a deserved death in a just war.[30] Christian European attacks on heathen Africans and Americans, for instance, were classed as "just wars" because the latter were not defending their property, but merely "waste land." Furthermore, Locke had the curious but convenient belief that

Africans and Americans did not practise agriculture and, according to him, the only entitlement to land came from cultivation.[31] The general scheme allowed for the taking of black slaves by Europeans. Moreover, the very existence of large numbers of African slaves led to the belief that they were "natural slaves" in the Aristotelian sense.

By the 1680s there was in fact a widespread opinion that Negroes were only one link above the apes—also from Africa—in the "great chain of being."[32] This type of thinking was made easier by Locke's nominalism: his denial of the objective validity of "species" and view of them as subjective concepts. He was particularly sceptical of the inconvenient category of "man":

> And I imagine none of the Definitions of the Word *man,* which we yet have, nor Descriptions of that sort of Animal, are so perfect and exact, as to satisfy a considerate inquisitive person; much less a general consent . . . [33]

This position is in sharp contrast not only to the biblical "God made man in his own image" but also to Descartes's insistence on a categorical distinction between unthinking animals and thinking man. Empiricism thus seems to remove an (admittedly flimsy) barrier against racism; however, there is no necessary connection between empiricism and racism.[34]

To recapitulate: it is certain that Locke and most eighteenth-century English-speaking thinkers like David Hume and Benjamin Franklin were racist: they openly expressed popular opinions that dark skin colour was linked to moral and mental inferiority. In Hume's case, racism so transcended conventional religion that he was a pioneer of the view that there had been not one creation of man but many different ones, because "Such a uniform and constant difference could not happen in so many countries and ages, if nature had not made an original distinction betwixt these breeds of men."[35] The centrality of racism to European society after 1700 is shown by the fact that this "polygenetic" view of human origins continued to grow in the early nineteenth century, even after the revival of Christianity.

Racism was not so clear-cut in eighteenth-century France. Nevertheless, the Aristotelian—and pseudo-Platonic—scheme of climatic and topographic determinism of races that had permeated the work of Jean Bodin in the sixteenth century was revitalized by Montesquieu in the eighteenth. Montesquieu became famous in 1721 through his *Persian Letters.* At one level he was using distinguished Persians to criticize and satirize Europe; at another, he was setting up the image of Europe as the "scientific" and "progressive" continent. This primacy was explained as the result of her beneficent, temperate climate. His pro-European views and hostility to Asia and Africa came out more clearly in his *Spirit of Laws,* which was published in 1748.[36]

Rousseau, in his *Social Contract,* published in 1762, violently attacked any justification of slavery. On the other hand, he followed the school of geographical determinism, believing that a people's virtue and political capacity depended on climate and topography. He was Europocentric and showed remarkably little interest in Egypt and China. This was a trait which persisted among later Romantics, whose predilections were nearly always for the misty and mountainous North of Europe, which was seen as the true repository of human virtue.

Romanticism

After the defence of Christianity and the idea of "progress," racism was, I believe, the third major force behind the overthrow of the Ancient Model; the fourth was Romanticism. To put it crudely, Romanticism maintains, against the Enlightenment and the Masonic tradition, that reason is inadequate to handle the important aspects of life and philosophy. Romanticism is concerned with the local and particular, rather than the global and general. There is also an oversimplified, but useful, contrast to be made between the eighteenth-century Enlightenment, with its interest in stability and the ordering of space, and the Romantic passion for movement, time and "progressive" development through history. Outstanding examples of Enlightenment achievement are the accurate mappings of the world's coasts, Linnaeus' systematic arrangement of natural species, and the American Constitution, which is supposed to last for ever.

Apart from the extraordinary achievements of natural science during the period of Romantic dominance from 1790 to 1890 there was an enormous interest in history, and in both the chief model used was that of the "tree." Trees, which are to be found in Darwinian evolution, Indo-European linguistics and most nineteenth-century histories, provide the ideal Romantic image. They are rooted in their own soils and nourished by their particular climates; at the same time they are alive and grow. They progress and never turn back. Like the image of history as biography, trees have a simple past and a complicated and ramified present and future. Nevertheless, the image of the tree had disadvantages in the description of European and Greek history.[37]

It should be borne in mind that despite the enormous influence of Rousseau, Romanticism was never as strong in France as it was in Britain and Germany, and it is in these regions that one should look for the movement's further development.

First, Germany: during the early part of the eighteenth century, Germany went through one of its most acute crises of national identity. In striking contrast to France, Holland and England, for more than a century following the end of the Thirty Years War in 1648 there was continued military devastation, political fragmentation and economic backwardness. The same period saw the military and cultural rise of France to a point where it seemed about to become a "New Rome," capable of absorbing all Europe.[38] The language and culture of the German courts, including that of Frederick the Great in Prussia, was French; most of the books published in Germany in the first half of the century were in Latin and

French. Thus there was a reasonable fear, voiced by the late-seventeenth-century philosopher and mathematician Leibniz and later patriots, that German would never develop into a language capable of being used for cultural and philosophical discourse; it might even, like the Germanic Frankish language spoken by the early rulers of France, disappear altogether in the face of French. German culture and the German people were seen as being in mortal danger.[39]

The most significant response to this crisis on the part of the German Romantics was the attempt to return Germans to their cultural roots, and to create an authentic German civilization from the German soil and the German people. According to the new Romantic and progressive views, peoples now had to be seen in their geographical and historical contexts. The racial genius or spirit belonging to the land and *its* people changed its forms according to the spirit of the age or, to use a term developed in the 1780s, its *Zeitgeist*; but a people always retained its immutable essence. The most powerful figure concerned with this aspect of the Romantic movement was Johann Gottfried Herder, who was also important in relation both to Neo-Hellenism and the development of linguistics. Herder himself stayed within the universalist bounds of the Enlightenment, maintaining that all peoples, not merely Germans, should be encouraged to discover and develop their own genii.[40] Nevertheless, the concern with history and local particularity, and the disdain for rationality or "pure reason" apparent in his views and those of other late-eighteenth- and early-nineteenth-century German thinkers including Kant, Fichte, Hegel and the Schlegels, provided a firm basis for the chauvinism and racism of the following two centuries.

N O T E S

1. Iversen (1961, pp. 5, 89–99); Blanco (1984, pp. 2263–64); Godwin (1979, esp. pp. 15–24).
2. Colie (1957, pp. 2–4); Pocock (1985, p. 12).
3. Pocock (1985, p. 13). This is not to say that the Cambridge Platonists were unconcerned by Spinoza and by what they saw as his pantheist or "hylozoick" atheism (Colie, 1957, pp. 96–97).
4. Westfall (1980, p. 815).
5. Ibid.; Manuel (1959, pp. 90–95).
6. Pocock (1985, p. 23); Colie (1957, p. 96).
7. See Josephus, *Against Apion*; Clement, *Stromata*.
8. Hare (1647, pp. 12–13), quoted in MacDougall (1982, p. 60).
9. For a survey of the historiography of this link between Protestantism and Greek studies, see Lloyd-Jones (1982, p. 19).
10. Pfeiffer (1976, pp. 143–58; Wilamowitz-Moellendorf (1982, pp. 79–81). It is generally considered that the *digamma* is an ancient letter because it does not exist in the Ionian alphabet, which became standard in Greece at the end of the Peloponnesian War in 403 B.C. I argue in Bernal (1987a; 1988) that the Ionian alphabet is much older than the Dorian

alphabets which contained the F, and that the letter was therefore introduced into the Greek alphabet around 1000 B.C.—much later than c. 1600, when I date the transmission of the alphabet as a whole. . . .

11. Bentley (1693).

12. Jacob (1981, p. 89).

13. Bentley (1693). For more on Bentley and the Boyle Lectures, see Pfeiffer (1976, pp. 146–47).

14. For the deist implications of Bentley's Boyle lectures themselves, see Force (1985, pp. 65–66). For further doubts about his orthodoxy, see Westfall (1980, pp. 650–51). There were, of course, Christians who objected to both Newton and Bentley; see Force (1985, p. 64).

15. Turgot (1808–15, vol. 2, pp. 52–92, 255–328).

16. Turgot (1808–15, vol. 2, pp. 55, 315).

17. Manuel (1959, p. 69).

18. Montesquieu (1748, Bk. 18, ch. VI). This is, of course, in direct contradiction to the later "hydraulic theory"—hinted at by Marx and developed by Wittfogel—that water control leads to "Oriental Despotism." Unlike the nineteenth- and twentieth-century thinkers, Montesquieu had the example of Holland on his side. For a bibliography on the Asiatic Mode of Production, see Bernal (1987b).

19. Turgot (1808–15, vol. 2, pp. 65, 253, 314–16). Elsewhere (p. 71) he wrote: "Plato sowed flowers; the charm of his eloquence even embellished his errors." For the persistence into the nineteenth century of the view of Plato as a seductive poet rather than a philosopher, see Wismann (1983, p. 496).

20. Turgot (1808–15, vol. 2, pp. 276–79).

21. Turgot (1808–15, vol. 2, p. 70).

22. Turgot (1808–15, vol. 2, pp. 66–67).

23. Turgot (1808–15, vol. 2, pp. 330–32).

24. Child (1882–98, vol. 3, pp. 233–54). This lack of concern with the Jews' colour is in stark contrast to Walter Scott's reconstruction of the period in *Ivanhoe,* in which their darkness is repeatedly emphasized. This, of course, was written in the early nineteenth century, when there was obsessive interest in "ethnic" or "racial" differences.

25. For a general survey of medieval attitudes to blacks, see Devisse (1979, pt. 1). See also Child (1882–98, vol. 1, pp. 119–21).

26. Child (1882–98, vol. 3, pp. 51–74).

27. *Politics,* VII. 7 (trans. Sinclair, 1962, p. 269).

28. Bracken (1973, pp. 81–96; 1978, pp. 241–60). See also Poliakov (1974, pp. 145–46).

29. See, for example, Locke (1689, Bk. 5, p. 41).

30. Locke (1689, Bk. 4).

31. Locke (1689, Bk. 5, pp. 25–45). For a discussion of this, see Bracken (1973, p. 86).

32. Jordan (1969, p. 229).

33. Locke (1688, Bk. 3, p. 6, quoted and discussed in Jordan, 1969, pp. 235–36). For other examples of Locke's racism, see Bracken (1978, p. 246).

34. See Bracken (1978, p. 253).

35. Footnote to "Of National Characters," cited in Jordan (1969, p. 253); Bracken (1973, p. 82); Popkin (1974, p. 143); and S. J. Gould (1981, pp. 40–41).

36. See, for instance, Montesquieu (1748, Bk. 8, p. 21).

37. For a more extended attack on trees, see Bernal (1988).

38. To some extent, the eighteenth-century French cultural conquest of Europe was shared by the Italians, who were generally acknowledged to be the finest musicians and painters, and still had a formidable scientific tradition.

39. See Blackall (1958, pp. 1–35).

40. Berlin (1976, pp. 145–216); Iggers (1968, pp. 34–37).

R E F E R E N C E S

Aristotle (1962). *Politics*. T. A. Sinclair, trans. London: Penguin.

Bentley, R. (1693). *A Confutation of Atheism from the Structure and Origin of Humane Bodies*. London.

Berlin, I. (1976). *Vico and Herder: Two Studies in the History of Ideas*. London: Hogarth.

Bernal, M. (1987a). "On the Transmission of the Alphabet to the Aegean before 1400 B.C.," *Bulletin of the American Schools of Oriental Research*.

—— (1987b). "First Land Then Sea: Thoughts about the Social Formation of the Mediterranean and Greece," in E. Genovese and L. Hochberg, eds., *Geography in Historical Perspective*. Oxford: Blackwell.

—— (1988). *Cadmean Letters: The Westward Diffusion of the Semitic Alphabet before 1400 B.C.* Winona Lake: Eisenbrauns.

Blackall, E. (1958). *The Emergence of German as a Literary Language, 1700–1775*. Cambridge University Press.

Blanco, A. G. (1984). "Hermeticism: Bibliographical Approach," in H. Temporini and W. Haase, eds. (1972–), *Aufstieg und Niedergang der römischen Welt: Geschichte und Kultur Roms im Spiegel der neueren Forschung*, 21 vols. Berlin/New York. Vol. 17.4. *Religion: (Heidentum: römische Götterkulte, orientalische Kulte in der römischen Welt [Forts.])*, ed. W. Haase, pp. 2240–81.

Bracken, H. (1973). "Essence, Accident and Race," *Hermathena* 116: 91–96.

—— (1978). "Philosophy and Racism," *Philosophia* 8: 241–60.

Child, F. J. (1882–98). *The English and Scottish Popular Ballads*. 5 vols. Boston.

Colie, R. L. (1957). *Light and Enlightenment: A Study of the Cambridge Platonists and the Dutch Arminians*. Cambridge University Press.

Devisse, J. (1979). *L'image du noir: Dans l'art occidental 2. Des premiers siècles chrétiens aux "grands découverts."* Pt. 1: *De la menace démoniaque à l'incarnation de la sainteté;* pt. 2: *Les Africains dans l'ordonnance chrétienne du monde (XIVᵉ–XVIᵉ siècle)*. Lausanne: Fondation de la Menil.

Force, J. E. (1985). *William Whiston: Honest Newtonian*. Cambridge University Press.

Godwin, J. (1979). *Athanasius Kircher: A Renaissance Man and the Quest for Lost Knowledge*. London: Thames & Hudson.

Gould, S. J. (1981). *The Mismeasure of Man*. New York: Norton.

Hare, J. (1647). *St. Edward's Ghost: or, Anti-Normanisme. Being a Patheticall Complaint and Motion in the behalfe of our English Nation against her grand (yet neglected) grievance, Normanisme*. London.

Iggers, G. I. (1968). *The German Conception of History: The National Tradition of Historical Thought from Herder to the Present*. Middletown, Conn.: Wesleyan University Press.

Iversen, E. (1961). *The Myth of Egypt and Its Hieroglyphs in European Tradition*. Copenhagen: Gad.

Jacob, M. C. (1976). *The Newtonians and the English Revolution 1689–1720*. Ithaca, N.Y.: Cornell University Press.

Jordan, W. D. (1969). *White over Black: American Attitudes toward the Negro: 1550–1812*. Baltimore: Penguin.

Kuhn, T. (1970). *The Structure of Scientific Revolutions*. 2d ed. University of Chicago Press.

Lloyd-Jones, H. (1982). *Classical Survivals: The Classics in the Modern World*. London: Duckworth.

Locke, J. (1688). *Essay concerning Human Understanding*. London.

—— (1689). *The True End of Civil Government*. London.

MacDougall, H. A. (1982). *Racial Myth in English History*. Montreal, Hanover, Vt., and London: Harvest House, University Press of New England.

Manuel, F. E. (1959). *The Eighteenth Century Confronts the Gods.* Cambridge, Mass.: Harvard University Press.

Montesquieu, C. de (1748). *L'esprit des lois.* Paris.

Pfeiffer, R. (1976). *History of Classical Scholarship: From 1300–1850.* Oxford: Clarendon.

Pocock, J. G A. (1985). "Gibbon as an Anglican Manqué: Clerical Culture and the *Decline and Fall.*" Miriam Leranbaum Memorial Lecture, SUNY, Binghamton, 17 April.

Poliakov, L. (1974). *The Aryan Myth: A History of Racist and Nationalist Ideas in Europe.* E. Howard, trans. London: Chatto & Windus and Heinemann for Sussex University Press.

Popkin, R. H. (1974). "The Philosophical Basis of Modern Racism," in C. Walton and J. P. Anton, eds., *Philosophy and the Civilizing Arts,* pp. 126–65.

Turgot, A. (1808–15). *Oeuvres de M. Turgot Ministre d'Etat, Précédées et accompagnées de Mémoires et de Notes sur sa Vie, son Administration et ses Ouvrages.* 9 vols. Paris.

Westfall, R. S. (1980). *Never at Rest: A Biography of Isaac Newton.* Cambridge University Press.

Wilamowitz-Moellendorf, U. von (1982). *History of Classical Scholarship.* A. Harris, trans. London and Baltimore: Johns Hopkins University Press.

Wismann, H. (1983). "Modus operandi, analyse comparé des études platoniciennes en France et en Allemagne au 19ème siècle," in Bollack and Wismann, pp. 490–513.

EARLY ANDEAN EXPERIMENTAL AGRICULTURE

Jack Weatherford

There is only one Machu Picchu, but it guards many mysteries. The ruins of this ancient Peruvian city sit perched eight thousand feet above sea level on a mountain overlooking the Urubamba River. Even though in size Machu Picchu barely surpasses a village, the ruins show a complexity indicative of a much more important place. The stone houses with trapezoidal doorways and simple lintel construction do not resemble the houses of the *puric,* the common peasants, and the public buildings surpass any administrative or religious building one might expect to see in a town of comparable size. The ruins show precision-crafted buildings with the neat regular lines, beveled edges, and mortarless seams that characterize the best of Inca architecture.

The spectacular setting combined with the exquisitely wrought buildings evoked much speculation and much romantic rubbish about the purpose of the city. The North American discoverer Hiram Bingham erroneously assumed that he had found Vilcabamba, the holdout capital of the Inca Empire after the fall of Cuzco. Lacking an explanation, many people assume that the purpose must have been religious and thus have dubbed the place "the sacred city of the Incas." Others claim that it was built as a city to protect the noble women from the Spanish, or that it served as a monastery associated with the sacred coca plant, or as a cult center.

None of this agrees with what we know about the Incas. Unlike the superstitious Aztecs, the Incas did not build large pyramids to perform massive blood sacrifices or pursue long wars to please their gods. Unlike the mystical Mayas, they did not build observatories to watch the endless patterns of the stars or write long, philosophical poems on the creation of the world. They displayed an austere practicality in every aspect of their lives, and they show little hint of religious fervor, no penchant for meditation, no tendency toward either the sentimental or the superstitious.

The supposedly practical peoples of ancient Rome, traditional Germany, and the contemporary United States seem almost like mystics compared to the Incas, and ancient Sparta seems like the home of the frivolous. The Incas' practicality shows in the precise and very angular style they used to construct buildings, in contrast to the more haphazard and rounder style of their predecessors. This same practicality and passion for organization shows in their economic system, which lacked money, markets, or merchants and yet managed to avoid the famine that stalks so many great empires.

In light of this practicality the very existence of Machu Picchu seems all the more puzzling. Why would the Incas build a city and line the mountain with terraces even though there was very little soil there? The builders used the best techniques known to them to make terraces that would last for eternity. Then the workers added layers of rock and clay as subsoil, and from the river below them they hauled up rich dirt over steep embankments half a mile deep. This task would be the equivalent of hauling dirt from the Colorado River to plant fields on top of the Grand Canyon.

The Incas built hundreds of the terraces, all of them quite small for any kind of extensive agriculture. Some of them narrow to as little as six inches in width. Yet these terraces climb up and down the mountain to great distances, and the Incas even built small terraces high up on the facing peak of Huayna Picchu, an hour's steep climb from the city. Such an arrangement makes no more sense than if Americans today decided to start farming the face of Mount Rushmore with plots the size of large flower boxes.

A hint of the possible function of Machu Picchu came to me while hiking around the area for two days with Charles Laughlin, a plant scientist from the University of Georgia. On one of our excursions, we returned to the ruined city by way of the Inca trail from the south. This trail enters the city through Inti Punuc, the stone gate of the sun, perched high up in the saddle of the mountain dividing the Machu Picchu side of the mountain from a dry inland valley. Standing in the gateway one sees two worlds, the brown and lifeless valley to one side and on the other side the lush, emerald-green valley watered by the thick fogs and mists of the Urubamba River far below the city ruins.

As we descended toward the city from this high pass, I stared out at the spectacular landscape. Why had the Incas built the city here at this point? Was it to guard the river? But what was there to guard? Perhaps it was a place to trade coca. But why would they need a monumental city for that? Why had they built the city up so far from the water of the river?

All the while I searched up and down the long vistas of the Urubamba and the surrounding mountains, Chuck was looking at the vegetation and naming everything growing along the path. I found this distracting from the big picture, but as we descended the mountain and passed from one terrace to another, the plants that he named changed. We were passing through a series of ecological layers, as one does on many mountains in the Andes. The mountainside is laid out in strips of vegetation and microzones. The place is a scientist's dream—the perfect place for all kinds of controlled experiments. Viewed in that context, the small terraces took on new meaning as experimental patches at a range of altitudes and built at so many different angles facing the morning sun, the evening sun, constant sun, or no sun. They are like a scientist's set of experiments all laid out in a field.

In my mind, Machu Picchu suddenly became an agricultural station. In that sense it was a sacred spot, because agriculture was a sacred activity for the Incas, who worshiped the life-giving Pachamama, the earth mother, and Inti, the sun, who together made the plants grow.

The ancient Peruvians had been among the world's greatest experimenters with agriculture, and they built numerous experimental areas where crops could be grown in different ways. It would not be surprising if they devoted a place such as Machu Picchu to just such activity. Whether this site actually functioned as an ancient experimental agricultural station or not, the Indians of the Andes probably did more plant experiments than any other people anywhere in the world.

Starting thousands of years before the Incas, the natives ascertained how to produce extremely high yields of potatoes from small plots of land. In the modern world, producing high yields has come about primarily through developing plants that can grow in different types of environments and, when necessary, through the manipulation of the immediate environment of the plant to ensure that it has just the right amount of moisture, nitrogen, and other requirements for maximum growth. Peruvians seem to have approached the problem in the opposite way. They sought to develop a different kind of plant for every type of soil, sun, and moisture condition. They prized diversity. They wanted potatoes in a variety of sizes, textures, and colors, from whites and yellows through purples, reds, oranges, and browns. Some tasted sweet and others too bitter for humans to eat, but the latter were useful as animal fodder.

They did not seek this diversity merely for the aesthetic pleasure of having so many shapes, colors, and textures, but rather for the practical reason that such variations in appearance also meant variation in other, less noticeable properties. Some potatoes matured fast and some slowly, an important consideration in a country where the growing season varies with the altitude. Some potatoes required a lot of water and some required very little, which made one variety or another more adaptable to the highly variable rainfalls of different valleys. Some potatoes stored easily for long periods of time, others made excellent food for livestock.

In addition to the potato, the Incas produced other tuber and root crops, such as *oca, añu, achira, papa liza, luki,* and *maca,* none of which even have names in English. The Peruvians grew corn in just as many varieties and diverse habitats, and they cultivated the native American grain crops that in Quechua they called *kiwacha* (or amaranth, *Amaranthus caudatus*) and *quinua* (or quinoa, *Chenopodium quinoa*).

The success of these early experimenters remains visible today, not only in the variety of food crops but in the extensive agricultural ruins of the Urubamba Valley stretching from Machu Picchu to the Inca capital city of Cuzco. As one goes along the valley, one is constantly in sight of Indian ruins remaining from the Spanish conquest. Crumbling watchtowers dot the high ridges like a row of decaying teeth, and empty citadels loom over nearly deserted villages. Irrigation canals once brought water down from the melting snows high in the mountains to the terraces. But the terraces now lie broken, and rock or mud long ago filled in the canals. It taxes the mind to imagine how magnificent this valley must have been before the conquest. Green terraced fields continued for miles, punctuated by filled warehouses; now, parched parcels of land, crumbling terraces, and destroyed bridges are all that remain to be seen.

As the Spanish armies, clergy, and diseases swept through the river valley, whole villages died or were taken away to work the mines of Potosí, and the rich valley soon gave way to decay and dim memories. This valley of the Urubamba River, which may have supported millions, now has only a fraction of its former population. While these fields lie neglected, the government of Peru, the land of the potato, imports potatoes from the Netherlands to feed the people.

Indians of the Andes have cultivated the potato on their mountain slopes and in their valleys for at least the last four thousand years. Apparently the potato descended from a tuberous *Solanum* that grew wild throughout the Americas and was used by Indian groups as far north as the southwestern United States, where the Navajos made it a major part of their diet. The Indians of the United States and of Mexico apparently were in the process of domesticating their own varieties of this potato when the Spanish arrived in the sixteenth century (Salaman, p. 1).

At the time of the Spanish conquest, Andean farmers already were producing about three thousand different types of potatoes in the Andes. This contrasts with the mere 250 varieties now grown in North America, and of those no more than twenty varieties constitute three-quarters of the total potato harvest in the contemporary United States. Under the guidance of the Indian farmers of the Andes, the potato became the basis for several great Andean empires, the last of which was that of the Incas whose empire fell to Francisco Pizarro in 1531.

The Andean farmers also devised and perfected the first freeze-dried method of preserving the potato. At night, farmers put their potatoes out in the freezing air of the high mountains. During the day the sun thawed the potatoes, and the farm family walked over them to press out the melting moisture. After several repetitions of this process, the potato dried into a white chunk which very much resembled modern plastic foam. In this very light form the Incas easily transported great numbers of potatoes to distant storehouses, where they could be preserved for five or six years without harm. When needed, the potato could be reconstituted by soaking it in water, and then it could be cooked. Cooks also ground it into meal for making soups and other dishes. Today this entire procedure continues exactly as before in thousands of hamlets scattered throughout the Andes. The resulting *ch'uño,* as the dried potatoes are called in Quechua, still serves as a staple of Andean cuisine throughout the year.

The Incas also used drying techniques on a variety of other vegetable crops and even on meat. The dried meat, or *charqui* as it was called in Quechua, also found favor among the Europeans as a convenient and light way to preserve and transport meat. The name *charqui* was taken over and corrupted into "*jerky,*" one of the few English words derived from Quechua.

Just as the silver of Potosí spread to Europe and then on to the Ottoman Empire, Timbuktu, and China to cause a major change in the world's economy, the humble potato spread to the rest of the world. The potato spread far more slowly than the silver, but in the end the potato and the other native crops of America have produced a far greater impact than the mountain of silver.

It is difficult to imagine what Ireland would be today without the potato. What would the Russians, the Germans, the Poles, and the Scandinavians eat? Without the potato the Soviet Union might never have become a world power, Germany would not have fought two world wars, and northern Europe and the Benelux countries would not have one of the world's highest standards of living.

Before the discovery of America, the Old World depended primarily on grain crops of domesticated grasses such as wheat, rye, barley, and oats in Europe and the Near East, rice in the Far East, and millet and sorghum in Africa. All of these plants, however, face numerous problems in their growing cycle. Because they grow on high stalks above the ground, they are easy prey to the destructive elements of wind, hail, heavy rain, and snow as well as to birds, insects, and animals.

For centuries the northern countries such as Russia and Germany suffered periodic famines when the grain crop failed because of unsuitable weather. For as long as the Old World depended on grain crops, the great population and power centers remained in the warmer southern nations around the Mediterranean, where the grains flourished. Greece, Rome, Persia, and Egypt all had successful empires primarily because of their control of grain production. Even a nation as far north as France was able to become a world power and a reasonably good producer of grain. But the unpredictable weather and food supply sat as a permanent burden on the German states, England, and Scandinavia, and on Russia, which sometimes exported grain and then sometimes imported it. These were all societies waiting for their chance to act on the cultural and political stage of world, but first they needed a consistent supply of nutritious and cheap food to sustain them.

This food finally arrived in the somewhat ugly form of the Andean potato. Together with maize corn from Mexico, potatoes were what French historian Fernand Braudel called "the miracle crops" (Braudel, vol. I, p. 74). The Europeans by no means greeted this new plant with general enthusiasm. The peasants of Europe despised the new plant. Aside from the occasional side dish of parsnips, turnips, and carrots, Europeans did not eat root crops. They certainly did not want to adopt one as a staple of their daily diet. For them the staples were the grains that they could mill and then bake into bread or more commonly could eat as a porridge, such as the oatmeal of the Scots and Irish or the gruel of the English. This was real food to the European peasant, not a knotty tuber grown by American savages.

European legends claimed potatoes caused leprosy because the potato grew in such a misshapen and ugly form. Some Orthodox sects in Russia called it the devil's plant and decreed it a sin to eat the potato, the tomato, and sugar, because they were not mentioned in the Bible. Even as authoritative a source as Denis

Diderot's *Encyclopédie* of 1765 accused the potato of being tasteless and of causing excess flatulence in the peasants who eat it (Braudel, vol. I, p. 170).

Adam Smith wrote one of the first defenses of the potato and theorized about the tremendous importance that its adoption portended for Europe. He accurately predicted that increased cultivation of potatoes would cause an increase in production, an increase in population, and an increase in the value of land. Based on his observation of Ireland, which was at that time the only country where the potato was already widely cultivated, Smith judged the tuber to be an excellent food, especially for the lower classes. In his opinion, the potato made men stronger and women more beautiful, and he based this opinion on his observations of the prostitutes and laborers imported from Ireland to London. Despite Smith's strong advocacy of potato cultivation, he doubted that potatoes would become very widespread because of the difficulty of preserving them for longer than a season (Smith, pp. 160–61).

For its first two centuries in Europe, the potato was little more than a curiosity grown in herbal gardens around monasteries and universities and eaten by the upper and middle classes as a novelty food; the masses steadfastly ignored the interloper. Not until the second half of the eighteenth century did the potato finally take root in fields of northern Europe. The peasants grudgingly accepted it only after their rulers forced them to plant it. Frederick the Great in Prussia, Catherine the Great in Russia, and similarly enlightened monarchs forced the peasants to grow potatoes or starve following a series of eighteenth-century famines, epidemics, and wars.

The archbishop of Mainz broke the dependence of the villagers of Kahl on grains through a number of strenuous laws. In Kahl and other villages, he outlawed construction of new home ovens and provided each village with only a single communal oven that the village women used in shifts. The large beehive-shaped oven still stands in the oldest part of Kahl near the church as a historical talisman uniting the contemporary villagers with the ancient community of their ancestors. The building of the communal oven markedly reduced the bread and baked goods available, because each housewife had only one turn per week at the oven, and she had to pay tax on each tray of foods she baked. Taxes on mills further reduced dependence on flour, and additional taxes on bakers and ovens raised the cost of bread. The peasants had to grow potatoes or face severe financial strain and possible hunger.

The monarchs and Adam Smith knew what the peasants would soon learn: a field of potatoes produces more food and more nutrition more reliably and with less labor than the same field planted in any grain. Even today, a hectare of land planted in potatoes produces 7.5 million calories. The same land planted in wheat produces only 4.2 million calories. The cultivation of potatoes also consumes far less calories or energy than does that of wheat. This means that each farmer could produce more hectares of food per worker, or that some of the workers could be freed for other tasks. The potato needed only three or four months to grow compared to almost double that for grains. The potato also needed far less attention and care while growing, and it grew in a variety of soils that were not otherwise productive (Farb and Armelagos, p. 76). Farmers found that the potato required none of the extensive milling and processing of grains, which necessitated a large capital investment in equipment and transportation. By contrast, potatoes could be pulled from the fields for immediate consumption or stored in the basement for nearly a year before being cooked.

The potato could be used for bread, although that was usually not necessary, since enough grain existed for the making of bread. Instead, cooks could make the potato into many new dishes to replace the limited breads, noodles, gruels, and porridges that could be made from grains. The potato could be served baked, boiled, roasted, or fried or could be made into soups, pancakes, dumplings, soufflés, and pies.

Once introduced into the fields of the European farmers, the potato thrived. Accustomed to the cool and often damp highland valleys of the Andes, the potato adapted easily to the cool and damp climates of Ireland, Germany, Poland, Russian, Scotland, England, the Netherlands, Belgium, and Scandinavia. Of the approximately three thousand varieties of potato grown in America, comparatively few were transplanted to Europe, but there were enough varieties to ensure that whatever region of Europe wanted a potato, at least one type possessed the traits that made it ideal for that climate and soil conditions. In Europe only the warmer areas of the Mediterranean proved inhospitable to the potato; there the natives continued with their traditional grains.

In the northern climates, where long winters without fresh vegetables were the rule, the potato offered a new source of vitamin C that greatly improved the health of the population. For a reason still not adequately understood, potatoes do not produce tooth cavities nearly as much as grains. When eaten as processed flour, the finely ground starches from grains stick to the teeth and rot them. On the other hand, when eaten as tough grains, they are very abrasive and wear out the teeth. By eating more potatoes, the northern Europeans retained strong teeth until an older age, and this improved their general health. Nutritional diseases declined steadily, and by early in the eighteenth century, they virtually disappeared as causes of death in Europe except during war (Petersen, p. 442).

In its gradual conquest of Europe the potato moved primarily from west to east. Ireland was the first nation to make an enthusiastic conversion to potato farming. As is often the case when reliable historical information is scarce, various legends arise to account for the origin or introduction of the potato. According to one such legend, Sir Walter Raleigh introduced the potato to Ireland in the sixteenth century on his way back to England from the Caribbean. Another legend claims that the Irish peasants discovered the potato in galleys of the ships of the Spanish Armada washed up on Irish beaches in 1588 after the Armada was attacked by the English navy and dispersed by a great storm. The timing for both legends seems more or less accurate; the latter half of the sixteenth century is usually accepted as the date of introduction. But another century passed before the plant took hold and won the widespread and fanatic devotion which the Irish have had for it ever since. By the end of the seventeenth century, it was the staple food of Ireland (Salaman, p. 222).

From Ireland, the potato as a staple crop of the field, rather than as a mere curiosity of the garden, spread through England, Scotland, and Wales, across the low countries and France, and through Germany and eastern Europe. The Russians did not adopt it very widely until the 1830s and 1840s, but then became no less devoted converts than the original Irish.

Despite the difficulties of introducing the potato to Europe, once the peasants became accustomed to it they loved it. In Flanders, between 1693 and 1791, grain consumption fell from 758 grams per person per day to 475 because of the introduction of potatoes. This means that potatoes replaced about 40 percent of the cereal consumption of Flanders (Braudel, vol. I, p. 170). The nutrition of the people improved markedly and the population grew accordingly.

One major problem encountered when tracing the history of the potato derives from its being misnamed from very early in the English-speaking areas. The Indians of the Andes have called it and still call it the *papa*. The word "potato" first came into English as the name of a very different plant imported from the Caribbean islands. The word *batata* came from the Taino Indians of what is now the Dominican Republic and Haiti; the Spanish made it *patata*, whence came the English "potato." This plant has since been called the "sweet potato" in English, but at the time of its introduction it was known simply as the potato. When the *papa* arrived from the Andes the English mistook it for the Caribbean sweet potato and consequently have called it "potato" ever since. To distinguish between the two unrelated tubers, one is often called the "sweet potato" now and the other is the "common potato" or sometimes the "white potato." In reading the early chronicles of plants and agriculture, it is often impossible to ascertain which of these plants is designated by the name "potato."

With the new calorie source and the new source of nutrition, the potato-fed armies of Frederick of Prussia and Catherine of Russia began pushing against their southern neighbors. During the Age of the Enlightenment these northern cultures wrestled free from the economic, cultural, and political domination of the south. Power shifted toward Germany and Britain and away from Spain and France, and finally all were eclipsed by Russia. Russia quickly became and remains the world's greatest producer of potatoes, and the Russians are among the world's greatest consumers of the potato. Their adoption of the potato as their staple food preceded their rise as a world power.

American foods brought about the miracle that centuries of prayer, work, and medicine had been unable to do: they cured Europe of the episodic famines that had been one of the major restraints on the population for millennia. Even France, the richest country of Europe, suffered acutely from numerous general famines and even more regional ones. The number of general famines in France varied from as few as two in the twelfth century to as many as twenty-six in the eleventh century. Even as recently as the eighteenth century, France succumbed to sixteen general famines, bringing the total number of famines to 111 for the years between 1371 and 1791 (Braudel, vol. I, p. 74).

As little as an acre and a half sufficed to nourish the average family if they planted the land in potatoes and supplemented these with milk, butter, or cheese.

With the revolutionary crop, the population of Ireland expanded from 3.2 million in 1754 to 8.2 million less than a century later in 1845. During this same century an additional 1.75 million Irish left Ireland for the New World. Thus in the first century after the introduction of the potato, the population of Ireland effectively tripled (Crosby, p. 183). Then when the potato blight hit, thousands of Irish starved or emigrated, because without the potato Ireland could not support such a massive population. Had the Irish followed the Indian technique of planting many different types of potatoes rather than just a few, the effect of the blight probably would have been considerably lessened.

Despite the Irish famine, the population of each country boomed as it adopted the potato. Possibly it was because of this effect of the potato on population that so many people accepted the notion that the potato was an aphrodisiac. The reputed aphrodisiac powers of the plant may also have been due to the tuber's somewhat phallic shape. Its erotic reputation further grew because of its similarity to the truffle, an extravagantly expensive delicacy associated with the rowdy and gluttonous life of the rich and aristocratic.

If we look at the larger population picture since the spread of American crops around the world, we see much the same process. In the three centuries between 1650 and 1950, the population of Europe (including the Soviet Union) climbed from just over 100 million to almost 600 million, a sixfold increase. In 1650 the population of Africa was probably about the same as that of Europe, but Africa's population only doubled, from 100 million to about 198 million in 1950. This comparatively slow growth reflects the slower incorporation of American food crops as well as the depopulation caused by the slave trade and colonization. Asia's population did not increase as rapidly as Europe's but did grow faster than Africa's. Asia went from 327 million to 1.3 billion in the same three centuries. In all, the Old World of Europe, Asia, and Africa increased in population from about half a billion people in 1650 to over two billion by 1950. In addition, tens of millions of people left Asia, Africa, and Europe to live in the New World as colonists or slaves (Crosby, p. 166).

On the world scene, the total population in 1750 has been estimated at 750 million. It reached a billion in 1830, two billion in 1930, and four billion in 1975 (Farb and Armelagos, p. 75). In recent decades, medical advances have accounted for some of the increase in population, but most of the population growth preceded the medical innovations. Improved nutrition accounts for most of the growth prior to this century. Only later did improvements in public health and sanitation have an impact, and only in the past century have any real gains in medicine affected the population.

The potato alone cannot claim full responsibility for the great population and health boom of the Old World. The American Indians cultivated over three hundred food crops, and many of these had dozens of variations. The people of the Old World gradually transplanted many of these crops from America, and each in turn contributed in various ways to improving the world diet in both quantity and quality of foods. The Indians gave the world three-fifths of the crops now in cultivation. Many of these grew in environments that had formerly been inaccessible to agriculture because of temperature, moisture, type of soil, or altitude.

Some of these plants spread through the world by way of Europe, but most of the tropical plants crossed directly to Africa and Asia. The African slave trade sent hundreds of ships laden with humans across the middle Atlantic to Brazil, the Caribbean, Virginia, and the Carolinas, but they had less cargo with which to return. In carrying food and supplies with them on the return voyage to Africa, the crews also carried American Indian foods and spices, many of which quickly took root in the similar soil and climate of Africa. At a slightly slower pace the tropical American foods spread to Asia aboard Spanish ships sailing from Acapulco, Mexico, to Spain's major Asian port at Manila in the Philippines. Other products were brought to Asia from the opposite direction by the Portuguese, who carried products from their Brazilian colony to their scattered holdings in Africa, around to Goa in India, and on to their easternmost colony of Macao in southern China.

The protein supply of the Old World also increased with the great variety of beans brought in from America, principally from Mexico, where beans, corn, and squashes had been the mainstay of the Indian diet. Different parts of the Old World eagerly adopted one or more of the American beans, including kidney beans, string beans, snap beans, the Mexican frijole, the common bean, butter bean, lima bean, navy bean, and pole bean. In addition, American Indian beans included many which took on very un-American names, such as the French bean, Rangoon bean, Burma bean, and Madagascar bean (Crosby, p. 172).

In Africa the American peanut or groundnut also helped to increase the protein intake. The peanut found a large following in Asia as well as in Africa, but in Europe it never became anything more than a novelty snack, a source of oil, and animal fodder. Even a food as common in the diet of the United States as peanut butter never found a European following, but it became common in West Africa, where peanut butter is mixed with hot peppers and sold in the streets as a tasty and nutritious snack.

Farther north in Europe where the cold hampers peanut cultivation, large amounts of oil and animal feed are made from another American staple, the sunflower, which is native to the United States plains and was domesticated by the Indians of North America. Next to the potato the sunflower is probably the most important plant that America gave to Russia. Neither olives nor oil-producing grains grew very well in Russia, and thus the sunflower finally gave the Russians a reliable source of edible oil. As with the potato, the Soviet Union is today the world's largest producer and consumer of sunflowers.

Of the many types of American grains, only maize corn found a use among the Europeans. The European farmers learned to grow corn, but most of them never learned to eat it. Only in a few areas of southern Europe, such as Italy, Greece, Yugoslavia, and Romania, is it sometimes used as a substitute for grains in making soupy porridges. Otherwise, the Europeans have largely ignored it. But corn did have a role to play. Many important products such as oil can be made from it, and it makes a nutritious food for most domesticated animals. Potatoes may be eaten by some animals, such as pigs, but not by others, such as cows or chickens. Corn, however, could be fed to all of these animals. Corn did for the animal population of Europe what the potato did for the human population. The new animal food not only increased the supply of meat and lard but also increased the supply of eggs, milk, butter, cheese, and all the animal products that constitute so important a part of the European diet. These foods substantially increased the European intake of protein.

The population impact of maize corn was much stronger in southern Europe than in the north. During the eighteenth century, when corn and other American crops were being widely cultivated in southern Europe, the population of Italy grew from eleven million to eighteen million, and the population of Spain doubled (Farb and Armelagos, p. 76). The impact on Africa is more difficult to measure, but corn grew more reliably than did the traditional African staples of millet and sorghum.

Corn grows easily in soils that receive too much or too little moisture for wheat or rice. While rice grows best in semitropical zones and wheat flourishes primarily in temperate zones, maize corn thrives in both. Indians cultivated rapid-growing varieties in areas as cold as Canada and Chile, while other types of corn flourished in the heat of the Amazon. Inca farmers cultivated it on the terraced sides of Andean mountains, and Hopi farmers irrigated it and made it grow in the hottest and driest deserts of the United States.

Even though the whites adopted corn slowly in comparison with the Chinese and Africans, they have not stopped finding new uses for it. The many varieties can be eaten directly or made into flour, starch, or syrup for cooking in other products. Particularly in its use as dextrose or as corn syrup it has steadily replaced cane sugar in processed foods. Unlike cane sugar, corn syrup can hold its moisture and thereby prevent crystallization of itself as well as any other sugars with which it is mixed. This unique resistance to drying out and crystallizing creates unusual uses for corn syrup, as in motion-picture studios, where special-effects artists dye it red and use it for blood in their films, since it will retain the appearance of fresh blood for hours of rehearsals and film shootings. This same quality has more practical applications, making corn syrup the ideal ingredient for sweetened drinks from baby formulas and chocolate milk to colas as well as for ice creams, catsup, syrups, candies, salad dressings, pies, and any dish for which moisture is desirable. Corn syrup can also do all of this much more cheaply than other sugars.

In Africa, maize corn and cassava together underlie the great population explosion which started in the last century and has continued throughout the twentieth century. Cassava assumed a particularly important role in Africa because it grows in poor soils that will not produce any other food crop; thus it does not compete with corn or the grains for land. Cassava has the added advantage that its roots can be harvested at any time within a two-year period after becoming mature. Thus they make an excellent food bank that can be preserved in the ground for times of scarcity. The climate and the numerous animal and insect pests of tropical Africa make food storage precarious. Cassava has one major drawback in that unlike the potato and corn it lacks substantial nutrition. Since the cassava root is almost pure starch, one hectare of land planted in cassava produces almost ten million calories, compared with less than half that for grains and three-fourths that for rice and potatoes. Cassava became a major source of calories and an important crop in preventing famine, but it did not improve the nutrition of the African diet.

Asians adopted the sweet potato with the same eagerness that Africans adopted cassava, and it had much the same impact on their diets as the common potato had on the Europeans'. Even though rice offers more nutrition than most grains, it still suffers from many of the shortcomings of the grains. It also showed high susceptibility to both droughts and floods, which caused frequent famines in China. The sweet potato enabled the Chinese to ameliorate the cycle of feast and famine that their dependence on rice had so long made inevitable. The sweet potato yields three to four times as much food as would rice planted on the same area of land, and the sweet potato thrives in weather and soils that kill rice (Crosby, p. 172).

Even though the stereotype of Oriental food is that it is all rice-based, the common people depend heavily on the sweet potato as well. China is the world's largest producer of sweet potatoes; the Chinese enjoy them plain or ground into flour to make noodles, dumplings, and other dishes. Rice is the prestige food of the Orient, but the sweet potato is the daily food for many of the peasants.

America also gave the world some new grains that offered more nutritional value than any of the Old World grains. For the most part the Europeans ignored the amaranth from Mexico and quinoa from the Andes. In the last years before the conquest of Mexico, the Aztec capital of Tenochtitlán received an annual tribute of twenty thousand tons of amaranth grain from its seventeen provinces (mostly in native Mexican varieties of *Amaranthus hypochondriacus* and *A. cruentus*). Because of its high protein content of 16 percent, compared with 7 percent for rice and 13 percent for wheat, amaranth is considerably more nutritious than most grains. It also has twice the lysine found in wheat and as much as is in milk, making it far more balanced in proteins than most plant foods. The Aztecs respected the grain so highly that each year they publicly celebrated it by eating amaranth cakes made with honey or human blood shaped into the forms of the gods. The Spanish interpreted this as a black mockery of the holy communion of the Christian church and consequently forbade the cultivation, sale, or consumption of amaranth under penalty of death (National Academy of Sciences, pp. 1–4). No matter how nutritious it might be, they already had enough grain crops and did not want more.

In the twentieth century, scientists discovered that Indian farmers in the high valleys of the Andes and in remote parts of Mexico still cultivate amaranth. Now international research organizations such as the National Academy of Sciences of the United States and UNICEF encourage its dissemination to help feed the Third World nations. Amaranth went on sale in health-food stores in the United States in the 1970s, and quinoa followed in 1986, but the great potentials of these two miracle grains of the Indians have not yet been tapped.

Amaranth has become one of the most important cereals in the diets of highland peoples in India, China, Pakistan, Tibet, and Nepal. Cultivation has spread so widely in the past century that Asia now cultivates and consumes more amaranth than do the Americas.

In the marshy ponds that dot the terrain of Minnesota and Wisconsin, the Indians for centuries gathered a water-grown grain which the whites later called "wild rice," even though it is not an Old World rice. Despite the emphasis on "wild," the plant grew under human care, for during the harvesting the Ojibwa farmers dispersed the seed for the next year's crop. The Ojibwas also introduced wild rice into ponds where it had not grown: In this way they spread the plant into new areas, but they also controlled the type of plant grown in ponds by selecting for particular characteristics preferred by various groups of Ojibwas. Thus lakes and ponds became associated with particular types of wild rice.

Unlike regular rice, which grows in semitropical areas, wild rice thrives in the coldest parts of the northern great plains. It grows after passing the winter in lakes that freeze for four or more months each year. This unusual crop has become popular as a luxury food, and cooks often mix it with white rices to accompany gourmet dishes. The full food potential of the plant is yet to be explored. Just as the potato was eaten only by the rich for the first two hundred years after its introduction to Europe and only later became a staple for common people, perhaps one day wild rice may find its role in the feeding of large populations in cold swampy areas such as the Siberian tundra which have shown little agricultural potential thus far.

Today the agricultural experimentation that began many centuries ago in the Andes continues at the International Potato Institute, located in the suburbs of Lima. The modern buildings of the institute spread out over the countryside like the new campus of a community college. Immaculate beds of potatoes in small, neat rows surround and run between the buildings. The site looks almost as though the beautiful mountain terraces of Machu Picchu had been flattened out and arranged in military formations across the plain. Funded by various international agencies, the institute serves as a bank of germ plasm for the approximately ten thousand varieties of domesticated and wild potatoes found in the Andes. In addition to the beds at this lowland center, the institute maintains a highland center and one in the jungle as well. In the bins of the institute one sees yellow, red, and purple potatoes as well as white, blue, green, black, and brown ones. Some are round or oval, others horn-shaped or squash-shaped. Some have smooth skins and others have gnarled skins. No matter how beautiful or ugly a potato may be, each one is carefully protected and nourished for the future treasure it may give the world.

The full array of scientists from agronomists and anthropologists through botanists, cartographers, demographers, economists, and on through the alphabet to zoologists all work together to study every aspect of the potato and its place in the environment and in human society. They study the way it grows, how the peasants prepare the soil, how it is harvested, and the ways of storing it in diverse climates. Looking at so many scientists puttering around the potato beds, working in the lab, conferring around coffee pots, and experimenting with diagrams on computers, I could not help but think of what it must have been like at Machu Picchu five hundred years earlier. I have no special knowledge of exactly what went on at Machu Picchu then, but perhaps the work done there now continues at this institute.

Like their predecessors, these scientists work to expand the range of the potato into new environments such as the tropics, to find ways of growing potatoes from seed rather than from the root, and to develop ways to preserve its nutrition longer. They hope that one day the potato might feed the peoples of Brazil, Botswana, or Bangladesh as it already feeds the peoples of Germany, Ireland, and Russia.

R E F E R E N C E S

Braudel, Fernand. *Civilization and Capitalism, 15th–18th Century.* 3 vols. Translated by Siân Reynolds. New York: Harper & Row, 1982–84. Vol. I, *The Structures of Everyday Life.*

Crosby, Alfred W., Jr. *The Columbian Exchange.* Westport, Conn.: Greenwood Press, 1972.

Drummond, J. C., and Anne Wilbraham. *The Englishman's Food.* London: Cape, 1957.

Farb, Peter, and George Armelagos. *Consuming Passions: The Anthropology of Eating.* New York: Washington Square Books, 1980.

Kalinowski, Luis Sumar. *Kiwicha, el pequeño gigante.* Lima, Peru: UNICEF.

National Academy of Sciences. *Amaranth: Modern Prospects for an Ancient Crop.* Washington, D.C.: National Academy Press, 1984.

Petersen, William. *Population.* 3d ed. New York: Macmillan.

Salaman, Redcliffe N. *The History and Social Influence of the Potato.* Cambridge: Cambridge University Press, 1949.

Smith, Adam. *The Wealth of Nations.* New York: Random House, 1937.

Stea, Vikkie. "High-Yield Corn from Ancient Seed Strains." *Christian Science Monitor,* August 20, 1985, p. 29.

Weatherford, Jack M. "Millennium of Modernization: A Changing German Village." In Priscilla Copeland Reining and Barbara Lenkerd, eds., *Village Viability in Contemporary Society.* AAAS Selected Symposium Series 34. Boulder, Colo.: Westview, 1980.

PART TWO

Science Constructs "Race"

In the last decades of the [nineteenth] century, both theories of racial supremacy and scientific and technological gauges of human worth were widely accepted by European politicians and intellectuals. . . . A tautological relationship developed: scientific and technological achievements were frequently cited as gauges of racial capacity, and estimates of racial capacity determined the degree of technical and scientific education made available to different non-Western peoples.

Michael Adas, *Machines as the Measure of Men: Science, Technology, and Ideologies of Western Dominance.*

Race is the phlogiston of our time.

Ashley Montagu, *The Concept of Race*

Orientalism depends for its strategy on this flexible *positional* superiority, which puts the Westerner in a whole series of possible relationships with the Orient without ever losing him the relative upper hand. And why should it have been otherwise, especially during the period of extraordinary European ascendancy from the late Renaissance to the present? . . . [T]here emerged a complex Orient suitable for study in the academy, for display in the museum, for reconstruction in the colonial office, for theoretical illustration in anthropological, biological, linguistic, racial, and historical theses about mankind and the universe, for instances of economic and sociological theories of development, revolution, cultural personality, national or religious character.

Edward Said, *Orientalism*

It is now almost forty years since biologists and anthropologists began to point out why explanations of human variability in terms of "racial"[1] inheritance were not useful. Moreover, for an even longer time scientists have recognized "the incompatibility between race and natural selection . . . so that if one's major aim were to discover the races of man, one has to disregard natural selection," as Frank B. Livingstone points out in his essay in this section.

In the first essay of this section, Stephen Jay Gould points to the cultural beliefs of David Hume, Thomas Jefferson, Benjamin Franklin, and other Enlightenment figures that shaped research on race differences prior to Darwin's writings. Then he reanalyzes the data of the founder of the science of craniometry,

Samuel George Morton, and identifies the "fudging and finagling" in Morton's interpretation of his data that enabled him to come up with spurious claims about the intellectual inferiority of blacks and Indians (and, not surprisingly, women). Since Morton published the data Gould uses, we may assume that he did not intend to deceive. Instead, the social expectations that he shared with the dominant scientific community shaped the way he understood his data. (Gould also reports on his subsequent discovery that *his own* beliefs evidently led him to a small bit of "fudging and finagling" in his reanalysis of Morton's figures!)

Anthropologist Gloria A. Marshall shows that the racial categories scientists use are highly shaped by the folklore of their particular cultures. For example, there is the case of a group of Japanese who do not differ biologically from their countrymen but who persistently have been perceived by them as racially different and inferior. In fact, it is a long history of class oppression that has made them different. S. L. Washburn analyzes the many ways in which culture shapes observable racial differences—in which culture shapes biology, we might say. Frank B. Livingstone explains why race is no longer a useful concept for modern biology; population genetics explains everything that can be explained about variations in populations. Livingstone's argument is not a secret to biologists and physical anthropologists. Why is this concept still used in biology, physical anthropology, medicine, and public health?

The persistence of the idea of race has unfortunate consequences in a number of scientific and policy areas. In the excerpt from *Not in Our Genes*, R. C. Lewontin, Steven Rose, and Leon J. Kamin review the history of the IQ controversy, drawing attention not only to the knowingly fraudulent claims of Cyril Burt's famous twin studies (originally exposed by Kamin) but also to the failure of scientific journals to exercise the level of critical scrutiny over the writings of Burt and his supporters that are standard for criticisms of racist claims as well as for research reports in less controversial fields. It is also clear, however, that while scientists have been among the most powerful legitimators of scientific racism, they have also been among its most devastating critics.

Nancy Krieger and Mary Bassett show that when it comes to explanations of racial differences in health levels, not only the persistence of the genetic model but also the uses of the supposedly more progressive environmental model demonstrate how "ideology and politics penetrate scientific theory and research." The genetic model blames black genes, and the environmental model is used to blame black life-style choices for low levels of black health. Neither focuses on "the social production of disease under conditions of capitalism and racial oppression."

In the final selection in this section, Nancy Leys Stepan and Sander L. Gilman show how Jews and African Americans fought back against the scientific discourses that defined them as biologically inferior; they did so by creating a "reverse discourse" that used the idioms of science against scientific claims. While these strategies alone could not succeed against the mighty forces of scientific racism arrayed against them, they were indispensable to the "psychological survival and political action" of these maligned groups.

Additional unsettling questions about scientific method and science education arise from reflecting on these accounts. The success of the methods and norms of the sciences in producing nonracist results depends ultimately on the abilities of scientists to detect racist beliefs and on their good intentions to do so. After all, no one but scientists is supposed to be capable of policing scientific methods and norms. Yet these studies make clear that good intentions are perfectly compatible with racist scientific research and racist consequences of science. Clearly, scientists who are members of a dominant race are no more able than nonscientists to detect widespread racist assumptions.

Is the solution to this problem to be found "outside" the sciences themselves? How entrenched have the sciences become in legitimating the dominant views of racial difference? And how is the power and authority of the sciences enhanced as a result of their serving such a legitimating role?

On the other hand, contributions toward a solution may also be found "inside" the sciences. It seems clear from these accounts that scientific method—at least as scientists are taught to conceptualize it—is not powerful enough to eliminate such distorting cultural biases. How can it be strengthened to enable scientists *systematically* to detect the assumptions shared by the dominant groups in society? Would the increased presence of peoples of Third World descent in the direction of "Western" science help in the project of detecting racist biases in the results of scientific research as well as in social life? Does this mean that affirmative action is not only an important moral and political issue but also a significant scientific and epistemological one? Should science education be transformed so that scientists are obligated to learn to think in a sophisticated way about race, racism, and the diversity of approaches to such topics so that they can detect how racist social structures will tend to shape their own work even when they have intentions to the contrary? These issues are discussed further in later sections.

N O T E

1. Hereafter, the terms *race* and *racial* are always to be understood as in quotes to remind us that these terms refer to human social constructions, not something given by nature. The matter is actually a bit more complex, since the whole culture-nature dichotomy is in fact part of this historically specific social construction, as several essays in this collection point out.

AMERICAN POLYGENY AND CRANIOMETRY BEFORE DARWIN
Blacks and Indians as Separate, Inferior Species

Stephen Jay Gould

Order is Heaven's first law; and, this confessed,
Some are, and must be, greater than the rest.

> Alexander Pope, *Essay on Man* (1733)

Appeals to reason or to the nature of the universe have been used throughout history to enshrine existing hierarchies as proper and inevitable. The hierarchies rarely endure for more than a few generations, but the arguments, refurbished for the next round of social institutions, cycle endlessly.

The catalogue of justifications based on nature traverses a range of possibilities: elaborate analogies between rulers and a hierarchy of subordinate classes with the central earth of Ptolemaic astronomy and a ranked order of heavenly bodies circling around it; or appeals to the universal order of a "great chain of being," ranging in a single series from amoebae to God, and including near its apex a graded series of human races and classes. To quote Alexander Pope again:

> Without this just gradation, could they be
> Subjected, these to those, or all to thee?
> • • •
> From Nature's chain whatever link you strike,
> Tenth, or ten thousandth, breaks the chain alike.

The humblest, as well as the greatest, play their part in preserving the continuity of universal order; all occupy their appointed roles.

This book treats an argument that, to many people's surprise, seems to be a latecomer: biological determinism, the notion that people at the bottom are constructed of intrinsically inferior material (poor brains, bad genes, or whatever). Plato cautiously floated this proposal in the *Republic*, but finally branded it as a lie.

Racial prejudice may be as old as recorded human history, but its biological justification imposed the additional burden of intrinsic inferiority upon despised groups, and precluded redemption by conversion or assimilation. The "scientific" argument has formed a primary line of attack for more than a century. In discussing the first biological theory supported by extensive quantitative data— early nineteenth-century craniometry—I must begin by posing a question of causality: did the introduction of inductive science add legitimate data to change or strengthen a nascent argument for racial ranking? Or did a priori commitment to ranking fashion the "scientific" questions asked and even the data gathered to support a foreordained conclusion?

A Shared Context of Culture

In assessing the impact of science upon eighteenth- and nineteenth-century views of race, we must first recognize the cultural milieu of a society whose leaders and intellectuals did not doubt the propriety of racial ranking—with Indians below whites, and blacks below everybody else (fig. 1). Under this universal umbrella, arguments did not contrast equality with inequality. One group—we might call them "hard-liners"—held that blacks were inferior and that their biological status justified enslavement and colonization. Another group—the "soft-liners," if you will—agreed that blacks were inferior, but held that a people's right to freedom did not depend upon their level of intelligence. "Whatever be their degree of talents," wrote Thomas Jefferson, "it is no measure of their rights."

Soft-liners held various attitudes about the nature of black disadvantage. Some argued that proper education and standard of life could "raise" blacks to a white level; others advocated permanent black ineptitude. They also disagreed about the biological or cultural roots of black inferiority. Yet, throughout the egalitarian tradition of the European Enlightenment and the American revolution, I cannot identify any popular position remotely like the "cultural relativism" that prevails (at least by lip-service) in liberal circles today. The nearest approach is a common argument that black inferiority is purely cultural and that it can be completely eradicated by education to a Caucasian standard.

All American culture heroes embraced racial attitudes that would embarrass public-school mythmakers. Benjamin Franklin, while viewing the inferiority of blacks as purely cultural and completely remediable, nonetheless expressed his hope that America would become a domain of whites, undiluted by less pleasing colors.

> I could wish their numbers were increased. And while we are, as I may call it, scouring our planet, by clearing America of woods, and so making this side of our globe reflect a brighter light to the eyes of inhabitants in Mars or Venus, why should we . . . darken its people? Why increase the Sons of Africa, by planting them in America, where we have so fair an opportunity, by excluding

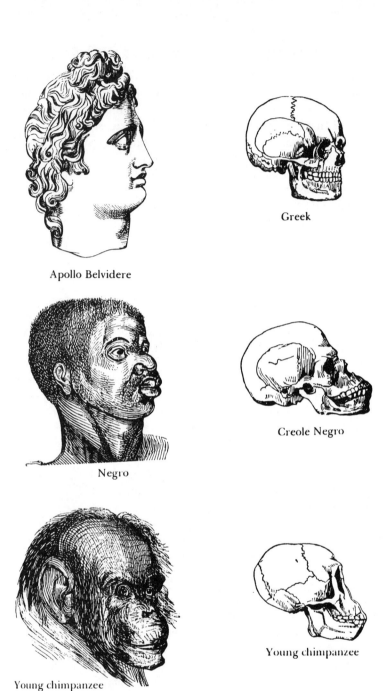

Apollo Belvidere

Greek

Negro

Creole Negro

Young chimpanzee

Young chimpanzee

The unilinear scale of human races and lower relatives according to Nott and Gliddon, 1868. The chimpanzee skull is falsely inflated, and the Negro jaw extended, to give the impression that blacks might even rank lower than the apes.

all blacks and tawneys, of increasing the lovely white and red?* (*Observations concerning the Increase of Mankind,* 1751)

Others among our heroes argued for biological inferiority. Thomas Jefferson wrote, albeit tentatively: "I advance it, therefore, as a suspicion only, that the blacks, whether originally a distinct race, or made distinct by time and circumstance, are inferior to the whites in the endowment both of body and of mind" (in Gossett, 1965, p. 44). Lincoln's pleasure at the performance of black soldiers in the Union army greatly increased his respect for freedmen and former slaves. But freedom does not imply biological equality, and Lincoln never abandoned a basic attitude, so strongly expressed in the Douglas debates (1858):

> There is a physical difference between the white and black races which I believe will forever forbid the two races living together on terms of social and political equality. And inasmuch as they cannot so live, while they do remain together there must be the position of superior and inferior, and I as much as any other man am in favor of having the superior position assigned to the white race.

Lest we choose to regard this statement as mere campaign rhetoric, I cite this private jotting, scribbled on a fragment of paper in 1859:

> Negro equality! Fudge! How long, in the Government of a God great enough to make and rule the universe, shall there continue knaves to vend, and fools to quip, so low a piece of demagogism as this (in Sinkler, 1972, p. 47).

I do not cite these statements in order to release skeletons from ancient closets. Rather, I quote the men who have justly earned our highest respect in order to show that white leaders of Western nations did not question the propriety of racial ranking during the eighteenth and nineteenth centuries. In this context, the pervasive assent given by scientists to conventional rankings arose from shared social belief, not from objective data gathered to test an open question. Yet, in a curious case of reversed causality, these pronouncements were read as independent support for the political context.

All leading scientists followed social conventions (fig. 2). In the first formal definition of human races in modern taxonomic terms, Linnaeus mixed character with anatomy (*Systema naturae,* 1758). *Homo sapiens afer* (the African black), he proclaimed, is "ruled by caprice"; *Homo sapiens europaeus* is "ruled by customs." Of African women, he wrote: *Feminis sine pudoris; mammae lactantes prolixae—*

---

*I have been struck by the frequency of such aesthetic claims as a basis of racial preference. Although J. F. Blumenbach, the founder of anthropology, had stated that toads must view other toads as paragons of beauty, many astute intellectuals never doubted the equation of whiteness with perfection. Franklin at least had the decency to include the original inhabitants in his future America; but, a century later, Oliver Wendell Holmes rejoiced in the elimination of Indians on aesthetic grounds: " . . . and so the red-crayon sketch is rubbed out, and the canvas is ready for a picture of manhood a little more like God's own image" (in Gossett, 1965, p. 243).

Algerian Negro   Saharran Negro

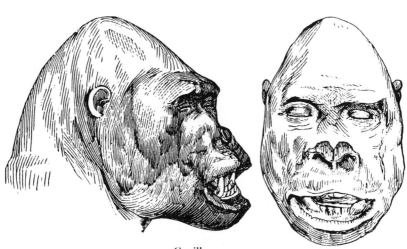

Gorilla

An unsubtle attempt to suggest strong affinity between blacks and gorillas. From Nott and Gliddon, 1854. Nott and Gliddon comment on
this figure: "The palpable analogies and dissimilitudes between an inferior type of mankind and a superior type of monkey require no
comment."

Women without shame, breasts lactate profusely. The men, he added, are indolent and anoint themselves with grease.

The three greatest naturalists of the nineteenth century did not hold blacks in high esteem. Georges Cuvier, widely hailed in France as the Aristotle of his age, and a founder of geology, paleontology, and modern comparative anatomy, referred to native Africans as "the most degraded of human races, whose form approaches that of the beast and whose intelligence is nowhere great enough to arrive at regular government" (Cuvier, 1812, p. 105). Charles Lyell, the conventional founder of modern geology, wrote:

> The brain of the Bushman . . . leads towards the brain of the Simiadae (monkeys). This implies a connexion between want of intelligence and structural assimilation. Each race of Man has its place, like the inferior animals (in Wilson, 1970, p. 347).

Charles Darwin, the kindly liberal and passionate abolitionist,* wrote about a future time when the gap between human and ape will increase by the anticipated extinction of such intermediates as chimpanzees and Hottentots.

> The break will then be rendered wider, for it will intervene between man in a more civilized state, as we may hope, than the Caucasian, and some ape as low as a baboon, instead of as at present between the negro or Australian and the gorilla (*Descent of Man,* 1871, p. 201).

Even more instructive are the beliefs of those few scientists often cited in retrospect as cultural relativists and defenders of equality. J. F. Blumenbach attributed racial differences to the influences of climate. He protested rankings based on beauty or presumed mental ability and assembled a collection of books written by blacks. Nonetheless, he did not doubt that white people set a standard, from which all other races must be viewed as departures:

> The Caucasian must, on every physiological principle, be considered as the primary or intermediate of these five principal Races. The two extremes into which it has deviated, are on the one hand the Mongolian, on the other the Ethiopian [African blacks] (1825, p. 37).

Alexander von Humboldt, world traveler, statesman, and greatest popularizer of nineteenth-century science, would be the hero of all modern egalitarians who

---

*Darwin wrote, for example, in the *Voyage of the Beagle:* "Near Rio de Janeiro I lived opposite to an old lady, who kept screws to crush the fingers of her female slaves. I have stayed in a house where a young household mulatto, daily and hourly, was reviled, beaten, and persecuted enough to break the spirit of the lowest animal. I have seen a little boy, six or seven years old, struck thrice with a horse-whip (before I could interfere) on his naked head, for having handed me a glass of water not quite clean. . . . And these deeds are done and palliated by men, who profess to love their neighbors as themselves, who believe in God, and pray that his Will be done on earth! It makes one's blood boil, yet heart tremble, to think that we Englishmen and our American descendants, with their boastful cry of liberty, have been and are so guilty."

seek antecedents in history. He, more than any other scientist of his time, argued forcefully and at length against ranking on mental or aesthetic grounds. He also drew political implications from his convictions, and campaigned against all forms of slavery and subjugation as impediments to the natural striving of all people to attain mental excellence. He wrote in the most famous passage of his five-volume *Cosmos:*

> Whilst we maintain the unity of the human species, we at the same time repel the depressing assumption of superior and inferior races of men. There are nations more susceptible of cultivation than others—but none in themselves nobler than others. All are in like degree designed for freedom (1849, p. 368).

Yet even Humboldt invoked innate mental difference to resolve some dilemmas of human history. Why, he asks in the second volume of *Cosmos,* did the Arabs explode in culture and science soon after the rise of Islam, while Scythian tribes of southeastern Europe stuck to their ancient ways; for both peoples were nomadic and shared a common climate and environment? Humboldt did find some cultural differences—greater contact of Arabs with surrounding urbanized cultures, for example. But, in the end, he labeled Arabs as a "more highly gifted race" with greater "natural adaptability for mental cultivation" (1849, p. 578).

Alfred Russel Wallace, codiscoverer of natural selection with Darwin, is justly hailed as an antiracist. Indeed, he did affirm near equality in the innate mental capacity of all peoples. Yet, curiously, this very belief led him to abandon natural selection and return to divine creation as an explanation for the human mind—much to Darwin's disgust. Natural selection, Wallace argued, can only build structures immediately useful to animals possessing them. The brain of savages is, potentially, as good as ours. But they do not use it fully, as the rudeness and inferiority of their culture indicates. Since modern savages are much like human ancestors, our brain must have developed its higher capacities long before we put them to any use.

Preevolutionary Styles of Scientific Racism: Monogenism and Polygenism

Preevolutionary justifications for racial ranking proceeded in two modes. The "softer" argument—again using some inappropriate definitions from modern perspectives—upheld the scriptural unity of all peoples in the single creation of Adam and Eve. This view was called *monogenism*—or origin from a single source. Human races are a product of degeneration from Eden's perfection. Races have declined to different degrees, whites least and blacks most. Climate proved most popular as a primary cause for racial distinction. Degenerationists differed on the remediability of modern deficits. Some held that the differences, though developed gradually under the influence of climate, were now fixed and could never be reversed. Others argued that the fact of gradual development implied reversibility in appropriate environments. Samuel Stanhope Smith, president of the College of New Jersey (later Princeton), hoped that American blacks, in a climate more suited to Caucasian temperaments, would soon turn white. But other degenerationists felt that improvement in benevolent climes could not proceed rapidly enough to have any impact upon human history.

The "harder" argument abandoned scripture as allegorical and held that human races were separate biological species, the descendants of different Adams. As another form of life, blacks need not participate in the "equality of man." Proponents of this argument were called "polygenists."

Degenerationism was probably the more popular argument, if only because scripture was not to be discarded lightly. Moreover, the interfertility of all human races seemed to guarantee their union as a single species under Buffon's criterion that members of a species be able to breed with each other, but not with representatives of any other group. Buffon himself, the greatest of eighteenth-century France, was a strong abolitionist and exponent of improvement for inferior races in appropriate environments. But he never doubted the inherent validity of a white standard:

> The most temperate climate lies between the 40th and 50th degree of latitude, and it produces the most handsome and beautiful men. It is from this climate that the ideas of the genuine color of mankind, and of the various degrees of beauty ought to be derived.

Some degenerationists cited their commitments in the name of human brotherhood. Etienne Serres, a famous French medical anatomist, wrote in 1860 that the perfectibility of lower races distinguished humans as the only species subject to improvement by its own efforts. He lambasted polygeny as a "savage theory" that "seems to lend scientific support to the enslavement of races less advanced in civilization than the Caucasian":

> Their conclusion is that the Negro is no more a white man than a donkey is a horse or a zebra—a theory put into practice in the United States of America, to the shame of civilization (1860, pp. 407–8).

Nonetheless, Serres worked to document the signs of inferiority among lower races. As an anatomist, he sought evidence within his specialty and confessed to some difficulty in establishing both criteria and data. He settled on the theory of recapitulation—the idea that higher creatures repeat the adult stages of lower animals during their own growth. Adult blacks, he argued, should be like white children, adult Mongolians like white adolescents. He searched diligently but devised nothing much better than the distance between navel and penis—"that ineffaceable sign of embryonic life in man." This distance is small relative to body height in babies of all races. The navel migrates upward during growth, but attains greater heights in whites than in yellows, and never gets very far at all in blacks. Blacks remain perpetually like white children and announce their inferiority thereby.

Polygeny, though less popular, had its illustrious supporters as well. David Hume did not spend his life absorbed in pure thought. He held a number of political posts, including the stewardship of the English colonial office in 1766. Hume advocated both the separate creation and innate inferiority of nonwhite races:

> I am apt to suspect the negroes and in general all the other species of men (for there are four or five different kinds) to be naturally inferior to the whites. There never was a civilized nation of any other complexion than white, nor even any individual eminent either in action or speculation.* No ingenious manufacturers amongst them, no arts, no sciences. . . . Such a uniform and constant difference could not happen in so many countries and ages, if nature had not made an original distinction betwixt these breeds of men. Not to mention our colonies, there are negroes slaves dispersed all over Europe, of which none ever discovered any symptoms of ingenuity, tho' low people without education will start up amongst us, and distinguish themselves in every profession. In Jamaica indeed they talk of one negroe as a man of parts and learning; but 'tis likely he is admired for very slender accomplishments like a parrot who speaks a few words plainly (in Popkin, 1974, p. 143; see Popkin's excellent article for a long analysis of Hume as a polygenist).

Charles White, an English surgeon, wrote the strongest defense of polygeny in 1799—*Account of the Regular Gradation in Man.* White abandoned Buffon's criterion of interfertility in defining species, pointing to successful hybrids between such conventionally separate groups as foxes, wolves, and jackals.† He railed against the idea that climate might produce racial differences, arguing that such ideas might lead, by extension, to the "degrading notion" of evolution between species. He disclaimed any political motivation and announced an untainted purpose: "to investigate a proposition in natural history." He explicitly rejected any extension of polygeny to "countenance the pernicious practice of enslaving mankind." White's criteria of ranking tended toward the aesthetic, and

---

*This "inductive" argument from human cultures is far from dead as a defense of racism. In his *Study of History* (1934 edition), Arnold Toynbee wrote: "When we classify mankind by color, the only one of the primary races, given by this classification, which has not made a creative contribution to any of our twenty-one civilizations is the Black Race" (in Newby, 1969, p. 217).

†Modern evolutionary theory does invoke a barrier to interfertility as the primary criterion for status as a species. In the standard definition: "Species are actually or potentially interbreeding populations sharing a common gene pool, and reproductively isolated from all other groups." Reproductive isolation, however, does not mean that individual hybrids never arise, but only that the two species maintain their integrity in natural contact. Hybrids may be sterile (mules). Fertile hybrids may even arise quite frequently, but if natural selection acts preferentially against them (as a result of inferiority in structural design, rejection as mates by full members of either species, etc.) they will not increase in frequency and the two species will not amalgamate. Often fertile hybrids can be produced in the laboratory by imposing situations not encountered in nature (forced breeding between species that normally mature at different times of the year, for example). Such examples do not refute a status as separate species because the two groups do not amalgamate in the wild (maturation at different times of the year may be an efficient means of reproductive isolation).

his argument included the following gem, often quoted. Where else but among Caucasians, he argued, can we find

> . . . that nobly arched head, containing such a quantity of brain. . . . Where that variety of features, and fulness of expression; those long, flowing, graceful ring-lets; that majestic beard, those rosy cheeks and coral lips? Where that . . . noble gait? In what other quarter of the globe shall we find the blush that overspreads the soft features of the beautiful women of Europe, that emblem of modesty, of delicate feelings . . . where, except on the bosom of the European woman, two such plump and snowy white hemispheres, tipt with vermillion (in Stanton, 1960, p. 17).

Louis Agassiz—America's Theorist of Polygeny

Ralph Waldo Emerson argued that intellectual emancipation should follow political independence. American scholars should abandon their subservience to European styles and theories. We have, Emerson wrote, "listened too long to the courtly muses of Europe." "We will walk on our own feet; we will work with our own hands; we will speak our own minds" (in Stanton, 1960, p. 84).

In the early to mid-nineteenth century, the budding profession of American science organized itself to follow Emerson's advice. A collection of eclectic amateurs, bowing before the prestige of European theorists, became a group of professionals with indigenous ideas and an internal dynamic that did not require constant fueling from Europe. The doctrine of polygeny acted as an important agent in this transformation; for it was one of the first theories of largely American origin that won the attention and respect of European scientists—so much so that Europeans referred to polygeny as the "American school" of anthropology. Polygeny had European antecedents, as we have seen, but Americans developed the data cited in its support and based a large body of research on its tenets. I shall concentrate on the two most famous advocates of polygeny—Agassiz the theorist and Morton the data analyst; and I shall try to uncover both the hidden motives and the finagling of data so central to their support.* For starters, it is obviously not accidental that a nation still practicing slavery and expelling its aboriginal inhabitants from their homelands should have provided a base for theories that blacks and Indians are separate species, inferior to whites.

Louis Agassiz (1807–1873), the great Swiss naturalist, won his reputation in Europe, primarily as Cuvier's disciple and a student of fossil fishes. His immigration to America in the 1840s immediately elevated the status of American natural history. For the first time, a major European theorist had found enough of value in the United States to come and stay. Agassiz became a professor at Harvard, where he founded and directed the Museum of Comparative Zoology until his

---

*An excellent history of the entire "American school" can be found in W. Stanton's *The Leopard's Spots.*

death in 1873 (I occupy an office in the original wing of his building). Agassiz was a charmer; he was lionized in social and intellectual circles from Boston to Charlestown. He spoke for science with boundless enthusiasm and raised money with equal zeal to support his buildings, collections, and publications. No man did more to establish and enhance the prestige of American biology during the nineteenth century.

Agassiz also became the leading spokesman for polygeny in America. He did not bring this theory with him from Europe. He converted to the doctrine of human races as separate species after his first experiences with American blacks.

Agassiz did not embrace polygeny as a conscious political doctrine. He never doubted the propriety of racial ranking, but he did count himself among the opponents of slavery. His adherence to polygeny flowed easily from procedures of biological research that he had developed in other and earlier contexts. He was, first of all, a devout creationist who lived long enough to become the only major scientific opponent of evolution. But nearly all scientists were creationists before 1859, and most did not become polygenists (racial differentiation within a single species posed no threat to the doctrine of special creation—just consider breeds of dogs and cattle). Agassiz's predisposition to polygeny arose primarily from two aspects of his personal theories and methods:

1. In studying the geographic distribution of animals and plants, Agassiz developed a theory about "centers of creation." He believed that species were created in their proper places and did not generally migrate far from these centers. Other biogeographers invoked creation in a single spot with extensive migration thereafter. Thus, when Agassiz studied what we would now regard as a single widespread species, divided into fairly distinct geographical races, he tended to name several separate species, each created at its center of origin. *Homo sapiens* is a primary example of a cosmopolitan, variable species.

2. Agassiz was an extreme splitter in his taxonomic practice. Taxonomists tend to fall into two camps—"lumpers," who concentrate on similarities and amalgamate groups with small differences into single species, and "splitters," who focus on minute distinctions and establish species on the smallest peculiarities of design. Agassiz was a splitter among splitters. He once named three genera of fossil fishes from isolated teeth that a later paleontologist found in the variable dentition of a single individual. He named invalid species of freshwater fishes by the hundreds, basing them upon peculiar individuals within single, variable species. An extreme splitter who viewed organisms as created over their entire range might well be tempted to regard human races as separate creations. Nonetheless, before coming to America, Agassiz advocated the doctrine of human unity—even though he viewed our variation as exceptional. He wrote in 1845:

> Here is revealed anew the superiority of the human genre and its greater independence in nature. Whereas the animals are distinct species in the different zoological provinces to which they appertain, man, despite the diversity of his races, constitutes one and the same species over all the surface of the globe (in Stanton, 1960, p. 101).

Agassiz may have been predisposed to polygeny by biological belief, but I doubt that this pious man would have abandoned the Biblical orthodoxy of a single Adam if he had not been confronted both by the sight of American blacks and the urgings of his polygenist colleagues. Agassiz never generated any data for polygeny. His conversion followed an immediate visceral judgment and some persistent persuasion by friends. His later support rested on nothing deeper in the realm of biological knowledge.

Agassiz had never seen a black person in Europe. When he first met blacks as servants at his Philadelphia hotel in 1846, he experienced a pronounced visceral revulsion. This jarring experience, coupled with his sexual fears about miscegenation, apparently established his conviction that blacks are a separate species. In a remarkably candid passage, he wrote to his mother from America:

> It was in Philadelphia that I first found myself in prolonged contact with negroes; all the domestics in my hotel were men of color. I can scarcely express to you the painful impression that I received, especially since the feeling that they inspired in me is contrary to all our ideas about the confraternity of the human type [*genre*] and the unique origin of our species. But truth before all. Nevertheless, I experienced pity at the sight of this degraded and degenerate race, and their lot inspired compassion in me in thinking that they are really men. Nonetheless, it is impossible for me to repress the feeling that they are not of the same blood as us. In seeing their black faces with their thick lips and grimacing teeth, the wool on their head, their bent knees, their elongated hands, their large curved nails, and especially the livid color of the palm of their hands, I could not take my eyes off their face in order to tell them to stay far away. And when they advanced that hideous hand towards my plate in order to serve me, I wished I were able to depart in order to eat a piece of bread elsewhere, rather than dine with such service. What unhappiness for the white race—to have tied their existence so closely with that of negroes in certain countries! God preserve us from such a contact! (Agassiz to his mother, December 1846.) (The standard *Life and Letters*, compiled by Agassiz's wife, omits these lines in presenting an expurgated version of this famous letter. Other historians have paraphrased them or passed them by. I recovered this passage from the original manuscript in Harvard's Houghton Library and have translated it, verbatim, for the first time so far as I know.)

Agassiz published his major statement on human races in the *Christian Examiner* for 1850. He begins by dismissing as demagogues both the divines who would outlaw him as an infidel (for preaching the doctrine of multiple Adams) and the abolitionists who would brand him as a defender of slavery:

> It has been charged upon the views here advanced that they tend to the support of slavery. . . . Is that a fair objection to a philosophical investigation? Here we have to do only with the question of the origin of men: let the politicians, let those who feel themselves called upon to regulate human society, see what they can do with the results. . . . We disclaim, however, all connection with any question involving political ⸻ It is simply with reference to the possi-

bility of appreciating the differences existing between different men, and of eventually determining whether they have originated all over the world, and under what circumstances, that we have tried to trace some facts respecting the human races (1850, p. 113).

Agassiz then presents his argument: The theory of polygeny does not constitute an attack upon the scriptural doctrine of human unity. Men are bound by a common structure and sympathy, even though races were created as separate species. The Bible does not speak about parts of the world unknown to the ancients; the tale of Adam refers only to the origin of Caucasians. Negroes and Caucasians are as distinct in the mummified remains of Egypt as they are today. If human races were the product of climatic influence, then the passage of three thousand years would have engendered substantial changes (Agassiz had no inkling of human antiquity; he believed that three thousand years included a major chunk of our entire history). Modern races occupy definite, nonoverlapping, geographic areas—even though some ranges have been blurred or obliterated by migration. As physically distinct, temporally invariant groups with discrete geographical ranges, human races met all Agassiz's biological criteria for separate species.

> These races must have originated . . . in the same numerical proportions, and over the same area, in which they now occur. . . . They cannot have originated in single individuals, but must have been created in that numeric harmony, which is characteristic of each species; men must have originated in nations, as the bees have originated in swarms (pp. 128–29).

Then, approaching the end of his article, Agassiz abruptly shifts his ground and announces a moral imperative—even though he had explicitly justified his inquiry by casting it as an objective investigation of natural history.

> There are upon earth different races of men, inhabiting different parts of its surface, which have different physical characters; and this fact . . . presses upon us the obligation to settle the relative rank among these races, the relative value of the characters peculiar to each, in a scientific point of view. . . . As philosophers it is our duty to look it in the face (p. 142).

As direct evidence for differential, innate value Agassiz ventures no further than the standard set of Caucasian cultural stereotypes:

> The indominable, courageous, proud Indian—in how very different a light he stands by the side of the submissive, obsequious, imitative negro, or by the side of the tricky, cunning, and cowardly Mongolian! Are not these facts indications that the different races do not rank upon one level in nature (p. 144).

Blacks, Agassiz declares, must occupy the bottom rung of any objective ladder:

It seems to us to be mock-philanthropy and mock-philosophy to assume that all races have the same abilities, enjoy the same powers, and show the same natural dispositions, and that in consequence of this equality they are entitled to the same position in human society. History speaks here for itself. . . . This compact continent of Africa exhibits a population which has been in constant intercourse with the white race, which has enjoyed the benefit of the example of the Egyptian civilization, of the Phoenician civilization, of the Roman civilization, of the Arab civilization . . . and nevertheless there has never been a regulated society of black men developed on that continent. Does not this indicate in this race a peculiar apathy, a peculiar indifference to the advantages afforded by civilized society? (pp. 143–144).

If Agassiz had not made his political message clear, he ends by advocating specific social policy. Education, he argues, must be tailored to innate ability; train blacks in hand work, whites in mind work:

What would be the best education to be imparted to the different races in consequence of their primitive difference. . . . We entertain not the slightest doubt that human affairs with reference to the colored races would be far more judiciously conducted if, in our intercourse with them, we were guided by a full consciousness of the real difference existing between us and them, and a desire to foster those dispositions that are eminently marked in them, rather than by treating them on terms of equality (p. 145).

Since those "eminently marked" dispositions are submissiveness, obsequiousness, and imitation, we can well imagine what Agassiz had in mind. I have treated this paper in detail because it is so typical of its genre—advocacy of social policy couched as a dispassionate inquiry into scientific fact. The strategy is by no means moribund today.

In a later correspondence, pursued in the midst of the Civil War, Agassiz expressed his political views more forcefully and at greater length. (These letters are also expurgated without indication in the standard version published by Agassiz's wife. Again, I have restored passages from the original letters in Harvard's Houghton Library.) S. G. Howe, a member of Lincoln's Inquiry Commission, asked Agassiz's opinion about the role of blacks in a reunited nation. (Howe, known best for his work in prison reform and education of the blind, was the husband of Julia Ward Howe, author of the "Battle Hymn of the Republic.") In four long and impassioned letters, Agassiz pleaded his case. The persistence of a large and permanent black population in America must be acknowledged as a grim reality. Indians, driven by their commendable pride, may perish in battle, but "the negro exhibits by nature a pliability, a readiness to accommodate himself to circumstances, a proneness to imitate those among whom he lives" (9 August 1863).

Although legal equality must be granted to all, blacks should be denied social equality, lest the white race be compromised and diluted: "Social equality I deem at all time impracticable. It is a natural impossibility flowing from the very character of the negro race" (10 August 1863); for blacks are "indolent, playful, sensuous, imitative, subservient, good natured, versatile, unsteady in their purpose, devoted, affectionate, in everything unlike other races, they may be compared to children, grown in the stature of adults while retaining a childlike mind. . . . Therefore I hold that they are incapable of living on a footing of social equality with the whites, in one and the same community, without being an element of social disorder" (10 August 1863). Blacks must be regulated and limited, lest an injudicious award of social privilege sow later discord:

> No man has a right to what he is unfit to use. . . . Let us beware of granting too much to the negro race in the beginning, lest it become necessary to recall violently some of the privileges which they may use to our detriment and their own injury (10 August 1863).

For Agassiz, nothing inspired more fear than the prospect of amalgamation by intermarriage. White strength depends upon separation: "The production of halfbreeds is as much a sin against nature, as incest in a civilized community is a sin against purity of character. . . . Far from presenting to me a natural solution of our difficulties, the idea of amalgamation is most repugnant to my feelings, I hold it to be a perversion of every natural sentiment. . . . No efforts should be spared to check that which is abhorrent to our better nature, and to the progress of a higher civilization and a purer morality" (9 August 1863).

Agassiz now realizes that he has argued himself into a corner. If interbreeding among races (separate species to Agassiz) is unnatural and repugnant, why are "halfbreeds" so common in America? Agassiz attributes this lamentable fact to the sexual receptiveness of housemaids and the naïveté of young Southern gentlemen. The servants, it seems, are halfbreeds already (we are not told how their parents overcame a natural repugnance for one another); young men respond aesthetically to the white half, while a degree of black heritage loosens the natural inhibitions of a higher race. Once acclimated, the poor young men are hooked, and they acquire a taste for pure blacks:

> As soon as the sexual desires are awakening in the young men of the South, they find it easy to gratify themselves by the readiness with which they are met by colored [halfbreed] house servants. . . . This blunts his better instincts in that direction and leads him gradually to seek more spicy partners, as I have heard the full blacks called by fast young men (9 August 1863).

Finally, Agassiz combines vivid image and metaphor to warn against the ultimate danger of a mixed and enfeebled people:

> Conceive for a moment the difference it would make in future ages, for the prospect of republican institutions and our civilization generally, if instead of the manly population descended from cognate nations the United States should hereafter be inhabited by the effeminate progeny of mixed races, half indian, half negro, sprinkled with white blood. . . . I shudder from the consequences.

We have already to struggle, in our progress, against the influence of universal equality, in consequence of the difficulty of preserving the acquisitions of individual eminence, the wealth of refinement and culture growing out of select associations. What would be our condition if to these difficulties were added the far more tenacious influences of physical disability. . . . How shall we eradicate the stigma of a lower race when its blood has once been allowed to flow freely into that of our children (10 August 1863).*

Agassiz concludes that legal freedom awarded to slaves in manumission must spur the enforcement of rigid social separation among races. Fortunately, nature shall be the accomplice of moral virtue; for people, free to choose, gravitate naturally toward the climates of their original homeland. The black species, created for hot and humid conditions, will prevail in the Southern lowlands, though whites will maintain dominion over the seashore and elevated ground. The new South will contain some Negro states. We should bow before this necessity and admit them into the Union; we have, after all, already recognized both "Haity and Liberia."† But the bracing North is not a congenial home for carefree and lackadaisical people, created for warmer regions. Pure blacks will migrate South, leaving a stubborn residue to dwindle and die out in the North: "I hope it may gradually die out in the north where it has only an artificial foothold" (11 August 1863). As for the mulattoes, "their sickly physique and their impaired fecundity" should assure their demise once the shackles of slavery no longer provide an opportunity for unnatural interbreeding.

Agassiz's world collapsed during the last decade of his life. His students rebelled; his supporters defected. He remained a hero to the public, but scientists began to regard him as a rigid and aging dogmatist, standing firm in his antiquated beliefs before the Darwinian tide. But his social preferences for racial segregation prevailed—all the more because his fanciful hope for voluntary geographic separation did not.

Samuel George Morton—Empiricist of Polygeny

Agassiz did not spend all his time in Philadelphia reviling black waiters. In the same letter to his mother, he wrote in glowing terms of his visit to the anatomical

---

*E. D. Cope, America's leading paleontologist and evolutionary biologist, reiterated the same theme even more forcefully in 1890 (p. 2054): "The highest race of man cannot afford to lose or even to compromise the advantages it has acquired by hundreds of centuries of toil and hardship, by mingling its blood with the lowest. . . . We cannot cloud or extinguish the fine nervous susceptibility, and the mental force, which cultivation develops in the constitution of the Indo-European, by the fleshly instincts, and dark mind of the African. Not only is the mind stagnated, and the life of mere living introduced in its stead, but the possibility of resurrection is rendered doubtful or impossible."
†Not all detractors of blacks were so generous. E. D. Cope, who feared that miscegenation would block the path to heaven (see preceding footnote), advocated the return of all blacks to Africa (1890, p. 2053): "Have we not burdens enough to carry in the European peasantry which we are called on every year to receive and assimilate? Is our own race on a plane sufficiently high, to render it safe for us to carry eight millions of dead material in the very center of our vital organism?"

collection of Philadelphia's distinguished scientist and physician Samuel George Morton: "Imagine a series of 600 skulls, most of Indians from all tribes who inhabit or once inhabited all of America. Nothing like it exists anywhere else. This collection, by itself, is worth a trip to America" (Agassiz to his mother, December 1846, translated from the original letter in Houghton Library, Harvard University).

Agassiz speculated freely and at length, but he amassed no data to support his polygenic theory. Morton, a Philadelphia patrician with two medical degrees—one from fashionable Edinburgh—provided the "facts" that won worldwide respect for the "American school" of polygeny. Morton began his collection of human skulls in the 1820s; he had more than one thousand when he died in 1851. Friends (and enemies) referred to his great charnel house as "the American Golgotha."

Morton won his reputation as the great data-gatherer and objectivist of American science, the man who would raise an immature enterprise from the mires of fanciful speculation. Oliver Wendell Holmes praised Morton for "the severe and cautious character" of his works, which "from their very nature are permanent data for all future students of ethnology" (in Stanton, 1960, p. 96). The same Humboldt who had asserted the inherent equality of all races wrote:

> The craniological treasures which you have been so fortunate as to unite in your collection, have in you found a worthy interpreter. Your work is equally remarkable for the profundity of its anatomical views, the numerical detail of the relations of organic conformation, and the absence of those poetical reveries which are the myths of modern physiology (in Meigs, 1851, p. 48).

When Morton died in 1851, the *New York Tribune* wrote that "probably no scientific man in America enjoyed a higher reputation among scholars throughout the world, than Dr. Morton" (in Stanton, 1960, p. 144).

Yet Morton gathered skulls neither for the dilettante's motive of abstract interest nor the taxonomist's zeal for complete representation. He had a hypothesis to test: that a ranking of races could be established objectively by physical characteristics of the brain, particularly by its size. Morton took a special interest in native Americans. As George Combe, his fervent friend and supporter, wrote:

> One of the most singular features in the history of this continent, is, that the aboriginal races, with few exceptions, have perished or constantly receded, before the Anglo-Saxon race, and have in no instance either mingled with them as equals, or adopted their manners and civilization. These phenomena must have a cause; and can any inquiry be at once more interesting and philosophical than that which endeavors to ascertain whether that cause be connected with a difference in the brain between the native American race, and their conquering invaders (Combe and Coates, in review of Morton's *Crania Americana,* 1840, p. 352).

Moreover, Combe argued that Morton's collection would acquire true scientific value *only if* mental and moral worth could be read from brains: "If this doctrine be unfounded, these skulls are mere facts in Natural History, presenting no particular information as to the mental qualities of the people" (from Combe's appendix to Morton's *Crania Americana,* 1839, p. 275).

Although he vacillated early in his career, Morton soon became a leader among the American polygenists. He wrote several articles to defend the status of human races as separate, created species. He took on the strongest claim of opponents—the interfertility of all human races—by arguing from both sides. He relied on travelers' reports to claim that some human races—Australian aborigines and Caucasians in particular—very rarely produce fertile offspring (Morton, 1851). He attributed this failure to "a disparity of primordial organization." But, he continued, Buffon's criterion of interfertility must be abandoned in any case, for hybridization is common in nature, even between species belonging to different genera (Morton, 1847, 1850). Species must be redefined as "a primordial organic form" (1850, p. 82). "Bravo, my dear Sir," wrote Agassiz in a letter, "you have at last furnished science with a true philosophical definition of species" (in Stanton, 1960, p. 141). But how to recognize a primordial form? Morton replied: "If certain existing organic types can be traced back into the 'night of time,' as dissimilar as we see them now, is it not more reasonable to regard them as aboriginal, than to suppose them the mere and accidental derivations of an isolated, patriarchal stem of which we know nothing?" (1850, p. 82). Thus, Morton regarded several breeds of dogs as separate species because their skeletons resided in the Egyptian catacombs, as recognizable and distinct from other breeds as they are now. The tombs also contained blacks and Caucasians. Morton dated the beaching of Noah's Ark on Ararat at 4,179 years before his time, and the Egyptian tombs at just 1,000 years after that—clearly not enough time for the sons of Noah to differentiate into races. (How, he asks, can we believe that races changed so rapidly for 1,000 years, and not at all for 3,000 years since then?) Human races must have been separate from the start (Morton, 1839, p. 88).

But separate, as the Supreme Court once said, need not mean unequal. Morton therefore set out to establish relative rank on "objective" grounds. He surveyed the drawings of ancient Egypt and found that blacks are invariably depicted as menials—a sure sign that they have always played their appropriate biological role: "Negroes were numerous in Egypt, but their social position in ancient times was the same that it is now, that of servants and slaves" (Morton, 1844, p. 158). (A curious argument, to be sure, for these blacks had been captured in warfare; sub-Saharan societies depicted blacks as rulers.)

But Morton's fame as a scientist rested upon his collection of skulls and their role in racial ranking. Since the cranial cavity of a human skull provides a faithful measure of the brain it once contained, Morton set out to rank races by the average sizes of their brains. He filled the cranial cavity with sifted white mustard seed, poured the seed back into a graduated cylinder and read the skull's volume in cubic inches. Later on, he became dissatisfied with mustard seed because he could not obtain consistent results. The seeds did not pack well, for they were too light and still varied too much in size, despite sieving. Remeasurements of single skulls might differ by more than 5 percent, or 4 cubic inches in skulls with an average capacity near 80 cubic inches. Consequently, he switched to one-eighth-inch-diameter lead shot "of the size called BB" and achieved consistent results that never varied by more than a single cubic inch for the same skull.

Morton published three major works on the sizes of human skulls—his lavish, beautifully illustrated volume on American Indians, the *Crania Americana* of 1839; his studies on skulls from the Egyptian tombs, the *Crania Aegyptiaca* of 1844; and the epitome of his entire collection in 1849. Each contained a table, summarizing his results on average skull volumes arranged by race. I have reproduced all three tables here (tables 1 to 3). They represent the major contribution of American polygeny to debates about racial ranking. They outlived the theory of separate creations and were reprinted repeatedly during the nineteenth century as irrefutable, "hard" data on the mental worth of human races. Needless to say, they matched every good Yankee's prejudice—whites on top, Indians in the middle, and blacks on the bottom; and, among whites, Teutons and Anglo-Saxons on top, Jews in the middle, and Hindus on the bottom. Moreover, the pattern had been stable throughout recorded history, for whites had the same advantage over blacks in ancient Egypt. Status and access to power in Morton's America faithfully reflected biological merit. How could sentimentalists and egalitarians stand against the dictates of nature? Morton had provided clean, objective data based on the largest collection of skulls in the world.

During the summer of 1977 I spent several weeks reanalyzing Morton's data. (Morton, the self-styled objectivist, published all his raw information. We can infer with little doubt how he moved from raw measurements to summary tables.) In short, and to put it bluntly, Morton's summaries are a patchwork of fudging and finagling in the clear interest of controlling a priori convictions. Yet—and this is the most intriguing aspect of the case—I find no evidence of conscious fraud; indeed, had Morton been a conscious fudger, he would not have published his data so openly.

Conscious fraud is probably rare in science. It is also not very interesting, for it tells us little about the nature of scientific activity. Liars, if discovered, are excommunicated; scientists declare that their profession has properly policed itself, and they return to work, mythology unimpaired, and objectively vindicated. The prevalence of *unconscious* finagling, on the other hand, suggests a general conclusion about the social context of science. For if scientists can be honestly self-deluded to Morton's extent, then prior prejudice may be found anywhere, even in the basics of measuring bones and toting sums.

The Case of Indian Inferiority: Crania Americana*

Morton began his first and largest work, the *Crania Americana* of 1839, with a discourse on the essential character of human races. His statements immediately expose his prejudices. Of the "Greenland esquimaux," he wrote: "They are

---

*This account omits many statistical details of my analysis. The complete tale appears in Gould, 1978. Some passages are taken from this article.

TABLE 1. **Morton's Summary Table of Cranial Capacity by Race**

Race	N	Internal Capacity (IN³)		
		Mean	Largest	Smallest
Caucasian	52	87	109	75
Mongolian	10	83	93	69
Malay	18	81	89	64
American	147	82	100	60
Ethiopian	29	78	94	65

TABLE 2. **Cranial Capacities for Skulls from Egyptian Tombs**

People	Mean Capacity (IN³)	N
Caucasian		
Pelasgic	88	21
Semitic	82	5
Egyptian	80	39
Negroid	79	6
Negro	73	1

crafty, sensual, ungrateful, obstinate and unfeeling, and much of their affection for their children may be traced to purely selfish motives. They devour the most disgusting aliments uncooked and uncleaned, and seem to have no ideas beyond providing for the present moment. . . . Their mental faculties, from infancy to old age, present a continued childhood. . . . In gluttony, selfishness, and ingratitude, they are perhaps unequalled by any other nation of people" (1839, p. 54). Morton thought little better of other Mongolians, for he wrote of the Chinese (p. 50): "So versatile are their feelings and actions, that they have been compared to the monkey race, whose attention is perpetually changing from one object to another." The Hottentots, he claimed (p. 90) are "the nearest approximation to the lower animals. . . . Their complexion is a yellowish brown, compared by travellers to the peculiar hue of Europeans in the last stages of jaundice. . . . The women are represented as even more repulsive in appearance than the men." Yet, when Morton had to describe one Caucasian tribe as a "mere horde of rapacious banditti" (p. 9), he quickly added that "their moral perceptions, under the influence of an equitable government, would no doubt assume a much more favorable aspect."

Morton's summary chart (table 1) presents the "hard" argument of the *Crania Americana*. He had measured the capacity of 144 Indian skulls and calculated a mean of 82 cubic inches, a full 5 cubic inches below the Caucasian norm. In

TABLE 3. **Morton's Final Summary of Cranial Capacity by Race**

Races and Families	N	Cranial Capacity (IN³)			
		Largest	Smallest	Mean	Mean
Modern Caucasian group					
Teutonic Family					
Germans	18	114	70	90	
English	5	105	91	96	92
Anglo-Americans	7	97	82	90	
Pelasgic Family	10	94	75	84	
Celtic Family	6	97	78	87	
Indostanic Family	32	91	67	80	
Semitic Family	3	98	84	89	
Nilotic Family	17	96	66	80	
Ancient Caucasian Group					
Pelasgic Family	18	97	74	88	
Nilotic Family	55	96	68	80	
Mongolian Group					
Chinese Family	6	91	70	82	
Malay Group					
Malayan Family	20	97	68	86	
Polynesian Family	3	84	82	83	85
American Group					
Toltecan Family					
Peruvians	155	101	58	75	
Mexicans	22	92	67	79	79
Barbarous Tribes	161	104	70	84	
Negro Group					
Native African Family	62	99	65	83	
American-born Negroes	12	89	73	82	83
Hottentot Family	3	83	68	75	
Australians	8	83	63	75	

addition, Morton appended a table of phrenological measurements indicating a deficiency of "higher" mental powers among Indians. "The benevolent mind," Morton concluded (p. 82), "may regret the inaptitude of the Indian for civilization," but sentimentality must yield to fact. "The structure of his mind appears to be different from that of the white man, nor can the two harmonize in the social relations except on the most limited scale." Indians "are not only averse to the restraints of education, but for the most part are incapable of a continued process of reasoning on abstract subjects" (p. 81).

Since *Crania Americana* is primarily a treatise on the inferior quality of Indian intellect, I note first of all that Morton's cited average of 82 cubic inches for

Indian skulls is incorrect. He separated Indians into two groups, "Toltecans" from Mexico and South America, and "Barbarous Tribes" from North America. Eighty-two is the average for Barbarous skulls; the total sample of 144 yields a mean of 80.2 cubic inches, or a gap of almost 7 cubic inches between Indian and Caucasian averages. (I do not know how Morton made this elementary error. It did permit him, in any case, to retain the conventional chain of being with whites on top, Indians in the middle, and blacks on the bottom.)

But the "correct" value of 80.2 is far too low, for it is the result of an improper procedure. Morton's 144 skulls belong to many different groups of Indians; these groups differ significantly among themselves in cranial capacity. Each group should be weighted equally, lest the final average be biased by unequal size of subsamples. Suppose, for example, that we tried to estimate average human height from a sample of two jockeys, the author of this book (strictly middling stature), and all the players in the National Basketball Association. The hundreds of Jabbars would swamp the remaining three and give an average in excess of six and a half feet. If, however, we averaged the averages of the three groups (jockeys, me, and the basketball players), then our figure would lie closer to the true value. Morton's sample is strongly biased by a major overrepresentation of an extreme group—the small-brained Inca Peruvians. (They have a mean cranial capacity of 74.36 cubic inches and provide 25 percent of the entire sample.) Large-brained Iroquois, on the other hand, contribute only 3 skulls to the total sample (2 percent). If, by the accidents of collecting, Morton's sample had included 25 percent Iroquois and just a few Incas, his average would have risen substantially. Consequently, I corrected this bias as best I could by averaging the mean values for all tribes represented by 4 or more skulls. The Indian average now rises to 83.79 cubic inches.

This revised value is still more than 3 cubic inches from the Caucasian average. Yet, when we examine Morton's procedure for computing the Caucasian mean, we uncover an astounding inconsistency. Since statistical reasoning is largely a product of the last one hundred years, I might have excused Morton's error for the Indian mean by arguing that he did not recognize the biases produced by unequal sizes among subsamples. But now we discover that he understood this bias perfectly well—for Morton calculated his high Caucasian mean by consciously eliminating small-brained Hindus from his sample. He writes (p. 261): "It is proper, however, to mention that but 3 Hindoos are admitted in the whole number, because the skulls of these people are probably smaller than those of any other existing nation. For example, 17 Hindoo heads give a mean of but 75 cubic inches; and the three received into the table are taken at that average." Thus, Morton included a large subsample of small-brained people (Inca Peruvians) to pull down the Indian average, but excluded just as many small Caucasian skulls to raise the mean of his own group. Since he tells us what he did so baldly, we must assume that Morton did not deem his procedure improper. But by what rationale did he keep Incas and exclude Hindus, unless it were the a priori assumption of a truly higher Caucasian mean? For one might then throw out the Hindu sample as truly anomalous, but retain the Inca sample (with the same mean as the Hindus, by the way) as the lower end of normality for its disadvantaged larger group.

I restored the Hindu skulls to Morton's sample, using the same procedure of equal weighting for all groups. Morton's Caucasian sample, by his reckoning, contains skulls from four subgroups, so Hindus should contribute one-fourth of all skulls to the sample. If we restore all seventeen of Morton's Hindu skulls, they form 26 percent of the total sample of sixty-six. The Caucasian mean now drops to 84.45 cubic inches, for no difference worth mentioning between Indians and Caucasians. (Eskimos, despite Morton's low opinion of them, yield a mean of 86.8, hidden by amalgamation with other subgroups in the Mongol grand mean of 83.) So much for Indian inferiority.

The Case of the Egyptian Catacombs: Crania Aegyptiaca

Morton's friend and fellow polygenist George Gliddon was United States consul for the city of Cairo. He dispatched to Philadelphia more than one hundred skulls from tombs of ancient Egypt, and Morton responded with his second major treatise, the *Crania Aegyptiaca* of 1844. Morton had shown, or so he thought, that whites surpassed Indians in mental endowment. Now he would crown his story by demonstrating that the discrepancy between whites and blacks was even greater, and that this difference had been stable for more than three thousand years.

Morton felt that he could identify both races and subgroups among races from features of the skull (most anthropologists today would deny that such assignments can be made unambiguously). He divided his Caucasian skulls into Pelasgics (Hellenes, or ancient Greek forebears), Jews, and Egyptians—in that order, again confirming Anglo-Saxon preferences (table 2). Non-Caucasian skulls he identified either as "negroid" (hybrids of Negro and Caucasian with more black than white) or as pure Negro.

Morton's subjective division of Caucasian skulls is clearly unwarranted, for he simply assigned the most bulbous crania to his favored Pelasgic group and the most flattened to Egyptians; he mentions no other criteria of subdivision. If we ignore his threefold separation and amalgamate all sixty-five Caucasian skulls into a single sample, we obtain an average capacity of 82.15 cubic inches. (If we give Morton the benefit of all doubts and rank his dubious subsamples equally— as we did in computing Indian and Caucasian means for the *Crania Americana*— we obtain an average of 83.3 cubic inches.)

Either of these values still exceeds the negroid and Negro averages substantially. Morton assumed that he had measured an innate difference in intelligence. He never considered any other proposal for the disparity in average cranial capacity—though another simple and obvious explanation lay before him.

Sizes of brains are related to the sizes of bodies that carry them; big people tend to have larger brains than small people. This fact does not imply that big people are smarter—any more than elephants should be judged more intelligent than humans because their brains are larger. Appropriate corrections must be made for differences in body size. Men tend to be larger than women; consequently, their brains are bigger. When corrections for body size are applied, men and women have brains of approximately equal size. Morton not only failed to correct for differences in sex or body size; he did not even recognize the relationship, though his data proclaimed it loud and clear. (I can only conjecture that Morton never separated his skulls by sex or stature—though his tables record these data—because he wanted so much to read differences in brain size directly as differences in intelligence.)

Many of the Egyptian skulls came with mummified remains of their possessors and Morton could record their sex unambiguously. If we use Morton's own designations and compute separate averages for males and females (as Morton never did), we obtain the following remarkable result. Mean capacity for twenty-four Caucasian skulls is 86.5 cubic inches; twenty-two female skulls average 77.2 (the remaining nineteen skulls could not be identified by sex). Of the six negroid skulls, Morton identified two as female (at 71 and 77 cubic inches) and could not allocate the other four (at 77, 77, 87, and 88).* If we make the reasonable conjecture that the two smaller skulls (77 and 77) are female, and the two larger male (87 and 88), we obtain a male negroid average of 87.5, slightly above the Caucasian male mean of 86.5, and a female negroid average of 75.5, slightly below the Caucasian value of 77.2. The apparent difference of 4 cubic inches between Morton's Caucasian and negroid samples may only record the fact that about half his Caucasian sample is male, while only one-third the negroid sample may be male. (The apparent difference is magnified by Morton's incorrect rounding of the negroid average down to 79 rather than up to 80. As we shall see again, all of Morton's minor numerical errors favor his prejudices.) Differences in average brain size between Caucasians and negroids in the Egyptian tombs only record differences in stature due to sex, not variation in "intelligence." You will not be surprised to learn that the single pure Negro skull (73 cubic inches) is a female.

The correlation of brain and body also resolves a question left hanging in our previous discussion of the *Crania Americana*: What is the basis for differences in average brain size among Indian peoples? (These differences bothered Morton considerably, for he could not understand how small-brained Incas had built such an elaborate civilization, though he consoled himself with the fact of their rapid conquest by the conquistadores.) Again, the answer lay before him, but Morton never saw it. Morton presents subjective data on bodily statures in his descriptions of the various tribes, and I present these assessments along with average brain sizes in table 4. The correlation of brain and body size is affirmed without exception. The low Hindu mean among Caucasians also records a difference in stature, not another case of dumb Indians.

---

*In his final catalogue of 1849, Morton guessed at sex (and age within five years!) for all crania. In this later work, he specifies 77, 87, and 88 as male, and the remaining 77 as female. This allocation was pure guesswork; my alternate version is equally plausible. In the *Crania Aegyptiaca* itself, Morton was more cautious and only identified sex for specimens with mummified remains.

TABLE 4. **Cranial Capacity of Indian Groups Ordered by Morton's Assessment of Body Stature**

Stature and Group	Cranial Capacity (IN³)	N
Large		
Seminole-Muskogee	88.3	8
Chippeway and related groups	88.8	4
Dacota and Osage	84.4	7
Middle		
Mexicans	80.2	13
Menominee	80.5	8
Mounds	81.7	9
Small		
Columbia River Flatheads	78.8	10
Peruvians	74.4	33

The Case of the Shifting Black Mean

In the *Crania Americana,* Morton cited 78 cubic inches as the average cranial capacity for blacks. Five years later, in the *Crania Aegyptiaca,* he appended the following footnote to his table of measurements: "I have in my possession 79 crania of Negroes born in Africa. . . . Of the whole number, 58 are adult . . . and give 85 cubic inches for the average size of the brain" (1844, p. 113).

Since Morton had changed his method of measurement from mustard seed to lead shot between 1839 and 1844, I suspected this alteration as a cause for the rising black mean. Fortunately, Morton remeasured most of his skulls personally, and his various catalogues present tabulations of the same skulls by both seed and shot (see Gould, 1978, for details).

I assumed that measures by seed would be lower. Seeds are light and variable in size, even after sieving. Hence, they do not pack well. By vigorous shaking or pressing of the thumb at the foramen magnum (the hole at the base of a skull), seeds can be made to settle, providing room for more. Measures by seed were very variable; Morton reported differences of several cubic inches for recalibrations of the same skull. He eventually became discouraged, fired his assistants, and redid all his measurements personally, with lead shot. Recalibrations never varied by more than a cubic inch, and we may accept Morton's judgment that measures by shot were objective, accurate, and repeatable—while earlier measures by seed were highly subjective and erratic.

I then calculated the discrepancies between seed and shot by race. Shot, as I suspected, always yielded higher values than seed. For 111 Indian skulls, measured by both criteria, shot exceeds seed by an average of 2.2 cubic inches. Data are not as reliable for blacks and Caucasians because Morton did not specify individual skulls for these races in the *Crania Americana* (measured by seed). For Caucasians, 19 identifiable skulls yield an average discrepancy of only 1.8 cubic inches for shot over seed. Yet 18 African skulls, remeasured from the sample reported in *Crania Americana,* produce a mean shot of 83.44 cubic inches, a rise of 5.4 cubic inches from the 1839 average by seed. In other words, the more "inferior" a race by Morton's a priori judgment, the greater the discrepancy between a subjective measurement, easily and unconsciously fudged, and an objective measure unaffected by prior prejudice. The discrepancy for blacks, Indians, and Caucasians is 5.4, 2.2, and 1.8 cubic inches, respectively.

Plausible scenarios are easy to construct. Morton, measuring by seed, picks up a threateningly large black skull, fills it lightly and gives it a few desultory shakes. Next, he takes a distressingly small Caucasian skull, shakes hard, and pushes mightily at the foramen magnum with his thumb. It is easily done, without conscious motivation; expectation is a powerful guide to action.

The Final Tabulation of 1849

Morton's burgeoning collection included 623 skulls when he presented his final tabulation in 1849—an overwhelming affirmation of the ranking that every Anglo-Saxon expected.

The Caucasian subsamples suffer from errors and distortions. The German mean, reported at 90 in the summary, is 88.4 from individual skulls listed in the catalogue; the correct Anglo-American average is 89 (89.14), not 90. The high English mean of 96 is correct, but the small sample is entirely male.* If we follow our procedure of computing averages among subsamples, the six modern Caucasian "families" yield a mean of 87 cubic inches.† The ancient Caucasian average for two subsamples is 84 cubic inches (table 5).

Six Chinese skulls provide Morton with a Mongolian mean of 82, but this low value records two cases of selective amnesia: First, Morton excluded the latest Chinese specimen (skull number 1336 at 98 cubic inches), though it must have been in his collection when he published his summary because he includes many Peruvian skulls with higher numbers. Secondly, although Morton deplored the absence of Eskimos from his collection (1849, p. iv), he did not mention the three

---

*To demonstrate again how large differences based on stature can be, I report these additional data, recovered from Morton's tabulations, but never calculated or recognized by him: (1) For Inca Peruvians, fifty-three male skulls average 77.5; sixty-one female skulls, 72.1. (2) For Germans, nine male skulls average 92.2; eight females, 84.3.

†My original report (Gould, 1978) incorrectly listed the modern Caucasian mean as 85.3. The reason for this error is embarrassing, but instructive, for it illustrates, at my expense, the cardinal principle of this book: the social embeddedness of science and the frequent grafting of expectation upon supposed objectivity. Line 7 in table 3 lists the range of Semitic skulls as 84 to 98 cubic inches for Morton's sample of 3. However, my original paper cited a mean of 80—an obvious impossibility if the smallest skull measures 84. I was working from a Xerox of Morton's original chart, and his correct value of 89 is smudged to look like an 80 on my copy. Nonetheless, the range of 84 to 98 is clearly indicated right alongside, and I never saw the inconsistency—presumably because a low value of 80 fit my hopes for a depressed Caucasian mean. The 80 therefore "felt" right and I never checked it. I am grateful to Dr. Irving Klotz of Northwestern University for pointing out this error to me.

TABLE 5. **Corrected Values for Morton's Final Tabulation**

People	Cranial Capacity (IN³)
Mongolians	87
Modern Caucasians	87
Native Americans	86
Malays	85
Ancient Caucasians	84
Africans	83

Eskimo skulls that he had measured for *Crania Americana*. (These belonged to his friend George Combe and do not appear in Morton's final catalogue.)

Morton never remeasured these skulls with shot, but if we apply the Indian correction of 2.2 cubic inches to their seed average of 86.8 we obtain a mean of 89. These two samples (Chinese with number 1336 added, and Eskimo conservatively corrected) yield a Mongolian average of 87 cubic inches.

By 1849 Morton's Indian mean had plummeted to 79. But this figure is invalid for the same reason as before, though now intensified—inequality of numbers among subsamples. Small-headed (and small-statured) Peruvians provided 23 percent of the 1839 sample, but their frequency had risen to nearly half (155 of 338 skulls) by 1849. If we use our previous criterion and compute the average of all subsamples weighted equally, the Indian average is 86 cubic inches.

For the Negro average, we should drop Morton's australoids because he wanted to assess the status of African blacks and we no longer accept a close relationship between the two groups—dark skin evolved more than once among human groups. I also drop the Hottentot sample of 3. All skulls are female, and Hottentots are very small in stature. Native and American-born blacks, amalgamated to a single sample, yield an average value between 82 and 83, but closer to 83.

In short, my correction of Morton's conventional ranking reveals *no* significant differences among races for Morton's own data (table 5). All groups rank between 83 and 87 cubic inches, and Caucasians share the pinnacle. If western Europeans choose to seek their superiority in high averages for their subsamples (Germanics and Anglo-Saxons in the Caucasian tabulations), I point out that several Indian subsamples are equally high (though Morton amalgamated all North American Indians and never reported averages by subgroup), and that all Teutonic and Anglo-Saxon averages are either miscalculated or biased in Morton's table.

Morton's finagling may be ordered into four general categories:

1. Favorable inconsistencies and shifting criteria: Morton often chose to include or delete large subsamples in order to match group averages with prior expectations. He included Inca Peruvians to decrease the Indian average, but deleted Hindus to raise the Caucasian mean. He also chose to present or not to

calculate the averages of subsamples in striking accord with desired results. He made calculations for Caucasians to demonstrate the superiority of Teutons and Anglo-Saxons, but never presented data for Indian subsamples with equally high averages.

2. Subjectivity directed toward prior prejudice: Morton's measures with seed were sufficiently imprecise to permit a wide range of influence by subjective bias; later measures with shot, on the other hand, were repeatable, and presumably objective. In skulls measured by both methods, values for shot always exceed values for the light, poorly packing seed. But degrees of discrepancy match a priori assumptions: an average of 5.4, 2.2, and 1.8 cubic inches for blacks, Indians, and whites, respectively. In other words, blacks fared poorest and whites best when the results could be biased toward an expected result.

3. Procedural omissions that seem obvious to us: Morton was convinced that variation in skull size recorded differential, innate mental ability. He never considered alternate hypotheses, though his own data almost cried out for a different interpretation. Morton never computed means by sex or stature, even when he recorded these data in his tabulations—as for Egyptian mummies. Had he computed the effect of stature, he would presumably have recognized that it explained all important differences in brain size among his groups. Negroids yielded a lower average than Caucasians among his Egyptian skulls because the negroid sample probably contained a higher percentage of smaller-statured females, not because blacks are innately stupider. The Incas that he included in the Indian sample and the Hindus that he excluded from the Caucasian sample both possessed small brains as a consequence of small body size. Morton used an all-female sample of three Hottentots to support the stupidity of blacks, and an all-male sample of Englishmen to assert the superiority of whites.

4. Miscalculations and convenient omissions: All miscalculations and omissions that I have detected are in Morton's favor. He rounded the negroid Egyptian average down to 79, rather than up to 80. He cited averages of 90 for Germans and Anglo-Saxons, but the correct values are 88 and 89. He excluded a large Chinese skull and an Eskimo subsample from his final tabulation for mongoloids, thus depressing their average below the Caucasian value.

Yet through all this juggling, I detect no sign of fraud or conscious manipulation. Morton made no attempt to cover his tracks and I must presume that he was unaware he had left them. He explained all his procedures and published all his raw data. All I can discern is an a priori conviction about racial ranking so powerful that it directed his tabulations along preestablished lines. Yet Morton was widely hailed as the objectivist of his age, the man who would rescue American science from the mire of unsupported speculation.

The American School and Slavery

The leading American polygenists differed in their attitude toward slavery. Most were Northerners, and most favored some version of Squier's quip: "[I have a] precious poor opinion of niggers . . . a still poorer one of slavery" (in Stanton, 1960, p. 193).

But the identification of blacks as a separate and unequal species had obvious appeal as an argument for slavery. Josiah Nott, a leading polygenist, encountered particularly receptive audiences in the South for his "lectures on niggerology" (as he called them). Morton's *Crania Aegyptiaca* received a warm welcome in the South (in Stanton, 1960, pp. 52–53). One supporter of slavery wrote that the South need no longer be "so much frightened" by "voices of Europe or of Northern America" in defending its "peculiar institutions." When Morton died, the South's leading medical journal proclaimed (R. W. Gibbs, *Charleston Medical Journal,* 1851, quoted in Stanton, 1960, p. 144): "We of the South should consider him as our benefactor, for aiding most materially in giving to the negro his true position as an inferior race."

Nonetheless, the polygenist argument did not occupy a primary place in the ideology of slavery in mid-nineteenth-century America—and for a good reason. For most Southerners, this excellent argument entailed too high a price. The polygenists had railed against ideologues as barriers to their pure search for truth, but their targets were parsons more often than abolitionists. Their theory, in asserting a plurality of human creations, contradicted the doctrine of a single Adam and contravened the literal truth of scripture. Although the leading polygenists held a diversity of religions attitudes, none were atheists. Morton and Agassiz were conventionally devout, but they did believe that both science and religion would be aided if untrained parsons kept their noses out of scientific issues and stopped proffering the Bible as a document to settle debates in natural history. Josiah Nott stated his goal in a forceful way (Agassiz and Morton would not have put it so baldly): " . . . to cut loose the natural history of mankind from the Bible, and to place each upon its own foundation, where it may remain without collision or molestation" (in Stanton, 1960, p. 119).

The polygenists forced defenders of slavery into a quandary: Should they accept a strong argument from science at the cost of limiting religion's sphere? In resolving this dilemma, the Bible usually won. After all, scriptural arguments for supporting slavery were not wanting. Degeneration of blacks under the curse of Ham was an old and eminently functional standby. Moreover, polygeny was not the only quasi-scientific defense available.

John Bachman, for example, was a South Carolina parson and prominent naturalist. As a committed monogenist, he spent a good part of his scientific career attempting to refute polygeny. He also used monogenist principles to defend slavery:

> In intellectual power the African is an inferior variety of our species. His whole history affords evidence that he is incapable of self-government. Our child that we lead by the hand, and who looks to us for protection and support is still of our own blood notwithstanding his weakness and ignorance (in Stanton, 1960, p. 63).

Among nonpolygenist, "scientific" defenses of slavery, no arguments ever matched in absurdity the doctrines of S. A. Cartwright, a prominent Southern physician. (I do not cite these as typical and I doubt that many intelligent Southerners paid them much attention; I merely wish to illustrate an extreme within the range of "scientific" argument.) Cartwright traced the problems of black people to inadequate decarbonization of blood in the lungs (insufficient removal of carbon dioxide): "It is the defective . . . atmospherization of the blood, conjoined with a deficiency of cerebral matter in the cranium . . . that is the true cause of that debasement of mind, which has rendered the people of Africa unable to take care of themselves" (from Chorover, 1979; all quotes from Cartwright are taken from papers he presented to the 1851 meeting of the Louisiana Medical Association.)

Cartwright even had a name for it—*dysesthesia,* a disease of inadequate breathing. He described its symptoms in slaves: "When driven to labor . . . he performs the task assigned to him in a headlong and careless manner, treading down with his feet or cutting with his hoe the plants he is put to cultivate—breaking the tools he works with, and spoiling everything he touches." Ignorant Northerners attributed this behavior to "the debasing influence of slavery," but Cartwright recognized it as the expression of a true disease. He identified insensibility to pain as another symptom: "When the unfortunate individual is subjected to punishment, he neither feels pain of any consequence . . . [nor] any unusual resentment more than stupid sulkiness. In some cases . . . there appears to be an almost total loss of feeling." Cartwright proposed the following cure:

> The liver, skin and kidneys should be stimulated to activity . . . to assist in decarbonizing the blood. The best means to stimulate the skin is, first, to have the patient well washed with warm water and soap; then to anoint it all over with oil, and to slap the oil in with a broad leather strap; then to put the patient to some hard kind of work in the open air and sunshine that will compel him to expand his lungs, as chopping wood, splitting rails, or sawing with the crosscut or whip saw.

Cartwright did not end his catalogue of diseases with dysesthesia. He wondered why slaves often tried to flee, and identified the cause as a mental disease called *drapetomania,* or the insane desire to run away. "Like children, they are constrained by unalterable physiological laws, to love those in authority over them. Hence, from a law of his nature, the negro can no more help loving a kind master, than a child can help loving her that gives it suck." For slaves afflicted with drapetomania, Cartwright proposed a behavioral cure: owners should avoid both extreme permissiveness and cruelty: "They have only to be kept in that state, and treated like children, to prevent and cure them from running away."

The defenders of slavery did not need polygeny. Religion still stood above science as a primary source for the rationalization of social order. But the American debate on polygeny may represent the last time that arguments in the scientific mode did not form a first line of defense for the status quo and the unalterable quality of human differences. The Civil War lay just around the corner, but so did 1859 and Darwin's *Origin of Species*. Subsequent arguments for slavery, colonialism, racial differences, class structures, and sex roles would go forth primarily under the banner of science.

R E F E R E N C E S

Agassiz, E. C. 1895. *Louis Agassiz: His Life and Correspondence*. Boston: Houghton, Mifflin.

Agassiz, L. 1850. The Diversity of Origin of the Human Races. *Christian Examiner* 49: 110–45.

Blumenbach, J. F. 1825. *A Manual of the Elements of Natural History*. London: W. Simpkin and R. Marshall.

Chase, A. 1977. *The Legacy of Malthus*. New York: Knopf.

Chorover, S. L. 1979. *From Genesis to Genocide*. Cambridge: Massachusetts Institute of Technology Press.

Combe, G., and B. H. Coates. 1840. Review of *Crania Americana*. *American Journal of Science* 38:341–75.

Cope, E. D. 1887. *The Origin of the Fittest*. New York: Macmillan.

———. 1890. Two Perils of the Indo-European. *The Open Court* 3:2052–54 and 2070–71.

Cuvier, G. 1812. *Recherches sur les ossemens fossiles*. Vol. 1. Paris: Deterville.

Darwin, C. 1871. *The Descent of Man*. London: John Murray.

Gossett, T. F. 1965. *Race: The History of an Idea in America*. New York: Schocken Books.

Gould, S. J. 1977. *Ever since Darwin*. New York: Norton.

———. 1977. *Ontogeny and Phylogeny*. Cambridge, Mass.: Harvard University Press.

———. 1978. Morton's Ranking of Races by Cranial Capacity. *Science* 200: 503–9.

Haller, J. S., Jr. 1971. *Outcasts from Evolution: Scientific Attitudes of Racial Inferiority, 1859–1900*. Urbana: University of Illinois Press.

Humboldt, A. von. 1849. *Cosmos*. London: H. G. Bohn.

Linnaeus, C. 1758. *Systema naturae*.

Meigs, C. D. 1851. *A Memoir of Samuel George Morton, M.D.* Philadelphia: T. K. and P. G. Collins.

Morton, S. G. 1839. *Crania Americana, or, a comparative view of the skulls of various aboriginal nations of North and South America*. Philadelphia: John Pennington.

———. 1844. Observations on Egyptian Ethnography, Derived from Anatomy, History, and the Monuments [separately reprinted subsequently as *Crania Aegyptiaca*, with title above as subtitle]. *Transactions of the American Philosophical Society* 9:93–159.

———. 1847. Hybridity in Animals, Considered in Reference to the Question of the Unity of the Human Species. *American Journal of Science* 3:39–50, and 203–12.

———. 1849. Observations on the Size of the Brain in Various Races and Families of Man. *Proceedings of the Academy of Natural Sciences Philadelphia* 4:221–24.

———. 1850. On the Value of the Word *Species* in Zoology. *Proceedings of the Academy of Natural Sciences Philadelphia* 5:81–82.

———. 1851. On the Infrequency of Mixed Offspring between European and Australian races. *Proceedings of the Academy of Natural Sciences Philadelphia* 5:173–75.

Newby, I. A. 1969. *Challenge to the Court: Social Scientists and the Defense of Segregation, 1954–1966*. Baton Rouge: Louisiana State University Press.

Nott, J. C., and G. R. Gliddon. 1854. *Types of Mankind*. Philadelphia: Lippincott, Grambo and Company.

———. 1868. *Indigenous Races of the Earth*. Philadelphia: J. B. Lippincott.

Popkin, R. H. 1974. The Philosophical Basis of Modern Racism. In *Philosophy and the Civilizing Arts,* ed. C. Walton and J. P. Anton.

Serres, E. 1860. Principes d'embryogénie, de zoogénie et de teratogénie. *Mémoire de l'Académie des Sciences* 25:1–943.

Sinkler, G. 1972. *The Racial Attitudes of American Presidents from Abraham Lincoln to Theodore Roosevelt*. New York: Doubleday Anchor Books.

Stanton, W. 1960. *The Leopard's Spots: Scientific Attitudes towards Race in America 1815–1859*. Chicago: University of Chicago Press.

Wilson, L. G. 1970. *Sir Charles Lyell's Scientific Journals on the Species Question*. New Haven: Yale University Press.

RACIAL CLASSIFICATIONS
Popular and Scientific

Gloria A. Marshall

I

Many scholars in the biological sciences agree that all typological divisions of mankind into discrete racial groups are to some extent arbitrary and artificial. Despite this widespread agreement, there appear to be two divergent views regarding the utility of the concept of race in studies of human biology. On the one hand, there are scholars who maintain that race as a statistically defined unit can and should be utilized in the description and analysis of intraspecific variation.[1] According to this view, the concept of race is applicable to clusters of populations, each of which can be genetically defined.

On the other hand, there are scholars who argue that in view of the arbitrariness of racial classifications, there can be little or no justification for the continued use of the race concept. Scientists who hold this view consider that the analysis and description of intraspecific variation in human and nonhuman populations can be most fruitfully pursued without reference to the concept of race.[2] Jean Hiernaux[3] has stated this position as follows:

> If any racial classification is arbitrary, for what purpose can it be of any use? Why spend so much time and effort building a classification, knowing that many others, not any worse, could be opposed to it, and that it runs the risk not only of being useless but also harmful by conveying the erroneous impression that it makes generalization possible?

Some of the anthropologists and biologists who favor continued use of the race concept have maintained that racial classifications are useful if they reflect the phylogenetic development of the species.[4] That such a purpose is not neces-

I wish to thank Karen Kerner for her assistance in the research on which this paper is based. I also wish to thank Miss Kerner, along with Robert LeVine, Joyce Riegelhaupt, Edward Riegelhaupt, Harold Conklin, Marvin Harris, Samuel Sutton, and David Feingold for their helpful comments at various stages in the preparation of this paper.

sarily served by *any* racial classification is noted by Ehrlich and Holm,[5] who caution that "there is no basis for assuming, without extensive genetic study, that any population or any taxonomic group is an evolutionary unit." On the same issue, Hiernaux[6] has argued that it would be extremely difficult to derive a phylogenetic tree from data on contemporary human populations since the species did not split into groups which were "exposed to different evolutionary forces and events under complete or effective genetic isolation," and he goes on to state:

> The general picture [of human evolution] is not one of isolated groups differentiating in circumscribed areas. Mixture occurred many times in many places between the most various populations brought into contact by human mobility. The tendency toward high adaptive specialization was balanced again and again by migration, and by man's power to transform his environment. Even if we could reconstruct the intricate succession of mixtures that contributed to each living population, the final picture would look like a reticulum more than a tree, and a reticulum defies dichotomizing subdivision.

It is not only the study of human variation that has led to a reappraisal of the utility of the concept of race for the analysis of intraspecific variation. Examination of the characters used in subspecific classifications of butterflies led N. W. Gillham[7] to conclude:

> In view of the prevailing discordance of geographical patterns followed by different variates, racial partition of butterfly species is not only arbitrary, but it must also necessarily weight some variates and ignore others, without regard for the biological significance of any of them. The best that can be hoped for now is an analysis of variation by individual characters, avoiding arbitrary subdivision of the species. Such analysis will eventually yield a less distorted picture of species formation than that to which the artificial subspecies now inevitably leads.

The debate regarding the relevance of the concept of race for the analysis and description of intraspecific variation has important implications for all sciences concerned with the study of mankind. However, it does not appear that this debate has had widespread impact on professionals in the fields of medicine, psychology, sociology, history, or political science. Moreover, the investigations and publications of many scholars in these and other fields often deal with populations that are termed "races" even though the distinctive attributes of these populations have no proven biological significance.

What is often unrecognized or ignored is the fact that the "races" about which many scientists speak and write are those perceived and delineated by particular groups of people who interact in given sociopolitical contexts. Comparative studies of these popular racial typologies show them to vary from place to place; studies of popular racial classifications also show them to vary from one historical period to another. In no instance are these classifications referable to competent genetic studies; rather, they are "concocted by human beings to explain or render intelligible their observations."[8] Whereas most scholars today acknowledge that it is necessary to make a distinction between popular and technical conceptions about human biology, they do not necessarily avoid confusion of the two. Hence, many scientists persist in the use of the term *race* to describe groups whose racial statuses are determined, and whose racial characteristics are defined, by sociopolitical expediencies.

This paper attempts to document the variability in the criteria upon which popular racial classifications are based and to show that scientific discussions of race often reflect and reinforce popular notions about human variation. It also intends to show that both scientific and popular conceptions about race are usually influenced by sociopolitical considerations. Many of the points raised in this paper have been discussed in various contexts by anthropologists and by scholars in other fields. That they must be repeated here indicates the difficulties involved in communicating on the subject of race.

II

Most laymen and many scientists in the United States hold that there are three "major races": Caucasian (white), Negro (black), and Mongolian (yellow). This typology has a scientific basis; it is a revision of that proposed by J. F. Blumenbach, a distinguished anatomist and physician of the eighteenth century.[9] But in some parts of the country Chinese Americans and other peoples from Asia are sometimes classed as "white."[10] However, almost nowhere in the United States is there any doubt that there are at least two "major races": namely, the Negro race and the white race.

In the United States, it is popularly held that descent is the basis upon which individuals are assigned to racial groups. However, Marvin Harris[11] has argued that it is a rule of *hypodescent* which governs the assignment of many individuals to the two major races distinguished by Americans. A rule of hypodescent operates when individuals whose parents belong to different "races" are assigned to the one that is politically subordinate. In America, individuals who have no known or acknowledged African ancestry constitute a politically and economically superordinate group. From this group has come the rule that individuals of both European and African parentage must be assigned to the politically subordinate group that is referred to as the Negro race.* "Thus, first generation children of interracial marriages in the United States are uniformly Negroes, when it is absolutely certain that such children have received half of their hereditary endowment from one parent and half from the other."

Even though the operation of the rule of hypodescent results in the application of the term *Negro* to American populations any of whose ancestors came

*In fact, it might be more accurate to say that it is known or demonstrable sub-Saharan African ancestry or "black African" ancestry which governs the assignment to the "negro race," since the populations of North Africa are not usually termed Negro.

from Africa, there is considerable ambiguity regarding the racial classification of peoples whose ancestors were European and Asian or African and Asian. Moreover, there does not appear to be popular consensus concerning the racial affiliation of people whose ancestors were African and European but who speak a language other than English. In New York, populations who speak Spanish are not usually referred to as belonging to the "Negro race" or to the "white race," but are simply designated as "Spanish," "Cuban," "Puerto Ricans," or "peoples of Puerto Rican descent." In many contexts, these appellations are used as if they were equivalent to the racial designations currently in use. Were the same people to speak only American English, they would be classed as Negro or as white, depending on the particular observer's perception of physical and behavioral "racial" cues.

Clearly, the popular racial typologies in America are not based on any competent genetic studies. It is also evident that observable phenotypical characteristics are often totally irrelevant in the assignment of individuals to the racial groups. There are Negroes who "can pass for white"; there are whites who "could pass for Negroes."

The popular American conceptions about race contrast sharply with those of contemporary Brazil, where descent plays a negligible role in establishing racial identity. Marvin Harris[12] has shown that full siblings whose phenotypes are markedly different are assigned to different racial categories. Harris's studies also indicate that more than forty racial categories are utilized in Brazil and that there are hundreds of racial terms constructed of combinations of these. In addition, there are alternative meanings for the same term, as well as a lack of consensus concerning the assignment of any particular term to a given individual.[13] Moreover, Harris points out that there is "a high frequency of passing out to other categories in conformity with the achievement of socio-economic success." Phenotypical attributes such as skin color, hair form, and nose or mouth shape enter into Brazilian racial classifications, but no combination of these variants is predictive of the "race" to which a person will be assigned since socio-economic position is one important determinant of racial status.

In Japan, skin color does not necessarily enter into popular racial classifications. The Burakumin or "outcastes" are popularly believed to be racially distinct from ordinary Japanese. They were formerly termed Eta—a word written with the characters for "defilement abundant"—and were officially emancipated in 1871 but remain a minority group set apart from other Japanese by low socio-economic status and by residential segregation.

The Eta are Japanese who descended from the lowest stratum in a hierarchical social system which existed in the earliest known period of Japanese history and was formalized by edict in the seventh century A.D. At that time, the Imperial House created two major categories: the free and the base. Included in the latter category were peasants, certain artisan guilds, and slaves. By the tenth century, most of the formalized class distinctions had become meaningless; social differences between the free and the unfree were no longer observable, and most of the base guilds were free.

It was during this period that Buddhism became accepted throughout Japan, and the Buddhist beliefs fused with indigenous Shinto beliefs concerning the avoidance of impurity. According to Donoghue,[14]

> The syncretic religious concepts that evolved associated the taking of life with ritual impurity, and the guilds whose livelihood depended upon animal slaughtering were physically and morally isolated from the "legitimate" society. The outcastes became known as Eta.

The Eta formed small enclaves on the outskirts of towns and villages, where they were joined by other marginal social groups such as beggars, criminals, vagabonds, and entertainers.

In Japan, some theories on the history of the outcastes suggest that they originated from a people different from the ancestors of the socially acceptable Japanese. One theory holds that the outcastes are descendants of the aboriginal inhabitants of the Japanese isles. Another theory maintains that they are descendants of Korean war captives brought to Japan in the late sixteenth century; a third considers the Eta to be the offspring of Negritoes of the Philippines.[15]

Most Western scholars regard the outcastes as physically identical to other Japanese. However, in the 1920s and 1930s a number of Japanese scholars described the Eta as a distinct race, and today many laymen still regard the outcastes as racially distinct from other Japanese. The outcastes' "distinctive racial heritage" is allegedly manifest in their behavior and appearance. Outcastes are popularly considered to be dirty; they are likened to hoodlums and gangsters. They are said to be afflicted with venereal diseases, tuberculosis, and leprosy. They are said to have one rib bone missing, to have distorted sexual organs, and to have defective excretory systems. Since they are animals, dirt does not stick to their feet when they walk barefooted.[16]

The data on popular racial classifications current in the United States, in Brazil, and in Japan indicate that any expedient set of physical and/or behavioral attributes may be taken as the basis for such classifications. In these and other popular racial taxonomies, there often is a fusion and/or confusion of behavioral and physical attributes, leading to the perpetuation of the notion of the inheritance of cultural characteristics.

The assignment of individuals to the various racial categories recognized in different societies is often based on perceived behavioral differences rather than on demonstrable physical differences. Even where physical differences exist between the "races" delineated, laymen usually make no attempt to ascertain the biological significance of these differences! Moreover, the physical and behavioral attributes which are perceived as characteristic of a group are usually "explained" as being racial in origin.

Despite the recognition by many scholars that popular racial classifications should not serve as a basis for scientific discussions of human variation and related topics, many scientific studies are based on these classifications. Moreover, many scholars provide support for these nonscientific classifications by stating or implying that the popularly and/or politically defined "races" can be distinguished on the basis of biologically relevant criteria.

"Scientific" justification for the classification of the Eta as a race was provided by Kikuchi Sanya, whose book on the outcastes was written "from an anthropological point of view." Ninomiya[17] summarizes Kikuchi's thesis as follows:

> There are many peculiarities of the *Eta*, such as (a) practice of eating meat when the Japanese proper despise it; (b) reddish tinge in eye color; (c) prominence of the cheekbone; (d) non-Mongolian type of the eyes; (e) dolichocephalic head; (f) shortness of stature; and (g) shortness of the neck.

In the 1930s, a professor of anthropology at Tokyo Imperial University also was of the opinion that "the *Eta* are not of the Mongolian type," although he did not "make this as a definite conclusion."

It is hardly necessary to document the fact that many scholars in the United States conduct research and write books which imply that the "white race" and the "Negro race" are genetically defined entities. It will suffice to point out that virtually all scholars who write about "race and intelligence" assume that the "races" which they study are distinguished on the basis of biologically relevant criteria. So accepted is this fact that most scholars engaged in such research never consider it necessary to justify their assignment of individuals to this or that "race."[18]

Even when scholars in the biological sciences devise or utilize racial classifications, these are generally no more than refinements of typologies used by laymen. Scientific racial typologies are usually based on presumptions about or intuitions regarding the distribution of genetic characteristics. The manifest bases for these typologies are variations in arbitrarily chosen phenotypical characteristics. Yet it is well known that the relationship between genotype and phenotype is not simple and that the effects of the operation of environmental forces on the phenotype are not genetically transmitted. Moreover, even when scientists make a serious attempt to base their racial typologies on genetic variants, they do not squarely face the problem that there should be some biologically relevant justification for the choice of the characters on whose variation the "races" are defined.[19]

It cannot be expected that the difficulties inherent in the construction of racial classifications will be appreciated by laymen when these problems are not often acknowledged by the scientists themselves. Normally, the layman who reads the literature on race and racial groupings is justified in assuming that the existent typologies have been derived through the application of theories and methods current in disciplines concerned with the biological study of human variation. Since the scientific racial classifications which a layman finds in the literature are not too different from popular ones, he can be expected to feel justified in the maintenance of his views on race.

It is not surprising, therefore, that scientific discourses on race serve to buttress the popular belief that discrete racial groups exist among mankind or that scientific racial typologies serve to legitimize popular racial classifications. On the one hand, scientists often base their studies of "racial differences" on popularly and/or politically defined races. On the other hand, they often take popular racial classifications as a point of departure for the construction of their own typologies, which, on close examination, appear just as spurious as those utilized by laymen.[20]

III

The literature on racial typologies of earlier historical periods in America further indicates that both scientific and popular racial classifications reflect prevailing sociopolitical conditions. Significant changes in the political status of some ethnic groups in America have led to reappraisals of their "racial" statuses and of the "racial" characteristics by which they were defined.

In contemporary America, there are a number of populations of European origin who comprise the "white race." Even though some laymen subdivide this race on the basis of national origin or religious affiliation, most Americans agree that there is essentially one "white race." That scientists concur in this opinion is illustrated by the fact that no present-day study that proposes to compare races would compare Americans who came from Ireland with those who came from England. But this was not always the case. Barbara Solomon's *Ancestors and Immigrants*,[21] which deals with racial ideologies in New England between the 1850s and 1920s, demonstrates that "white" people who are now regarded as members of one "race" were formerly divided into several "races." In the second half of the nineteenth century and the early decades of the twentieth century, various American scholars published works which divided and redivided peoples now termed white or Caucasian into the following "races": Anglo-Saxons, Celts, Teutons, Jews, and southern Europeans or "brownish races." Scandinavians were regarded as a branch of the Teutonic "race," and Teutons and Anglo-Saxons were regarded as cousins, "racially" speaking.

Between the 1830s and 1870s the industrial expansion of New England brought waves of immigrants from Europe to Boston and the surrounding areas. Most were from Ireland. In the early phases of immigration, the self-styled Brahmins, who comprised the New England aristocracy, decried the "racial inferiority" of these Irish immigrants. In the 1840s and 1850s many prominent New Englanders shared C. E. Norton's apprehensions about the "sudden influx of people so long misgoverned . . . [and] of a race foreign to our own."[22] Charles F. Adams, Jr., remarked that "the Irish race," being "quick of impulse, sympathetic, ignorant, and credulous . . . have as few elements in common with native New Englanders as one race of men well can have with another."[23]

By the 1870s, the Irish, representative of the so-called Celtic race, gained dominance in some service industries in Boston and nearby mill towns; by the

1880s, they wrestled the political leadership of Boston from the old New England aristocracy. The political supremacy of the Brahmins having been challenged, various academicians from this aristocracy sought to prove that the increased influx of members of the Celtic and other "inferior races" undermined the chances for the survival of democratic institutions which were Teutonic in origin and transmitted "through the blood."

During the 1870s, Francis A. Walker, a noted social scientist who was to become a university president, was a leading spokesman for those who were alarmed by the rising power of the alien Celts. The census of 1880 confirmed Walker's suspicions that the birth rate among the urbanized immigrant populations was exceeding that of the native Anglo-Saxons, and he became obsessed by the "fecundity of the foreign elements in the United States." During the 1880s Walker wrote many articles on the evils of immigration and used his academic affiliations to appeal to younger scholars to support his thesis that the arrival of foreigners in the United States had caused a "shock to the principle of population among the native element." By the end of the 1880s, "the happy ideal of assimilation, which [John] Fiske had spread over the land, disintegrated under Walker's cogent proofs, and, for old New Englanders, immigration became a matter of racial preservation."[24]

Support for New England raciology had come from academic circles in Europe. During the latter half of the nineteenth century one of the most influential books was *The Races of Men*, written in 1850 by Robert Knox, a professor of anatomy at the Edinburgh College of Surgeons, which proclaimed that all of civilization depended on race. To the Celts, Knox attributed the following characteristics: "furious fanaticism; a love of war and disorder; a hatred for order and patient industry; no accumulative habits; restless, treacherous, uncertain; [one need only] look at Ireland." Knox saw the American Know-Nothing riots as a prelude to the inevitable conflict between Saxons and Celts. He said that "the war of race will some day shake the Union to its foundation. They never will mix—never commingle and unite."[25]

Edward A. Freeman, an Oxford historian, was another scholar who favored racial explanations of history. In 1881 when Freeman made a lecture tour of the United States, he proposed that "the best remedy for whatever is amiss in America would be if every Irishman should kill a Negro and be hanged for it."[26]

During the late nineteenth and early twentieth centuries, the appeals to limit European immigration were increasingly based on racial as well as economic arguments. The Immigration Restriction League of Boston, founded in 1894, was in the forefront of the battle to ensure that the Anglo-Saxon-Teutonic racial strains would not be overwhelmed by "Slav, Latin, and Asiatic races, historically down-trodden, atavistic, and stagnant."[27]

Solomon points out that historians, economists, sociologists, and physical scientists synthesized the earlier diffuse Teutonist sentiments into a pseudoscientific ideology of racial superiority. These academicians were influenced by the League's opinions; in turn, Brahmin restrictionist views were reinforced by the scholars' presentations. The eugenics movement, which crystallized in America in the early twentieth century, argued that the influx of alien races had increased the rate of "insanity, imbecility, and feeblemindedness" in the population of the United States.

By the early twentieth century, however, less attention was being paid to the inferiority of the Celts than to that of the south-eastern Europeans, who, according to the eugenicists, "had hereditary passions which were unalterable, regardless of public schools and economic opportunities in the United States."[28] Restrictions on the immigration of these undesirables would be the initial step in the creation of a race of supermen in America.

The Anglo-Saxon, Teutonic, southern European, Jewish, and other "races" defined during this period of American history were considered immutable; the characteristics which distinguished them were endowed by heredity. As might be predicted, these "racial" characteristics were as often behavioral as physical. Despite the alleged immutability of these "races" and of the characteristics attributed to them, New Englanders did in fact change their evaluation of the so-called "races of Europe."

Between the 1830s and 1890s, the Celts were described as ignorant, shiftless, credulous, impulsive, and mechanically inept; they were inclined toward drinking and related crimes. By the 1890s, when the Irish were the political leaders of the hub of New England and large numbers of southern Europeans were coming to the United States, the Irish had become tolerated aliens. The shift in attitude toward the Celtic race reflected the change in the political situation. The Irish were said to have "a remarkable race trait of adaptability which explained the achievement of the more intelligent and prosperous of the Boston group." Moreover, the Irish "above all races [had] the mixture of ingenuity, firmness, human sympathy, comradeship, and daring that [made them] the amalgator of races."[29]

That there were no proven biologically significant differences among the "races of Europe" did not prevent New Englanders from perceiving European immigrant populations as separate races. So-called racial differences were said to be manifest in life-styles; racial affiliation could be determined by listening to individuals speak or by hearing their names. In any case, even without perceptible clues, the relative backwardness of the immigrants was "proof" of their inferior intellectual capabilities and characters, both of which were reputedly determined by "racial" heritage.

IV

Solomon's *Ancestors and Immigrants*, Gossett's *Race: The History of an Idea in America*, Stanton's *The Leopard's Spots*,[30] and Curtin's *Image of Africa*[31] provide abundant documentation for the statement that at various historical periods, racial typologies and/or ideologies have reflected prevailing sociopolitical conditions. Historically, both scientific and lay concepts of race have served to support the economic and political privileges of ruling groups who regarded themselves as superior by virtue of phylogenetic heritage rather than because of the accidents of culture history.

From the preceding discussion it should be apparent that popular racial classifications are based on a wide range of emotional, political, and other evaluative criteria that are not relevant to the biological study of human variation. The differences in popular racial typologies become apparent when one shifts in time or place from one society to another. Therefore, it is obvious that there can be no justification for the elevation of any popular racial classification to the status of an analytic system in science.

Studies which purport to demonstrate the genetic basis for this or that behavioral characteristic observed among persons who make up popularly defined races are essentially nonscientific and should be labeled as such. Hence, to presume to study the genetic basis for some behavioral attribute of the "Negro race" in America is to ignore the fundamental difficulty of defining that "race." It is entirely probable that any biogenetically significant division of Americans would include some groups comprised of *both* so-called Negroes and so-called whites. But to isolate such groups would violate the folk theory that there is a pure white race and a Negro race which includes some so-called racial hybrids.

In conclusion, it must be made clear that this paper is not aimed at the deprecation of the study of human variation. The directions for future research into the genetics of human variation have been indicated by various writers, including the contributors to the volume entitled *The Concept of Race*, edited by Ashley Montagu. The isolation of those genetic characters that constitute the most variable array of features in mankind, the determination of the characters that admit of biologically significant clustering of breeding populations, the study of the relationship between genotype and phenotype, including the investigation of genetic characters as they are represented in different life stages of individuals—these are some of the problems which have to be pursued.

These problems can and should be studied without reference to race, which has never been and never will be a primarily biological concept. The history of the use of the race concept by scientists and laymen alike makes it apparent that race could probably never be accepted as a purely statistical concept. Race is a biopolitical concept, the continued use of which will serve only to obfuscate the problems entailed in the study of human variation. As Livingstone[32] has pointed out,

> Just as Galileo's measurements and experiments paved the way for Newton's laws of motion, which totally replaced the Aristotelian laws of motion concerned as they were with describing the nature of bodies and their "essences," our newer genetic knowledge and the measurement of gene frequencies will replace the studies on the nature or essence of race and the mathematical theory of population genetics will replace the Linnaean system of nomenclature.

NOTES AND REFERENCES

1. This position is exemplified by Theodosius Dobzhansky in *Mankind Evolving* (New Haven, Yale University Press, 1965), 266–69. It also appears to be the view of William Boyd, *Genetics and the Races of Man* (Boston, Little, Brown and Co., 1950), and of C. S. Coon, S. M. Garn, and J. B. Birdsell in *Races* (Springfield, Ill., C. C. Thomas, Publisher, 1950).

2. This point of view is represented by a number of contributors to the volume *The Concept of Race*, edited by Ashley Montagu (New York, The Free Press, 1964). For a critical examination of the theoretical and methodological problems involved in racial classifications, see especially the articles by Jean Hiernaux, "The Concept of Race and the Taxonomy of Mankind," 29–45; Frank B. Livingstone, "On the Nonexistence of Human Races," 46–60; Paul R. Ehrlich and Richard W. Holm, "A Biological View of Race," 153–79; and Nigel A. Barnicot, "Taxonomy and Variation in Modern Man," 180–227.

3. Hiernaux, in *The Concept of Race*, 40.

4. See, for example, S. L. Washburn, "The Study of Race," in *The Concept of Race*, 242–60.

5. Ehrlich and Holm, in *The Concept of Race*, 175; see also 154–55, 161–62, and 177–78.

6. Hiernaux, in *The Concept of Race*, 41–42.

7. N. W. Gillham, "Geographic Variation and the Subspecies Concept in Butterflies," *Systematic Zoology* 5 (1956), 110–20, quoted by Ehrlich and Holm in *The Concept of Race*, 167.

8. Livingstone, in *The Concept of Race*, 56.

9. See Thomas F. Gossett, *Race: The History of an Idea in America* (Dallas, Southern Methodist University Press, 1963), 37–39, 69–70, and 80.

10. *New York Times*, October 20, 1966, p. 21, reported that "Chinese-American public school children in Boston have been officially declared white by the School Committee ['the official city agency in charge of Boston's public schools'] in the latest phase of the controversy over racial imbalance in schools." One week later, it was reported that the Massachusetts State Board of Education had rejected the ruling of the Boston School Committee, and that Chinese-American children who had been classed as white would be reclassified as nonwhite. *New York Times*, October 27, 1966, p. 40.

11. Marvin Harris, *Patterns of Race in the Americas* (New York, Walker and Co., 1964), 56.

12. Marvin Harris, "Race," in *International Encyclopedia of the Social Sciences*.

13. Marvin Harris and Ruth Martinez, "Referential Ambiguity in the Calculus of Brazilian Racial Identity," unpublished manuscript.

14. This account of the history of the Eta is based upon John Donoghue, "An Eta Community in Japan: The Social Persistence of Outcaste Groups," *American Anthropologist* 59 (1957), 1000–1017. For additional data on this group, see George DeVos and Hiroshi Wagatsuma, eds., *Japan's Invisible Race: Caste in Culture and Personality* (Berkeley, The University of California Press, 1966).

15. See Shigeaki Ninomiya, "An Inquiry concerning the Origin, Development, and Present Situation of the *Eta* in Relation to the History of Social Classes in Japan," *Transactions of the Asiatic Society of Japan*, 2d series, vol. 10 (1933), 47–154.

16. Kikuchi Sanya, *Eta-Zoku ni Kansuru Kenkyù* (A study concerning the *Eta* race, Tokyo, 1923), cited in Ninomiya, "An Inquiry," 56.

17. Ninomiya, "An Inquiry," 56.

18. This is exemplified by the comments of Audrey M. Shuey in *The Testing of Negro Intelligence* (Lynchburg, Va., J. P. Bell Co., 1958), and by comments of the authors whose studies are reviewed by Shuey.

19. For a discussion of the methodological problems involved here, see Hiernaux, 30–40, and Ehrlich and Holm, 160–61 and 163–64, in *The Concept of Race*.

20. For a sample of scientific racial typologies, see those summarized in Dobzhansky, *Mankind Evolving*, 256–66.

21. Barbara Solomon, *Ancestors and Immigrants* (Cambridge, Harvard University Press, 1956).

22. Charles Eliot Norton, "Goldwin Smith," *North American Review* 205 (1864), 536, quoted in Solomon, *Ancestors*, 12.

23. Charles Francis Adams, *Three Episodes of Massachusetts History* (Boston, Houghton Mifflin and Co., 1892), vol. II, 957, quoted in Solomon, *Ancestors*, 29.

24. Solomon, *Ancestors*, 69–79.

25. Robert Knox, *The Races of Men* (Philadelphia, 1850), 26–27 and 177, quoted in Gossett, *Race*, 96.

26. Edward A. Freeman, *Lectures to American Audiences* (Philadelphia, 1882), quoted in Gossett, *Race*, 109.

27. Solomon, *Ancestors*, 111.

28. Ibid., 151.

29. Ibid, 154.

30. William Stanton, *The Leopard's Spots* (Chicago, University of Chicago Press, 1960).

31. Philip D. Curtin, *The Image of Africa* (Madison, University of Wisconsin Press, 1964).

32. Livingstone, in *The Concept of Race*, 55.

THE STUDY OF RACE

S. L. Washburn

Discussion of the races seems to generate endless emotion and confusion. I am under no illusion that this paper can do much to dispel the confusion; it may add to the emotion. The latest information available supports the traditional findings of anthropologists and other social scientists—that there is no scientific basis of any kind for racial discrimination. I think that the way this conclusion has been reached needs to be restated. The continuation of antiquated biological notions in anthropology and the oversimplification of facts weakens the anthropological position. We must realize that great changes have taken place in the study of race over the last twenty years and it is up to us to bring our profession into the forefront of the newer understandings, so that our statements will be authoritative and useful.

• • •

Beginning with agriculture and continuing at an ever-increasing rate, human customs have been interposed between the organism and the environment. The increase of our species from perhaps as few as five million before agriculture to three billion today is the result of new technology, not of biological evolution. The conditions under which the races evolved are mainly gone, and there are new causes of mutation, new kinds of selection, and vast migration. Today the numbers and distribution of the peoples of the world are due primarily to culture. Some people think the new conditions are so different that it is better no longer to use the word *race* or the word *evolution,* but I personally think this confuses more than it clarifies.

All this does not mean that evolution has stopped, because the new conditions will change gene frequencies, but the conditions which produced the old races are gone. In this crowded world of civilization and science, the claim has been made repeatedly that one or another of the races is superior to the others. Obviously, this argument cannot be based on the past; because something was useful in times past and was selected for under conditions which are now gone, does not mean that it will be useful in the present or in the future.

Delivered as the presidential address at the annual meeting of the American Anthropological Association, November 16, 1962, in Chicago.

The essential point at issue is whether the abilities of large populations are so different that their capacity to participate in modern technical culture is affected. Remember in the first place that no race has evolved to fit the selective pressures of the modern world. Technical civilization is new and the races are old. Remember also that all the species of *Homo* have been adapting to the human way of life for many thousands of years. Tools even antedate our genus, and our human biological adaptation is the result of culture. Man and his capacity for culture have evolved together, as Dr. Dobzhansky has pointed out. All men are adapted to learn language—any language; to perform skillful tasks—a fabulous variety of tasks; to cooperate; to enjoy art; to practice religion, philosophy, and science.

Our species only survives in culture, and, in a profound sense, we are the product of the new selection pressures that came with culture.

Infinitely more is known about the language and culture of all the groups of mankind than is known about the biology of racial differences. We know that the members of every racial group have learned a vast variety of languages and ways of life. The interaction of genes and custom over the millennia has produced a species whose populations can learn to live in an amazing variety of complex cultural ways.

Racism is based on a profound misunderstanding of culture, of learning, and of the biology of the human species. The study of cultures should give a profound respect for the biology of man's capacity to learn. Much of the earlier discussion of racial inferiority centered on the discussion of intelligence; or, to put the matter more accurately, usually on that small part of biological intelligence which is measured by the IQ. In the earlier days of intelligence testing, there was a widespread belief that the tests revealed something which was genetically fixed within a rather narrow range. The whole climate of opinion that fostered this point of view has changed. At that time animals were regarded as primarily instinctive in their behavior, and the genes were supposed to exert their effects in an almost mechanical way, regardless of the environment. All this intellectual climate has changed. Learning has proved to be far more important in the behavior of many animal species, and the action of the complexes of genes is now known to be affected by the environment, as is, to a great degree, the performance that results from them. For example, Harlow has shown that monkeys learn to learn. Monkeys become test wise. They become skillful in the solution of tests—so monkeys in Dr. Harlow's laboratories are spoken of as naive or as experienced in the use of tests. To suppose that humans cannot learn to take tests is to suppose that humans are rather less intelligent than monkeys.

Krech and Rosenzweig have shown that rats raised in an enriched environment are much more intelligent and efficient as maze-solvers than rats that have been given no opportunity to learn and to practice before the testing. To suppose that man would not learn through education to take tests more efficiently, is to suppose that our learning capacities are rather less than those of rats.

The human is born with less than a third of the adult brain capacity, and there is tremendous growth of the cortex after birth. There is possibly no mammalian species in which the environment has a longer and more direct effect on the central nervous system than man. We should expect, then, that test results are going to be more affected by the environment of man than in the case of any other animal. Deprivation studies of monkeys and chimpanzees and clinical investigations of man show that the lack of a normal interpersonal environment may be devastating to the developing individual.

Today one approaches the study of intelligence expecting to find that environment is important. The intellectual background is very different from that of the '20s. The general results on testing may be briefly summarized as follows:

> The average IQ of large groups is raised by education. I believe the most important data on this are the comparisons of the soldiers of World War I and of World War II. More than 80 per cent of the soldiers tested in World War II were above the mean of those tested in World War I. This means a wholesale massive improvement, judged by these tests, in the sons of the people who fought in World War I.

In the states where the least educational effort is made, the IQ is the lowest. In fact, as one looks at the review in Anastasi, it is exceedingly difficult to see why anyone ever thought that the IQ measured innate intelligence, and not the genetic constitution as modified in the family, in the schools, and by the general intellectual environment.

I would suggest that if the intelligence quotients of Negroes and Whites in this country are compared, the same rules be used for these comparisons as would be used for comparisons of the data between two groups of Whites. This may not seem a very extreme thing to suggest, but if you look at the literature, you will find that when two groups of Whites differ in their IQs, the explanation of the difference is immediately sought in schooling, environment, economic positions of parents, and so on, but that when Negroes and Whites differ in precisely the same way the difference is said to be genetic.

Let me give you but one example of this. Klineberg showed years ago in excellent studies that the mean test scores of many northern Negro groups were higher than those of certain groups of southern Whites. When these findings were published, it was immediately suggested that there had been a differential migration and the more intelligent Negroes had moved to the North. But the mean of northern Whites test results is above that of southern Whites. Are we to believe that the intelligent Whites also moved to the North?

There is no way of telling what the IQ would be if equal opportunity were given to all racial and social groups. The group which is sociologically classified as Negro in the United States, about one-third of whose genes are of European origin, might well test ahead of the Whites. I am sometimes surprised to hear it stated that if Negroes were given an equal opportunity, their IQ would be the same as the Whites'. If one looks at the degree of social discrimination against Negroes and their lack of education, and also takes into account the tremendous amount of overlapping between the observed IQs of both, one can make an equally good case that, given a comparable chance to that of the Whites, their

IQs would test out ahead. Of course, it would be absolutely unimportant in a democratic society if this were to be true, because the vast majority of individuals of both groups would be of comparable intelligence, whatever the mean of these intelligence tests would show.

We can generalize this point. All kinds of human performance—whether social, athletic, intellectual—are built on genetic and environmental elements. The level of all kinds of performance can be increased by improving the environmental situation so that every genetic constitution may be developed to its full capacity. Any kind of social discrimination against groups of people, whether these are races, castes, or classes, reduces the achievements of our species, of mankind.

The cost of discrimination is reflected in length of life. The Founding Fathers were wise to join life, liberty, and the pursuit of happiness, because these are intimately linked in the social and cultural system. Just as the restriction of social and economic opportunity reduces intelligence so it reduces length of life.

In 1900 the life expectancy of White males in the United States was forty-eight years, and in that same year the expectancy of a Negro male was thirty-two years; that is a difference of 50 per cent, or sixteen years. By 1940 the difference had been reduced to ten years, and by 1958 to six. As the life expectancy of the Whites increased from forty-eight to sixty-two to sixty-seven years, that of the Negroes increased from thirty-two to fifty-two to sixty-one years. They died of the same causes, but they died at different rates.

Discrimination, by denying equal social opportunity to the Negro, made his progress lag approximately twenty years behind that of the White. Somebody said to me, "Well, sixty-one, sixty-seven, that's only six years." But it depends on whose six years it is. There are about nineteen million people in this country sociologically classified as Negroes. If they die according to the death rate given above, approximately 100 million years of life will be lost owing to discrimination.

In 1958 the death rate for Negroes in the first year of life was fifty-two per thousand and for Whites twenty-six. Thousands of Negro infants died unnecessarily. The social conscience is an extraordinary thing. A lynching stirs the whole community to action, yet only a single life is lost. Discrimination, through denying education, medical care, and economic progress, kills at a far higher rate. A ghetto of hatred kills more surely than a concentration camp, because it kills by accepted custom, and it kills every day in the year.

A few years ago in South Africa, the expectation of life for a Black man was forty years, but it was sixty at the same time for a White man. At that same time a White woman could expect twenty-five more years of life than a Black woman. Among the Blacks the women lived no longer than the men. People speak of the greater longevity of women, but this is only because of modern medicine. High birth rates, high infant mortality, high maternal mortality—these are the hallmarks of the history of mankind.

Of course there are biological differences between male and female, but whether a woman is allowed to vote, or the rate that she must die in childbirth, these are a matter of medical knowledge and of custom. Biological difference only expresses itself through the social system.

Who may live longer in the future—Whites or Negroes? There's no way of telling. Who may live longer in the future—males or females? There is no way of telling. These things are dependent on the progress in medical science and on the degree to which this progress is made available to all races and to both sexes.

When environment is important, the only way genetic difference may be determined is by equalizing the environment. If you believe in mankind, then you will want mankind to live on in an enriched environment. No one can tell what may be the ultimate length of life, but we do know that many people could live much longer if given a chance.

Whether we consider intelligence, or length of life, or happiness the genetic potential of a population is only realized in a social system. It is that system which gives life or death to its members, and in so doing changes the gene frequencies. We know of no society which has begun to realize the genetic potential of its members. We are the primitives living by antiquated customs in the midst of scientific progress. Races are products of the past. They are relics of times and conditions which have long ceased to exist.

Racism is equally a relic supported by no phase of modern science. We may not know how to interpret the form of the Mongoloid face, or why Rh° is of high incidence in Africa, but we do know the benefits of education and of economic progress. We know the price of discrimination is death, frustration, and hatred. We know that the roots of happiness lie in the biology of the whole species and that the potential of the species can only be realized in a culture, in a social system. It is knowledge and the social system which give life or take it away, and in so doing change the gene frequencies and continue the million-year-old interaction of culture and biology. Human biology finds its realization in a culturally determined way of life, and the infinite variety of genetic combinations can only express themselves efficiently in a free and open society.

R E F E R E N C E S

Anastasi, Anne. 1958. *Differential Psychology: Individual and Group Differences in Behavior*. New York, Macmillan.

Dobzhansky, Theodosius. 1962. *Mankind Evolving: The Evolution of the Human Species*. New Haven and London, Yale University Press.

Klineberg, Otto. 1935. *Race Differences*. New York and London, Harper & Brothers.

Krech, David, Mark R. Rosenzweig, and Edward L. Bennett. 1962. Relations between Brain Chemistry and Problem-Solving among Rats Raised in Enriched and Impoverished Environments. *Journal of Comparative and Physiological Psychology* 55:801–7.

ON THE NONEXISTENCE OF
HUMAN RACES

Frank B. Livingstone

In the last decade there has been a remarkable increase in our knowledge of the complexities of human genetic variability. To an increasing number of anthropologists the concept of race seems to be losing its usefulness in describing this variability. In fact, for the human populations among which some of us have worked, it seems impossible even to divide these populations into races. At the same time a growing minority of biologists in general are advocating a similar position with regard to the usefulness of the concept of subspecies for classifying such diverse organisms as grackles, martens, and butterflies (Brown, 1957; Hagmeier, 1958; Gillham, 1956). Although there appears to have been a minimum of communication between anthropologists and biologists on this common problem, many of the arguments of the two groups are quite similar. It should be pointed out that the two similar positions on subspecific variation do not imply that there is no biological or genetic variability among the populations of organisms which comprise a species, but simply that this variability does not conform to the discrete packages labelled races or subspecies. For man the position can be stated in other words: There are no races, there are only clines.[1]

The term *race* has had a long history of anthropological usage and it can be generally defined as referring to a group of local or breeding populations within a species. Thus, it is a taxonomic term for subspecific groupings greater than the local population. Most anthropologists today use a genetic definition of races as populations which differ in the frequency of some genes.

The term *race,* or its newer synonym, *geographical race,* is used in a similar way with reference to biological species other than man. Where the term is used, it can be considered as approximately synonymous with the term *subspecies.* In 1953 Wilson and Brown first suggested discarding the concept of subspecies since it did not accord with the facts. Their main argument was that the genetic variation among the local populations of a species was discordant.

Variation is concordant if the geographic variation of the genetic characters is

---

[1][A cline is a continuous gradation over space in the form or frequency of a trait. Thus clinal variation is continuous, not abrupt.—Ed.]

correlated, so that a classification based on one character would reflect the variability in any other. Such a pattern of variation is almost never found among the local populations of a wide-ranging species, although it is usually found among related relatively allopatric species.[2]

Thus, although it is possible to divide a group of related species into discrete units, namely the species, it is impossible to divide a single species into groups larger than the panmictic[3] population. The causes of intraspecific biological variation are different from those of interspecific variation and to apply the term subspecies to any part of such variation is not only arbitrary or impossible but tends to obscure the explanation of this variation.[4] If one genetic character is used, it is possible to divide a species into subspecies according to the variation in this character. If two characters are used, it may still be possible, but there will be some "problem populations," which, if you are an anthropologist, will be labelled composite or mixed. As the number of characters increases it becomes more nearly impossible to determine what the "actual races really are."

In addition to being a concept used to classify human variability, race has also been overworked as an explanation of this variability. When a particular blood group gene or hair form is found to be characteristic of the populations of a particular region, it is frequently "explained" as being a "racial" character. This type of explanation means, in other words, that this particular set of human populations possesses this character, while it is absent in the rest of humanity, because of the close common ancestry of the former. At times many characteristics which were thought to be racial have been found in many widely separated populations, so that the explanation in terms of race required the assumption of lengthy migrations. In this way race or common ancestry and migration have been used to explain much of the genetic variability among human populations. Unfortunately such explanations neither accord with our knowledge of the population structure and movements of hunters and gatherers, nor take into consideration the basic cause of biological variation, natural selection.

The incompatibility between race and natural selection has been recognized for a long time; so that if one's major aim were to discover the races of man, one has to disregard natural selection. Thus, nonadaptive characters were sought and, in some instances, considered found. But the recognition of the role of natural selection has in the past ten years changed the course of research into human variability; or at least it has changed the thinking of the "aracial ultrapolymorphists."

Recently there have been two somewhat different attempts to resolve the dilemmas created by our new knowledge and outlook and still retain the term *race*. On the one hand, Dobzhansky (1962) appears to want to apply the term *racial variability* to any differences in gene frequencies among human populations, a usage which accords with the genetic definition of race as stated above.

[2][Allopatric species are ones which occupy different geographic regions.—Ed.]
[3][A panmictic population is one with random mating among its members.—Ed.]
[4][Intraspecific variation is within a single species; interspecific variation is between different species.—Ed.]

Since all human populations most likely differ in the frequency of some gene, this position implies that each population would be a separate race; but to Dobzhansky it is a matter of convenience as to how many we call races. Such a usage also implies that any number of racial classifications of the same populations but based on different gene frequencies are "equally valid" or useful. It should be noted that this is a quite different concept of race than previous usage and seems as unfortunate to Hiernaux (1963) as it does to me. But if applied rigorously to the human populations of the world it would result in much the same description of human genetic variability as the clinal analysis advocated in this paper but with the description in words and not in numbers as a clinal analysis would be.

On the other hand, Garn (1961), although paying homage to the genetic definition of race, has attempted to demonstrate the existence of nine specific geographical races, but the question of whether there are nine or nineteen such races is not arbitrary or up to the classifier or dependent on the genetic character used in the classification. These are taxonomic races, but "taxonomic races must bear correspondence to natural races, mirroring nature rather than lecturing her" (Garn, 1963, p. 197), which I think it is fair to say, Garn thinks his geographical races do. Also some of these geographic races "approach true subspecies" (p. 198), and these races, and not others, exist because "the first and foremost fact governing the existence of a geographical race is that it has distinct geographical limits coinciding with major reproductive barriers" (p. 198), which Garn's races presumably do. Thus, according to Garn, there are natural races to which our taxonomic races should correspond, and although the number of races may vary through time, it is still fixed at any one time. Since the existence, validity, or utility of this racial classification is almost entirely dependent on the existence of these major reproductive barriers to gene flow, it seems to me that Garn should present a careful, detailed analysis of these barriers to demonstrate the existence of his geographical races. Aside from a few vague references to the "scarcely inhabited uplands" (Garn, 1961, p. 15), in Western Asia or the deserts of Africa, however, such a demonstration is not forthcoming. Thus, it is rather difficult to contest the existence of the nine geographical races, but I think it can be argued that at present these "major reproductive barriers" do not exist and most likely have existed even less in the past. For example, an analysis of the populations and/or genes in the Sahara Desert certainly indicates that the desert is not a major reproductive barrier, although there may be fewer people or populations inhabiting it. In addition, the utter wasteland which characterizes most parts of the Sahara today is a rather recent phenomenon and due in large part to human occupation. A short 5,000 years ago pastoralists occupied much of the Sahara, and it was perhaps one of the most populated parts of Africa. Prior to these pastoralists, the rich African fauna inhabited most of the Sahara and North Africa and provided probably the best hunting in the whole continent, as the great numbers of archaeological finds attest (Mauny, 1957; Forde-Johnston, 1959). The concept of race seems to me to be of no use in describing or explaining human genetic variability in this region today. The retention of this obsolete concept has caused a recent analysis of the genetic variability among Saharan populations to label the Teda as having "Berber blood in Negro bodies" and the Moors as having "negroid blood in morphologically Berber bodies" (Briggs, 1957, pp. 20–21). Such a description only confuses the issue and hence is worse than useless.

Such a description of the bodies and blood of a human population also implies an explanation of their particular characteristics, which is based on common ancestry and/or mixture with the race involved. The advocates of the validity of the concept of race recognize the great genetic variability which occurs among the populations of the Sahara, Sudan, and Ethiopia, and even refer to these areas as a "clinal zone." The usual explanation of these clines in terms of race and mixture is so widely accepted—even among cultural anthropologists and the general public—that Murdock (1959, p. 9) can state baldly with respect to Ethiopians, "The Cushites have long since incorporated a not insubstantial infusion of Negroid blood. This reveals itself in different ways in different tribes. Thus the lowland Somali are much darker than the peoples of Highland Ethiopia but have hair that is wavy or occasionally straight and only rarely kinky, whereas this typically Negroid form prevails in sixty to seventy percent of the plateau population." This statement clearly indicates that the clines in these characters are discordant. For this reason it is impossible to explain these clines or this genetic variability solely in terms of race and mixture. If a population is X percent Negro in one characteristic it must be X percent in all characters for this to be an adequate explanation. If it is not, other factors of evolutionary change must be involved. One could invoke random genetic drift but the more likely explanation is natural selection. I think this analysis of human genetic variation in racial terms aptly illustrates the inadequacy of this kind of analysis. As an illustration of how our increasing knowledge of biochemical genetics increases this inadequacy, I refer the reader to a recent series of papers on Ethiopian populations (*American Journal of Physical Anthropology,* 1962, pp. 168–208B). Furthermore, this increase in knowledge clearly contradicts Coon's statement that "To me, at least, it is encouraging to know that biochemistry divides us into the same subspecies that we recognize on the basis of other criteria" (Coon, 1962, p. 663). It is discouraging, to me at least, that anyone would make such a statement.

Garn (1961) also seems to regard some biological characteristics as having a similar racial explanation. Garn (1961, p. 16) states that while "Certain human differences transcend geographical race, and are more meaningfully distributed with respect to climate or disease. . . . A geographical race is a collection of populations whose similarities are due to long-continued confinement within set geographical limits." Although these similarities are not outlined in detail, Garn does imply that some biological characteristics are due to natural selection through climate and disease, while others—the racial traits—are not. Natural races thus only reflect variability in certain traits, and any racial classification can only describe a part of human genetic variability and seemingly explain it.

For animal populations other than man, Mayr (1963) has also considered the problems associated with the concept of subspecies, although Mayr feels that

"These questions are of little evolutionary interest" (p. 350). He gives a definition of subspecies as "an aggregate of local populations of a species, inhabiting a geographic subdivision of the range of the species, and differing taxonomically from other populations of the species" (p. 348). Mayr thinks that the subspecies category is such a convenient taxonomic device, this accounts for the great reluctance to abandon it. Although it is still convenient, Mayr (1963, p. 349) warns "It must be realized at all times, however, that in many cases the subspecies is an artifact and that it is not a 'unit of evolution.' Nor should the subspecies be confused with phenomena of a very different nature, such as character gradients (clines)." I think it is fair to say that both Garn (1961) and Coon (1962) conceive of human races as "units of evolution," in fact the major units of human evolution, which is the major source of confusion as Mayr says.

Mayr continues his discussion of genetic variation within a species by separating this variation into three categories: (1) clinal variation, (2) geographic isolates, (3) hybrid belts or zones of intergradation, which he further divides into primary and secondary zones of intergradation (p. 360). According to Mayr, "Whether a subspecies is part of a cline or is isolated completely by geographic barriers is, however, of decisive influence on its evolutionary potential" (p. 366). Thus, some genetic variation within species is subspecific, some clinal, and some associated with primary or secondary zones of intergradation, which, however, might exist between subspecies.

In addition to being a method of describing genetic variability among the populations of a species, each of Mayr's concepts implies an explanation of the variability which it labels. This seems to be particularly so when such variability is said to be associated with primary or secondary zones of intergradation (Mayr, 1963, p. 369). Mayr's different concepts of the way in which to explain genetic variability among the populations of a species accord with the mathematical theory of population genetics, which is advocated here, but again, like Dobzhansky, Mayr's analysis attempts to apply words or labels to different kinds of variability or "phenomena." However, the major argument of this paper is that at present we can be much more precise and, further, that these obsolete labels are inhibiting scientific advances in this field.

I do not think these arguments or the problems they face are of "little evolutionary significance" but quite the opposite. The explanation of the genetic variability among human populations is a central problem of physical anthropology, and there are other methods of describing and explaining this variability which do not utilize the concept of race or which simply attempt to label different kinds of genetic variability. Human genetic variability can be described in terms of the concepts of cline and morphism (Huxley, 1955) or polymorphism which is becoming more widely used to denote the same thing.[5] The variability in the frequency of any gene can be plotted in the same way that temperature is plotted on

[5][Polymorphism refers to discontinuous traits which are at least partly genetically based (e.g., blood type); thus polymorphism is the existence within a population of two or more genotypes, the rarest of which exceeds some arbitrarily chosen frequency (like 1 percent).—Ed.]

a weather map, and this description of genetic variability can describe all of it and implies no explanation whatsoever. Then one can attempt to explain this variability by the mathematical theory of population genetics. This is a very general theory and is capable of explaining all racial or gene frequency differences, although of course for any particular gene the exact magnitudes of factors, mutation, natural selection, gene drift, and gene flow, which control gene frequency differences are not known. All genes mutate, drift, flow, and for a given environment have fitnesses associated with their various genotypes.[6] Hence differences in the frequency of any gene among a series of populations can be explained by these general factors which control gene frequency change. Gene frequency clines can result from many different types of interaction between the general factors which control gene frequencies. For example, a cline may be due to: (1) the recent advance of an advantageous gene; (2) gene flow between populations which inhabit environments with different equilibrium frequencies for the gene; or (3) a gradual change in the equilibrium value of the gene along the cline. The theoretical analysis of clines has barely begun but there seems to be no need for the concept of race in this analysis.

I want to emphasize that in contrast to racial analysis, clinal analysis is a method which can describe all gene frequency differences. Even if one or several genes are completely absent in one population and 100 percent in the next adjacent population, these differences can still be described as clines albeit very steep ones. But if the variability of a particular gene is continuous from Cairo to Cape-town, its variability cannot be described in terms of race, or if two genes vary discordantly, the races set up on the basis of one do not describe the variability in the other. Just as Galileo's measurements and experiments paved the way for Newton's laws of motion, which totally replaced the Aristotelian laws of motion concerned as they were with describing the nature of bodies and their "essences," our newer genetic knowledge and the measurement of gene frequencies will replace the studies on the nature or essence of race and the mathematical theory of population genetics will replace the Linnaean system of nomenclature. Newton's laws can describe and explain all motion, just as clines can describe all genetic variability and coupled with the modern theory of evolution explain it. Linnaeus was given a medal two hundred years ago for "discovering the essence of genera" which I think is an apt expression of the Aristotelian mode of thought and concept of the universe. In 1963 Newman and Dobzhansky are still attempting to discover the nature of race or as Dobzhansky says (1950, p. 101) "defining the essence of race. . . . " Dobzhansky (1963) has characterized my position as having "discovered that races of man do not exist," but I have never "discovered" anything. The concepts of a culture are primarily a function of the level of measurement and observation within the culture. "Races" of man unfortunately exist in the United States, and race as a concept of Western Civilization exists

---

[6][Gene flow is the incorporation of genes from one population to another, either by actual movement of individuals or by breeding between adjacent populations. Genetic drift is fluctuations in frequencies in the various possible forms of genes (the alleles) in a population due to chance events. Genotype is the genetic basis for a particular trait.—Ed.]

just as much as God or the $\sqrt{-1}$. Much of the discussion on the existence of race reminds me of the obituary in *Time* magazine (January 11, 1963) of Arthur O. Lovejoy. When the late Professor Lovejoy was asked at a government investigation if he believed in God, he promptly rattled off thirty-three definitions of God and asked the questioner which one he had in mind. But of course it really didn't matter to the questioner. To avow a belief in the existence of God simply assured one's participation in the sociocultural system, in which everyone knows that God exists out there but we humans are just too ignorant to perceive or define Him accurately. It is likewise with races; they exist but we haven't discovered or defined them yet.

Just as races do not exist but are only part of a general theory concocted by human beings to explain or render intelligible their observations, so the concepts and theorems of the mathematical theory of population genetics do not exist in the same sense. Any scientific theory can be considered as a mathematical or logical system with no reference to reality. It consists of certain basic or primitive terms and axioms from which are derived the major statements or content of the theory, the theorems. Such a theory is fitted to reality by operational definitions of the basic terms so that there are rules to measure random mating or the mutation rate just as there are rules to measure mass or acceleration (see R. L. Wilder, 1952, for an exposition of the nature of scientific theories). In this way the application of any scientific theory is a function of the measuring instruments and experiments of the culture at that time. According to this particular view, I don't think it is legitimate to say that anthropologists and geneticists have "discovered" breeding populations in the last twenty years.

The concept of breeding population when considered as part of the mathematical theory of population genetics pertains to nothing in reality. But when combined with the concepts of gene frequency, random mating, etc., further concepts such as the Hardy-Weinberg Law or the principle of random gene drift can be logically derived. The latter are more or less the theorems of population genetics and are the logical outcomes of the more basic concepts or axioms. The science of population genetics then attempts to apply this theory to bodies of data and to attempt to determine which group of individuals in a particular area fits most closely the concept of breeding population, but the function of this concept of the theory is not to divide up or label reality, but to explain it. Of course, the concepts of the mathematical theory of population genetics have been developed from the data and findings of a particular sphere of reality and are approximations to these data. But they can also be considered solely as logical concepts and studied as a formal system with no reference to this reality. As Medawar (1960) has remarked, this theory has great generality in biology and in that science occupies a position analogous to Newton's Laws in physical science. An infinite population randomly mating without selection, mutation, or gene flow is analogous to Newton's body moving without friction at a constant velocity.

In applying the theory of population genetics to humanity, the species is divided into breeding populations although for any area or group of people this concept may be difficult to apply. It is likely that each breeding population will prove to be genetically unique, so that all will be racially distinct in Dobzhansky's terms. But this is not the general use of the concept of race in biology, and the concept has not in the past been associated with this theory of human diversity. Race has instead been considered as a concept of the Linnaean system of classification within which it is applied to groups of populations within a species. To apply a concept of the Linnaean system to a group of populations implies something about the evolutionary history of these populations, and it also implies that these populations are similar in whatever characters were used to classify them together because of close common ancestry.

For years such racial traits were considered to be relatively nonadaptive and were the property of the physical anthropologists, while at the same time the geneticists were concerned with characters which were due to the presence of a single gene and which were for the most part deleterious.[7] Much of the early work in human genetics was done on such characters as achondroplasia, albinism, alcaptonuria, and brachydactyly. Most of these deleterious genes occur in low frequencies in most populations and their explanation seems to be a balance of mutation to them and selection against them. These were considered "bad" genes but once in a great while a "good" gene would appear and completely replace its allele. Although the sickle cell gene has changed the outlook of geneticists, the idea that there are different kinds of inherited traits which require different explanations persists today. Coon (1962) has even introduced a new division into racial and evolutionary characters. But to use an overworked cliché, a gene is a gene is a gene, and all genes are subject to the factors outlined previously which control gene frequencies. Hence the mathematical theory of population genetics applies to all genes, racial, deleterious, evolutionary, etc.

But science progresses. Just as the theory of population genetics is gaining acceptance, the pace of biological research is such that our measuring instruments are beginning to reach beyond the concepts. Newton's Laws when first accepted were considered to be "truth" or "facts," but when the measuring instruments began to get above and below their sphere of application, Einstein's equations replaced them. Similarly the mathematical theory of population genetics evolved around and was based on the concept of a gene as a bead on a chromosomal string. It was the unit which mutated, recombined, and functioned—at first to produce one enzyme but now one polypeptide chain. And it was a satisfactory unit for the experimental genetics of the day which consisted of animal breeding and observation of hereditary characters. But now as these discrete units have become a rather continuous strand of DNA, the question can be asked, do these units with the aforementioned properties exist? Obviously not (Benzer, 1962), and it has been suggested that we discuss mutons, recons, and cistrons in place of genes. It would appear that any unit above the individual base pair is arbitrary. Hence the mathematical theory of population genetics is almost obsolete before it begins to be accepted. But to me this is only one vivid example

---

[7][Deleterious genes are ones that natural selection acts against, i.e., ones that result in an individual bearing fewer than average number of offspring.—Ed.]

of the maxim that "Yesterday's science is today's common sense and tomorrow's nonsense." For the concept of race and the intraspecific application of the Linnaean system of classification, tomorrow is here.

R E F E R E N C E S

American Journal of Physical Anthropology. 1962. A Survey of Some Genetical Characteristics in Ethiopian Tribes. 20:168–208B.

Benzer, S. 1962. The Fine Structure of the Gene. *Scientific American* 206:70–84.

Briggs, L. C. 1957. A Review of the Physical Anthropology of the Sahara and Its Prehistoric Implications. *Man* 57:20–23.

Brown, W. L., Jr. 1957. Centrifugal Speciation. *Quarterly Review of Biology* 32:247–77.

Coon, C. S. 1962. *The Origin of Races.* New York, Knopf.

Dobzhansky, T. 1950. The Genetic Nature of Differences among Men, in S. Persons, ed., *Evolutionary Thought in America.* New Haven, Yale, 86–155.

———. 1962. Comment on Livingstone. *Current Anthropology* 3:279–80.

———. 1963. Comment on Newman. *Current Anthropology* 4:197–98.

Forde-Johnston. 1959. *Neolithic Cultures of North Africa.* Liverpool, Liverpool University Press.

Garn, S. M. 1961. *Human Races.* Springfield, Thomas.

———. 1963. Comment on Newman. *Current Anthropology* 4:197–98.

Gillham, N. W. 1956. Geographic Variation and the Subspecies Concept in Butterflies. *Systematic Zoology* 5:110–20.

Hagmeier, E. M. 1958. The Inapplicability of the Subspecies Concept in the North American Marten. *Systematic Zoology* 7:1–7.

Hiernaux, J. 1963. Comment on Newman. *Current Anthropology* 4:198–99.

Huxley, J. S. 1955. Morphism and Evolution. *Heredity* 9:1–52.

Mauny, R. 1957. Répartition de la grande "faune ethiopienne" du Nord-Ouest Africain du Paléolithique à nos jours. Proceedings of the 3d Pan African Congress of Prehistory, 1955, 102–5.

Mayr, E. 1963. *Animal Species and Their Evolution.* Cambridge, Harvard.

Medawar, P. B. 1960. *The Future of Man.* London, Methuen.

Murdock, G. P. 1959. *Africa.* New York, McGraw-Hill.

Newman, M. T. 1963. Geographic and Microgeographic Races. *Current Anthropology* 4:189–92.

Wilder, R. L. 1952. *Introduction to the Foundations of Mathematics.* New York, John Wiley.

Wilson, E. O., and W. L. Brown., Jr. 1953. The Subspecies Concept and Its Taxonomic Application. *Systematic Zoology* 2:97–111.

IQ: THE RANK ORDERING OF THE WORLD

R. C. Lewontin, Steven Rose, and Leon J. Kamin

The Roots of IQ Testing

Social power runs in families. The probability that a child will grow into an adult in the highest 10 percent of income earners is ten times greater for children whose parents were in the top 10 percent than for children of the lowest 10 percent.[1] In France, the school failure rate of working-class children is four times that for children of the professional class.[2] How are we to explain hereditary differences in social power in a society that claims to have abolished hereditary privilege in the eighteenth century? One explanation—that hereditary privilege is integral to bourgeois society, which is not structurally conducive to real equality—is too disquieting and threatening; it breeds disorder and discontent; it leads to urban riots like those in Watts and Brixton. The alternative is to suppose that the successful possess an intrinsic merit, a merit that runs in the blood: Hereditary privilege becomes simply the ineluctable consequence of inherited ability. This is the explanation offered by the mental testing movement, whose basic argument can be summarized in a set of six propositions that, taken as a whole, form a seemingly logical explanation of social inequality. These are:

1. There are differences in status, wealth, and power.
2. These differences are consequences of different intrinsic ability, especially different "intelligence."
3. IQ tests are instruments that measure this intrinsic ability.
4. Differences in intelligence are largely the result of genetic differences between individuals.
5. Because they are the result of genetic differences, differences in ability are fixed and unchangeable.
6. Because most of the differences between individuals in ability are genetic, the differences between races and classes are also genetic and unchangeable.

While the argument begins with an undoubted truth that demands explanation, the rest is a mixture of factual errors and conceptual misunderstandings of elementary biology.

The purposes of Alfred Binet, who in 1905 published the first intelligence test, seem to have been entirely benign. The practical problem to which Binet addressed himself was to devise a brief testing procedure that could be used to help identify children who, as matters then stood, could not profit from instruction in the regular public schools of Paris. The problem with such children, Binet reasoned, was that their "intelligence" had failed to develop properly. The intelligence test was to be used as a diagnostic instrument. When the test had located a child with deficient intelligence, the next step was to increase the intelligence of such a child. That could be done, in Binet's view, with appropriate courses in "mental orthopedics." The important point is that Binet did not for a moment suggest that his test was a measure of some "fixed" or "innate" characteristic of the child. To those who asserted that the intelligence of an individual is a fixed quantity that one cannot augment, Binet's response was clear: "We must protest and react against this brutal pessimism."[3]

The basic principle of Binet's test was extraordinarily simple. With the assumption that the children to be tested had all shared a similar cultural background, Binet argued that older children should be able to perform mental tasks that younger children could not. To put matters very simply, we do not expect the average three-year-old to be able to recite the names of the months, but we do expect a normal ten-year-old to be able to do so. Thus, a ten-year-old who cannot recite the months is probably not very intelligent, while a three-year-old who can do so is probably highly intelligent. What Binet did, quite simply, was to put together sets of "intellectual" tasks appropriate for each age of childhood. There were, for example, some tasks that the average eight-year-old could pass, but which were too difficult for the average seven-year-old and very easy for the average nine-year-old. Those tasks defined the "mental age" of eight years. The intelligence of a child depended upon the relation his or her mental and chronological ages bore to each other. The child whose mental age was higher than his or her chronological age was "bright" or accelerated, and the child whose mental age was lower than his or her chronological age was "dull" or retarded. For most children, of course, the mental and chronological ages were the same. To Binet's satisfaction, the mental ages of children in a school class, as measured by his test, tended to correspond with teachers' judgments about which children were more or less "intelligent." That is scarcely surprising, since for the most part Binet's test involved materials and methods of approach similar to those emphasized in the school system. When a child lagged behind its age-mates by as much as two years of mental age, it seemed obvious to Binet that remedial intervention was called for. When two Belgian investigators reported that the children whom they had studied had much higher mental ages than the Paris children studied by Binet, Binet noted that the Belgian children attended a private school and came from the upper social classes. The small class sizes in the private school, plus the kind of training given in a "cultured" home, could explain, in Binet's view, the higher intelligence of the Belgian children.

The translators and importers of Binet's test, both in the United States and in England, tended to share a common ideology, one dramatically at variance with Binet's. They asserted that the intelligence test measured an innate and unchangeable quantity, fixed by genetic inheritance. When Binet died prematurely in 1911, the Galtonian eugenicists took clear control of the mental testing movement in the English-speaking countries and carried their determinist principles even further. The differences in measured intelligence not just between individuals but between social classes and races were now asserted to be of genetic origin. The test was no longer regarded as a diagnostic instrument, helpful to educators, but could identify the genetically (and incurably) defective, those whose uncontrolled breeding posed a "menace . . . to the social, economic and moral welfare of the state."[4] When Lewis Terman introduced the Stanford-Binet test to the United States in 1916 he wrote that a low level of intelligence

> is very common among Spanish-Indian and Mexican families of the Southwest and also among negroes. Their dullness seems to be racial, or at least inherent in the family stocks from which they come. . . . The writer predicts that . . . there will be discovered enormously significant racial differences in general intelligence, differences which cannot be wiped out by any scheme of mental culture.
>
> Children of this group should be segregated in special classes. . . . They cannot master abstractions, but they can often be made efficient workers. . . . There is no possibility at present of convincing society that they should not be allowed to reproduce, although from a eugenic point of view they constitute a grave problem because of their unusually prolific breeding.[5]

Though Terman's Stanford-Binet test was basically a translation of Binet's French items, it contained two significant modifications. First, a set of items said to measure the intelligence of adults was included, as well as items for children of different ages. Second, the ratio between mental and chronological age, the "intelligence quotient," or IQ, was now calculated to replace the simple statement of mental and chronological ages. The clear implication was that the IQ, fixed by the genes, remained constant throughout the individual's life. "The fixed character of mental levels" was cited by another translator of Binet's test, Henry Goddard, in a 1919 lecture at Princeton University, as the reason why some were rich and others poor, some employed and others unemployed. "How can there be such a thing as social equality with this wide range of mental capacity? . . . As for an equal distribution of the wealth of the world, that is equally absurd."[6]

The major translator of Binet's test in England was Cyril Burt, whose links to Galtonian eugenics were even more pronounced than those of his American contemporaries. Burt's father was a physician who treated Galton, and Galton's strong recommendations hastened Burt's appointment as the first school psychologist in the English-speaking world. As early as 1909 Burt had administered some crude tests to two very small groups of schoolchildren in the town of Oxford. The children at one school were the sons of Oxford dons, fellows of the Royal Society, etc., while children at the other school were the sons of ordinary townspeople. Burt claimed that the children from the higher-class school did better on his tests and that this demonstrated that intelligence was inherited. This scientifically stated conclusion, published in the 1909 *British Journal of Psychology,*[7] might have been predicted from Burt's handwritten entry, six years earlier, in his Oxford undergraduate notebook: "The problem of the very poor— chronic poverty: Little prospect of the solution of the problem without the forcible detention of the wreckage of society or other preventing them from propagating their species."

Burt continued his eugenic researches into the inheritance of IQ until he died in 1971, knighted by his monarch and bemedaled by the American Psychological Association. The masses of data that he published helped to establish the "eleven-plus" examination in England, linked to the postwar system of selective education. "Intelligence," Burt wrote in 1947, "will enter into everything the child says, thinks, does or attempts, both while he is at school and later on. . . . If intelligence is innate, the child's degree of intelligence is permanently limited." Further, "Capacity must obviously limit content. It is impossible for a pint jug to hold more than a pint of milk; and it is equally impossible for a child's educational attainments to rise higher than his educable capacity permits."[8] There could be no clearer statement of what had happened to Binet's test in the hands of the Galtonians. The test designed to alert educators that they must intervene with special educational treatment was now said to measure "educable capacity." When a child did poorly in school, or when an adult was unemployed, it was because he or she was genetically inferior and must always remain so. The fault was not in the school or in the society, but in the inferior person.

The IQ test, in practice, has been used both in the United States and England to shunt vast numbers of working-class and minority children onto inferior and dead-end educational tracks.* The reactionary impact of the test, however, has extended far beyond the classroom. The testing movement was clearly linked, in the United States, to the passage, beginning in 1907, of compulsory sterilization laws aimed at genetically inferior "degenerates." The categories detailed included, in different states, criminals, idiots, imbeciles, epileptics, rapists, lunatics, drunkards, drug fiends, syphilitics, moral and sexual perverts, and "diseased and degenerate persons." The sterilization laws, explicitly declared constitutional by the U.S. Supreme Court in 1927, established as a matter of legal fact the core assertion of biological determinism: that all these degenerate characteristics were transmitted through the genes. When the IQ testing program of the United States Army in World War I indicated that immigrants from Southern and Eastern Europe had low test scores, this was said to demonstrate that "Alpines" and "Mediterraneans" were genetically inferior to "Nordics." The army of IQ data figured prominently in the public and congressional debates over the Immigration Act of 1924. That overtly racist act established as a feature of American

---

*"Tracking" in the U.S. educational system is more or less synonymous with "streaming" in Britain.

immigration policy a system of "national origin quotas." The purpose of the quotas was explicitly to debar, as much as possible, the genetically inferior peoples of Southern and Eastern Europe, while encouraging "Nordic" immigration from northern and western Europe. This tale has been told in full elsewhere.[9]

Today many (if not most) psychologists recognize that differences in IQ between various races and/or ethnic groups cannot be interpreted as having a genetic basis. The obvious fact is that human races and populations differ in their cultural environments and experiences, no less than in their gene pools. There is thus no reason to attribute average score differences between groups to genetic factors, particularly since it is so obviously the case that the ability to answer the kinds of questions asked by IQ testers depends heavily on one's past experience. Thus, during World War I, the Army Alpha test asked Polish, Italian, and Jewish immigrants to identify the product manufactured by Smith & Wesson and to give the nicknames of professional baseball teams. For immigrants who could not speak English, the Army Beta test was designed as a "nonverbal" measure of "innate intelligence." That test asked the immigrants to point out what was missing from each of a set of drawings. The set included a drawing of a tennis court, with the net missing. The immigrant who could not answer such a question was thereby shown to be genetically inferior to the tennis-playing psychologists who devised such tests for adults.

What IQ Tests Measure

How do we know that IQ tests measure "intelligence"? Somehow, when the tests are created, there must exist a prior criterion of intelligence against which the results of the tests can be compared. People who are generally considered "intelligent" must rate high and those who are obviously "stupid" must do badly or the test will be rejected. Binet's original test, and its adaptations into English, were constructed to correspond to teachers' and psychologists' a priori notions of intelligence. Especially in the hands of Terman and Burt, they were tinkered with and standardized so that they became consistent predictors of school performance. Test items that differentiated boys from girls, for example, were removed, since the tests were not meant to make that distinction; differences between social classes, or between ethnic groups or races, however, have not been massaged away, precisely because it is these differences that the tests are *meant* to measure.

IQ tests at present vary considerably in their form and content, but all of them are validated by how well they agree with older standards. It must be remembered that an IQ test is published and distributed by a publishing company as a commercial item, selling hundreds of thousands of copies. The chief selling point of such tests, as announced in their advertising, is their excellent agreement with the results of the Stanford-Binet test. Most combine tests of vocabulary, numerical reasoning, analogical reasoning, and pattern recognition.

Some are filled with specific and overt cultural references: Children are asked to identify characters from English literature ("Who was Wilkins Micawber?"); they are asked to make class judgments ("Which of the five persons below is most like a carpenter, plumber, and bricklayer? 1) postman, 2) lawyer, 3) truck driver, 4) doctor, 5) painter"); they are asked to judge socially acceptable behavior ("What should you do when you notice you will be late to school?"); they are asked to judge social stereotypes ("Which is prettier?" when given the choice between a girl with some Negroid features and a doll-like European face); they are asked to define obscure words (sudorific, homunculus, parterre). Of course, the "right" answers to such questions are good predictors of school performance.

Other tests are "nonverbal" and consist of picture explanations or geometric pattern recognition. All—and most especially the nonverbal tests—depend upon the tested person having learned the ability to spend long periods participating in a contentless, contextless mental exercise under the supervision of authority and under the implied threat of reward or punishment that accompanies all tests of any nature. Again, they necessarily predict school performance, since they mimic the content and circumstances of schoolwork.

IQ tests, then, have not been designed from the principles of some general theory of intelligence and subsequently shown to be independently a predictor of social success. On the contrary, they have been empirically adjusted and standardized to correlate well with school performance, while the notion that they measure "intelligence" is added on with no independent justification to validate them. Indeed, we do not know what that mysterious quality "intelligence" is. At least one psychologist, E. G. Boring, has defined it as "what intelligence tests measure."[10] The empirical fact is that there exist tests that predict reasonably well how children will perform in school. That these tests advertise themselves as "intelligence" measures should not delude us into investing them with more meaning than they have.

Reifying Behavior

The possibility of behavioral measurements rests upon certain basic underlying assumptions, which should now be clarified. First, it is assumed that it is possible to define, absolutely or operationally, a particular "quality" to be measured. Some such qualities, like height, are relatively unproblematic. To the question, "How tall are you?" the answer in centimeters, feet, or inches is easy to give. To the question "How angry are you?" no such easy answer can be given. Anger has to be defined operationally, as, for instance, how often an individual placed in a given test situation and asked the question by the experimenter responds by hitting him on the nose. This is not a flippant example. "Aggression" in a rat is measured by putting a mouse in a cage with it and observing the behavior and time taken for the rat to kill the mouse. Sometimes this is described under the name "muricidal" behavior in the literature, which presumably makes the experimenters happier that they are measuring something really scientific. Research in this area thus becomes forced into Boring's circularity: Intelligence "is" what intelligence tests measure.

The "quality" is then taken to be an underlying object that is merely reflected in varying aspects of an individual's behavior under widely different circumstances. Thus "aggression" is what individuals express when a man beats his wife, pickets boycott scabs during a strike, teenagers fight after a football game, black Africans struggle for independence from their colonial masters, generals press buttons unleashing thermonuclear war, or America and the Soviet Union compete in the Olympic Games or the space race. The underlying quality is identical with that which underlies muricide in rats.

Second, it is assumed that the quality is a fixed property of an individual. Aggression and intelligence are seen not as processes that emerge from a situation and are part of the relationships of that situation, but rather exist like reservoirs each of defined amount, inside each of us, to be turned on or off. Instead of seeing the anger or aggression expressed in inner city riots as emerging from the interaction between individuals and their social and economic circumstances and as expressive of collective action—therefore a social phenomenon—the biological determinist argument defines inner city violence as merely the sum of individual units of aggressiveness. . . .

Thus verbs are redefined as nouns: processes of interaction are reified and located inside the individual. Further, reified verbs, like aggression, are assumed to be rigid, fixed things that can be reproducibly measured. Like height, they will not vary much from day to day; indeed, if the tests designed to measure them show such variations they are regarded as poor tests. It is assumed not that the "quality" being measured is labile, but that our instruments need greater precision.

Psychometry and the Obsession with the Norm

Implicit in reification is the third and crucial premise of the mental testing movement. If processes are really things that are the properties of individuals and that can be measured by invariant objective rules, then there must be scales on which they can be located. The scale must be metric in some manner, and it must be possible to compare individuals across the scale. If one person has an aggression score of 100 and the next of 120, the second is therefore 20 percent more aggressive than the first. The fault in the logic should be clear: The fact that it is possible to devise tests on which individuals score arbitrary points does not mean that the quality being measured by the test is really metric. The illusion is provided by the scale. Height is metric, but consider, for instance, color. We could present individuals with a set of colors ranging from red to blue and ask them to rank them as 1 (reddest) to 10 (bluest). But this would not mean that the color rated 2 was actually twice as blue as the color rated 1. The ordinal scale is an arbitrary one, and most psychometric tests are actually ordinals of this sort. If one rat kills ten mice in five minutes and a second rat kills twelve in the same time, this does not automatically mean that the second is 20 percent more aggressive than the first. If one student scores 80 in an exam and a second 40, this does not mean the first is twice as intelligent as the second.

Surmounting or disguising the scaling problem is integral to the grand illusion of psychometry. Individuals vary in height, and if heights for a hundred or so individuals drawn at random from a population are plotted, they will likely fall into the normal distribution, or bell-shaped curve. If the divisions in one's scale are very fine—say, inches—the bell curve is quite wide. If we had no measures less than feet, and we measured each individual to the nearest foot, the curve would be much narrower at the bottom. The vast majority of individuals in Western society would lie between the five- and six-foot measure. While we know the relationship of inches to feet and could under appropriate circumstances convert from one scale to another, and we know when to use each, as when we are finding a pair of shoes that fit or deciding the best size to make a door opening, we do not know the comparable relationships between different ways of measuring aggression or intelligence. Which scale is chosen depends on whether one wants to make differences of scale appear large or small, and these decisions are those that psychometry arbitrarily makes. The decision that a "good" scale is one in which two-thirds of the population should lie within 15 percent of the mean score of the entire population—the famous normal distribution—is arbitrary, but its power is such that psychometrists chop and change their scales till they meet this criterion.

Yet the power of the "norm," once established, is that it is used to judge individuals who have been located along its linear scale. Deviations from the norm are regarded with alarm. Parents who are told that their child is two standard deviations from the norm on some behavioral score are led to believe that he or she is "abnormal" and should be adjusted in some way to psychometry's Procrustean bed. Psychometry, above all, is a tool of a conformist society that, for all its professed concern with individuals, is in reality mainly concerned to match them against others and to attempt to adjust them to conformity.

Pressure to conform to social norms, and institutions that propagate and reinforce these norms, are, of course, characteristic of all human societies. In advanced capitalist societies and today's state capitalist societies like the Soviet Union or those in Eastern Europe, the norm becomes an ideological weapon in its own right, foreshadowed by Huxley's *Brave New World* and Orwell's *1984* but cloaked in the benign language of those who only wish to help, to advise, but not to control and manipulate. Let us be clear: norms are statistical artifacts; they are not biological realities. Biology is not committed to bell-shaped curves.

IQ Tests as Predictors of Social Success

The claim that IQ tests are good predictors of eventual social success is, except in a trivial and misleading sense, simply incorrect. It is true that if one measures social success by income or by what sociologists call socioeconomic status (SES)—a combination of income, years of schooling, and occupation—then people with higher incomes or higher SES did better on IQ tests when they were children than did people with low incomes or low SES. For example, a person whose childhood IQ was in the top 10 percent of all children is fifty times more likely to wind up in the top 10 percent of income than a child whose IQ was in the lowest 10 percent. But that is not really quite the question of interest. What we really should ask is: How much more likely is a high-IQ child to wind up in the top 10 percent of income, *all other things being equal?* In other words, there are multiple and complex causes of events which do not act or exist independently of each other. Even where *A* looks at first sight as if it is the cause of *B*, it sometimes really turns out on deeper examination that *A* and *B* are both effects of some prior cause, *C.* For example, on a worldwide basis, there is a strong positive relationship between how much fat and how much protein the population of a particular country consumes. Rich countries consume a lot of each, poor countries little. But fat consumption is neither the cause nor the result of eating protein. Both are the consequence of how much money people have to spend on food. Thus, although fat consumption per capita is statistically a predictor of protein consumption per capita, it is not a predictor when all other things are equal. Countries that have the same per capita income show no particular relation between average fat and average protein consumption, since the real causal variable, income, is not varying between countries.

This is precisely the situation for IQ performance and eventual social success. They go together because both are the consequences of other causes. To see this, we can ask how good a predictor IQ is of eventual economic success when we hold constant the person's family background and the number of years of schooling. With these constant, a child in the top 10 percent of IQ has only twice, not fifty times, the chance of winding up in the top 10 percent of income as a child of the lowest IQ group. Conversely, and more important, a child whose family is in the top 10 percent of economic success has a 25 times greater chance of also being at the top than the child of the poorest 10 percent of families, even when both children have average IQ.[11] Family background, rather than IQ, is the overwhelming reason why an individual ends up with a higher than average income. Strong performance on IQ tests is simply a reflection of a certain kind of family environment, and once that latter variable is held constant, IQ becomes only a weak predictor of economic success. If there is indeed an intrinsic ability that leads to success, IQ tests do not measure it. If IQ tests do measure intrinsic intelligence as is claimed, than clearly it is better to be born rich than smart.

The Heritability of IQ

The next step in the determinist argument is to claim that differences between individuals in their IQ arise from differences in their genes. The notion that intelligence is hereditary is, of course, deeply built into the theory of IQ testing itself because of its commitment to the measurement of something that is intrinsic and unchangeable. From the very beginning of the American and British mental testing movement, it was assumed that IQ was biologically heritable.

There are certain erroneous senses of "heritable" that appear in the psychometricians' writings on IQ, mixed up with the geneticists' technical meaning of heritability, and which contribute to false conclusions about the consequences of heritability. The first error is that genes themselves determine intelligence. Neither for IQ nor for any other trait can genes be said to determine the organism. There is no one-to-one correspondence between the genes inherited from one's parents and one's height, weight, metabolic rate, sickness, health, or any other nontrivial organic characteristic. The critical distinction in biology is between the *phenotype* of an organism, which may be taken to mean the total of its morphological, physiological, and behavioral properties, and its *genotype,* the state of its genes. It is the genotype, not the phenotype, that is inherited. The genotype is fixed; the phenotype develops and changes constantly. The organism itself is at every stage the consequence of a developmental process that occurs in some historical sequence of environments. At every instant in development (and development goes on until death) the next step is a consequence of the organism's present biological state, which includes both its genes and the physical and social environment in which it finds itself. This comprises the first principle of developmental genetics: that every organism is the unique product of the interaction between genes and environment at every stage of life. While this is a textbook principle of biology, it has been widely ignored in determinist writings. "In the actual race of life, which is not to get ahead, but to get ahead of somebody," wrote E. L. Thorndike, the leading psychologist of the first half of the century, "the chief determining factor is heredity."[12]

The second error—even if admitting that genes do not determine the actual developmental outcome—is to claim that they determine the effective limit to which it can go. Burt's metaphor of the pint jug that can hold no more than a pint of milk is a precise image of this view of genes as the determinants of capacity. If the genetic capacity is large, the argument runs, then an enriched environment will result in a superior organism, although in a poor environment the same individual will not show much ability. If the genetic capacity is poor, however, then an enriched environment will be wasted. Like the notion of the absolute determination of organisms by genes, this view of genetic "capacity" is simply false. There is nothing in our knowledge of the action of genes that suggests differential total capacity. In theory, of course, there must be *some* maximum height, say, to which an individual could grow; but in fact there is no relationship between that purely theoretical maximum, which is never reached in practice, and the actual variations among individuals. The lack of relationship between actual state and theoretical maximum is a consequence of the fact that growth rates and growth maxima are not related. Sometimes it is the slowest growers that reach the greatest size. The proper description of the difference between genetic types is not in some hypothetical "capacity" but in the specific phenotype that will develop for that genotype as a consequence of some specific chain of environmental circumstances.

Nor, of course does the phenotype develop linearly from the genotype from birth to adulthood. The "intelligence" of an infant is not merely a certain small percentage of that of the adult it will become, as if the "pint jug" were being steadily filled. The process of growing up is not a linear progression from incompetence to competence: To survive, a newborn baby must be competent at being a newborn baby, not at being a tiny version of the adult it will later become. Development is not just a quantitative process but one in which there are transformations in quality—between suckling and chewing solid food, for instance, or between sensorimotor and cognitive behavior. But such transitions are not permitted in the rank-ordered view of the universe that determinism offers.

The total variation in phenotype in a population of individuals arises from two interacting sources. First, individuals with the same genes still differ from each other in phenotype because they have experienced different developmental environments. Second, there are different genotypes in the population which differ from each other on the average even in the same array of environments. The phenotype of an individual cannot be broken down into the separate contributions of genotype and of environment, because the two interact to produce the organism; but the total variation of any phenotype in the population can be broken down into the variation between the average of the different genotypes and the variation among individuals with the same genotype. The variation between the average performance of different genotypes is called the *genetic variance* of the trait (that is, the aspect of the phenotype under study—eye color, height, or whatever) in the population, while the variation among individuals of the same genotype is called the *environmental variance* of the trait in the population. It is important to notice that the genetic and environmental variances are not universal properties of a trait but depend upon which population of individuals is being characterized and under which set of environments. Some populations may have a lot of genetic variance for a character, some only a little. Some environments are more variable than others.

The *heritability* of a trait, in the technical sense in which geneticists understand it, is the proportion of all the variation of a trait in a population that is accounted for by the genetic variance. Symbolically,

$$\text{Heritability} = H = \frac{\text{genetic variance}}{\text{genetic variance} + \text{environmental variance}}$$

If the heritability is 100 percent, then all of the variance in the population is genetic. Each genotype would be phenotypically different, but there would be no developmental variation among individuals of the same genotype. If the heritability is zero, all of the variation is among individuals within a genotype, and there is no average variation from genotype to genotype. Characters like height, weight, shape, metabolic activity, and behavioral traits all have heritabilities below 100 percent. Some, like specific language spoken or religious and political affiliation, have heritabilities of zero. The claim of biological determinists has been that the heritability of IQ is about 80 percent. How do they arrive at this figure?

Estimating the Heritability of IQ

All genetic studies are studies of the resemblances of relatives. If a trait is heritable, that is, if different genotypes have different average performances, then relatives ought to resemble each other more closely than unrelated persons do, since relatives share genes from common ancestors. Brothers and sisters ought to be more like each other than aunts and nephews, who ought to be more similar than totally unrelated people. The standard measure of similarity between things that vary quantitatively is their *correlation,* which measures the degree to which larger values for one variable go together with larger values of a second variable, and smaller values with smaller values. The correlation coefficient, r, ranges from $+ 1.0$ for perfect positive correlation, through zero for no relationship, to $- 1.0$ for perfect negative correlation. So, for example, there is a positive correlation between father's income and child's years of schooling. Richer fathers have better-educated children while poorer fathers have less-educated children, on the average. The correlation is not perfect, since some families produce children who go to graduate school, but it is positive. In contrast, in the United States there is a negative correlation between family income and the number of visits per year to hospital emergency rooms. The lower your income, the more likely you are to use the emergency room as a medical service instead of a private doctor.

One important point about correlation is that it measures how two things vary together but does not measure how similar their average levels are. So the correlation between the heights of mothers and their sons could be perfect in that taller mothers had the taller sons and shorter mothers had the shorter sons, yet all the sons could be taller than all the mothers. Covariation is not the same as identity. The significance of this fact for the heritability of IQ and its meaning is considerable. Suppose a group of fathers had IQs of 96, 97, 98, 99, 100, 101, 102, and 103, while their daughters, separated from their fathers at birth and raised by foster parents, had IQs respectively of 106, 107, 108, 109, 110, 111, 112, and 113. There is a perfect correspondence between the IQs of fathers and daughters, and we might judge the character to be perfectly heritable because, knowing a father's IQ, we could tell without error which of the daughters was his. The correlation is, in fact, $r = + 1.0$, yet the daughters are ten points above their fathers in IQ, so the experience of being raised by foster parents had a powerful effect. There is thus no contradiction between the assertion that a trait is perfectly heritable and the assertion that it can be changed radically by environment. As we shall see, this is not a hypothetical example.

Second, a correlation between two variables is not a reliable guide to causation. If A and B are correlated, one may be the cause of the other, they may both be the consequence of a common cause, or they may be entirely accidentally related. The number of cigarettes smoked per day is correlated with the chance of lung cancer because smoking is a cause of lung cancer. The floor area of a person's house and the average age to which he or she lives are positively correlated not because living in a big house is conducive to health but because both characteristics are a consequence of the same cause—high income. For that matter, the distance of the Earth from Halley's comet and the price of fuel are negatively correlated in recent years because one has been decreasing while the other increased, but for totally independent reasons.

In general, heritability is estimated from the correlation of a trait between relatives. Unfortunately, in human populations two important sources of correlation are conflated: Relatives resemble each other not only because they share genes but also because they share environments. This is a problem that can be circumvented in experimental organisms, where genetically related individuals can be raised in controlled environments, but human families are not rat cages. Parents and their offspring may be more similar than unrelated persons because they share genes but also because they share family environment, social class, education, language, etc. To solve this problem, human geneticists and psychologists have taken advantage of special circumstances that are meant to break the tie between genetic and environmental similarity in families.

The first circumstance is adoption. Are particular traits in adopted children correlated with their biological families even when they have been separated from them? Are identical (i.e. monozygotic, or one-egg) twins, separated at birth, similar to each other in some trait? If so, genetic influence is implicated. The second circumstance holds environment constant but changes genetic relationship. Are identical twins more alike than fraternal (i.e. dizygotic, or two-egg) twins? Are two biological brothers or sisters (sibs) in a family more alike than two adopted children in a family? If so, genes are again implicated because, in theory, identical twins and fraternal twins have equal environmental similarity but they are not equally related genetically.

The difficulty with both these kinds of observations is that they only work if the underlying assumptions about environment are true. For the adoption studies to work, it must be true that there is no correlation between the adopting families and the biological families. There must not be selective placement of adoptees. In the case of one-egg and two-egg twins, it must be true that identical twins do not experience a more similar environment than fraternal twins. As we shall see, these problems have been largely ignored in the rush to demonstrate the heritability of IQ.

The theory of estimating heritability is very well worked out. It is well known how large samples should be to get reliable estimates. The designs of the observations to avoid selective adoptions, to get objective measures of test performance without bias on the part of the investigator, to avoid statistical artifacts that may arise from unrepresentative samples of adopting families, are all well laid out in textbooks of statistics and quantitative genetics. Indeed, these theories are constantly put into practice by animal breeders who would be unable to have their research reports published in genetics journals unless they adhered strictly to the standard methodological requirements. The record of psychometric observations on the heritability of IQ is in remarkable contrast. Inadequate sample sizes, biased subjective judgments, selective adoption, failure to separate so-called "separated twins," unrepresentative samples of adoptees, and gratuitous and untested assumptions about similarity of environments are all standard characteristics in the literature of IQ genetics. There has even been, as we shall see, massive and influential fraud. We will review in some detail the state of psychometric genetic observations—not simply because it calls into question the actual heritability of IQ, but because it raises the far more important issue of why the canons of scientific demonstration and credibility should be so radically different in human genetics than in the genetics of pigs. Nothing demonstrates more clearly how scientific methodology and conclusions are shaped to fit ideological ends than the sorry state of the heritability of IQ.

The Cyril Burt Scandal

The clearest evidence, by far, for the genetic determination of IQ was the massive life's work of the late Sir Cyril Burt. In 1969 Arthur Jensen quite correctly referred to Burt's work as "the most satisfactory attempt" to estimate the heritability of IQ. When Burt died, Jensen referred to him as "a born nobleman," whose "larger, more representative samples than any other investigator in the field has ever assembled" would secure his "place in the history of science."[13] Hans Eysenck wrote that he drew "rather heavily" on Burt's work, citing "the outstanding quality of the design and the statistical treatment in his studies."[14]

The Burt data seemed so impressive for a number of very good reasons. First, one of the simplest ways, at least in theory, of demonstrating the heritable basis of a trait is to study separated identical twins. The separated twin pairs have identical genes, and they are assumed not to have shared any common environment. Thus, if they resemble one another markedly in some respect, the resemblance must be due to the only thing they share in common: their identical genes. The largest IQ study of separated identical twins ever reported, supposedly based on fifty-three twin pairs, was that of Cyril Burt. The IQ correlation of separated twin pairs reported by Burt was strikingly high, more so than that reported in the three other studies of separated twins. The most important aspect of Burt's study, however, was that he alone had been able to measure quantitatively the similarity of the environments in which the separated twin pairs had been reared. The incredible (and convenient) result reported by Burt was that there was no correlation at all between the environments of the separated pairs.

Further, in order to fit a genetic model to IQ data, it is necessary to know what the IQ correlations are for a considerable number of types of relatives—some close and some not so close. Burt was the only investigator in history who claimed to have administered the same IQ test, in the same population, to the full gamut of biological relatives of all degrees of closeness. In fact, for some types of relatives (grandparent-grandchild, uncle-nephew, second cousin pairs), the IQ correlations reported by Burt are the *only* such correlations *ever* to have been reported. The Burt correlations for all types of relatives corresponded with remarkable precision to the values expected if IQ were almost entirely determined by the genes.

The blunt fact is that Burt's data, which have played so important a role, were reported and published in what is clearly a truly scandalous and suspicious fashion. The implausibility of Burt's claims should have been noted at once by any reasonably alert and conscientious scientific reader. To begin with, Burt never provided even the most elementary description of how, when, or where his "data" had been collected. The normal canons of scientific reporting were ignored entirely by Burt, and by the editors of the journals that published his papers. He never even identified the "IQ test" he supposedly administered to untold thousands of pairs of relatives. Within many of his papers, even the sizes of his supposed samples of relatives were not reported. The correlations were given without any supporting details. The 1943 paper that first reported many of the correlations between relatives made only the following reference to procedural details: "Some of the inquiries have been published in LCC reports or elsewhere; but the majority remain buried in typed memoranda or degree theses."[15] Conscientious scientists usually do not refer interested readers to their primary sources and documentation in such a cavalier way. The reader should not be surprised by the fact that none of the London County Council reports, typed memoranda, or degree theses glancingly referred to by Burt have ever come to light.

The very few occasions when Burt made specific statements about his procedure should have provoked some doubts in his scientific readers. For example, in a 1955 paper Burt described the procedure by which he obtained IQ test results for parent-child, grandparent-grandchild, uncle-nephew, etc. The IQ data for children were supposedly obtained by revising (on the basis of teacher's comments) the results of unspecified IQ tests given in school. But how did Burt obtain "IQs" for adults? He wrote: "For the assessments of the parents we relied chiefly on personal interviews; but in doubtful or borderline cases an open or a camouflaged test was employed."[16] That is, in measuring the "IQs" of adults Burt did not even *claim* to have administered an objective, standardized IQ test. The IQ was said to have been guessed at during an interview! The spectacle of Professor Burt administering "camouflaged" IQ tests while chatting with London grandparents is the stuff of farce, not of science. The correlations reported by Burt on this claimed basis, however, were routinely presented as hard scientific truths in textbooks of psychology, of genetics, and of education. Professor Jensen referred to precisely this work as "the most satisfactory attempt" to estimate the heritability of IQ. When Burt's procedure was publicly criticized, Hans Eysenck was able to write in Burt's defense: "I could only wish that modern workers would follow his example."[17]

The collapse of Burt's claims within the scientific community began when attention was drawn to some numerical impossibilities in Burt's published papers.[18] For example, Burt in 1955 claimed to have studied twenty-one pairs of separated identical twins and reported that, on some unnamed group test of intelligence, their IQ correlation was .771. By 1958 the number of pairs had been increased to "over 30"; surprisingly, the IQ correlation remained precisely .771. By 1966, when the sample size had been increased to fifty-three pairs, the correlation was still exactly .771! This remarkable tendency for IQ correlations to remain identical to the third decimal place was also true of Burt's studies of nonseparated identical twin pairs: as the sample size increased progressively with time, the correlation failed to change. The same identity to the third decimal place was also true of IQ correlations for other types of relatives published by Burt, as sample sizes increased (or in some cases decreased) over time. These and other characteristics indicated that, at the very least, Burt's data and claimed results could not be taken seriously. As one of us in 1974 concluded after surveying Burt's work: "The numbers left behind by Professor Burt are simply not worthy of our current scientific attention."[19]

The scientific exposure of Burt prompted Professor Jensen to execute a brisk about-face. Two years earlier Jensen had described Burt as a born nobleman, whose large and representative samples had secured his place in the history of science. But in 1974 Jensen wrote, after citing the absurdities that critics had already documented, that Burt's correlations were "useless for hypothesis testing"—that is to say, worthless.[20] But Jensen maintained that Burt's work had merely been careless, not fraudulent; and he also maintained that the elimination of Burt's data did not substantially reduce the weight of the evidence demonstrating a high heritability of IQ. That incredible claim was made despite Jensen's earlier assertion that Burt's was "the most satisfactory attempt" to calculate the heritability of IQ.[21]

The argument over Burt's data might have remained a discreet academic affair and might have tiptoed around the question of Burt's fraudulence were it not for the medical correspondent of the London *Sunday Times,* Oliver Gillie. Gillie tried to locate two of Burt's research associates, the Misses Conway and Howard, who had supposedly published papers in a psychological journal edited by Burt. According to Burt, they were responsible for the IQ testing of the separated identical twins, for the testing of other types of relatives, and for much of Burt's published data analyses. But Gillie could uncover absolutely no documentary record of the existence of these research associates. They had not been seen by, and were wholly unknown to, Burt's closest co-workers. When asked about them by his housekeeper, Burt had replied that they had emigrated to Australia or New Zealand, this at a time *before,* according to Burt's published papers, they were testing twins in England. Burt's secretary indicated that Burt had sometimes written papers signed by either Conway or Howard. These facts led Gillie to suggest, in a front-page article in 1976, that Conway and Howard may never have existed.[22] The article flatly accused Burt of perpetrating a major scientific fraud, a charge subsequently supported by two of Burt's former students, now themselves prominent psychometricians, Alan and Ann Clarke.

The public exposure of Burt's fraudulence seemed to strike a raw hereditarian nerve. Professor Jensen wrote that the attack on Burt was designed "to wholly discredit the large body of research on the genetics of human mental abilities. The desperate scorched-earth style of criticism we have come to know in this debate has finally gone the limit, with charges of 'fraud' and 'fakery' now that Burt is no longer here to . . . take warranted legal action against such unfounded defamation."[23] Professor Eysenck joined in by pointing out that Burt had been "knighted for his services" and that the charges against him contained "a whiff of McCarthyism, of notorious smear campaigns, and of what used to be known as character assassination."[24]

The attempt to defend Burt by assaulting his critics soon collapsed. The eulogy at Burt's memorial service had been delivered by an admirer, Professor Leslie Hearnshaw, and had prompted Burt's sister, in 1971, to commission Hearnshaw to write a biography of her distinguished brother and to make Burt's private papers and diaries freely available to him. When the fraud charges exploded, Hearnshaw wrote to the *Bulletin* of the British Psychological Society, indicating that he would assess all the available evidence and warning that the charges of Burt's critics could not be lightly dismissed. This warning seems to have muted the tone of Burt's more militant hereditarian defenders. Thus, by 1978, Eysenck wrote of Burt: "On at least one occasion he invented, for the purpose of quoting it in one of his articles, a thesis by one of his students never in fact written; at the time I interpreted this as a sign of forgetfulness."[25]

The Hearnshaw biography, published in 1979, has put to rest any lingering doubts about Burt's wholesale faking.[26] The painstaking searches and inquiries made by Hearnshaw failed to unearth any substantial traces of Miss Conway, or Miss Howard, or of any separated twins. There were many instances of dishonesty, of evasion, and of contradiction in Burt's written replies to correspondents who had inquired about his data. The evidence made clear that Burt had collected no data at all during the last thirty years of his life, when, supposedly, most of the separated twins had been studied. With painful reluctance, Hearnshaw found himself forced to conclude that the charges made by Burt's critics were "in their essentials valid." The evidence demonstrated that Burt had "fabricated figures" and had "falsified." There is now no doubt whatever that all of Burt's "data" on the heritability of IQ must be discarded. The loss of these incredibly clear-cut "data" has been devastating to the claim that a substantial IQ heritability was demonstrated.

But what are we to make of the additional fact that Burt's transparently fraudulent data were accepted for so long, and so uncritically, by the "experts" in the field? Perhaps the clearest moral to be drawn from the Burt affair was spelled out by N. J. Mackintosh in his review of the Hearnshaw biography in the *British Journal of Psychology*:

> Ignoring the question of fraud, the fact of the matter is that the crucial evidence that his data on IQ are scientifically unacceptable does not depend on any examination of Burt's diaries or correspondence. It is to be found in the data

themselves. The evidence was there . . . in 1961. It was, indeed, clear to any-one with eyes to see in 1958. But it was not seen until 1972, when Kamin first pointed to Burt's totally inadequate reporting of his data and to the impossible consistencies in his correlation coefficients. Until then the data were cited, with respect bordering on reverence, as the most telling proof of the heritability of IQ. It is a sorry comment on the wider scientific community that "numbers . . . simply not worthy of our current scientific attention" . . . should have entered nearly every psychological textbook.[27]

We do not view the uncritical acceptance of Burt's data as an unusual or inexplicable "sorry comment on the wider scientific community." The fraud per-petrated by Burt, and unwittingly propagated by the scientific community, served important social purposes. Professor Hearnshaw's biography essentially saves the face of psychometry by probing the individual psychology of Burt to ask why he should have been moved to such fraudulence. Burt, no longer a nobleman but now victim of a debilitating and psychiatrically distressing disor-der, has become the bad apple of psychometry. By 1980, when the British Psy-chological Society was prepared to draw up its "Balance Sheet on Burt,"[28] there had been a closing of the ranks; the psychometric doyens reiterated their belief that, despite the eviction of Burt, the residual evidence for the heritability of intelligence was strong. The social function of IQ ideology was still dominant.

N O T E S

1. S. Bowles and V. Nelson, "The Inheritance of IQ and the Intergenerational Trans-mission of Economic Inequality." *Review of Economics and Statistics* 54, no. 1 (1974).

2. M. Schiff, M. Duyme, A. Dumaret, and S. Tomkiewicz, " 'How Much *Could* We Boost Scholastic Achievement and IQ Scores?' Direct Answer from a French Adoption Study." *Cognition* 12 (1982):165–96.

3. A. Binet. *Les Idées modernes sur les enfants* (Paris: Flammarion, 1913), pp. 140–41.

4. L. M. Terman, "Feeble-minded Children in the Public Schools of California." *School and Society* 5 (1917) 165.

5. L. M. Terman, *The Measurement of Intelligence* (Boston: Houghton Mifflin, 1916), pp. 91–92.

6. H. H. Goddard, *Human Efficiency and Levels of Intelligence* (Princeton, N.J.: Prince-ton University Press, 1920), pp. 99–103.

7. C. Burt, "Experimental Tests of General Intelligence." *British Journal of Psychology* 3 (1909):94–177.

8. C. Burt, *Mental and Scholastic Tests,* 2d ed. (London: Staples, 1947); and *The Back-ward Child,* 5th ed. (London: University of London Press, 1961).

9. L. Kamin, *The Science and Politics of IQ* (Potomac, Md.: Erlbaum, 1974); K. Ludmerer, *Genetics and American Society* (Baltimore: Johns Hopkins University Press, 1972); M. Haller, *Eugenics: Hereditarian Attitudes in American Thought* (New Brunswick, N.J.: Rutgers University Press, 1963); C. Karier, *The Making of the American Educational State* (Urbana: University of Illinois Press, 1973); and N. Stepan, *The Idea of Race in Sci-ence* (London: Macmillan, 1982).

10. E. G. Boring, "Intelligence as the Tests Test It." *New Republic* 34 (1923):35–36.

11. S. Bowles and V. Nelson, "The Inheritance of IQ and the Intergenerational Reproduction of Economic Inequality." *Review of Economics and Statistics* 56 (1974):39–51.

12. E. L. Thorndike, *Educational Psychology* (New York: Columbia University Teachers College, 1903) p. 140.

13. A. R. Jensen, "Sir Cyril Burt" (obituary), *Psychometrika* 37 (1972):115–17.

14. H. J. Eysenck, *The Inequality of Man* (London: Temple Smith, 1973).

15. C. Burt, "Ability and Income," *British Journal of Educational Psychology* 13 (1943):83–98.

16. C. Burt, "The Evidence for the Concept of Intelligence," *British Journal of Educational Psychology* 25 (1955):167–68.

17. H. J. Eysenck, "H. J. Eysenck in Rebuttal," *Change* 6, no. 2 (1974).

18. L. Kamin, "Heredity, Intelligence, Politics and Psychology," unpublished presidential address to meeting of the Eastern Psychological Association (1972).

19. Kamin, *Science and Politics of IQ.*

20. A. R. Jensen, "Kinship Correlations Reported by Sir Cyril Burt," *Behavior Genetics* 4 (1974):24–25.

21. A. R. Jensen, "How Much Can We Boost IQ and Scholastic Achievement?" *Howard Educational Review* 39 (1969):1–123.

22. O. Gillie, *Sunday Times* (London), 24 October 1976.

23. A. R. Jensen, "Heredity and Intelligence: Sir Cyril Burt's Findings," letters to the *Times* (London), 9 December 1976, p. 11.

24. H. J. Eysenck, "The Case of Sir Cyril Burt," *Encounter* 48 (1977):19–24.

25. H. J. Eysenck, "Sir Cyril Burt and the Inheritance of the IQ," *New Zealand Psychologist* (1978).

26. L. S. Hearnshaw, *Cyril Burt: Psychologist* (London: Hodder & Stoughton, 1979).

27. N. J. Mackintosh, book review of *Cyril Burt: Psychologist* by J. S. Hearnshaw, *British Journal of Psychology* 71 (1980):174–75.

28. A Balance Sheet on Cyril Burt, *Supplement to the Bulletin of the British Psychological Society* 33 (1980):i.

THE HEALTH OF BLACK FOLK
Disease, Class, and Ideology in Science

Nancy Krieger and Mary Bassett

Since the first crude tabulations of vital statistics in colonial America, one stark fact has stood out: black Americans are sicker and die younger than whites. As the epidemic infectious diseases of the nineteenth century were vanquished, the black burden of ill health shifted to the modern killers: heart disease, stroke, and cancer. Today black men under age forty-five are ten times more likely to die from the effects of high blood pressure than white men. Black women suffer twice as many heart attacks as white women. A variety of common cancers are more frequent among blacks—and of cancer victims, blacks succumb sooner after diagnosis than whites. Black infant mortality is twice that of whites. All told, if the mortality rates for blacks and other minorities today were the same in the United States as for whites, more than 60,000 deaths in minority communities could be avoided each year.

What is it about being black that causes such miserable odds? One answer is the patently racist view that blacks are inherently more susceptible to disease— the genetic model. In contrast, environmental models depict blacks as victims of factors ranging from poor nutrition and germs to lack of education and crowded housing. Initially formulated as an alternative to the genetic model by liberals and much of the Left, the environmental view has now gained new support from the Right and becomes a major prop for Reagan administration health policies: instead of blaming the victims' genes, these conservatives blame black life-style choices as the source of the racial gap in health.

We will argue that these analytic models are seriously flawed, in essence as well as application. They are not the product of a racist use of allegedly "neutral" science, but reflect the ways in which ideology and politics penetrate scientific theory and research. Typically, they deny or obscure that the primary source of black/white health disparities is the social production of disease under conditions of capitalism and racial oppression. The "facts of being black" are not, as these

Both authors would like to thank the following people for taking the time to critique this article: Melanie Tervalon, Mark Nelson, Ruth Hubbard, Linda Burnham, Margo Sercarz, David Himmelstein, and Steffie Woolhandler.

models suggest, a genetically determined shade of skin color, or individual deprived living conditions, or ill-informed life-style choices. The facts of being black derive from the joint social relations of race and class: racism disproportionately concentrates blacks into the lower strata of the working class and further causes blacks in all class strata to be racially oppressed. It is the Left's challenge to incorporate this political reality into how we approach racial differences in health.

The Genetic Model

Despite overwhelming evidence to the contrary, the theory that "race" is primarily a biological category and that black-white differences in health are genetically determined continues to exert profound influence on both medical thinking and popular ideology. For example, an editorial on racial differences in birth weight (an important determinant of infant mortality) in the January 1986 *Journal of the American Medical Association* concluded: "Finally, what are the biologic or genetic differences among racial or ethnic groups? Should we shrink from the possibility of a biologic/genetic influence?" Similarly, a 1983 handbook prepared by the International Epidemiologic Association defined "race" as "persons who are relatively homogeneous with respect to biological inheritance." Public health texts continue to enshrine "race" in the demographic triad of "age, race, and sex," implying that "race" is as biologically fundamental a predictor of health as aging or sex, while the medical literature remains replete with studies that examine racial differences in health without regard to class.

The genetic model rests on three basic assumptions, all of which are flawed: that "race" is a valid biological category; that the genes which determine "race" are linked to the genes which affect health; and that the health of any community is mainly the consequence of the genetic constitution of the individuals of which it is composed. In contrast, we will argue that the health of the black community is not simply the sum of the health of individuals who are "genetically black" but instead chiefly reflects the social forces which create racially oppressed communities in the first place.

It is of course true that skin color, hair texture, and other visible features used to identify "race" are genetically encoded—there is a biologic aspect to "race." The importance of these particular physical traits in the spectrum of human variation, however, has been determined historically and politically. People also differ in terms of stature and eye color, but these attributes are rarely accorded significance. Categories based primarily on skin color correlate with health because race is a powerful determinant of the location and life-destinies of individuals within the class structure of U.S. society. Ever since plantation owners realized that differences in skin color could serve as a readily identifiable and permanent marker for socially determined divisions of labor (black runaway slaves were easier to identify than escaped white indentured servants and convicts, the initial workforce of colonial America), race and class have been inextricably intertwined. "Race" is not a neutral descriptive category, but a social category both of the antagonistic relation of white supremacy and black oppression. The basis of the relative health advantage of whites is not to be found in their genes but in the relative material advantage whites enjoy as a consequence of political prerogative and state power. As Richard Lewontin has pointed out, "If, after a great cataclysm, only Africans were left alive, the human species would have retained 93 percent of its total genetic variation, although the species as a whole would be darker skinned." The fact that we all know which race we belong to says more about our society than about our biology.

Nevertheless, the paradigm of a genetic basis for black ill health remains strong. In its defense, researchers repeatedly trot out the few diseases for which a clear-cut link of race is established: sickle cell anemia, G&PD deficiency, and lactose intolerance. These diseases, however, have a tiny impact on the health of the black population as a whole—if anything, even less than those few diseases linked to "whiteness," such as some forms of skin cancer. Richard Cooper has shown that of the tens of thousands of excess black deaths in 1977, only 277 (0.3 percent) could be attributed to diseases such as sickle cell anemia. Such uncommon genetic maladies have become important strictly because of their metaphorical value: they are used to support genetic explanations of racial differences in the "big diseases" of the twentieth century—heart disease, stroke, and cancer. Yet no current evidence exists to justify such an extrapolation.

Determined nonetheless to demonstrate the genetic basis of racial health differences, investigators today—like their peers in the past—use the latest techniques. Where once physicians compared cranial capacity to explain black-white inequalities, now they scrutinize surface markers of cells. The case of hypertension is particularly illustrative. High blood pressure is an important cause of strokes and heart attacks, contributing to about 30 percent of all deaths in the United States. At present, the black rate of hypertension in the United States is about twice that of whites. Of over five hundred recent medical journal articles on the topic, fewer than a dozen studies explored social factors. The rest instead unsuccessfully sought biochemical-genetic explanations—and of these, virtually none even attempted to "define" genetically who was "white" and who was "black," despite the alleged genetic nature of their enquiry. As a consequence of the wrong questions being asked, the causes of hypertension remain unknown. Nonetheless, numerous clues point to social factors. Hypertension does not exist in several undisrupted hunter-gatherer tribes of different "races" but rapidly emerges in these tribes after contact with industrial society; in the United States, lower social class begets higher blood pressure.

Turning to cancer, the authors of a recent major government report surmised that blacks have poorer survival rates than whites because they do not "exhibit the same immunologic reactions to cancerous processes." It is noteworthy, however, that the comparably poor survival rates of British breast cancer patients have never elicited such speculation. In our own work on breast cancer in Washington state, we found that the striking "racial" difference in survival evaporated when we took class into account: working-class women, whether black or white, die sooner than women of higher social class standing.

To account for the persistence of the genetic model, we must look to its political significance rather than its scientific content. First used to buttress biblical arguments for slavery in a period when science was beginning to replace religion as sanction for the status quo, the genetic model of racial differences in health emerged toward the end of the eighteenth century, long before any precise theory of heredity existed. In well-respected medical journals, doctors debated whether blacks and whites were even the same species (let alone race), and proclaimed that blacks were intrinsically suited to slavery, thrived in hot climates, succumbed less to the epidemic fevers which ravaged the South, and suffered extraordinary rates of insanity if allowed to live free. After the Civil War effectively settled the argument about whether blacks belonged to the human species, physicians and scientists began elaborating hereditarian theories to explain the disparate health profiles not only of blacks and whites, but of the different white "races"—as defined by national origin and immigrant status. Virtually every scourge, from TB to rickets, was postulated to be inherited. Rheumatic fever, now known to be due to strep bacteria combined with the poverty which permits its expression in immunocompromised malnourished people, was long believed to be linked with the red hair and pale complexions of its Irish working-class victims. Overall, genetic explanations of differences in disease rates have politically served to justify existing class relations and excuse socially created afflictions as a result of immutable biology.

Nowadays the genetic model—newly dressed in the language of molecular genetics—continues to divert attention from the class origin of disease. Genetic explanations absolve the state of responsibility for the health profile of black America by declaring racial disparities (regrettably) inevitable and normal. Intervention efforts based on this model founder for obvious reasons: short of recombinant DNA therapies, genetic screening and selective reproduction stand as supposed tools to reduce the racial gap in health.

Unfortunately, the genetic model wields influence even within the progressive health movement, as illustrated by the surge of interest in sickle cell anemia in the early 1970s. For decades after its initial description in 1925, sickle cell anemia was relegated to clinical obscurity. It occurs as often in blacks as does cystic fibrosis in whites. By linking genetic uniqueness to racial pride, such groups as the Black Panther party championed sickle cell anemia as the number one health issue among blacks, despite the fact that other health problems—such as infant mortality—took a much greater toll. Because the sickle cell gene provides some protection against malaria, sickle cell seemed to link blacks to their African past, now three centuries removed. It raised the issue of racist neglect of black health in a setting where the victims were truly blameless: the fault lay in their genes. From the point of view of the federal government, sickle cell anemia was a uniquely black disease which did not raise the troubling issues of the ongoing oppression of the black population. In a period of political turmoil, what more could the government ask for? Small wonder that President Nixon jumped on the bandwagon and called for a national crusade.

The Environmental Model

The genetic model's long history and foundations in the joint race and class divisions of our society assure its continued prominence in discussions on the racial gap in health. To rebut this model, many liberals and progressives have relied upon environmental models of disease causation—only to encounter the Right on this turf as well.

Whereas the rise of slavery called forth genetic models of diseases, environmental models were born of the antagonistic social relations of industrial capitalism. In the appalling filth of nineteenth-century cities, tuberculosis, typhus, and infant diarrhea were endemic in the newly forming working class; periodically, epidemics of yellow fever and cholera would attack the entire populace. A sanitary reform movement arose, advocating cleaner cities (with sewer systems and pure water) to protect the well-being of the wealthy as well as the poor, and also to engender a healthier, more productive work force.

In the United States, most of the reformers were highly moralistic and staunchly procapitalist, seeing poverty and squalor as consequences of individual intemperance and ignorance rather than as necessary correlates of capital accumulation. In Europe, where the working-class movement was stronger, a class-conscious wing of the sanitary reform movement emerged. Radicals such as Frederick Engels and Rudolph Virchow (later the founder of modern pathology) argued that poverty and ill health could only be eliminated by resolving the antagonistic class relations of capitalism.

The early sanitary reform movement in the United States rarely addressed the question of racial differences in health per se. In fact, environmental models to explain black-white disparities emerged only during the mid-twentieth century, a consequence of the urban migration of blacks from the rural South to the industrial North and the rise of the civil-rights movement.

Today's liberal version of the environmental model blames poverty for black ill health. The noxious features of the "poverty environment" are catalogued and decried—lead paint from tenement walls, toxins from work, even social features like discrimination. But as in most liberal analyses, the unifying cause of this litany of woes remains unstated. We are left with an apparently unconnected laundry list of problems and no explanation of why blacks as a group encounter similar sickening conditions.

The liberal view fetishizes the environment: individuals are harmed by inanimate objects, physical forces, or unfortunate social conditions (like poverty)—by *things* rather than by people. That these objects or social circumstances are the *creations* of society is hidden by the veil of "natural science." Consequently, the "environment" is viewed as a natural and neutral category, defined as all that is external to individuals. What is not seen is the ways in which the underlying structure of racial oppression and class exploitation—which are relationships among people, not between people and things—shape the "environments" of the groups created by these relations.

The debilitating disease pellagra serves as a concrete example. Once a major health problem of poor southern farm and mill laborers in the United States, pellagra was believed to be a genetic disease. By the early 1920s, however, Joseph Goldberger had proved that the disease stemmed from a dietary deficiency in niacin and had also demonstrated that pellagra's familial nature existed because of the inheritance of nutritional options, not genes. Beyond this, Goldberger argued that pellagra, in essence, was a *social* disease caused by the single cash-crop economy of the South: reliance on cotton ensured seasonal starvation as food ran out between harvests, as well as periodic epidemics when the cotton market collapsed. Southern workers contracted pellagra because they had limited diets—and they had limited diets *because* they were southern workers. Yet governmental response was simply to supplement food with niacin: according to this view, vitamin deficiency—not socially determined malnutrition—was the chief cause of pellagra.

The liberal version of the environmental model also fails to see the causes of disease and the environment in which they exist as a historical product, a nature filtered through, even constructed by, society. What organisms and chemicals people are exposed to is determined by both the social relations and types of production which characterize their society. The same virus may cause pneumonia in blacks and whites alike, just as lead may cause the same physiologic damage—but *why* the death rate for flu and pneumonia and *why* blood lead levels are consistently higher in black as compared to white communities is not addressed. While the liberal conception of the environment can generate an exhaustive *list* of its components, it cannot *comprehend* the all-important assemblage of features of black life. What explains why a greater proportion of black mothers are single, young, malnourished, high-school dropouts, and so on?

Here the Right is ready with a "life-style" response as a unifying theme: blacks, not racism, are the source of their own health woes. Currently, the Reagan administration is the chief promoter of this view—as made evident by the 1985 publication of the Report of the Secretary's Task Force on Black and Minority Health. Just one weapon among many in the government's vicious ideological war to justify its savage gutting of health and social service programs, the report shifts responsibility for the burden of disease to the minority communities themselves. Promoting "health education" as a panacea, the government hopes to counsel minorities to eat better, exercise more, smoke and drink less, be less violent, seek health care earlier for symptoms, and in general be better health-care consumers. This "life-style" version of the environmental model accordingly is fully compatible with the genetic model (i.e., genetic disadvantage can be exaggerated by life-style choices) and echoes its ideological messages that individual shortcomings are at the root of ill health.

In focusing on individual health habits, the task force report ironically echoes the language of many "health radicals," ranging from iconoclasts such as Ivan Illich to counterculture advocates of individually oriented self-help strategies. United in practice, if not in spirit, these apparently disparate camps all take a "holistic" view, arguing that disease comes not just from germs or chemicals but from life-style choices about food, exercise, smoking, and stress. Their conflation of life-style choices and life circumstance can reach absurd proportions. Editorializing on the task force report, the New York Times agreed that "Disparities may be due to cultural or lifestyle differences. For example, a higher proportion of blacks and hispanics live in cities, with greater exposure to hazards like pollution, poor housing, and crime." But what kind of "life-style" causes pollution, and who chooses to live in high-crime neighborhoods? Both the conservative and alternative "life-style" versions of the environmental model deliberately ignore or distort the fact that economic coercion and political disenfranchisement, not free choice, locate minority communities in the most hazardous regions of cities. What qualitatively constrains the option of blacks to "live right" is the reality of being black and poor in the United States.

But liberals have had little response when the Right points out that even the most oppressed and impoverished people make choices affecting their health: it may be hard to eat right if the neighborhood grocer doesn't sell fresh vegetables, but teenage girls do not have to become pregnant. For liberals, it has been easier to portray blacks as passive, blameless victims and in this way avoid the highly charged issue of health behaviors altogether. The end result is usually just proposals for more health services for blacks, Band-Aids for the gaping wounds of oppression. Yet while adequate health services certainly are needed, they can do little to stem the social forces which cause disease.

Too often the Left has been content merely to trail behind the liberals in campaigns for health services, or to call only for social control of environmental and occupational exposures. The Right, however, has shifted the terrain of battle to the issue of individual behavior, and we must respond. It is for the Left to point out that society does not consist of abstract individuals, but rather of people whose life options are shaped by their intrinsic membership in groups defined by the social relations of their society. Race and class broadly determine not only the conditions under which blacks and whites live, but also the ways in which they can respond to these conditions and the political power they have to alter them. The material limits produced by oppression create and constrain not only the type of housing you live in, but even the most intimate choices about what you do inside your home. Oppression and exploitation beget the reality and also the belief that bad health and personal failure are ineluctable facts of life.

Frantz Fanon wrote eloquently of the fatalistic hopelessness engendered by oppression in colonial Algeria. Eliminating self-destructive behaviors, like drug addiction or living in a battering relationship, requires that they be acknowledged as the subjective reflection of objective powerlessness. As Bylle Avery, director of the National Black Women's Health Project, has said, wellness and empowerment are linked. School-based birth control clinics, however necessary as part of the strategy to reduce teen pregnancy, will be ineffective as long as the social motivation for young black women to get pregnant remains unaddressed; for black women to improve their health, they must individually choose to act collectively in order to transform the social conditions which frame, constrain, and devalue their lives as black women.

Toward a Marxist Conception

The ideological content of science is transparent in disease models now rejected as archaic or indisputably biased. The feudal view of disease as retribution of God and the eugenist science underlying Nazi racial hygiene clearly resonated well with the dominant politics and ideology of their respective societies. But it is far more difficult to discern the ideological content of scientific theory in one's own time and place.

Criticism of the ideology underlying existing paradigms is an important tool in undermining reactionary science. It can help us sort out the apparent riddle of the Reagan administration's embrace of "holistic" health. Such criticism also points the way toward alternative concepts. To construct a new paradigm, however, requires painstaking work. Moreover, the goal is not a "neutral" science, but one which openly acknowledges the ways in which ideology inevitably is incorporated *into* scientific concepts and theories. Accurate elucidation and prevention of the material and ideological components of disease processes necessitates the explicit adoption of an antiracist and class-conscious standpoint.

We have only a hint of how a Marxist analysis of the social relations of race and class can illuminate the processes involved in the social production of disease. Such an approach has already shown that many "racial" differences in disease are actually attributable to differences in class. Similarly, the finding of some Marxist researchers that an absentee landlord, rather than race, is the best predictor of lead poisoning points to what this new science can offer in the way of prevention.

But these are small, isolated observations. Too often we are constrained by assumptions built into existing techniques and methodologies. The intimidating mathematics of multiple regression which dominate public health research cannot even contemplate an effect which becomes its own cause—such as the way in which malnutrition opens the way for infections, which cause diarrhea, which causes malnutrition. Further, existing analytic techniques cannot address phenomena like class relations or racial oppression which cannot be expressed as numbers. True, we can calculate the health effect of more or less income or education, but these are pale reflections of class relations, outcomes and not essences. Similarly, we are limited by disease definitions geared toward individual etiology. Treating the problems of substance abuse, infectious disease, infant mortality, and occupational exposure in the black community as separate maladies obscures their common social antecedent. Clearly, we need basically new approaches to understand the dialectical interpenetration of racism, class relations, and health.

To unravel and eliminate black-white differences in disease, we must begin by politically exposing, not merely describing, the social roots of suffering and disease. Throughout U.S. history, the functioning of capitalism has been bound up with the exploitation and racial oppression of blacks, and the racial stratification of the working class has meant that within the context of the ill health of the working class as a whole, that of blacks has been the worst.

To improve black health, progressive health-care activists must not only fight to restore and expand urgently needed health services. We must also expose the class essence of the disease models which the federal government uses to rid itself of responsibility for social intervention to deal with the problem. In order to target the social forces which produce disease, we must begin to develop an antiracist model of disease causation. Ultimately, to call for an antiracist science is to demand a class-conscious science. We cannot afford to do with less.

APPROPRIATING THE IDIOMS OF SCIENCE

The Rejection of Scientific Racism

Nancy Leys Stepan and Sander L. Gilman

This paper considers some writings of minority groups, as they responded to and resisted the claims of scientific racism. In exploring the relationship between language and resistance we focus on two very different groups of individuals stereotyped as different and inferior in the biological, medical, and anthropological sciences, namely African-Americans and Jews. We concentrate specifically on the period of transition to modern science between 1870 and 1920, when the claims of scientifically established inferiority were pressed most insistently by the mainstream scientific community. Our analysis reveals a body of literature by minorities and the marginal *about* the sciences of themselves that has been virtually untouched by historians of science. What did the men and women categorized by the biological and medical sciences as racially distinct and inferior say about the matter? How did they respond to the claims made about them in the name of science?

Limitations of space have made us very selective with materials. Examples have been chosen for their effective illustration of points, and the goal is to open up a problem for discussion in the history of science and racism that has hitherto been almost entirely ignored.

The Problem Defined

This paper derives from a consideration of two intertwined issues: the centrality of scientific racism to the Western intellectual tradition, and the absence of sustained criticism of scientific racism from within mainstream science in the period under study. Historians have long been aware of the existence of scientific racism in Western societies, especially its intensification and institutionalization in the second half of the nineteenth century. Scientific racism was significant because it provided a series of lenses through which human variation was constructed, understood, and experienced from the early nineteenth century until well into the twentieth century, if not until the present day.[1] We assume in this paper that the races that peopled the texts of science in the past were "artifactual," constructed categories of social knowledge. These categories had material weight in the lives of individuals and groups; racial identities were embodied in political practices of discrimination and law, and affected people's access to education, forms of employment, political rights, and subjective experience. Scientific language was one of the most authoritative languages through which meaning was encoded, and as a language it had political and social, as well as intellectual, consequences.[2]

In studying the history of scientific racism, we have been struck by the relative absence of critical challenges to its claims from within mainstream science. This absence is in itself an interesting problem in the sociology of scientific knowledge, since controversy and contention are often taken to be characteristic of science and the route by which empirical certainty is established. When it came to the sciences of race difference, however, disagreements tended to be minor and technical.[3] Since racial science was invariably a science of inequality, produced by European men in an age of widespread racism, to a large (but not predetermined) extent the scientists' own racial identities and identifications prevented them from asking critical questions about their own science—its assumptions, its methods, its content. The concepts within racial science were so congruent with social and political life (with power relations, that is) as to be virtually uncontested from inside the mainstream of science.[4]

One place one encounters a "critical tradition" in relation to scientific racism is in the writings of those stereotyped by the sciences of the day. These writings had a problematic relation to the mainstream, since by the very definitions of racial science the stigmatized were largely outside, or at the margins, of science. Their exclusion was part of the very process of the construction of the sciences of difference and inequality, a result of the scientific expectation that the so-called lower races served mainly as objects of study, but not as scientific truth-seekers themselves. Yet many individuals reacted to scientific racism by actively seeking to enter the relatively closed circle of science, or to use its tools and techniques, to define and defend themselves.

There is far more writing by such individuals than is generally recognized by historians of science. Much of the historical work of uncovering the "struggles and strategies" (in Margaret Rossiter's words) of minority writers, as they confronted a hostile and stereotyping science of race, remains to be done. Our purpose here is to reflect generally on such writing, and to present some examples of the "textual" strategies we have uncovered.[5]

The problem of resistance to imposed meaning and identity in the human sciences is only beginning to be articulated by scholars. The situation contrasts markedly with the issue of social and political resistance, long considered an essential part of historical analysis, for example in the brilliant work on slave revolts and runaway slave communities, or the fight for black or female suffrage. These studies are indispensable to the study of intellectual resistance, since the capacity to formulate challenges to dominant discourses is closely tied to the political and social resources of the groups making the challenges. Often, the strategies of intellectual resistance—struggles over meaning— mirror or are part of the same process of political struggle. Confronting scientific racism necessitated acquiring a degree of control over the elements of an intellectual idiom, their reassemblage and employment for new ends. How could science be used to transform the racial valuations built into discussions of human variation? Can we discern in the writings of minorities a variety of different tactics, and if so, what were they? As a genre of writing, does it have distinctive features? What effect did the resistance of minorities to negative scientific claims have on the dominant discourse? What does the study of such writings offer the historian of scientific change?

In the history of science, the reasons for theoretical neglect of such questions are rather straightforward. The temptation to think of science as a neutral and universal form of knowledge is still strong, despite many years of criticism of traditional scientific epistemology. By thinking of science as objective, scientists have been in a position to dismiss areas of knowledge from the past that are now viewed as obviously out of date and biased—such as scientific racism—as nothing but "pseudoscience." Studying the resistance of men and women to what has been labeled a pseudoscience is then seen as a narrow endeavor, of interest primarily to the "victims" themselves, but not central to the story of modern science. Furthermore, calling scientific racism a pseudoscience also allows scientists to refuse to confront the issue of the inherently political nature of much of the biological and human sciences, and to ignore the problem of the persistence of racial metaphors of inferiority in the sciences of today.

Critical approaches from outside the history of science have been more useful to our work on oppositional, cognitive strategies, even though scientific writing usually lies outside their purview. Antonio Gramsci's explorations of cultural hegemony and the role of the "organic" intellectual in his *Prison Notebooks;* the deconstructionists' attacks on essentialism and metaphysics, and their emphasis on the radically heterogeneous nature of the text; Michel Foucault's projects on the inherently political character of knowledge, his analysis of power as something dispersed discursively through entire systems of discourses and practices, and the problematic character of resistance from within the regime of power and knowledge; recent analyses of minority writing that examine the degree to which female and minority literary traditions represent explicit or implicit subversions of the dominant discourse: all of these developments are relevant to analyzing scientific racism.[6] Our study can be seen as a contribution to the debate about how people use languages to constitute themselves as self-conscious subjects, or find a self-representation that is not sexualized or racialized.[7] Our work is distinctive in its focus on science as an especially weighty discourse of identity, whose appropriation by oppositional groups was extremely problematic. The period from 1870 to 1920 has been chosen on purpose because, as we shall show, science acquired its modern epistemological, institutional, and cultural forms during this period. Our interest in this paper lies in the interplay between these cultural forms, scientific racism, and scientific resistance. Strategies and meanings are always historically specific and cannot be given transcendent value; our focus throughout is on a particular kind of discourse in a particular moment in history, and the strategies open to resisting individuals and groups.

The Authority of Modern Science

Responding to scientific racism was peculiarly difficult because of certain characteristics of the emerging discourse of science itself. Our argument is that from the mid-nineteenth century onward, scientific claims could be effectively rebutted only by scientific discourses to which resisting groups stood in an especially disadvantaged and problematic position.

Our period situates scientific racism in a moment of elaboration and institutional embodiment of modern science and its epistemology. It was the time in which, as Morrell and Thackray have remarked in their history of the British Association for the Advancement of Science (BAAS), science became consolidated as "the dominant mode of cognition of industrial society." As a mode of cognition, science was conceptualized as "a sharply edged and value-neutral domain of knowledge"—as an apolitical, nontheological, universal, empirical, and uniquely objective (in part because uniquely methodological) form of knowledge unlike any other.[8] The result was the self-definition of science as *the* nonpolitical, unbiased arena of knowledge.

This conceptualization was not a "natural" outcome of the unproblematic study of nature, but a social outcome of a process whereby science was historically and materially constituted to have certain meanings, functions, and interests. In a complex series of innovations, science's epistemological claims were given definition and institutional representation in the form of new scientific societies and organizations sharply delimited from other institutions. These innovations were tied not only to industrialization, but to the politics of class, and the closing of ranks of bourgeois society in the face of challenges from the working class in the 1830s and 1840s. Race and gender were also crucial to the construction of modern science, in that science was defined as "masculine" and European in its abstraction, detachment, and objectivity.[9]

Morrell and Thackray point out that appeals to an impersonal "nature" are common in times of turmoil; what made the mid-nineteenth century distinctive was the successful institutionalization of a particular view of that "nature."[10] The processes of boundary setting were contested at many points, since they meant the delegitimization of many areas of knowledge and redefinition of those areas as "nonscience" or "pseudoscience." Morell and Thackray, for instance, demonstrate that between 1832 and 1870, as the BAAS created a new ideology of science, practitioners in fields of inquiry ruled "unscientific" were excluded from the association and thereby from representation within "science." Areas fraught with moral and/or political controversy kept a place within the boundaries of science only when purged of those concerns, as scientists adopted the value-neutral, empirical language now seen as defining science itself. Science as a form of knowledge separated itself from other knowledge systems; in the process, the dichotomies between the pure and the impure (or the applied sciences), the rational and the irrational, the objective and the subjective, the hard and the soft, the male and the female, were given material form. Such polarities, and the institutional boundaries that created and maintained them, were not the inevitable results of a nature merely "discovered" and described; they were the products of active institution creation, demarcation setting, and the successful use of political and cultural resources to achieve these ends.[11]

The formation of the scientific *text* as a new, standardized cultural genre, replacing the more open, varied, metaphorically porous, literary forms of science, is a further aspect of scientific modernization that bears on the problem of the responses to scientific racism. It was in the late nineteenth century that the modern scientific text as we know it stabilized to become the standard, accepted form of writing in nearly all branches of the natural sciences. We are referring here to the scientific paper—the short, depersonalized, empirical paper that is still the hallmark of science today. In a persuasive account of the scientific paper as a cultural and literary genre that emerged in the specific, historically contingent conditions of the late nineteenth century, Gyorgy Markus argues that the scientific text served normative goals, and through its form—its depersonalized authorship, its demand for a peculiarly competent scientific reader—successfully satisfied the expectations of science for constant innovation and accumulation of knowledge.[12] The neutral style of the scientific paper, the absence of a strong, individualized, authorial "I," the emphasis on the factuality of nature, on a nature revealed by specific methods (experimental, technical)—all these features rendered the scientific text problematic for the nonscientific writer and reader and successfully circumscribed the process of contestation.

The new cultural genre of science was an added impediment to opposition in the realm of scientific racism, since it delegitimized the cultural forms of the earlier period.[13] The scientific text became more sharply distinguished from the literary; in the process the range of literary repertoires of meaning—the opportunity for literary play and hermeneutics—was reduced. One thinks, for example, of the charged and metaphoric language of Charles Darwin's *Origin of Species* compared to the dry, limited vocabulary of the sciences of evolution by the 1920s and 1930s. Darwin could not keep control over the metaphors he introduced (such as natural selection, struggle for survival, survival of the fittest). Nearly every term he used was multivalent and was appropriated in selective and varied ways by very different groups for very different purposes.[14] Though Darwin endeavored in later editions of *The Origin of the Species* to reduce the metaphoric ambiguities of his science, his attempts failed, and until well into the twentieth century Darwinism served as a metadiscourse that opened up, rather than merely closed off, the discussion of nature. By the 1900s in the physical sciences, and by the 1920s in the biological sciences, however, the metaphors of scientific language had become much more tightly controlled. The modern scientific text had

replaced the expansive scientific book, and the possibilities of multivalent meanings being created out of scientific language were thereby curtailed.

The Marginalization of Moral/Political Argument in Science

The result of the various processes of transformation of science that accompanied
industrialization and modernization was that, from 1870 to 1920, science became
both more specialized and authoritative as a cultural resource and language of
interpretation. It began to replace theological and moral discourse as the appropriate discourse with which to discuss nature. Science also encroached heavily
on political discourse, as many political issues were transposed into the realm of
neutral "nature," the scientists' province. The outcome was a narrowing of the
cultural space within which, and the cultural forms by which, the claims of biological determinism could be effectively challenged.

The effects of this narrowing can be seen in the marginalization and delegitimization of a number of forms of oppositional writing that had been used before
about 1860. We will give a few examples. One was to keep in the foreground the
moral issues of rights and justice, and to refuse to separate them from scientific
ones. These rights, belonging to individuals as members of the human family,
rights debated in political and theological terms until the 1850s and 1860s, were
increasingly reduced to questions about the racial "natures" of individuals, questions that scientists now claimed had objective, neutral answers. Moral rights
were thereby translated into matters of anatomy and physiology.

In the mid-1800s, African-Americans, confronting a "purely factual" science
whose message was apparently ever more racialistic in its conclusions concerning themselves, tried to resist the process of reduction and "naturalization" associated with science. In 1854, for instance, the abolitionist Frederick Douglass, in
an address titled "The Claims of the Negro Ethnologically Considered," attacked
the scientific racists by questioning their logic, their data, and their conclusions
concerning the supposed gulf separating the white and black races. He proved to
his audience that anatomically and craniologically the similarities between the
Negro and the white race far outweighed the differences, that the human species
was one, and that the Negro could therefore claim full membership in the human
family. But at the end of his address, Douglass made a crucial move from the
discourse of anatomy to the discourse of morality and rights: "What, if . . . the
case [of anatomical similarity between whites and blacks] is not made out? Does
it follow, that the Negro should be held in contempt?" He answered with a re-
sounding "No," because the title to freedom, liberty, and knowledge was not a
question of "natural" difference or similarity, but an issue of natural rights and
morality. "It is registered in the Courts of Heaven, and is enforced by the eloquence of the God of all the earth." Douglass here asked a question that would
virtually disappear from science: What difference does difference make to human

rights? Douglass's answer was that it made no difference, because equality and rights were moral, political, and religious issues.[15] The silence of most scientific texts on this matter after 1860 suggests the power of science to occupy the terrain formerly held by moral discourse, and to disguise the political projects that helped constitute the scientific field.

African-American intellectuals continued to infuse discussions of race with theological, moral, and political concerns. They continued, especially, to evoke the older tradition of Christian monogenism long after it had lost ground as an acceptable *style* of scientific argumentation in mainstream science. Christian monogenism was one of the few powerful traditions linked to science on which they could draw in self-defense; moreover, theological discourse was one of the most significant intellectual productions of the black community. A notable example of the genre is the work of the Harvard-trained physician and Pan-Africanist Dr. Martin R. Delany. He used the Mosaic story of the Deluge to structure a scientific study of race unity in his *Principia of Ethnology* (1879). His strategy made sense within the black tradition but it rendered his book a cultural and linguistic hybrid unlike white scientific writings on race in the same period, a hybrid reflected in its very title, half-English and half Latin. Religiously oriented ethnography survived as a form because it served the political and psychological needs of the African-American. Isolation from the norms of science meant that those norms were less internalized. The creation of a different narrative form resisted the conventions of science, but as a strategy of resistance, theological arguments had the disadvantage of seeming illegitimate or "unscientific" when measured by the canons of mainstream science.[16]

Another strategy of resistance was the employment of wit, irony, or parody. These literary devices became marginalized and delegitimized in the second half of the nineteenth century precisely because they did not fit the depersonalized, nonauthorial style of modern science. As a style, humor had the advantage of distancing and subverting the claims of science, thereby serving as a strategy of empowerment. An exceptional use of the ironic voice is found in an anonymous article in the black American periodical, the *Anglo-African Magazine,* in 1860. The article, which was almost certainly the work of the black Scottish-trained physician Dr. James McCune Smith, is especially interesting because it represents, as far as we know, the first account of Darwinian ideas by an African-American. Titled "A Word for the 'Smith' Family," the article put Darwin's new science to witty use to defend the unity and success of the black people named Smith. The very commonness of the name Smith was taken as proof of the evolutionary success of black people, who were shown to have thrived, adapted, and multiplied through natural selection and the struggle for survival. The theory of common descent was also used implicitly to poke fun at the pretensions of all the white Smiths who thought they were distinct and superior to black Smiths. All Smiths, the author suggested, were linked together in an evolutionary kinship.[17]

Wit and irony gave a writer control and power over language and content. Parody could perform a similar task of distancing in relation to the claims of science. But all three literary (or cultural) styles, because they impressed directly the author's own personality on the text, had less and less place in scientific discourse as the century wore on. As strategies of resistance, they too became marginal to the scientific enterprise.[18]

Using the Scientific Idiom

Despite the continuing resort to political and moral written arguments to challenge the claims of the scientific racists, the professionalization of science made such tactics less effective. By the last third of the century, effective strategies of resistance were often structured by the dominant discourse. Science's conceptual categories, rhetorical styles, and methodologies were adopted.

Of course, science had always been used as a source of ideas and arguments by people challenging the conventional wisdom and dominant ideologies of their day. Feminists in the eighteenth century defended the rights of women in the language of Newton; artisanal socialists in the early nineteenth century called upon Lamarckian evolutionism to serve their antibourgeois, confrontational needs.[19] After the mid-1800s, however, writers were forced to use the sciences of the day more narrowly to challenge scientific claims if they wished to have a hearing within science. As minorities moved into the scientific arena, their own competencies in the scientific idiom grew, as did their ability to meet science on its own terms. It is no surprise, then, to find that evolutionism, hereditarianism, the new Mendelism, and even "eugenics" (which in the United States was racist almost by definition) were embraced by African-Americans, Jews, and other minorities to counter the charges of racial inferiority.[20] The cultural forms of scientific texts were imitated in a necessary process of identification with the norms and standards of science. Blacks produced texts of blackness, with anthropological illustrations of heads, cranial measurements, and scientific tables of racial health and illness.[21] Jewish scientists particularly used scientistic representations of self because of their greater access to scientific education and greater commitment to the norms of science.

The use of science to dismantle the claims of science involved the authors in complex processes of transformation of the meaning of terms. Any discussion of the critical responses to scientific racism in the late nineteenth and early twentieth century must acknowledge how the need to meet science on its own terms limited the nature of the response. This was also true of other discourses—for example, literary discourse—but scientific discourse was distinguished by its high barriers of entry.[22] By the end of the nineteenth century, professionalization separated science from both "high" literary culture and popular culture. Science acquired technical procedures and practices, as well as new vocabularies unfamiliar to the nonscientist; these could only be acquired in the professional scientific academy. Only the trained scientist, it was claimed, was able to speak coherently and legitimately about scientific matters. Disciplinary boundaries were a further disincentive to the kind of critical inquiry that dismantling scientific racism and sexism required.[23]

Exclusion from the academy meant exclusion from the authoritative use of the idioms of science. Whenever racial minorities and women wrote critically about the sciences of themselves, their writing ran the risk of being ignored or dismissed because it came from "outside" professional science, and was therefore by definition "unscientific." Furthermore, resisting the claims of scientific racism by pointing out its subjective, metaphorical, particular, or politically biased nature (namely, that science was articulated around notions of race) was extraordinarily difficult because many minority writers shared the belief of the mainstream scientists in science as a progressive, instrumental, and objective form of knowledge. Given the epistemological status of science, to admit that race, especially one's own, was an issue in science was to make the writer immediately less than fully "objective" and therefore less than fully "scientific."[24] For the African-American or Jew writing *as* a scientist, or from *within* science, the writer's own status as objective observer of nature was at stake. The problem of both using science as a language of self-assertion and identity, while exposing its essentially *political* character in relation to racial claims, was rarely addressed by resisting groups because rarely recognized.[25]

Some Tactics and Responses to Scientific Racism

In relation to the terrain and idioms of science, different groups were very differently situated. Access to education and the languages of science varied, and was indeed a part of the social construction *of* race as a category of human and political difference. Yet even when the barriers were very great, as was the case for African-Americans, critical engagement with scientific racism long predated the Civil War; the way this critical response influenced black periodical writings is relatively unstudied. Jews as a group had far greater access to education in general and were strongly attracted to the scientific professions. In some branches of science, in fact, Jews made up 6 to 10 percent of all scientists, a figure much higher than their total representation in the population.[26]

What is not generally realized is the degree to which Jews themselves engaged with racial science, because of its potentially harmful implications for themselves as a "race." Their cultural production has barely been studied in the context proposed here. As Jews (and other groups stereotyped in the biological and social sciences of the day) were drawn more deeply into the sciences of racial difference, whether in measuring themselves as a race by craniometry and other methods, or by comparing one fraction of the Jewish "race" with another, or by commenting on or contesting the thesis of Jewish pathology and illness, they were tempted simultaneously to embrace and reject the field: to embrace science's methods, concepts, and the promise it held out for discovering knowledge, and to reject, in a variety of ways, the conclusions of science as they appeared to apply negatively to themselves.

Audre Lorde has stated that "the master's tools will never dismantle the master's house."[27] Yet our studies suggest that when minorities took on the matter of racial science, in the idioms of science, that science was inevitably changed. Even for the most oppressed, science created spaces for self-definition and self-representation. It is these interstices—or more precisely, the strategies that created them—to which we turn now.

Our discussion takes the form of a simple typology. One of the typology's functions is to draw attention to a variety of responses to scientific racism and a range of textual materials that are usually overlooked. By providing a simple classification of these materials, we show that despite the individuality of the responses, despite the very different social experiences of the writers analyzed, despite the fact that "race" was not a unitary category but had multiple meanings, certain similarities in textual strategies can be found in minority responses. These similarities indicate the power of scientific racism to map the terrain within which, and the terms by which, resistance and challenge could be carried out. Recurring tropes, recurring techniques of reenvisioning identity, certain patterns in the tactics of re-representation, characterize the critical tradition we examine.

The kinds of responses illustrated here are not exhaustive or mutually exclusive. We find that a writer employed a number of responses or strategies, either simultaneously or successively over the course of a writing career. Since the dominant ideology of scientific racism was itself heterogeneous, and fueled by contradictory impulses, so were the resisting discourses that echoed, commented upon, and modified them. "Cannibalization," disarticulation and reassemblage, and the employment of multiple modes of attack were the tactics that made sense.[28] Our typology, then, is a highly dynamic one, employed mainly to point out how responses placed the writer in different relations to the dominant discourse, with varying consequences psychologically, intellectually, and scientifically.

The most pernicious effect of racial science was the profound *internalization* of the negative terms and norms of the discourse itself. Insofar as resisting discourses are necessarily tied to, reflective of, and constructed in similar terms to dominant discourses, "internalization" is to a certain extent characteristic of all strategies of intellectual resistance. "Internalization" here, however, means more than this—we refer to the very profound psychological and social introjection of negative images and meanings contained in the stereotypes, in the construction and understanding of one's self-identity. Such internalization was recognized by the stereotyped people as a common and profoundly problematic outcome of stereotyping discourses. "In the psychology of the human mind, suggestion plays an important part," wrote the African-American George Parker in 1908: "If it be true that as a man thinketh, so he is, then the self-making power becomes proportionately more powerful when applied to a whole race. For years it has been constantly affirmed and reaffirmed that races of African blood have contributed nothing to humanity's store of knowledge and civilization, and this incessant affirmation has produced a conviction of truth not only in the minds of those who affirm it, but also in the minds of those whom it wrongs."[29]

The psychological processes of identification with and internalization of the dominant discourses of "otherness" are extremely complex and varied. Gilman has discussed the fragmentation of identity that internalization of the norms of "otherness" entails, and the conflicts that arise when we use on ourselves the discourse that labels us as different and unacceptable.[30] Our interest here is in the special weight of scientific discourses of otherness and inequality on individual and group self-consciousness in the late nineteenth and early twentieth centuries, in which the self was understood and represented through a preexisting, racialized science. Absolute application, without qualification, of the dominant discourse to oneself or to one's group is for rather obvious reasons relatively rare. Psychologically the outcome is extreme and potentially devastating self-hatred. The publication of one such self-hating text, by the Jewish student of philosophy Otto Weininger in 1903, was followed a few months later by his suicide. Weininger, a student of the Viennese philosophers Laurenz Müller and Friedrich Jodl, attempted to combine a biology of human sexuality with a philosophy of sexual and racial identity. His self-inflicted death, in the house in which Beethoven had died, reveals the profound conflict he experienced when biological determinism came into direct contact with self-definition.

No matter how bizarre Weininger's attempt to place himself within the discourses of race may appear to be, in his own times he was understood as a scientific investigator whose ideas, though controversial, were nevertheless taken as contributions to scholarship, not as examples of psychosis. His well-known text was called *Sex and Character,* a title not unrelated to the problem of internalization. For even in the case of such self-hating texts, it is evident there must always be a way out of extreme negative self-stereotyping, whether or not the step is taken. As a male author, Weininger tried to rescue himself from complete negativity by projecting onto the female sex all the most negative qualities found in the science of biological determinism. Women were portrayed as biologically predisposed to illness, hysteria, and to an inferior and incomplete form of speaking and thinking. Such strategies of internalization and projection in principle provide a form of psychological rescue for the author. But for Weininger, both homosexual and Jewish, it proved a failure.[31]

The choice of the female as the site of negative projection in Weininger's text was not idiosyncratic but deeply structured by the stereotyping discourses of the day, as is shown in texts by male authors writing in very different social and racial circumstances. For example, the African-American William Hannibal Thomas wrote *The American Negro* in 1901, just two years before Weininger's book, during the height of American scientific racism. Thomas's work provoked an immediate angry reaction within the African-American intellectual community. Kelly Miller, professor of mathematics at Howard University, commented that the book had been "more widely noticed than any other recent work on the race problem," and he drew attention to its similarity to Jewish self-hating texts.[32]

Thomas, a northerner who went to the South to study the Negro and did not like what he found, wrote a text that might have been produced by the most racist white scientist. Yet here too processes of projection, of "self-rescue," and re-representation similar to those in Weininger can be discerned, despite the differences in personality, nationality, and the terms of the dominant, scientific, stereotyping discourse. First, Thomas maintained that the women of the Negro race embodied all of the corrupting sensuality that scientists had attributed to the entire Afro-American race. In this way Thomas implicitly exonerated the male author from the most negative aspects of the stereotyping discourse of science. Second, like Weininger, Thomas attempted to shift the definition of "race" away from a permanent, outwardly visible "sign" such as color, to a subjective, psychological condition within. To Thomas, the term "Negro" referred negatively to a "characteristic form of thought and action" (the equivalent to Weininger's "psychological constitution" of Jewishness), so that any person, of whatever hue, who exhibited such characteristic traits was to be considered a "Negro." The inclusion of all people of a particular color (such as blackness) in the same category was an unjust classification "which acts with great severity against a saving remnant of good men and true women."[33] By projecting blackness onto women and away from color per se, the mulatto author both internalized the terms of racialized and scientized discourse, and distanced himself from complete application of the negative elements of racialist discourse to himself.

A second response to racial science was to accept the terms set by the dominant discourse, but to change the valuations attached to them. The significance of biological race differences was accepted, but the "inferior" element in the hierarchy revalued and renamed. This strategy entailed a transvaluation of the terms of the dominant discourse. For example, blackness became an oppositional structure to whiteness, and negativity was thereby transformed into positivity.

Once again, this kind of strategy is familiar in discourses other than scientific ones; we mean to call attention here to the authority of scientific language in structuring such reversals. We call this strategy "transvaluation" because in such writing the response was always couched in terms similar to the dominant discourse, so that one mythology of identity was in a sense replaced by another. Though as a type, the form of writing moved the resisting author further away from total acceptance or accommodation to the dominant discourse of difference, the terms of the dominant discourse were very far from being transcended. In addition, the reverse stereotype that was created had many of the disadvantages of stereotyping in general—it failed to give space to individuality and variation, and could therefore be circumscribing. Furthermore, the simple process of transvaluation of the terms from negative to positive was not always convincing, since the resisting minority voice was always in a position of lesser legitimacy than that of the dominating voice. For the writer, however, such transvaluations often had considerable weight. Reactive and defensive though transvaluations may have been, the result was often empowerment. Upon the basis of such reversals, political solidarities were created. At times, too, they could result in telling criticisms of the science of race of the times.[34]

Since the strategy of reversal and transvaluation echoed the dominant discourse—indeed it appropriated the binary opposition upon which the dominant terms themselves depended—these reversals had somewhat predictable forms. What is important is to connect the use of such reversals to the politics of discrimination and assimilationism. When patterns of discrimination and negative stereotypes circulated widely in discourses, a dialectical politics of self-segregation, solidarity, and reversals was set in motion. We can see this clearly in the use of reversals and transvaluations in the African-American intellectual and political tradition. The "romantic racialism" espoused by some white abolitionists before the Civil War (a romanticism that included a great deal of condescension, as George Fredrickson has remarked), was embraced by African-American writers themselves in periods of intensified racism. August Meier notes the appearance of such racialism in the 1890s, at a time when anti-immigration sentiment was growing and racial categorization and exclusion were widespread.[35] Marcus Garvey's Back to Africa movement involved this kind of reversal and transvaluation.

These reversals were sometimes grounded in the idioms of science. W. E. B. Du Bois, in an early (1897) and controversial statement, "The Conservation of Races," countered the charge of biologically based racial inferiority of the black population by asserting a distinctive and positive psychic-biological identity for African-Americans.[36] Anthony Appiah, in a recent commentary on Du Bois's text, describes this transvaluation as the "classic dialectic," in that it is the antithesis to the thesis of the "American Negro denial of difference." Instead of rejecting the biological concept of race of the time, Du Bois accepted it and proposed that the different biological races of the world were complementary and necessary to each other. Appiah remarks that, as the dialectic required, Du Bois's reevaluation occurred "in the face of the sciences of inferiority."[37]

The results of such transvaluations of a binary opposition were complex. Reversals sometimes involved not only racial "essences" but the narrative histories of self and the group. For instance, B. F. Lee, in an article on "Selection, Environment and the Negro's Future," argued, as Du Bois did later, that race was not effaced or altered by changes in the environment. Lee posited the "Ethiopian" as a noble type of race which, through its "wonderful primitive instinct of adaptation" would survive to take its turn as the ruling race, when dark skin, as well as all the other traits of the Negro, would become "the highest concept of the beautiful."[38]

Among Jewish scientists, transvaluations were often tied closely to scientific anti-Semitism and the politics of antiassimilationism, especially Zionism. Theodor Herzl set the tone when he accepted the pejorative label "Oriental" for the Jews of Europe, and turned it into the basis for a new political ideology, Zionism. Martin Buber's emphasis on the positive racial identity of the Jew, or Max Nordau's call for a "muscle Jew," must be read in this context and seen as the antithesis of stereotyped Jewish feminization, weakness, mental illness, and degeneracy.[39]

A third response to scientific racism moved the speakers even further from the dominant discourses. This textual strategy involved "recontextualizations." Writings of this kind were associated with a growing empowerment of minorities in science, an increased familiarity with its idioms and technologies, and, therefore, a new authority in challenging the claims of science on its own terms.

Two rather different aspects of the process of recontextualization can be discerned. First, the tools of science were used either to prove that the supposed factual data upon which the stereotypes of racial inferiority were based were wrong, or to generate new "facts" on which different claims could be made. Second, scientific reasoning was used to question the *explanation* of the facts. "Recontextualization" resulted in new interpretations, new narratives of self and identity, which amounted to a scientific counterdiscourse.

For example, the high mortality and morbidity figures of Afro-Americans were cited repeatedly by white physicians as evidence of "racial" susceptibilities and in exoneration of white inaction in the face of the poverty and misery of the black population. Two issues confronted the Afro-American scholar. Were the facts and figures of mortality and morbidity correct? And, to the extent that accurate information about the Negro was available, what was the meaning of the statistics? A superb example of the process of recontextualization was Dr. Kelly Miller's sophisticated critique of the highly racialistic tract on supposed Negro racial inferiority by the statistician Fredrick Hoffman, *Race Traits and Tendencies of the American Negro.*[40] The German origin of the author made him, Hoffman said, "impartial" in his approach. The factual, impersonal form in which Hoffman couched his argument also made the book's impact powerful. It was, said Miller, "by far the most thorough and comprehensive treatment of the Negro problem, from a statistical standpoint, which has yet appeared."[41] As a *scientific* statement, it demanded an answer in scientific terms.

Miller's long review of Hoffman's work was the first paper to be published by the newly founded American Negro Academy, established in 1897 in Washington, D.C., as a forum for intellectual discussion, and more specifically to refute or challenge the assertions of white scientists.[42] Miller used the occasion to point out the many errors in Hoffman's data. Hoffman's main thesis was that the Negro race was dying out in America because of racially based morbidity exacerbated by conditions of political "freedom." Miller, using data collected from a wide variety of sources from several cities, showed that the African-American population had actually grown in absolute numbers, that its birthrate was greater than that of whites in many places, and that the data "proving" the death of the black race were so selectively assembled by Hoffman as to be completely fallacious.

Miller also recontextualized the actual statistics of death and disease, establishing a very different understanding of the meaning of the figures. Here the most significant figures concerned high black morbidity and mortality from diseases such as tuberculosis, which Hoffman, in keeping with the science of race of the times, presented as the result of innate racial susceptibilities to illness and degeneration. Miller used comparable data on working-class whites in Europe to make the case that high rates of disease and death were a function not of innate racial susceptibilities but of social conditions (whites in parts of Europe were as poorly off in housing, employment, education, medical care and health as Afri-can-Americans). Miller also neatly turned to advantage some of Hoffman's own arguments and data—for instance, by citing Hoffman's assertion that 50 percent of all Negro children who died under the age of five received *no* medical atten-tion. Miller's conclusion was that the Afro-American should not be discouraged by scientific inquiry, for "it is a condition and not a theory that confronts him."[43]

W. E. B. Du Bois's *The Health and Physique of the Negro American* (1906), was the first of the Atlanta University publications on black Americans that was su-pervised by Du Bois himself, after he was invited to Atlanta in 1897. This project was more ambitious than Miller's in that it not only attacked the data on which many of the claims of the white scientists were founded, but collected new data as a means of narrating in a new way the history and condition of the Afro-American people.[44] Du Bois was the most imposing black intellectual of the time, and a pioneer of the new sociology, which he saw as an essential tool in the fight against racism. In addition to combing the U.S. Census records for information, Du Bois arranged to have measured, craniometrically and otherwise, some 1,000 students at Hampton Institute in Atlanta, in strict accordance with the techniques of contemporary racial science.

On the existing data of blacks, the study attacked the conclusions concerning the supposed low brain weights of African-Americans, showing they were based on insufficient numbers (the total number of Afro-American brains that had been measured and weighed in America at the time was 500, from which generaliza-tions about more than 20 million persons of Negro descent in the West had been formed). Furthermore, Du Bois pointed out that no account was given of the age, stature, social class, occupation, nutrition, or cause of death of the individuals whose heads and brains had been measured, all of which separately or together affected the structure of the brain. In cases in which morbidity and mortality rates in the Afro-American race were accepted as correct, Du Bois recontextual-ized the data, emphasizing social conditions, economic environment, and the political realities of discrimination, as their cause. The evidence showed, for in-stance, that tuberculosis was "not a racial disease but a social disease," and that high infant mortality in the cities was "not a Negro affair, but an index of social conditions." "If the population were divided as to social and economic conditions the matter of race would be almost entirely eliminated," the report concluded.[45]

Jewish scientists also produced a plethora of statistical data of their own—on Jewish disease rates and head shapes—in order to contribute to, and rewrite, the scientific study of their own identity. Of special interest were the scientific data on the supposed high rates of illness. As trained scientists, many employed by municipal and state mental hospitals, Jewish physicians were in a position to gather their own data on rates of mental illness, and to recontextualize the prob-lem as one not of biology but of the history of Jews in Europe. Raphael Becker, a student of Eugen Bleuler and resident physician of the Zurich University psychi-atric clinic, for example, produced a monograph that was widely cited by Jews, demonstrating that the higher incidence of mental illness among Western Euro-pean Jews compared with non-Jews was the result of a "Jewish inferiority complex," itself a product of "two thousand years of persecution."[46] Biological race, Becker asserted, was not the causal factor. Other Jewish scientists challenged the existing information on supposed Jewish mental illness, much as Miller had challenged the data on black racial susceptibilities to disease, and set out to gather their own, more accurate, statistics.

By such recontextualizations, rejection of the *meaning* of the dominant scientific discourses of difference could be achieved, and efforts at explanation could be steered in innovative directions.[47] The new social sciences, with their growing identity as "sciences," their accessibility, and their early connection to reform projects, were important weapons in the fight against biological racism and sexism, although they could also be used in the elaboration of racial and sexual stereotypes.

Another form of recontextualization was "universalization," whereby a trait or character labeled as peculiar to one race and designated as negative, was relabeled instead as a universal trait of all human beings, so that the racial marker was removed as a sign of inferiority. We see it at work in Delany's universalization of color in his *Principia of Ethnology,* where he argued that the black skin, the supposed "sign" of black inferiority, was the result not of features unique to the black race, but merely of a subtle elaboration of a universal, underlying color process in the skin shared by all human beings. The blackness of the black was therefore only a "concentrated" form of something universal in humans. As Delany put it, "The color of the blackest African is produced by *identically the same* essential coloring matter that gives the 'rose cheeks and ruby lips' to the fairest and most delicate beautiful white lady."[48] Similarly we see a strategy of universalization in the rejection, early in the twentieth century, of the very concept of "tropical" diseases, which scientists in the newly emerging discipline of "tropical medicine" attributed to tropical places and "tropical" (racially dark or racially mixed) peoples.[49] Some Latin American physicians removed the stigma of tropicalization by embracing a "universal" theory of disease causation, namely germ theory. A racial theory of illness was thereby replaced by a nonracial theory of disease etiology.[50]

A last category we want to discuss is one that, theoretically at least, moves the writer to a position of greatest distance from the terms of the dominant discourse. This category involves the creation of an "alternative ideology" that serves to place the minority writer outside the terms of the discourse of scientific racism. Such an alternative ideology functions as (and produces) a genuine oppositional discourse or set of discourses, but this is accomplished not through the appropriation and reassemblage of elements of the existing science, but by positing a radically different world view, with different perceptions of reality, goals, and points of reference. It effectively dissolves the relevance of the stereotyping discourse of science, by conceptualizing the issue of human variation in different, and essentially egalitarian, terms.

It is interesting to ask whether the individuals and groups in the period we have been examining could have created such alternatives to science, and thereby "stepped outside" the discourse and ignored science's claims about human difference and inequality. Today such alternatives seem attractive and even possible. In our so-called postmodern world, many of the projects of modernism are under attack. Among them is science itself, and its epistemology. Thomas Kuhn's investigations into scientific paradigms, the "strong program" in the social construction of science, the study of the fundamental metaphors that structure science, the feminist examination of gender in the development of scientific epistemology—all of these themes are part of the postmodern reevaluation of science, and all cast doubt on the claims of science to be a value-free, apolitical, universal, or purely empirical form of knowledge. The consensus that once underlay the scientific enterprise has gone, and questions arise about the relativity of scientific knowledge, the fundamentally political character of science, the problems of its rationalistic claims. The fragmentation of the consensus surrounding scientific positivism, a fragmentation that is itself a product of political and social changes since the 1950s, has in turn created political and intellectual possibilities for seeing science in new ways and of imagining a science put to different political ends.

In the period between 1870 and 1920, however, the consensus about science was relatively strong. As we noted earlier, until the middle of the nineteenth century, several world views and discourses about human identity, difference, and destiny competed for cultural and political authority. Theological and political discourses, for example, rivaled science for legitimacy, and potentially offered alternative world views for the representation of human variation along lines different from that of the new scientific racism. By the middle of the century, however, science replaced other discourses in the authoritative representation of the facts of nature. As science acquired status as the preeminently empirical, value-free, and objective type of knowledge, its power to settle political issues concerning "nature" was increased. Theological, ethical, and political approaches to what scientists now presented as problems of mere empirical nature were reduced in their authority. Thus scientists effectively removed from science the most powerful defense against scientific racism and sexism—namely, the assertion that individual and group variation made no difference to issues of justice and rights. As Douglass had said, rights were grounded not in putatively neutral "facts" of different natures, but on other, political and moral, principles.

This is not to say that men and women stereotyped as different and inferior in the sciences of the late nineteenth century, and denied equality and fair treatment on the grounds of their "natures," stopped talking about and fighting for rights—for equal treatment in the law, for political representation, or the right to education. The politically motivated and biased characters of the charges made against them by supposedly "objective" scientists were often intensely felt by the stereotyped. Even as minorities at the turn of the century pinned their hopes on the possibilities inherent in the sciences for uncovering the truth about themselves, many of them saw clearly that racial science violated the standards of neutrality, and that scientists' ideas were fundamentally marked by the relations of power between the dominating and the dominated. The African-American physician, monogenist, and trenchant critic of scientific racism C. V. Roman, in 1916 (quoting the French journalist, Jean Finot) wrote: "The science of inequality is emphatically a science of white people. It is they who have invented it, and set it agoing, who have maintained, cherished, and propagated it, thanks to *their* observations and *their* deductions."[51]

To the mainstream scientists, however, such criticisms were contaminated by their language of engagement and passion, and by their source in the stereotyped or injured parties. By the norms of modern science, passion was taken to be an inappropriate stance in relation to nature and scientific argument. Science called for detachment, neutrality, a depoliticization of the terms of the debate, and the achievement of the suitably scholarly tone—even in matters of such extreme urgency and political consequence as one's own individuality and meaning. This meant, therefore, that when the stereotyped engaged in the scientific study of difference, they too found it difficult to introduce the question asked by Douglass—what difference does difference make?—and to transform the discourses of science into ones of morality and politics.[52]

What we are arguing is that in the era of the successful establishment of science as a epistemologically neutral and instrumentally successful form of knowledge, standing "outside of" or ignoring science was very difficult. With the triumph of "positive" science and positivist ideology, even those with the most radical intellectual and political philosophies and programs—alternative world views—tended to exempt science from their criticisms and to posit science as the one positive form of knowledge that escaped contamination from political and personal factors. A hard-hitting critique of science, as itself a political form of knowledge reflective of power, was, relatively speaking, absent.[53]

Operating within the circle of science, expressing themselves in the terms of the debate set by science, the stereotyped groups' best defense in the heyday of scientific racism was, as we have seen, to use science to point out the errors, the questionable data, and the specious logic of the discourses on human difference and inequality. The dominant discourse of race within science was not without its contradictions and fractures; it did not and could not wholly determine how individuals saw themselves. Even within the confining space and languages of science, Afro-Americans and Jews found opportunities to represent themselves in alternative yet "scientific" terms. In acting *as* scientists and intellectuals, in insisting on gaining a foothold within the scientific academy, even if on "separate and unequal" terms, they kept open and contested arenas of knowledge that otherwise might have become completely "naturalized" and uncontested.

It is true that the challenges mounted by the minorities we have examined here often made relatively little difference to mainstream science. The white, male academy usually ignored the contributions of minorities to the sciences of themselves. For instance, only one of W. E. B. Du Bois's many articles on the sociology of the African-American was published in the journal of the new profession of sociology, *The American Journal of Sociology,* even during the time when the journal was actively involved in the discussion of race (and even though its editors shared to some degree the antiracist outlook of Du Bois).[54] Similarly,

Jewish scientific writing on the Jewish race and self-identity was more important to Jews themselves than to the establishment circles of science.

But despite the apparently marginal status of the counterwriting produced by Afro-Americans and Jews within scientific racism before the 1930s, their efforts were not without significance. Their work created modes of representation and knowledge essential for the stereotyped themselves. Swedish sociologist Gunnar Myrdal, for instance, in his massive study of race in America in the late 1930s undertaken very much in the spirit of an objective and scientific investigation, found that he was able to call upon a long tradition of scientific work produced by African-American physicians, educators, and social scientists about their own identity, meaning, and status. Myrdal remarked upon the environmentalist emphasis found in these black scientific studies of the Negro, in contrast to the innatist tendencies of the white academy. That emphasis gave black writing, he said, a much more modern tone than white writings of the same period. Myrdal also stressed that black intellectual resistance to the dogma of Negro racial inferiority had a significant impact on the black community itself. By being widely disseminated in the black press, their counterformulation of the issue of race had emerged as a fundamental belief of all black communities, he said, allowing them to refuse to accommodate themselves to white beliefs.[55] The history of resistance to dominant scientific discourses of inequality suggests that, for the stereotyped, challenges to intellectual discourses of difference and inequality were indispensable to their psychological survival and political action.

N O T E S

1. On scientific racism, see Nancy Stepan, *The Idea of Race in Science: Great Britain, 1800–1960* (London, 1982); George Mosse, *Toward the Final Solution: A History of European Racism* (New York, 1981); and Stephen Jay Gould, *The Mismeasure of Man* (New York, 1981).

2. For an interesting discussion of how ideological-linguistic formulations of race have material consequences, see K. J. Anderson, "Cultural Hegemony and the Race-Definition Process in Chinatown, Vancouver: 1880–1980," *Environment and Planning: Science and Society* 6 (1988):127–49.

3. Before 1850 there was an active tradition of scientific antiracism, albeit one with its own racialist condescensions. See Stepan, *The Idea of Race,* chaps. 1–2. After 1850, critics of scientific racism and/or sexism from within science were often themselves in one way or another members of marginal groups (for example, Franz Boas in the United States was Jewish). As for the "technical" disagreements about race, many disputes arose among scientists about *which* measurement accurately demonstrated the essential differences between human races—facial angle, cephalic index, overall brain weight, brain volume, or some other index. These disputes generated a large literature, but the fundamental principle underlying the science of race difference—that some measurement would indeed reveal categorically the essential racial types—was generally accepted.

4. As an example, one could contrast the caution, care, and argumentative skill with

which Darwin defended his general position on the evolution of species by natural selection, with the broad assumptions and lack of caution with which he discussed male and female differences in the human species in the *Descent of Man*. On this point see Susan Mosedale, "Science Corrupted: Victorian Biologists Consider the 'Woman Question,'" *Journal of the History of Biology* 11 (1978): 1–55; and Evelleen Richards, "Darwin and the Descent of Woman," in *The Wider Domain of Evolutionary Thought*, ed. D. Oldroyd and I. Langham (Dordrecht, Holland, 1983), pp. 57–111.

5. Margaret W. Rossiter, *Women Scientists in America: Struggles and Strategies to 1940* (Baltimore, 1982). Our focus in this paper is not on the many groups categorized as "inferior" races but on those few individuals with access to education or scientific writings who challenged the claims about their "race."

6. Gramsci's *Prison Notebooks* has many striking passages: see Michael Walzer, "The Ambiguous Legacy of Antonio Gramsci," *Dissent* 35 (Fall 1988): 444–56. Also valuable is Edward Said's work on Orientalism, especially his comments in "Orientalism Reconsidered," in *Cultural Critique* I (Fall 1985): 89–108, and his introduction in Said and Christopher Hitchens, eds., *Blaming the Victims: Spurious Scholarship and the Palestinian Question* (London, 1988), pp. 1–19. See also the two issues on the theme "The Nature and Context of Minority Discourse," in *Cultural Critique* 6 (Spring 1987) and 7 (Fall 1987); Gayatri Chakravorty Spivak, *In Other Worlds: Essays in Cultural Politics* (New York, 1987); and Henry Louis Gates, Jr., *Figures in Black: Words, Signs, and the "Racial Self"* (New York, 1987).

7. See the reflections of Joan Wallach Scott, in *Gender and the Politics of History* (New York, 1988); Teresa de Lauretis, "The Technology of Gender," in *Technologies of Gender* (Bloomington, Ind., 1987), pp. 1–30.

8. Jack Morrell and Arnold Thackray, *Gentlemen of Science: Early Years of the British Association for the Advancement of Science* (Oxford, 1981), p. 32.

9. The relation of gender to the emergence of modern scientific epistemology has been explored by a number of historians. See Carolyn Merchant, *The Death of Nature: Women, Ecology and the Scientific Revolution* (San Francisco, 1980); and Londa Schiebinger, *The Mind Has No Sex? Women in the Origins of Modern Science* (Cambridge, 1989).

10. In Britain, science was represented as a "gentlemen's" pursuit (hence the title of Morrell and Thackray's book). Class and gender exclusions from science followed from the social structure of science. The long persistence of the "amateur" in science—one consequence of the gentlemanly and aristocratic nature of British high culture—made British science organizationally distinctive and postponed professionalization. For American science, see Alexandra Oleson and John Voss, *The Organization of Knowledge in Modern America, 1860–1920* (Baltimore, 1979); for aspects of the new epistemology in Vienna, see Erna Lesky, *Die Wiener medizinische Schule im 19. Jahrhundert* (Graz, 1965).

11. Boundary setting in areas of knowledge other than science was not dissimilar—between "high" and "low," elite and popular, the canonical and noncanonical in literature and the visual arts, for example. An especially interesting analysis is Andreas Huyssen's "Mass Culture as Woman: Modernism's Other," in *After the Great Divide: Modernism, Mass Culture, Postmodernism* (Bloomington, Ind., 1986), chap. 3.

12. Gyorgy Markus, "Why is There No Hermeneutics of Natural Sciences? Some Preliminary Theses," *Science in Context* I (March 1987): 5–51. In a very different vein, see Mary Louise Pratt, "The Face of the Country," *Critical Inquiry* 12 (Autumn 1985): 119–43, on the emergence of the informational, depersonalized, scientistic form of travel literature as a new genre of the late eighteenth century, a form whose lack of vivid and personalized narrative was resisted by the continued use of older forms of travel literature as heroic adventures of personal and geographical discovery.

13. The neutral, universal forms of science disguise the way science is nevertheless grounded on the metaphors and practices of racism and sexism. See for example Luce Irigaray's "Is the Subject of Science Sexed?" *Cultural Critique* I (Fall 1985): 73–88.

14. See Gillian Beer, *Darwin's Plots: Evolutionary Narrative in Darwin, George Eliot, and*

Nineteenth-Century Fiction (London, 1983); Robert M. Young, *Darwin's Metaphor: Nature's Place in Victorian Culture* (Cambridge, 1985); Ted Benton, "Social Darwinism and Socialist Darwinism in Germany: 1860–1900," *Rivista di Filosofia* 73 (1982): 79–121.

15. The speech was a commencement address before the literary societies of Western Reserve College (Rochester, N.Y., 1854). Reprinted in Philip S. Foner, ed., *The Life and Writings of Frederick Douglass,* 5 vols. (New York, 1975), 2:289–309.

16. Martin R. Delany, *Principia of Ethnology: The Origin of Races and Color, with an Archeological Compendium of Ethiopian and Egyptian Civilization from Years of Careful Examination and Enquiry* (Philadelphia, 1879). A great deal could be said about the survival of older cultural scientific forms among groups who needed to resist the growing racialism and the narrowing of the languages within which racialism was expressed in the transition period from about 1830 to 1930. For example, Casely Hayford's *Ethiopia Unbound: Studies in Race Emancipation* (1911), the first African novel, fused fiction with factual "studies" to create a tale of black emancipation and power. Other uses of monogenism by blacks were less religious in tone. A powerful statement was made by C. V. Roman, *American Civilization and the Negro* (Freeport, N.Y., 1971, rpt. of 1916 ed.); the chapter "Racial Differences" engaged directly in rebutting racialism and Roman used the scientific argument for monogenism as the necessary and sufficient foundation for political and moral equality. The survival of traditional environmentalist explanations of difference, dating back to the Enlightenment, is also worth exploring.

17. "A Word for the 'Smith' Family," *Anglo-African Magazine* 2 (March 1860): 77–83. In addition to its irony, the article is interesting for the accurate account of the main points of Darwin's themes in relation to human beings, and for the association McCune Smith makes between Darwinism and monogenism. Within a few years, Darwinism would be successfully integrated into scientific polygenism and put to the service of disunity and inequality. Black writers often resisted Darwinism for this reason, and because it destroyed the religious basis of ethnology and anthropology by stressing humankind's common heritage with animals.

18. For an interesting account of the uses of parody as a strategy of resistance to medical authority and expertise, as well as the limits of this strategy in the face of increasing success and professionalization of science, see Judith R. Walkowitz, "Science and Seance: Transgressions of Gender and Genre in Late Victorian London," *Representations* 22 (Spring, 1988):3–29.

19. Lois N. Magner, "Women and the Scientific Idiom: Textual Episodes from Wollstonecraft, Fuller, Gilman and Firestone," *Signs* 4 (1986):61–80; Adrian Desmond, "Artisan Resistance and Evolution in Britain, 1819–1848," *Osiris,* 2d ser., 3 (1987):77–110.

20. As we show later, the use of idioms of science usually associated with, or carrying, racialist meanings, such as eugenics, demanded a huge effort of transformation of meanings. Some examples of the use of the language of eugenics by African-Americans can be found in the black *Journal of the National Medical Association (JNMA)*; see for example, Dr. John A. Kenney, "Eugenics and the School Teacher," *JNMA* 7.4 (1915):253–59; Dr. Barnett M. Rhetta, "A Plea for the Lives of the Unborn," *JNMA* 7.3 (1915):200–205; C. V. Roman, "Some Ramifications of the Sexual Impulse," *JNMA* 12.4 (1920):14–17. In nearly every case, African-American doctors accepted the importance of good heredity in health and emphasized the need for care in reproduction. They called this "eugenics." At the same time, they rejected the antiblack and sterilization themes characteristic of white eugenics. Many women and Jews also embraced the themes and conclusions of eugenics.

21. For an example, see *The Health and Physique of the Negro American,* ed. W. E. Burghardt Du Bois (Atlanta, 1906), especially its plates of "Typical Negro-Americans" prefacing the text.

22. For valuable work on the problem of how dominant discourses in literature structure minority writing and the degree to which the Jewish, female, and black literary traditions represent implicit or explicit forms of resistance to the dominant discourse, see Sandra M. Gilbert and Susan Gubar, *The Madwoman in the Attic: The Woman Writer and*

the Nineteenth-Century Literary Imagination (New Haven, Conn., 1979); Mary Poovey, *The Proper Lady and the Woman Writer: Ideology as Style in the Works of Mary Wollstonecraft, Mary Shelley and Jane Austen* (Chicago, 1984); Deirdre David, *Intellectual Women and Victorian Patriarchy* (Ithaca, N.Y., 1987); Henry Louis Gates, Jr., *Figures in Black;* and Sander L. Gilman, *Jewish Self-Hatred: Anti-Semitism and the Hidden Language of the Jews* (Baltimore, 1986).

23. A sign of this separation was the translation of increasingly specialized knowledge of great cultural, symbolic, and material power into more accessible forms for the general public. Journals such as *Nature* and *Popular Science Monthly* were established to carry out this task of translation, initially by scientists themselves. The social circumstances in which successful attacks on scientific racism and sexism could be made also need to be studied in far greater detail. When disciplinary structures are not stabilized, or where new fields come into being that are not fully professionalized, the opportunities for minorities in science are increased.

24. The defensive tone characteristic of critical writing by minorities is explained by the high barriers to entry science had erected. See Evelyn Fox Keller, "The Gender/ Science System: or, Is Sex to Gender as Nature Is to Science?" *Hypatia* 2 (Fall 1987): 37–49.

25. This problem is addressed, however, by feminists writing on science today. As Rossiter (*Woman Scientists*) and others have noted, accepting the prevailing ideology of science as unmarked by gender did not protect women and/or minorities in science from discrimination and exclusion. Instead, it only perpetuated and masked the material conditions of that exclusion.

26. According to Willie Pearson, about 950 African-Americans earned doctorates in the natural sciences between 1876 and 1976; the percentage of all natural scientists who are African-American has remained the same for over a century, namely 1 percent. About 1 percent of all PhDs in the social sciences in the United States are African-American. See Willie Pearson, Jr., *Black Scientists, White Society and Colorless Science: A Study of Universalism in American Science* (Millwood, N.Y., 1985), pp. 31–33. For the size of the African-American medical population in the period under study, see Todd Savitt, "Entering a White Profession," *Bull. Hist. Med.* (1987):516. By 1920, African-American physicians represented 2.7 percent of all doctors, compared to only 0.9 percent in 1890. European medical schools opened to Jewish males at the very beginning of the emancipation of the Jews, with the Act of Tolerance of 1782 promulgated by Joseph II of Austria. Jews tended to be clustered in the medical specialties with the lowest status (for example, syphilogy, dermatology, and so on); when Ferdinand von Hebra took over the dermatological clinic in Vienna in the 1860s, he was able to recruit only Jewish assistants. See Monika Richarz, *Der Eintritt der Juden in die akademischen Berufe* (Tübingen, 1974), pp. 28–43; and Erna Lesky, *Die Wiener medizinische Schule im 19. Jahrhundert* (Graz, 1978).

27. Quoted in Barbara Johnson, *A World of Difference* (Baltimore, 1987), pp. 1–2.

28. Obviously, the social differences fracturing race (and gender) affected the emphases within the dominant discourse of "natural" difference, as it was applied to particular groups. Thus both black males and Jewish males were described in nineteenth-century anthropological and medical science as "female" in traits and character. How African-Americans and Jews supposedly manifested this femaleness was distinctive. Any study of the reactions to racial science must be alert to the nuances and emphases within the scientific stereotypes, since the responses were fundamentally structured by them, echoing, commenting upon, and modifying the specifics of particular themes. See Desmond ("Artisan Resistance") for the use of the word "cannibalization" to mean the selective use of elements of science whereby "stolen fragments were . . . re-constituted" in such a way as to legitimate an alternative program.

29. George W. Parker, "The Negroid Line in History," *American Methodist Episcopal Review* 25 (October 1908):28.

30. See Gilman, *Jewish Self-Hatred.*

31. Otto Weininger's *Sex and Character* appeared in English translation in 1906. Weininger conceived of both sex and racial character as a continuum, qualities of maleness and femaleness were, therefore, not absolutes, and both aspects could be found in an individual. Nevertheless, the extreme end of the continuum of sex, the female, was postulated as unchangeable and negative. Freud was one scientist who acknowledged the basic validity of Weininger's concept of bisexuality. See Peter Heller, "A Quarrel over Bisexuality," in *The Turn of the Century: German Literature and Art, 1890–1915,* ed. Gerald Chapple and Hans H. Schulte (Bonn, 1981), pp. 87–116.

32. William H. Thomas, *The American Negro: What He Was, What He Is, and What He May Become: A Critical and Practical Discussion* (New York, 1901). Chapter 5, "Characteristic Traits," is of special interest. Kelly Miller, "Review of W. Hannibal Thomas' Book 'The American Negro,' " *Hampton Negro Conference* 5 (July 1901):64–74; the quotations are from pp. 64–65. See also Du Bois's review in *Book Reviews by W. E. B. Du Bois,* comp. and ed. Herbert Aptheker (Millwood, N.Y., 1977), pp. 1–3. Other reviews were by Charles W. Chestnutt, "A Defamer of His Race," *The Critic* (April 1901):350–51; Charles T. Walker, "Reply to William H. Thomas: The Twentieth Century Slander of the Negro Race—Address" (New York, n.d.).

33. Thomas, *American Negro,* p. xxiii.

34. Gates, *Figures in Black,* emphasizes the reactive and negative side of such reversals, and the bizarre stereotypes that can result.

35. George M. Fredrickson, *The Black Image in the White Mind: The Debate on Afro-American Character and Destiny, 1817–1914* (New York, 1971), pp. 97ff. August Meier, *Negro Thought in America, 1880–1915: Racial Ideologies in the Age of Booker T. Washington* (Ann Arbor, Mich., 1966), pp. 22ff.

36. W. E. B. Du Bois, "The Conservation of Races" (1897), in Andrew G. Paschal, ed., *A W. E. B. Du Bois Reader* (New York, 1971), pp. 19–31. An earlier statement of the theme is Du Bois's Harvard Address of 1890, where he posited the African-American as the opposite race to the Teuton, and suggested that the Teuton needed the more submissive Negro for the full development of civilization. See his *Against Racism: Unpublished Essays, Papers, Addresses, 1887–1961,* ed. Herbert Aptheker (Amherst, Mass., 1985), p. 16.

37. Anthony Appiah, "The Uncompleted Argument: Du Bois and the Illusion of Race," *Critical Inquiry* 12 (Autumn 1985):21–35. A similar example is provided by Kelly Miller's "The Artistic Gifts of the Negro," in his *Race Adjustment: Essays on the Negro* (New York, 1908), pp. 246–57. The political context of Du Bois's embrace of biology was not only scientific racism, but the need to oppose Booker T. Washington's accommodationism. In a period in which there was much discussion of "pure races," of race sentiment as binding nations together, of the need to preserve the integrity of race, it is not surprising to find many minorities embracing for themselves these notions. Du Bois's "biologism" was exceptional in his overall endeavor; he is generally known for his steadfast opposition to biological racism. Other strategies employed by Du Bois in countering scientific racism are discussed later.

38. B. F. Lee, "Selection, Environment and the Negro's Future," *AME Church Review* 20.4 (1904):388–90. The rewriting of African history, from one of nullity or "blank darkness," to use Christopher Miller's arresting title (*Blank Darkness: Africanist Discourse in French* [Chicago, 1985]), to a densely filled history of African civilization, is another aspect of the process of reversals.

39. See Gilman, *Jewish Self-Hatred,* p. 291.

40. Fredrick L. Hoffman's book was published for the American Economic Association. Hoffman, *Race Traits and Tendencies of the American Negro* (New York, 1896). A short variation of this tract appeared earlier as "The Vital Statistics of the Negro," *The Arena* 24 (1892):529–42.

41. Kelly Miller, "A Review of Hoffman's *Race Traits and Tendencies of the American Negro,*" *The American Negro Academy, Occasional Papers,* No. 1 (Washington, D.C., 1897), pp. 3–36.

42. Alfred A. Moss, Jr., *The American Negro Academy: Voice of the Talented Tenth* (Baton Rouge, 1981), gives a detailed account of this institution.

43. Miller, "Review of Hoffman's *Race Traits*," p. 36.

44. See Du Bois, *Health and Physique*. Du Bois "singlehandedly initiated serious research on blacks in America," says Elliot Rudwick, in "W. E. B. Du Bois as Sociologist," in *Black Sociologists: Historical and Contemporary Perspectives*, ed. James E. Blackwell and Morris Janowitz (Chicago, 1974), p. 46.

45. Du Bois, *Health and Physique*, p. 89. Several white scientists contributed data to the Atlanta University publications. Du Bois revised drastically the themes of African-American difference put forward in the Atlanta University publication no. 2, which had been published in 1897 before Du Bois became director of the conferences and publications on the Negro. In the second publication, the excessive Negro mortality and morbidity were attributed not to the environment but to ignorance of health laws and immorality, a theme that reflected the self-help outlook of the period.

46. Raphael Becker, *Die jüdische Nervosität: Ihre Art, Entstehung und Bekämpfung* (Zurich, 1918).

47. The noted Swedish sociologist Gunnar Myrdal, in studying the problem of American racism and its grounding in the idioms of science, gave pride of place to the new social sciences in dismantling racism, and noted that from the beginning black social scientists took the stand that the American dogma of race inequality was a scientific falsehood. See Gunnar Myrdal, *An American Dilemma: The Negro Problem and Modern Democracy*, 2 vols. (New York, repr. 1972), 1:93. Myrdal's emphasis on the liberating effects of the social sciences reflects the time in which he was writing (the late 1930s and 1940s); he could not foresee how many of the stereotypes of race would be reformulated, following the collapse of the older biological discourse of racism, in the new language of sociology, cultural and social anthropology, and developmental political science.

48. Delany, *Principia of Ethnology*, p. 23, Delany's italics.

49. See Thomas E. Skidmore, *Black into White: Race and Nationality in Brazilian Thought* (New York, 1974), p. 183.

50. See Nancy Stepan, *Beginnings of Brazilian Science: Oswaldo Cruz, Medical Research, and Policy, 1880-1920* (New York, 1976), pp. 57–58.

51. C. V. Roman, *American Civilization and the Negro* (Philadelphia, 1916), p. 149. Jean Finot, a naturalized Frenchman of Polish birth, wrote two of the more remarkable anti-racist and antisexist books of the late nineteenth and early twentieth centuries: *Race Prejudice*, trans. Florence Wade-Evans (Miami, 1969, rpr. of Eng. ed. of 1906), and *Problems of the Sexes*, trans. Mary J. Safford (New York, 1913).

52. This difficulty remains within the field of sex differences. Usually the argument about sex or gender difference is couched in terms of "the actual facts of difference," whether the issue is brain anatomy or function, hormonal or reproductive differences, or differences in psychic or mental operations. What is rarely broached within science is why apparently small differences between the sexes (often so small they remain disputed matters to this day) are nevertheless seen as neutral *answers* to complex problems of modern social life.

53. For example, Marxists treated science as an unproblematical and highly desirable feature of modern society. The most important exceptions to the relative dearth of strong criticism of the political agendas of science were the socialist scientists, who maintained that science was part of a complex political and social system.

54. Challenges to scientific racism rarely came from within mainstream science, or from those individuals whose own status was most closely tied to science. Resistance came from the marginalized and works critical of biological determinism were rarely accepted by well-known publishers of scientific books; critics rarely held chairs of science in universities; and works of criticism were rarely reviewed seriously except by the stereotyped. On Du Bois, see Blackwell and Janowitz, *Black Sociologists*, pp. 50–52.

55. Myrdal, *American Dilemma*, 1:96.

PART THREE

Who Gets to Do Science?

[T]he establishment of democracy on the American continent was scarcely as radical a break with the past as was the necessity, which Americans faced, of broadening this concept to include black men. . . . [T]he Negro in America . . . is not a visitor to the West, but a citizen there, an American; as American as the Americans who despise him, the Americans who fear him, the Americans who love him—the Americans who became less than themselves, or rose to be greater than themselves by virtue of the fact that the challenge he represented was inescapable.

> James Baldwin, "Stranger in the Village," in
> *Notes of a Native Son*

My way of discovering sciences goes far to level men's wits, and leaves but little to individual excellence; because it performs everything by surest rules and demonstrations.

> Sir Francis Bacon

Whatever we do, we always look to the West and see what they are doing. Suppose I want a new subject, I go on looking through new journals to find out what are the new lines coming up. I suddenly see surface physics coming up and start working on it. . . . We draw up projects by looking through papers in *Physical Review, Journal of Physics* etc. to find out what types of things are being done because if you don't do that, you don't get a job here. You have to publish in these journals, so you must do something which they are doing.

> From interviews with two physicists in V. Shiva and
> J. Bandyopadhyaya, *Science in India*

Science is supposed to be the most universal of all human products. It is supposed to make no difference whether a scientist is Japanese or British, white or black, male or female, of working class or wealthy origins. Scientific method is supposed to be powerful enough to eliminate from the results of research any social biases that may have crept into scientific work because of the obvious social values and interests that we all have as members of historical communities. This is fundamentally Bacon's image of scientific method as a kind of mechanism that can function without intellectual brilliance and regardless of the social peculiarities of the individual scientist. Consequently, one might think that science would be more welcoming to minorities (and women) than other professions that do not so emphasize the universality of their methods.

Of course, in racially stratified societies such as the United States, most African Americans, Native Americans, and other peoples of color have not had access to the scarce resources—educational, economic, social—that would enable them even to imagine having a career in the sciences. When they have tried to enter science, white men have often responded with what appears to be paranoia, as in the example from Harvard Medical School in the nineteenth century reported by historian Ronald Takaki in the first essay in this section. Nevertheless, more African Americans than most European Americans imagine have gained access to at least some of those resources. Beginning in 1980, a few biographical accounts of African American scientists have revealed the triumphs and difficulties of racially marked individuals who enter Western sciences and medicine. Excerpts from several are included here. Unfortunately, accounts by racial minorities other than African Americans of their hoped-for or actual careers in U.S. science are hard to come by.

Ernest Everett Just, the African American embryologist, gained a national and international reputation in the 1930s for his contributions to the study of marine organisms. However, he could never get the kind of appointment at a top research university that went to equally (and less) accomplished European Americans. As a result, he did not have access to well-equipped laboratories, the possibility of training and gaining assistance from graduate students, or the foundation support that was necessary for maintaining a research career. Nor could he then become a teacher and patron for another generation of scientists—either white or black—who would carry on his work. The story of the vicious circle of individual, university, and foundation racism and of his superhuman efforts to fulfill his powerful sense of obligation to his students, the Howard University administration, the white scientists and foundations that did support him, his family and "his people" is told in the selection from his biography by Kenneth R. Manning.

Darlene Clark Hine debunks the assumption that only since the civil rights movement of the 1960s have African American women begun to gain advanced degrees in the sciences. "In the quarter century after the demise of slavery and during the height of racial segregation and discrimination, 115 black women had become physicians in the United States," gaining advanced degrees from the same institutions as did their European American sisters and their African American brothers. She tells the story of their social origins, their struggles against discrimination, how they founded an important array of health care institutions for African Americans, and how they combined family life with their professional and community activities.

Unfortunately, the patterns of racist discrimination in science fields have by no means disappeared. Even in the last two decades, when it has been illegal to discriminate against women and people of color in many of the ways experienced by the Harvard Medical School students, Just, and the first African American women physicians, many forms of subtle and not so subtle discrimination succeed in keeping to a minuscule number the African Americans—and especially the African American women—who receive advanced science degrees. In Aimee Sands's interview, historian of science Evelynn Hammonds reports on her experiences as a physics student at Spelman College, Georgia Tech, and MIT. Shirley Malcom, who heads the Directorate for Education and Human Resources of the American Association for the Advancement of Science, writes about strategies to meet the special needs of minority women in science and engineering. How effective will Malcom's proposed strategies be in breaking down the kinds of barriers reported by Manning, Hine and Hammonds? Recently, the changing demography of the United States has forced science institutions and the U.S. government to consider the possibility that racial minorities and women will have to be recruited and trained as scientific workers in far greater numbers unless the scientific work force is to shrink drastically in the years ahead. Eileen M. O'Brien's account of the 1987 final report of the U.S. government Task Force on Women, Minorities, and the Handicapped in Science and Technology reveals the magnitude of this problem and the heroic efforts that will be required to resolve it. How effective will the task force's proposals be?

Western science is now international in its scope. Eurocentric assumptions and institutions keep non-Western science institutions, work forces, and practices dependent upon dominant groups in the North Atlantic. Susantha Goonatilake, a Sri Lankan engineer turned political economist, here shows how Asian scientists are kept dependent on the concerns and institutions of North Atlantic scientists and thus scientific creativity in the Third World is stifled.[1] Indigenous scientific traditions still are practiced in these areas, however, and their creativity sharply contrasts with the unoriginal and mundane science that Western-trained scientists must do. Goonatilake's essay challenges the reader to ask who are the creative scientists under these conditions and how does this situation illuminate our understanding of the evident fact that social conditions are a cause of "good science" and, consequently, of better descriptions and explanations of nature.

Reflecting on the earlier accounts, one can say that in failing to notice or to question the racism (and imperialism) of the social structure of the sciences locally or internationally, the vast majority of historians, sociologists, and philosophers of science and technology mimic racist social analyses in other fields. Their refusal to treat racial stratification as a social matter—not a matter of individual prejudice but of social meanings and social structure—leaves them producing a view of the sociology, history, and philosophy of the sciences that dos not differ significantly from the one an overt biological determinist would produce: they either overtly treat race as biological or implicitly do so when they write as if it were beyond the borders of their concern with science as a social enterprise.

Are the sciences *alone* responsible for the discrimination and discouragement minorities have experienced there? Of course not. It would be absurd to expect the social structure of science to be far more democratic than that of the larger society, even though the sciences persistently claim to have special talents for resisting antidemocratic forces whenever they seek funding or other forms of public resources. The issue, instead, is a different one: what keeps the sciences so resistant to democratizing tendencies? How should this resistance be understood in light of the way the sciences stake their integrity on the power of scientific method to eliminate social biases?

Several of these analyses, as well as ones in earlier sections of this book, make clear that not only are different economic and social resources made available to different races; they are always also portioned out by gender within any race or class. This is one clue to the fact that in societies stratified by gender, race, and class, each is used to construct the others. Gender, race, and class are not parallel and independent social phenomena but interweaving and mutually constructing ones.

It cannot be emphasized enough that it is not primarily those who have been denied access to the sciences who need to be changed in order to achieve racial balance in the sciences. The causes of that exclusion are to be found in the institutional racism of U.S. society and its sciences and in the narrow and ignorance-producing nature of what are regarded as the very best science educations. It is not only those excluded from the best science educations who exhibit "scientific illiteracy."[2]

We need more non-Western peoples involved in the direction of sciences in the West to assist in eliminating Eurocentrism. Those who are the victims of scientific racism are often far more sensitive to subtle forms of racist belief than are those who have less at stake. They are more stimulated to exercise their critical imaginations, to generate new ways of thinking. Of course whites can recognize racist errors, as so many of the essays in this collection demonstrate. But if the goal of the sciences is to maximize access to truths—or, at least, to gain less partial and distorted beliefs—then a diverse body of scientists is important in fields where different groups have different things at stake. Affirmative action in the direction of science is a scientific and epistemological issue.[3] However, as Goonatilake made clear, sciences in the West are not the only ones that need transformation.

N O T E S

1. But see Marcos Cueto, "Andean Biology in Peru: Scientific Styles on the Periphery," *Isis* 80 (1989), 640–58 for an account of original research "that was both locally important and significant to specialists working at the international level on the frontier of knowledge" (658). Anne Fausto-Sterling brought this account to my attention.

2. This point is discussed in the introduction to this collection.

3. I thank Anthony Appiah for this way of putting the point.

AESCULAPIUS WAS A WHITE MAN
Race and the Cult of True Womanhood

Ronald T. Takaki

During his travels in America, Tocqueville observed how blacks were degraded and assigned animal or brutish qualities, and how white women were elevated and praised for their morality. While blacks were segregated and enslaved, white women were placed within a narrow circle of domestic life and in a condition of dependency. Had Tocqueville reflected more deeply on these two developments, he would have noticed how the subordination of blacks in the ideology of the black "child/savage" and the confinement of white women in the cult of "true womanhood" were interdependent, and how both of them interacted dynamically in a process of mutual reinforcement. During the age of Jackson, America became more virulently than ever before a "white man's country" as institutional and ideological patterns of white over black and male over female were strengthened.

Recently, due to the social ferment of our times, scholars have begun to give unprecedented attention to the racial and sexual patterns that Tocqueville noted. But one of the effects of these studies has been evasive: They have tended to focus on the outgroups rather than those responsible for the plight of the oppressed. While studies by scholars like C. Wright Mills and G. William Domhoff have demonstrated that power in America has been almost exclusively a monopoly of white men, they have neither analyzed the relationship of the oppressions of different outgroups nor explored adequately the motivations of white men in power in America. While studies by historians like Eugene Genovese and Eleanor Flexnor have advanced our understanding of the subordination of blacks and women respectively, they have tended to analyze the two groups separately. Such a fragmented approach has precluded a comparative analysis of the stereotypes applied to blacks and women, and fails to recognize how the oppression of different groups served common needs of white men. Thus a fascinating and disturbing question still remains largely unanswered: Why have white men historically relegated people unlike themselves to specially defined "places"? This relationship between racial and sexual domination has been apparent at times. One such moment occurred in 1850 at Harvard Medical School where Oliver

Wendell Holmes was dean and where faculty were seeking to professionalize medicine.[1]

Traditionally Harvard Medical School had been an institution for white men only. But in November 1850, the faculty admitted three black men—Martin Delany, Daniel Laing, and Isaac Snowden—and a white woman—Harriot K. Hunt. Actually the admissions were hardly expressions of enlightened views on race and sex. The faculty understood that the black students would emigrate and practice medicine in Africa after graduation. Their application for admission probably would have been denied had they wished to remain in America. The conditionality of their admission was suggested in the correspondence between Dean Holmes and Dr. H. H. Childs of the Pittsfield Medical School. Asked for advice on the admission of black students, Dr. Childs told Dean Holmes that he was willing to train blacks sponsored by the American Colonization Society. "We have had applications," he added, "to educate colored students to practice medicine in this country which have been uniformly refused." Hunt's admission was also conditional: Allowed to attend lectures, she would not be permitted to take the examination for the degree.[2]

The admission of the four students provoked a storm of protest. At a meeting held on December 10, Harvard medical students demanded the dismissal of the blacks and Hunt. The faculty quickly capitulated. "Leading members of the faculty" met privately with Hunt and persuaded her to withdraw her application. Meeting at the home of Dean Holmes, the faculty deemed it "inexpedient" to allow blacks to attend medical lectures. The professors argued that their commitment to teaching and academic excellence required the exclusion of blacks from the school. The "intermixing of the white and black races in the lecture rooms," they pointed out, was "distasteful to a large portion of the class, & injurious to the interests of the school." The presence of blacks was a "source of irritation and distraction" and interfered with "the success of their teaching."[3]

In the judgment of these worried Harvard students and professors, the honorable calling of Aesculapius, the ancient physician consecrated to holy mysteries, should be reserved for white men only. The exclusion of blacks and white women from Harvard Medical School helped students as well as faculty identify themselves as white and male.[4] What is important here is the way in which Harvard white men defined Delany and Hunt as people unlike themselves—how they imaged those who should not be admitted to one of the foremost educational institutions in America. Their images of blacks and white women not only told them who they were but also what kind of society America was and should be.

In their protest, Harvard students denounced blacks as intellectual inferiors. Here they were reflecting notions of black inferiority in intelligence which were ubiquitous in mid-nineteenth century American society and which their own professors promoted. Dr. Morton's *Crania Americana,* which contained the Philadelphia physician's findings on the differential cranial capacities of whites and blacks, was in the private libraries of Harvard medical professors. Dean Holmes had such a high regard for the writings of Dr. Morton that he considered Morton's research "permanent data for all future students of Ethnology. . . . "[5] Thus, for Harvard students, black men might have had strong bodies, but mind or intelligence was a monopoly of the white race, especially the males of that race.

The presence of Delany and the other black students in the lecture room was a disturbing contradiction to the belief in white intellectual superiority. Delany, as the letters of recommendation from his private instructors Dr. Joseph Gazzam and Dr. Julius Le Moyne indicated, had shown impressive competence in the study of medicine. As editor of the *Pittsburgh Mystery* and then as coeditor of the *Rochester North Star* during the 1840s, Delany had attacked segregated education in his struggle to topple oppressive notions of white over black. But Harvard students could not or did not want to admit that black men like Delany could compete with them intellectually. To have done so would have been disastrous for their own self-image. Instead they complained that the admission of blacks would lower academic standards. "For the reputation of the school," they argued, " . . . it is to be hoped that the professors will not graduate their instructions according to their estimation of the intellectual abilities of the negro race; at least, not until the number of blacks preponderate!" And the protesters anxiously warned that the admission of blacks was "but the beginning of an Evil, which, if not checked will increase, and that the number of *white* students will, in future, be in inverse ratio, to that of *blacks*." The angry students also claimed the admission of blacks jeopardized caste lines in society, and refused "to be identified as fellow-students, with blacks, whose company we would not keep in the streets, and whose society as associates we would not tolerate in our houses."[6] In their demand for the exclusion of blacks and in their defense of academic standards, Harvard men were reinforcing the caste lines of northern Jacksonian society and reaffirming their claims to membership in a race of superior intelligence.

Significantly Harvard men viewed intelligence as a matter of sex as well as race. For them, mind was masculine. This belief was an important underpinning of the ethos of American white male society. Early nineteenth-century white male claims of female intellectual inferiority often bore a curious resemblance to the racist theory of Dr. Morton: It was "almost universally believed that a woman's brain was smaller in capacity and therefore inferior in quality to that of a man." In his book *Females and Their Diseases* (1848), Dr. Charles Meigs noted that a woman had "a head almost too small for intellect but just big enough for love." But the idea of masculine intelligence required vigilant defense in an age when women like Margaret Fuller were demanding greater educational opportunities and threatening to prove to white male America that women were intellectually equal, even superior, to men. The relationship between Fuller and Holmes has some relevance to our analysis here. Arrogantly brilliant, Fuller had made Holmes feel uncomfortable. As a boy, Oliver had tried to compete with "smart" Margaret in school. "Some themes were brought home from the school for examination by my father," he recalled, "among them one of hers. I took it up with a certain emulous interest . . . and read the first words. 'It is a trite remark,' she began. I stopped. Alas! I did not know what *trite* meant. How could I ever judge Margaret fully after such a crushing discovery of her superiority?"[7]

Like Margaret Fuller, Harriot Hunt threatened masculine white America.

Deeply involved in the women's rights movement, Hunt complained that the American Revolution had given freedom to the "white man only," and called for "another revolution" to realize "freedom for all." Already a practicing physician (defiantly "undegreed") in Boston for more than twelve years, she was refusing to be what men like Holmes thought women should be—nurses rather than doctors. Hunt's admission to the medical school distressed Harvard men because she was repudiating their images of women as "modest" and "delicate" beings. She was "unsexing" herself. She was impudently violating their cherished dichotomy between the world of men and that of women. She was revolting against the confining role men had assigned to her, and insisting that "mind was not sexual." In her letter requesting admission, she bluntly challenged: "Shall mind or sex, be recognized in admission to medical lectures?"[8] Obviously she threatened what white men at Harvard thought was their "self-respect" and "dignity."

The Harvard student protest against Hunt's admission reflected some of the significant developments in male-female relationships which occurred during the Market Revolution. The tremendous economic changes of this era transformed patterns of work and relations between the two sexes. In an agrarian society, work was to a large extent nonsexual: It belonged to both men and women. The factory system and urbanization, however, tended to undermine this pattern. Women were employed in factories, but at this time, at least, on a temporary basis, their employment taking place during a brief period before marriage. Increasingly industrial and urban work became largely male, and men's work was located away from home. As the *Monthly Religious Magazine* observed in 1860, the need for business and professional men to travel long distances to their places of "duty," produced "little short of an absolute separation from their families."[9]

As middle-class men were separated from home and family, they increasingly worshipped the "cult of true womanhood." No doubt for ages men had been claiming that woman's place was in the home, but during the 1840s and 1850s, this claim became a cult. In books, magazines, speeches, and sermons, men sang praises to woman and her sacred place—the home. Women were told to be "feminine," "domestic," "modest," and "delicate"; they were exalted as moral guardians of the hearth and radiant sources of purity in a moneymaking and enterprising society.[10] Given a "lofty" place, white women were confined to the home, segregated from the marketplace and from the professions, including medicine.

The relationship between Dr. Holmes and his wife, Amelia, illustrates this "cult of true womanhood." One of Mr. Holmes's biographers described Mrs. Holmes as the "kindest, gentlest, and tenderest of women," "a *helpmate* the most useful, whose abilities seemed to have been arranged by happy foresight for the express purpose of supplying *his* wants." Mrs. Holmes "took care of him and gave him every day the fullest and freest chance to be always at his best, always able to do his work amid cheerful surroundings. She contributed immensely to *his* success. . . . She eschewed the idea of having wit or literary and critical capacities. . . . " Indeed, Mrs. Holmes was "an ideal wife." She was what

Mr. Holmes wanted a wife to be. In a letter to Harriet Beecher Stowe (whose prolificness as a writer made Holmes feel "ashamed") written long after the admissions controversy, Mr. Holmes remarked: "Men are out-of-door and office animals; women are indoor creatures essentially. . . . "[11]

The dichotomy between the marketplace and the home which developed during the Market Revolution served an important psychological function for enterprising and career-oriented men: It enabled them to make raids into the anarchistic business world of men, then retreat into what they thought or wished to think was the calm and moral world of women. This need to dichotomize life was especially intense in a society where the pressure upon "a multitude of business and professional men" was "really frightful," and where Americans thought it was not "uncommon for the same man in the course of his life to rise and sink again through all the grades that lead from opulence to poverty."[12]

Harvard medical men had a particular reason for insisting on a separation between the office and the home. Research on cadavers, Professor John Ware warned in his introductory lecture in 1850, could make young men forget that "the object" before them was "anything but a mere subject of our art." Thus the pursuit of scientific knowledge could make them callous. A woman was particularly vulnerable in this regard. Convinced that the practice of medicine would be found unsuitable to woman's "physical, intellectual, and moral constitution," Professor Ware declared that it was "difficult to conceive that she should go through all that we have to encounter in the various departments of the study of medicine, without tarnishing that *delicate* surface of the female mind, which can hardly be imagined even to reflect what is gross without somewhat defilement."[13]

But men, too, were susceptible to this danger. Thus white men of enterprise needed white women to be moral and delicate custodians of the home, which became a counterpoint to the market and a safety valve for its pressures. Leading and respected ministers, like the Reverend Horace Bushnell, advised women to stay in the home: "Let us have a place of quiet, and some quiet minds which the din of our public war never embroils. Let a little of the sweetness and purity, and, if we can have it, of simple religion of life remain. God made woman to be a help for man, not to be a wrestler with him." In his novel, *Elsie Venner,* published nine years after the admissions controversy, Dr. Holmes also located the woman's place in the home for similar reasons. He noted how the education of the community to "beauty" flowed mainly through its women, and how female educational institutions served an important function in the inculcation of "higher tastes" among them. Surrounded by "practical and every-day working youth," women had a particular responsibility for the preservation of culture. "Our young men come into active life so early," Holmes warned, "that, if our girls were not educated to something beyond mere practical duties, our material prosperity would outstrip our culture; as it often does in large places where money is made too rapidly."[14] Thus, in a market society, the home was to be the domain of "true women," the sanctuary of "sweetness," "purity," and "beauty," where busy and weary businessmen could rest from the pressurized labor of the office and where insensitive doctors could restore their humanity away from the "defiling" laboratories.

The racial and sexual divisions which prevailed in Jacksonian society and which surfaced at Harvard Medical School in 1850 were dialectically involved in a powerful cultural and psychological process. A clue to the understanding of this process may be found in a letter published in the *Boston Journal* during the admissions controversy. This letter, signed "Common Sense," attempted to justify the exclusion of the blacks and the white woman from Harvard Medical School. The presence of the three black men in the lecture room, he explained, "occasioned a good deal of feeling in the school . . . and, anon, the report was circulated that a *woman* had taken tickets for the lectures! The pent up indignation now broke forth, and two series of resolutions were passed, remonstrating against this *amalgamation of sexes and races*."[15] Thus the admission of nonmale and nonwhite students meant not only the "unsexing" of women (and implicitly also of men), but also the mixing of white women and black men.

Such "amalgamation" also constituted a symbolic mixing of the "savagery" and "culture" which blacks and white women respectively represented in the minds of white men. Like the old black servant Sophy in Holmes's *Elsie Venner,* blacks were viewed as "cannibals," "terrible wild savages," or their descendants, while white women represented the force of culture; they were preservers of all that was "beautiful" in society. Living in the highly competitive and constantly changing conditions of the Market Revolution, white men like the students of Harvard felt compelled to bifurcate society on the basis of race and sex. The image of the black "child/savage" and the image of the "true woman" served as reference points for these nervous white men. Together, racial and sexual imagery enabled them to delineate their own white male identity—to affirm, through the degradation of blacks, the virtues of self-control and industry, and to protect, through the elevation of white women, the culture and beauty which white men feared were in danger in a society where blacks were present and where science and the rapid making of money could "defile" white men themselves.[16]

Thus, in the eyes of uneasy Harvard students, Delany and his black colleagues and Hunt threatened the social and cultural divisions which supported white male supremacy, and had to be excluded from the temples of knowledge and power. This need to separate themselves from black men and white women, however, did not preclude the possibility or even the desire for integration, if integration could be achieved on a hierarchical basis—white over black, male over female. White Harvard students were upset because Delany and Hunt had been permitted to attend lectures as fellow students. They would not have objected to the presence of black janitors or female nurses. Frederick Douglass, an astute analyst of the white male psychology, painfully understood the reality of this hierarchical integration. "While we are servants," he explained, "we are never offensive to the whites. . . . On the very day we were brutally assaulted in New York for riding down Broadway in company with ladies, we saw several white ladies riding with *black servants*."[17] This kind of hierarchical integration, involving physical proximity but in a definite superior-inferior relationship, helped to reinforce the identity of white men.

But more than white male identity was at stake in the Harvard Medical School admissions controversy. The exclusion of Delany and Hunt was related to the professionalization of medicine in America. During the 1840s, medicine in this country became increasingly professionalized: The American Medical Association was founded in 1847 and medical schools emphasized the importance of formal training and degrees. One of the leaders of this effort, Dr. Holmes called for greater recognition for scholarly and professionally trained doctors, and denounced the "self-taught genius" and the "fancy practitioner." While this professionalization indicated a desire to provide scientific, skilled, and responsible medical services, it developed from a concern for the intense competition which existed in the medical business. Doctors thought their numbers were already excessive; in 1848, a committee of the American Medical Association reported that the ratio of physicians to the population in the United States was five times as high as in France. Two years later, in his introductory lecture, Professor Ware told Harvard medical students that the medical field was "always filled by eager and aspiring competitors," and that young men were anxious about their chances for "success"—a "large practice" and "large income." Resentful toward competition from "ignorant novices," the graduates of *"inferior medical schools,"* Harvard medical men feared black admissions would "lessen" the "value" of their diplomas. Thrust into the nervous struggle for "success," they were also apprehensive about competition from women, especially in the areas of gynecology and obstetrics, where women had traditionally provided services as midwives. After Hunt had been forced to withdraw from Harvard, she bitterly remarked: "If we could follow those young men [Harvard medical students] into life, and see them subjecting woman to examinations *too often unnecessary*—could we penetrate their secret feelings, should we not find in some, that female practitioners *are needed* . . . ?"[18]

Professionalized, medicine in America would become the monopoly of university-trained white men: It would maintain the exclusion of blacks and remove the competition of white women from medical practice. Given the responsibility and power to train and credential a professional elite, universities would institutionalize the reproduction of a stratified class structure in American society based on both race and sex. But what Harvard students and professors did not fully realize was how the professionalization of medicine was part of the development of a "culture of professionalism,"[19] and how the hegemony of experts based on their exclusive control of specialized knowledge was penetrating all the professions in America. Neither did they foresee how professional elites would become integrated into bureaucratic corporate structures and their needs in a technological society, or how their republican "iron cages" which demanded strenuous competitive activity and the domination of the black "child/savage" and the "true woman" would give way to the corporate "iron cage" in America.

N O T E S

1. Alexis de Tocqueville, *Democracy in America*, 2 vols. (New York, 1945), originally published in 1835), vol. 2, pp. 225, 209. See also Burton J. Bledstein, *The Culture of Professionalism: The Middle Class and the Development of Higher Education in America* (New York, 1976).

2. Childs to Holmes, December 12, 1850, Martin Delany file, Countway Library, Harvard Medical School; Records of the Medical Faculty of Harvard University, vol. 2, Minutes for November 4, 23, 1850, Countway Library.

3. Records of the Medical Faculty, vol. 2, Minutes for December 26, 1850, Countway Library; drafts of letters of the Massachusetts Colonization Society and to Abraham R. Thompson, Countway Library; letter signed "E. D. L.," published in the *Boston Evening Transcript,* January 1, 1851; Records of the Medical Faculty, vol. 2, Minutes for December 13, 1850, Countway Library.

4. Kai Erikson, *Wayward Puritans: A Study in the Sociology of Deviance* (New York, 1966), p. 64. See also Winthrop D. Jordan, *White over Black: American Attitudes toward the Negro, 1550–1812* (Chapel Hill, N.C., 1968).

5. Holmes to Morton, November 27, 1849, quoted in Thomas F. Gossett, *Race: The History of an Idea in America* (Dallas, Tex., 1963), p. 59. For an informative study of science and race, see William Stanton, *The Leopard's Spots: Scientific Attitudes toward Race in America, 1815–1859* (Chicago, 1960).

6. See Delany, *North Star,* April 28, 1848, and March 30, 1849; student petition, December 10, 1850: letter signed "Common Sense," published in the *Boston Journal,* clipping in Delany file, Countway Library. There was a student counterpetition favoring admission of the blacks, but even there students admitted that "their prejudices would perhaps lead them to wish that no occasion had occurred for the agitation of this question" (student petition, December 11, 1850, Countway Library).

7. Quote on size of woman's brain, in Eleanor Flexnor, *Century of Struggle: The Women's Rights Movement in the United States* (New York, 1968), p. 23; Dr. Charles Meigs, quoted in Richard H. Shryock, *Medicine and Society in America, 1660–1860* (New York, 1960), p. 121; Holmes, *Pages from an Old Volume of Life* (Cambridge, Mass., 1892), pp. 243–44.

8. Harriot K. Hunk, *Glances and Glimpses* (Boston, 1856), pp. 217, 263–64; letter from Hunt to the Harvard Medical Faculty, November 12, 1850, reprinted in *Boston Evening Transcript,* January 7, 1851. See also student resolutions, in letter signaled "Scapel," published in *Boston Evening Transcript,* January 3, 1851; Hunt to Elizabeth Cady Stanton, June 30, 1852, Stanton Papers, Library of Congress, Washington, D.C., and "Protest of Harriot K. Hunt, M.D.," in *Frederick Douglass's Paper,* November 25, 1853.

9. *Monthly Religious Magazine* (1860), quoted in William E. Bridges, "Family Patterns and Social Values in America, 1825–1875," *American Quarterly,* vol. 17 (Spring 1965), p. 8. See also Carl N. Degler, "Revolution without Ideology: The Changing Place of Women in America," in R. J. Lifton, ed., *The Woman in America* (Boston, 1967), p. 194.

10. See the well-documented study by Barbara Welter, "The Cult of True Womanhood, 1820–1860," *American Quarterly,* vol. 18 (Summer 1966), pp. 151–74. See also Lawrence Friedman, *Inventors of the Promised Land* (New York, 1976), part two, "Woman's Role in the Promised Land," for a sophisticated study of the subtle and complex roles assigned to the "true woman." The subject has recently been given a full-scale treatment in Ann Douglas, *The Feminization of American Culture* (New York, 1977).

11. John T. Morse, Jr., *Life and Letters of Oliver Wendell Holmes,* 2 vols. (Boston, 1896), vol. 1, pp. 170–71 (italics added); Holmes to Harriet Beecher Stowe, March 31, 1872, in Morse, *Life and Letters,* vol. 2, pp. 233–34.

12. *Monthly Religious Magazine,* in Bridges, "Family Patterns," p. 8; Tocqueville, *Democracy in America,* vol. 2, p. 213.

13. John Ware, *Success in the Medical Profession: An Introductory Lecture delivered at the Massachusetts Medical College, November 6, 1850* (Boston, 1851), pp. 24–25 (italics added).

14. Horace Bushnell, "American Politics," *The American National Preacher* (1840), quoted in Ronald W. Hogeland, "Horace Bushnell's Concept of the American Woman: A Case Study in Masculine Ambivalence," paper read at the American Historical Association Meeting, December 1969; Holmes, *Elsie Venner—A Romance of Destiny* (Boston, 1888, originally published in 1859), p. 172.

15. "Common Sense," *Boston Journal,* clipping in Delany file, Countway Library.

16. Holmes, *Elsie Venner,* p. 240.

17. Douglass, *North Star,* June 13, 1850.

18. Holmes, *The Benefactors of the Medical School of Harvard University* (Boston, 1850), p. 10: Ware, *Success in the Medical Profession,* pp. 3–4; Hunt, *Glances and Glimpses,* p. 271. See also Shryock, *Medicine and Society in America,* p. 147; Holmes, *An Introductory Lecture delivered at the Massachusetts Medical College, November 3, 1847* (Boston, 1847), pp. 8–9. On the rise of male domination in the field of gynecology, see Graham John Barker-Benfield, *The Horrors of the Half-Known Life: Male Attitudes toward Women and Sexuality in Nineteenth-Century America* (New York, 1976). On the question of examination of women by male doctors, see Holmes's comment, in Holmes, *The Position and Prospects of the Medical Student* (Boston, 1844), pp. 20–21.

19. See Bledstein, *Culture of Professionalism.* The induction of professionalism, particularly the scientific and technical fields into the service of corporations, is studied in David F. Noble, *America by Design: Science, Technology, and the Rise of Corporate Capitalism* (New York, 1977).

CO-LABORERS IN THE WORK OF THE LORD
Nineteenth-Century Black Women Physicians

Darlene Clark Hine

The Afro-American woman physician of the late nineteenth and early twentieth centuries remains an enigma. Today only scattered bits and pieces of evidence—an occasional biographical sketch, a random name in an old medical school catalogue—attest to the existence of this first generation of black women doctors. In spite of this negligible evidence, we know that in the quarter century after the demise of slavery and during the height of racial segregation and discrimination, 115 black women had become physicians in the United States.[1]

An examination of their lives and experiences will illuminate the conditions in and the transformations of the American medical profession in the last half of the nineteenth and the first quarter of the twentieth century. If white women, black men, and poor whites, as many scholars argue, were outsiders in medicine, then black women, belonging as they did to two subordinate groups, surely inhabited the most distant perimeters of the profession.[2] Yet it is precisely because of this dual—sexual and racial—marginality that any examination of their lives and careers bears the possibility of shedding new light on many conventional interpretations in American medical history.

To be sure, the history of black women physicians is one worthy of study in its own right. From an analysis of factors ranging from family background, to medical education, to medical practice, to social status, to marriage, to Victorian sex role definitions, a portrait of one of the earliest and most significant groups of black professional women emerges. Finally, insights gleaned from looking at the early black women doctors will further the reconstruction of a more inclusive and, perhaps, more accurate picture of the opportunities and restrictions that all women and black male physicians encountered in pursuit of medical careers.

In 1864, one year before the Civil War ended and fifteen years after Elizabeth

The author wishes to thank Professor William C. Hine of South Carolina State College for his thoughtful and helpful comments on this essay. A special word of thanks is owed to Ms. Cynthia Fitz Simmons for her research and typing assistance and to Ms. Ruth Abram and Ms. Margaret Jerrido, for their encouragement and support.

Blackwell became the first American woman medical graduate, the first black woman graduate, Rebecca Lee, received an M.D. degree from the New England Female Medical College in Boston. Three years later, one year before the ratification of the Fourteenth Amendment to the United States Constitution, the second black American woman physician, Rebecca J. Cole (1846–1922), was graduated from the Woman's Medical College of Pennsylvania. They were followed by Susan Smith McKinney Steward (1848–1919), who completed her studies at New York Medical College for Women in 1870.[3] Lee, Cole, and Steward signaled the emergence of black women in the medical profession.

During this era, white women, like blacks in general, challenged traditional subservient roles and demanded improved educational opportunities and greater individual autonomy. Medical school matriculation statistics reflect the efforts and desires of many middle-class white and black women to expand restrictive private spheres to encompass areas outside of the home. The late nineteenth century witnessed a dramatic increase of women doctors in America. Their numbers rose from a mere 200 or fewer in 1860 to 2,423 in 1880 and to more than 7,000 by 1900. During this period nineteen medical schools for women were founded, although by 1895 eleven had disbanded.[4] By the 1920s the United States Census listed only 65 black women as actually practicing physicians. Not surprisingly, black male physicians far outnumbered their female counterparts. In 1890 there were 909 black physicians; by 1920 the number had jumped to 3,885.[5]

The increase in the numbers of black physicians was due largely to the existence of several medical schools founded for blacks in the post-Reconstruction South. At one time seven such institutions flourished. Four of the seven schools were considered by black and white observers to be adequate. According to one contemporary black male physician, M. Vandehurst Lynk, the big four—Howard University School of Medicine in Washington, D.C.; Meharry Medical School in Nashville, Tennessee; Leonard Medical School of Shaw University in Raleigh, North Carolina; and Flint Medical College (originally known as the Medical Department of New Orleans University) in New Orleans, Louisiana—labored to keep up with quickly evolving medical standards. They "not only extended the instruction over four years, but have increased the number of subjects to be taught and have better equipped facilities," Lynk wrote in 1893.[6] By 1914, however, of the approved medical schools only Howard and Meharry remained open. These two institutions played the most significant role in the education of black women physicians.

The Howard University Medical School, chartered in 1868 and supported by the United States government as an institution to train blacks for the medical profession, actually had more white students than black during the early years. The founders of the Howard Medical School had all been officers in the Union Army, including Dr. Alexander T. Augusta, the only black on the original faculty. The first woman faculty member was Isabel C. Barrows, who was graduated from the Woman's Medical College in New York City and who studied ophthalmology in Vienna. She lectured on this subject at Howard in 1872 and 1873.[7]

Dr. Susan Smith McKinney Steward, 1848–1919 (1890s). Brooklyn
Historical Society.

By 1900 Howard University had graduated 552 physicians, 35 of whom, or 5 percent of the total, were women. Only 25 of the 35 women, however, were black. The first 2 women to be graduated from the medical school, Mary D. Spackman (1872) and Mary A. Parsons (1874), were white.[8]

Howard's gender-blind policy sparked outright hostility and retaliation from some medical colleges. In 1873, the school's Medical Alumni Association denounced discrimination against women "as being unmanly and unworthy of the [medical] profession," and declared, "we accord to all persons the same rights and immunities that we demand for ourselves."[9] Four years later, however, the Association of American Medical Colleges, spurred by objections of the Jefferson Medical College of Philadelphia faculty, refused to seat the Howard delegation at its annual convention, in part because the Howard Medical School permitted men and women to be taught in the same classes.[10]

Meharry Medical College in Nashville, Tennessee, actually graduated the largest number of black women physicians (thirty-nine by 1920). Beginning in 1876 as the medical department of Central Tennessee College, Meharry was the first medical school in the South to provide for the education of black physicians. In light of the fact that the majority of blacks still resided in the eleven southern states of the old Confederacy, where racial segregation and exclusionism prevailed, Meharry's location made it the logical place for the majority of black women to pursue a medical education. In 1893, seventeen years after its opening, Meharry graduated its first black women physicians, Annie D. Gregg and Georgia Esther Lee Patton. Three black women had reached junior class status in 1882 but for reasons unknown they were never graduated.[11] Meharry had a penchant for hiring its own graduates. The first woman to teach at Meharry and the first to attain a position of leadership there was Josie E. Wells, a member of the class of 1904. Wells had received prior training as a nurse. Specializing in diseases of women and children, Wells gave freely of her time and resources. She dispensed free medicine and treatment to poor blacks in Nashville two afternoons a week. As superintendent of Hubbard Hospital, the teaching facility associated with Meharry, Wells executed her duties with skill. A black male colleague wrote of her, "She was really a remarkable woman, and under a more favorable environment might have risen to fame."[12]

By the turn of the century the Woman's Medical College of Pennsylvania, established in 1850 as the first regular medical school for females, had graduated approximately a dozen black women physicians. The Woman's Medical College blazed a new trail of providing medical training to women of every race, creed, and national origin. Indeed, all of the women's medical colleges, which in most instances were founded as temporary expediencies, enabled women to escape social ostracism, subtle discrimination, and overt hostility throughout their training in a male-dominated profession. Still, integration with male medical schools remained the guiding aspiration of most women in the medical profession. Unfortunately, the trend toward coeducation in the 1870s did not signal much change in the percentage of black female physicians. Only one or two ever attended the integrated coeducational institutions.[13]

Among the early black women graduates of the Woman's Medical College were Rebecca J. Cole (1867), Caroline Still Wiley Anderson (1878), Verina Morton Jones (1888), Halle Tanner Dillon Johnson (1891), Lucy Hughes Brown (1894), Alice Woodby McKane (1894), Matilda Arabella Evans (1897), and Eliza Anna Grier (1897). Of this group a large proportion became pioneers in establishing, simultaneously, a female and a black presence in the medical profession in several southern states. Three of the early black women graduates from the Woman's Medical College—Johnson, Jones, and Brown—became the first of their sex to practice medicine in Alabama, Mississippi, and South Carolina, respectively.[14] It is open to speculation whether the successes achieved by the Woman's Medical College's black graduates attest to a high quality of education or simply underscore the advantage of a more nurturing and supportive, sex-segregated environment, in which students learned from female faculty role models. Closer scrutiny suggests other factors, including family background, prior education, and social status, may have influenced their securing a medical education in the first place and subsequently their success.

That family background and prior education were important determinants of success in acquiring a medical education is reflected in the lives of a few of the early black women physicians, such as Caroline Still Wiley Anderson and Halle Tanner Dillon Johnson. The majority of the early black women physicians were the daughters of socially privileged or "representative" black families who, perhaps to protect them from menial labor or domestic servitude, encouraged their daughters to educate themselves. Of the few career options open to black women, teaching was the most accessible profession. Indeed, outside of the professions of teaching, medicine, and nursing, black women possessed scant opportunity for white- or pink-collar jobs as sales clerks, elevator operators, or typists. Ironically, they either entered the professions at the outset or remained mired in service occupations; there was little in between.[15]

Caroline Still Wiley Anderson (1848–1919) was the daughter of William and Letitia Still of Philadelphia. Her father had achieved widespread fame as a founder of the Underground Railroad and Vigilance Committee in antebellum Philadelphia and as the author of *The Underground Railroad,* which chronicled the means and patterns of escape for runaway slaves. Anderson received her primary and secondary education at Mrs. Henry Gordon's Private School, The Friends Raspberry Alley School, and the Institute for Colored Youth. She entered Oberlin College, in 1874, the only black woman in a class of forty-six. Upon graduation she married a black classmate; after his premature death she moved to Washington, D.C., where she taught music and gave instruction in drawing and elocution at Howard University. She completed one term at the Howard University Medical School before entering, in 1876, the Woman's Medical College in Philadelphia. In 1880 she married a prominent minister and educator, Matthew Anderson.[16]

Halle Tanner Dillon Johnson, born in 1864 in Pittsburgh, was also a member of an outstanding family. She was the daughter of Bishop B. T. Tanner of the African Methodist Episcopal Church in Philadelphia.[17] Sarah Logan Fraser, a

New York native, was the daughter of Bishop Logan of the Zion Methodist Episcopal Church. Like William Still, Bishop Logan had aided and harbored escaping slaves in his home, in Syracuse, New York.[18] Unlike Caroline Still Wiley Anderson and Halle Tanner Dillon Johnson, Fraser received her medical degree from the Medical School of Syracuse University. Another New Yorker, Susan Smith McKinney Steward, the seventh of ten children born to Sylvanus and Anne Springsteel Smith, was the daughter of a prosperous Brooklyn pork merchant. One of her sisters was married to the noted antislavery leader Reverend Henry Highland Garnett.[19] Among southern black women doctors, Sarah G. Boyd Jones is a good example of a daughter of a representative black family who enjoyed a highly successful medical career. Her father, George W. Boyd, was reputed to be the wealthiest black man in Richmond. A native of Albemarle County, Virginia, Sarah attended the Richmond Normal School before completing medical training in 1893 at Howard University Medical School. After graduation she returned to Richmond, where she became the first woman to pass the Virginia medical board examinations. She later founded the Richmond Hospital and Training School of Nurses, which in 1902 was renamed the Sarah G. Jones Memorial Hospital.[20]

To be sure, not all of the first generation of black women physicians belonged to illustrious and socially prominent families. They had, however, received the best undergraduate preparations then available to blacks. Some, such as Eliza Anna Grier, were former slaves who worked their way through college and medical school, occasionally receiving minimal financial assistance from parents and siblings.

It took Eliza Anna Grier seven years to work and study her way through Fisk University in Nashville, Tennessee. In 1890 she wrote to the Woman's Medical College concerning her financial straits, "I have no money and no source from which to get it only as I work for every dollar." She continued, "What I want to know from you is this. How much does it take to put one through a year in your school? Is there any possible chance to do any work that would not interfere with one's studies?" Grier apparently completed the medical program by working every other year, for it took her seven years to earn the degree. She was graduated in 1897.[21]

Even those black families who for various reasons could not afford to assist their daughters financially did, nevertheless, provide much-needed moral support and encouragement. May E. Chinn, who in 1892 became the first black woman graduate of the University of Bellevue Medical Center, noted the importance of her mother's support. Interviewed at the age of eighty-one, she recalled that her father, who had been a slave, opposed her even going to college, but her mother, who "scrubbed floors and hired out as a cook," became the driving force behind her educational effort.[22]

Black women who were fortunate enough to secure medical education in spite of limited access to and segregation and gender discrimination in the schools did so only to encounter additional obstacles. For most black women the establishment of a financially and professionally rewarding medical practice proved a most formidable challenge. Racial customs and negative attitudes to-

Dr. Eliza Grier, d. 1902 (1890s). Archives and Special Collections on
Women in Medicine, Medical College of Pennsylvania.

ward women dictated that black women physicians practice almost exclusively among blacks, and primarily with black women, for many of whom the payment of medical fees was a great hardship. Poverty usually was accompanied by superstition and fear. Consequently, the newly minted black woman doctor frequently had to expend considerable effort persuading, cajoling, and winning confidence before being allowed to treat physical illness. May E. Chinn's experiences are again illustrative of the problems encountered. She observed that one of the peculiar problems she had to overcome as late as the 1920s was the negative attitude of some black women toward her. In one instance a black woman patient wept as Chinn approached because "she felt she had been denied the privilege of having a white doctor wait on her." Not surprisingly, few black women doctors enjoyed the support of or were consulted by their white male colleagues in the communities in which they practiced. They were, however, frequently taken aback by the actions of some of their black male colleagues. According to Chinn, black male doctors could be divided into three groups, "those who acted as if I wasn't there; another who took the attitude 'what does she think she can do that I can't do?'; and the group that called themselves supporting me by sending me their night calls after midnight."[23]

It is significant that many black women who were able to establish private practices also had to found hospitals, nursing training schools and social service agencies. These institutions became adjuncts to their medical practices and simultaneously addressed the needs of the black communities. By custom, black professionals and patients were prohibited from using or were segregated within local health care facilities. As late as 1944 one black physician remarked, "Within the past five years, I have seen colored patients quartered in a subbasement separated from the coal-fire furnace, of a white denominational hospital, by a thin plaster board partition not extending to the ceiling." He added, "There is much credence to be placed in the constantly repeated charge that even this concession was made only because Negro patients furnished material for the training of the white surgical staff."[24]

Several black graduates of the Woman's Medical College, most notably Lucy Hughes Brown (1863–1911) and Matilda Arabella Evans (1869–1935), journeyed south to launch medical careers. Brown, a North Carolinian by birth, moved after her 1894 graduation to Charleston, South Carolina, becoming the first black woman physician in that state. In 1896 she joined a small group of eight black male physicians led by Alonzo C. McClellan and established the Hospital and Nursing Training School.

Matilda Arabella Evans returned after graduation to her native South Carolina, where she practiced medicine for twenty years in Columbia. Inasmuch as there were no hospital facilities open to blacks in the city, Evans initially cared for patients in her own home. Eventually, as the number of clients grew, she was able to rent a separate building with a bed capacity for thirty patients and to establish a full-scale hospital and nurses' training school. During her tenure in Columbia, she also founded the Negro Health Association of South Carolina.[25]

Black women physicians such as Rebecca J. Cole and Caroline Still Wiley

Dr. Matilda Evans, 1869–1935. Archives and Special Collections on Women in Medicine, Medical College of Pennsylvania.

Anderson skillfully combined private medical practice with community service work among white and black women. Cole worked for a time with Elizabeth and Emily Blackwell at the New York Infirmary for Women and Children as a "sanitary visitor." The Blackwells' Tenement House Service, begun in 1866, was the earliest practical program of medical social service in the country. As a sanitary visitor or "tenement physician," Cole made house calls in slum neighborhoods, teaching indigent mothers the basics of hygiene and "the preservation of health of their families." Elizabeth Blackwell described Cole as "an intelligent young coloured physician," who conducted her work "with tact and care," and thus demonstrated that the establishment of a social service department "would be a valuable addition to every hospital."[26]

After a stint in Columbia, South Carolina, during the Reconstruction, Cole returned to Philadelphia. There, with the aid of physician Charlotte Abbey, she launched a new effort on behalf of destitute women and children. In 1893 Cole and Abbey founded the Woman's Directory, a medical and legal aid center. The purpose of the Woman's Directory was, according to its charter, "the prevention of feticide and infanticide and the evils connected with baby farming by rendering assistance to women in cases of approaching maternity and of desertion or abandonment of mothers and by aiding magistrates and others entrusted with police powers in preventing or punishing [such] crimes. . . . " During the latter part of her fifty-year career, Cole served as superintendent of the Government House, for children and old women, in Washington, D.C.[27]

A sister Philadelphian, Caroline Still Wiley Anderson, combined her private medical practice with the dispensary and clinic operated in conjunction with the Berean Presbyterian Church, of which her husband was the pastor. For forty years, Anderson managed the church clinic, or Berean Dispensary, as it was called, "for the benefit of women and children within the immediate neighborhood of the Church." A community activist, Anderson played a major role in establishing the first black YWCA in Philadelphia, served as treasurer of the Woman's Medical College Alumnae Association, was a member of the Women's Medical Society, and for several years occupied the position of president of the Berean Women's Christian Temperance Union. Anderson performed all of these services while maintaining her position of assistant principal and instructor in elocution, physiology, and hygiene at the Berean Manual Training and Industrial School. In 1888 she read a paper entitled "Popliteal Aneurism," which was published in the alumnae journal of the Woman's Medical College.[28]

Given the uncertainty, costs, and emotional strain of establishing a successful private practice, it is understandable that several black women physicians initially accepted appointments as resident physicians in segregated black colleges and universities established in the South during Reconstruction. Such appointments provided small but steady stipends and much-needed experience at working in an institutional setting. Moreover, these appointments assured a degree of professional autonomy, status, and visibility and enabled the development of greater confidence.

During the 1890s and early 1900s, black women physicians Halle Tanner

Dillon Johnson, Ionia R. Whipper, Verina Morton Jones, and Susan Smith McKinney Steward became resident physicians at black colleges. Not only did they minister to the health care needs of the college students and faculties, but they often taught courses and lectured on health subjects. Johnson served as a resident physician at Tuskegee Institute from 1891 to 1894. During her tenure she was responsible for the medical care of 450 students as well as for 30 officers and teachers and their families. Johnson was expected to make her own medicines, while teaching one or two classes each term. For her efforts she was paid six hundred dollars per year plus room and board; she was allowed one one-month vacation per year.[29]

In 1903, Ionia R. Whipper, a member of the 1903 graduating class of Howard Medical School, succeeded Johnson and became the second black woman resident physician at Tuskegee Institute. Reflecting social change, however, Whipper was restricted to the care of female students at the institute. After leaving Tuskegee, Whipper returned to Washington, D.C., where she established a home to care for unwed, pregnant, school-age black girls. Aided by a group of seven friends, Whipper commenced this work in her home. In 1931 she purchased some property and opened the Ionia R. Whipper Home Inc. for Unwed Mothers, which had a policy of nondiscrimination as to race, religion, or residence.[30]

After completing her education at the Woman's Medical College, Verina Morton Jones accepted an appointment as a resident physician of Rust College in Holly Springs, Mississippi. Like Johnson and Whipper, Morton doubled as a teacher, giving classes to the students enrolled in the industrial school connected with the university.[31] Jones and Dillon shared another characteristic in that they both were the first women to pass their states' medical board examinations, in Alabama and Mississippi respectively.

To be sure, acquiring a medical education and establishing a practice before the turn of the century was difficult, but later generations of black women physicians were further encumbered in their pursuit of medical careers. Entrance into the medical profession became more difficult as the requirements for certification were raised. Medical graduates were increasingly expected to secure internships and residencies for specialization and to pass state medical board examinations for certification. Only a small number of the highly rated hospitals in the country accepted blacks or women for internships and residencies. Consequently, black women faced fierce competition for available slots. Most of the all-black hospitals preferred to grant internships and residencies to black men, while the few women's hospitals usually selected white women. The confluence of sexual and racial segregation strengthened the barriers blocking the aspirations and careers of black woman physicians.[32]

The experiences of Isabella Vandervall, who studied at the Woman's Medical College, reveal the difficulties involved in securing internships. Vandervall wrote in an article detailing her frustrations, "I had almost given up hope of securing an internship when one day, I saw a notice on the college bulletin board saying the Hospital for Women and Children in Syracuse, New York, wanted an interne. Here I thought was another chance. So I wrote, sent in my application, and was

Dr. Halle Tanner Dillon Johnson with the Class of 1891, Woman's Medical College of Pennsylvania. Archives and Special Collections on Women in Medicine, Medical College of Pennsylvania.

accepted without parley. . . . So to Syracuse I went with bag and baggage enough to last me for a year. I found the hospital; I found the superintendent. She asked me what I wanted. I told her I was Dr. Vandervall, the new interne. She simply stared and said not a word. Finally, when she came to her senses, she said to me: 'You can't come here; we can't have you here! You are colored! You will have to go back.' "[33]

As the professionalization of medicine progressed, so too increased the exclusion and ostracism of outside groups. For example, black women physicians, like their black male counterparts, chafed under the denial of membership in the leading professional organization, the American Medical Association. In response to this exclusion, black physicians met in 1895 in Atlanta, Georgia, to create the National Medical Association (NMA). From the outset, black women participated in the NMA. Although few were elected or appointed to prominent positions, they nevertheless, on occasion, held offices, attended the annual conventions, and periodically published papers in the *Journal of the National Medical Association*. For example, Georgia R. Dwelle, a graduate of Meharry who began her practice in Atlanta, Georgia, in 1906, was a vice-president of the NMA during the 1920s.[34]

In addition to their struggles with race-related problems within the medical profession, black women physicians had also to be concerned with gender-related issues. Like their white women counterparts, black women physicians remained sensitive to the prevailing social attitude that higher education and professional training threatened a woman's femininity. To be sure, black Americans, more so than white Americans, tended to tolerate women working outside the home. Economic necessity and racism so circumscribed the opportunities of black males that black women, regardless of marital status, had to contribute to the well-being of the family. Indeed, the black woman physician was frequently a much sought-after marriage partner. Many black women physicians married black ministers, fellow black physicians, or educators. Susan Smith McKinney Steward, commenting on the marriageability of black women physicians, observed, "Fortunate are the men who marry these women from an economic standpoint at least. They are blessed in a three-fold measure, in that they take unto themselves a wife, a trained nurse, and a doctor." She went on, however, to point out the necessity for the black woman physician to avoid becoming "unevenly yoked." She cautioned that "such a companion [would] prove to be a millstone hanged around her neck." Steward concluded on an optimistic note, asserting that "the medically educated women are generally good diagnosticians in this direction also."[35]

Actually, nineteenth-century medical practice permitted the best of both worlds. Offices were frequently located in the home. Thus, marriage and career could be conducted in the same location. Aspiring black middle-class women, especially those associated with the black women's club movement and authors of the inspirational biographies of the time, vacillated in their praise of professional black women. They celebrated the accomplishments of the black women physicians and at the same time applauded the fact that these professional role models successfully fulfilled their obligations as wives and mothers. Of Steward, for example, the author of one black women's club publication declared, "She had fairly outdone her white sisters in proving that a married woman can successfully follow more than one profession without neglecting her family." In the same publication Caroline Still Wiley Anderson was hailed as a wife, mother, physician, teacher, clubwoman, and "co-laborer in the work of the Lord."[36]

Susan Smith McKinney Steward married another minister after her first husband, Reverend William C. McKinney, died. Her second husband, Reverend Theophilus G. Steward, was a former chaplain of the United States Army. An extremely successful physician, she had offices in Brooklyn and Manhattan and served on the staffs of the New York Hospital for Women, the Brooklyn Women's Homeopathic Hospital, and the Brooklyn Home for Aged Colored People. She was also a church organist and choirmaster and founded the Woman's Local Union, which was black New York's leading women's club, and the Equal Suffrage League of Brooklyn.[37]

Verina Morton Jones was also held up for commendation. She married W. A. Morton in 1890 and, after she resigned from her position as resident physician at Rust College, she and her husband established a practice in Brooklyn together, although they specialized in different areas.[38] The Brooklyn *Times* noted in 1891, "they do not interfere with each other in the least. They are a handsome young couple, intelligent and refined looking."[39] Alice Woodby McKane and her husband, Cornelius McKane, also practiced medicine as a team. In 1895 they traveled to Monrovia, Liberia, where they opened and operated the first hospital in that republic. In 1896 they returned to Savannah, Georgia, and together established the McKane Hospital for Women and Children, which was renamed Charity Hospital in the 1920s.[40]

This brief examination of black women physicians underscores the fact that much more research and discovery of additional primary source materials needs to be done before definite conclusions can be drawn concerning the impact of their work and experiences on the larger medical profession. The lives of the few women discussed reveal the depth and breadth of their struggle to overcome gender and race barriers thwarting their access to medical schools, internships, and residencies and impeding subsequent professional development. It is fair to say that in an age in which the standards of medical practice were low and the backgrounds of most physicians were wanting, these black women doctors defied, for the most part, traditional stereotypes and characterizations. This dedicated, albeit small, group of professionals was drawn, with few exceptions, from the upper echelons of black society.

Several points distinguish black women physicians, the most obvious one being that they were an integral part of the black communities in which they practiced. Moreover, these women not only administered to the health care needs of blacks but also founded an array of related health care institutions. They established hospitals and clinics, trained nurses, taught elementary health rules to students and patients, and founded homes and service agencies for poor women and unwed girls of both races. They were self-reliant, committed, and talented women who successfully combined a multiplicity of roles as physicians, wives, mothers, daughters, and community leaders. Although they were, by any standard, elite black women, each of them employed her education and skills to the advantage of her people. It is reasonable to conclude that the convergence of the triple forces of racism, sexism, and professionalization resulted in a significant reduction in the number of black women physicians in the 1920s. It is also likely, however, that instead of entering the medical profession the aspiring, career-oriented, black women began focusing on nursing as a more viable alternative for a professionally rewarding place in the American health care system. Thus, these early black professional women played an undeniably significant role in the overall survival struggle of all black people. For their contributions, sacrifices, and services, all black Americans owe to them a great debt of gratitude, one that is only beginning to be acknowledged.

Medical Colleges for Blacks

Howard University Medical School
Washington, D.C...1868
Meharry Medical School
Nashville, Tenn. 1876
Leonard Medical School (Shaw University)
Raleigh, N.C. 1882–1914
New Orleans University Medical College, renamed Flint Medical College
New Orleans, La. 1887–1911
Chattanooga Medical College
Chattanooga, Tenn... 1902
Knoxville Medical College
Knoxville, Tenn. 1895
University of West Tennessee College of Physicians and Surgeons
Memphis, Tenn...1904–23

Total number of M.D. degrees awarded: 216

Note: Seven schools for blacks were established between 1868 and 1904. By 1923 only two approved schools existed, Howard and Meharry.

R E C O M M E N D E D   S O U R C E S

John Duffy, *The Healers: A History of American Medicine* (Urbana: University of Illinois Press, 1979): pp. 260–88.
Mary Roth Walsh, *"Doctors Wanted: No Women Need Apply": Sexual Barriers in the Medi-*

cal Profession, 1835–1975 (New Haven, Conn.: Yale University Press, 1977), pp. 179, 180–83.

Herbert M. Morais, *The History of the Negro in Medicine* (New York: Association for the Study of Afro-American Life and History, 1967), pp. 57–67.

N O T E S

1. Dorothy Sterling, ed., *We Are Your Sisters: Black Women in the Nineteenth Century* (New York: W. W. Norton & Company, 1984), p. 450.

2. Mary Roth Walsh, *"Doctors Wanted: No Women Need Apply": Sexual Barriers in the Medical Profession, 1835–1975* (New Haven, Conn.: Yale University Press, 1977), pp. 194, 225, 236–37; M. O. Bousfield, "An Account of Physicians of Color in the United States," *Bulletin of the History of Medicine* 17 (January 1945): pp. 62, 70, 80; E. Richard Brown, *Rockefeller Medicine Men: Medicine and Capitalism in America* (Berkeley: University of California Press, 1979), pp. 88, 153; Paul Starr, *The Social Transformation of American Medicine: The Rise of a Sovereign Profession and the Making of a Vast Industry* (New York: Basic Books, 1982), pp. 124–25.

3. Bettina Aptheker, "Quest for Dignity: Black Women in the Professions, 1885–1900," in her *Woman's Legacy: Essays on Race, Sex, and Class in American History* (Amherst: University of Massachusetts Press, 1982), pp. 97–98; Sara W. Brown, "Colored Women Physicians," *Southern Workman* 52 (1923): p. 586; Sterling, *We Are Your Sisters*, pp. 440–41; Leslie L. Alexander, "Early Medical Heroes: Susan Smith McKinney Steward, M.D., 1847–1918: First Afro-American Woman Physician in New York State, *Journal of the National Medical Association* 67 (March 1975): pp. 173–75.

4. Walsh, *"Doctors Wanted,"* p. 186; Cora Bagley Marrett, "On the Evolution of Women's Medical Societies," *Bulletin of the History of Medicine* 53 (1979): p. 434.

5. Bousfield, "An Account of Physicians of Color," p. 592; Numa P. G. Adams, "Sources of Supply of Negro Health Personnel: Section A: Physicians," *Journal of Negro Education* 6 (July 1937): p. 468.

6. *Medical and Surgical Observer* (October 1893): p. 184. M. Vandehurst Lynk was the editor of this first black medical journal. He also founded the medical department of the University of West Tennessee in Memphis.

7. Rayford W. Logan, *Howard University: The First Hundred Years, 1867–1967* (New York: New York University Press, 1969), pp. 42, 47.

8. Daniel Smith Lamb, *Howard University Medical Department: A Historical, Biographical and Statistical Souvenir* (Washington, D.C.: R. Beresford, 1900), p. 142; Brown, "Colored Women Physicians," p. 592; Bousfield, "An Account of Physicians of Color," p. 70; Aptheker, *Woman's Legacy*, p. 100; *Catalogue of Officers and Students of Howard University, 1971–1872*, pp. 54, 62.

9. Cited in Herbert M. Morais, *The History of the Negro in Medicine* (New York: Association for the Study of Negro Life and History, 1967), p. 43; *Catalogue of the Officers and Students of Howard University from March 1887 to March 1879*, pp. 12–13. All catalogues found in the Moorland-Spingarn Library of Howard University, Washington, D.C.

10. Morais, *The History of the Negro in Medicine*, p. 43; Logan, *Howard University*, p. 47.

11. James Summerville, *Educating Black Doctors: A History of Meharry College* (University: The University of Alabama Press, 1983), pp. 31–32; Darlene Clark Hine, "The Pursuit of Professional Equality: Meharry Medical College, 1921–1938, A Case Study," *New Perspectives in Black Educational History*, Vincent P. Franklin and James D. Anderson, eds., (Boston: G. K. Hall, 1978), pp. 173–92.

12. Charles Victor Roman, *Meharry College: A History* (Nashville, Tenn.: Sunday School Publishing Board of the National Baptist Convention, 1934), pp. 64, 76, 107; Summerville, *Educating Black Doctors*, p. 33.

13. Walsh, *"Doctors Wanted"*, pp. 62, 181, 195.

14. Aptheker, *Woman's Legacy*, pp. 98–99; Sterling, *We Are Your Sisters*, pp. 443–49; Brown, "Colored Women Physicians," p. 591; Margaret Jerrido, "Black Women Physicians: A Triple Burden," *Alumnae News*, The Woman's Medical College of Pennsylvania, now the Medical College of Pennsylvania (Summer 1979): p. 45; Ruth Abram, "Daughters of Aesculapius," *Alumnae News*, The Woman's Medical College of Pennsylvania, now the Medical College of Pennsylvania (Fall 1983): p. 10.

15. E. Wilber Block, "Farmer's Daughter Effect: The Case of the Negro Female Professional," *Phylon* 30 (Spring 1969): pp. 17–26; Elizabeth R. Haynes, "Negroes in Domestic Service in the United States," *Journal of Negro History* 8 (1923): pp. 422–28; Lawrence B. de Graff, "Race, Sex and Region: Black Women in the American West," *Pacific Historical Review* 49 (May 1980): pp. 285–313.

16. G. R. Richings, *Evidences of Progress Among Colored People* (Philadelphia: George S. Ferguson Co., 1905), p. 412; L. A. Scruggs, *Women of Distinction: Remarkable in Works and Invincible in Character* (Raleigh, N.C.: L. A. Scruggs, 1982), pp. 177–78; Matthew Anderson, *Presbyterianism: Its Relation to the Negro* (Philadelphia: John McGill, White & Company, 1899), contains sketches of the Berean Church, Caroline Still Wiley Anderson, and the author; Brown, "Colored Women Physicians," p. 585.

17. Brown, "Colored Women Physicians," p. 591; Richings, *Evidences of Progress*, pp. 411–12.

18. Richings, *Evidences of Progress*, pp. 411–12; Brown, "Colored Women Physicians," pp. 585–86.

19. Sterling, *We Are Your Sisters*, pp. 441–43; Scruggs, *Women of Distinction*, pp. 100–103.

20. Brown, "Colored Women Physicians," p. 588; Aptheker, *Woman's Legacy*, p. 98; Elizabeth L. Davis, *Lifting As They Climb: The National Association of Colored Women* (Washington, D.C.: National Association of Colored Women's Clubs, 1933), p. 292; Sterling, *We Are Your Sister*, pp. 443–448.

21. Quoted in Sterling's *We Are Your Sisters*, pp. 445–46; Richings, *Evidences of Progress*, p. 413; Scruggs, *Women of Distinction*, pp. 364–65; Brown, "Colored Women Physicians," p. 591.

22. Quoted in Charlayne Hunter-Gault's "Black Women M.D.'s: Spirit and Endurance," *New York Times*, November 16, 1977.

23. Ibid.

24. Bousfield, "An Account of Physicians of Color," p. 72; E. H. Beardsley, "Making Separate Equal: Black Physicians and the Problems of Medical Segregation in the Pre-World War II South," *Bulletin of the History of Medicine* 57 (Fall 1983): pp. 382–96.

25. Sterling, *We Are Your Sisters*, pp. 444–45.

26. Elizabeth Blackwell, *Pioneer Work in Opening the Medical Profession to Women: Autobiographical Sketches* (New York: Schocken Books, 1977 reprint of 1895 edition), p. 228; Jerrido, "Black Women Physicians," pp. 4–5.

27. *Directory of the Philanthropic, Educational and Religious Association of Churches of Philadelphia*, 2d ed. (Lancaster, Pa.: New Era Printing Company, 1903), p. 158; Philadelphia City Hall, Wills. Inventory and Appraisement, filed, January 11, 1923; Sterling, *We Are Your Sisters*, pp. 440–41; Brown, "Colored Women Physicians," p. 586.

28. Anderson, *Presbyterianism: Its Relation to the Negro*, 5ff; Margaret Jerrido, "In Recognition of Early Black Women Physicians," *Women and Health* 5 (Fall 1980); pp. 1–3.

29. Aptheker, *Woman's Legacy*, pp. 98, 99, 101; *Atlanta University Bulletin*, November 1891.

30. Logan, *Howard University*, p. 136; Brown, "Colored Women Physicians," pp. 589–90; Aptheker, *Women's Legacy*, p. 99.

31. Scruggs, *Women of Distinction,* pp. 267–68.

32. Sister M. Anthony Scally, *Medicine, Motherhood and Mercy: The Story of a Black Woman Doctor* (Washington, D.C.: Associated Publisher, 1979), pp. 23–27.

33. Isabella Vandervall, "Some Problems of the Colored Woman Physician," *Woman's Medical Journal* 27 (July 1917): pp. 156–58.

34. Aptheker, *Woman's Legacy,* p. 99.

35. Quoted in Sterling's *We Are Your Sisters,* pp. 440, 441, 443.

36. Scruggs, *Women of Distinction,* pp. 100–103, 177–78; Brown, "Colored Women Physicians," p. 585.

37. Maritcha Lyons, "Dr. Susan S. McKinney Steward," *Homespun Heroines and Other Women of Distinction,* Hallie Quinn Brown, editor (Xenia, Ohio, Aldine Publishing Company, 1926; reprint 1971), p. 162; Alexander, "Early Medical Heroes: Susan Smith McKinney Steward," pp. 21–23; Davis, *Lifting As They Climb,* p. 292; Sterling, *We Are Your Sisters,* pp. 440–43; William Peper, "Boro Had 1st Negro Woman M.D. in 1870s," *Sun,* May 9, 1960; Brooklyn *Times,* June 27, 1891.

38. Scruggs, *Women of Distinction,* pp. 267–68.

39. Brooklyn *Times,* June 27, 1891; Scruggs, *Women of Distinction,* pp. 267–68.

40. Brown, "Colored Women Physicians," p. 582.

ERNEST EVERETT JUST

The Role of Foundation Support for Black Scientists 1920–1929

Kenneth R. Manning

[Ernest Everett Just—the "Black Apollo of Science" in the biography by Kenneth R. Manning—was born in Charleston, South Carolina, in 1883 and died in Washington, D.C., in 1941. He graduated from South Carolina State College, then was admitted to Dartmouth. Immediately after earning his undergraduate degree in 1907, he began teaching at Howard University in Washington and at its medical school—appointments he would hold more or less continuously for the rest of his life. Soon he returned to graduate school and received his doctoral degree at the University of Chicago under the distinguished biologist, Frank Lillie. Lillie sponsored him for many summers of research at the famous Marine Biology Laboratory (MBL) at Woods Hole, Massachusetts, both during and after his doctoral studies. Just's work increasingly gained national and international attention.

By 1918, Just recognized that he needed to cut back on his teaching at Howard if he was to continue his scientific career. He tried to get financial support from outside the university. In this account, Manning explains the importance of foundation support for scientific careers, Howard University's relative poverty, the history of foundations' refusal to provide research support for black scientists, and how Just tried to deal with the convergence of these three elements in his life.—Ed.]

Money has always been crucial to a career in science. Even in the early part of this century, the initial investment in undergraduate and graduate education was costly, as were the ongoing expenditures for laboratories and equipment. The bills were often footed by a university, a scientific society, a philanthropic foundation, or a private benefactor—but often also by the scientists themselves. Most scientists, including the independently wealthy, sought and received some outside support. Frank Lillie, for instance, obtained funds from various sources throughout his career, even though he was married to the Crane fortune.[1]

As a result, scientists frequently presented themselves as geniuses with colossal talents, an image that helped them in their pursuit of financial backing. Benefactors in both the public and private sectors were suitably impressed. Nonscientists themselves for the most part, they did not understand atoms and gases and enzyme functions, but they were fascinated by the mystery of what went on in the laboratory and especially by the idea that science held the key to knowledge and power in a flourishing industrial state. They gave liberally to scientists, convinced that the returns would more than justify the expenditures.

Blacks did not benefit from all this. The extensive education and rigorous training required of anyone who chose a career in science could be found only in white universities, where blacks were at best admitted only in exceptional cases. Even if a black was lucky enough to get the training, there was no hope of long-term support for his work. He had no chance of a post in a white institution, so he was obliged to seek employment as a teacher in one of the black colleges. And the philanthropic Establishment, on advice from the white scientific community, did not think of black colleges as a good investment for the training of scientists and the production of high-quality research. Only the most niggardly support was extended to blacks and their institutions, and since science required such a great deal of money, few black colleges had viable science departments and few blacks pursued science as a career.

• • •

Howard was a poor institution. It started out with funds from the Bureau of Refugees, Freedmen and Abandoned Lands set up by Congress after the Civil War to aid in educating the freed slaves and other destitute persons. At first it was merely a high school, but its administration strove hard to make it more, by developing programs as quickly as possible in medicine, law, education, theology, and agriculture. Financial support flowed in swiftly and the prospects for the future seemed encouraging. But in the early 1870s funds began to dwindle. The Freedmen's Bureau closed, and private donations fell off during the panic that crippled the nation's economy in 1873. Howard suffered enormous financial strains, but it kept afloat with the help of dedicated faculty and staff. Run mostly by whites in the service of blacks, the institution attracted leaders imbued with missionary zeal. Its first twelve presidents, in fact, were all white northerners connected to the church in one way or another. Much of the faculty was white too, dedicated to the cause of black education. The black professors were the cream of the black intelligentsia, highly educated men and women often trained at white northern schools. Barred from jobs in white colleges, they found their niche at Howard, the only black institution with a wide, growing range of collegiate and professional programs.

• • •

[When Just decided to look for support outside Howard University,] it was a pioneering move. No other black had ever received foundation support for research in pure science, let alone substantial funding. As a result, no black had achieved an outstanding career in science. Edward Bouchet, the first black Ph.D. from Yale in 1870, remained a high school physics teacher in New Haven for his entire career; Charles Henry Turner, a Ph.D. in biology from Chicago in 1907, taught high school in St. Louis until his premature death in 1923. Turner's case was particularly tragic. The black community knew him as a struggling and frustrated scientist who died of "neglect and overwork," who had once been denied a university position because "the head professor . . . would not have a 'Nigger.' "[2] Without money, support, and position, men like Bouchet and Turner were unable to enter, let alone compete in, the world of American science. So it might have been with Just.

But as we shall see, Just turned out to be adept at winning support. He acquired the art of getting money, studied and learned the ins and outs of presenting persuasive proposals to philanthropists and foundations. He convinced donors of the worth of his research—for himself, Howard, science, the black race, and mankind—and people backed his work. Just managed to keep their enthusiasm and support, but he also kept his dignity at a time when charity and philanthropy were often confused, especially for blacks.

• • •

[After strenuous efforts to obtain funding from several sources, it became clear to Just that his best help would come from Julius Rosenwald, "a philanthropist with a strong and longstanding commitment to improving the lot of blacks." Rosenwald had begun building a great personal fortune when he bought Sears, Roebuck and Company. Later, he created the Rosenwald Fund to promote "the well-being of mankind." It funded a variety of projects intended to meet primarily the educational needs of blacks.—Ed.]

For years Rosenwald had received hundreds of applications for financial assistance, so many, in fact, that as early as 1912 he had found it necessary to hire a special assistant, W. C. Graves, to deal with such matters. Graves had had wide experience as an administrator with charitable organizations in Illinois. Under Rosenwald, his job was to put together summaries of each case that came through the office. Just's case was handled no differently. Graves prepared it by summarizing the letters of recommendation and highlighting the purpose of the support Just sought. In his dossier, [C. E.] McClung's emotional portrayal of Just as wearing himself out in "a hopeless struggle" to continue his research was complemented by [Abraham] Flexner's measured advice that "service would be rendered to humanity through giving a fitting opportunity and support to a really able scientist of the Negro race."[3] It was a solid case, and before the end of February Rosenwald had decided to help Just for three years at $1,500 per year. A little later he increased the amount to $2,000 per year, adding $500 per year for summers at Woods Hole. The decision was straightforward, but the ramifications were not.

The grant went into effect on 1 July 1920. Rosenwald would supply the money; the National Research Council would administer it and send Rosenwald progress reports on Just's work; Abraham Flexner would be the liaison, the middleman and pivotal force of the whole arrangement. The importance of Flexner's role became clear very early. President Durkee agreed to accept the gift and alter

Just's teaching arrangements at Howard only on condition that the General Education Board make a contribution to the Howard Medical School.[4] His condition was accepted: Flexner gave Howard a large grant, $250,000 out of the $50 million Rockefeller fund he administered for the reorganization of American medical education. The way was clear for Just's fellowship, and plans could be made to reduce his teaching load. Apparently, he had more clout than he knew. Behind the scenes high-level officials were using his situation to haggle over huge sums.

Setting up the new arrangement was problematic, however. Lillie and Mc-Clung wanted Just to have a whole semester off from teaching, so that he could devote a period of uninterrupted time to his research. In their view, teaching and research could not be mixed; half days devoted to each would cause one or the other to suffer, most likely the research. It would be difficult for Just to go into Howard without being disturbed at all hours, they argued. Students from his afternoon classes would inevitably find their way to his laboratory in the morning, and such interruptions would hamper his high-powered, nerve-straining microscopic work. The National Research Council had a responsibility to maximize the advantages of the fellowship, to insure that Just was allowed "sufficient time free from teaching in order to continue his important investigations."[5] The entire fellowship program was in fact being taken to task. On the other hand, if Just succeeded with the Rosenwald grant, finding money for other scientists would become easier.

But Durkee did not like the idea of giving Just a semester off. He thought it would be best if Just spent the year doing research in the mornings and holding classes in the afternoons.[6] He was adamant on this point. Perhaps he feared that other faculty members would also want leaves of absence, and hoped that if Just could be kept busy throughout the year, less attention would be called to his privileged status. Flexner vacillated. When he was with McClung or Lillie he would agree with them; but with Durkee, he would note that the "free morning" arrangement Durkee proposed was more liberal than that under which his own brother, Simon, had been doing research. Rather unfairly, he likened the circumstances of a fledgling scientist and those of a seasoned administrator, assuming that what was good for the one was good for the other.

The controversy went on, with Lille and McClung, Flexner and Durkee each setting forth his viewpoint. Even Rosenwald stepped in on one occasion, asking Flexner for an opinion on Lillie's suggestion that Just teach half a year and do research the other half, instead of dividing the day between the two.[7] For his own part, Just agreed with Lillie and McClung, and he told Heilbrunn privately that there had been "much damn foolishness" in the arrangement of research conditions under the grant.[8] But he was so delighted to have the fellowship at all that he was content to let Flexner and Durkee win out, at least for a while.

Except for minor routine mix-ups, the first year of the fellowship (1920–21) went well. As usual, Just spent the summer at Woods Hole. He was "sour as a goat" because he could not get away from Howard until mid-June, but once at the MBL his research went better than ever.[9] He found himself "going strong" on the fertilization work, and felt particularly pleased that his starfish slides were "looking good" and promising to help advance the general theory of the role of the cortex in fertilization.[10] He spent day and night in his laboratory observing the fertilization process, which sometimes took as much as thirty hours from the moment of insemination to complete development.

Back at Howard in mid-September, he began a regimen of four hours in the morning in the laboratory and four hours in the afternoon in the classroom. Even though he managed to do more research in a single quarter than in "all ten years previously" at Howard,[11] his responsibilities to the university were not substantially lessened. He taught at least 750 students, and was responsible for counseling some 300 prospective medical and dental students in the college and junior college. Part of his time was spent thinking about "pedagogical" questions, such as the need to maintain "the personal element" in the classroom.[12] Also, he became "one of the most careful and painstaking" advisors to the administration on matters relating to science, making an effort to bring to the university the special knowledge he had gained from his outside experiences concerning the place of science in American education and life, and its directions for the future.[13] The university would have been unable to meet the larger responsibilities of the science curriculum without Just's "wise counsel" and "eager and hearty cooperation." His fellowship had put him in a very special position. He was also in demand to do committee work, which turned out to be as time-consuming, if less exhausting, than teaching. He contributed so much, in fact, that Durkee relaxed restrictions and allowed him time off in the spring before the close of the academic year.

In early May he went to Woods Hole again and worked hard at his research for four months. Progress was slow at first because unusually bad weather had depleted the fauna along the Massachusetts coastline. But things picked up by mid-June, and the summer turned out to be one of Just's most productive to date. Glowing reports went to Rosenwald from all concerned: Just, the National Research Council, Lillie, and Durkee.[14] There was little chance that Rosenwald would discontinue his three-year commitment. Just seemed set.

One problem, though, was that he and Flexner got off on the wrong foot. Whenever they met anywhere, at Woods Hole in particular, Flexner would remind Just that the grant was "tentative and conditional," and that its continuation depended on satisfactory report cards from Lillie and McClung.[15] He seemed to harbor, or so Just thought, a deep-seated fear that Just's head would become "swollen" and that he would quit work, especially on his "sudden accession of wealth." This whole attitude was "a bit childish" and "the whole business . . . irksome," as far as Just was concerned. Flexner was, however, the line to sources of money, and too powerful a man to be crossed directly. Just had to be careful lest he jeopardize future help for himself and other blacks. But he also had his pride, and he was not going to stand for paternalism. He was an established scientist, not an inexperienced student, so why should others be "responsible" for him and his work?[16] He let Flexner know his feelings obliquely, through McClung and Lillie. He could not change what Flexner thought privately, but he could at least try to change what he said and did publicly.

As Just must have expected, Flexner was intelligent enough not to continue in the same vein. He more or less called a truce, stressing at the same time that he did not want Just to read into his statements meanings that were not there.[17] Over the course of the next two years they worked out a mutually respectful relationship, though Flexner never truly became the "friend and advisory sponsor" Just had hoped for.[18] Flexner expressed concern, offered advice, and promised to do everything in the world to promote Just's welfare and progress. But he never seemed completely sincere.

Flexner was a southerner, albeit a Jewish one.[19] Born and bred in Louisville, Kentucky, he had the outlook of a typical educated southern white. Though he acknowledged that blacks deserved some opportunity to better themselves, he was a paternalistic segregationist. He believed that segregation would work if blacks were given a chance to develop their own institutions. Just would work at Howard, Rosenwald Fund recipient W. S. Quinland at Meharry—and that was that.[20] It did not matter what black professionals wanted for themselves. Flexner had decided that everyone, black and white, would be better off if blacks kept to themselves.

Flexner's goal was constructive in a way. At least he was attempting to help blacks and to solicit support for Howard, which was more than most whites were doing at the time. He had a point when he once linked himself and Rosenwald as "two Jews of liberal spirit and lofty purposes" who might be able to "do something to encourage tolerance in this country—and perhaps in other countries." [21] Without doubt he was one of the best allies a black could find among whites in that era. As a result, there was hardly any black other than Just who insisted on being treated with real respect by Flexner—for most blacks it was satisfying enough to find a white man who was even cautiously progressive.

Still, Flexner's attitude left much to be desired. Despite his importance as an administrator, he spent much time talking about blacks in a small-minded manner. Even in his professional correspondence with Rosenwald he did not refrain from passing on racial slurs. A case in point involves W. S. Quinland, the black doctor from Meharry. Wallace T. Buttrick, president of the General Education Board, had interviewed Quinland concerning fellowship support. These are his comments, as reported to Rosenwald by Flexner: "I believe he is a real find. To begin with—he is about my height, not yet having attained to my equational dimensions. He is as black as Major Moton. Close your eyes and you'd think you were talking with or rather listening to a refined country gentleman."[22] For Buttrick and Flexner, Quinland was the day's comic relief. True, Quinland, a Jamaican, spoke with a British accent and had a complexion as dark as that of Major Moton, president of Tuskegee Institute. But what did these facts have to do with awarding him a fellowship? Such petty considerations, deeply ingrained in the American mentality, were part and parcel of the larger problem of support for blacks. That Flexner quoted these remarks without condemning them is revealing; that he might have thought them complimentary is appalling. Blacks knew remarks like these were being made everywhere, though they did not usually know the details. The best way for them to deal with such things, most felt, was to ignore them if at all possible or, like Just, complain through third parties. Most often they suffered silently, in the interest of winning support for themselves and their race.

Just's problems were not limited to the slurs and paternalism of white philanthropists and donors. The low-keyed intellectual life at Howard also weighed heavily on his mind. He was an oddity in that environment. Few Howard faculty members were actively pursuing research in any field, scientific or otherwise; even fewer were receiving fellowship support. Most, including Durkee at first, believed research was "merely time off to do nothing."[23] And those who did consider research worthwhile employment were jealous of anyone who had time off to do it. Evidently there was no pleasing anybody.

Just had difficulty pursuing his work under these conditions. He felt guilty whenever he spent time in his laboratory rather than in the classroom, and ill at ease when he saw how much newspaper publicity his grant was receiving. Therefore, during the first three years of his fellowship he found himself giving in more and more to requests that he teach large classes and serve on numerous committees. Even though the restrictive "free morning" arrangement was abandoned after the first year in favor of leave for the entire spring term, Durkee was still making extra demands on Just's time and energy during the fall and winter terms, involving him in work far removed from biology.[24] Just complied willingly. In part, his intensive devotion to university affairs was a means of offsetting adverse criticism at Howard and the only way he could feel free to go to Woods Hole early in the spring; in part, it was a response to the serious needs of his students.[25] He had no obligation to squeeze in more work during the fall and winter quarters; the official arrangement now simply called for him to do a *normal* amount of work during the fall and winter, and to use the spring for research. No one intended him to cram three quarters of work into two. The burden was of his own making—with a little pressure from Durkee.

Just felt as strong a responsibility to the National Research Council as he did to Howard. He knew that he and two other scientists—Albert Mann, a specialist on unicellular algae, and Carl H. Eigenmann, an ichthyologist—were test cases for the council's Division of Biology and Agriculture, that they were the first three biologists to receive grants from the council, and that the success or failure of their work would be a crucial factor in determining whether the grant program was continued.[26] The pressure was on, and Just had to produce. Unfortunately, the gimmicks he devised to keep his time for himself were often not effective. During the 1921–22 academic year, for example, he scheduled his larger courses at eight o'clock in the morning to try and cut down on the enrollment.[27] Fewer students, less work. The scheme had only limited effect, however, and he continued to work on university matters throughout the day and evening, able to snatch only bits and pieces of time here and there for science. He was unable to find time for in-depth research. All he could do was perform mechanical chores such as slide sectioning; real experiments and serious writing had to be left for Woods Hole. Even publication was becoming a problem. In the early 1920s Just and most other scientists had to worry about getting their work into print: American journals were cutting back their expenditures drastically, and the *Biological Bulletin* in particular had instituted a frustrating policy of "cold storage for a year before publication."[28] A scientist either had to canvass far and wide for a place to publish or give up in despair. As might have been expected, Just opted to make the extra effort needed to find journals with space available. At one point he considered publishing privately, but the cost was clearly prohibitive.

Just's regimen brought on periods of great mental and physical fatigue. As early as the fall and winter of 1920 he was having such "a hard time" with his health that Lillie became quite concerned.[29] To make matters worse, Just's home life was in confusion. Some time in the spring of 1921, Ethel learned she was pregnant, but she did not want another child. She and the two children, Margaret and Highwarden, spent the summer on Martha's Vineyard, an island five miles south of Woods Hole. Just visited them on weekends and tried to placate Ethel, but he was unable to relieve her distress. Throughout the fall he worried about her so much that teaching became a painful routine and research impossible. His low output was making him feel guilty about the Rosenwald stipend.

At two o'clock in the morning on 9 December Just had to rush Ethel to a private hospital.[30] Her two previous children had been born at home without complication, but this time she went through a difficult ten-hour labor before giving birth to a daughter, Maribel. It took her three weeks in the hospital to recuperate. Just, unable to find domestic help—his maid had quit and Ethel's mother, Bamba, could not take a leave of absence from her post at the State College in Orangeburg, South Carolina—had to "look after the kids . . . cook, wash, do every damn thing."[31] In addition, he held classes daily from eight to noon. There was no escaping the pressures, and Lillie voiced concern that Just would "burn himself out" unless he found a way to relax his pace.[32] Still, Just kept hoping that he would be able to "buckle down to good work for the rest of the year."[33]

The spring of 1922 brought a further reason for anxiety. Just was about to put ten papers into press: one in *American Naturalist*, one in *Science*, six in the *Biological Bulletin*, and two in the *American Journal of Physiology*. He also had four others in the final stages of preparation. To top it off, he was trying to make up for "time lost" from research owing to duties at school and pressures at home.[34] His experiments were under way again. Results were coming in, but only after "extremely hard" work which could not be kept up "indefinitely."[35] In three months he cut, mounted, stained, and examined 635 sections of twelve stages of *Arbacia* eggs. His hectic research schedule was complicated by his personal sense of duty "to his University and the people of his race." He was still carrying out heavy committee assignments, teaching as much as thirty hours a week, and carrying the "onerous burden" of responsibility for the study programs of over five hundred premedical students. Many people, Lillie included, did not think he should relinquish the commitment to the education of his people. Others disagreed, arguing that a sense of racial duty "should not mean either suicide or abandonment of research."[36]

Just was simply working too hard—going to Woods Hole in mid-April, rushing back to Washington for end-of-term duties at the end of May, returning to Woods Hole in early June. In 1922 he had to leave Woods Hole for a rest around mid-August, before the end of the MBL session. He had worked every day, including Sundays, for four months, and wound up the experiments for no less than sixteen separate research problems.[37] He was badly worn out and on the verge of a nervous breakdown, causing much worry among the administrators in charge of his grant. They admired productivity and had let Just know this, but they did not want a breakdown on their consciences. At one point Graves urgently asked an official at the National Research Council whether Just was "undertaking too much," whether his health might "break under the strain."[38] What they feared materialized in the summer of '24, when Just had to take two months of complete relaxation in order to recover his health.[39]

N O T E S

The manuscript and records collections listed below are cited in the notes by the code letters on the left.

EGC   Edwin Grant Conklin Papers, Firestone Library, Princeton, N.J.

FRL(C)   Frank R. Lillie Papers, Archives, University of Chicago, Chicago, Ill.

GEB   Papers of the General Education Board, Rockefeller Archive Center, Pocantico Hills, N.Y.

JR   Julius Rosenwald Papers, Archives, University of Chicago, Chicago, Ill.

LVH   Lewis V. Heilbrunn Papers, letters and manuscripts in the possession of Constance Tolkan.

RF   Rosenwald Fellowship Files, National Research Council, National Academy of Sciences Archives, Washington, D.C.

WJC   William J. Crozier Papers, Archives, Harvard University, Cambridge, Mass.

1. The general history of American philanthropy, particularly as it relates to the development of universities and research institutions, has been well documented in Merle Curti and Roderick Nash, *Philanthropy in the Shaping of American Higher Education* (New Brunswick, N.J.: Rutgers University Press, 1965); Warren Weaver, *U.S. Philanthropic Foundations: Their History, Structure, Management, and Reward* (New York: Harper and Row, 1967); Waldemar A. Nielson, *The Big Foundations* (New York: Columbia University Press, 1972); Abraham Flexner, *Funds and Foundations: Their Policies Past and Present* (reprint ed., New York: Arno Press, 1976); Frederick P. Keppel, *The Foundation: Its Place in American Life* (New York: Macmillan, 1930). See also Stanley Coben, "Foundation Officials and Fellowships: Innovation in the Patronage of Science," *Minerva* 14 (1976): 225–40.

2. *Crisis* 36 (1929): 203.

3. McClung to Rosenwald, 7 Jan. 1920, JR, box 19, folder 3; Abraham Flexner to Graves, 23 Jan. 1920, JR, box 19, folder 3, and Graves to Rosenwald, 18 Feb. 1920, ibid.

4. See Abraham Flexner to Rosenwald, 13 Feb. and 16 March 1920, ibid.; Emmett J. Scott to Flexner, 25 August 1920, GEB, box 695, folder 6967.

5. McClung to Durkee, 9 and 25 March 1920; RF; McClung to Lillie, 26 March 1920, ibid.

6. Durkee to McClung, 17 and 30 March 1920, ibid.

7. Rosenwald to Flexner, 5 Oct. 1920, JR, box 19, folder 3.

8. Just to Heilbrunn, 8 June 1920, LVH.

9. Ibid.

10. Just to Lillie, 18 Sept. 1920, FRL(C) box 4, folder 20.

11. Just to McClung, 16 Feb. 1921, RF.

12. Just to Heilbrunn, 11 Dec. 1920. LVH.

13. Durkee to L. R. Jones, 19 Oct. 1921, RF; see also Durkee to Lillie, 21 July 1922, ibid.

14. Just to Graves, 15 Oct. 1921, JR, box 19, folder 3; L. R. Jones to Graves, 26 Oct. 1921 (with enclosures: letter from Durkee and report from Just, 19 Oct. 1921), RF; Lillie to Graves, 31 Oct. 1921, FRL(C), box 4, folder 20. The progress of Just's work in the early part of the summer is well plotted in his letters to Heilbrunn, 14 and 22 May and 4 June 1921, LVH.

15. See Just to Lillie, 18 Sept. 1920, FRL(C), box 4, folder 20.

16. Just to McClung, 18 Sept. 1920, RF.

17. Flexner to Just, 23 Oct. 1920, GEB, box 695, folder 6967.

18. Just to Flexner, 16 July 1926, RF.

19. The only adequate summary of Flexner's life and work is an autobiography entitled *I Remember* (New York: Simon & Schuster, 1940). A good brief sketch is "Abraham Flexner," in Maxine Block, ed., *Current Biography: Who's News and Why, 1941* (New York: H. W. Wilson, 1941), pp. 289–91. See also Franklin Parker, "Abraham Flexner, 1866–1959" *History of Education Quarterly* 2 (1962): 199–209, and the obituary in the *New York Times*, 22 Sept. 1959, p. 1. A series of interviews done with Flexner as part of the New York Times Oral History Project has been published on microfiche as *Reminiscences* (Glen Rock, N.J.: Microfilming Corp., 1972).

20. For the relationship between Flexner and Quinland, see "William Quinland, 1919–22," GEB, box 702, folder 7024. See also Flexner to Graves, 21 March 1923, JR, box 19, folder 3.

21. Flexner to Rosenwald, 10 May 1930, JR, box 4, folder 2.

22. Flexner to Rosenwald, 25 July 1919, GEB, box 702, folder 7024.

23. See Just to Lillie, 15 May 1922, RF. The reference is to a letter Durkee wrote James R. Angell, National Research Council chairman (1919–20). This letter apparently does not survive: it cannot be found in the council's files on Just, and there is no copy of it in the Angell Papers at Yale University.

24. Just to Lillie, 15 May 1922, RF: see also Just to L. R. Jones, 17 March 1922, RF.

25. Just to Lillie, 15 May 1922, RF; Just to Abraham Flexner, 21 Oct. 1920, GEB, box 695, folder 6967.

26. Details on "projects from individuals" in the Division of Biology and Agriculture can be found in the various annual reports submitted to the National Research Council executive by division chairmen. A MS. copy of the complete report for 1920–21, written by the chairman, C. E. McClung, is preserved in the Conklin papers, EGC, box 42. A summary was published in *Report of the National Academy of Sciences for the Year 1920* (Washington, D.C.: Government Printing Office, 1921), pp. 76–80.

27. Just to Lillie, 15 May 1922, RF.

28. Just to Heilbrunn, [April 1921], LVH; also Just to Rosenwald, 16 April 1922, JR, box 19, folder 3. For the reaction of another scientist, see B. H. Willier to W. J. Crozier, 15 April 1922, WJC.

29. See Lillie to Just, 20 Dec. 1920, FRL(C), box 4, folder 20.

30. Just to Heilbrunn, 4 Jan. 1922, LVH; also interview with Maribel Just Butler, 29 July 1979.

31. Just to Heilbrunn, 4 Jan. 1922, LVH.

32. Lillie to W. C. Graves, 31 Oct. 1921, FRL(C), box 4, folder 20.

33. Just to Heilbrunn, 4 Jan. 1922, LVH.

34. Just to J. R. Schramm, 16 June 1922, RF.

35. Lillie to L. R. Jones, 22 May 1922, RF; see also Just to Jones, 17 March 1922, ibid.

36. Jones made this comment in the margin at the bottom of the letter from Lillie cited in note 62.

37. Just to J. R. Schramm, 16 June 1922; Just to Lillie, 19 Aug. 1922, RF.

38. W. C. Graves to J. R. Schramm, 25 March 1922, RF; also Lillie to Just, 12 May 1922, FRL(C), box 4, folder 20.

39. See Lillie to Rosenwald, 14 July 1924, JR, box 19, folder 3: Graves to J. R. Schramm, 29 July 1924, ibid: W. C. Curtis to Just, 1 Jan. 1925, EEJ(H), box 125-3, folder 54: Just to the National Research Council, 13 March 1925, RF; Just to Edwin R. Embree, 16 July 1930, JR, folder 3.

NEVER MEANT TO SURVIVE

A Black Woman's Journey

An Interview with Evelynn Hammonds
by Aimee Sands

Aimee. What was it that sparked becoming a scientist in your mind?

Evelynn. I thought I'd like to be a scientist when at nine I had my first chemistry set. I had such a good time with all the experiments. I wanted to know more, and I wanted to get the advanced Gilbert chemistry set so I could do more interesting experiments.

A. Who gave you the chemistry set?

E. My father. And he gave me a microscope a year later. I always had sets like that. I had chemistry sets or microscopes or building sets or race car sets or different kinds of project-kit things to build stuff. My father and I always spent some time together working on them, and he was always interested in what I was finding out . . . figuring out. . . .

A. When did you start doing science in school?

E. We always had science in elementary school. The, you know, "go out and look at the plants," and the general basic (I guess in elementary school) science curriculum that I took along with everything else. I didn't think of taking more science courses than just the requirements until I was in high school. But I really liked science, I always did. But my basic interest was that I wanted to go to a good college. So I wanted to have a good background to do that. And I felt that the more science and math I could take the better off I would be.

So I started seriously . . . I guess in my high school we had to take up through chemistry, but then I went on and took physics. We only had math up through trigonometry, but I begged my math teacher to let us have a pre-calculus class because I wanted to go on. And that pre-calculus class came about because in my junior year in high school I was accepted into a National Science Foundation summer program for high achievers in mathematics for high school students. So I spent the summer in Emory University studying math.

There were three Black students in the program, and we were all just totally

The phrase "never meant to survive" is from a line in the poem "A Litany for Survival" by Audre Lorde, published in *A Black Unicorn* (New York: Norton, 1978).

baffled by what was going on. We were taking a course in analytical geometry when we didn't know what analytical geometry was. We were taking an introductory course in group theory, and I can't remember the third course, but, some of the concepts it seemed all the other students had studied before and we hadn't studied at all, 'cause all three of us had gone to segregated high schools or recently integrated high schools. And it was a very painful experience because I felt that I was as smart as the other kids, the white kids in the class, but I had this gap in my background. I didn't know what to do about it, how to go and find the information I didn't have, and I didn't know how to prove I was still good, even though I didn't understand what was going on in class.

A. Did you know what the gap was even called? What you were missing?

E. No, I didn't have any words for it. It was just very painful. The three of us sort of haunted the libraries trying to find the books that would help us understand what was going on. It was supposed to be a summer program, so we were supposed to have fun, but the three of us weren't having fun at all. We were miserable and scared, and wondered if we were going to make it. And I was also completely angry at my parents and at my teachers that I'd had at my high school, who I felt hadn't pushed me and hadn't given me the right preparation. And that was the beginning for me to begin to understand that I'd had a deficient education . . . because I'd gone to predominantly Black schools, that that deficiency showed up most strongly in math and science. So it made me angry and made me start looking over what had happened to me.

A. What did you see?

E. I felt I'd been cheated . . . I felt I'd been denied that opportunity to have a good education because I was a Black person and I lived in the South. So I went back to my high school, and I took another year of science when I didn't have to. And I took another year of math and asked my teacher for the pre-calculus course.

A. Did that turn out to be what you were missing? Pre-calculus?

E. In part.

A. I want to go back a little before the Emory experience, when you were in grade school and high school. Were there teachers that encouraged your interest in science? I mean you said you took what everyone else took, and you implied by that you didn't have any special interest in school and it sounds like your special interest was more outside of school with the chemistry stuff. Is that right?

E. Yeah, uh . . . in elementary school and probably in junior high and the early years of high school I pursued my interest outside. I'd read books, science books and books about science and ideas just on my own, and I would talk to the few friends that I had who were interested in those things.

A. Were there teachers who encouraged or discouraged you or did they just not know anything about that side of your life?

E. Most of my teachers didn't know that I was doing it. It would show up when I'd come back to school that I had read all this interesting stuff, and I'd talk about it in class. They were very encouraging but they didn't push or anything. I always had—particularly math and science—teachers who took an interest in me most of the way—*except* , I have to say, for a couple of the times when I was being bused. I had two teachers, both math, one science, who were just outright racist and . . . one math teacher, who would, if I raised my hand for a question (I was the only Black student in the class) she would stop, call the roll, ask everybody if they had a question, skip my name and *then* ask me what my question was at the end. So I had those kinds of experiences. Or I never quite had enough points to make an A on a test or . . . I always seemed to get an A −. It always seemed there were points to be taken off for something—you know that kind of stuff—and I noticed. Those were the kinds of things I didn't know how to fight, at that time.

A. Why do you think it was that those kinds of experiences didn't discourage you from pursuing science?

E. Because I was angry, and I wasn't going to let that stop me. And . . . because my parents wouldn't have let me stop, to a certain extent. If I had given that kind of reason they wouldn't have—they would have thought I was unacceptable—especially my mother.

A. What would she have said?

E. She would have said that I could stop it if I didn't *like* it, but I couldn't stop because someone was discriminating against me—or making it difficult for me— because I had to understand people were going to make it difficult for me in the world because I was Black. . . .

A. Describe the remainder of your college years and what happened?

E. I entered Spelman College in the Dual Degree Program, which was a program between the five Black colleges and the Atlanta University Center and Georgia Tech where students would spend 2 ½ years at one of the Black colleges and then 2½ years at Georgia Tech and at the end of that time have bachelors degrees from both schools.

It was important to me to have the experience of being at Spelman. Even though I rebelled at first, I began to like being there. At the end of my junior year at Spelman, I was about to begin my time at Georgia Tech. I had declared at Spelman that I was a physics major, so I was predominantly taking most of my physics classes at Morehouse because Spelman College actually didn't have a Physics Department. So there I was again—there were about four women in my class, at Morehouse.

It was in the spring of that year, that I really came to terms with what it was going to mean to be a female and be a serious scientist, because at that time we had a speaker who was Shirley Jackson, who had just gotten her Ph.D. in physics from MIT and was the first Black woman to do so. She came and spoke, and it created quite a furor in our department and a whole conversation engendered about whether or not women could be women and scientists at the same time.

It was really an ugly way that it all came about. In choosing officers for a society of physics students organization, the men students in the class fought really seriously against any women being officers of the organization. In the midst of that election all the faculty members, who were male, voted for the male students. Afterwards they apologized to me for doing so. It just started coming out more and more that you couldn't be a serious scientist and a woman. That was a prevailing attitude in the department. I was startled, I was completely shocked. I had never had anybody, the Black students I had gone to school with, question whether or not I could do what I wanted to do. I expected opposition from white people, and I expected that to be because I was a Black person, but I never expected opposition because I was a woman. In my usual fashion I went to the library to find out about Black women in science and women scientists . . . and there was *nothing!* Then I started getting worried.

At the end of that school term I went for a summer at Bell Laboratories to the Summer Research Program for Minorities and Women. It was a great program! We would go up to the labs, and we were given scientists to work with. We had a project for the summer, and we could report on it at a big presentation we had at the end of the summer, or lots of us were able to get our names on the work published in scientific journals. So it was a really good program. That also really honed my interest in being a scientist because I really like the projects that I worked on there, and I did well. I got a paper published with my name on it as one of the authors. It was exciting to be around famous people. The labs were well equipped so I got to see I . . . I remember saying to the person who was my advisor for the summer, that I was really interested in lasers, and he pointed to a laser sitting on the table, and I didn't know that was what a laser looked like [laugh]. I had only seen really small ones because we didn't have that kind of equipment at Morehouse. We had minimal equipment. So here I am saying, "I love lasers," and "I'm really interested in them," and I don't know what they look like! I was really embarrassed.

But I didn't encounter any opposition at Bell Labs. All of us were there because we were bright, and we were encouraged to do well and to take the opportunity we were being given there seriously. Though among the students themselves there was still *a lot* of talk about women not being serious scientists, and that was difficult, and I began to see it as more and more of a problem. I was *very* angry about it, and I thought of myself as a feminist for the first time as a result of that experience, both in the spring at school and the summer at Bell Labs.

A. What year was this?

E. This was 1974. . . .

A. What about your family, were they of any help at this point?

E. Let me clarify at this point. I wasn't getting discouraged by teachers or other scientists at Bell Labs at all. I was getting a lot of encouragement, also from my professors at Morehouse. I wasn't getting encouraged by my *peers*, though. That's where it was coming from. . . . All the social pressure. To give up going out with someone because I wanted to stay home and work was seen as weird. *I was seen as weird and different, and wrong!*—somehow not being a "right kind of woman." And *that* was what was disturbing me a lot.

And what I got by reading about the women's movement and reading all those books was that I wasn't the only woman in this world that was having this problem. That helped me tremendously, even though I was one of the few . . . I didn't know any other feminists! I was a—you know—bookstore feminist. Certainly there were women around me beginning to call into question men making outrageous sexist remarks. So reading about the women's movement helped me a lot, and the women that I met in the summer program at Bell Labs were also beginning to think of themselves seriously as having careers in science—going to graduate school, getting a Ph.D., and being serious scholars. So we were beginning to talk about it, beginning to see what was happening in terms of our relationships in the social world that we lived in.

So I left Bell Labs at the end of that summer and came back to face Georgia Tech. And that was something. What I faced there was that I was the only woman in my engineering class and one of the three Black students. The racism was unbelievable! . . .

A. So you moved from Spelman and Morehouse which were sister/brother Black colleges over to a predominantly white college?

E. Predominantly male. And the students in the Dual Degree Program were viewed by many people as only there because of affirmative action programs. It was felt if we didn't have good enough grades to come to Georgia Tech from the beginning, then we weren't as strong as other students, and we didn't deserve to be there. We were only there because the government was forcing them to let us in—that was the prevailing view of us.

A. So, on the whole, your experience at Georgia Tech—how would you sum it up insofar as your experience as a Black woman in science?

E. I think it was an extremely *difficult* period for me. If I hadn't had the support to pursue physics, if I hadn't had (after my first year at Georgia Tech) another summer at Bell Labs where I had that same nurturing, encouraging environment, I would not have gone on. At Georgia Tech the people there were *not* interested in Black students' development at all. So just basic things—like going into somebody to ask, "what's going to be on a test"—you could *never* get that information from people. We were being *denied* that kind of information; we were being left out of the environment there in really serious ways. It was as if you—and there were Black students who did *well* and they were *really bright*—they could really get the information on their own and didn't need to have other students to bounce ideas off and help them understand. They really basically did it on their own, and they were real bright—the students who did it. Those who weren't struggled *a lot*, with no encouragement whatsoever, I think. The people in the Dual Degree Program administration basically told us we were going to have a tough time, and nobody was going to help us out. Being a woman— nobody wanted to address that at all.

A. Wasn't that an issue there?

E. For me it was. I was going to lab and having a male lab partner who would set up the experiment. What we would usually do is set the experiment up, run the experiment, and get our data. They'd usually come in and set it up and want me to take notes. If I got in and *I* set it up, usually they would take it apart, and I would have to fight with some guy about "Don't take it apart." They just assumed I couldn't set it up correctly!

A. These were white *and* Black guys?

E. Yes. So I had to deal with that all the time, and it was very hard. But I wasn't the only Black woman in that program who started out; I was the only Black woman in my class, in the Dual Degree Program, who finished. And I was not the brightest woman. I know that. The other three women were stronger in math than me, and two of them were certainly stronger in chemistry. I was definitely the strongest in physics, but they didn't finish because of the lack of encouragement. I feel that very strongly. I don't think it was anything intellectual. I think it was the lack of encouragement. One woman—the other woman who was a physics major—when it was time to transfer to Georgia Tech, she was so terrified of what we heard about how hard it was—about the pressures—that she refused to go. She stayed at Spelman where it was more comfortable for her.

A. It sounds as if the fact that you majored in physics was ultimately what saved you. You also mentioned a professor who helped you along at Georgia Tech, and the other woman, I guess, didn't have that person?

E. No, they didn't and they didn't finish. I think it was the lack of encouragement from professors, what people felt was going to be a hostile atmosphere at Georgia Tech that they didn't want to face. *And* the fact that again, what was happening in our personal lives was that more and more we were experiencing "you can't be a woman and do this." That pull from boyfriends, from male friends, was causing a lot of conflict. And there was nobody to talk to about that who wasn't just saying "you have to be tough," and that was the only solace that we had. So it was very hard . . . and I'd always look around to see who was there and wonder why people weren't with me now that I'd started out with. And I know that for those women, that's why they weren't there.

A. It seems like you got to be tough in terms of racism but not in terms of sexism, how come? I mean it worked as a way to keep going for you when you were facing racism, not when you were facing sexism, is that right?

E. Ah, both. I guess I was prepared to face the fact that I was going to be having difficulties because I was Black. I wasn't *prepared* to face difficulties because I was female. And there were just too few people around to even acknowledge it and help me understand it. I think that there were lots of people around to talk to about how tough it was to be Black and do this. There were just too few people around, I think, until I came to MIT.

A. And it also sounds like, starting with your family, there was a real strong identification of racism as white people's problem, but sexism was *not* strongly identified as men's problem so that you would more easily internalize that.

E. I did internalize a lot of that and see it as my own deficiency. And that created a lot of doubt for me and was just hard for me to deal with. But I was still excited enough about science and physics to keep going. I had *no* intention of being an electrical engineer, at all. So I applied to MIT and was accepted, and I received a fellowship from Xerox. So, I was ready to leave Atlanta and turn my back on that and start. I really saw myself as a serious science student at that time, and I really saw coming to MIT as a big adventure.

And being at MIT was very difficult; again, I faced the racism and the sexism.

And even in some ways it was as overt as at Georgia Tech, and in other ways that I felt in the end was more damaging . . . it was very subtle. I think the sexual, the male/female issues were probably stronger then. And my growing, *growing* consciousness as a feminist was almost like—at first I had no words and no one to talk to, and then, when I found them, my whole way of looking at the world changed. I think it's difficult for women students to continue in graduate school, to go onto the Ph.D. without being very single-minded and not let themselves be distracted . . . it's real important to do that. But the nature of the system . . . I have to say sometimes that the feminism distracted me. It made it hard for me to tolerate what I saw around me. It made it hard for me to tolerate the way I saw women treated when they came to speak. And I'd sit there in the back of the room and hear professors and fellow students talk about how the woman was dressed, and not ever talk about the content of her presentation. And there were very few women who came to talk at MIT in the Physics Department. So that was real disheartening. As my feminist consciousness grew, I was in great conflict about this. Did I really want to be involved with these people? The *culture* of physics was beginning to bother me a lot when I saw what was happening. And the work was hard, and I was beginning to have a lot of doubts about whether I could do the work.

A. But you were really a success as a young physicist.

E. I was. My research was successful. As a physics student, I was not successful. I was having a hard time with my courses, for the most part. I was having a hard time with my exams. But I was doing good research.

A. Did your problems in the courses and exams have to do with the atmosphere that you were experiencing there in terms of the sexism you described before?

E. I think a lot of it, again, is not being prepared for MIT in certain kinds of ways . . .

A. In the educational holes again?

E. Yeah, the educational holes. My first week at MIT, the first person I had as a sort of advisor on which courses to take suggested that I start with freshman physics . . . essentially saying I should start all over!

A. This is graduate school?

E. Graduate school. And I was angry. I was very angry. I was insulted. What that meant was that instead of taking . . . you know looking at the educational holes and saying where do I really need to build up . . . I was mad! I was determined that I was going to take what every other graduate student was going to take. And the hell with them! Which was a mistake. Because there were some things I shouldn't have taken. I remember there were times when people said I had a chip on my shoulder. But, I remember that all of us Black students that came in that year, there were four of us, felt the same way; we felt we had been insulted. We felt we were being . . . um . . . we couldn't ask anybody and get a *reasonable* answer. It was an *unreasonable* answer to say to me I had to take freshman physics. We didn't want to be seen as deficient! We didn't want to be seen as, you know, not supposed to be there once again! This whole thing I think, really results from affirmative action; there are a lot of people who are resentful about affirmative action and they tended to label us. We didn't want to be labeled as deficient students. We wanted to be students and pursue our work like everybody else. There was lots of students . . . in fact, there was a student I had gone to Georgia Tech with, who came in and had (you know) educational holes in the same areas because . . .

A. Was he a white student?

E. Yeah, a white student. Because if you go to a . . . anybody who went to say a small college coming to MIT may not have the whole range of courses, or the background that lots of students that have gone to larger research institutions as undergraduates might have had. That's true across the board. And white students are given more reasonable, and in this case, the white student that I knew, was given more reasonable advice—"You should take junior-level this, or the senior undergraduate course in this." *Not* that he should take freshman physics. If someone had said to me, "take junior level quantum mechanics or junior or senior level this," I would have said, "fine." You know, uh, but we didn't get that kind of advice. Because I knew it was racist, it angered me. And I went with the anger—I went with the emotional response. And I didn't have any way to distance myself and say, "wait a minute, what do I really need to do?"

A. And once again, there was nobody to help you distance yourself?

E. Yeah, exactly.

A. You were again on your own?

E. Yeah. We were on our own. We were the other Black students that we had for support. There were very few people around that had just been through the department. Cheryl Jackson was the only Black woman who had ever been through the department and managed to survive, through to the Ph.D., and she had studied under the only *Black* professor in the department. There was nobody who had that step back and was there to say, "take this approach to being successful."

A. Why were the Black students isolated? How did that come about?

E. I don't know how it comes about anywhere, but we were. In certain ways, we banded together. We all knew each other—except for one. Three of us had been at Bell Labs together—the summer program. So we stuck together because we knew each other. And we were isolated because it took us a long time to be willing to reach out of our group to other people and nobody reached towards us. So I don't see on white campuses, it's simply that Black students isolate themselves. The few Black students there who are in a class stick together; the other white students don't feel like they can reach across into that group and make alliances and work with people. So I think it's on both sides, because I think when *I* reached outside of that group there were people willing to be friends with me and study with me and stuff. But they didn't reach out.

A. What do you mean "they didn't reach out?" I missed what you meant.

E. When I was ready to reach outside of my group of Black students, there were people who were receptive to that. But there weren't white students who were coming around who were trying to reach into *our* group.

A. What was the role of your advisor in encouraging you to get through or not encouraging you to get through this time at MIT?

E. My advisor was very encouraging in a sense. He wanted me to get through, but I thought he was real tough on me, and that was hard. And I don't know if I can say that it's a lot more complicated than that. I think in part it was difficult for him to know *how* to advise a student like me.

A. Like *you* meaning what?

A. Black and female. And not just advise, I mean to move to the next step. An *advisor* just imparts information to you. A *mentor* really prepares you in a larger way to become a part of the profession in the same way that they are. I think that was difficult for him.

A. How long did you stay at MIT?

E. 3½ years.

A. And did you in fact get a Ph.D.?

E. No.

A. What happened?

E. I chose to leave.

A. Why?

E. I chose to leave because I finished my Master's degree work, and I had to prepare for my Ph.D. exams, and I really came to a crisis. I didn't know if I really wanted to go on. I questioned whether I really wanted to be a physicist.

A. Is that because you questioned that you wanted to do physics?

E. I didn't question . . . I don't think I really questioned whether or not I wanted to do physics. I questioned whether or not I could really *be* a physicist. I questioned whether or not I had the skills. I questioned whether or not I was going to make it through my exams. I had a lot of doubts, and it was a real crisis for me. So I decided to leave.

A. What about the factor that you mentioned before, the social milieu of doing science? Did that play a role in this decision?

E. Oh yeah. I mean it was clear to me that I was going to be the only Black woman. You know, the social experience of going to an international conference and being the only Black woman there was difficult. That's the kind of isolation that was beginning to bother me tremendously. People were very nice to me, but I didn't have any friends. I didn't have anybody that I was close to that I could share my work with. And I knew that it wasn't going to get any better; it was going to continue, and I was going to continue to be isolated. And that isolation . . . that's what I mean by the culture of it was bothering me. It was the isolation. It was the fact that Black scientists are questioned more severely. Our work is held up to greater scrutiny; we have a difficult time getting research, getting university positions. All of that, and I didn't really want to fight that. One of my friends, the other Black woman who finished MIT, was supposed to come to a particular international conference, so I was feeling ok. "Well, she was going to be there, I'll be fine." And she decided not to come, because a piece of work that she was doing wasn't finished, and she knew that she was going to be given a really difficult time and asked very pointed questions about her work that she was not prepared to face. So she chose not to come. But that meant I was there alone. Ok, so what does that mean? That the three Black women in physics that I knew in the entire country at that time if we weren't all at the same conference we were going to be alone. And as I said before, my consciousness as a feminist was growing and growing. I wanted to become more active. Raising the issues of racism and sexism and trying to get my degree out of that department seemed to be at odds and more and more difficult for me. I would spend more time on those kinds of issues than I would on my science sometimes. So I was in a lot of conflict and that's why I chose to leave.

A. You said that you experienced sexism as an overriding problem at MIT when we first started talking about it. But the way you talked about it since then it really sounds like it was racism that really affected you the most.

E. They are *not* separate. Because they aren't separate in me. I am always Black and female. I can't say "well, that was just a sexist remark" without wondering would he have made the same sexist remark to a white woman. So, does that make it a racist, sexist remark? You know, I don't know. And that takes a lot of energy to be constantly trying to figure out which one it is. I don't do that anymore, I just take it as, you know, somebody has some issues about *me* and who *I am* in the world. *Me* being Black, female and wanting to do science and be taken seriously. That's it.

INCREASING THE PARTICIPATION OF BLACK WOMEN IN SCIENCE AND TECHNOLOGY

Shirley Malcom

I first came to the American Association for the Advancement of Science, Office of Opportunities in Science as a research assistant in 1975. The Office had received a grant from the National Science Foundation to develop an inventory of special programs which had been undertaken to increase the participation of minorities in science, mathematics, engineering and health. The inventory of programs was published in 1976 and listed over 300 efforts nationwide to affect the number of American Indians, Blacks, Mexican Americans and Puerto Ricans as science, engineering and health professionals. After two and a half years as a program officer at the National Science Foundation, I returned to AAAS in 1979 to head the Office of Opportunities in Science. Staff members of the Project on Women in Science were completing an inventory of such intervention programs for women. This inventory, published in 1980, listed over 300 efforts across the full extent of the educational pipeline to affect the flow of women into science and engineering.

And where were minority women? Minority women were prominent neither in efforts for women nor those for minorities, though more prevalent in the latter projects than the former. Staff of the AAAS Project on Women in Science made determinations about including some of the minority-focused projects in the women's inventory based on the extent to which special activities were undertaken to deal with issues specific to minority women, such as recruitment, and making a conscious effort to provide female role models or career materials which prominently featured women. Enrollment figures could not be used alone as indicators of "special effort" since many of the projects, especially those focused on Blacks, had large participation rates by girls or women students. In some cases these programs had a majority of female participants. But rather than reflecting the effort of the project staff, these ratios more often reflected an opting out by minority males who chose sports, work or some other activity in place of a science-focused activity. But in some of these female majority projects of the late

1970s, all too often minority women found little that spoke specifically to their particular needs.

And what of the needs of minority women in science and engineering? How do these differ from the needs of all women and those of minority males? The special problems faced by minority women in science and engineering were subjects of a late 1975 conference convened by AAAS and chaired by Dr. Jewel Plummer Cobb. The resulting conference proceedings, *The Double Bind: The Price of Being a Minority Woman in Science* , increased the visibility of the issues which minority women uniquely face. Perhaps these reflections for the conference participants can be summed up in an essay written in 1976 which was incorporated into *The Double Bind*.

> There seems therefore to be a range of costs to the individual in the attainment of a professional science career. The more an individual resembles the "typical scientist" the lower are his costs. Each factor of deviation from the norm raises the costs so that, as a group, minority women must pay a tremendous price for a career in science. This "differentness" of the minority woman in science may not only be a factor in the scientific community but also in the context of her culture. The tremendous personal cost that results from the combined effect of being a scientist, a woman and a member of a minority racial or ethnic group was frequently alluded to in the conference discussions. The toll of foregone social and personal activity, highly valued in traditionally defined cultural roles, was for many severe. The scarcity of companions of their own racial or ethnic group and gender, progressively greater as the degree of specialization in science increased, was a source of isolation and loneliness. Majority males and, to a lesser degree, females are not required to bear this burden. The feeling of differentness, which for most of the conferees began to develop as early as their interest in science, was reinforced continually by the recurrent experience of being the only woman in so many situations.

Perhaps more than anything else it was the isolation (being "the only") that led to the formation of the National Network of Minority Women in Science in 1978. Meeting at the AAAS annual meeting in Washington, some of the Double Bind conference participants and others decided that a network could provide a vehicle for communication and, where sufficient numbers of women were present in a locale, the basis for local organizing and local activity. The first chair of the group was Yolanda Scott George, then at Lawrence Livermore Laboratory, who served in that capacity until she joined the AAAS Office of Opportunities staff as Co-Director of our national Linkages Project. Local chapters were established in Washington, D.C., Atlanta, Ga., Selma, Ala., and more recently in Baton Rouge, La., and Greensboro, N.C. These chapters are independent units which operate their own programs and raise their own funding. Included among activities which have been undertaken are career days for minority students (male and female) and workshops for science teachers.

In 1981 a grant to AAAS from the Women's Educational Equity Act Program of the Department of Education led to the development of career booklets in

TABLE 1

	Male	Female	Total
Engineering, Math & Physical Science	33	8	41
Life Sciences	35	43	78
Social/Behavioral Science	54	82	136
Total Science	122	133	255
Non-Science	193	315	508
Other/unspecified	2	0	2
Total	317	448	765

engineering, mathematics and the physical sciences aimed specifically at minority girls and young women. This project responded directly to a recommendation made by participants in the 1975 conference. The small number of minority women in science and engineering, they reasoned, meant that few minority girls would likely meet real people like themselves who had chosen such careers. The career materials attempted to convey a sense of the kind of life one led, on a day-to-day and long-term basis as a minority woman who had made such a nontraditional choice. The series was aptly entitled, "A Day's Work . . . A Life's Work."

MWIS stirred mixed reactions among minority women, a way to respond to the feelings of isolation, to work together to develop programs on behalf of minority youth, to add to their lives a group specifically aimed at women of color—this put on top of other organizations for women (mostly dominated by whites) and minorities (mostly dominated by males) to which they committed their time. Among minority men there was sometimes misunderstanding, sometimes hostility—a feeling that by having a separate organization, minority women were distancing themselves somehow. As the female advantage grew among Blacks enrolled in college, it became harder to explain why special efforts on behalf of Black women were needed. And it was hard to explain that the female majority in higher education had more to do with what was happening *to* Black males than what was happening *for* Black females. In the early 1980s a landmark was reached, when Black women citizens received over 50 percent of doctorates awarded to all Black American citizens, a first time achievement for women of any group. But in spite of the female advantage among Black high school and college graduates and Ph.D. recipients, the problems for Black women in science and engineering were and are subtle and pervasive.

In 1987, Black citizens received 765 doctorates, 255 of which were in the sciences and engineering. Black women received a majority of the degrees in both these categories. But if we look at broad fields we find a different story (Table 1). Black women received a smaller proportion of their science degrees in the fields of engineering, mathematics and physical sciences (EMP) than women of any other racial/ethnic group—6 percent of science and engineering doctorates.

TABLE 2 **Science Degrees Awarded in EMP Fields (U.S. Citizens)**

	Percent
All	35
All Women	16
American Indian Women	13
Asian American Women	27
Black Women	6
Hispanic Women	16

Table 2 gives figures for women of other races for percentage of science degrees received in EMP fields.

One cannot reasonably expect to raise the EMP doctorate levels of Blacks overall without getting greater participation from Black women, who receive the overwhelming majority of high school diplomas and total bachelor's degrees. We must intervene in the life experiences of these young women to make sure that they do not leave these fields by default—because of inadequate preparation in mathematics and lack of exposure to topics in the physical sciences and technology consistently from pre-K throughout the educational pipeline.

Early and appropriate exposure to physical sciences, mathematics and technology is essential. Topics in physics, chemistry and technology should not be optional in our schools. It is now possible in many places to finish high school having taken no course work in the physical sciences. The failure to provide quality science education routinely at elementary and middle school levels is a national problem. But its consequences are greater for children who have no other way of accessing science in their lives: who are unlikely to have scientist parents, neighbors or social contacts; who may not go, outside of a school field trip, to the science museum; for whom science and engineering are things done by people who do not look like them. Intervention programs out of school are needed to provide early access to science until we can move forward in a national resolve to fix the science and mathematics which students receive in school.

What kinds of interventions can promote participation in science and engineering careers by minority females? Our experience from successful programs suggests:

- starting early
- a continuing focus on rigorous preparation in science and especially mathematics throughout the pipeline
- promoting hands-on involvement through activities such as science fairs and projects
- contact with role models who are minority women
- availability of appropriate career information
- early exposure to research

- directly addressing gender and race specific issues, such as combining marriage and family, addressing clash of culture
- an opportunity for early work experience in science-related employment

Perhaps one of the most important factors is the support of family, friends, peers, and for Black women, support for science and engineering careers by Black men.

The declining levels of participation by Black males in higher education is a challenge which all of America must address. We must explore the possible roots of this decline. This includes looking at the following issues and others: differential and lower expectations for minority males by teachers, parents, peers; different and fewer demands, i.e., failure to challenge; signals sent by the media with its focus on sports figures and entertainers as Black male heroes; lack of access to role models in science and so on. Perhaps we need to expand the growing network of organizations established by Black men to help the next generation of Black men—groups that focus on decision making, leadership and choice in an atmosphere of teamwork and acquisition of skills and knowledge, that stress what Black manhood means for a technological future. These problems must be addressed. But addressing these problems for Black men must not come at the expense of current efforts on behalf of Black women. We cannot allow anyone to force us into a trade off of this kind. We are and must continue to be a part of the solution—each other's solution.

WITHOUT MORE MINORITIES, WOMEN, DISABLED, U.S. SCIENTIFIC FAILURE CERTAIN, FED STUDY SAYS

Eileen M. O'Brien

Washington, D.C.—To combat the projected shortage of scientists and engineers, the nation must encourage women, minorities and disabled individuals to earn three times as many bachelor's degrees and ten times as many Ph.D.s in these fields over the next decade, a new federal report says.

Changing America: The New Face of Science and Engineering, the final report of the Task Force on Women, Minorities and the Handicapped in Science and Technology,* details the current underrepresentation in science and engineering of white women, Native Americans, Blacks, Hispanics and individuals with disabilities and suggests specific actions for all sectors of society in addressing the crisis.

Currently, white women, Native Americans, Blacks and Hispanics account for only 14.5 percent of all employed scientists and engineers, yet these groups represent 64.6 percent of the total population, the report says. Citing figures from the National Science Foundation, *Changing America* adds that in 1986, only 94,000 Americans with disabilities were working as scientists or engineers.

"The urgency is obvious. Remedies are available. Fast action, long-term commitment and new partnerships are needed now," according to the report. *Changing America* urges involvement from the president, governors, industry, the federal government, state legislators, universities and colleges, school boards, PreK-12 educators, the media and parents.

Releasing the report earlier this month, task force Executive Director Sue Kemnitzer said the federal government and the administration were expected to act on the recommendations immediately. Secretary of energy, Adm. James D. Watkins, was expected to issue plans this month for carrying through on the report's recommendations, and the National Aeronautics and Space Administration was expected to endorse the report and present 68 steps it will take in response to the report.

*[Released in September 1988.—Ed.]

"The Office of Science and Technology Policy will set up an interagency committee to follow through on the kind of coordination that the task force has achieved and recommends should continue," Kemnitzer added. In addition, the president's fiscal 1991 budget should include new funding for some of the recommendations, she said.

In general, the report noted that minorities' pursuit of science and engineering careers is hindered by inadequate mathematical and science education in grades K-12. American Indians suffer because they are concentrated in Bureau of Indian Affairs schools, with "generally poor" teaching in these subjects, and Blacks and Hispanics—primarily concentrated in large urban school districts—receive "an inadequate basic education," the report says.

Kemnitzer said Asian Americans were not studied because "as a whole they are not underrepresented in science and engineering" and disaggregated data did not exist in the areas they examined.

Changing America offered the following statistics on current and future degrees in science and engineering for underrepresented groups.

American Indians

American Indians represent .6 percent of the national population and hold .3 percent of all bachelor's degrees and .11 percent of all Ph.D.s in science and engineering; they represent .5 percent of all employed scientists and engineers. The report projects that for American Indians, the number of bachelor's degrees in science and engineering must triple from about 700 in 1987 to 2,200 in 2000, and doctorate degrees must increase eleven-fold, from 15 in 1987 to 160 in 2000.

As a recent study by Dr. Robert Wells of St. Laurence University demonstrated, almost three-quarters of American Indian students who enroll in college drop out. The task force notes "strong support programs which reflect family and tribal ties are crucial to success in college."

Blacks

While Blacks comprise 12 percent of the general population, they account for only 2 percent of all employed scientists and engineers, earn just 5 percent of the bachelor's degrees and 1 percent of the Ph.D.s in science and engineering. By 2000, three times as many bachelor's degrees and 16 times as many doctorate degrees should be awarded to Blacks in these fields, the task force said. "In 1986, the 25 largest school districts were 45 percent Black," said the report. These large, urban school districts "must be helped to prepare Black young people for careers in science and engineering."

Hispanics

The fastest growing minority group, Hispanics represent 9 percent of the total population. However, only 2 percent of employed scientists and engineers are Hispanic, and only 3 percent of all bachelor's and 2 percent of all Ph.D.s in science and engineering are earned by Hispanics. Because of their continued growth, the report projects Hispanics must earn seven times as many bachelor's degrees and 11 times as many doctorates in these fields.

"Many Hispanic parents have high hopes for their children but often do not encourage them to go to college, especially if this requires that they move away from home," according to the task force.

Disabled Individuals

An estimated 22 million Americans of working age have some physical disability, yet only 7.2 million are employed, the report says. Kemnitzer noted, "Unfortunately, no one collects nationwide statistics on degrees earned by people with disabilities, so we cannot present the same analysis." The report calls students with disabilities "the largest minority," citing Education Department statistics showing that 10.5 percent or more than 1.3 million of 12.5 million students enrolled in postsecondary education institutions report having at least one disability.

According to the report, "Low expectations and lack of encouragement are keeping students with disabilities from participating fully in mathematics and science, particularly in the science laboratory courses."

White Women

White women account for 43 percent of the population, yet they represent only 10 percent of all employed scientists and engineers, and earned 22 percent of bachelor's degrees and 13 percent of Ph.D.s in these fields. However, because they have the highest representation of the groups studied, the report calls for only a 60 percent increase in the number of bachelor's degrees and three times the number of doctorate degrees in science and engineering by the year 2000.

"Young women must be encouraged to pursue science and engineering studies at every point along the education pipeline, especially because negative attitudes toward women in these careers can discourage them all too easily," according to the report. "However, special efforts should be focused on supporting graduate training because a far smaller proportion of women than men complete the Ph.D."

Based on these statistics and testimony on public hearings in six major U.S. cities, the task force developed a number of recommendations aimed at all sectors. "This crisis is not going to be solved just by federal actions," she said. "Everyone should feel a responsibility and see a role for themselves. We wanted each agency and sector to take ownership [of addressing the shortage], rather than us coming in with some grand scheme telling people how much they should spend and where."

Recommendations

- The President should establish national education goals, performance standards and timetables for meeting the goals, with special emphasis placed on mathematics and science capabilities of all students. Also, the president should convene an annual meeting of chief executive officers of leading U.S. corporations to report on the state of the nation's science and engineering education and the efforts of the business sector to develop a fully competitive workforce.
- Governors must ensure that their colleges and universities recruit and graduate sufficient numbers of science and engineering students, especially those traditionally underrepresented in these fields. Kemnitzer pointed out, "Governors are the heads of these enormous state university systems and they're in a real leadership position." She suggested that states offer scholarships in science and engineering and in science and math education to minorities, women and disabled individuals.
- State legislators should give special financial incentives to those students who plan to teach mathematics and science.
- Also, state legislators along with school boards should require high standards for high school graduation, including four years of math and four years of laboratory science. "Very few states require such high standards," Kemnitzer said. "Many have upped it to two years math and two years science, and some even require up to three."

  Kemnitzer said that so many years are needed "because if students stop taking math and science courses, they lose interest and proficiency, and they fall off the learning curve. They're not hopelessly lost, but they definitely are slowed down."
- The task force also called upon both industry and the media to launch a national campaign to increase science literacy, and especially in the media, to provide a more positive image of scientists and engineers. Kemnitzer criticized toy stores and toy manufacturers for their sex role stereotyping marketing strategies. In toy stores, she said, "the boys' department has all the erector sets, the trains and all the things that develop the skills you'll need for engineering. From the very beginning, you're predisposing the sexes to different kinds of activities."

- All agencies of the federal government must collect and maintain data to evaluate the participation of minorities, women and persons with disabilities in their research and development programs. Currently, NSF is the only agency that does, Kemnitzer said.
- Universities and colleges should set quantitative goals for recruiting and graduating more U.S. students in the sciences and engineering, especially from underrepresented groups. Higher education institutions also should offer forgivable educational loans to students from underrepresented groups who agree to pursue faculty careers.
- Institutions at the K-12 level, as well as postsecondary level, need to remove barriers for students with disabilities. "Treat every student with a physical disability as a potential scientist or engineer, and provide the necessary technical aids to minimize physical obstacles," the report urges Pre-K-12 educators. Postsecondary schools need to make labs accessible and adapted to persons with disabilities, particularly for students who are hearing or visually impaired. Kemnitzer said, "An alarmingly few number of schools have the accommodations for students who are disabled."

While some have said that the fruits of any program to expand the pipeline will not be evident for five to ten years, Kemnitzer argued otherwise. "At the undergraduate level, there are a lot of people in the pipeline who we don't seem to encourage and they drop out, not out of school altogether, but out of science and engineering programs. We could almost double the output simply by reaching out to these people," she said.

Kemnitzer said the task force, mandated by Congress in 1987 to produce a "long-range plan for broadening participation in science and engineering," already has inspired legislation. Before Congress adjourned in November, Sens. Mark Hatfield (R-OR) and John Glenn (D-OH) introduced bills which incorporate the recommendations of the task force's interim report, released in September 1988.

MODERN SCIENCE AND THE PERIPHERY

The Characteristics of Dependent Knowledge

Susantha Goonatilake

Scientific Knowledge in the Third World

The modern sciences that rose in Europe from the seventeenth century spread in the subsequent centuries to the rest of the world and began to occupy a dominant position. The peripheral countries were mostly the colonies of those countries where modern science had developed. This intimate colonial link directed and distorted the development of science within the peripheral countries. The impact of modern science on these latter countries varied according to the different socio-economic contexts that changed over time within Europe, as well as the socio-economic conditions within the individual countries in the periphery, and according to the relationship between the two sets of countries.

The mapping of science in the dependent countries thus varied from the mercantilist colonial period (corresponding roughly to the period of the Renaissance), to the period of industrial capitalism and the emergence of a new division of labour in the world, and then to the present period of transnational capitalism. It also varied according to the physical, economic and political characteristics of the individual colonized country and according to the level of its pre-colonial scientific and intellectual traditions. The sciences in the colonies were also affected by the time of incorporation into the colonial economy—whether for example it was during the mercantilist era or the Industrial Revolution. As I have indicated in earlier chapters, some aspects of the sciences and technologies which came to be legitimized in the European countries were known already or simultaneously in countries of Asia.

The imposition of science on the periphery was similar to the imposition of other knowledge and cultural systems. Thus the mercantile period, an era of extreme violence, was characterized by intolerance in the cultural transfer, while the corresponding situation in the period of industrial capitalism and transnational capitalism was different. (For a detailed treatment of cultural transfer, see my *Crippled Minds—An Exploration into Colonial Culture,* 1982.) The period of the industrialization of Europe required a more complete integration of the economic and social systems of the periphery into the dominant centre. The periphery now became raw material producers and/or markets for the new industrial order and these required subtler forms of knowledge transfer.

• • •

The knowledge that has emerged through the transfer of science and technology over a period of more than 150 years, and especially the large transfer in the post-independence period, thus raises certain vital issues. Even in the case of India, with the third largest scientific work force in the world, questions can legitimately be raised as to the productivity in qualitative terms of the scientific knowledge generated. The words, "satellitic" science and technology, have been used (Rahman 1977) to describe the situation even by Indian observers close to the officialdom of science.

I have earlier attempted (Goonatilake 1975; 1976) to examine the structure of this knowledge and analyse why it was not creative. The general thrust of this analysis was that in spite of differences at a detailed level, colonial or dependent scientific knowledge had certain constant characteristics. What is considered scientific knowledge in a dependent context is only that which has been made legitimate in the centre. It is then imitated in the periphery through the operation of pervasive dependent social and cultural mechanisms. Generally in such a model of knowledge as fitting dependent countries, the process of knowledge acquisition is largely a diffusionist one, even though the diffusion is sometimes limited only to the broad paradigms and not to minor variations within a paradigm. The fundamental and the basic core knowledge grows largely in the West and is transferred to developing countries in the context of a dependent intellectual relationship. The major paradigms in the sciences, as well as the major problematics in the West were developed in the West and still continue to be (or in the alternative are at least legitimized there) and only the minor variations of the major viewpoints are handled locally.

This diffusion model of knowledge that operates between the centre and the periphery really leads to a colonial division of labour in the academic world, paralleling divisions in the economic and political worlds. Most of the important works, the major issues and paradigms in the sciences are developed and undertaken in the centre while mostly only minor professional issues and subproblems are tackled by scientists in the dependent country.

Many other general characteristics in the working of the Third World's particular system of knowledge can be described in a formal model. Thus, because of the high degree of formal learning and imitative knowledge acquisition, the problems and concerns of the intelligentsia are oriented towards the external (i.e., the Western world), in what Shils (1957) called a system of "Xenophilia." Commenting on the situation, broad outlines of which can still be discerned within the sub-continent, Shils remarked:

It is not only the man who has studied at Oxford, Cambridge, Heidelburg or Paris who is referred to, but the person who, whether he has studied abroad or not, is intimate with the contents of the *New Statesman* and *Economist,* who knows about Bertrand Russell, T. S. Eliot, Sartre, Graham Greene, Camus, Auden and Faulkner, who is at home with the conflicts within the British Labour Party, and the plays of Christopher Fry. Even among scientists in these countries work seems to be done for an invisible jury of scientists in England, the United States and Germany while other scientists, working in the same field within their own country, are less frequently thought of or referred to. (Shils 1957)

This, we may add, is partly on account of the lack of a viable community among local scientists.

Arunachalam (1979) has shown—apparently contradicting this external orientation—that the majority of Indian scientists cite each other, but Shiva and Bandyopadhyay's study indicates that this apparent local scientific community has only developed among second-level scientists not working on research frontiers. This second-level scientific community in essence works on the micro problems set elsewhere by the external reference groups. What is considered major, relevant and worthy of research is already determined in the West.

If on the other hand a major breakthrough occurs in a peripheral region, for example in Latin America, it is then usually transferred to other peripheral regions only after legitimization and acceptance in the centre. The consequence is that academics in the dependent countries limit their methodologies and approaches to what are perceived as the most recent scientific fashions of the Western world, and, because of time lags, these are always outdated fashions. Creativity and originality among local scientists are inevitably stifled as a result. (See Goonatilake 1975.)

The legitimization of knowledge—the process by which a particular knowledge output is stamped as correct and relevant—takes a different form in the centre from that in the periphery (Goonatilake 1976). In the centre legitimization is by intense debate and social negotiation on scientific issues by scientists of the centre. In the dependent periphery, significant knowledge accretions are by diffusion of ideas from the centre, and legitimization is by recourse to writings and authors in the centre. Scientific reputations within a peripheral country are often formed not on scientific criteria, but on personal–political ones. Scientific knowledge in the centre is therefore potentially liberating knowledge in that it is generated in a creative and organic process; in the periphery, the dependent structures give rise to mimicked knowledge or to knowledge legitimitized on non-scientific criteria; knowledge therefore no longer portrays reality. In addition it acts as a suppressor of creativity (ibid.).

The satellitic nature of the science created in the periphery, where the most important thinking and major paradigms are those emanating from the West, has other implications. It implies that apart from those scientists who interact frequently with the centre, there is usually a time-lag in the level of debate in the sciences between the West and the dependent countries. Where ample literature is available and staff and students carry out frequent exchanges with the metropolitan centre, time-lags can be relatively small and could be of a few years or a few months' duration. But where academic exchanges are infrequent and library material is lacking—as in most Third World countries—time-lags can sometimes be extended literally to decades.

Often, particular theories current in the centre would be mapped in the periphery by individuals who have visited the centre. They then continue to teach and practise in the periphery the particular paradigm and/or school of thought which they were exposed to in the centre. New developments or new paradigms, because of the lack of organic interaction in a scientific community, are often not mapped by the individual socialized through the earlier tradition. Another individual going to the centre at a later time and being socialized in the later intellectual fashions similarly maps the later school of thought faithfully in the periphery. There is very little interaction between these successive waves of mapping and so the mapped fashions exist, as it were, in layers in the periphery. They are similar to the strata found in archaeology or geology. Taking this process to its logical conclusion, one can say that if one wants to discover petrified and fossilized knowledge of the European past surviving in the present, one perhaps has only to go to the periphery. There, by interacting with different Third World gurus, one can savour the different time-layers of the Western past, albeit in a diluted and emasculated form.

Because of the imitative process, when the knowledge of the centre is itself in a state of flux, different aspects of this changing scientific culture—with all its cross-currents—are mapped in the periphery. The social sciences have been in a state of deep flux and crisis over the last decade and a half and therefore one sees mappings of several strands indicating this flux. Many of the positions developed in the centre from both the right and the left have been reproduced recently. One finds right-wing monetary economics and left-wing dependency theory, as well as various other perspectives mapped almost simultaneously in different, isolated groups. This mimicking is not limited only to conservative groups which one would normally expect to follow Western cues but also exists on the left. As Jha (1977) has commented somewhat cruelly on this left-wing mapping,

> Marx, of course, all of them swore by, but each sect claimed to know more about what Marx had written or implied than the other. Each sect obviously was founded upon a particular Marxist hero, from Lenin and Stalin down to Mao, Minh and Che Guevara. The influence and power of the contestants was proved by their ability to quote from their intellectual-revolutionary heroes and, above all, in their capacity for combining militant slogans. (Jha 1977, p. 66)

The fragmented nature of the knowledge mapped from the centre in the scientific neo-colony or satellite means that organic interaction within it is impossible. Consequently one has the amusing situation of a guru cult growing up around professors, whose students uncritically absorb the notes that they accumulated earlier in the West but which are now outdated scientific fashions. Such a *guru-shisya* tradition demands personal loyalty of the *shisya* as in the old guru tradition. Yet the knowledge which the guru purveys as modern is actually as petrified and sanctified as the knowledge transmitted through 1,000-year-old Sanskrit texts.

The social milieu within which education is acquired and the social context in which the scientific endeavour is pursued by an individual influences further aspects of this knowledge system. Education and the search for science in South Asia now come largely from a desire for general social mobility, without an intellectual and scientific commitment *per se*. The acquired legitimized knowledge is often used mainly as a ladder for social advancement—measured in normal subcontinental terms such as jobs, dowries and social status. And as advancement is not generally related to real scientific production, the scientists do not enter fully into the real science-generating process.

From the pockets of fragmented knowledge that is mapped in the periphery from the centre, the dependent scientist and intellectual often forages in a superficial manner in search of legitimization and social advances. The existence of several pockets of fragmented knowledge transferred from the centre to the periphery sometimes allows several parallel frames of scientific and intellectual legitimacy. This gives a pseudo-scientist interested in social climbing an almost complete freedom of action to fraudulently legitimize his scientific results on several—sometimes even contradictory—frames of scientific reference.

The necessary outcome of the general colonial division of knowledge between the centre and periphery is that contrary perceptions and solutions of problems arise, the periphery giving rise to "unreal" and "disorganic" perceptions. This is because the perceptions are determined by macro-level views and by scientific and social relations determined from the centre; as the centre can never mirror the social realities at the periphery, such perceptions carry an air of unreality about them. The social scientific world of the periphery is marginalized and does not enter science theory building. Such an international division of knowledge also engenders habits of subservience among scientists in the periphery because they constantly have to look over their shoulders to the centre to have knowledge created at the periphery stamped as legitimate.

Scientific knowledge in such cases is authenticated principally by the fact (or the semblance) that it is recognized by the centre rather than by the actual organic development of scientific knowledge.

A more insidious consequence of this diffusion model is the creation of a dependent class of intelligentsia who, through an apparently neutral scientific ethos, look for scientific solutions on the basis of the version of reality emanating from the metropolitan centre. With the weakening of classic colonial political and economic ties, domination through knowledge structures becomes crucial.

It should be emphasized that the conditioning of the Third World scientist and intellectual described above is a contextual one; the fact that the Third World scientist is imprisoned and output limited does not imply criticism of the individual. The Third World scientist is imprisoned by a set of paradigms that are defined elsewhere, a legitimization and reward system that is defined elsewhere and a system of science which by nature is imitative and noncreative. These prison walls bind most Third World scientific workers, whether in Africa, Asia or Latin America, occasional breakthroughs notwithstanding. There are many instances of Third World scientists and intellectuals who are unproductive in Third World social conditions, but, once transferred to First World centres of learning and integrated into an organic scientific community, become prolific and begin to work on knowledge frontiers.

In my description of the social context of science, I evoked the image of science as a snake-like tube advancing on the terrain of physical reality. The tube was propelled by social forces internal to the scientific community while being buffeted by external socio-economic forces. How does this image of the advancing knowledge tube fit into our description of Third World science? In the first place, knowledge generation in the periphery is marginal, being of a routine kind, while the major knowledge fronts are in the centre. Therefore the knowledge tube still remains in the centre, buffeted by the centre's socio-economic forces. Occasionally the tube may take as conceptual fodder elements from the periphery but as legitimization takes place in the centre, the tube still moves essentially on a terrain whose guidelines are set by the socio-economic process of the centre. Thus the tube of knowledge does not interact very much with the periphery; it keeps the Third World marginal to the major scientific advances. Only the shadow of the advancing tube is cast on the scientific milieu of the periphery, not the tube itself.

Creativity in the Periphery

I have sketched above a more or less formal model of knowledge in the periphery. Being a model, our description does not necessarily fit completely all Third World countries at all times, but it is a useful guide for orientation. A general conclusion is that creativity is rare because of the particular structure of the Third World scientific community. If acts of creativity occur in the Third World, they are not legitimized as new knowledge because legitimization at the periphery is reached not by organic processes but by imitation of the centre. But are there any pockets of creativity beyond what we have surveyed?

Creativity can be sought in the former non-Western organic intellectual tradition of the region. But here, because of the sheer productivity of the Western tradition and the legitimacy attached to it, the output and visibility of the non-Western traditional system have continued to weaken in both quantity and creativity. The traditional system was a formalized one with a structured system for training newcomers as well as formal procedures for knowledge creation and legitimization. The emasculation of this tradition has removed from serious consideration the old "great" traditions of scientific endeavour. Surprisingly, it is often from the practitioners of earlier great traditions that the new Western intellectual strata were drawn. Thus sons of Brahmins entered the new intelligentsia or, in the case of Sri Lanka, sons of Ayurvedic physicians aspired to become Western doctors (Srinavas 1971; Goonatilake 1976). Yet the earlier "great traditions" are not the only traditions in the Third World. There are little traditions more associated with folk culture than with great civilizations.

In such little traditions, in knowledge pockets untouched by either the old great traditions or the newer Western one, virility and creativity can still be found. These pockets still continue to create and develop knowledge systems from their environments, in a manner reminiscent of Schrodinger's (1957, p. 88) primitive groups of proto-scientists, which I have already referred to. These groups for example have developed certain classifications and taxonomies of plants and animals which, though not necessarily identical with the Western systems, are intellectually serious and in practise very useful.

The claim to a systematic status for this knowledge—although it is less sophisticated than the modern scientific or the past great tradition—is best illustrated by the following words from the introduction to a textbook on taxonomy: " . . . the most basic postulate of science is that nature itself is orderly. . . . All theoretical science is ordering and if systematic is equated with ordering, the systematics is synonymous with theoretical science" (Simpson 1961).

If these criteria are followed, then one finds that systematic classifications relevant to their environment have been made by very many little traditions, as is indicated by examples taken from a number of simple cultures. Thus Amerindians have taken pains to observe and systematize scientific facts concerning lower animal life (Speck 1923, p. 273), although these animals do not afford any direct economic benefit to this culture, the interest in classification being purely intellectual. Thus for another simple culture, B. E. Smith (1954) notes "every plant, wild or cultivated had a name and a use, and where every man, woman and child knew literally hundreds of plants . . . (my instructor) simply could not realize that it was not the words but the plants which baffled me" (p. 19). In yet another culture, any child could identify

> the kind of tree from which a tiny wood fragment has come and furthermore, the sex of that tree, as defined by Kabiran notions of plant sex, by observing the appearance of its wood and bark, its smell, its hardness and similar characteristics. Fish and shell fish by the dozen are known by individually distinctive terms, and their separate features and habits as well as the sexual difference within each type, are well recognized. (A. H. Smith 1960)

Other instances of systematic classification and accumulation of rational knowledge of the environment have been given by several writers, for example from Hawaii (Handy et al. 1953); the Hanunoo (Conklin 1954) and the Filipino Negrito (Fox 1953). But what should be emphasized is that this systematic thinking and process of classification are not static but are based on the constant expansion of existing knowledge and on experimentation. As Ackernecht (1942) has forcefully noted, "in my investigations, I have found that there is more than enough evidence to indicate that experimentation in the old fashioned trial and error system is not unique to Western European societies or even to civilized societies" but exists also in the simplest ones.

That this experimentation goes on continually is indicated by the fact that many simple societies continually develop from local plants medicines that have been estimated as at least 25–50 percent effective (Grollig et al. 1976). Further, these isolated, simple cultures have often developed medicines for diseases introduced by Western man, a notable example being the development of a cure for malaria using the cinchona bark by Amerindians. The manner in which this process of continual experimentation goes on at the tribal level is best indicated by the following observation by Fox (1953) regarding the Negritos of the Philippines:

> The Negrito is an intrinsic part of his environment and what is still more important, continually studies his surroundings. Many times I have seen a Negrito, who, when not being certain of the identification of a particular plant, will taste the fruit, the leaves, break and examine the stem, comment upon its habitat, and only after all of this, pronounce whether he did or did not know the plant.

Further if a plant introduced to the environment is found to be useful "it will be quickly utilised. The fact that many Philippino groups such as the Pinatubo Negritos, constantly experiment with plants hastens the process of the recognition of the potential usefulness, as defined by the culture, of the introduced flora" (pp. 212–13).

I have given in conclusion this example of creativity from the Negritos (Aeta) because I myself, in discussions with Aeta groups in the Philippines, have listened to several instances of this process of experimentation. The Aetas' bold experimentation and new discoveries in medicine are best contrasted with the research of a major medical products company in the Philippines—"research" which is in the dependent, modern sector. This company produces a wide variety of medical products under licence from Western multinationals and also has a research department in the firm consisting of several MDs and PhDs; this by Philippino standards is a large research department. The "research" of the company, however, was very routine and pre-programmed. Most of the "research" was limited to sampling the population that used its products for quality control. The medical products tested, it should be noted, were well known and accepted in the US and the testing was routine and hardly worthy to be called "research." The lack of creativity of these highly trained, expensive scientists in this major pharmaceutical firm contrasted with the incessant curiosity and constant creativity of the more "primitive" Negritos. The moral is that creativity could exist—although in an unsophisticated fashion—in groups not yet covered by the repressive blanket of dependent knowledge.

R E F E R E N C E S

Ackernecht, E. H. (1942), *Bulletin of the History of Medicine,* 11, pp. 503–21. Reprinted 1958 in *Reader in Comparative Religion: An Anthropological Approach,* William A. Lessa and Evon S. Vogt, pp. 343–753. Evanston, Illinois, White Plains, New York.

Arunachalam, S. (1979), "Why Is Indian Science Mediocre," *Science Today,* February.

Conklin, H. C. (1954), *The Relation of Hanunoo Culture to the Plant World,* doc. dissertation, Yale (microfilm).

Fox, R. B. (1953), "The Pinatubo Negritos: Their Useful Plants and Material Culture," *The Philippine Journal of Science,* nos. 3–4, vol. 81, Manila.

Goonatilake, Susantha (1975), "Development Thinking as Cultural Neo-Colonialism," *Bulletin* of the Institute of Development Studies, Sussex, April (with a reply by Michael Lipton). The debate continued in the *Bulletin,* October 1975, with further comments by Rita Cruise O'Brien, Michael Lipton and Susantha Goonatilake. A reply also by Godfrey Goonatilake in *Marga,* vol. 2, no. 4, 1975.

————. (1976), "Technology and the Societal Context," *Engineer,* Colombo, March 1976.

————. (1976), "Towards a Study of Europology," presidential address, section "F," Sri Lanka Association for the Advancement of Science, Annual Sessions, December.

Grollig, Francis, and Harold B. Haley, (1976), *Medical Anthropology,* Mouton Publishers, The Hague.

Handy, E. S., Craighill and Pukui, M. Kawena (1953), "The Polynesian Family System in Ka'-u Hawaii," parts VI, VII, VIII, *Journal of the Polynesian Society,* vols. 62 and 64, Wellington, N.Z.

Jha, Akhilshwar (1977), *Intellectuals at the Crossroads,* Vikas Publishing House Pvt. Ltd., New Delhi.

Rahman, A. (1977), *Triveni: Science, Democracy and Socialism,* Indian Institute of Advanced Study, Simla.

Schrodinger, E. C. (1957), *Science, Theory and Man,* Dover Publications, New York.

Shils, Edward (1957), "The Intellectuals, Public Opinion and Economic Development," *Economic Development and Cultural Change,* vol. VI, no. 1.

Shiva, V. and J. Bandyopadhyay (1980), *Science in India—Research without Programmes, Scientists without a Community,* Indian Institute of Management, Bangalore.

Simpson, G. G. (1961), *Principles of Animal Taxonomy,* Columbia University Press, New York.

Smith, A. H. (1960), "The Culture of Kabira, Southern Byuku Islands," *Proceedings of the American Philosophical Society,* vol. 104, no. 2, Philadelphia.

Smith, Bowen E. (1954), *Return to Laughter,* Natural History Press, New York.

Speck, F. G. (1923), "Reptile Lore of the Northern Indians," *Journal of American Folk Lore,* vol. 36, no. 141, Boston and New York.

Srinavas, M. N. (1971), *Social Change in Modern India,* University of California Press, Berkeley.

PART FOUR

Science's Technologies and Applications

Western science at its foundations, as promoted by its most brilliant as well as its most ordinary exponents, never questioned the usefulness of scientific knowledge for warmaking. I know of no text from the early modern period which suggests that the scientist should withhold his knowledge from any government, at any time, but especially in the process of preparing for warmaking. Indeed most texts that recommend science also propose its usefulness in improving the state's capacity to wage war more effectively, to destroy more efficiently.

> Margaret Jacob, *The Cultural Meanings of the Scientific Revolution*

[M]odern science and technology are indivisible. The particular character of modern science ushered in with the Galilean revolution is precisely that it is directed towards experiment, use, technology itself; it is this which sets modern science apart from that of classical Greece, Babylon or India. The contemporary production of scientific knowledge is predominantly through the method of experiment, inherently committed to acting on the natural world, in order to understand and control it. At the level of consciousness of individual scientists, a quite contrary view was commonly expressed from the nineteenth through to the mid-twentieth century. This emphasized the disinterested and non-utilitarian nature of the work of the "man of science". . . . Their belief that they were pursuing knowledge for knowledge's sake savours more of the social functions of pre-modern science, where science is on a par with other intellectual and aesthetic activities such as music or poetry, than those of contemporary science.

> Hilary Rose and Steven Rose, "The Incorporation of Science," *Ideology of/in the Natural Sciences*

Modern science . . . is a threat to democracy, the quality of human life, and even the very capacity of our planet to support life at all. Moreover, modern science is a *social problem* because it is part of modern society, which itself is a social problem. . . . The scientific revolution was one of an interrelated set of *parallel* organizational responses within the major institutional spheres of Western Europe from the fifteenth century onwards (including Protestantism in the religious sphere and modern capitalism in the economic sphere) to an underlying set of ecological, demographic, and political economic conditions. This perspective does not readily yield a conception of modern science as an autonomous social system.

> Sal Restivo, "Modern Science as a Social Problem,"
> *Social Problems* 35:3 (1988)

[I]n the fifteen years following the war, the central fact of scientific life in physics was unprecedented growth based upon military funding. Yet however "significant" the funds made available for basic research, the total of such funds for all fields of science represented only a relatively insignificant fraction—roughly 5%—of the military's outlays for research and development. This rule of the twentieth arose in the earliest efforts to attach basic research to military missions. . . . The observance of this rule almost religiously even unto the present day results not from any intrinsic quantitative dependence of technical development upon "basic" research, but because a twentieth is the largest amount still relatively insignificant. It is the highest still inappreciable rate of taxation on social investment in advanced technological enterprise. . . . [T]oday even the 5% is encumbered by an explicit mission orientation.

> Paul Forman, "Behind Quantum Electronics," *Historical Studies in Physical and Biological Sciences* 18 (1987)

Should the strengths and weaknesses of the sciences, on the one hand, and of scientific technologies, applications and consequences, on the other hand, be evaluated independently? As was discussed in the introductory essay, the older view has been that they are discrete, and that it is important not to confuse the two. (This directive has sometimes, bizarrely, been interpreted to mean that no one should try to describe the causal relations *between* sciences and their technologies, applications, and consequences.) According to the older view, scientists and science institutions—foundations, universities, laboratories, journals, and so on—bear no responsibility for what society does with the information about nature and the social order that the sciences provide. Since World War II, however, this older view has come to seem more and more mistaken about the way contemporary science is located and practiced in contemporary society—and in earlier ones, as well.

Of course there have been many good consequences of scientific technologies and applications. In contrast to Sal Restivo's important argument stated in the epigraph, science should not be regarded *only* as a social problem, although it is illuminating to follow his recommendation and consider how it is one. But if sciences should get credit for their great achievements and good consequences, then they must take equal responsibility for the "bad science" and bad results that they also produce. Even better, we should articulate a more sophisticated account of the causes and consequences of scientific activity than this utopian–dystopian dichotomy permits. Sciences are, among other things, the meanings and uses of their institutions, practices, languages, and products. Their origins, the values they carry, and their consequences are not something different from "real sciences" but, instead, an intrinsic part of what they are. Sciences can change direction and critically distance their current projects from older origins, uses, and meanings; but that is what they must do, and they must figure out how to do it effectively in order to avoid the criticisms that appear in this section.

Many essays in other sections of this book discuss scientific technologies and applications in other contexts. The following selections review just a few more—in addition to the warmaking sciences Margaret Jacob and Paul Forman point to above—that have had especially regressive effects on people of non-European origin, and that raise disturbing questions about the legitimacy of scientific institutions' claims to autonomy from social control. Each of these critiques arose from a specific historical context, as the selections reveal. All were published first in the 1980s.

James Jones's 1981 account of the infamous Tuskegee syphilis experiment tells how poor African Americans were used in medical experiments of dubious scientific value and of which they had no knowledge or control. Many U.S. scientific institutions played a role in generating, funding, and maintaining this project. Perhaps we should expect no less in an era when so many European Americans tolerated the exploitation of African Americans in many other ways.

The new reproductive technologies have increased the ability of the privileged race, class, and gender to make policy decisions about who will live and who will not, as Phillida Bunkle's account of the international politics of birth control shows. The corporate construction and ownership of knowledge has life and death consequences. Should research to produce such technologies be done at all when the chances are so low that those on whom they will be used will have any say in the matter? (Wouldn't it go far to solve the economic problems of Third World countries if birth control were strictly enforced for wealthy and high-consuming elites in the North Atlantic? How many dozens of impoverished Africans—or Americans—could live well off the natural resources and human labor that one wealthy American consumes?)

Vandana Shiva argues that Western so-called scientific development created primarily maldevelopment in the Third World. For example, scientific forestry has caused ecological ruin, the impoverishment of the indigenous peoples, and the spread of unjust social relations. Women especially have suffered from this process. She reports also on over a century of women's organized political resistance to this kind of immiseration. Shiva here constructs a "reverse discourse" that persistently uses the colonial, capitalist, and sexist association of women with nature and "natives" against its original intentions; she uses it to criticize colonial, capitalist, and sexist practices that have had such tragic consequences for the Indian groups who have lived in the forests—especially for the women in these groups—and for the ecology of those regions. Some readers will find this set of associations disturbing, even when used for such progressive ends. Does Shiva's analysis inadvertently reinstate just the colonial framework she wishes to undermine? Does she invite Westerners to "demonize" Western science and dream of escapes to "elsewhere," rather than to learn how to block its regressive tendencies and advance its progressive ones? Or can such reverse discourses help to dismantle the power of the original sexist and racist assumptions?

Biologists Richard Levins and Richard Lewontin point to four main approaches to science in the Third World, none of which is drawing the disturbing conclusion Levins and Lewontin do, namely that " 'modern' high-technology agriculture is a successional stage ecologically, an unstable relationship to nature that is rapidly running its course and must be replaced by a radically different system of production."

Finally, Karl Grossman, who is the author of three books on energy and environmental issues, reports the growing resistance among people of color in the United States to environmental racism—discriminatory practices in environmental policy. This issue is not likely to disappear quickly since the United States and the West have not figured out what to do about polluting industries or the existing accumulations of toxic wastes. (In whose "backyards" will the toxic weaponry and other residue of the Cold War be laid to rest?) One target of their criticism is the restrictive vision of the environmental movement that has limited its concern to the preservation of "the wild" while ignoring how toxic dumps and polluting industries are systematically located in the neighborhoods of people of color. Grossman's account makes clear the importance of grass-roots organizing in drawing national attention to these practices.

In societies so stratified by race, class, and gender, should we expect their sciences and technologies to contribute to the progress of the humankind from which they draw their material and intellectual resources?

THE TUSKEGEE SYPHILIS EXPERIMENT
"A Moral Astigmatism"

James Jones

In late July of 1972, Jean Heller of the Associated Press broke the story: for forty years the United States Public Health Service (PHS) had been conducting a study of the effects of untreated syphilis on black men in Macon County, Alabama, in and around the county seat of Tuskegee. The Tuskegee Study, as the experiment had come to be called, involved a substantial number of men: 399 who had syphilis and an additional 201 who were free of the disease chosen to serve as controls. All of the syphilitic men were in the late stage of the disease when the study began.[1]

Under examination by the press the PHS was not able to locate a formal protocol for the experiment. Later it was learned that one never existed; procedures, it seemed, had simply evolved. A variety of tests and medical examinations were performed on the men during scores of visits by PHS physicians over the years, but the basic procedures called for periodic blood testing and routine autopsies to supplement the information that was obtained through clinical examinations. The fact that only men who had late, so-called tertiary, syphilis were selected for the study indicated that the investigators were eager to learn more about the serious complications that result during the final phase of the disease.

The PHS officers were not disappointed. Published reports on the experiment consistently showed higher rates of mortality and morbidity among the syphilitics than the controls. In fact, the press reported that as of 1969 at least 28 and perhaps as many as 100 men had died as a direct result of complications caused by syphilis. Others had developed serious syphilis-related heart conditions that may have contributed to their deaths.[2]

The Tuskegee Study had nothing to do with treatment. No new drugs were tested; neither was any effort made to establish the efficacy of old forms of treatment. It was a nontherapeutic experiment, aimed at compiling data on the effects of the spontaneous evolution of syphilis on black males. The magnitude of the risks taken with the lives of the subjects becomes clearer once a few basic facts about the disease are known.

Syphilis is a highly contagious disease caused by the *Treponema pallidum,* a delicate organism that is microscopic in size and resembles a corkscrew in shape. The disease may be acquired or congenital. In acquired syphilis, the spirochete (as the *Treponema pallidum* is also called) enters the body through the skin or mucous membrane, usually during sexual intercourse, though infection may also occur from other forms of bodily contact such as kissing. Congenital syphilis is transmitted to the fetus in the infected mother when the spirochete penetrates the placental barrier.

From the onset of infection syphilis is a generalized disease involving tissues throughout the entire body. Once they wiggle their way through the skin or mucous membrane, the spirochetes begin to multiply at a frightening rate. First they enter the lymph capillaries where they are hurried along to the nearest lymph gland. There they multiply and work their way into the bloodstream. Within days the spirochetes invade every part of the body.

Three stages mark the development of the disease: primary, secondary, and tertiary. The primary stage lasts from ten to sixty days starting from the time of infection. During this "first incubation period," the primary lesion of syphilis, the chancre, appears at the point of contact, usually on the genitals. The chancre, typically a slightly elevated, round ulcer, rarely causes personal discomfort and may be so small as to go unnoticed. If it does not become secondarily infected, the chancre will heal without treatment within a month or two, leaving a scar that persists for several months.[3]

While the chancre is healing, the second stage begins. Within six weeks to six months, a rash appears signaling the development of secondary syphilis. The rash may resemble measles, chicken pox, or any number of skin eruptions, though occasionally it is so mild as to go unnoticed. Bones and joints often become painful, and circulatory disturbances such as cardiac palpitations may develop. Fever, indigestion, headaches, or other nonspecific symptoms may accompany the rash. In some cases skin lesions develop into moist ulcers teeming with spirochetes, a condition that is especially severe when the rash appears in the mouth and causes open sores that are viciously infectious. Scalp hair may drop out in patches, creating a "moth-eaten" appearance. The greatest proliferation and most widespread distribution of spirochetes throughout the body occurs in secondary syphilis.[4]

Secondary syphilis gives way in most cases, even without treatment, to a period of latency that may last from a few weeks to thirty years. As if by magic, all symptoms of the disease seem to disappear, and the syphilitic patient does not associate with the disease's earlier symptoms the occasional skin infections, periodic chest pains, eye disorders, and vague discomforts that may follow. But the spirochetes do not vanish once the disease becomes latent. They bore into the bone marrow, lymph glands, vital organs, and central nervous systems of their victims. In some cases the disease seems to follow a policy of peaceful coexistence, and its hosts are able to enjoy full and long lives. Even so, autopsies in such cases often reveal syphilitic lesions in vital organs as contributing causes of death. For many syphilitic patients, however, the disease remains latent only two or three years. Then the delusion of a truce is shattered by the appearance of signs and symptoms that denote the tertiary stage.

It is during late syphilis, as the tertiary stage is also called, that the disease inflicts the greatest damage. Gummy or rubbery tumors (so-called gummas), the characteristic lesions of late syphilis, appear, resulting from the concentration of spirochetes in the body's tissues with destruction of vital structures. These tumors often coalesce on the skin forming large ulcers covered with a crust consisting of several layers of dried exuded matter. Their assaults on bone structure produce deterioration that resembles osteomyelitis or bone tuberculosis. The small tumors may be absorbed, leaving slight scarred depressions, or they may cause wholesale destruction of the bone, such as the horrible mutilation that occurs when nasal and palate bones are eaten away. The liver may also be attacked; here the result is scarring and deformity of the organ that impede circulation from the intestines.

The cardiovascular and central nervous systems are frequent and often fatal targets of late syphilis. The tumors may attack the walls of the heart or the blood vessels. When the aorta is involved, the walls become weakened, scar tissue forms over the lesion, the artery dilates, and the valves of the heart no longer open and close properly and begin to leak. The stretching of the vessel walls may produce an aneurysm, a ballonlike bulge in the aorta. If the bulge bursts, and sooner or later most do, the result is sudden death.

The results of neurosyphilis are equally devastating. Syphilis is spread to the brain through the blood vessels, and while the disease can take several forms, the best known is paresis, a general softening of the brain that produces progressive paralysis and insanity. Tabes dorsalis, another form of neurosyphilis, produces a stumbling, foot-slapping gait in its victims due to the destruction of nerve cells in the spinal cord. Syphilis can also attack the optic nerve, causing blindness, or the eighth cranial nerve, inflicting deafness. Since nerve cells lack regenerative power, all such damage is permanent.

The germ that causes syphilis, the stages of the disease's development, and the complications that can result from untreated syphilis were all known to medical science in 1932—the year the Tuskegee Study began.

Since the effects of the disease are so serious, reporters in 1972 wondered why the men agreed to cooperate. The press quickly established that the subjects were mostly poor and illiterate, and that the PHS had offered them incentives to participate. The men received free physical examinations, free rides to and from the clinics, hot meals on examination days, free treatment for minor ailments, and a guarantee that burial stipends would be paid to their survivors. Though the latter sum was very modest (fifty dollars in 1932 with periodic increases to allow for inflation), it represented the only form of burial insurance that many of the men had.

What the health officials had told the men in 1932 was far more difficult to determine. An officer of the venereal disease branch of the Centers for Disease Control in Atlanta, the agency that was in charge of the Tuskegee Study in 1972, assured reporters that the participants were told at the beginning that they had syphilis and were told what the disease could do to them, and that they were given the opportunity to withdraw from the program any time and receive treatment. But a physician with firsthand knowledge of the experiment's early years directly contradicted this statement. Dr. J. W. Williams, who was serving his internship at Andrews Hospital at the Tuskegee Institute in 1932 and assisted in the experiment's clinical work, stated that neither the interns nor the subjects knew what the study involved. "The people who came in were not told what was being done," Dr. Williams said. "We told them we wanted to test them. They were not told, so far as I know, what they were being treated for or what they were not being treated for." As far as he could tell, the subjects "thought they were being treated for rheumatism or bad stomachs." He did recall administering to the men what he thought were drugs to combat syphilis, and yet as he thought back on the matter, Dr. Williams conjectured that "some may have been a placebo." He was absolutely certain of one point: "We didn't tell them we were looking for syphilis. I don't think they would have known what that was."[5]

A subject in the experiment said much the same thing. Charles Pollard recalled clearly the day in 1932 when some men came by and told him that he would receive a free physical examination if he appeared the next day at a nearby one-room school. "So I went on over and they told me I had bad blood," Pollard recalled. "And that's what they've been telling me ever since. They come around from time to time and check me over and they say, 'Charlie, you've got bad blood.' "[6]

An official of the Centers for Disease Control (CDC) stated that he understood the term "bad blood" was a synonym for syphilis in the black community. Pollard replied, "That could be true. But I never heard no such thing. All I knew was that they just kept saying I had the bad blood—they never mentioned syphilis to me, not even once." Moreover, he thought that he had been receiving treatment for "bad blood" from the first meeting on, for Pollard added: "They been doctoring me off and on ever since then, and they gave me a blood tonic."[7]

The PHS's version of the Tuskegee Study came under attack from yet another quarter when Dr. Reginald G. James told his story to reporters. Between 1939 and 1941 he had been involved with public health work in Macon County—specifically the diagnosis and treatment of syphilis. Assigned to work with him was Eunice Rivers, a black nurse employed by the Public Health Service to keep track of the participants in the Tuskegee Study. "When we found one of the men from the Tuskegee Study," Dr. James recalled, "she would say, 'He's under study and not to be treated.' " These encounters left him, by his own description, "distraught and disturbed," but whenever he insisted on treating such a patient, the man never returned. "They were being advised they shouldn't take treatments or they would be dropped from the study," Dr. James stated. The penalty for being dropped, he explained, was the loss of the benefits that they had been promised for participating.[8]

Once her identity became known, Nurse Rivers excited considerable interest, but she steadfastly refused to talk with reporters. Details of her role in the experiment came to light when newsmen discovered an article about the Tuskegee Study that appeared in *Public Health Reports* in 1953. Involved with the study from its beginning, Nurse Rivers served as the liaison between the researchers and the subjects. She lived in Tuskegee and provided the continuity in personnel that was vital. For while the names and faces of the "government doctors" changed many times over the years, Nurse Rivers remained a constant. She served as facilitator, bridging the many barriers that stemmed from the educational and cultural gap between the physicians and the subjects. Most important, the men trusted her.[9]

As the years passed the men came to understand that they were members of a social club and burial society called "Miss Rivers' Lodge." She kept track of them and made certain that they showed up to be examined whenever the "government doctors" came to town. She often called for them at their homes in a shiny station wagon with the government emblem on the front door and chauffeured them to and from the place of examination. According to the *Public Health Reports* article, these rides became "a mark of distinction for many of the men who enjoyed waving to their neighbors as they drove by." There was nothing to indicate that the members of "Miss Rivers' Lodge" knew they were participating in a deadly serious experiment.[10]

Spokesmen for the Public Health Service were quick to point out that the experiment was never kept secret, as many newspapers had incorrectly reported when the story first broke. Far from being clandestine, the Tuskegee Study had been the subject of numerous reports in medical journals and had been openly discussed in conferences at professional meetings. An official told reporters that more than a dozen articles had appeared in some of the nation's best medical journals, describing the basic procedures of the study to a combined readership of well over a hundred thousand physicians. He denied that the Public Health Service had acted alone in the experiment, calling it a cooperative project that involved the Alabama State Department of Health, the Tuskegee Institute, the Tuskegee Medical Society, and the Macon County Health Department.[11]

Apologists for the Tuskegee Study contended that it was at best problematic whether the syphilitic subjects could have been helped by the treatment that was available when the study began. In the early 1930s treatment consisted of mercury and two arsenic compounds called arsphenamine and neoarsphenamine, known also by their generic name, salvarsan. The drugs were highly toxic and often produced serious and occasionally fatal reactions in patients. The treatment was painful and usually required more than a year to complete. As one CDC officer put it, the drugs offered "more potential harm for the patient than potential benefit."[12]

PHS officials argued that these facts suggested that the experiment had not been conceived in a moral vacuum. For if the state of the medical art in the early 1930s had nothing better than dangerous and less than totally effective treatment to offer, then it followed that, in the balance, little harm was done by leaving the men untreated.[13]

Discrediting the efficacy of mercury and salvarsan helped blunt the issue of withholding treatment during the early years, but public health officials had a great deal more difficulty explaining why penicillin was denied in the 1940s. One PHS spokesman ventured that it probably was not "a one-man decision" and added philosophically, "These things seldom are." He called the denial of penicillin treatment in the 1940s "the most critical moral issue about this experiment" and admitted that from the present perspective "one cannot see any reason that they could not have been treated at that time." Another spokesman declared: "I don't know why the decision was made in 1946 not to stop the program."[14]

The thrust of these comments was to shift the responsibility for the Tuskegee Study to the physician who directed the experiment during the 1940s. Without naming anyone, an official told reporters: "Whoever was director of the VD section at that time, in 1946 or 1947, would be the most logical candidate if you had to pin it down." That statement pointed an accusing finger at Dr. John R. Heller, a retired PHS officer who had served as the director of the division of venereal disease between 1943 and 1948. When asked to comment, Dr. Heller declined to accept responsibility for the study and shocked reporters by declaring: "There was nothing in the experiment that was unethical or unscientific."[15]

The current local health officer of Macon County shared this view, telling reporters that he probably would not have given the men penicillin in the 1940s either. He explained this curious devotion to what nineteenth-century physicians would have called "therapeutic nihilism" by emphasizing that penicillin was a new and largely untested drug in the 1940s. Thus, in his opinion, the denial of penicillin was a defensible medical decision.[16]

A CDC spokesman said it was "very dubious" that the participants in the Tuskegee Study would have benefited from penicillin after 1955. In fact, treatment might have done more harm than good. The introduction of vigorous therapy after so many years might lead to allergic drug reactions, he warned. Without debating the ethics of the Tuskegee Study, the CDC spokesman pointed to a generation gap as a reason to refrain from criticizing it. "We are trying to apply 1972 medical treatment standards to those of 1932," cautioned one official. Another officer reminded the public that the study began when attitudes toward treatment and experimentation were much different. "At this point in time," the officer stated, "with our current knowledge of treatment and the disease and the revolutionary change in approach to human experimentation, I don't believe the program would be undertaken."[17]

Journalists tended to accept the argument that the denial of penicillin during the 1940s was the crucial ethical issue. Most did not question the decision to withhold earlier forms of treatment because they apparently accepted the judgment that the cure was as bad as the disease. But a few journalists and editors argued that the Tuskegee Study presented a moral problem long before the men were denied treatments with penicillin. "To say, as did an official of the Centers for Disease Control, that the experiment posed 'a serious moral problem' after penicillin became available is only to address part of the situation," declared the *St. Louis Post-Dispatch*. "The fact is that in an effort to determine from autopsies what effects syphilis has on the body, the government from the moment the experiment began withheld the best available treatment for a particularly cruel disease. The immorality of the experiment was inherent in its premise."[18]

Viewed in this light, it was predictable that penicillin would not be given to the men. *Time* magazine might decry the failure to administer the drug as "almost beyond belief or human compassion," but along with many other publications it failed to recognize a crucial point. Having made the decision to withhold treatment at the outset, investigators were not likely to experience a moral crisis when a new and improved form of treatment was developed. Their failure to administer penicillin resulted from the initial decision to withhold all treatment. The only valid distinction that can be made between the two acts is that the denial of penicillin held more dire consequences for the men in the study. The *Chicago Sun Times* placed these separate actions in the proper perspective: "Whoever made the decision to withhold penicillin compounded the original immorality of the project."[19]

In their public comments, the CDC spokesmen tried to present the Tuskegee Study as a medical matter involving clinical decisions that may or may not have been valid. The antiseptic quality of their statements left journalists cold, prompting an exasperated North Carolina editor to declare: "Perhaps there are responsible people with heavy consciences about their own or their organizations' roles in this study, but thus far there is an appalling amount of 'So what?' in the comments about it." ABC's Harry Reasoner agreed. On national television, he expressed bewilderment that the PHS could be "only mildly uncomfortable" with an experiment that "used human beings as laboratory animals in a long and inefficient study of how long it takes syphilis to kill someone."[20]

The human dimension dominated the public discussions of the Tuskegee Study. The scientific merits of the experiment, real or imagined, were passed over almost without comment. Not being scientists, the journalists, public officials, and concerned citizens who protested the study did not really care how long it takes syphilis to kill people or what percentages of syphilis victims are fortunate enough to live to ripe old age with the disease. From their perspective the PHS was guilty of playing fast and loose with the lives of these men to indulge scientific curiosity.[21]

Many physicians had a different view. Their letters defending the study appeared in editorial pages across the country, but their most heated counterattacks were delivered in professional journals. The most spirited example was an editorial in the *Southern Medical Journal* by Dr. R. H. Kampmeir of Vanderbilt University's School of Medicine. No admirer of the press, he blasted reporters for their "complete disregard for their abysmal ignorance," and accused them of banging out "anything on their typewriters which will make headlines." As one of the few remaining physicians with experience treating syphilis in the 1930s, Dr. Kampmeir promised to "put this 'tempest in a teapot' into proper historical perspective."[22]

Dr. Kampmeir correctly pointed out that there had been only one experiment dealing with the effects of untreated syphilis prior to the Tuskegee Study. A Norwegian investigator had reviewed the medical records of nearly two thousand untreated syphilitic patients who had been examined at an Oslo clinic between 1891 and 1910. A follow-up had been published in 1929, and that was the state of published medical experimentation on the subject before the Tuskegee Study began. Dr. Kampmeir did not explain why the Oslo Study needed to be repeated.

The Vanderbilt physician repeated the argument that penicillin would not have benefited the men, but he broke new ground by asserting that the men themselves were responsible for the illnesses and deaths they sustained from syphilis. The PHS was not to blame, Dr. Kampmeir explained, because "in our free society, antisyphilis treatment has never been forced." He further reported that many of the men in the study had received some treatment for syphilis down through the years and insisted that others could have secured treatment had they so desired. He admitted that the untreated syphilitics suffered a higher mortality rate than the controls, observing coolly: "This is not surprising. No one has ever implied that syphilis is a benign infection." His failure to discuss the social mandate of physicians to prevent harm and to heal the sick whenever possible seemed to reduce the Hippocratic oath to a solemn obligation not to deny treatment upon demand.[23]

Journalists looked at the Tuskegee Study and reached different conclusions, raising a host of ethical issues. Not since the Nuremberg trials of Nazi scientists had the American people been confronted with a medical *cause célèbre* that captured so many headlines and sparked so much discussion. For many it was a shocking revelation of the potential for scientific abuse in their own country. "That it has happened in this country in our time makes the tragedy more poignant," wrote the editor of the *Philadelphia Inquirer*. Others thought the experiment totally "un-American" and agreed with Senator John Sparkman of Alabama, who denounced it as "absolutely appalling" and "a disgrace to the American concept of justice and humanity." Some despaired of ever again being able to hold their heads high. A resident of the nation's capital asked: "If this is true, how in the name of God can we look others in the eye and say: 'This is a decent country.' "[24]

Perhaps self-doubts such as these would have been less intense if a federal agency had not been responsible for the experiment. No one doubted that private citizens abused one another and had to be restrained from doing so. But the revelation that the Public Health Service had conducted the study was especially distressing. The editor of the *Providence Sunday Journal* admitted that he was shocked by "the flagrant immorality of what occurred under the auspices of the United States Government." A curious reversal of roles seemed to have taken place in Alabama: Instead of protecting its citizens against such experiments, the government was conducting them.[25]

Memories of Nazi Germany haunted some people as the broader implications of the PHS's role in the experiment became apparent. A man in Tennessee reminded health officials in Atlanta that "Adolf Hitler allowed similar degradation of human dignity in inhumane medical experiments on humans living under the

Third Reich," and confessed that he was "much distressed at the comparison." A New York editor had difficulty believing that "such stomach-turning callousness could happen outside the wretched quackeries spawned by Nazi Germany."[26]

The specter of Nazi Germany prompted some Americans to equate the Tuskegee Study with genocide. A civil rights leader in Atlanta, Georgia, charged that the study amounted to "nothing less than an official, premeditated policy of genocide." A student at the Tuskegee Institute agreed. To him, the experiment was "but another act of genocide by whites," an act that "again exposed the nature of whitey: a savage barbarian and a devil."[27]

Most editors stopped short of calling the Tuskegee Study genocide or charging that PHS officials were little better than Nazis. But they were certain that racism played a part in what happened in Alabama. "How condescending and void of credibility are the claims that racial considerations had nothing to do with the fact that 600 [all] of the subjects were black," declared the *Afro-American* of Baltimore, Maryland. That PHS officials had kept straight faces while denying any racial overtones to the experiment prompted the editors of this influential black paper to charge "that there are still federal officials who feel they can do anything where black people are concerned."[28]

The *Los Angeles Times* echoed this view. In deftly chosen words, the editors qualified their accusation that PHS officials had persuaded hundreds of black men to become "human guinea pigs" by adding: "Well, perhaps not quite that [human guinea pigs] because the doctors obviously did not regard their subjects as completely human." A Pennsylvania editor stated that such an experiment "could only happen to blacks." To support this view, the *New Courier* of Pittsburgh implied that American society was so racist that scientists could abuse blacks with impunity.[29]

Other observers thought that social class was the real issue, that poor people, regardless of their race, were the ones in danger. Somehow people from the lower class always seemed to supply a disproportionate share of subjects for scientific research. Their plight, in the words of a North Carolina editor, offered "a reminder that the basic rights of Americans, particularly the poor, the illiterate and the friendless, are still subject to violation in the name of scientific research." To a journalist in Colorado, the Tuskegee Study demonstrated that "the Public Health Service sees the poor, the black, the illiterate and the defenseless in American society as a vast experimental resource for the government." And the *Washington Post* made much the same point when it observed, "There is always a lofty goal in the research work of medicine but too often in the past it has been the bodies of the poor . . . on whom the unholy testing is done."[30]

The problems of poor people in the rural South during the Great Depression troubled the editor of the *Los Angeles Times,* who charged that the men had been "trapped into the program by poverty and ignorance." After all, the incentives for cooperation were meager—physical examinations, hot lunches, and burial stipends. "For such inducements to be attractive, their lives must have been savagely harsh," the editor observed, adding: "This in itself, aside from the experiment, is an affront to decency." Thus, quite apart from the questions it raised about human experimentation, the Tuskegee Study served as a poignant reminder of the plight of the poor.[31]

Yet poverty alone could not explain why the men would cooperate with a study that gave them so little in return for the frightening risks to which it exposed them. A more complete explanation was that the men did not understand what the experiment was about or the dangers to which it exposed them. Many Americans probably agreed with the *Washington Post's* argument that experiments "on human beings are ethically sound if the guinea pigs are fully informed of the facts and danger." But despite the assurances of PHS spokesmen that informed consent had been obtained, the Tuskegee Study precipitated accusations that somehow the men had either been tricked into cooperating or were incapable of giving informed consent.[32]

An Alabama newspaper, the *Birmingham News,* was not impressed by the claim that the participants were all volunteers, stating that "the majority of them were no better than semi-literate and probably didn't know what was really going on." The real reason they had been chosen, a Colorado journalist argued, was that they were "poor, illiterate, and completely at the mercy of the 'benevolent' Public Health Service." And a North Carolina editor denounced "the practice of coercing or tricking human beings into taking part in such experiments."[33]

The ultimate lesson that many Americans saw in the Tuskegee Study was the need to protect society from scientific pursuits that ignored human values. The most eloquent expression of this view appeared in the *Atlanta Constitution.* "Sometimes, with the best of intentions, scientists and public officials and others involved in working for the benefit of us all, forget that people are people," began the editor. "They concentrate so totally on plans and programs, experiments, statistics—on abstractions—that people become objects, symbols on paper, figures in a mathematical formula, or impersonal 'subjects' in a scientific study." This was the scientific blindspot to ethical issues that was responsible for the Tuskegee Study—what the *Constitution* called "a moral astigmatism that saw these black sufferers simply as 'subjects' in a study, not as human beings." Scientific investigators had to learn that "moral judgment should always be a part of any human endeavor," including "the dispassionate scientific search for knowledge."[34]

Many editors attributed the moral insensitivity of PHS officers to the fact that they were bureaucrats, as well as scientists. Distrust of the federal government led a Connecticut editor to charge that the experiment stemmed from "a moral breakdown brought about by a mindless bureaucracy going through repeated motions without ever stopping to examine the reason, cause and effects." To a North Carolina editor, the experiment had simply "rolled along of its own inhuman momentum with no one bothering to say, 'Stop, in the name of human decency.' " In a sense, then, the government's scientific community itself became a casualty of the Tuskegee Study.

N O T E S

1. *New York Times,* July 26, 1972, pp. 1, 8.

2. Because of the high rate of geographic mobility among the men, estimates of the mortality rate were confusing, even in the published articles. PHS spokesmen in 1972 were reluctant to be pinned down on an exact figure. An excellent example is the Interview of Dr. David Sencer by J. Andrew Liscomb and Bobby Doctor for the U.S. Commission on Civil Rights, Alabama State Advisory Committee, September 22, 1972, unpublished manuscript, p. 9. For the calculations behind the figures used here, see *Atlanta Constitution,* September 12, 1972, p. 2A.

3. During this primary stage the infected person often remains seronegative: A blood test will not reveal the disease. But chancres can be differentiated from other ulcers by a dark field examination, a laboratory test in which a microscope equipped with a special indirect lighting attachment can view the silvery spirochetes moving against a dark background.

4. At the secondary stage a blood test is an effective diagnostic tool.

5. Dr. Donald W. Prinz quoted in *Atlanta Journal,* July 27, 1972, p. 2; *Birmingham News,* July 27, 1972, p. 2.

6. *New York Times,* July 27, 1972, p. 18.

7. Dr. Ralph Henderson quoted in ibid.; *Tuskegee News,* July 27, 1972, p. 1.

8. *New York Times,* July 27, 1972, p. 2.

9. Eunice Rivers, Stanley Schuman, Lloyd Simpson, Sidney Olansky, "Twenty Years of Followup Experience in a Long-Range Medical Study," *Public Health Reports* 68 (April 1953): pp. 391–95. (Hereafter Rivers et al.)

10. Ibid., p. 393.

11. Dr. John D. Millar quoted in *Birmingham News,* July 27, 1972, pp. 1, 4: *Atlanta Journal,* July 27, 1972, p. 2.

12. Prinz quoted in *Atlanta Journal,* July 27, 1972, p. 2.

13. Millar quoted in *Montgomery Advertiser,* July 26, 1972, p. 1.

14. Ibid.; Prinz quoted in *Atlanta Journal,* July 27, 1972, p. 2.

15. Millar quoted in *Montgomery Advertiser,* July 26, 1972, p. 1; *New York Times,* July 28, 1972, p. 29.

16. Dr. Edward Lammons quoted in *Tuskegee News,* August 3, 1972, p. 1.

17. Prinz quoted in *Atlanta Journal,* July 27, 1972, p. 2; Millar quoted in *Montgomery Advertiser,* July 26, 1972, p. 1.

18. *St. Louis Dispatch,* July 30, 1972, p. 2D.

19. *Time,* August 7, 1972, p. 54; *Chicago Sun Times,* July 29, 1972, p. 23.

20. *News and Observer,* Raleigh, North Carolina, August 1, 1972, p. 4; ABC Evening News, August 1, 1972.

21. Their reactions can be captured at a glance by citing a few of the legends that introduced newspaper articles and editorials that appeared on the experiment. The *Houston Chronicle* called it "A Violation of Human Dignity" (August 5, 1972, section 1. p. 12); *St. Louis Post-Dispatch,* "An Immoral Study" (July 30, 1972, p. 2D); *Oregonian,* an "Inhuman Experiment" (Portland, Oregon, July 31, 1972, p. 16); *Chattanooga Times,* a "Blot of Inhumanity" (July 28, 1972, p. 16); *South Bend Tribune,* a "Cruel Experiment" (July 29, 1972, p. 6); *New Haven Register,* "A Shocking Medical Experiment" (July 29, 1972, p. 14); and Virginia's *Richmond Times Dispatch* thought that "appalling" was the best adjective to describe an experiment that had used "Humans as Guinea Pigs" (August 6, 1972, p. 6H). To the *Los Angeles Times* the study represented "Official Inhumanity" (July 27, 1972, part II, p. 6); to the *Providence Sunday Journal,* a "Horror Story" (July 30, 1972, p. 2G); and to the *News and Observer* in Raleigh, North Carolina, a "Nightmare Experiment"

(July 28, 1972, p. 4). The *St. Petersburg Times* in Florida voiced cynicism, entitling its editorial "Health Service?" (July 27, 1972, p. 24), while the *Milwaukee Journal* made its point more directly by introducing its article with the legend "They Helped Men Die" (July 27, 1972, p. 15).

22. R. H. Kampmeir, "The Tuskegee Study of Untreated Syphilis," *Southern Medical Journal* 65 (1972): pp. 1247–51.

23. Ibid., p. 1250.

24. *Philadelphia Inquirer,* July 30, 1972, p. 4H; *Montgomery Advertiser,* August 12, 1972, p. 13; letter to the editor signed A. B., *Evening Star,* Washington, D.C., August 10, 1972, p. 18A; for examples of a similar reaction, see the *Gazette,* Charleston, West Virginia, July 30, 1972, p. 2D, and Salley E. Clapp to Dr. Merlin K. Duval, July 26, 1972, Tuskegee Files, Centers for Disease Control, Atlanta, Georgia. (Hereafter TF-CDC).

25. *Providence Sunday Journal,* July 30, 1972, p. 2G; for the same view, see *Evening Sun,* Baltimore, Maryland, July 26, 1972, p. 26A.

26. Roderick Clark Posey to Millar, July 27, 1972, TF-CDC; *Daily News,* July 27, 1972, p. 63; see also *Milwaukee Journal,* July 27, 1972, p. 15; *Oregonian,* July 31, 1972, p. 16; and Jack Slater, "Condemned to Die for Science," *Ebony* 28 (November 1972), p. 180.

27. *Atlanta Journal,* July 27, 1972, p. 2; *Campus Digest,* October 6, 1972, p. 4.

28. *Afro-American,* August 12, 1972, p. 4. For extended discussions of the race issue, see Slater, "Condemned to Die," p. 191, and the three-part series by Warren Brown in *Jet* 43, "The Tuskegee Study," November 9, 1972, pp. 12–17, November 16, 1972, pp. 20–26, and, especially, November 23, 1972, pp. 26–31.

29. *Los Angeles Times,* July 27, 1972, part II, p. 6; *New Courier* also stated, "No other minority group in this country would have been used as 'Human Guinea Pigs,' " and explained, "because those who are responsible knew that they could do this to Negroes and nothing would be done to them if it became known," August 19, 1972, p. 6.

30. *Greensboro Daily News,* August 2, 1972, p. 6; *Gazette-Telegraph,* Colorado Springs, August 3, 1972, p. 8A; *Washington Post,* July 31, 1972, p. 20A. See also *Arkansas Gazette,* July 29, 1972, p. 4A.

31. *Los Angeles Times,* July 27, 1972, p. 20A.

32. *Washington Post,* July 31, 1972, p. 20A.

33. *Birmingham News,* July 28, 1972, p. 12; *Gazette-Telegraph,* August 3, 1972, p. 8A; *Greensboro Daily News,* August 2, 1972, p. 6A.

34. *Atlanta Constitution,* July 27, 1972, p. 4A.

CALLING THE SHOTS?

The International Politics of Depo-Provera

Phillida Bunkle

Depo-Provera, the three-monthly contraceptive injection, is a case study in the dilemmas posed to women by the development of the new reproductive technology. On the one hand Depo's easy administration and contraceptive efficacy makes contraception potentially convenient for millions of underprivileged women; on the other hand these very features make it a powerful tool for the control of women.

Depo is exclusively manufactured by the multinational Upjohn Corporation. Upjohn not only manufactures the drug—it also manufactures most of the information about it. Responding "rationally" to the economic system, naturally they promote knowledge favourable to their product.

Depo, or medroxyprogesterone acetate, is a progestogen, that is, an artificially created drug which has some properties similar to naturally occurring sex hormones called progesterones. Upjohn started testing Depo as a contraceptive in the early 1960s.

In 1967 Upjohn applied to the United States Food and Drug Administration (FDA) for a licence to sell Depo as a contraceptive (*The Depo-Provera Debate,* 1978). In the following year Upjohn began the seven-year dog and ten-year monkey studies required by FDA.

The dog trials showed dose-related increases in both benign breast nodules and breast cancer. As a result of initial findings in dogs, the oral form of the drug, called Provest, and four other progestogen contraceptive preparations were withdrawn in 1970. Controversy has surrounded the use of the injectable long-acting Depo form ever since.

In 1974 FDA responded to the licensing application by allowing marketing with very stringent restrictions (ibid.: 223–27). Even with these conditions final permission was stayed on request from a congressional committee. The debate continued with a series of Congressional Hearings. In 1978 FDA finally rejected the application to market Depo as a contraceptive in the United States. In an extraordinary move Upjohn appealed against the decision. A Public Board of Enquiry heard this appeal in early 1983 (*Science,* 1982; *Time,* 1983). As of September 1983 the results of this and a similar appeal in the United Kingdom are not known.

The FDA ban meant effectively that Depo could not be manufactured in the USA. New Zealand, which had approved it for use in 1968, imports its supplies from an Upjohn subsidiary in Belgium. Not only was the company denied the lucrative U.S. market, but, more importantly, because State Department policy prevented USAID (the main channel for American overseas aid) from supplying drugs banned in the United States, Upjohn could not manufacture there for the huge Third World market (*Export of Hazardous Products,* 1980; Shaikh and Reich, 1981). Until President Reagan changed this policy in 1981 this was the primary cause of the company's concern. The ban not only inhibited willingness to buy by making the product look suspect, it cut off the large market that AID funds would make available.

Various population agencies were led, by their perception of the overriding need to make contraception available to all women, to evade this restriction (Ehrenreich, Dowie, and Minkin, 1979; Sarra, 1982). It is alleged, for instance, that AID funds passed to International Planned Parenthood Federation (IPPF), whose headquarters are in London. IPPF purchased Depo for worldwide supply to national family planning associations. In this way family planning associations (FPA) became major sources of Depo, although many of their well-intentioned medical workers are not aware of this background. When the propriety of laundering funds was questioned, IPPF defended their actions by convening an international committee of medical experts especially to consider Depo. Some committee members had worked with FPA supplying Depo in their various countries. Their report was highly reassuring, as were the expert evaluations provided by other interested parties, the World Health Organization and AID (*Bulletin of the World Health Organization,* 1982; *IPPF Medical Bulletin,* 1980, 1982; AID, *Report to USAID of the Ad Hoc Consultative Panel,* 1978). Sometimes FPA doctors who prescribe Depo in New Zealand appear to have only information from these reports and package inserts supplied by the company.

Who Uses Depo-Provera?

The market potential of Depo was enormous. With half the world's population as potential users and manufacturing costs low, the market for contraceptive drugs is particularly large and profitable. In the West market saturation for contraceptive pharmaceuticals was reached with the pill by the late 1960s. Thereafter development of new products slowed. Market expansion depended on developing methods of administering contraceptives that would reach new populations. Here the interests of the drug companies and population controllers coincided. Unlike other expensive drugs, contraceptives are ones which Third World governments and international agencies are willing to spend money on. Although long-acting injectable drugs were ideal, the U.S. ban meant that Upjohn had to work hard to develop the market potential. Between 1971 and 1974 Upjohn spent over $4 million in bribes to foreign governments and family planning officials to encourage the use of the drug (*Export of Hazardous Products,* 1980: 184–87). Upjohn's persistence in challenging FDA decisions kept the safety issue "open" and kept the debate focused on the distant issue of cancer rather than more immediate adverse effects, until Depo was firmly established as brand leader.

Sales increased throughout the 1970s, reaching 7 million doses per year in 1978 and 8 million by 1983 (*Population Reports,* 1983, K-21). Of the countries with the highest rates of use, Jamaica, Thailand, New Zealand, Mexico and Sri Lanka, only New Zealand is not a Third World country (ibid.). In most rich countries, for example, in the USA, Australia and Great Britain, Depo is banned or heavily restricted (Rakusen, 1981). In these countries there is, however, significant use in sections of the population which most resemble Third World stereotypes. Depo is, for example, reportedly used extensively on West Indian and Asian women in Britain and Aboriginals in Australia (*Cultural Survival,* 1981; Floreman, 1981: 17; Lucas and Ware, 1981; Savage, 1983; Thomas, 1982; *The Times,* 1981).

In New Zealand it is used disproportionately on Polynesian women. One statistically reliable survey of family practice found that

> Maori and Non-Maori women had similar overall contraception consultation rates, but there was a striking difference between races in the type of contraception used. Maori women were much more likely to get the Depo Provera injection. (Gimore and Madarasz, 1983: 8)

In this study Depo was prescribed to Maori women more often than any other form of contraception.

Company sales figures suggest that between 80,000 to 100,000 injections are sold in New Zealand each year. Dr. Charlotte Paul of the University of Otago Medical School has estimated from surveys of contraceptive use that approximately 15 percent of Pakeha (paleface) and 25 percent of Maori women have used it at some time (Paul, 1981). A disturbing proportion of us, especially Maoris, will be at risk from any long-term effects Depo may turn out to have.

Debate over the Safety of Depo-Provera

Upjohn's assertion that Depo "is probably the safest hormonal contraceptive drug available" is based on their claim that after fifteen years' use and millions of prescriptions there is a "low reported incidence of side effects" (Upjohn Corporation, 1980: 314). The company has a vested interest in not looking for such evidence. But the absence of information does not establish the safety of a drug.

Upjohn claims that Depo is one of the most studied drugs available. None of these studies, however, conclusively answers vital safety questions. This is apparent even from an exhaustive evaluation of the medical evidence that is very favourable to Depo by Ian Fraser, Australia's foremost advocate of Depo and consultant to WHO and FPA (Fraser and Weisberg, 1981).

The example of this review shows why the medical evidence does not answer women's questions. Fraser's review was published as part of the *Medical Journal of Australia*. Printing costs were, however, paid by Upjohn. Having paid for production, Upjohn distributes this "reputable" medical opinion as part of their promotional literature. Corporate production of "academic" knowledge is not usually so blatant. Political science journals do not carry party manifestos even as supplements. The medical literature is generally reassuring about Depo, not because the drug is safe, but because of the way medical knowledge is constructed and disseminated.

The claim made by medical literature that Depo is safe cannot in fact be scientifically evaluated because the evidence available is either (1) the result of experiments performed or funded by the corporation and constructed to give them favourable results, (2) is "proprietary information," or (3) has never been systematically examined at all. To illustrate this I shall examine each of the safety issues using these three categories.

1. The Corporate Construction of Knowledge

Cancer. Three cancer sites are involved, the breast, cervix and uterus. There are questions about the carcinogenicity of oestrogen pills and IUDs, especially copper IUDs, but if Depo were licensed it would be the first contraceptive drug accepted by FDA which is known to have caused cancer in test animals.

Controversy has centered on the applicability of the findings of cancer in the dog and monkey studies to women. Upjohn argued, and the population control agencies echoed, that the dog study is not significant because in Upjohn's view the beagles used in the dog studies were uniquely susceptible to breast cancers. Critics reply that while these results do not prove that Depo causes breast cancer in humans it must nevertheless be treated as presumptive evidence. Since animal tests have proved predictive for other known carcinogens, at the very least they shift the onus of proof of safety onto the manufacturer (Epstein, 1977).

When the results of the monkey study became available they added fuel to the controversy. At the end of the ten years, two of the high dose animals had endometrial cancers, and it was later revealed that three had had breast lumps. The debate on the validity of species-to-species extrapolation was promptly repeated for the monkeys. There has been little independent study of a possible cancer link in women. The evidence on breast cancer is described as "sparse" (Fraser and Weisberg, 1981: 11). Upjohn rebuts the possibility that Depo causes uterine cancer by citing a "study" done by Malcolm Potts in Thailand (McDaniel and Potts, 1979). In 1978 Potts, former medical director of IPPF, joined the International Fertility Research Program (IFRP), an organization funded by USAID with lesser contributions from IPPF, Upjohn and others. IFRP has led the campaign for Depo. Potts went to Thailand for one month and with Edward McDaniel, the main distributor of Depo in northern Thailand, he was able to trace nine of the sixty women who had been admitted to the region's hospital with uterine cancer (Minkin, 1981). He ascertained that none of the nine had had Depo. The inadequacies of the "study" are obvious, indeed laughable, yet it has been cited repeatedly as "evidence" that Depo does not cause cancer in women.

Very recently, Dr. Potts, Dr. Shelton from AID and others have published evidence from 5,000 black American Depo users showing no increase in breast, uterine or ovarian cancers (Liang et al., 1983). Unfortunately, short exposure, a limited follow-up period and wide "confidence limits" prevent the study from being anything other than inconclusive.

In the meantime, however, concern had arisen over a possible relation in humans between Depo and cervical cancer, which is a much greater cause of concern than relatively rare uterine cancer. This is the shakiest, but in some ways most suggestive, human evidence on the carcinogenicity of Depo.

The human trials required from Upjohn were reported with no control, little information of concurrent drug usage and zero follow-up. In 1974 an FDA analyst giving testimony to a congressional subcommittee showed, however, that if the Third National Cancer Survey was used as a control to the Upjohn supplied data then it appeared that women on Depo had rates of cervical cancer in situ much greater than expected (Johnson, 1976).

FDA rejected the validity of using the National Cancer Survey as a control because the Upjohn group had been subject to more intense diagnostic scrutiny. Feminists were dissatisfied with FDA's dismissal of such suggestive evidence. They found two similarly screened groups to use as controls for the Upjohn data. Both suggested elevated rates of cervical cancer in Depo users (Corea, 1980).

Upjohn now needed evidence to refute the suspicion. The New Zealand Contraception and Health Study was the response. The "primary objective" of the study "is to examine the relative association between contraceptive practices and the development of dysplasia, carcinoma in situ, or invasive carcinoma of the cervix" (Protocol, 1982:2). The study has a most prestigious executive committee, including the senior obstetrics/gynaecology professors from both New Zealand medical schools. The chairperson of the executive, Professor Liggins, from the National Women's Hospital, vehemently maintains that the study is independent and was initiated by him (Close Up, 1983). This is disputed by some scientists who were first consulted by Upjohn personnel. The fragmentary documentary history made public at a recent Statistical Association conference would seem to support the view that the early stages were initiated and designed by Upjohn (Renner, 1983a). The company seems less concerned than academics to maintain the appearance of independence from the study; their "media package" says "Upjohn is currently conducting long range studies in New Zealand" (Upjohn Interview, 1982). There appears to be no other study to which they might be referring.

New Zealand is convenient for an investigation of a possible link between

Depo and cervical cancer. New Zealand has a higher rate of use than any other country with a social and ethnic composition similar to the United States and a comparable standard of health care. An internal Upjohn memo notes the public health care system as an advantage, presumably because it will relieve the company from having to pay for any medical treatment incurred by subjects (Weisblat, 1977). The minister of health, dedicated to the "free market" of ideas, eschews any regulation of privately funded research, even on human subjects. More significantly, welfare state legislation precludes the possibility of suing a doctor or drug company for damages. Regulatory freedom and legal immunity must be extremely attractive to a company which is a party to multi-million-dollar suits for damages from American women who feel they have been injured by DES or Depo.

The New Zealand Contraception and Health Study is a prospective observational study following three groups of 2,500 subjects using Depo, IUDs, or combined pills for five years. A PAP smear is taken at each annual examination and a questionnaire completed by the doctor. Completed questionnaires are forwarded to the study office located in a partitioned section of the Upjohn warehouse in Auckland, which is leased by the Executive Committee from Upjohn, with Upjohn funds. "Sealed patient questionnaires are not opened in New Zealand" (*Protocol,* 1982: 13) but are sent direct to Upjohn headquarters in Kalamazoo, Michigan, where data are stored on the company computer (ibid.: 21). Data will be analysed by company scientists under the director of an Upjohn "project manager" (ibid.). There is no undertaking to publish all or any results.

Professor Liggins maintains that this constitutes complete independence from the Upjohn Corporation (*Close Up,* 1983). There has been some discussion internal to the medical profession about why the pathology for the study is not being handled in New Zealand, where the capacity to process PAP smears is well developed. Similarly the protocol says that "All data processing and analysis will be performed in Kalamazoo" (*Protocol,* 1982: 21). Some biostatisticians have asked why the statistical analysis has not been designed and carried out in New Zealand. The report of the Survey Appraisals Committee of the New Zealand Statistical Association, which is critical of the study, draws attention to the fact that there will be no independent access to data to facilitate "peer review" (Deely, 1983).

The design of the study will crucially affect its results. Papers by a statistical consultant at recent Statistical Association and Epidemiological conferences show that the duration and sample size are too small to allow the study the statistical power to discriminate even large increases in cervical dysplasia or cancer (Renner, 1983a, 1983b, 1983c). Study design will therefore ensure reassuring results, justified or not. Only one medical doctor in New Zealand has publicly voiced concern about the study (*Close Up,* 1983). Next day he was verbally assailed by the head of National Women's Hospital and told that his professional standing was in jeopardy. These remarks were later withdrawn but the collective silence of the medical profession is perhaps not surprising. It is unlikely that aspiring obstetricians and gynaecologists will risk their career prospects by publicly criticising senior professors of both medical schools, on an issue of little personal concern to themselves.

The most outspoken medical advocate of Depo in New Zealand is John Hutton, formerly junior colleague of Professor Liggins, and recently promoted to the chair of obstetrics and gynaecology at Wellington Clinical School. At his aptly entitled inaugural lecture, "Depo-Provera: Are the Critics Justified?" (Hutton, 1981, 1983), Professor Hutton defended Upjohn paying for a study in which they have a vested interest, on the grounds that 80 percent of all medical research worldwide is funded by drug companies. Upjohn funding for this study was, he said, comparable to the annual budget of the Medical Research Council, the government source of medical research funds in New Zealand. Of course, such funds are important to those whose careers and prestige depend upon attracting them. By lending their names to research funded by drug companies, academics notch up the publication titles essential to career success. The more they do this, the more successful and powerful they will become, and the more able to attract funds (Mangold, 1983).

Upjohn money may also have influenced liberal doctors, many of whom work for FPA. Through affiliation with IPPF, FPA became the single largest supplier of Depo in New Zealand. FPA is chronically poorly funded. The company pays them $25 plus a consultation fee for each woman recruited into the study.

Upjohn has spent a great deal of money on the New Zealand Contraceptive and Health Study. It is unlikely that its funds will be wasted.

2. Corporate Control of Knowledge

Cancer is not, however, the only safety issue with Depo-Provera. In 1979 Stephen Minkin published a critical review of the evidence on Depo in which he claimed that company reports of the animal studies spoke of cancers but did not reveal other very important adverse effects, in particular that many dogs actually died of uterine disease (Minkin, 1979). Minkin's work has been widely discredited, especially for lax citation (Hutton, 1980). Some of these criticisms are justified, but nevertheless the central charge that important evidence of side effects was not released remains unrefuted (Corea, 1980). Since the company "owns" the evidence it is not available for scrutiny and the charge cannot be evaluated. The safety debate has focused on cancer with little investigation on other health risks to women.

Depo has been promoted worldwide as the ideal contraceptive for lactating mothers. This is a critical issue for Third World women. In New Zealand this is when it is likely to be prescribed for white, middle-class women. Apart from one study on rats, there is no evidence about the effect on neonates of Depo, absorbed from breast milk (Satayasthit et al., 1976). That Depo should have been promoted for this purpose before its effects on infants was established is another example of unwillingness to look for evidence that might injure prime markets.

Teratogenic effects. The concern arises because of the known teratogenic effects of progestogens (Shapiro, 1978). Exposure during gestation is different and more significant but is nevertheless reasonable grounds for caution in exposing breast-fed neonates. As with cancer the evidence is a pattern of suggestive animal studies, backed by fragmentary human evidence.

In animal studies progestogens given in utero cause masculinisation of female foetuses. There is some slight but disturbing corroborative evidence from children who have been treated with Depo during gestation. Girl babies exposed to large doses of Depo in utero have been found to have "clitoral hypertrophy." "Clitoral hypertrophy is an increase in the size of the clitoris in relationship to the size of the baby." (*The Depo-Provera Debate,* 1978: 75–80). The doctors who gave this evidence to a congressional committee, however, testified that they found no evidence of birth defects. Clitoral enlargement "becomes less obvious as the girl grows up" (ibid.) so that although it was a defect apparent at birth it was not a "birth defect."

Upjohn has used this remarkable logic to discredit critics concerned about a possible link between Depo and growth abnormalities (*Export of Hazardous Products,* 1980: 332). Now-you-see-it-now-you-don't definitions enable them to evade disturbing evidence and at the same time discredit opposition.

A recent evaluation in the prestigious *Journal of the American Medical Association* turns the lack of research on this issue into an argument for wider use to facilitate further experimentation (Rosenfield et al., 1983: 2925).

Upjohn recognises that more evidence is needed. In their submission to the FDA Board of Enquiry Upjohn says: "follow-up of children exposed in utero is one aspect of the prospective observational study being conducted in New Zealand." (Upjohn Corporation, 1982: 5)

The study protocol, however, has no mention of such children. The protocol simply provides no evidence for the existence of this aspect of the study (*Protocol,* 1982: 5, 10). This is similar to the "six years of clinical trials" that the Upjohn consumer information pamphlet claims have taken place in New Zealand, but of which there is no trace (*Close Up,* 1983).

3. The Invisibility of Women's Experience in Medical Research

If advocates of Depo discount animal evidence because it is animal, they also discount women's experience with the drug because it is "subjective."

When women report to their doctors effects of the drug unrelated to its contraceptive efficacy it does not appear to raise doubts about the drug, but, rather, reinforces the stereotype of women as "complaining" or "over-anxious." Effects may be attributed to women's nature rather than recognised as drug-related. Many women have been told that the problems they report are "most unusual." The implication is that the problems are "in" the women rather than "in" the drug.

Women's experience has not been heard at all in the Depo debate. The definition of medical knowledge excludes the personal and invalidates our testimony. I have been part of a New Zealand feminist health group evaluating the medical evidence and asserting the primacy of women's experience in the debate. By gathering together many women's accounts of how they were prescribed Depo and their experience using it we have been able to reassure many women that they are not alone or unusual in experiencing adverse effects. For many women it has been a huge relief to feel it is not something "wrong" with them.

In trying to gather information about the use of Depo in New Zealand, our group has been hampered not only by our lack of resources but also by the belief that we are paranoid or neurotic. Not being scientists or doctors, we are made to feel that we have no "right" to such information. Our health and our bodies are none of our business. The chief O & G (obstetrician/gynecologist) of New Zealand described the letters that come to National Women's Hospital on "forced sterilization and Depo-Provera" as "not usually true, grossly distorted or psychotic" (Bonham, 1980). Feminist research is seen as the exaggeration of distorted minds having problems with "authority." This may seem like rather primitive abuse of psychiatric labels but it is effective in discrediting our individual and collective experience.

Some of the women who shared their experience with us found Depo helpful and experienced few side effects; others experienced side effects but considered them worthwhile for effective contraception; others experienced very severe effects. Because it is important that negative experiences be made visible I draw on them here.

Bleeding. The medical literature recognises that bleeding "disturbances" are the most common side effect of Depo. What is unacknowledged is how disabling these "disturbances" can be.

> *Ruth:* Within 24 hours of the injection I started bleeding. I flooded for 14 weeks. In that time I lost 3 stone (42 lbs). I couldn't go out. Sometimes I could only crawl around.

Upjohn does now admit that 1–2 percent of women will have heavy bleeding on Depo. Bleeding is difficult to quantify. It has therefore been consistently minimised. Few studies investigate it. One study which does do so speaks of bleeding "episodes" of eleven–thirty days a month (Nash, 1975; Toppozada, 1978). But how heavy, for how many months? Bleeding is perceived as a problem because it is the main reason of "discontinuance." The significance of side effects is measured by the effect on "acceptance ratios." This orientation is reflected in a World Health Organization study which set out to test how "legitimate" women's reasons were for discontinuing Depo. They found that stopping Depo was positively correlated with bleeding "episodes" of eighty days or more (WHO, 1978)!

There is no recognition in the medical literature of the meaning to otherwise healthy women of these "disturbances," or of the utter debility they can cause. One "expert" said "one woman a week was admitted to National Women's Hospital with uncontrollable bleeding from Depo Provera" (Taylor, 1980). The issue is not just how many incapacitated women this adds up to, but that it trivialises women's sometimes devastating experience.

> *Christine:* Christine is a maths teacher. She is married to a senior lecturer (assistant professor) of accountancy. She was given Depo in the maternity hospital after the birth of her second child. She believed it was administered routinely to all her doctor's patients and did not feel she had a choice. It seemed to make all her post-natal symptoms worse. She felt debilitated by the following eighteen months spotting and bleeding which was accompanied by sharp stabbing pains in the uterus. But it was feeling afraid to go out of the house because she had to be near a toilet that contributed most to her depression. She was prescribed psycho-active drugs but the gynaecologist offered no treatment for the bleeding.

When we talk openly of women's experiences and what they mean we are said to be "sensationalising" the issue. The fact that they are often accompanied by acute distress and depression is used to discredit the testimony. We are accused of "frightening" women but their months of fear are ignored.

There seems to be a discrepancy between what women experience and the evidence in the medical literature. The New Zealand Contraception and Health Study provides an example of how this discrepancy can come about. The study devises useful measures of bleeding "disturbances." The "exclusion criteria," however, exclude subjects who stop their method of contraception within ninety days (*Protocol*, 1982: 7). Ninety days is only relevant to Depo. It means that women who only have one shot will be dropped from the study. Although heavy bleeding sometimes occurs when the drug is withdrawn, usually the worst bleeding occurs immediately after the first shot. The most severe bleeding will therefore be excluded by the study and will not be measured at all.

Such knowledge is constructed to discount women's actual experience. "Objective facts" like these are used to show how feminists exaggerate.

Science is projected as "pure," that is, independent of the interests that produce it. The authority of science obscures the political process in the construction of scientific knowledge. The "facts," however, directly reflect the structures that create them.

The process by which facts are validated is very important in defining what is "known." Only events recorded in medical literature are recognised, yet such documentation is quite haphazard. The experience of our group suggests significant underreporting of serious effects. Fraser's review of the medical literature found "one case of anaphylactic shock has been reported" and "there does not appear to be a single well substantiated case" of permanent infertility "in the literature" (Fraser and Weisberg, 1981: 8). Our group knows of four women who have had life-threatening anaphylactic reactions. Two followed the first and two followed the second injection. The ninety-day "exclusion criterion" will predictably result in under-representation of anaphylaxis in the New Zealand Contraception and Health Study, which will contribute to "knowledge" about the rarity of such events.

Infertility. Similarly, we know of four women, two of "proven fertility," who, having been regular before, have not had a period since taking Depo.

> *Gail* had previously had a child. "I took Depo 8 years ago and my cycle has never returned to normal. I have never had a period since then unless I took the pill." Gail was later able to conceive with the help of fertility drugs.

> *Jane* had previously had a child. "I had two shots of Depo 7 years ago. I have not had a period since." Jane has recently had some treatment with fertility drugs. She hopes they will make her fertile again as she felt that being made infertile was one reason why her relationship broke up.

The absence of "objective" evidence of permanent infertility is used to show that continuing concern about Depo is irrational. Four women may not be many, but for them being unusual is no comfort.

The long delay in the return of fertility can cause havoc in women's lives. It is hard to plan your life when you are waiting in limbo to conceive, or worrying that you may be either pregnant or sterile.

The manufacturers do admit that there is a lengthy delay in the return of fertility. Two studies are quoted which show that, two years after stopping Depo injections, conception rates are comparable to the pill and higher than the IUD (Pardthaisong et al., 1980; Gardner and Mischell, 1970). The medical literature shows that, eighteen months after discontinuance, 85 percent of women are menstruating again (*Population Reports,* 1983). The 15 percent who are not disappear from the literature. Reversibility is of vital concern to women, yet it is given little attention in the research. Women's needs do not determine scientific priorities.

Depression and permanent weight gain. No attempt at all is made to gather information on some "side effects," no matter how important they are to women. Medical research tends to equate "real" with "quantifiable." "Real" means you can add it up. Everything else is psychosomatic or subjective. Evidence that does not fit into the objective quantifiable mode, such as depression, cannot be measured and is readily dismissed. There is an assumption that only clearly physical effects can be caused by a drug. It is a short step to seeing the person who reports such "unreal" effects as unreal or unstable too.

Many women have told us how depressed they seemed to become while taking Depo. Most women recognised that it was difficult to tell whether Depo was a "cause" of their depressed mood, although some said that they had never felt depressed before taking it. Quite a few women had treatment for depression while taking Depo. Depo is frequently given to women who are experiencing difficulties. It is routinely given to many mental hospital patients. No one knows how much it may contribute to keeping them in this state.

Women who are given Depo postnatally may have weight gain, sexual turn-off and depression anyway, but Depo isn't going to help the situation. These women may have to struggle harder to climb out of their condition. The medical literature shows that the average weight gain is 5–10 lbs. (*Population Reports,* 1983: K-27). Quite a lot of women are, however, really distressed by very large weight gains which they find hard to reverse. The literature shows gains of up to 45 lbs. in a year. For some women this was associated with a sense of helplessness that contributed to depression.

Sexual turn-off. The effect of Depo about which most women complained to us was that of being sexually turned off. Depo is used in two American clinics to chemically castrate male sex offenders (Barry and Ciccone, 1975), but it is used on millions of women without any consideration of its effects on their sex lives. In the medical literature on Depo, the only discussion of this as a problem I have found was from a Chilean doctor who said that they gave up using six-monthly injections of a double dose because "it caused a rather marked regression of the internal genitals that was accompanied frequently by poor libido and lack of orgasm, a matter that meant some conflict with the husband" (Zanartu, 1978). What it meant for the women themselves is not considered. It simply isn't important that women experience sexual pleasure. Is contraception for women, but sex for men? Only sexist science sees the chemical castration of women as a technical advance.

Two women who shared their experiences with us said they thought Depo was a good contraceptive but also said that they lost interest in sex. Some women are so concerned about pregnancy that they find being turned off an acceptable price to pay for secure contraception. That some of us do not feel free not to have sex we do not enjoy is probably a comment on how closely sex is associated with our dependence on men, rather than our pleasure. It is a telling measure of our powerlessness in a sexist society.

I have been told repeatedly that being turned off cannot be investigated at all because it would rely on what women say. It would mean believing that women actually know whether they are turned on or not. Such a belief cannot be incorporated into science. "Hard" science has "objective" evidence that women do not know the difference between an orgasm and a shiny floor.

Who Calls the Shots?

Depo is not unique. It is one example of the creation of authoritative knowledge in our society (Spender, 1981: 1–9). Technological knowledge is both a function and a source of power. Women must insist upon becoming informed participants in public debate over technology. But it is hard. We have been told we are incapable of this type of understanding. Not only do we have to convince ourselves that we can crack the medical code but be confident enough to offer a basic criticism of the distortions of male-defined science (Elston, 1981; Overfield, 1981).

Committed to an empirical, value-free mode, medics find it hard to perceive the basic contamination of the "objectivity" of their data by the processes and structures within which it is defined and constructed (Fee, 1982; Whitbeck, 1982). From the industry's point of view the health care system exists only to market its products. The integration of the medical profession and corporate enterprise is obvious in marketing but is actually cemented in the production of medical data itself.

Contraception is an example of the technology created by the structures of capitalist patriarchy. The "knowledge" on which it is based reflects these interests. It is not "value-free" but generated to serve the interests that create it. Many doctors pass on the fruits of this knowledge in good faith because they do not see their own place in the structure that perpetuates such "truths." They then find themselves unable to treat the problems it creates.

The overwhelming reason most women who spoke to us use Depo is that they cannot solve the contraception problem. Many had run the gauntlet of contraceptive methods. All the other methods demand that we face the conflict over and over again, every day. Here at last is a method that promises we will not have to face the problem for a few weeks. No wonder it sounds attractive. For some it worked, but for some it was a false promise. For most of those of us who need birth control there is no answer to the problem.

The technology is the end product of the system that produced it. That system has nothing at all to do with women's needs. No wonder our needs are not met by it. Depo-Provera gives the illusion that women can control their reproductive destiny. Our need for that control is exploited. Our desire for that control is used against us. We are made to pay an enormous price for our reproductive "power."

R E F E R E N C E S

Agency for International Development. 1978. *Report to USAID of the Ad Hoc Consultative Panel on Depot Medroxyprogesterone Acetate.* AID, New York.

Barry, D., and J. Ciccone, 1975. "Use of Depo-Provera in the Treatment of Aggressive Sexual Offenders: Preliminary Report of Three Cases." *Bulletin of the American Academy of Psychiatry and the Law* 3 (179).

Bonham, Professor. 1980. Family Planning Course for Counsellors and Nursing Staff. Auckland. 22 September.

Bulletin of the World Health Organization (WHO). 1982. Vol. 60, no. 2, pp. 199–210.

Close Up. 1983. TVNZ. 13 April. Producer Chris Mitson.

Continho, Elsimai. 1978. "Statement of Dr. Elsimai Continho, Professor of Obstetrics and Gynaecology, Federal University of Baluci, Brazil." *The Depo-Provera Debate:* pp. 75–80.

Corea, Gena. 1980. "The Depo-Provera Weapon." In Helen B. Holmes, ed. *Birth Control and Controlling Birth: Women Centered Perspectives.* Humana Press, New Jersey: pp. 107–16.

Cultural Survival. 1981. 5(4): p. 6.

Deely, J. J., Convenor, Survey Appraisals Committee of New Zealand Statistical Association. "The New Zealand Contraception and Health Study: The Appraisal of the Protocol." *New Zealand Statistician* 18, no. 2, Dec. 1983. pp. 6–11.

The Depo-Provera Debate: Hearings before the Select Committee on Population, United States House of Representatives. 1978. Ninety-fifth Congress, Second Session, August 8, 9, 10. Chairman Scheuer.

Ehrenreich, Barbara, Mark Dowie, and Stephen Minkin. 1979. "The Charge: Gynocide, the Accused: the U.S. Government." *Mother Jones,* November.

Elston, Mary Ann. 1981. "Medicine as 'Old Husband's Tales': The Impact of Feminism." In Dale Spender, ed., *Men's Studies Modified: The Impact of Feminism on the Academic Disciplines.* Pergamon, Oxford: pp. 189–211.

Epstein, Samuel. 1977. "Cancer and the Environment." *Bulletin of the Atomic Scientists,* pp. 24, 25, 29.

Export of Hazardous Products: Hearings before a Subcommittee on International Economic Policy and Trade of the Committee of Foreign Affairs, United States House of Representatives, 1980. Ninety-Sixth Congress, Second Session, June 5, 12 and Sept. 9.

Fee, Elizabeth. 1982. "A Feminist Critique of Scientific Objectivity." *Science for the People.* July/August: pp. 5–33.

Floreman, Ylra. 1981. *Lyckopillret.* Reportage, Falun, Sweden.

Fraser, Ian, and Edith Weisberg. 1981. "A Comprehensive Review of Injectable Contraception with Special Emphasis on Depot Medroxyprogesterone Acetate." *Medical Journal of Australia* 1 (1). Supplement 1: pp. 1–20.

Gardner, J., and D. Mischell. 1970. "Analysis of bleeding patterns and resumption of fertility following discontinuation of a long acting injectable contraceptive." *Fertility and Sterility* 21 (4): pp. 286–91.

Gimore, Lyn, and Judith Madarasz. 1983. "Women's Involvement in Primary Health Care." *A Report on the Women's Health Network National Conference.* New Zealand Women's Health Network, Tauranga.

Holmes. Helen B., ed. 1980. *Birth Control and Controlling Birth: Women Centered Perspectives.* Humana Press, New Jersey.

Hutton, John. 1980. "Depo-Provera: A Critical Analysis of the Published References." Typescript. Postgraduate School of Obstetrics and Gynaecology, National Women's Hospital, Auckland.

Hutton, John. 1981. DMPA and the Press in New Zealand in Edwin McDaniel, ed., *Second Asian Regional Workshop on Injectable Contraceptives, Chiang Mai, Thailand.* World Neighbours, Oklahoma.

Hutton, John. 1983. "Depo-Provera: Are the Critics Justified?" Inaugural address to the Wellington Clinical School, Wellington, Aug. 3.

IPPF Medical Bulletin. 1980. 14 (6).

IPPF Medical Bulletin. 1982. 16 (6).

Johnson, Anita. 1976. "Depo-Provera—A Contraceptive for Poor Women." *Public Citizen.* Washington, D.C., Health Research Group.

Liang, Arthur, et. al. 1983. "Risk of Breast, Uterine Corpus, and Ovarian Cancer in Women Receiving Medroxyprogesterone Injections." *Journal of the American Medical Association* 249 (21): pp. 2902–12.

Lucas, David, and Helen Ware. 1981. "Fertility and Family Planning in the South Pacific." *Studies in Family Planning* 12 (8/9): pp. 303–15.

McDaniel, Edwin, ed. 1981. *Second Asian Regional Workshop on Injectable Contraceptives, Chiang Mai, Thailand,* World Neighbours, Oklahoma.

McDaniel, Edwin and Malcolm Potts. 1979. "International Forum Update: Depot Medroxyprogesterone Acetate and Endometrial Carcinoma." *International Journal of Gynaecology and Obstetrics* 17 (3): pp. 297–99.

Mangold, Tom. 1983. "Relationships between Doctors and Salesmen Are Lurching Out of Control" *Listener,* London, Jan. 2.

Minkin, Stephen. 1979. *Depo-Provera: A Critical Analysis.* Institute for Food and Development Policy, San Francisco.

Minkin, Stephen. 1981. "Nine Thai Women Had Cancer . . . None of Them Took Depo-Provera: Therefore Depo-Provera Is Safe . . . This Is Science?" *Mother Jones,* November: pp. 34–50.

Nash, H. 1975. "Depo-Provera: A Review." *Contraception* 2 (4): pp. 377–94.

Overfield, Kathy. 1981. "Dirty Fingers, Grime and Slag Heaps: Purity and the Scientific Ethic." In Dale Spender, ed., *Men's Studies Modified: The Impact of Feminism on the Academic Disciplines.* Pergamon, Oxford.

Pardthaisong, T. et al. 1980. "Return of Fertility after Discontinuation of Depot Medroxy-progesterone Acetate and Intra-uterine Devices in Northern Thailand." *Lancet* 1 (8167): pp. 509–12.

Paul, Charlotte. 1981. Unpublished paper. Department of Preventative and Social Medicine, Medical School, Otago University, Dunedin.

Population Reports. 1983. "Injectables and Implants." May. Series K no. 2. N.B. This publication is "supported by" USAID.

Potts, Malcolm. 1978. "Statement by Dr. Malcolm Potts. Executive Director, International Fertility Research Programme." *The Depo-Provera Debate:* pp. 15–18.

Protocol, New Zealand Contraception and Health Study. 1982. Auckland.

Rakusen, Jill. 1981. "Depo-Provera: The Extent of the Problem—A Case Study in the Politics of Birth Control." In Helen Roberts, ed., *Women, Health and Reproduction.* Routledge & Kegan Paul, London.

Renner, Ross. 1983a. *Depo-Provera: A Study in Weak Design.* A paper delivered on 29 June 1983 at the 34th Annual Conference of the New Zealand Statistical Association.

Renner, Ross. 1983b. *Scientific Objectivity and Social Responsibility: A Critique of the Protocol of the New Zealand Contraception and Health Study.* A paper presented to ANZSERCH Annual Conference, 25–27 May, at the Clinical School, Wellington.

Renner, Ross. 1983c. "Depo-Provera: The New Zealand Contraceptive and Health Study." *New Zealand Statistician* 18, no. 2, Dec. 1983, pp. 20–33.

Roberts, Helen, ed. 1981. *Women, Health and Reproduction.* Routledge & Kegan Paul, London.

Rosenfield, Allan, et al. 1983. "The Food and Drug Administration and Medroxyprogesterone Acetate: What Are the Issues?" *Journal of the American Medical Association,* 249 (21): p. 2925.

Sarra, Janis. 1982. "The Case against Depo-Provera." *Healthsharing.* Fall: pp. 20–23.

Satayasthit, N., et al. 1976. "The Effect of Medroxyprogesterone Acetate, Administered to the Lactating Rat, on the Subsequent Growth, Maturation and Reproductive Function of the Litter." *Journal of Reproduction and Fertility* 46 (2): pp. 411–12.

Savage, Wendy. 1983. "Taking Liberties with Women: Abortion, Sterilization, and Contraception." *New Zealand Women's Health Network Newsletter,* April, 1 (36).

Science. 1982. "Depo-Provera Debate Revs Up at FDA." July 30, 217: pp. 424–28.

Shaikh, Rashid, and Michael Reich. 1981. "Haphazard Policy on Hazardous Exports." *Lancet,* October 3: pp. 740–42.

Shapiro, Samuel. 1978. "Evidence concerning Possible Teratogenic Effects of Exogenous Female Hormones and Statement of Dr. Samuel Shapiro, Drug Epidemiology Unit, Boston University Medical Center." *The Depo-Provera Debate:* pp. 87–91.

Spender, Dale, ed. 1981. *Men's Studies Modified: The Impact of Feminism on the Academic Disciplines.* Pergamon, Oxford.

Stimpson, Catharine, and Ethel Spector Person, eds. 1980. *Women: Sex and Sexuality.* University of Chicago Press, Chicago.

Taylor, John. 1980. Statement at Family Planning Course for Counsellors and Nurses, Auckland. September 18.

Thomas, Helen. 1982. "Girls Injected with Contraceptive U.S. Has Banned." *National Times.* October 31.

Time. 1983. 212 (4): p. 49.

The Times. 1981. "Aborigines Given Birth Control Banned in U.S." March 23.

Toppozada, Mokhtav. 1978. "Effects of Depo-Provera on Menstruation." *The Depo-Provera Debate:* pp. 438–77.

Upjohn Corporation, 1980. Commentary of Depo-Provera, submitted by the Upjohn Corporation. Appendix 8. *The Export of Hazardous Products.*

Upjohn Corporation. 1982. *Depo-Provera for Contraception: Information for the Public Board of Inquiry for Depo-Provera: Response to the Board's Questions,* June 25: p. 5.

Upjohn Interview. 1982. *Controversy Continues to Cloud Facts about Depo-Provera.* Upjohn Interview is a trademark of the Upjohn Company.

Weisblat, D. 1977. *Memo to D. Weisblat, from N. Mohberg, J. Assenzo, and P. Schwallie, Subject: Review of Depo-Provera Study Proposed,* November 1: pp. 1–7.

Whitbeck, Caroline. 1982. "Women and Medicine: An Introduction." *Journal of Medicine and Philosophy* 7 (2): pp. 119–32.

World Health Organization. 1978. "Multinational Comparative Evaluation of Two Long-Acting Injectable Contraceptive Steroids: Norethisterone Enanthate and Medroxyprogesterone Acetate." *The Depo-Provera Debate*: pp. 662–85.

Zanartu, J. 1978. *The Depo-Provera Debate*: p. 79.

COLONIALISM AND THE EVOLUTION OF MASCULINIST FORESTRY

Vandana Shiva

Let them come and see men and women and children who know how to live, whose joy of life has not yet been killed by those who claimed to teach other nations how to live.

Chinua Achebe, No Longer at Ease

Science and Development: Progress for Whom?

The Age of Enlightenment and the theory of progress to which it gave rise were centred on the sacredness of two categories: modern scientific knowledge and economic development. Somewhere along the way, the unbridled pursuit of progress, guided by science and development, began to destroy life without any assessment of how fast and how much of the diversity of life on this planet is disappearing. The act of living and of celebrating and conserving life in all its diversity—in people and in nature—seems to have been sacrificed to progress, and the sanctity of life been substituted by the sanctity of science and development.

Throughout the world, a new questioning is growing, rooted in the experience of those for whom the spread of what was called "enlightenment" has been the spread of darkness, of the extinction of life and life-enhancing processes. A new awareness is growing that is questioning the sanctity of science and development and revealing that these are not universal categories of progress, but the special projects of modern Western patriarchy. This book [*Staying Alive: Women, Ecology and Development*] has grown out of my involvement with women's struggles for survival in India over the last decade. It is informed both by the suffering and insights of those who struggle to sustain and conserve life, and whose struggles question the meaning of a progress, a science, a development which destroys life and threatens survival.

The death of nature is central to this threat to survival. The earth is rapidly dying: her forests are dying, her soils are dying, her waters are dying, her air is dying. Tropical forests, the creators of the world's climate, the cradle of the world's vegetational wealth, are being bulldozed, burnt, ruined or submerged. In 1950, just over 100 million hectares of forests had been cleared—by 1975, this figure had more than doubled. During 1950–75, at least 120 million hectares of tropical forests were destroyed in South and Southeast Asia alone; by the end of the century, another 270 million could be eliminated. In Central America and Amazonia, cattle ranching for beef production is claiming at least 2.5 million hectares of forests each year; in India 1.3 million hectares of forests are lost every year to commercial plantation crops, river valley projects, mining projects and so on. Each year, twelve million hectares of forests are being eliminated from the face of the earth. At current rates of destruction, by the year 2050 all tropical forests will have disappeared, and with tropical forests will disappear the diversity of life they support.

Up to 50 percent of all living things—at least five million species—are estimated to live in tropical forests. A typical four-square-mile patch of rainforest contains up to 1,500 species of flowering plants, 750 of trees, 125 of mammals, 400 of birds, 100 of reptiles, 60 of amphibians and 150 of butterflies. The unparalleled diversity of species within tropical forests means relatively few individuals of each; any forest clearance thus disrupts their life cycles and threatens them with rapid extinction. Current estimates suggest that we are losing one species of life a day from the five–ten million species believed to exist. If present trends continue, we can expect an annual rate of loss as high as 50,000 species by the year 2000. In India alone, there exist 7,000 species of plant life not found anywhere else in the world; the destruction of her natural forests implies the disappearance of this rich diversity of animal and plant life.

Forests are the matrix of rivers and water sources, and their destruction in tropical regions amounts to the desiccation and desertification of land. Every year twelve million hectares of land deteriorate into deserts and are unable to support vegetation or produce food. Sometimes land is laid waste through desertification, at other times through ill-conceived land use which destroys the fertility of fragile tropical soils. Desertification in the Sahel in Africa has already killed millions of people and animals. Globally, some 456 million people today are starving or malnourished because of the desertification of croplands. Most agricultural lands cropped intensively with green revolution techniques are either water-logged or desiccated deserts. Nearly seven million hectares of land in India brought under irrigation have already gone out of production due to severe salinity, and an additional six million hectares have been seriously affected by water-logging. Green revolution agriculture has decreased genetic diversity and increased the vulnerability of crops to failure through lowering resistance to drought and pests.

With the destruction of forests, water and land, we are losing our life-support systems. This destruction is taking place in the name of "development" and progress, but there must be something seriously wrong with a concept of progress that threatens survival itself. The violence to nature, which seems intrinsic to the dominant development model, is also associated with violence to women who depend on nature for drawing sustenance for themselves, their families, their societies. This violence against nature and women is built into the very mode of perceiving both, and forms the basis of the current development paradigm. This chapter is an attempt to articulate how rural Indian women, who are still embedded in nature, experience and perceive ecological destruction and its causes, and how they have conceived and initiated processes to arrest the destruction of nature and begin its regeneration. From the diverse and specific grounds of the experience of ecological destruction arises a common identification of its causes in the developmental process and the view of nature with which it is legitimised. This chapter focuses on science and development as patriarchal projects not as a denial of other sources of patriarchy, such as religion, but because they are thought to be class, culture and gender neutral.

Seen from the experiences of Third World women, the modes of thinking and action that pass for science and development, respectively, are not universal and humanly inclusive, as they are made out to be; modern science and development are projects of male, Western origin, both historically and ideologically. They are the latest and most brutal expression of a patriarchal ideology which is threatening to annihilate nature and the entire human species. The rise of a patriarchal science of nature took place in Europe during the fifteenth and seventeenth centuries as the scientific revolution. During the same period, the closely related industrial revolution laid the foundations of a patriarchal mode of economic development in industrial capitalism. Contemporary science and development conserve the ideological roots and biases of the scientific and industrial revolutions even as they unfold into new areas of activity and new domains of subjugation.

The scientific revolution in Europe transformed nature from *terra mater* into a machine and a source of raw material; with this transformation it removed all ethical and cognitive constraints against its violation and exploitation. The industrial revolution converted economics from the prudent management of resources for sustenance and basic needs satisfaction into a process of commodity production for profit maximization. Industrialism created a limitless appetite for resource exploitation, and modern science provided the ethical and cognitive license to make such exploitation possible, acceptable—and desirable. The new relationship of man's domination and mastery over nature was thus also associated with new patterns of domination and mastery over women, and their exclusion from participation *as partners* in both science and development

Contemporary development activity in the Third World superimposes the scientific and economic paradigms created by Western, gender-based ideology on communities in other cultures. Ecological destruction and the marginalisation of women, we know now, have been the inevitable results of most development programmes and projects based on such paradigms; they violate the integrity of one and destroy the productivity of the other. Women, as victims of the violence of patriarchal forms of development, have risen against it to protect nature and preserve their survival and sustenance. Indian women have been in the forefront of ecological struggles to conserve forests, land and water. They have challenged the Western concept of nature as an object of exploitation and have protected her as Prakriti, the living force that supports life. They have challenged the Western concept of economics as production of profits and capital accumulation with their own concept of economics as production of sustenance and needs satisfaction. A science that does not respect nature's needs and a development that does not respect people's needs inevitably threaten survival. In their fight to survive the onslaughts of both, women have begun a struggle that challenges the most fundamental categories of Western patriarchy—its concepts of nature and women, and of science and development. Their ecological struggle in India is aimed simultaneously at liberating nature from ceaseless exploitation and themselves from limitless marginalisation. They are creating a feminist ideology that transcends gender, and a political practice that is humanly inclusive; they are challenging patriarchy's ideological claim to universalism not with another universalising tendency, but with diversity; and they are challenging the dominant concept of power as violence with the alternative concept of non-violence as power.

The everyday struggles of women for the protection of nature take place in the cognitive and ethical context of the categories of the ancient Indian worldview in which nature is Prakriti, a living and creative process, the feminine principle from which all life arises. Women's ecology movements, as the preservation and recovery of the feminine principle, arise from a non-gender-based ideology of liberation, different both from the gender-based ideology of patriarchy which underlies the process of ecological destruction and women's subjugation, and the gender-based responses which have, until recently, been characteristic of the west.

Inspired by women's struggles for the protection of nature as a condition for human survival, this book goes beyond a statement of women as special victims of the environmental crisis. It attempts to capture and reconstruct those insights and visions that Indian women provide in their struggles for survival, which perceive development and science from outside the categories of modern Western patriarchy. These oppositional categories are simultaneously ecological and feminist: they allow the possibility of survival by exposing the parochial basis of science and development and by showing how ecological destruction and the marginalisation of women are not inevitable, economically or scientifically.

Colonizing the Forests Creates Maldevelopment

When the British colonised India, they first colonised her forests. Ignorant of their wealth and of the wealth of knowledge of local people to sustainably manage the forests, they displaced local rights, local needs and local knowledge and reduced this primary source of life into a timber mine. Women's subsistence economy based on the forest was replaced by the commercial economy of British colonialism. Teak from Malabar was extracted for the King's Navy, and the *sal* of Central India and the conifers of the Himalaya were exploited for the railway system. Although it is always local people who are held responsible for deforestation, it is commercial demands that have more frequently resulted in large-scale forest destruction. In the Himalayan region there is evidence that it was the needs of the Empire and not the local people that led to rapid forest denudation. According to Atkinson's *Gazetteer,*

> the forests were denuded of good trees in all places. The destruction of trees of all species appears to have continued steadily and reached its climax between 1855 and 1861, when the demands of the Railway authorities induced numerous speculators to enter into contracts for sleepers, and these men were allowed, unchecked, to cut down old trees very far in excess of what they could possibly export, so that for some years after the regular forest operations commenced, the department was chiefly busy cutting up and bringing to the depot the timber left behind by the contractors.[1]

When the British started exploiting Indian timber for military purposes, they did it rapaciously and in ignorance, because the "great continent appeared to hold inexhaustible tracts covered with dense jungles, but there was no apparent necessity for their detailed exploration, even had this been a possibility. In the early years of our occupation the botany of the forests, the species of trees they contained and their respective values was an unopened book."[2]

To the colonial government and its officials the critical role that forests play in nature and the great influence they exercise on the physical well-being of a country went unrecognised. In view of the large forest wealth that existed, the government for some years obtained its full requirement without difficulty, while local needs were also met. The early administrators appear to have been convinced that this state of affairs could go on for an unlimited period. In many localities forests were viewed as an obstruction to agriculture, which was taxed, and were seen therefore as a limiting factor to the prosperity of the coloniser. The policy was to extend agriculture and the watchword was to clear the forests with this end in view. Virgin forests of the Doon Valley were thus clearfelled for land grants made exclusively to British settlers.[3]

The military requirement for Indian teak led to an immediate proclamation declaring that the royalty right in teak trees claimed by the former government in the south of the continent was vested in the East India Company. In the year 1799 alone, 10,000 teak trees were brought down the Beypur River in Malabar. Under further pressure from the Home Government to ensure the maintenance of the future strength of the King's Navy, a decision was taken to appoint a special officer to superintend forest work—his duties were to preserve and improve the production of teak and other timber suitable for shipbuilding. Captain Watson of the police was appointed the first Conservator of Forests in India on November 10, 1806. Under the proclamation of April 1807, he wielded great powers. He soon established a timber monopoly throughout Malabar and Travancore and furnished the government, as did his immediate successors, with a plentiful supply of cheap timber. But the methods by which this was done were intolerable and gradually gave rise to seething discontent amongst both local peasants and proprietors. The feeling rose to such a pitch that the conservatorship was abolished in 1823.[4]

The introduction of colonial forestry was thus established not because of superior forestry knowledge or scientific management, but through dominant military need and power. It was only after more than half a century of uncontrolled forest destruction by British commercial interests that an attempt was made to control exploitation. In 1865 the first Indian Forest Act (VII of 1865) was passed by the Supreme Legislative Council, which authorised the government to declare forests and wastelands (*benap,* or unmeasured lands) as reserved forests.

The introduction of this legislation marks the beginning of what is called the "scientific management" of forests; it amounted basically to the formalisation of the erosion both of forests and of the rights of local people to forest produce. Commercial forestry, which is equated with "scientific forestry" by those narrow interests exemplified by Western patriarchy, is reductionist in intellectual content and ecological impact, and generates poverty at the socio-economic level for those whose livelihoods and productivity depend on the forest. Reductionism has been characteristic of this forestry because it sunders forestry from water management, from agriculture and from animal husbandry. Within the forest ecosystem it has reduced the diversity of life to the dead product, wood, and wood in turn to commercially valuable wood only. A commercial interest has the primary objective of maximising exchange value on the market through the extraction of commercially valuable species—forest ecosystems are therefore reduced to the timber of such species. By ignoring the complex relationship within the forest community and between plant life and other resources like soil and water, this pattern of resource use generates instabilities in the ecosystem and leads to counterproductive use of nature as a living and self-reproducing resource. The destruction of the forest ecosystem and the multiple functions of forest resources in turn hurts the economic interest of those groups of society, mainly women and tribals, who depend on the diverse resource functions of the forests for their survival. These include soil and water stabilisation and the provision of food, fodder, fuel, fertilizer, etc. In the alternative feminine forestry science which has been subjugated by the masculinist science, forests are not viewed as merely a stock of wood, isolated from the rest of the ecosystem, nor is their economic value reduced to the commercial value of timber. "Productivity," "yield" and "economic value" are defined for nature and for women's work as *satisfying basic needs through an integrated ecosystem managed for multipurpose utilisation.* Their meaning and measure is therefore entirely different from the meaning and measure employed in reductionist masculinist forestry. In a shift from ecological forestry to reductionist forestry all scientific terms are changed from ecosystem-dependent to ecosystem-independent ones. Thus while for women, tribals and other forest communities a complex ecosystem is productive in terms of water, herbs, tubers, fodder, fertilizer, fuel, fibre and as a genepool, for the forester, these components are useless, unproductive waste and dispensable. Two economic perspectives lead to two notions of "productivity" and "value." As far as women's productivity in survival and overall productivity are concerned, the natural tropical forest is a highly productive ecosystem. Examining the forests of the humid tropics from an ecological perspective Golley has noted, "A large biomass is generally characteristic of tropical forests. The quantities of wood especially are large in tropical forests and average about 300 tons per ha. compared with about 150 tons per ha. for temperate forests."[5] However, in reductionist commercial forestry, overall productivity is subordinated to industrial use, and large biomass to species that can be profitably marketed—industrial and commercial biomass prevail; all the rest is waste. As Bethel, an international forestry consultant says, referring to the large biomass typical of forests in the humid tropics,

> It must be said that from a standpoint of industrial material supply, this is relatively unimportant. The important question is how much of this biomass represents trees and parts of trees of *preferred species that can be profitably marketed.* . . . By today's utilisation standards, *most of the trees in these humid tropical forests are, from an industrial materials standpoint, clearly weeds.*[6]

The "industrial materials standpoint" is the standpoint of a capitalist and patriarchal reductionist forestry which splits the living diversity and democracy of the forest into commercially useful dead wood, which it valorises, and ecologically valuable weeds, which it characterises as waste. This waste, however, is the wealth of biomass that maintains nature's water and nutrient cycles and satisfies the needs of food, fuel, fodder, fertilizer, fibre and medicine of agricultural communities.

Since it is women's work that protects and conserves nature's life in forestry and in agriculture, and through such conservation work, sustains human life through ensuring the provision of food and water, the destruction of the integrity of forest ecosystems is most vividly and concretely experienced by peasant women. For them forestry is married to food production; it is essential for providing stable, perennial supplies of water for drinking and for irrigation, and for providing the fertility directly as green manure or as organic matter cycled through farm animals. Women's agricultural work in regions like the Himalaya is largely work in and with the forest, yet it is discounted both in forestry and in agriculture. The only forestry-related work that goes into census data is lumbering and tree-felling; cutting trees then becomes a source of *roti* or food for the men engaged in lumbering operations; for the women, however, forests are food, not in death, but in life. The living forest provides the means for sustainable food production systems in the form of nutrients and water, and women's work in the forest facilitates this process. When, for example, women lop trees they enhance the productivity of the oak forest under stable conditions and under common ownership and control. While an unlopped tree has leaves that are too hard for cattle, lopping makes them soft and palatable, especially in early spring. Maintaining the diversity of living resources is critical to the feminine use of the forest; thus oak-leaf along with a mixture of dried grasses and agricultural by-products is fed to cattle through the late autumn, winter and into spring. In the monsoon, the green grass becomes the dominant fodder, and in October and November, agricultural waste such as rice straw, *mandua* straw and *jangora* straw become the primary supply of fodder. Lopping has never been viewed as a forest management strategy for using tree produce while conserving the tree. Yet, as Bandy-opadhyay and Moench[7] have shown, lopping under appropriate conditions can actually *increase* the forest density and fodder productivity of the forest. Groups of women, young and old, go together to lop for fodder, and expertise develops by participation and through learning-by-doing. These informal forestry colleges of the women are small and decentred, creating and transferring knowledge about how to maintain the life of living resources. The visible forestry colleges by contrast are centralised and alienated: they specialise in a forestry of destruction, on how to transform a living resource into a commodity and subsequently, cash.

The dispossession of the local people of their rights, their resources and their knowledge has not gone unchallenged. Forest struggles have been taking place throughout the country for over two centuries to resist the colonisation of the people's forests in India. The access and rights of the people to forests were first severely encroached upon with the introduction of the Forest Acts of 1878 and 1927. The following years witnessed the spread of forest satyagrahas throughout India, as a protest against the reservation of forests for exclusive exploitation by British commercial interest, and their concommitant transformation from a common resource into a commodity. Villagers ceremonially removed forest products from the reserved forests to assert their right to satisfy their basic needs. The forest satyagrahas were especially successful in regions where survival of the local population was intimately linked with access to the forests, as in the Himalaya, the Western Ghats, and the Central Indian hills. These non-violent protests were systematically crushed by the British; in Central India, Gond tribals were gunned down for participating in the protests; in 1930 dozens of unarmed villagers were killed and hundreds injured in Tilari village in Tehri Garhwal, when they gathered to protest against the Forest Laws of the local rulers. After enormous loss of life, the satyagrahis were successful in reviving some of the traditional rights of the village communities to various forest products.[8] The Forest Policy of post-colonial India continued on the colonial path of commercialisation and reductionism, and with it continued people's resistance to a denial of their basic needs, both through alienation of rights and through ecological degradation.

In the mountain regions of the Himalaya, the women of Garhwal started to protect their forests from commercial exploitation even at the cost of their lives, by starting the famous Chipko movement, embracing the living trees as their protectors. Beginning in the early 1970s in the Garhwal region of Uttar Pradesh, the methodology and philosophy of Chipko has now spread to Himachal Pradesh in the north, to Karnataka in the south, to Rajasthan in the west, to Orissa in the east, and to the Central Indian highlands.

· · ·

The main thrust of conservation struggles like Chipko is that forests and trees are life-support systems, and should be protected and regenerated for their bio-spheric functions. The crisis mind on the other hand sees the forest and trees as weed, valued commercially, and converts even afforestation into deforestation and desertification. From life-support systems, trees are converted into green gold—all planting is motivated by the slogan, "Money grows on trees." Whether it is schemes like social forestry or wasteland development, afforestation pro-grammes are conceived at the international level by "experts" whose philosophy of tree-planting falls within the reductionist paradigm of producing wood for the market, not biomass for maintaining ecological cycles or satisfying local needs of food, fodder and fertilizer. All official programmes of afforestation, based on heavy funding and centralised decision making, act in two ways against the feminine principle in forestry—they destroy the forest as a diverse and self-reproducing system, *and* destroy it as commons, shared by a diversity of social groups with the smallest having rights, access and entitlements.

"Greening" with Eucalyptus

Social forestry projects are a good example of single-species, single-commodity production plantations, based on reductionist models which divorce forestry from agriculture and water management, and needs from markets.

A case study of World Bank sponsored social forestry in Kolar district of Karnataka[9] is an illustration of reductionism and maldevelopment in forestry being extended to farmland. Decentred agroforestry, based on multiple species and private and common treestands, has been India's age-old strategy for main-taining farm productivity in arid and semi-arid zones. The *honge*, tamarind, jack-fruit and mango, the *jola, gobli, kagli*** and bamboo traditionally provided food and fodder, fertilizer and pesticide, fuel and small timber. The backyard of each rural home was a nursery, and each peasant woman the sylviculturalist. The invisible, decentred agroforestry model was significant because the humblest of species and the smallest of people could participate in it, and with space for the small, *everyone* was involved in protecting and planting.

The reductionist mind took over tree planting with "social forestry." Plans were made in national and international capitals by people who could not know the purpose of the *honge* and the *neem,* and saw them as weeds. The experts decided that indigenous knowledge was worthless and "unscientific," and pro-ceeded to destroy the diversity of indigenous species by replacing them with row after row of eucalyptus seedlings in polythene bags, in government nurseries. Nature's locally available seeds were laid waste; people's locally available knowl-edge and energies were laid waste. With imported seeds and expertise came the import of loans and debt and the export of wood, soils—and people. Trees, as a

---

*Pongamia globra, Azadirachta indica, Tamarindus indica, Autocarpus integrifolia, Mangifera indica, Acacia fernesiana and *Acacia catechu.*

TABLE 1. **Area and Production of Ragi in Kolar District**

Year	Area (ha)	Production (tons)
1977–78	141,772	175,195
1978–79	146,361	165,174
1979–80	140,862	99,236
1980–81	48,406	13,340

living resource, maintaining the life of the soil and water and of local people, were replaced by trees whose dead wood went straight to a pulp factory hundreds of miles way. The smallest farm became a supplier of raw material to industry and ceased to be a supplier of food to local people.Women's work, linking the trees to the crops, disappeared and was replaced by the work of brokers and middlemen who brought the eucalyptus trees on behalf of industry. Industrialists, foresters and bureaucrats loved the eucalyptus because it grows straight and is excellent pulp-wood, unlike the *honge* which shelters the soil with its profuse branches and dense canopy and whose real worth is as a living tree on a farm. The *honge* could be nature's idea of the perfect tree for arid Karnataka. It has rapid growth of precisely those parts of the tree, the leaves and small branches, which go back to the earth, enriching and protecting it, conserving its moisture and fertility. The eucalyptus, on the other hand, when perceived ecologically, is unproductive, even negative, because this perception assesses the "growth" and "productivity" of trees in relation to the water cycle and its conservation, in relation to soil fertility and in relation to human needs for food and food production. The eucalyptus has destroyed the water cycle in arid regions due to its high water demand and its failure to produce humus, which is nature's mechanism for conserving water. Most indigenous species have a much higher biological productivity than the eucalyptus, when one considers water yields and water conservation. The non-woody biomass of trees has never been assessed by forest measurements and quantification within the reductionist paradigm, yet it is this very biomass that functions in conserving water and building soils. It is little wonder that Garhwal women call a tree *dali* or branch, because they see the productivity of the tree in terms of its non-woody biomass, which functions critically in hydrological and nutrient cycles within the forest, and through green fertilizer and fodder in cropland.

In the context of ecological cycles and of the food needs of people and livestock, the eucalyptus actually makes negative contributions. It is destructive to nature's work and women's work in agriculture, for by destroying the water and land and organic matter base for food production, women's productivity in sustenance is killed. Kolar, which is the most successful social forestry district in Karnataka, has already lost more than 13 percent of its agricultural land to eucalyptus cultivation; most of this has been at the cost of its staple food, the millet, *ragi,* and associated food crops. Table 1 gives the decline in the area under *ragi* cultivation since the beginning of the social forestry programme. Today Kolar is

TABLE 2. **Food Availability per Day per Individual**

	Korategere		Malur	
Land Holdings	Cereals (gms)	Pulses (gms)	Cereals (gms)	Pulses (gms)
1 ha	.55	.06	.21	.03
1–2 ha	.58	.07	.29	.01
2–4 ha	1.23	.07	.47	.03
4 ha	3.65	3.65	1.60	.06

the most severely hit by drought and food scarcity, for eucalyptus undermines not just food production but the long-term productivity of the soil.

Mular, a region in Kolar district which has 30 percent of its land under eucalyptus, was compared to Korategere in neighbouring Tumkur, where indigenous farm forestry continues to provide a diversity of organic inputs to agriculture. Table 2 shows how eucalyptus has induced food and nutrition deficiencies in Mular.

"Greening" with eucalyptus is a violence against nature and its cycles, and it is a violence against women who depend on the stability of nature's cycles to provide sustenance in the form of food and water. Eucalyptus guzzles nutrients and water and, in the specific conditions of low rainfall zones, gives nothing back but terpenes to the soil. These inhibit the growth of other plants and are toxic to soil organisms which are responsible for building soil fertility and improving soil structure.[10] The eucalyptus certainly increased cash and commodity flows, but it resulted in a disastrous interruption of organic matter and water flows within the local ecosystem. Its proponents failed to calculate the costs in terms of the destruction of life in the soil, the depletion of water resources and the scarcity of food and fodder that eucalyptus cultivation creates. Nor did they, while trying to shorten rotations for harvesting, see that tamarind, jackfruit and *honge* have very short rotations of one year in which the biomass harvested is far higher than that of eucalyptus, which they nevertheless declared a "miracle" tree. The crux of the matter is that fruit production was never the concern of forestry in the reductionist paradigm—it focused on wood, and wood for the market, alone. Eucalyptus as an exotic, introduced in total disregard of its ecological appropriateness, has thus become an exemplar of anti-life afforestation.

Women throughout India have resisted the expansion of eucalyptus because of its destruction of water, soil and food systems. On August 10, 1983, the women and small peasants of Barha and Holahalli villages in Tumkur district (Karnataka) marched en masse to the forest nursery and pulled out millions of eucalyptus seedlings, planting tamarind and mango seeds in their place. This gesture of protest, for which they were arrested, spoke out against the virtual planned destruction of soil and water systems by eucalyptus cultivation. It also silently challenged the domination of a forestry science that had reduced all species to one (the eucalyptus), all needs to one (that of the pulp industry), and all knowledge to one (that of the World Bank and forest officials). It challenged the myth of the miracle tree: tamarind and mango are symbols of the energies of nature and of local people, of the links between these seeds and the soil, and of the needs that these trees—and others like them—satisfy in keeping the earth and the people alive. Forestry for food—food for the soil, for farm animals, for people—all women's and peasants' struggles revolve around this theme, whether in Garhwal or Karnataka, in the Santhal Parganas or Chattisgarh, in reserved forests, farmlands or commons. Destruction of diversity and life and colonisation of the commons are built into reductionist forestry and its new avatar, "wasteland development."

N O T E S

1. E. T. Atkinson, *Himalayan Gazetteer,* vol. III, Allahabad: Government Press, 1882, p. 852.

2. E. P. Stebbing, *The Forest of India* (reprint), New Delhi: A. J. Reprints Agency, 1982, p. 61.

3. J. Bandyopadhyay et al., *The Doon Valley Ecosystem,* mimeo, 1983.

4. Stebbing, op. cit., p. 65.

5. F. B. Golley, *Productivity and Mineral Cycling in Tropical Forests' Productivity of World Ecosystems,* Washington: National Academy of Sciences. 1975. pp. 106–15.

6. James A. Bethel. "Sometimes the Word is 'Weed,' " in *Forest Management,* June, 1984, pp. 17–22.

7. J. Bandyopadhyay and M. Moench, "Local Needs and Forest Resource Management in the Himalaya," in Bandyopadhyay et al., *India's Environment: Crisis and Responses,* Dehradun: Natraj Publishers, 1985, p. 56.

8. J. Bandyopadhyay and V. Shiva, "Chipko Politics of Ecology," in *Seminar,* no. 330, 1987.

9. V. Shiva, H. C. Sharatchandra and J. Bandyopadhyay, *The Social, Ecological and Economic Impact of Social Forestry in Kolar,* mimeo, Indian Institute of Management, Bangalore, 1981; V. Shiva, H. C. Sharatchandra and J. Bandyopadhyay, "The Challenge of Social Forestry," in W. Fernandes and S. Kulkarni, eds. *Towards a New Forest Policy,* New Delhi: Indian Social Institute, 1983; and V. Shiva, H. C. Sharatchandra and J. Bandyopadhyay, "No Solution within the Market," in *Ecologist,* October 1982.

10. V. Shiva and J. Bandyopadhyay, *Ecological Audit of Eucalyptus Cultivation,* Dehradun: EBD Publishers, 1985.

APPLIED BIOLOGY IN THE THIRD WORLD

The Struggle for Revolutionary Science

Richard Levins and Richard Lewontin

Debates about the nature of science in the Third World are very different from those in Europe and North America. In the industrial capitalist countries, science is already deeply entrenched in institutions, intellectual life, public policy, and technology. It is a fact of life: even debates about science policy accept science as given and argue mostly about the uses and abuses of or access to science. Modern science was created in these countries. If the earlier glow of a science linked to liberation has become increasingly tarnished, there is still pride in its achievements and nostalgia for its promise.

In some ways, the fate of science parallels that of bourgeois democracy: both were born as exuberant forces for liberation against feudalism, but their very successes have turned them into caricatures of their youth. The bold, antiauthoritarian stance of science has become docile acquiescence; the free battle of ideas has given way to a monopoly vested in those who control the resources for research and publication. Free access to scientific information has been diminished by military and commercial secrecy and by the barriers of technical jargon; in the commoditization of science, peer review is replaced by satisfaction of the client as the test of quality. The internal mechanisms for maintaining objectivity are, at their best—in the absence of sycophancy toward those with prestige, professional jealousies, narrow cliques, and national provincialism—able to nullify individual capricious errors and biases, but they reinforce the shared biases of the scientific community. The demand for objectivity, the separation of observation and reporting from the researchers' wishes, which is so essential for the development of science, becomes the demand for separation of thinking from feeling. This promotes moral detachment in scientists which, reinforced by specialization and bureaucratization, allows them to work on all sorts of dangerous and harmful projects with indifference to the human consequences. The idealized egalitarianism of a community of scholars has shown itself to be a rigid hierarchy

This essay is based on a paper presented at the Gramsci Institute, Palermo, Italy, in October 1983.

of scientific authorities integrated into the general class structure of the society and modeled on the corporation. And where the pursuit of truth has survived, it has become increasingly narrow, revealing a growing contradiction between the sophistication of science in the small within the laboratory and the irrationality of the scientific enterprise as a whole.

Euro–North American science, like democracy, has been marketed to much of the Third World. Its advocates praise its values, bemoan its deficiencies, and assert its superiority over all alternatives. But if European and North American science is already a caricature of the "science" seen by its enthusiastic advocates, it comes to the Third World as a caricature of that caricature. Science appeared on its shores as the technology of conquest. Knowledge of plants and minerals provided the means of exploitation, and every new advance in the understanding of soils or flora allowed new and deeper penetration by the colonizers. Even the disinterested collecting of specimens or artifacts was a plundering of resources for the enrichment of the intellectual life of the metropolis: it filled their museums.

British plant breeding increased the yield of the rubber plant tenfold, making possible the plantation system in Malaya. Sugar technology meant slavery. Research in tropical medicine was aimed first at protecting the health of the administrators and their troops; later, when the high mortality of laborers could no longer be replaced by recruiting immigrants, medicine turned to diseases that impaired labor efficiency. Finally, in the wake of colonial rebellion, public health became an instrument of pacification and was closely tied to private health industry as a new profitable investment.

Science came into the Third World as a rationale for domination with theories of racial superiority, of "progress," and of its own intellectual superiority:

> If in the first instance one could speak of the expansion and conquest as a result of the technological superiority of some peoples over others, in a second stage the technological superiority and the greater military capacity was made synonymous with rationality; and in the final stage the rationality was no longer presented as a cause of the domination to be converted directly in its justification. The historic fact of European expansion is transformed into a natural phenomenon, a necessary consequence of the expansion of Reason over the world. A rationality was transformed into *Rationality,* a way of knowing was transformed into Science, a procedure for knowing became the Scientific Method. The vast enterprise of dominating the world in a few centuries was sufficient argument to demonstrate the imposition of European reason as a universal and necessary development. (Gutierrez 1974)

Finally, science entered the Third World as a form of intellectual domination. After the troops depart, the investments remain; after direct ownership is removed, managerial skills, patents, textbooks, and journals remain, repeating the message that only by adopting their ways can we progress, only by going to their universities can we learn; only by emulating their universities can we teach. One student of science development even calculated the optimum structure of a research establishment for Latin America by averaging the ratios of full professors to associate professors to assistant professors to graduate students and technicians for all the countries of Western Europe and North America!

It is our thesis that many of the critical theoretical issues—the class versus universal nature of science, its relation to other kinds of knowledge, the role of the dialectic in natural science and of class struggle within science—which are treated as philosophical problems in Europe, will be fought out in Third World countries as part of the political struggle for complete, real independence and as part of the struggle to build science in socialist countries.

There are four main approaches to science in the heterogeneous assemblage of colonies, semicolonies, neocolonies, and former colonies with different degrees of independence, which we refer to loosely as the Third World. These approaches differ in the ways they cope with the contradiction of science as imperialist domination and science as progress. The least critical approach is sycophantic pragmatism. It accepts not only "science" but also its agendas as progress. It considers that a fully developed national science is a luxury incompatible with Third World poverty and therefore opts to limit research investment to narrowly defined secondary modifications of the results of world science, to local research and development. This approach is common in the most colonized of Third World countries. Its consequences are reinforcement of economic and intellectual dependence, economic policies based on subordination to international capital, intellectual dependence, and often the emigration of scientists who want to do fundamental research on a world level.

The next two approaches are "developmentalist." Developmentalism looks at progress as occurring along a single axis from less to more. The task of the less developed is to catch up with the more developed and even surpass them on their own terms. Developmentalists are uncritical of the structure and ideology of science, although they see that in foreign hands science may work against national interests. Therefore they seek an independent example of world science. There are conservative and radical branches of developmentalism with very different social bases and political perspectives. They share the view that science is progress, but they differ about whom the progress is for.

The conservative branch of developmentalism is strongest in countries where a national bourgeoisie is in power. They are allies but not "tools" of imperialism, manifesting an entrepreneurial nationalism while oppressing their own peasants and workers. This branch is also powerful in countries where a colonial civil service became a ruling bureaucracy in a relatively smooth manner and aspires to become a national bourgeoisie. Conservative developmentalism faces a contradiction: maintaining a competitive position requires encouraging scientific creativity. It needs universities in which not all students concentrate in law, medicine, or civil engineering. But universities are also dangerous—when students are encouraged to think, they may think about things you don't want them to think about.

Different regimes have attempted to solve this problem in different ways. Specialization in academic pursuits is one strategy. "A compartmentalized knowledge means not only disciplinary specialization and the differentiation of the scientists among themselves, but also the impossibility of a connected grasp of reality and a critical judgment of it. The application of the specialists to the study of small realities, connected to whole at best by abstract and formal relations, impedes the critical evaluation of this totality" (Gutíerrez 1974, p. 36). This specialization is achieved by stressing applied physical sciences, engineering, and mathematics, as in Brazil; abolishing whole academic departments, such as philosophy (Chile); or founding private scientific-technical colleges physically removed from the ferment of the national university (Mexico).

But such specialized education is not only a question of curriculum; it carries with it a view of the world as well. Specialists begin to see nature as subdivided into domains that parallel the table of organization of their university, ministry, or company. Problems are recognized, but in isolation from each other, to be solved by separate interventions that leave the whole unchanged. Thus to the technocratic specialist, malnutrition is treated with dietary supplements; pollution, with standards for each molecule; pest problems with the right poison. Impressed by the importance of precise scientific information, the technocrat is equally adamant in refusing to pursue a problem beyond the narrowest possible boundaries of his or her speciality and in refusing to allow considerations from the broader areas to inform his or her own work.

Conservative developmentalist regimes also make use of direct force; the alternate subsidizing of universities and military intervention in them has spread Argentine scholars all over Latin America. The more secure regimes can adopt a strategy of cooptive liberty in which scientists can think and discuss all questions within the confines of the national university and can publish scholarly tracts, but cannot circulate their conclusions as popular pamphlets (Colombia) or organize to carry out their programs (Mexico). This strategy results in a curious kind of abstract applied science in which innovative plans are created to improve agriculture, promote health, and protect the environment, with the tacit understanding that they will never be put into practice.

Radical developmentalism starts from different political premises. It is anti-imperialist, committed to serving the people, even socialist. Radical developmentalists accept part of the critique of science, that it has become commoditized, that it is used for profit and war, that it tries to monopolize knowledge. Radical developmentalists want a national, fully developed science with an agenda determined by the needs of the people. They typically promote the popularization and participation in science, and they open the doors to scientific education to everyone. They call for expanded health services, improved standards for occupational health, and conservation programs.

In capitalist countries radical developmentalists are dissident critical voices against the plunder of their national resources, against the hegemony of foreign intellectuals, against profit-oriented health services. But in revolutionary societies, where they are usually the dominant voice in science, radical developmentalists play an ambiguous and often harmful role. The ideology of "modernization," of undirectional progress has a powerful hold on their thinking. This often combines with a deeply felt sense of urgency to meet the needs of the people and results in a narrow pragmatism, the promotion of specialization, and the enthusiastic adoption of the already proven "successful" methods of production and of research. They are impressed by the flashiness of "advanced" science (the more molecular and expensive, the more impressed they are). This approach allows them to plant monocultures of timber to get wood for housing as fast as possible, but it underestimates the dangers of pest outbreaks. They will clear forests to plant food for the people and dismiss the warnings of erosion. They will import toxic pesticides and hope to prevent poisonings by improving protection of farm laborers, but they remain unconvinced of suggested ecological impacts.

The one major difference between the short-sightedness of radical and that of conservative developmentalists is that the radicals have no real interest in hiding the harm caused by "modern" technologies, while the conservatives have a direct or indirect commitment to corporate profit. Radical developmentalists can be convinced by argument that a course of action is socially harmful; once they become aware of particular ecological issues, they are concerned. For example, at the first national ecology conference in Cuba in 1980, representatives of the food industry were the ones who raised the problems of environmental deterioration caused by the accumulation of rice husks near the mills and of mango seeds near juice factories. In contrast, the economically rational but socially irrational actions of the conservative developmentalists can be reversed only by political confrontation, in which scientific argument is merely one weapon.

But radical developmentalism is unable to cope with the contradiction between science as growth of human knowledge and science as class product. They concentrate on the first part of the contradiction and reduce its opposite to a concern about the uses and abuses of science. The other part of the contradiction is represented by other movements separately, by the humanist and mystical antiscience ideologies. These approaches see only the oppressive, imperialist aspect of science and reject it more or less completely. They see quantification and abstraction as dehumanizing, and technological application of science as destructive. They counterpose a gentle, spiritual, or humanistic holism to the reductionism, compartmentalization, and aggressive exploitation of Euro–North American science and often stress its foreign, alien character.

Within the world Marxist movement, radical developmentalism has coexisted with the revolutionary, dialectical critique of science. It has been reinforced by that passive acceptance of necessary stages of (mostly material) progress which often passes for historical materialism. This approach is strengthened by revulsion at Lysenko's efforts to create a self-consciously distinct Marxist science and by the role of international scientific cooperation in promoting peaceful coexistence or fighting hunger and disease. In Europe radical developmentalism fits in with the Eurocommunist plea for respectability and acceptance by saying, "See, we aren't really all that outrageous. We may differ *within* science but not *about* science, which is part of our common heritage. In fact, only we can free science to come into its own!"

In contrast to radical developmentalism is the revolutionary, dialectical critique of science which attempts to recognize both aspects of the contradictory nature of science. Although Marxists have contributed to this critique as individuals, it has developed mostly outside of institutionalized Marxism in the context of the movements for feminism, the new Left, ecology, alternative health care, and radical science in industrial capitalist countries and around the edges of national liberation movements in the Third World.

This viewpoint has not yet found a coherent, integral programmatic expression. Its main idea is that modern science is a product of the bourgeois revolution and the age of imperialism. It was created mostly by Euro–North American white middle-class males in ways that meet their own material and ideological needs, and it is supported, encouraged, and tolerated mostly by Euro–North American white bourgeois males. These conditions of its origin and existence cannot but penetrate all aspects of science. In particular, the social determination of science operates both locally and on a world historic scale. On the one hand, the science of each country is part of world science, a product of the international development of capitalism and, on the other, it reflects the particular history of that country, its position in the international system, the origins and functions of its own scientific community. The result is not some homogenized "universal science" that smooths out national particulars, but rather a pattern of uneven development of science paralleling that of capitalism. We must understand this uneven development before we can engage constructively in international scientific cooperation.

The science of the industrial capitalist countries is a privileged science, made possible by the economic surplus accumulated from the whole world. The abundance of physical resources, libraries, universities, and scientists permits both extensive research aimed at practical goals and theoretical explorations aimed at more general understanding of nature. But this science is crippled because it is subordinated to the general (and often also very particular) interests of the bourgeoisie and deprived of the opportunity of working toward truly human goals by commercialization, militarism, internal organization, and ideology. It is bourgeois science. The designation "bourgeois" is not a judgment of the validity of any of its conclusions but a recognition of its historical contingencies.

Marxist scientists in the industrial capitalist countries share in the privileges afforded by the economic surplus. We cannot use these resources, however, to develop a science that really serves the long-range and global needs of our peoples. Our best analyses are often "unrealistic"—that is, incompatible with capitalist relations or implausible within the constraints of the dominant ideologies. In association with political movements we can struggle for improved health, more rational agriculture, and better environmental protection. And we can polemicize against the most oppressive ideological creations used to justify oppression. At the same time, we are free of the daunting responsibilities of constructing the new socialist societies, which dominate the lives of our comrades in the revolutionary countries. This isolation and privilege allow us to pursue investigations and to elaborate theory in a way that is often quite general, subtle, and powerful but that is also condemned to overabstraction.

Third World science is also incomplete and one-sided. It is limited by lack of physical resources, libraries, and communication with world science. It suffers from the intellectual hegemony of world (bourgeois) science. In the capitalist Third World, science suffers from the simultaneous under- and overproduction of scientists—underproduction compared to the country's needs but overproductions in relation to the country's capacity to equip and support science and to carry its research results into practice. It is distorted by the process of recruiting scientists into a civil service where upward mobility is conditional on prudence before daring.

The revolutionary societies of the Third World have the same shortage of resources, an overwhelming disparity between the urgent needs of the people and the limited material and intellectual resources to meet them. The planners' Marxist intellectual commitment to long-range and global issues comes into partial conflict with this urgent political commitment.

When Marxist scientists from industrial capitalist countries and revolutionary Third World nations collaborate in socialist development, we bring different strengths and weaknesses, and we are equally products of our very different social conditions. The typical errors of those from capitalist countries are overabstraction and long-range concerns; Marxists from revolutionary nations are more likely to err toward pragmatism. We meet to build a solidarity against two common distortions: on the one hand, the repetition of old patterns of Euro–North American arrogance and domination, complemented by Third World deference toward the "advanced" and titled experts, and, on the other hand, the guilt-driven passivity of the Western scientists complemented by the revolutionary nationalism of the host country.

The basis for cooperation is that world science, although concentrated in some countries, was made possible by the labor of the whole world and legitimately belongs to all peoples. Revolution anywhere in the world is heir not only to the history of struggle of that people but also to over a century of international political and intellectual struggles; therefore the revolution belongs to all of us who oppose imperialism and fight for socialism.

A central task for a Marxist program of international solidarity in science is to examine the contradiction of science as class product and science as progress in human knowledge to recognize the historicity of science and therefore not to assume that the science developing now in the Third World must recapitulate the history of Euro–North American science. We have to raise anew the questions of conducting practical research in a fundamental way, finding the appropriate subdivisions of the sciences, reconciling the conflicting needs for specialized knowledge and broad overview, integrating professional and popular knowledge, and training revolutionary scientists.

Scientific collaboration is the locus of both cooperation and conflict. When Marxist scientists work with nonsocialist scientists in the United Nations, or in national and private development or aid programs, the relationship is one of cooperation within conflict. The cooperation is founded on a shared scientific culture and the stated objectives of the programs, say, improving health or agriculture. But this takes place within a conflict: while we see the struggles for health and agriculture and environmental protection as aimed toward building a new society with basically different relations among people and with nature, the sponsors of these programs see them more as means to preserve the existing societies (usually expressed as promoting stability). The working scientists usually do not deal with these global objectives but, rather, see themselves as pursuing humanitarian, nonpolitical objectives such as reducing hunger. But a precondition for their employment is that they will pursue these goals subject to the constraints of "realism": nutritional programs must not ask about the distribution of wealth, plant pathologists do not touch land tenure, agricultural economists assume production for profit. At different times the cooperative or the conflictive aspects may be in the forefront, but the basic relationship is one of cooperation within conflict.

On the other hand, relationship between revolutionary scientists of industrial capitalist and socialist Third World countries is one of conflict within cooperation. The cooperation derives from the common goals of building socialism and opposing imperialism. The conflict arises from our different experiences within our own societies. While those who have been excluded in the past from world science stress the need to join in and share its fruits, we who have been immersed in the most modern bourgeois science are more impressed with the need to criticize it. While socialist planners suffer from the lack of expertise in hundreds of specialities, we are more aware of the oppressiveness of the cults of expertise. While they see the production of scientists with advanced degrees as triumphs of human labor and therefore honor titles as measures of progress, we more often see the degrees and titles as part of a system for the regulation of privilege and cooptation and therefore often scorn them. While we struggle for a science that negates the most oppressive features of the scientific life of our own countries, our comrades have a greater sense of the urgencies of their nascent economies.

These differences are of course neither universal nor absolute, and listing them is already a step toward resolving them. But they indicate some of the dimensions of conflict within cooperation that must be understood as a prerequisite for effective international solidarity. Needless to say, the processes of conflict within cooperation are possible only if embedded in the broader solidarity of anti-imperialist struggle.

This critique, unlike more nationalist responses to science, does not automatically reject the findings of science as false or irrelevant because they are foreign or historically contingent. But it insists that that contingency must be explored at each point before decisions are made about what to adopt from world science for the revolutionary societies of the Third World.

The major problems of applied ecology in Third World countries are linked to agriculture, public health, environmental protection, and resource management. Here we concentrate on agriculture and refer only briefly to other areas.

The pragmatists and the conservative developmentalists agree in their approach to agriculture: a modern, progressive agriculture would attract foreign investment through agribusiness; transfer and adapt a capital-intensive high-technology approach based on plant breeding, chemical fertilizers, pesticides, irrigation, and mechanizations; and draw the peasants into the national and international market through specialization in cash crops. The political goals are the creation of a technically progressive and aggressive rural bourgeoisie, to be the political base of support for dependent capitalism, and a rural proletariat, which may struggle for economic goals but may not challenge the system. The increased food production or earnings on exchange would cheapen wage goods in the cities as well.

This model for agriculture has been implanted unevenly in many areas of the Third World and has been subject to many kinds of criticism. Most of these criticisms apply also to the industrial societies, but they are especially important to the Third World. First, high-technology agriculture destroys its own productive base. Increased erosion, lowering of water tables, salinization, compaction of soils, depletion of nutrients, and destruction of soil structure are threatening agriculture everywhere, but under the tropical conditions of most Third World regions, these problems are exacerbated. In more prosperous regions they can be hidden for a while by increased investment. In regions of deep soils and adequate rainfall distribution, they can be ignored for decades. But in the fragile habitats into which commercial agriculture is expanding, this is less possible. It must be recognized that capital-intensive high-technology agriculture is an ecologically unstable system.

The high-technology monocultures increase the vulnerability of production to natural and economic fluctuations. The plant varieties developed for the green revolution give superior yields only under optimal conditions of fertilizers, water, and pest management. They have been selected to put most of their energy into grain rather than vegetative parts, and the resulting stout dwarf stems make it easier for weeds to outgrow them, making herbicide use mandatory. Their reduced root growth increases the plants' sensitivity to shortage of water. Irrigation buffers the crop against the vagaries of rainfall but increases the farmers' sensitivity to the price of fuel. High-nitrogen fertilizers and the growth-stimulating effects of herbicides make the plants more vulnerable and attractive to insects. The use of fertilizers offsets local variations in soil nutrients but makes fertilizer prices part of the environment of the roots of plants. And monoculture removes diversity as one of the traditional hedges against uncertainty.

Despite modern agricultural technology, crop loss to pests has not been reduced since 1900 and probably is increasing. With increased areas sown to a single highest-yielding crop, more species of pests invade the crops; the use of pesticides often creates new pest problems by destroying the predators of pests. Commercial seed production reduces varietal diversity and disrupts the processes of local adaptation and diffusion that created our present crops.

Modern technology adversely affects the health of populations. Pesticides are poisons; the World Health Organization (WHO) estimated some years ago that 500,000 people are poisoned, and some 5,000 die, from pesticides each year.

Where government regulation of chemicals is weakest, where protective measures are not available, where children accompany their parents into the fields, where illiteracy makes warning labels irrelevant, where aircraft carry out the spraying, pesticide poisoning is at its worst.

The diversity of crops has declined as farmers have opted for the most profitable product. Grass crops (wheat, rice, sorghum) respond better to the new technologies and therefore have pushed out chickpeas and other legumes. Soybeans produced for cattle feed displace black beans, so protein production increases but available food protein declines. Selection of crops for total yield and measurement of the value of chemical inputs for their effect on yield often result in declining nutritional value of crops.

Modern technology in agriculture under capitalism alters the rural class structure: tenants are evicted and replaced by wage laborers who have no land for supplementing subsistence production, land is increasingly concentrated, and the surplus rural people move to the cities, where they join the masses of the unemployed. Particular innovations have particular consequences: herbicides replace hand weeding and therefore increase unemployment among women; monoculture generally increases the unevenness of demand for labor. While young men are relatively free to follow the crop cycle, unmarried women with children are able to farm independently only on the basis of a crop mixture that spreads the labor requirements. And since new technologies are almost always made available only to men, technical progress in agriculture promotes sexist inequality.

Modern agricultural technology results in environmental deterioration. Runoff of fertilizers leads to eutrophication of lakes; the added nutrients favor the growth of edible species of algae, which then decay, absorbing oxygen and leading to oxygen-deficient conditions that kill fish and invertebrates. Increased erosion speeds up the silting of lakes and ponds and increases turbidity, so production of aquatic life declines. Pesticides penetrate the whole ecosystem, killing wildlife and often favoring not only agricultural pests but also disease vectors. When cotton, which is very dependent on pesticides, is introduced into new regions, malaria often increases. The promise of high yields encourages farmers to expand cultivation of annual row crops into forests, up slopes, and in general into more fragile habitats.

Most agricultural development schemes attempt to overwhelm nature by technology and to dismiss indigenous knowledge, thus guaranteeing unpleasant surprises, undermining the capacity of farmers to understand what is happening, and reinforcing ideological domination. The intellectual foundations of modern agricultural science are dominated by short-range pragmatism, narrow specialization, and reductionism, which prevent the kind of broad vision that could anticipate the problems, which otherwise come as surprises. This viewpoint is rooted both in the prevailing philosophy of science and in the commoditization of science.

The final, disturbing conclusion is that "modern" high-technology agriculture is a successional stage ecologically, an unstable relationship to nature that is rapidly running its course and must be replaced by a radically different system of production. But neither conservative nor radical developmentalists draw this conclusion.

R E F E R E N C E

Gutierrez, G. 1974. *Ciencia-cultura y dependencia.* Buenos Aires: Editorial Guadalupe.

ENVIRONMENTAL RACISM

Karl Grossman

"We're sitting in a center of a donut surrounded by a hazardous waste incinerator that gives off PCBs, seven landfills that are constantly growing—they look like mountains," Hazel Johnson was saying. "There are chemical plants, a paint factory, two steel mills which give off odors, and lagoons filled with all kinds of contaminants that emit 30,000 tons of poison into the air each year. And there's a water reclamation district where they dry sludge out in the open. The smell is horrible, like bodies decomposing."

Mrs. Johnson was describing Atgeld Gardens, a housing project in which 10,000 people, nearly all African-Americans, reside on the Southeast Side of Chicago, surrounded on every side by sources of pollution.

The result: environmental diseases and death.

"We have lots of cancer, respiratory problems, birth deformities," Mrs. Johnson went on. "Just the other day, there were three cancer deaths. Then more. We've been having babies born with brain tumors. One baby was born with her brain protruding from her head. She's two now, blind and she can't walk. My daughter was five months pregnant. She took ultra-sound and the doctors found the baby had no behind, no head," said Mrs. Johnson, the mother of seven. "The baby had to be aborted."

Mrs. Johnson has no doubt that "the terrible health problems we have in our community are related to the pollution," the product of trying to live amid one of the most concentrated areas of environmental contamination in the United States.

And she is clear about why her area gets dumped on: because it is largely inhabited by African-Americans and Hispanics. "In Chicago, everything is mostly dumped out in this area where we are. They figure that we're not going to come out and protest and disagree." But Mrs. Johnson has, for ten years now, as the head of People for Community Recovery, been fighting back.

"Atgeld Gardens symbolizes environmental racism," the Reverend Benjamin Chavis, Jr., the noted civil rights leader and executive director of the United Church of Christ's Commission for Racial Justice, declared. "The community is surrounded on all four sides by pollution and has one of the highest cancer rates in the nation. The public officials in Chicago are well aware of the circumstances that these people are forced to live in, yet, because of their race, the city has no priority in stopping this type of environmental injustice."

Reverend Chavis was the first to use the term *environmental racism* in 1987 with the release of what has become a landmark study by the commission, "Toxic Wastes and Race in the United States." It has taken several years for the import of the report, notes Reverend Chavis, to take hold.

But now that has well begun. There have been a series of important events, including a week-long tour by the Reverend Jesse Jackson, shortly before Earth Day 1990, of low-income minority communities struck by pollution. He stressed the "relationship between environment and empowerment" and declared it "a new day and a new way. No longer will corporations be allowed to use job blackmail to poison poor people be they black, brown, yellow, red, or white. We are demanding that all corporate poisoners sign agreements to stop the poisoning of our communities."

Reverend Jackson was accompanied by Dennis Hayes, a principal organizer of both the original Earth Day, in 1970, and last year's event, and John O'Connor, executive director of the National Toxics Campaign, who emphasized that "for the environmental movement to be successful in saving the planet, it must include all races, ethnic groups, rich and poor, black and white, and young and old. When our movement to clean up the nation is truly a reflection of all people in the country, it is at that point that we will succeed in stopping the poisoning of America."

Issuing a report in 1990 at a National Minority Health Conference in Washington on environmental contamination, describing how "a marriage of the movement for social justice with environmentalism" was taking place, was the Panos Institute. "Organizing for environmental justice among people of color has grown from a small group of activists in the 1970s to a movement involving thousands of people in neighborhoods throughout the U.S.," said Dana A. Alston, director of the Environment, Community Development and Race Project of Panos, an international group that works for "sustainable development." She added in the report, "We Speak for Ourselves: Social Justice, Race and Environment," that "communities of color have often taken a more holistic approach than the mainstream environmental movement, integrating 'environmental' concerns into a broader agenda that emphasizes social, racial, and economic justice."

In Atlanta in 1990, at a conference on environmental problems in minority areas sponsored by the federal Agency for Toxic Substances and Disease Registry and others attended by 300 community leaders, doctors and governmental officials. Dr. Aubrey F. Manley, deputy assistant secretary of the Department of Health and Human Services, stated, "Poor and minority organizations charged eight major national environmental groups with racism in their hiring practices and demanded that they substantially increase the number of people of color on their staffs. The environmental groups acknowledged the problem—"The truth is that environmental groups have done a miserable job of reaching out to minorities," said Frederick D. Krupp, executive director of the Environmental Defense Fund—and set up an Environmental Consortium for Minority Outreach.

And last year, too, the Commission for Racial Justice organized a workshop on racism and the environment for the Congressional Black Caucus, whose members, unbeknownst to many, are rated as having among the best pro-environmental voting records in Congress by the League of Conservation Voters, which scores congressional representatives on their environmental records.

A key event to be held this year [1991] will be the first National Minority Environmental Leadership Summit in Washington, D.C., in October. "We want to bring together leaders of community groups, environmental groups, civil rights organizations and academic, scientific, governmental and corporate organizations to participate in this three-day corporate meeting," says Charles Lee, research director of the Commission for Racial Justice, which is organizing the gathering. "The purpose of this summit is to develop a comprehensive and tangible national agenda of action that will help reshape and redirect environmental policy-making in the United States to fully embrace the concerns of minority Americans."

People of color have been the worst victims of environmental pollution for a long time. Lee tells of the building of the Gauley Bridge in West Virginia in the 1930s: "Hundreds of African-American workers from the Deep South were brought in by the New Kunawha Power Company, a subsidiary of the Union Carbide corporation, to dig the Hawks Nest tunnel. Over a two-year period, approximately 500 workers died and 1,500 were disabled from silicosis, a lung disease similar to black lung. Men literally dropped on their feet breathing air so thick with microscopic silica that they could not see more than a yard in front of them. Those who came out for air were beaten back into the tunnel with ax handles." At subsequent congressional hearings, New Kanawha's contractor revealed, "I knew I was going to kill these niggers, but I didn't know it was going to be this soon."

Lee relates how "an undertaker was hired to bury dead workers in unmarked graves" and of his agreeing "to perform the service for an extremely low rate because the company assured him there would be a large number of deaths."

But it was not until recent years that this and other horror stories of environmental racism started to be examined in their systematic context.

It was in 1982 that residents of predominantly African-American Warren county, North Carolina, asked the Commission for Racial Justice for help in their protests against the siting of a dump for PCBs—the acronym for polychlorinated biphenyls, a carcinogen. In a campaign of civil disobedience that ensued, there were more than 500 arrests, including the commission's Reverend Chavis, Dr. Joseph Lowery of the Southern Christian Leadership conference, and Congressman Walter Fauntroy of Washington.

It was during that effort that Reverend Chavis began considering the connection between the dumping in Warren County; the federal government's Savannah River nuclear facility, long a source of radioactive leaks and located in a heavily African-American area of South Carolina; and the "largest landfill in the nation" in the mainly black community of Emelle, Alabama. "We began to see evidence of a systematic pattern which led us to a national study," recounted Reverend Chavis.

That study—"Toxic Wastes and Race in the United States"—clearly shows what Reverend Chavis suspected: communities of color are where most of America's places of poison are located. In detail, the analysis looked at a cross section of the thousands of U.S. "commercial hazardous waste facilities" (defined by the U.S. Environmental Protection Agency as places licensed for "treating, storing or disposing of hazardous wastes") and "uncontrolled toxic waste sites" (defined by EPA as closed and abandoned sites), and correlated them with the ethnicity of the communities in which they are located.

Some of the study's minor findings:

- "Race proved to be the most influential among variables tested in association with the location of commercial hazardous waste facilities. This represented a consistent national pattern."
- "Communities with the greatest number of commercial hazardous waste facilities had the highest composition of ethnic residents."
- "Although socio-economic status appeared to play an important role in the location of commercial hazardous waste facilities, race still proved to be more significant."
- "Three out of every five black and Hispanic Americans lived in communities with uncontrolled toxic waste sites."
- "Blacks were heavily overrepresented in the populations of metropolitan areas with the largest number of uncontrolled toxic waste sites"—Memphis, St. Louis, Houston, Cleveland, Chicago, and Atlanta.
- "Approximately half of all Asian/Pacific Islanders and American Indians lived in communities with uncontrolled toxic waste sites."

The analysis called for change. "This report firmly concludes that hazardous wastes in black, Hispanic and other racial and ethnic communities should be made a priority issue at all levels of government. This issue is not currently at the forefront of the nation's attention. Therefore, concerned citizens and policymakers, who are cognizant of this growing national problem, must make this a priority concern."

It called for the U.S. president "to issue an executive order mandating federal agencies to consider the impact of current policies and regulations on racial and ethnic communities"; state governments "to evaluate and make appropriate revisions in their criteria for the siting of new hazardous waste facilities to adequately take into account the racial and socio-economic characteristics of potential host communities"; the U.S. Conference of Mayors, the National Conference of Black Mayors and the National League of Cities "to convene a national conference to address these issues from a municipal perspective"; and "civil rights and political organizations to gear up voter registration campaigns as a means to further empower racial and ethnic communities to effectively respond to hazardous wastes in racial and ethnic communities at the top of state and national legislative agendas."

Environmentalist Barry Commoner commented that the report showed the "functional relationship between poverty, racism and powerlessness and the chemical industry's assault on the environment."

It was in 1978 that sociologist Robert Bullard first began exploring environmental racism. He was asked by Linda McKeever Bullard, his wife, to conduct a study on the siting of municipal landfills and incinerators in Houston for a class-action lawsuit challenging a plan to site a new landfill in the "solid middle class" mostly African-American Houston neighborhood of Northwood Manor, notes Bullard. Just out of graduate school, a new professor at Texas Southern University, he found that from the 1920s to that time, all five of Houston's landfills and six out of eight of its incinerators were sited in black neighborhoods. That led to wider studies by Dr. Bullard on how "black communities, because of their economic and political vulnerability, have been routinely targeted for the siting of noxious facilities, locally unwanted land uses and environmental hazards."

He wrote several papers, and last year his book, *Dumping in Dixie: Race, Class, and Environmental Quality,* came out. Black communities are consistently the ones getting dumped on "because of racism, plain and simple," says Dr. Bullard, now a professor at the University of California at Riverside.

Often it is a promise of "jobs, jobs, and jobs that are held out as a savior" for these communities although, in fact, "these are not labor-intensive industries." The companies involved, meanwhile, figure they can "minimize their investment" by avoiding the sort of lawsuit more likely to be brought by a white community faced with having a toxic dump, an incinerator, a paper mill, a slaughterhouse, a lead smelter, a pesticide plant, "you name it," said Dr. Bullard. Also, with planning and zoning boards commonly having "excluded people of color," the skids are further greased. And to top it off, "because of housing patterns and limited mobility, middle-income and lower-income blacks," unlike whites, often cannot "vote with their feet" and move out when a polluting facility arrives. "Targeting certain communities for poison is another form of discrimination," charged Dr. Bullard.

He tells in *Dumping in Dixie* of how African-Americans in Houston and Dallas; in Alsen, Louisiana; Institute, West Virginia, and Emelle, Alabama, "have taken on corporate giants who would turn their areas into toxic wastelands." He is enthused by how "literally hundreds of environmental justice groups are made up of people of color."

One of the many organizations is the Gulf Coast Tenants Association. "We have not only the dumping here, but we get the upfront stuff; this is where much of the petrochemical industry is centered, and where they produce a lot of the stuff," says Darryl Malek-Wiley, the New Orleans-based group's director of research. "Cancer Alley is the nickname for this area," he says, speaking of the seventy-five-mile swath along the Mississippi from Baton Rouge to New Orleans. The group offers courses in environmental education and assists people to fight environmental hazards in their communities and block the siting of new ones. The placement of hazardous facilities in black communities in the South follows a pattern of subjugation going back "hundreds of years," notes Malek, with "the industrial age" giving this a new translation. And, he says, it should be viewed in connection with the dumping of hazardous waste in Third World countries.

Up north, in the middle of America's biggest city, New York—Peggy Shepard has been challenging environmental racism as a leader of West Harlem Environmental Action (WHE ACT). Obnoxious, "exploitive" facilities placed in her area in recent years, she notes, have included a huge sewage treatment plant, a "marine transfer station" for garbage, and yet another bus storage depot. "We organized around a series of issues in our community that turned out to be all environmental in nature." WHE ACT has been "networking with organizations around" New York City and found that what had happened to West Harlem is typical of what has occurred to other African-American and Hispanic neighborhoods. "We get so used to the stereotype that what environmentalism means is wildlife and the preservation of open space. There had not been sufficient movement on urban environmental problems: incinerators, sewage treatment plants, factories polluting the air, devastating occupational exposure."

Sulalman Mahdi is southeast regional director of the Center for Environment, Commerce and Energy in Atlanta. "Our work involves educating the African-American community around the whole question of the environment. I am particularly interested in bridging the civil rights movement and the environmental justice movement," says Mahdi.

He became involved in the "green" movement while working in the campaign for reparations in land for African-Americans for the injustices committed against them. Living in southern Georgia near Brunswick, a papermill town, and "smelling the sulfur all the time" from the papermill lands, he concluded, as he choked on the putrid air, that "we need to fight for environmental protection or the land we seek might not be of any real value once it's returned."

He takes the African-American perspective on nature right back to Africa, and indeed is writing a book on African ecology. The African approach to nature "is very similar to that of the Native Americans," says Mahdi. He speaks of the "founder of agriculture, the founder of botany," both ancient Egyptians. He sees a solid "relationship between our freedom struggle" and battling the environmental abuse subjected on African-Americans, what he terms "environmental genocide."

Genocide is also the word used by Lance Hughes of Native Americans for a Clean Environment. "As states and various municipalities have been closing down a lot of dumps because of public opposition, the companies have been descending on the reservations across the country," says Hughes. Indian reservations are seen as good dump sites by the firms because they are considered sovereign entities not subject to local or state environmental restrictions.

The group of which he is director was formed six years ago because of radioactive contamination caused by a twin set of nuclear production facilities run by Kerr-McGee in northeast Oklahoma amid a large concentration of Native Americans. One produces nuclear fuel for weaponry, the other for nuclear power plants. Further, some of the nuclear waste generated at them is put in fertilizer throughout the state, and also by Kerr-McGee on 10,000 acres surrounding the nuclear facilities.

"The hay and cattle from that land is sold on the open market," says Hughes. The Native Americans who live in the area have many "unusual cancers" and a high rate of birth defects from "genetic mutation. It gets pretty sad," says Hughes, "with babies born without eyes, babies born with brain cancers."

Wildlife is also born deformed. "We found a nine-legged frog and a two-headed fish. And there was a four-legged chicken." Hughes emphasizes that the subjugation of Native Americans "is still going on. The name of the game has been changed, but I would call it the same—genocide, because that is exactly what the result is."

The Southwest Organizing Project (SWOP) is a multi-ethnic, multi-issue organization which began a decade ago in a predominantly Chicano area of Albuquerque, New Mexico. "We have a municipal landfill, the largest pig farm in the city of Albuquerque, a dogfood plant, Texaco, Chevron, General Electric, a sewage plant," says Richard Moore, SWOP co-director. This, he said, is typical of Hispanic and African-American communities in the Southwest.

"Wherever you find working-class, ethnic communities you find environmental injustice," say Moore, whose group has grown to fight environmental racism throughout New Mexico. "We have been organizing door-to-door, building strong organizations, going up against pretty major organizations." Nonpartisan voter registration has been a key tool. The group was also the founding organization of the Southwest Network of Environmental and Economic Justice, which Moore co-chairs, that brings together people in seven Southwest states also on a multi-ethnic, multi-issue basis.

Moore was one of the signatories of the letter sent to eight major environmental organizations protesting their lack of minority representation (example: of the 315 staff members of the Audubon Society, only three were black).

Importantly, not scored in that letter were three prominent national environmental groups: Greenpeace, the National Toxics Campaign, and Earth Island Institute. In a breakthrough, in contradiction to the pattern elsewhere, the president of Earth Island Institute is an African-American.

Carl Anthony is not only president of Earth Island Institute, headquartered in San Francisco, but director of its Urban Habitat program. "We're very interested in issues at two ends of the spectrum: global warming, the ozone layer, depletion of global resources—and the negative environmental impacts on communities of poor people and people of color. In order to bring these two concerns together," says Anthony, "we have to develop a new kind of thrust and a new kind of leadership in communities of color to address the needs of our communities and also the larger urban community in making a transaction to more sustainable urban patterns." Urban Habitat is "basically a clearinghouse for a lot of people all over the country who want to work on these issues. And it helps alert people from our community to the issues that concern them: toxics, energy issues, air quality, water quality."

Anthony, an architect, says he has "always been aware of environmental issues." He is a designer of buildings and is a professor of architecture at the University of California at Berkeley, where he is now teaching a new course for the school: Race, Poverty, and the Environment. He speaks with great pleasure of his involvement with Earth Island Institute but is dubious about whether some of the other national environmental groups will become fully multi-ethnic. They have long taken an "elitist perspective. I doubt that Audubon, for instance, will ever make a big push in this direction."

Chicago's Hazel Johnson has worked closely with Greenpeace, the national environmental group most committed to direct action. "I have a very good working relationship with Greenpeace. It is more than an action group. I have gone with Greenpeace to many places and they have come out to assist us." She spoke of one recent demonstration carried on by her People for Community Recovery against yet one more incinerator planned for her community in which, with Greenpeace, "we chained ourselves to trucks."

"Unequivocally," says Lee, of the Commission for Racial Justice, "minority communities are the communities most at risk to environmental pollution." He paints in words the panorama of pollution. There is the heavy exposure to pesticides of Hispanic farm workers, including those in Delano, California, where "there is an estimated 300,000 pesticide-related cancers among farm workers each year."

There are the effects of radioactive contamination on Native Americans, especially the Navajos, the nation's primary work force in the mining of uranium—who have extreme cancer rates as a result. "There is lead poisoning of children in urban areas—with an estimated 55 percent of the victims being African-Americans," says Lee. There is the mess in Puerto Rico, "one of the most heavily polluted areas in the world," with U.S. petrochemical and pharmaceutical companies long having discharged toxics on a massive scale. All the people in the island's town of La Cuidad Cristiana were forced to be relocated due to mercury poisoning. The terrible stories go on and on. Says Lee: "We still have a long way to go in truly addressing this issue."

"To understand the causes of these injustices, it is important to view them in a historical context," he notes. "Two threads of history help to explain the disproportionate impact of toxic pollution on racial and ethnic communities. The first is the long history of oppression and exploitation of African-Americans, Hispanic Americans, Asian-Americans, Pacific Islanders, and Native Americans. This has taken the form of genocide, chattel slavery, indentured servitude, and racial discrimination in employment, housing and practically all aspects of life in the United States. We suffer today from the remnant of this sordid history, as well as from new and institutionalized forms of racism. The other thread of history is the massive expansion of the petrochemical industry since World War II."

"Environmental racism is racial discrimination in environmental policymaking," says Reverend Chavis. "Wherever you find non-white people, that's where they want to dump stuff. And it's spreading all over the world. A lot of toxic chemicals have been going for dumping in the Pacific Islands and Africa; it recently was revealed that Kenya has been allowing us to dump nuclear wastes." (The Organization of African Unity has denounced the dumping by the United States and European countries of hazardous waste in Africa as "toxic terrorism" and "a crime against Africa and the African people.")

"I think when we define the freedom movement, it now includes the environmental issues," says Reverend Chavis. "We now understand the insidious nature of racism. Fighting it does not just involve getting civil rights laws on the books. It goes beyond that. Racism has so permeated all facets of American society. We see the struggle against environmental racism as being an ongoing part of the civil rights and freedom movement in this country, something we are going to make part of our agenda, not a side issue but a primary issue. We must be just as vigilant in attacking environmental racism in health care, housing, and schools."

PART FIVE

Objectivity, Method, and Nature: Value Neutral?

Nature is part of history and culture, not the other way around. Sociologists and historians of science tend to know that. Most scientists do not. Because I was trained as a scientist, it has taken me many years to understand that "in science, just as in art and in life, only that which is true to culture is true to nature."

Ruth Hubbard, *The Politics of Women's Biology*

[S]cientists who retreat behind the screen of pure science are passively abandoning their social responsibility; those who choose to become actively involved risk being seen as no longer "objective." Here the notion of "objectivity" becomes merely a code word for the political passivity of those scientists who have tacitly agreed to accept a privileged social position and freedom of inquiry within the laboratory in return for their silence in not questioning the social uses of science or the power relations that determine its direction.

Elizabeth Fee, "Women's Nature and Scientific Objectivity," in *Woman's Nature: Rationalizations of Inequality*

We now have a much clearer idea of what it is to follow scientists and engineers in action. We know that they do not extend "everywhere" as if there existed a Great Divide between the universal knowledge of the Westerners and the local knowledge of everyone else, but instead that they travel inside narrow and fragile networks, resembling the galleries termites build to link their nests to their feeding sites. Inside these networks, they make traces of all sorts circulate better by increasing their mobility, their speed, their reliability, their ability to combine with one another. We also know that these networks are not built with homogeneous material but, on the contrary, necessitate the weaving together of a multitude of different elements which renders the question of whether they are "scientific" or "technical" or "economic" or "political" or "managerial" meaningless. Finally, we know that the results of building, extending and keeping up these networks is to act at a distance, that is to do things in the centres that sometimes make it possible to dominate spatially as well as chronologically the periphery.

Bruno Latour, *Science in Action*

By now, it is widely held that objectivity, method, and, indeed, nature-as-an-object-of-knowledge cannot possibly be value free. Scientific method was supposed to ensure the elimination of social values from the results of scientific research. In the selection presented here, the National Academy of Sciences adopts the enlarged understanding of scientific method for which so many science observers have argued. It states that scientific method itself inevitably will be shaped by social values, since scientific "methods include the judgments scientists make about the interpretation or reliability of data, . . . the decisions scientists make about which problems to pursue or when to conclude an investigation, . . . the ways scientists work with each other and exchange information." As so many essays in this book have argued, it is no longer reasonable to regard scientific method as value neutral. Moreover, although science training has historically avoided exposing young scientists to anything but the most minimal history, philosophy and sociology of science, the academy here recommends such studies, arguing that such accounts provide important resources for scientists in learning to identify their own and their culture's values. The academy's statement reflects its concern to preserve scientific "property" in the face of scientific scandals that threaten to deteriorate its value. It wants to preserve the economic, political, and social value of the information produced by the sciences and their authority to produce these accounts. Obviously, many historians, philosophers, and sociologists of science do not share these goals or values.

The other selections in this section, like many others in this collection, provide important examples of the kind of social studies of the sciences called for by the National Academy of Sciences. Robert Proctor points out that Nazi science and "medicine" were perfectly consistent with highly regarded scientific tendencies in the United States and elsewhere at the time, including not only eugenics but also an increasing authoritarianism in scientific and medical practices. Moreover, he argues that while Nazis obviously politicized science in one sense, in another sense the problem was that they *depoliticized* it "by destroying the possibility of political debate and controversy. Authoritarian science based on the 'Führer principle' replaced what had been, in the Weimar period, a vigorous spirit of politicized debate in and around the sciences."

Historian Nancy Leys Stepan considers the widely used analogy that linked race to gender in both nineteenth- and twentieth-century scientific theorizing about human variation. She challenges the conventional view holding that the metaphors, analogies, and models of science are merely heuristic devices or unnecessary decorations of pure descriptions of nature, and thus that they are not in any way essential to the advance of scientific knowledge. To the contrary, she argues that metaphors, analogies, and models, through their capacity to construct similarities, serve as programs of research that both create new knowledge and suppress old knowledge. Thus the growth of knowledge depends upon scientific use of socially meaningful metaphors, analogies, and models.

Consequently, when these metaphors change, so too will the research programs that they guide.

Donna Haraway contrasts the images of nature provided by Anglo-American versus Japanese primatology, showing how national preoccupations shape the problems primatologists want to study, and consequently nature-as-an-object-of-knowledge and even their distinctive philosophies of science. Nature-as-an-object-of-knowledge is multilingual, we could say: it speaks not only in the mathematical language that Bacon recommended scientists learn if they wished to "converse" with nature, but also and always in the many cultural accents of the societies in which scientists conduct their scientific conversations. What kinds of science education will enable scientists to recognize, critically evaluate, and use as a resource this multilinguality of "nature," the sciences and philosophies of science?

The kinds of cultural influences on scientific method Haraway reports are by no means restricted to the borders between natural and social sciences occupied by primatology, for anthropologist Sharon Traweek shows that cultural differences in how the work of high-energy physics is socially organized by the scientists at the Stanford Linear Accelerator and at KEK, the accelerator in Tsubuka, Japan, lead, in the view of the physicists involved, to "different physics." Finally, Jack Stauder points out that the unusual popularity of functionalist anthropology in England compared to the United States, France, and Germany in the 1920s and '30s is accounted for by the fact that England, in contrast to Germany, was faced with the problem of learning how local African societies worked so as to be able to establish and maintain the form of colonialism known as "indirect rule." "Sciences will tend toward their uses," he argues. His analysis leads us to consider how contemporary physics, chemistry, and biology also tend toward their uses. Would other uses lead us to other sciences?

Like other essays in this collection, these show that if a scientific project doesn't effectively distance itself from regressive politics, it can easily end up complicit with them. Scientists need better ways to evaluate the relationship between their work and regressive social policies. The "ostrich strategy" of attempting to achieve less partial and distorted results of research by turning one's back to antidemocratic politics evidently is not an effective technique. While "whistle blowing" can sometimes be effective, the cases presented here suggest the limits of that approach. Commitment to far more comprehensive standards of objectivity—a "strong objectivity"—could help to provide the tools to undertake such critical evaluations.[1] But such commitments require that sciences explicitly and effectively be committed to advancing democracy in order to achieve their "purely scientific" ends—paradoxical as this may sound. Is democracy a goal of science? Should it be? (What form of democracy?) Should we go further than the National Academy of Sciences and say that such a commitment should be part of scientific method?

N O T E

1. I discuss what is wrong with the conventional notion of objectivity that links it to value neutrality and the need, instead, to formulate systematic methods that can achieve "strong objectivity" in chap. 6 of *Whose Science? Whose Knowledge? Thinking from Women's Lives* (Ithaca, N.Y: Cornell University Press, 1991).

METHODS AND VALUES IN SCIENCE

National Academy of Sciences

Over the years, scientists have developed a vast array of methods that are designed to minimize problems [of researcher bias]. At the most familiar level, these methods include techniques such as double-blind trials, randomization of experimental subjects, and the proper use of controls, which are all aimed at reducing individual subjectivity. Methods also include the use of tools in scientific work, both the mechanical tools used to make observations and the intellectual tools used to manipulate abstract concepts.

The term *methods* can be interpreted more broadly. Methods include the judgments scientists make about the interpretation or reliability of data. They also include the decisions scientists make about which problems to pursue or when to conclude an investigation. Methods involve the ways scientists work with each other and exchange information. Taken together, these methods constitute the craft of science, and a person's individual application of these methods helps determine that person's scientific style.

Some methods, such as those governing the design of experiments or the statistical treatment of data, can be written down and studied. (The bibliography includes several books on experimental design.) But many methods are learned only through personal experience and interactions with other scientists. Some are even harder to describe or teach. Many of the intangible influences on scientific discovery—curiosity, intuition, creativity—largely defy rational analysis, yet they are among the tools that scientists bring to their work.

Although methods are an integral part of science, most of them are not the product of scientific investigation. They have been developed and their use is required in science because they have been shown to advance scientific knowledge. However, even if perfectly applied, methods cannot guarantee the accuracy of scientific results. Experimental design is often as much an art as a science; tools can introduce errors; and judgments about data inevitably rest on incomplete information.

The fallibility of methods means that there is no cookbook approach to doing science, no formula that can be applied or machine that can be built to generate scientific knowledge. But science would not be so much fun if there were. The skillful application of methods to a challenging problem is one of the great

pleasures of science. The laws of nature are not apparent in our everyday surroundings, waiting to be plucked like fruit from a tree. They are hidden and
unyielding, and the difficulties of grasping them add greatly to the satisfaction of
success.

Values in Science

When methods are defined as all of the techniques and principles that scientists
apply in their work, it is easier to see how they can be influenced by human
values. As with hypotheses, human values cannot be eliminated from science,
and they can subtly influence scientific investigations.

The influence of values is especially apparent during the formulation or judgment of hypotheses. At any given time, several competing hypotheses may explain the available fact equally well, and each may suggest an alternate route for
further research. How should one select them?

Scientists and philosophers have proposed several criteria by which promising scientific hypotheses can be distinguished from less fruitful ones. Hypotheses
should be internally consistent, so that they do not generate contradictory conclusions. Their ability to provide accurate predictions, sometimes in areas far
removed from the original domain of the hypothesis, is viewed with great favor.
With disciplines in which prediction is less straightforward, such as geology or
astronomy, good hypotheses should be able to unify disparate observations. Also
highly prized are simplicity and its more refined cousin, elegance.

The above values relate to the epistemological, or knowledge-based, criteria
applied to hypotheses. But values of a different kind can also come into play in
science. Historians, sociologists, and other students of science have shown that
social and personal values unrelated to epistemological criteria—including philosophical, religious, cultural, political, and economic values—can shape scientific
judgment in fundamental ways. For instance, in the nineteenth century the geolo-
gist Charles Lyell championed the concept of uniformitarianism in geology, arguing that incremental changes operating over long periods of time have
produced the Earth's geological features, not large-scale catastrophes. However,
Lyell's preference for this still important idea may have depended as much on his
religious convictions as on his geological observations. He favored the notion of a
God who is an unmoved mover and does not intervene in His creation. Such a
God, thought Lyell, would produce a world where the same causes and effects
keep cycling eternally, producing a uniform geological history.

The obvious question is whether holding such values can harm a person's
science. In many cases the answer has to be yes. The history of science offers
many episodes in which social or personal values led to the promulgation of
wrong-headed ideas. For instance, past investigators produced "scientific" evidence for overtly racist views, evidence that we now know to be wholly erroneous. Yet at the time the evidence was widely accepted and contributed to
repressive social policies.

Attitudes regarding the sexes also can lead to flaws in scientific judgments. For instance, some investigators who have sought to document the existence or absence of a relationship between gender and scientific abilities have allowed personal biases to distort the design of their studies or the interpretation of their findings. Such biases can contribute to institutional policies that have caused females and minorities to be underrepresented in science, with a consequent loss of scientific talent and diversity.

Conflicts of interest caused by financial considerations are yet another source of values that can harm science. With the rapid decrease in time between fundamental discovery and commercial application, private industry is subsidizing a considerable amount of cutting-edge research. This commercial involvement may bring researchers into conflict with industrial managers—for instance, over the publication of discoveries—or it may bias investigations in the direction of personal gain.

The above examples are valuable reminders of the danger of letting values intrude into research. But it does not follow that social and personal values necessarily harm science. The desire to do accurate work is a social value. So is the belief that knowledge will ultimately benefit rather than harm humankind. One simply must acknowledge that values do contribute to the motivations and conceptual outlook of scientists. The danger comes when scientists allow values to introduce biases into their work that distort the results of scientific investigations.

The social mechanisms of science act to minimize the distorting influences of social and personal values. But individual scientists can avoid pitfalls by trying to identify their own values and the effects those values have on their science. One of the best ways to do this is by studying the history, philosophy, and sociology of science. Human values change very slowly, and the lessons of the past remain of great relevance today.

NAZI MEDICINE AND THE POLITICS OF KNOWLEDGE

Robert Proctor

Science is not an end in itself; every science has
certain tasks to fulfill.

Karl Kötschau, 1936

The triumph of National Socialism coincides with the most rapid demise of the scientific culture of a people in recent history. In 1930 Germany led the world in the physical, life, and social sciences. By 1935, however, one in five scientists had been driven from their posts; in some universities (the University of Berlin, for example) this figure approached one in three.[1] National Socialists forced the emigration or imprisonment of some of Germany's most eminent scientists: Einstein, Schrödinger, and Franck in physics: Goldschmidt in biology; Haber and Pauli in chemistry—and these are only some of the better known. In medicine, where Jewish representation was large, the toll was especially great. Between 1933 and 1938, 10,000 German physicians were forced from their jobs; many of these were compelled to flee the country, and others were killed in concentration or death camps.[2] Physicians driven from Germany or Austria included five men who either had won or would eventually win Nobel Prizes: Ernst Boris Chain, Max Delbrück, Hans A. Krebs, Otto Loewi, and Otto Meyerhof. The Nazis forced the dispersal of the world-famous Institute of Physiology headed by Meyerhof, and stripped the famous veterinary college in Berlin of most of its staff. Leading medical figures such as Sigmund Freud, Käte Frankenthal, Rudolf Nissen, Hermann Zondek, Selmer Aschheim, and Friedrich Dessauer were all either fired or forced to emigrate. Other physicians driven from their jobs included von Bayer, Blumenthal, Borschardt, Goldstein, Klemperer, Roesle, and Teleky. The Nazis forced socialist and communist physicians into exile or concentration camps. In countries occupied by German armies, the story was similar. In Poland the medical philosopher Ludwik Fleck was deported to Auschwitz, where he was forced to work on vaccines for the SS.[3] The Nazis destroyed the University of Cracow and forced the majority of its faculty into the camps. In Paris medical scholars such as Langevin were imprisoned.

Charlatans and Quacks or "Normal Science"?

In one sense, the persecution of Jewish, socialist, and communist intellectuals can be seen as part of a larger attack on German intellectual life. Nazi philosophers reoriented schooling from intellectual to manual labor; Education Minister Bernhard Rust shortened the high school week from six to five days and ordered that Saturdays be devoted to sports. Nazi philosophers cultivated the virtues of brawn over those of brain, naming as their first official playwright a man (Hans Johst) whose most memorable phrase appears to have been his boast: "When I hear the word 'culture,' I release the safety catch on my gun."

And yet it is only partially true, and in more than one sense misleading, to characterize the phenomenon of National Socialism as anti-intellectual. The image of the Nazis as irrational, jack-booted fanatics fails to appreciate (1) the extent to which the National Socialist movement appealed to academics and intellectuals; (2) the extent to which the Nazis were able to draw upon the imagery, results, and authority of science; and (3) the extent to which Nazi ideology informed the practice of science.

Academics in every field gave support to the Nazi regime. The Nazis, in return, provided support for various forms of intellectual endeavor, and in some instances quite handsomely. Certain fields, such as psychology, anthropology, and human genetics, actually expanded under the Nazis.[4] The Nazis provided substantial support for research in fields such as criminal biology, genetic pathology, and comparative physical anthropology. The German government provided financial support for twin studies and genealogical research, in an attempt to isolate the effects of nature and nurture, heredity and environment. More than a dozen new medical journals were founded in the Nazi period, and a host of new scientific institutes and academies were established.[5] The Nazis expanded Germany's public health facilities and state health offices. Health authorities implemented public health reforms with a zeal rarely equaled in modern times; millions of persons were X-rayed as part of a nationwide effort to combat tuberculosis; health authorities initiated a program to provide dental examinations for an entire generation of German youth. One could name many other programs implemented on this scale.

Nazi physicians frequently boasted of the growth of public health and medical science under the Hitler regime. Leonardo Conti, for example, on a trip to Denmark in 1942, maintained that "never before has the importance of science been so recognized as in Germany today," especially in his own area of work: medicine.[6] In 1936, when the first volume of the journal *Öffentlicher Gesundheitsdienst* was published, Hans Rinne of the Nazi party's Office for Public Health claimed that there was no area in which the National Socialist state had undertaken greater efforts of construction than in public health.[7] The same conclusion was reached by Franz Orsós, president of Hungary's National Association of Physicians, after a survey of German medical institutions at the height of Nazi power. Orsós traveled to Germany in 1937 as head of a delegation to evaluate

German medical science. On the basis of his visit, he concluded that "no country in the world can compare with German achievements in the field of medicine." Germany, according to Orsós, was "unsurpassed in the health of its people; never before has a nation so thoroughly protected its people from disease; never before has a nation concerned itself to such a degree with the health of 'normal people'—the people who will be useful in the future." He marveled at the new scientific institutions founded in the Nazi period, institutions unique in the extent to which they concentrated on preventive medical care: "Special institutes deal with racial protection and racial care, or with genetics and criminal biology. In genetics institutes, there are special divisions devoted to statistical, etiological, and therapeutic research, and research on genetic diseases. . . . There is research on genetic idiocy and mental illness, and all designed to serve the German people."[8]

Nazi racial theory and practice were not the product of a tiny band of marginal or psychotic individuals. Nazi racial hygienists were among the top professionals in their fields and saw themselves in the tradition of Virchow, Semmelweis, Koch, Lister, Pasteur, and Ehrlich. Racial hygienists like Lenz, Fischer, and Verschuer were not men whose scientific or medical credentials were in doubt. Individuals we today remember as men of high ideals and wide learning—like Sauerbruch the surgeon or Diepgen the historian—celebrated Nazi programs and ideals. These were serious and respected scholars and physicians; the same might be said for many others in the Nazi medical apparatus. Rudolf Ramm was not a marginal figure in his profession. Nor was Kurt Blome, or Gerhard Wagner, or Walter Gross. Nazi racial theory was supported not only by cranks and quacks but also by men at the highest levels of German biomedical science. Racial science was "normal science," in the sense that Kuhn has given this expression.[9]

How Could It Happen?

Many of the racial medical policies of the Nazis were both legal and public— open, that is, to public scrutiny. Legislators codified policies into law; the courts rendered judgments based on these laws, and prisons or hospitals carried out the orders of the courts. The Nazis formed a government only after being elected to power; they were careful to construct racial policies in accordance with the rule of law. By October 30, 1938, the Office of Racial Policy of the NSDAP could publish a list of more than 250 separate "Legal Measures for the Solution of the Jewish Question." Doctors cooperated with lawyers in administrating the new policies. Medical journals reported in a businesslike fashion on the confinement of alcoholics to concentration camps, recommending such measures as a means to prevent "hysterical disorders."[10] In the war years, Germany's leading medical journal carried a regular column on "The Solution of the Jewish Question."

How could such ideas come to dominate a community of scholars and physicians dedicated to serving and preserving life? Each of Germany's doctors had taken the Hippocratic oath; each had sworn never to do harm knowingly. These were men who, in the words of one physician at the Nuremberg trials, were supposed to be "nearer humanity than other men." There are several possible answers to this question, none of which is completely satisfactory, but some of which may help throw light on the matter.

First, it is important to recognize that many elements of racial hygiene were not restricted to Germany. Eugenics movements flourished in England, Norway, Sweden, France, the Soviet Union, the United States, and many other countries.[11] German racial hygienists modeled their science on movements in other countries, imploring their fellow Germans to follow these examples, lest Germany be surpassed in racial purity. Racial hygienists drew upon the examples of American immigration, sterilization, and miscegenation laws to formulate their own policies in these areas. German scholars took notice when American eugenicists helped push through emigration restriction laws; Germany's foremost racial hygiene journal reported on the refusal of the American Medical Association to admit black physicians.[12] German scholars also took notice when British and American journals openly considered the question of euthanasia. Racial hygiene, in short, was an international phenomenon and by no means restricted to Germany.

A second element is of a more philosophical nature. One of the pillars of Nazi medical ideology was the "hereditarian" assumption that nature is more important than nurture in the shaping of human character and institutions. Racial hygienists followed Eugen Fischer's claim that the science of genetics had shown that "all human traits—normal or pathological, physical or mental—are shaped by hereditary factors." They argued that the environment—whether climate, nutrition, or education—played a relatively minor role in the development of human character, and that modern science had "destroyed the theory of the equality of men."[13] This hereditarian bias was part of a broader conception of the place of science in society, one that was shared by eugenics movements in other countries. Common to racial hygiene movements throughout the world was the view that it is to *biology* that we must look to solve social problems. Knowledge of (and control over) the human genetic future was the key to human destiny; racial hygiene would eliminate human disease—not just schizophrenia or flatfeet or epilepsy, but also criminality, alcoholism, and homosexuality. The Nazis took major problems of the day—problems of race, gender, crime, and poverty—and transformed them into medical or biological problems. Nazi philosophers argued that Germany was teetering on the brink of racial collapse, and that racial hygiene was needed to save Germany from "racial suicide." Racial hygiene thus combined a philosophy of biological determinism with a belief that science might provide a technical fix for social problems. Harnessed to a political party mandated to root out all forms of racial, social, or spiritual "disease," the ideology of biological determinism helped drive the kinds of programs for which the Nazis have become infamous.

The willingness of Nazi authorities to "medicalize" or "biologize" a host of social problems may well be one of the primary reasons National Socialism so appealed to physicians. The Nazis saw their movement as applied biology and conceived their program of "cleansing" in medical terms. Nazi racial programs were seen as public health programs, involving the participation of doctors in state policy on an unprecedented scale. National Socialism promised to place medicine on a new and higher level in society; it may even be true that under the Nazis the medical profession achieved a higher status than at any other time in history.

A further dimension to the question of how such things could come to pass concerns the codes and canons of the profession. Central in the medical code of ethics was (and is) that physicians should stand up for one another, especially in the face of criticism or adversity. Rudolf Ramm, for example, instructed German medical students that a physician should always defend his colleagues against criticisms from outside the profession:

> It often happens that a patient, dissatisfied by the treatment he has received, goes to another doctor and attempts to portray the first doctor as incompetent, ill-willed, or derelict in his duties. It is the duty of the physician, however, to give no credence to such accusations. One should instead attempt to excuse and defend one's colleagues. . . . One should always keep in mind that problems faced by a colleague today, you yourself may one day have to face, and further, that your own reputation, and the reputation of the entire profession may depend on the reputation of one single physician.[14]

One might well wonder whether an ethic that *encouraged* criticism might not have served the profession better.

Why Germany? If eugenics movements flourished outside Germany, then what was special about the German experience? If resistance and antiracialist alternatives existed in Germany, then how did racial science gain the upper hand to a degree not found in other countries? One factor is the relative impoverishment of the German medical profession in the years prior to the rise of the Nazis. The collapse of the German economy in 1929–32 polarized the profession, driving many from the center to the far Left and Right. (Recall in this context that communism as well as fascism grew in the years before the Nazi rise to power.) Between 1928 and 1932, liberal parties (DVP, Deutsche Demokratische Partei, Wirtschaftspartei) lost nearly 80 percent of their votes, falling from nearly a quarter of the entire vote to fewer than 3 percent. Physicians were among many of those who shifted from the center to the Right because they felt that Germany's other political parties were not addressing their needs. Physicians found it difficult to identify with either proletarian socialism or the interests of Germany's landed, conservative parties. Many found hope in the "third path" of National Socialism.

Professional opportunism also played a role in physicians' support for the Nazis. Overcrowding led to severe competition for jobs, especially among younger physicians. Many entering the job market for the first time saw the elimination of Jews as a way to advance their careers; and in fact, many a Nazi doctor saw his career advance as a direct result of attacks on Jews in the profession. As Jewish physicians fled or were forced from the clinics and the universities, thousands of new positions opened up. Those who stood most to gain from this were younger physicians, and these were the people who were most enthusiastic in their support for National Socialism. Professional opportunism, exacerbated by the reality and threat of unemployment, must be considered one of the chief causes for the attraction of physicians to National Socialism.

There is also a philosophical dimension to this attraction. The decades before the rise of National Socialism saw both the rise of bureaucratic, scientific, and socialized medicine in Germany and an increase in the number of Jews in the profession; many linked the two phenomena as cause and effect. Jews became a scapegoat for all that was wrong with medicine—they were accused of importing abstract science into medicine, of transforming medicine from an art into a business. Jews were blamed for the problems of both capitalist and socialist medicine; Jewish physicians were blamed for the excessive use of drugs or the suppression of natural and folk medicines. Physicians rallied around the Nazis for their promise to return to an earlier, more personal or organic kind of medicine.

Nazi medicine was *authoritarian* medicine. The 1930s–1950s mark a period when medicine achieved unprecedented power and authority in European and Anglo-American culture:[15] the same period that gave us Nazi medicine also witnessed the invention of the lobotomy (in Spain and the United States), the chordotomy (in Germany), electric shock treatment (in the United States), sensory deprivation techniques (in the Soviet Union), and the first use of physicians to administer capital punishment. This is a period when psychiatrists were given increased powers forcibly to confine individuals judged mentally ill or dangerous to the public.

One further element is crucial in understanding medicine under the Nazis, especially those practices we consider criminal. In times of war or economic crisis things can happen that otherwise—in times of peace or economic stability—would never be tolerated. The Nazis gave new meaning to the idea of sacrifice in time of war. Doctors in the Nazi period recalled that nearly 2,000 German physicians lost their lives in World War I. Alfred Hoche, author of the treatise *The Destruction of Lives Not Worth Living,* lost his first and only son in the war, and used this to argue that if the healthy could make such a sacrifice, then why should the sick and inferior not make similar sacrifices? The "euthanasia" of Germany's "less fit elements" was defended as a measure that would balance the counterselective effects of the war and free up beds for the German war effort; the cloak of war also provided the secrecy necessary for the massive programs of human destruction.

There are many different theories on the ultimate causes of the rise of fascism as a whole. Some have argued that fascism is a form of totalitarianism, and that the same forces responsible for the rise of Hitler can be seen at work in the rise of other dictatorships. Others have argued that fascism is a particularly virulent and imperialistic form of monopoly capitalism. Still others have argued that National

Socialism was the product of neither capitalism nor totalitarianism but rather of the particular social and economic interests of the distressed middle and lower-middle classes.[16]

Whatever the explanation for the rise of National Socialism, one fact is clear: scientists and physicians were not exempt from the pressures that led to the triumph of the movement. That most of Germany's medical professionals followed Hitler's "revolution" is probably ultimately traceable to the same kinds of forces responsible for the triumph of National Socialism in German society as a whole. This is not to say that physicians blindly followed the political aims of their leaders. Physicians, and the body of intellectuals associated with them, did not follow blindly, but actually helped cast the light and clear the path.

Did the Nazis Depoliticize Science?

It is possible to distinguish different conceptions of what might be called the political philosophy of science. In the liberal view, predominant in twentieth-century liberal democracies, science is political only in its applications. Science in this view is (ideally) neutral or value free, and becomes "tainted" when politics directs the course of intellectual inquiry. This is the view expressed, for example, in the writings of the analytic philosophical tradition that flourished in Britain and the United States in the middle decades of this century; it is also found among philosophers influenced by the so-called Vienna Circle and among many conservative economic theorists such as Ludwig Mises or F. A. von Hayek. The racialist orientation of Nazi science represented (in this view) a violation of the norms of "neutral" and objective science. The Nazis politicized science—twisting it to serve racial or political goals, striking out against the traditional ideal of knowledge for its own sake.[17]

And yet the characterization of Nazi science as an illegitimate "politicization" captures only part of what happened. It is certainly true that, in one important sense, the Nazis sought to politicize the sciences. Nazi doctors sought a National Socialist revolution in medicine; and in this sense Nazi racial science represented a revolt against the liberal ideal of value-free science, against the vision of science and scholarship as ideally detached and apolitical. The Nazis made no secret of their distrust of traditional ideals of academic freedom and expressed scorn for those who remained within the ivory tower in times of political need. Nazi racial theorists attacked the "apathetic equanimity" of parliamentarian, Weimar Republican "liberal-Jewish-Bolshevist science" and contrasted this with the German, volkish science that was to ally itself with the values of nation and race. Jews were accused of attempting to create a state within a state, isolating themselves from the broader community. This accusation extended to art as well as science. In 1938 the in-house journal of the Office of Racial Policy argued that the doctrine of art for art's sake (*l'art pour l'art*) was a characteristically "Jewish and homosexual" philosophy; the office defended this association on the grounds that such groups "shut themselves off" either from the broader community (as in the case of the Jews) or from the reproductive life process (as in the case of homosexuals).[18] Volkish science and medicine were to overcome such "one-sidedness" by rooting science once again in blood and earth.

But the political philosophy of science under the Nazis was by no means consistent in this regard. On the one hand, science was to be brought into accord with certain national (and racial) goals and values; the ideal of "objective science" in this view was simply an excuse to eliminate the "volkish and blood-bound personality" in favor of some mythical thing in itself (*Ding an sich*). Races do not work with the same reality; science therefore cannot be some "value-free and worthless truth"; science must serve the racial spirit of a people. (This concept was articulated by a man who saw the Nazi revolution as completing a process begun not just by Nietzsche but also by Darwin, Mendel, Galton, and Weismann—men whose ideas when properly applied would help put a halt to the decline of the West into "racial chaos, Africanism, and Orientalism.")[19] Nazi philosophers cited Nietzsche's words to the effect that "science, too, is founded upon belief; there is no such thing as a science free of suppositions." Nazi philosophers contrasted this conception of science as assumptive and value laden with what they called a Jewish conception of science—a conception of science as value free and independent of any particular culture or race. Jews were accused of advocating an abstract, neutral, and internationalist (or cosmopolitan) science, in contrast with German earth-rooted science; Nazi racial scientists advocated a "medical-biological revolution" that would reorient science around racial values.[20]

Yet racial philosophers often sought to portray their work as neutral science, standing above all politics. Section 2 of the statutes of the Society for Racial Hygiene announced that the society would "avoid all political and religious tendencies"; the Nordic supremacist *Politisch-anthropologische Revue* similarly claimed to reject any allegiance to particular philosophical doctrines or political parties.[21] When Fritz Lenz attempted to discover the moral and physical qualities of the various races, he saw his work as continuing Darwin's attempts to elucidate the origin of species. Lenz defended his elaborate racial typology as "neutral" with regard to the *value* of the various races; racial science merely described objectively existing racial realities. This was a common argument among racial hygienists prior to 1933. In 1917, for example, Eugen Fischer presented the specter of racial degeneration, not as the product of pessimism on the part of racial hygienists, but as "a binding consequence of naked facts."[22] After 1933, medical societies continued to pledge their allegiance to the ideal of political neutrality at the same time that they proclaimed their willingness to collaborate with the new regime. Germany's leading psychotherapy society, for example, claimed in its 1934 statutes that the society considered itself "neutral in regard to political and religious affairs." The society's journal printed these statutes only two pages after one of its most influential members proclaimed *Mein Kampf* "required reading" for all psychotherapists in the new Germany.[23]

Racial hygienists defended the innocence of their science with respect to politics on other grounds as well. Fritz Lenz, for example, contended that in the broader scale of things, the importance of maintaining racial health far out-weighed particular questions of political organization. The maintenance of the genetic quality of the race was "a hundred times more important than the strug-gle between capitalism and socialism"; indeed, "worse than the political impo-tence of our Fatherland, worse even than the lost war is the degeneration of our race. The conflict over whether "republican" or "monarchical" government is superior fades into insignificance, compared with the problem of maintaining the fitness of the race."[24] Lenz's view was not an uncommon one. *Ziel und Weg,* the journal of the National Socialist Physicians' League, announced in 1932 that "eu-genics is a science that has nothing to do with politics, and especially with party politics."[25] A writer for *Die Medizinische Welt* declared in a similar vein that "eugenics dares not become a partisan issue; it cannot. Biological or eugenic value has nothing to do with status, profession, religion, income, financial condi-tion, or any other way in which one discriminates among men: there are inferior, genetically diseased people everywhere and in all classes."[26]

The desire felt by many intellectuals in this period to remain above party politics (*überparteilich*) can be seen in the fact that several of Germany's leading racial hygienists never joined the party or only joined late in the regime. Fritz Lenz edited the most important racial hygiene journal (the *Archiv Für Rassen-und Gesellschaftsbiologie*) and helped construct Nazi racial and population policy without becoming a party member until 1937. Eugen Fischer directed Germany's most prestigious eugenics institute until his retirement in 1942 and did not be-come a member until January 1940. Ernst Rüdin directed one of the most presti-gious racial hygiene institutes in the country (the Rüdin Institut at Munich) and helped draft the 1933 Sterilization Law without becoming a member until 1937. Otmar von Verschuer, Mengele's mentor and one of Germany's most influential racial hygienists, did not join until July 1940. Alfred Ploetz, father of racial hy-giene and winner of a number of Nazi honors and awards, did not join the party until 1937, when he was seventy-seven years old.

After the war, of course, it became especially important for scholars to be able to claim that their work in science or medicine had remained above party poli-tics. The ideal of science as neutral and apolitical translated into the assumption that, as long as one had concentrated solely on one's science, one was exempt from blame; indeed, in 1945 some German scholars considered it a form of resis-tance simply to have kept the flame of science alive. The quiet pursuit of science constituted a kind of "inner emigration" that separated one from the culpability of government actions.[27] Even some of those most actively involved in the devel-opment of racial science defended their work in these terms. Hans F. K. Günther, author of at least seventeen books on racial science and the period's most widely read racial theorist, reported in his postwar autobiography that he had never mixed science and politics—this despite his widely recognized status as father of German *Rassenkunde* and the Nordic movement.[28]

One might well question the motives of postwar claims to neutrality among Nazi racial theorists.Yet in an important sense the Nazis might indeed be said to have "depoliticized" science (and many other areas of culture). The Nazis depoliticized science by destroying the possibility of political debate and controversy. Authoritarian science based on the "Führer principle" replaced what had been, in the Weimar period, a vigorous spirit of politicized debate in and around the sciences. The Nazis "depoliticized" problems of vital human interest by reducing these to scientific or medical problems, conceived in the narrow, reductionist sense of these terms. The Nazis depoliticized questions of crime, poverty, and sexual or political deviance by casting them in surgical or otherwise medical (and seemingly apolitical) terms. Confronting crime with the knife of the surgeon, justifying genocide on the grounds of quarantine, racial hygienists allowed a reductionist biologism to obscure the political character of social problems.

Politics pursued in the name of science or health provided a powerful weapon in the Nazi ideological arsenal. Important in this was not only a particular conception of science but also a particular conception of *politics*.

Nazi medical philosophers defended their revolution as one in accord with the latest results of science. The appeal to science is not surprising, given the place of science in German society at this time. National Socialism took root in a culture supporting the greatest scientific tradition of the century, one that ranks with the greatest of all times. By 1933 Germany and Austria had been awarded more than one-third of all Nobel Prizes—nearly as many as England, France, and the United States combined. It is not surprising, then, that science should have been drawn upon by any group wishing to stake out its legitimacy. "Politics" by contrast had a bad name, and in this sense the desire of scientists and physicians to appear apolitical represented a desire to move beyond (or avoid) the issues that had divided German society since before World War I. National Socialism was itself supposed to transcend all political differences, to end the squabbles between landlord and peasant, worker and industrialist, and to replace the divisive emphasis on class by a unifying emphasis on race. The Nazi state was supposed to be a *Volksstaat,* and not a *Parteistaat.* The Nazi party was supposed to be not just a party but a movement (*Bewegung*). Nazi medical philosophers praised Hitler for his attempts to address the needs of the German people *as a whole* and to abolish, once and for all, the demands of "special interests."[29] When the Nazis claimed they wanted their philosophy to appear scientific, it was on similar grounds. Science would unite, where politics had divided. Nazi medical periodicals thus cited Hitler's assertion that National Socialism was "no mystical doctrine, but rather a realistic doctrine of a strictly scientific nature."[30] Theobald Lang, we should recall, as early as 1930 declared National Socialist methods strictly scientific (*streng wissenschaftlich*).

Nazi science was also ambivalent on the question of academic freedom. Prior to the rise of National Socialism, the importance of science in Europe had generated a tradition of respect for its freedom. The Prussian Constitution of 1843 declared that the pursuit of science is free; article 142 of the Weimar Constitution reaffirmed this commitment to the freedom of science and of teaching. National Socialism suspended many of the civil liberties won in Weimar and in Wilhelmine Germany, but not without maintaining a certain facade of tolerance. Alfred

Rosenberg, in *Die Freiheit der Wissenschaft,* defended freedom of teaching (*Lehrfreiheit*), but distinguished this from freedom to agitate (*Agitationsfreiheit*), noting that because the universities were *national* institutions, neither treason not "antisocial" activity could be permitted in the classroom.[31] Absolute freedom of thought or of science was regarded by the Nazis as symptomatic of a society in the midst of chaos and despair. Freedom was to be replaced by the Führer principle, according to which science, like other social activity, was to be hierarchically organized and subordinated to a single, powerful authority.

In 1935 Walter Gross of the Office of Racial Policy said, "National Socialism does not intend to interfere with 'purely scientific matters,' " but qualified this by asserting that tolerance could only go so far and that any attempt on the part of "pseudoscience" to hinder Nazi goals would not be tolerated.[32] In 1937, as calls for "Deutsche Wissenschaft" reached their peak, Alfred Rosenberg issued an order that the Nazi party was not to take sides on questions of cosmology, experimental chemistry, or prehistoric geology; such questions, he proclaimed, must remain free for every individual researcher to decide according to the dictates of "serious scientific investigation."[33]

This same ideological largess did not, of course, apply equally to all sciences or to all scientists. Yet for many—especially those in the vanguard of German racial science—science and National Socialism moved in harmony with each other. Otmar von Verschuer, in a May 1939 speech to the Kaiser Wilhelm Gesellschaft in Breslau, reflected on the fact that

> the parallel development of political and scientific ideas is not by chance but rather by internal necessity. . . . We geneticists and racial hygienists have been fortunate to have seen our quiet work in the scholar's study and the scientific laboratory find application in the life of the people. Our responsibility has thereby become enormous. We continue quietly with our research, confident that here also, battles will be fought which will be of greatest consequence for the survival of our people.[34]

A Question of Abuse?

In the 1920s American writers on eugenics commonly considered two possible dangers of eugenic sterilization. Some worried that sterilization "might prevent the birth of a genius"; others, that sterilization might allow one to engage in sex with abandon, without fear of pregnancy. Rarely, however, did eugenicists consider the possibility that their science might be used by one group to persecute another. In 1929, for example, Harry H. Laughlin maintained that "the possibility that sterilization might become a political tool that might be used by one race against another, by one religion against another, or by one social class against another, is extremely remote."[35]

In Germany also, physicians dismissed the possibility that their science and skills might be abused. Racial hygienists as late as 1939 mocked warnings of "the

Jewish press" that Germany was "once again on the road to barbarism," that Germany was about to "eliminate" persons in political disfavor under the pretense that they were genetically diseased. Germany, like other states, had embarked on a program of racial cleansing. But what made Germany special was that

> in contrast to other states, the German [sterilization] laws have been administered through the large-scale mediation of genetic health courts, with the possibility of appeals to appellate genetic health courts, excluding for all time the possibility of the *abuse* of these laws. Furthermore, criteria for genetic health and sickness have been so thoroughly and clearly formulated that the possibility of error on human grounds has been completely eliminated. Countless safeguards have been built into the law and the procedures for its implementation—safeguards which, taken together, prevent improper diagnosis by a doctor and effectively protect the person to be sterilized.[36]

Carefully administered scientific expertise, in other words, together with the appropriate legal apparatus, would guarantee the execution of the racial task in accord with the rule of law; this was supposed to exclude forever the possibility of abuse.

There is often talk of the "abuse of science" under National Socialism. Yet there may be a problem in conceiving Nazi racial science primarily in such terms. One could well argue that the Nazis were not, properly speaking, abusing the results of science but rather were merely putting into practice what doctors and scientists had themselves already initiated. Nazi racial science in this sense was not an abuse of eugenics but rather an attempt to bring to practical fruition trends already implicit in the structure of this branch of science. Dr. Friedrich Zahn, in his article "Racial Research," intended something of this sort in 1940 when he claimed that "the theory of today becomes the practice of tomorrow."[37]

I do not mean to say that science was *not* abused under the Nazis, or that the quality of science under the Nazis did not suffer, in both a moral and an intellectual sense. There can be no doubt that this was the case. But many scientists of the time did not perceive this to be the case. On the contrary, many—and perhaps most—scientists in the various fields of biomedicine saw no contradiction between the aspirations of science and the goals of the Nazi regime.

There is something missing, then, when we characterize National Socialism as simply "anti-intellectual." The Nazis opposed certain kinds of science and supported others. Many academics and intellectuals found the ideology of Nazism attractive; the Nazis were thereby able to draw upon the imagery, results, and authority of science. Nazi ideology also informed the practice of science; indeed scientists were intimately involved in the construction of racial policy. It is probably as fair to say that Nazi racial policy emerged from *within* the scientific community as to say that it was imposed *upon* the scientific community.

One should not conclude, however, that Nazi medicine rose to power unopposed or that everyone was a Nazi. Alternatives were articulated and institutionalized within the medical profession, and many paid with their lives for expressing or acting upon those alternatives. The fact that these alternatives were ultimately crushed does not lessen the valiancy of their efforts. There *was* resistance—however too little or too late; the example of the Association of Socialist Physicians must not be forgotten. The moral, then, is not just that the Nazis supported science or that science supported the Nazis, but that there was a struggle that led to the triumph of Nazi racial policy, and this struggle was played out, at least in part, in the spheres of science and medicine.

In his 1954 *Destruction of Reason*, Georg Lukács noted that biological determinism (biologism) in the fields of philosophy and sociology has always provided a basis for reactionary world views. Perhaps this has not always been the case—certainly one can find examples in other centuries where appeals to nature or to biology have been used in the service of moral progress or liberation. In the twentieth century, however, the appeal to biology to structure human society has tended to have unfortunate and sometimes tragic consequences. The experience of science and medicine under the Nazis represents an extreme case of the dangers of such a philosophy, but it is by no means the first, and certainly not the last, time intellectuals have hoisted a banner proclaiming that biology is destiny. It is a history, one might say, we have yet to conquer.

N O T E S

1. In 1937 Edward Hartshorne reported that 1,684 scholars had been dismissed from their posts. This included not only professors but also scientists at the Kaiser Wilhelm institutes, assistants, and the like. See his *German Universities and National Socialism* (London, 1937), p. 93. In 1938 Hartshorne revised the proportion of all scholars dismissed from 14 percent to 20 percent. See his *German Universities and the Government* (Chicago, 1938), pp. 13–14.

2. Stephan Leibfried, "Stationen der Abwehr," *Leo Baeck Institute Bulletin* 62 (1982): 3.

3. On the life of Ludwik Fleck, see the introduction to his *Die Entstehung und Entwicklung einer wissenschaftlichen Tatsache* (1935) (Frankfurt, 1983).

4. For the case of psychology, see Ulfried Geuter, *Die Professionalisierung der deutschen Psychologie im Nationalsozialismus* (Frankfurt, 1984). For the case of anthropology, see my "From *Anthropologie* to *Rassenkunde* in the German Anthropological Tradition," in *History of Anthropology*, ed. George Stocking, vol. 5 (Madison, Wis., 1988).

5. New medical institutions established in the Nazi period include the Academy of Medicine in Munich, the Medical Academy in Danzig, and the Kaiser Wilhelm Institute for Biophysics in Frankfurt (from the older Institut für physikalische Grundlagen der Medizin). The Nazi period saw the establishment of institutes for general medicine at Berlin and Vienna, an institute for colonial medicine at Hamburg, and an institute for rural hygiene in Lichtenheim. The Nazi government funded the establishment of an Institute for Natural Healing (Neue Deutsche Heilkunde) at Dresden and a new Staatsakademie des öffentlichen Gesundheitsdienst in Berlin.

6. Conti rejected as "enemy propaganda" reports that the freedom of science had been restricted under the Nazis. See *Deutsches Ärzteblatt*, 72 (1942): 51.

7. Hans Rinne, "Die Aufgaben des Amtes für Volksgesundheit der NSDAP," Der Öffentliche Gesundheitsdienst, 2 (1936): 857.

8. Franz Orsós, "1st der Stand der deutschen Wissenschaft gesunken?" Deutsches Ärzteblatt, 67 (1937): 1119. German medical journals celebrated technical achievements in other fields besides medicine. In 1939 the Ärzteblatt für Berlin celebrated the Wunder des Vierjahresplans, including synthetic rubber, flexible glass, and prefabricated auto frames (Presskarosserien). See Ärzteblatt für Berlin, 44 (1939): 94. Other achievements of the Nazi period include the synthesis of polyvinyl chloride, the fabrication of paper from oil, the harnessing of power from geothermal energy, the production of atomic fission in the laboratory (Hahn and Meitner), the electron microscopy of viruses, ultraviolet irradiation of milk in order to control spoilage, and of course the rocket-powered bombs (V1 and V2) that wreaked havoc over England.

9. See Thomas Kuhn, The Structure of Scientific Revolutions (Chicago, 1962).

10. See Ärzteblatt für Pommern, Mecklenburg und Lübeck, 1 (1934): 107; also Zeitschrift für die gesamte Neurologie und Psychiatrie (1935): 177.

11. In 1914 eugenics was taught in 44 American colleges and universities; by 1928 the number had grown to 376—"racial hygiene" was thus taught in nearly three-quarters of all American colleges and universities. See Garland Allen, "A History of Eugenics," in Biology as Destiny, ed. Science for the People Sociobiology Study Group (Cambridge, Mass., 1984), p. 14.

12. See "Keine Negerärzte in der amerikanischen Standesorganisation," Archiv für Rasen- und Gesellschaftsbiologie, 33 (1939): 276.

13. Eugen Fischer, Der völkische Staat biologisch gesehen (Berlin 1933), pp. 11–12.

14. Rudolf Ramm, Ärztliche Rechts- und Standeskunde, der Arzt als Gesundheitserzieher, 2d ed. (Berlin, 1943), 88–89.

15. For the American case, see Paul Starr, The Social Transformation of American Medicine (New York, 1982); also Elliot S. Valenstein, Great and Desperate Cures (New York, 1986), and Barbara Ehrenreich and Deirdre English, For Her Own Good: 150 Years of Experts' Advice to Women (New York, 1978).

16. For a review of theories of fascism, see Richard Saage, Faschismustheorien, 2d ed. (Frankfurt, 1977).

17. For a historical analysis of the ideal of value-free science, see my "Politics of Purity: Origins of the Ideal of Neutral Science," Ph.D. diss., Harvard University, 1984.

18. Informationsdienst, June 20, 1938.

19. Ziel und Weg, 9 (1939): 5.

20. The claim that "Es gibt keine voraussetzungslose Wissenschaft!" was a common one in the Nazi period; the expression was generally traced to Houston Stewart Chamberlain; see his Natur und Leben, ed. J. von Uexküll (Munich, 1928).

21. See Politisch-anthropologische Revue, 1 (1902): 1–2.

22. R 86/2371, fol. 1, p. 94, Bundesarchiv Koblenz.

23. See Zentralblatt für Psychotherapie und Ihre Grenzgebiete, 7 (1934): 132–34.

24. Fritz Lenz, "Biologie als staatliche Notwendigkeit der Rassentüchtigkeit," Der Biologe, 1 (1931–32): 97.

25. Ziel und Weg, 2 (1932): 8.

26. Struve, "Die Eugenik im Staatsrat," Die Medizinische Welt, 6 (1932): 1076.

27. Alan D. Beyerchen, Scientists under Hitler: Politics and the Physics Community in the Third Reich (New Haven, 1977), 68, 208.

28. Hans F. K. Günther, Mein Eindruck auf Hitler (Pähl, 1969), 19. Günther claimed that since 1919, he had found party politics "tasteless and dirty."

29. "Ausschaltung von Interessengruppen," report of the Verein der Ärzte, Halle, in the July 28, 1934, issue of the Klinische Wochenschrift. Ludwig Liebl, in the first issue of Ziel und Weg, denounced "interest-group politics." See Ziel und Weg, 1 (1931): 4.

30. Compare also Hitler's boast at the 1938 Reichsparteitag that National Socialism

was "eine kühle Wirklichkeitslehre schärfster wissenschaftlicher Erkenntnisse," cited in the frontispiece to *Ziel und Weg,* 9 (1939): 29.

31. Hauptamt Wissenschaft, file no. 56595 T-81, roll 54, National Archives, Washington, D.C.

32. Walter Gross, "Die Idee bleibt rein," *Ziel und Weg,* 5 (1935): 37; also *Ärztin,* 17 (1941): 29.

33. "Reichsleiter Rosenbergs parteiamtliche Stellungnahme zur naturwissenschaftlichen Forschung," *Der Biologe* 8 (1939). See also *Informationsdienst,* May 20, 1938.

34. Otmar von Verschuer, "Das Erbbild des Menschen," *Der Erbarzt* 7 (1939): 12, cited in Karl Heinz Roth, "Schöner neuer Mensch," in *Der Griff nach der Bevölkerung,* ed. Heidrun Kaupen-Haas (Hamburg, 1986), 11.

35. Harry H. Laughlin, "Die Entwicklung der gesetzlichen rassenhygienischen Sterilisierung in den Vereinigten Staaten," *Archiv für Rassen- und Gesellschaftsbiologie,* 23 (1929): 261. See also *Journal of the American Medical Association,* 101 (1933): 866, 877, where the twin dangers of the Sterilization Law are listed as the unwitting destruction of "valuable biologic material" and the fact that a man might have himself sterilized in order "to secure unrestrained sexual gratification without fear of consequences."

36. Erich Berger, "Das deutsche Beispiel macht Schule," *Ziel und Weg,* 9 (1939): 44. Otmar von Verschuer, in his "Erbpflege in der deutschen Gesetzgebung," *Archiv der Julius Klaus-Stiftung* (10 [1935]: '59), expressed similar views.

37. "Die Theorie von heute wird die Praxis von Morgen." See Friedrich Zahn, "Rassenforschung und Statistik," in *Die Statistik in Deutschland,* ed. Josef Götz (Berlin, 1940).

RACE AND GENDER
The Role of Analogy in Science

Nancy Leys Stepan

Metaphor occupies a central place in literary theory, but the role of metaphors, and of the analogies they mediate, in scientific theory is still debated.[1] One reason for the controversy over metaphor, analogy, and models in science is the intellectually privileged status that science has traditionally enjoyed as the repository of nonmetaphorical, empirical, politically neutral, universal knowledge. During the scientific revolution of the seventeenth century, metaphor became associated with the imagination, poetic fancy, subjective figures, and even untruthfulness and was contrasted with truthful, unadorned, objective knowledge—that is, with science itself.[2]

In the twentieth century logical positivists also distinguished between scientific and metaphoric language.[3] When scientists insisted that analogies or models based on analogies were important to their thinking, philosophers of science tended to dismiss their claims that metaphors had an *essential* place in scientific utterances. The French theoretical physicist Pierre Duhem was well known for his criticism of the contention that metaphor and analogies were important to *explanation* in science. In his view, the aim of science was to reduce all theory to mathematical statements; models could aid the process of scientific discovery, but once they had served their function, analogies could be discarded as extrinsic to science, and the theories made to stand without them.[4]

One result of the dichotomy established between science and metaphor was that obviously metaphoric or analogical science could only be treated as "prescientific" or "pseudoscientific" and therefore dismissable.[5] Because science has been identified with truthfulness and empirical reality, the metaphorical nature of much modern science tended to go unrecognized. And because it went unrecognized, as Colin Turbayne has pointed out, it has been easy to mistake the model in science "for the thing modeled"—to think, to take his example, that nature *was* mechanical, rather than to think it was, metaphorically, seen as mechanical.[6]

More recently, however, as the attention of historians and philosophers of science has moved away from logical reconstructions of science toward more "naturalistic" views of science in culture, the role of metaphor, analogies, and models in science has begun to be acknowledged.[7] In a recent volume on metaphor, Thomas S. Kuhn claims that analogies are fundamental to science; and Richard Boyd argues that they are "irreplaceable parts of the linguistic machinery of a scientific theory," since cases exist in which there are metaphors used by scientists to express theoretical claims "for which no adequate literal paraphrase is known."[8] Some philosophers of science are now prepared to assert that metaphors and analogies are not just psychological aids to scientific discovery, or heuristic devices, but constituent elements of scientific theory.[9] We seem about to move full circle, from considering metaphors mere embellishments or poetic fictions to considering them essential to scientific thought itself.

Although the role of metaphor and analogy in science is now recognized, a critical theory of scientific metaphor is only just being elaborated. The purpose of this article is to contribute to the development of such a theory by using a particular analogy in the history of the life sciences to explore a series of related questions concerning the cultural sources of scientific analogies, their role in scientific reasoning, their normative consequences, and the process by which they change.

Race and Gender: A Powerful Scientific Analogy

The analogy examined is the one linking race to gender, an analogy that occupied a strategic place in scientific theorizing about human variation in the nineteenth and twentieth centuries.

As has been well documented, from the late Enlightenment on students of human variation singled out racial differences as crucial aspects of reality, and an extensive discourse on racial inequality began to be elaborated.[10] In the nineteenth century, as attention turned increasingly to sexual and gender differences as well, gender was found to be remarkably analogous to race, such that the scientist could use racial difference to explain gender difference, and vice versa.[11]

Thus it was claimed that women's low brain weights and deficient brain structures were analogous to those of lower races, and their inferior intellectualities explained on this basis.[12] Woman, it was observed, shared with Negroes a narrow, childlike, and delicate skull, so different from the more robust and rounded heads characteristic of males of "superior" races. Similarly, women of higher races tended to have slightly protruding jaws, analogous to, if not as exaggerated as, the apelike, jutting jaws of lower races.[13] Women and lower races were called innately impulsive, emotional, imitative rather than original, and incapable of the abstract reasoning found in white men.[14] Evolutionary biology provided yet further analogies. Woman was in evolutionary terms the "conservative element" to the man's "progressive," preserving the more "primitive" traits found in lower races, while the males of higher races led the way in new biological and cultural directions.[15]

Thus when Carl Vogt, one of the leading German students of race in the middle of the nineteenth century, claimed that the female skull approached in many respects that of the infant, and in still further respects that of lower races, whereas the mature male of many lower races resembled in his "pendulous" belly a Caucasian woman who had had many children, and in his calves and flat thighs the ape, he was merely stating what had become almost a cliché of the science of human difference.[16]

So fundamental was the analogy between race and gender that the major modes of interpretation of racial traits were invariably evoked to explain sexual traits. For instance, just as scientists spoke of races as distinct "species," incapable of crossing to produce viable "hybrids," scientists analyzing male-female differences sometimes spoke of females as forming a distinct "species," individual members of which were in danger of degenerating into psychosexual hybrids when they tried to cross the boundaries proper to their sex.[17] Darwin's theory of sexual selection was applied to both racial and sexual difference, as was the neo-Lamarckian theory of the American Edward D. Cope.[18] A last, confirmatory example of the analogous place of gender and race in scientific theorizing is taken from the history of hormone biology. Early in the twentieth century the anatomist and student of race Sir Arthur Keith interpreted racial differences in the human species as a function of pathological disturbances of the newly discovered "internal secretions" or hormones. At about the same time, the apostle of sexual frankness and well-known student of sexual variation Havelock Ellis used internal secretions to explain the small, but to him vital, differences in the physical and psychosexual makeup of men and women.[19]

In short, lower races represented the "female" type of the human species, and females the "lower race" of gender. As the example from Vogt indicates, however, the analogies concerned more than race and gender. Through an intertwined and overlapping series of analogies, involving often quite complex comparisons, identifications, cross-references, and evoked associations, a variety of "differences"—physical and psychical, class and national—were brought together in a biosocial science of human variation. By analogy with the so-called lower races, women, the sexually deviate, the criminal, the urban poor, and the insane were in one way or another constructed as biological "races apart" whose differences from the white male, and likenesses to each other, "explained" their different and lower position in the social hierarchy.[20]

It is not the aim of this article to provide a systematic history of the biosocial science of racial and sexual difference based on analogy. The aim is rather to use the race-gender analogy to analyze the nature of analogical reasoning in science itself. When and how did the analogy appear in science? From what did it derive its scientific authority? How did the analogy shape research? What did it mean when a scientist claimed that the mature male of many lower races resembled a mature Caucasian female who had had many children? No simple theory or resemblance or substitution explains such an analogy. How did the analogy help construct the very similarities and differences supposedly "discovered" by scientists in nature? What theories of analogy and metaphor can be most effectively applied in the critical study of science?

The Cultural Sources of Scientific Metaphor

How particular metaphors or analogies in science are related to the social production of science, why certain analogies are selected and not others, and why
certain analogies are accepted by the scientific community are all issues that
need investigation.

In literature, according to Warren Shibles, striking metaphors just come,
"like rain."[21] In science, however, metaphors and analogies are not arbitrary, nor
merely personal. Not just any metaphors will do. In fact, it is their lack of perceived "arbitrariness" that makes particular metaphors or analogies acceptable
as science.

As Stephen Toulmin recently pointed out, the constraints on the choice of
metaphors and analogies in science are varied. The nature of the objects being
studied (e.g., organic versus nonorganic), the social (e.g., class) structure of the
scientific community studying them, and the history of the discipline or field
concerned all play their part in the emergence of certain analogies rather than
others and in their "success" or failure.[22] Sometimes the metaphors are strikingly
new, whereas at other times they extend existing metaphors in the culture in
new directions.

In the case of the scientific study of human difference, the analogies used by
scientists in the late eighteenth century, when human variation began to be studied systematically, were products of long-standing, long-familiar, culturally endorsed metaphors. Human variation and difference were not experienced "as
they really are, out there in nature," but by and through a metaphorical system
that structured the experience and understanding of difference and that in essence created the objects of difference. The metaphorical system provided the
"lenses" through which people experienced and "saw" the differences between
classes, races, and sexes, between civilized man and the savage, between rich
and poor, between the child and the adult. As Sander Gilman says in his book
Seeing the Insane, "We do not see the world, rather we are taught by representations of the world about us to conceive of it in a culturally acceptable manner."[23]

The origin of many of the "root metaphors" of human difference are obscure.
G. Lakoff and M. Johnson suggest that the basic values of a culture are usually
compatible with "the metaphorical structure of the most fundamental concepts
in the culture."[24] Not surprisingly, the social groups represented metaphorically
as "other" and "inferior" in Western culture were socially "disenfranchised" in a
variety of ways, the causes of their disenfranchisement varying from group to
group and from period to period. Already in ancient Greece, Aristotle likened
women to the slave on the grounds of their "natural" inferiority. Winthrop Jordan has shown that by the early Middle Ages a binary opposition between blackness and whiteness was well established in which blackness was identified with
baseness, sin, the devil, and ugliness, and whiteness with virtue, purity, holiness,
and beauty.[25] Over time, black people themselves were compared to apes, and
their childishness, savageness, bestiality, sexuality, and lack of intellectual ca-

pacity stressed. The "Ethiopian," the "African," and especially the "Hottentot" were made to stand for all that the white male was not; they provided a rich analogical source for the understanding and representation of other "inferiorities." In his study of the representation of insanity in Western culture, for instance, Gilman shows how the metaphor of blackness could be borrowed to explicate the madman, and vice versa. In similar analogical fashion, the laboring poor were represented as the "savages" of Europe, and the criminal as a "Negro."

When scientists in the nineteenth century, then, proposed an analogy between racial and sexual differences, or between racial and class differences, and began to generate new data on the basis of such analogies, their interpretations of human difference and similarity were widely accepted, partly because of their fundamental congruence with cultural expectations. In this particular science, the metaphors and analogies were not strikingly new but old, if unexamined and diffuse. The scientists' contribution was to elevate hitherto unconsciously held analogies into self-conscious theory, to extend the meanings attached to the analogies, to expand their range via new observations and comparisons, and to give them precision through specialized vocabularies and new technologies. Another result was that the analogies became "naturalized" in the language of science, and their metaphorical nature disguised.

In the scientific elaboration of these familiar analogies, the study of race led the way, in part because the differences between blacks and whites seemed so "obvious," in part because the abolition movement gave political urgency to the issue of racial difference and social inequality. From the study of race came the association between inferiority and the ape. The facial angle, a measure of hierarchy in nature obtained by comparing the protrusion of the jaws in apes and man, was widely used in analogical science once it was shown that by this measure Negroes appeared to be closer to apes than the white race.[26] Established as signs of inferiority, the facial angle and blackness could then be extended analogically to explain other inferior groups and races. For instance, Francis Galton, Darwin's cousin and the founder of eugenics and statistics in Britain, used the Negro and the apish jaw to explicate the Irish: "Visitors to Ireland after the potato famine," he commented, "generally remarked that the Irish type of face seemed to have become more prognathous, that is, more like the negro in the protrusion of the lower jaw."[27]

Especially significant for the analogical science of human difference and similarity were the systematic study and measurement of the human skull. The importance of the skull to students of human difference lay in the fact that it housed the brain, differences in whose shape and size were presumed to correlate with equally presumed differences in intelligence and social behavior. It was measurements of the skull, brain weights, and brain convolutions that gave apparent precision to the analogies between anthropoid apes, lower races, women, criminal types, lower classes, and the child. It was race scientists who provided the new technologies of measurement—the callipers, cephalometers, craniometers, craniophores, craniostats, and parietal goniometers.[28] The low facial angles attributed by scientists starting in the 1840s and 1850s to women, criminals, idiots, and the degenerate, and the corresponding low brain weights, protruding jaws, and incompletely developed frontal centers where the higher intellectual faculties were presumed to be located, were all taken from racial science. By 1870 Paul Topinard, the leading French anthropologist after the death of Paul Broca, could call on data on sexual and racial variations from literally hundreds of skulls and brains, collected by numerous scientists over decades, in order to draw the conclusion that Caucasian women were indeed more prognathous or apelike in their jaws than white men, and even the largest women's brains, from the "English or Scotch" race, made them like the African male.[29] Once "woman" had been shown to be indeed analogous to lower races by the new science of anthropometry and had become, in essence, a racialized category, the traits and qualities special to woman could in turn be used in an analogical understanding of lower races. The analogies now had the weight of empirical reality and scientific theory. The similarities between a Negro and a white woman, or between a criminal and a Negro, were realities of nature, somehow "in" the individuals studied.

Metaphoric Interactions

We have seen that metaphors and analogies played an important part in the science of human difference in the nineteenth century. The question is, what part? I want to suggest that the metaphors functioned as the science itself—that without them the science did not exist. In short, metaphors and analogies can be constituent elements of science.

It is here that I would like to introduce, as some other historians of science have done, Max Black's "interaction" theory of metaphor, because it seems that the metaphors discussed in this essay, and the analogies they mediated, functioned like interaction metaphors, and that thinking about them in these terms clarifies their role in science.[30]

By interaction metaphors, Black means metaphors that join together and bring into cognitive and emotional relation with each other two different things, or systems of things, not normally so joined. Black follows I. A. Richards in opposing the "substitution" theory of metaphor, in which it is supposed that the metaphor is telling us indirectly something factual about the two subjects—that the metaphor is a *literal comparison,* or is capable of a literal translation in prose. Richards proposed instead that "when we use a metaphor, we have two thoughts of different things active together and supported by a single word or phrase, whose meaning is the resultant of their interaction." Applying the interaction theory to the metaphor "The poor are the negroes of Europe," Black paraphrases Richards to claim that "our thoughts about the European poor and American negroes are 'active together' and 'interact' to produce a meaning that is a resultant of that interaction."[31] In such a view, the metaphor cannot be simply reduced to literal comparisons or "like" statements without loss of meaning or cognitive content, because meaning is a product of the interaction between the two parts of a metaphor.

How do these "new meanings" come about? Here Black adds to Richards by suggesting that in an interaction metaphor, a "system of associated common-places" that strictly speaking belong only to one side of the metaphor are applied to the other. And he adds that what makes the metaphor effective "is not that the commonplaces shall be true, but that they should be readily and freely evoked."[32] Or as Mary Hesse puts it in *Models and Analogies in Science,* these implications "are not private, but are largely common to a given language community and are presupposed by speakers who intend to be understood."[33] Thus in the example given, the "poor of Europe" are seen in terms strictly applicable only to the "Negro" and vice versa. As a consequence, the poor are seen like a "race apart," savages in the midst of European civilization. Conversely, the "Negro" is seen as shiftless, idle, given to drink, part of the social remnant bound to be left behind in the march toward progress. Both the ideas of "savagery" and of "shiftlessness" belong to familiar systems of implications that the metaphor itself brings into play.

Black's point is that by their interactions and evoked associations both parts of a metaphor are changed. Each part is seen as more like the other in some characteristic way. Black was primarily interested in ordinary metaphors of a culture and in the commonplace associations. But instead of commonplace associations, a metaphor may evoke more specially constructed systems of implications. Scientists are in the business of constructing exactly such systems of implications, through their empirical investigations into nature and through their introduction into discourse of specialized vocabularies and technologies.[34] It may be, indeed, that what makes an analogy suitable for scientific purposes is its ability to be suggestive of new systems of implications, new hypotheses, and therefore new observations.[35]

In the case of the nineteenth-century analogical science of human difference, for instance, the system of implications evoked by the analogy linking lower races and women was not just a generalized one concerning social inferiority, but the more precise and specialized one developed by years of anthropometric, medical, and biological research. When "woman" and "lower races" were analogically and routinely joined in the anthropological, biological, and medical literature of the 1860s and 1870s, the metaphoric interactions involved a complex system of implications about similarity and difference, often involving highly technical language (for example, in one set of measurements of the body in different races cited by Paul Topinard in 1878 the comparisons included measures in each race of their height from the ground to the acromion, the epicondyle, the styloid process of the radius, the great trochanter, and the internal malleolus). The systems of implications evoked by the analogy included questions of comparative health and disease (blacks and women were believed to show greater degrees of insanity and neurasthenia than white men, especially under conditions of freedom), of sexual behavior (females of "lower races" and lower-class women of "higher races," especially prostitutes, were believed to show similar kinds of

bestiality and sexual promiscuity, as well as similar signs of pathology and degeneracy such as deformed skulls and teeth), and of "childish" characteristics,
both physical and moral.[36]

As already noted, one of the most important systems of implications about
human groups developed by scientists in the nineteenth century on the basis of
analogical reasoning concerned head shapes and brain sizes. It was assumed that
blacks, women, the lower classes, and criminals shared low brain weights or
skull capacities. Paul Broca, the founder of the Société d'Anthropologie de Paris
in 1859, asserted: "In general, the brain is larger in mature adults than in the
elderly, in men than in women, in eminent men than in men of mediocre talent,
in superior races than in inferior races. . . . Other things being equal, there is a
remarkable relationship between the development of intelligence and the volume
of the brain."[37]

Such a specialized system of implications based on the similarities between
brains and skulls appeared for the first time in the phrenological literature of the
1830s. Although analogies between women and blackness had been drawn before,
women's place in nature and her bio-psychological differences from men had been
discussed by scientists mainly in terms of reproductive function and sexuality, and
the most important analogies concerned black females (the "sign" of sexuality)
and lower-class or "degenerate" white women. Since males of all races had no
wombs, no systematic, apparently scientifically validated grounds of comparison
between males of "lower" races and women of "higher" races existed.

Starting in the 1820s, however, the phrenologists began to focus on differences in the shape of the skull of individuals and groups, in the belief that the
skull was a sign faithfully reflecting the various organs of mind housed in the
brain, and that differences in brain organs explained differences in human behavior. And it is in the phrenological literature, for almost the first time, that we find
women and lower races compared directly on the basis of their skull formations.
In their "organology," the phrenologists paid special attention to the organ of
"philoprogenitiveness," or the faculty causing "love of offspring," which was
believed to be more highly developed in women than men, as was apparent from
their more highly developed upper part of the occiput. The same prominence,
according to Franz Joseph Gall, was found in monkeys and was particularly well
developed, he believed, in male and female Negroes.[38]

By the 1840s and 1850s the science of phrenology was on the wane, since the
organs of the brain claimed by the phrenologists did not seem to correspond with
the details of brain anatomy as described by neurophysiologists. But although the
specific conclusions of the phrenologists concerning the anatomical structure and
functions of the brain were rejected, the principle that differences in individual
and group function were products of differences in the shape and size of the head
was not. This principle underlay the claim that some measure, whether of cranial
capacity, the facial angle, the brain volume, or brain weight, would be found that
would provide a true indicator of innate capacity, and that by such a measure
women and lower races would be shown to occupy analogous places in the scale
of nature (the "scale" itself of course being a metaphorical construct).

By the 1850s the measurement of women's skulls was becoming an established part of craniometry and the science of gender joined analogically to race. Vogt's *Lectures on Man* included a long discussion of the various measures available of the skulls of men and women of different races. His data showed that women's smaller brains were analogous to the brains of lower races, the small size explaining both groups' intellectual inferiority. (Vogt also concluded that within Europe the intelligentsia and upper classes had the largest heads, and peasants the smallest.)[39] Broca shared Vogt's interest; he too believed it was the smaller brains of women and "lower" races, compared with men of "higher" races, that caused their lesser intellectual capacity and therefore their social inferiority.[40]

One novel conclusion to result from scientists' investigations into the different skull capacities of males and females of different races was that the gap in head size between men and women had apparently widened over historic time, being largest in the "civilized" races such as the European, and smallest in the most savage races.[41] The growing difference between the sexes from the prehistoric period to the present was attributed to evolutionary, selective pressures, which were believed to be greater in the white races than the dark and greater in men than women. Paradoxically, therefore, the civilized European woman was less like the civilized European man than the savage man was like the savage woman. The "discovery" that the male and female bodies and brains in the lower races were very alike allowed scientists to draw direct comparisons between a black male and a white female. The male could be taken as representative of both sexes of his race and the black female could be virtually ignored in the analogical science of intelligence, if not sexuality.

Because interactive metaphors bring together a *system* of implications, other features previously associated with only one subject in the metaphor are brought to bear on the other. As the analogy between women and race gained ground in science, therefore, women were found to share other points of similarity with lower races. A good example is prognathism. Prognathism was a measure of the protrusion of the jaw and of inferiority. As women and lower races became analogically joined, data on the "prognathism" of females were collected and women of "advanced" races implicated in this sign of inferiority. Havelock Ellis, for instance, in the late nineteenth-century bible of male-female differences *Man and Woman,* mentioned the European woman's slightly protruding jaw as a trait, not of high evolution, but of the lower races, although he added that in white women the trait, unlike in the lower races, was "distinctly charming."[42]

Another set of implications brought to bear on women by analogy with lower races concerned dolichocephaly and brachycephaly, or longheadedness and roundheadedness. Africans were on the whole more longheaded than Europeans and so dolichocephaly was generally interpreted as signifying inferiority. Ellis not surprisingly found that on the whole women, criminals, the degenerate, the insane, and prehistoric races tended to share with dark races the more narrow, dolichocephalic heads representing an earlier (and by implication, more primitive) stage of brain development.[43]

Analogy and the Creation of New Knowledge

In the metaphors and analogies joining women and the lower races, the scientist was led to "see" points of similarity that before had gone unnoticed. Women became more "like" Negroes, as the statistics on brain weights and body shapes showed. The question is, what kind of "likeness" was involved?

Here again the interaction theory of metaphor is illuminating. As Black says, the notion of similarity is ambiguous. Or as Stanley Fish puts it, "Similarity is not something one finds but something one must establish."[44] Metaphors are not meant to be taken literally but they do imply some structural similarity between the two things joined by the metaphor, a similarity that may be new to the readers of the metaphoric or analogical text, but that they are culturally capable of grasping.

However, there is nothing obviously similar about a white woman of England and an African man, or between a "criminal type" and a "savage." (If it seems to us as though there is, that is because the metaphor has become so woven into our cultural and linguistic system as to have lost its obviously metaphorical quality and to seem a part of "nature.") Rather it is the metaphor that permits us to see similarities that the metaphor itself helps constitute.[45] The metaphor, Black suggests, "selects, emphasizes, suppresses and organizes features" of reality, thereby allowing us to see new connections between the two subjects of the metaphor, to pay attention to details hitherto unnoticed, to emphasize aspects of human experience otherwise treated as unimportant, to make new features into "signs" signifying inferiority.[46] It was the metaphor joining lower races and women, for instance, that gave significance to the supposed differences between the shape of women's jaws and those of men.

Metaphors, then, through their capacity to construct similarities, create new knowledge. The full range of similarities brought into play by a metaphor or analogy is not immediately known or necessarily immediately predictable. The metaphor, therefore, allows for "discovery" and can yield new information through empirical research. Without the metaphor linking women and race, for example, many of the data on women's bodies (length of limbs, width of pelvis, shape of skull, weight or structure of brain) would have lost their significance as signs of inferiority and would not have been gathered, recorded, and interpreted in the way they were. In fact, without the analogies concerning the "differences" and similarities among human groups, much of the vast enterprise of anthropology, criminology, and gender science would not have existed. The analogy guided research, generated new hypotheses, and helped disseminate new, usually technical vocabularies. The analogy helped constitute the objects of inquiry into human variation—races of all kinds (Slavic, Mediterranean, Scottish, Irish, yellow, black, white, and red), as well as other social groups, such as "the child" and "the madman." The analogy defined what was problematic about these social groups, what aspects of them needed further investigation, and which kinds of measurements and what data would be significant for scientific inquiry.

The metaphor, in short, served as a program of research. Here the analogy comes close to the idea of a scientific "paradigm" as elaborated by Kuhn in *The Structure of Scientific Revolutions;* indeed Kuhn himself sometimes writes of paradigms as though they are extended metaphors and has proposed that "the same interactive, similarity-creating process which Black has isolated in the functioning of metaphor is vital also in the function of models in science."[47]

The ability of an analogy in science to create new kinds of knowledge is seen clearly in the way the analogy organizes the scientists' understanding of causality. Hesse suggests that a scientific metaphor, by joining two distinct subjects, implies more than mere structural likeness. In the case of the science of human difference, the analogies implied a similar *cause* of the similarities between races and women and of the differences between both groups and white males. To the phrenologists, the cause of the large organs of philoprogenitiveness in monkeys, Negroes, and women was an innate brain structure. To the evolutionists, sexual and racial differences were the product of low, adaptive changes involving variation and selection, the results being the smaller brains and lower capacities of the lower races and women, and the higher intelligence and evolutionarily advanced traits in the males of higher races. Barry Barnes suggests we call the kind of "redescription" involved in a metaphor or analogy of the kind being discussed here an "explanation," because it forces the reader to "understand" one aspect of reality in terms of another.[48]

Analogy and the Suppression of Knowledge

Especially important to the functioning of interactive metaphors in science is their ability to neglect or even suppress information about human experience of the world that does not fit the similarity implied by the metaphor. In their "similarity-creating" capacity, metaphors involve the scientist in a selection of those aspects of reality that are compatible with the metaphor. This selection process is often quite unconscious. Stephen Jay Gould is especially telling about the ways in which anatomists and anthropologists unself-consciously searched for and selected measures that would prove the desired scales of human superiority and inferiority and how the difficulties in achieving the desired results were surmounted.

Gould has subjected Paul Broca's work on human differences to particularly thorough scrutiny because Broca was highly regarded in scientific circles and was exemplary in the accuracy of his measurements. Gould shows that it is not Broca's measurements per se that can be faulted, but rather the ways in which he unconsciously manipulated them to produce the very similarities already "contained" in the analogical science of human variation. To arrive at the conclusion of women's inferiority in brain weights, for example, meant failing to make any correction for women's smaller body weights, even though other scientists of the period were well aware that women's smaller brain weights were at least in part a function of their smaller body sizes. Broca was also able to "save" the scale of ability based on head size by leaving out some awkward cases of large-brained but savage heads from his calculations, and by somehow accounting for the occasional small-brained "geniuses" from higher races in his collection.[49]

Since there are no "given" points of measurement and comparison in nature (as Gould says, literally thousands of different kinds of measurements can theoretically be made of the human body), scientists had to make certain choices in their studies of human difference. We are not surprised to find that scientists selected just those points of comparison that would show lower races and women to be nearer to each other and to other "lower" groups, such as the anthropoid apes or the child, than were white men. The maneuvers this involved were sometimes comical. Broca, for instance, tried the measure of the ratio of the radius to the humerus, reasoning that a high ratio was apish, but when the scale he desired did not come out, he abandoned it. According to Gould, he even almost abandoned the most time-honored measure of human difference and inferiority, namely, brain weights, because yellow people did well on it. He managed to deal with this apparent exception to the "general rule of nature" that lower races had small heads by the same kind of specious argumentation he had used with small-brained geniuses. Broca claimed that the scale of brain weights did not work as well at the upper end as at the lower end, so that although small brain weights invariably indicated inferiority, large brain weights did not necessarily in and of themselves indicate superiority![50]

Since most scientists did recognize that the brain weights of women were in fact heavier in proportion to their body weights than men's, giving women an apparent comparative advantage over men, not surprisingly they searched for other measures. The French scientist Léonce Pierre Manouvrier used an index relating brain weight to thigh bone weight, an index that gave the desired results and was in confirmation with the analogies, but that even at the time was considered by one scientist "ingenious and fantastic but divorced from common sense."[51] Even more absurd when viewed from the distance of time was the study mentioned by Ellis by two Italians who used the "prehensile" (i.e., apish) character of the human toe to compare human groups and found it was greater in normal white women than in white men, and also marked in criminals, prostitutes, idiots, and of course lower races.[52]

One test of the social power (if not the scientific fruitfulness) of an analogy in science seems in fact to be the degree to which information can be ignored, or interpretation strained, without the analogy losing the assent of the relevant scientific community. On abstract grounds, one would expect an analogy of the kind being discussed here, which required rather obvious distortions of perception to maintain (at least to our late twentieth-century eyes), to have been abandoned by scientists fairly quickly. Since, however, interactive metaphors and analogies direct the investigators' attention to some aspects of reality and not others, the metaphors and analogies can generate a considerable amount of new information about the world that confirms metaphoric expectations and direct attention away from those aspects of reality that challenge those expectations.

Given the widespread assent to the cultural presuppositions underlying the analogy between race and gender, the analogy was able to endure in science for a long time.

For instance, by directing attention to exactly those points of similarity and difference that would bring women and lower races closer to apes, or to each other, the race-gender metaphor generated data, many of them new, which "fit" the metaphor and the associated implications carried by it. Other aspects of reality and human experience that were incompatible with the metaphor tended to be ignored or not "seen." Thus for decades the Negro's similarity to apes on the basis of the shape of his jaw was asserted, while the white man's similarity to apes on the basis of his thin lips was ignored.

When contrary evidence could not be ignored, it was often reinterpreted to express the fundamental valuations implicit in the metaphor. Gould provides us with the example of neoteny, or the retention in the adult of childish features such as a small face and hairlessness. A central feature of the analogical science of inferiority was that adult women and lower races were more childlike in their bodies and minds than white males. But Gould shows that by the early twentieth century it was realized that neoteny was a positive feature of the evolutionary process. "At least one scientist, Havelock Ellis, did bow to the clear implication and admit the superiority of women, even though he wriggled out of a similar confession for blacks." As late as the 1920s the Dutch scientist Louis Bolk, on the other hand, managed to save the basic valuation of white equals superior, blacks and women equal inferior by "rethinking" the data and discovering after all that blacks departed more than whites from the most favorable traits of childhood.[53]

To reiterate, because a metaphor or analogy does not directly present a preexisting nature but instead helps "construct" that nature, the metaphor generates data that conform to it, and accommodates data that are in apparent contradiction to it, so that nature is seen via the metaphor and the metaphor becomes part of the logic of science itself.[54]

Changing Metaphors

Turbayne, in *The Myth of Metaphor,* proposes as a major critical task of the philosopher or historian of science the detection of metaphor in science. Detection is necessary because as metaphors in science become familiar or commonplace, they tend to lose their metaphorical nature and to be taken literally. The analogical science of human difference is a particularly striking example. So familiar and indeed axiomatic had the analogies concerning "lower races," "apes," and "women" become by the end of the nineteenth century that in his major study of male-female differences in the human species, Ellis took almost without comment as the standards against which to measure the "typical female" on the one hand "the child," and on the other "the ape," "the savage," and the "aged human." The tendency for metaphors to become dogmatic and to be seen as literally true and nonmetaphoric is particularly strong in science because of the identification of the language of science with the language of objectivity and reality.

The confusion of metaphor for reality in science would be less important if metaphors did not have social and moral consequences in addition to intellectual ones. This aspect of metaphoric and analogic science is often overlooked in discussions of paradigms, models, and analogies in science, in which the main focus tends to be on the metaphor as an intellectual construct with intellectual consequences for the doing of science. But metaphors do more than this. Metaphors shape our perceptions and in turn our actions, which tend to be in accordance with the metaphor. The analogies concerning racial and gender and class differences in the human species developed in the biosocial sciences in the nineteenth century, for instance, had the social consequences of helping perpetuate the racial and gender status quo. The analogies were used by scientists to justify resistance to efforts at social change on the part of women and "lower races," on the grounds that inequality was a "fact" of nature and not a function of the power relations in a society.

Another reason, then, for uncovering or exposing metaphor in science is to prevent ourselves from being used or victimized or captured by metaphors.[55] The victims of the analogical science of human difference were the women and the human groups conceptualized as "lower" races. Their exclusion from the community of scientists doing the analogizing was, to a large extent, part of the same social division of labor that produced scientific theories of natural inferiority. It was an exclusion that made identifying and challenging metaphors of natural inequality very difficult.

That the analogy between race and gender was eventually discarded (though not until well into the twentieth century) raises the interesting question of how metaphors in science change. For if metaphors are part of the logical structure of science, changes in metaphor will bring about changes in science. Ever since Kuhn published *The Structure of Scientific Revolutions* in 1962, of course, the problem of change has been central to any critical theory of science. Kuhn's contribution was to show that the substitution of one "paradigm" (defined as the belief, values, or techniques of a scientific community) by another was a complex historical event that could not be reduced to straightforward questions concerning the increased rationality, comprehensiveness, or logic of one paradigm over another. His work raised important questions about the relationship between scientific theories and empirical reality, about the grounds on which one paradigm is accepted and another rejected, and about the roots of change. He proposed that paradigms were not in fact simple reflections of reality but complex human constructions. Above all, Kuhn stressed the idea that all scientific knowledge is "embedded in theory and rules" which the scientist learns as a member of a scientific community.

Nevertheless, despite the emphasis he gave to the scientific community, Kuhn's own explanation of scientific revolutions tended toward the "intellectualist" rather than the sociological. He concentrated attention on the ways in which the scientific paradigm itself generates, through the normal process of puzzle solving within the paradigm, anomalies that eventually cause the breakdown of the paradigm and its replacement by another. On his own admission, Kuhn paid little attention to the role of social, political, or economic factors in the generation of new metaphors, and therefore new meanings, in science.

Recent work in the history and sociology of science, however, in part under the stimulus of Kuhn's work, has tended to stress the importance of the scientific community itself, as a sociological and political as well as scientific entity, for the generation and rejection of metaphors and analogies. The hope is that close historical and sociological investigation will begin to indicate in what ways particular representations or metaphors of nature are related to the social structure— class organization, professional socialization, interests—of the scientific community. The suggestion is being made that the root metaphors held by a particular scientific community or school of thought can become unsatisfactory, not merely because the data generated by the metaphor do not "fit" the metaphor, but because, for political or social or economic reasons, social formations change and new aspects of reality or human experience become important, are "seen," and new metaphors introduced.

The full implication of my own studies of the changes that eventually occurred in the analogical science of human difference is indeed along these lines— namely, that changes in political and social life were closely tied to the new metaphors of human similarity and equality, as opposed to metaphors of difference and inequality, that were proposed in the human sciences after World War II.[56] The subject of metaphoric change is obviously one requiring much further study.

A Brief Conclusion

In this essay I have indicated only some of the issues raised by a historical consideration of a specific metaphoric or analogical science. There is no attempt at completeness or theoretical closure. My intention has been to draw attention to the ways in which metaphor and analogy can play a role in science, and to show how a particular set of metaphors and analogies shaped the scientific study of human variation. I have also tried to indicate some of the historical reasons why scientific texts have been "read" nonmetaphorically, and what some of the scientific and social consequences of this have been.

Some may argue I have begged the question of metaphor and analogy in science by treating an analogical science that was "obviously pseudoscientific." I maintain that it was not obviously pseudoscientific to its practitioners, and that they were far from being at the periphery of the biological and human sciences in the nineteenth and early twentieth centuries. I believe other studies will show that what was true for the analogical science of human difference may well be true also for other metaphors and analogies in science.

My intention has also been to suggest that a theory of metaphor is as critical to science as it is to the humanities. We need a critical theory of metaphor in science in order to expose the metaphors by which we learn to view the world scientifically, not because these metaphors are necessarily "wrong," but because they are so powerful.

N O T E S

1. A metaphor is a figure of speech in which a name or descriptive term is transferred to some object that is different from, but analogous to, that to which it is properly applicable. According to Max Black, "every metaphor may be said to mediate an analogy or structural correspondence": see Black, "More About Metaphor," in *Metaphor and Thought,* ed. Andrew Ortony (Cambridge: Cambridge University Press, 1979), pp. 19–43, on p. 31. In this article, I have used the terms *metaphor* and *analogy* interchangeable.

2. G. Lakoff and M. Johnson, *Metaphors We Live By* (Chicago: University of Chicago Press, 1980), p. 191. Scientists' attacks on metaphor as extrinsic and harmful to science predate the Scientific Revolution.

3. See A. J. Ayer, *Language, Truth and Logic* (New York: Dover, 1952), p. 13.

4. On Duhem, see Carl H. Hempel, *Aspects of Scientific Explanation and Other Essays in the Philosophy of Science* (New York: Free Press, 1965), pp. 433–77. Hempel agrees with Duhem's view that "all references to analogies or analogical models can be dispensed with in the systematic statement of scientific explanations" (p. 440).

5. For this point see Jamie Kassler, "Music as a Model in Early Science," *History of Science,* 1982, 20: 103–39.

6. Colin M. Turbayne, *The Myth of Metaphor* (Columbia: University of South Carolina Press, 1970), p. 24.

7. General works on metaphor and science include Philip Wheelwright, *Metaphor and Reality* (Bloomington: Indiana University Press, 1962); Max Black, *Models and Metaphor* (Ithaca, N.Y: Cornell University Press, 1962); Mary Hesse, *Models and Analogies in Science* (Notre Dame, Ind.: University of Notre Dame Press, 1966); Richard Olson, ed., *Science as Metaphor* (Belmont, Calif.: Wadsworth, 1971); W. M. Leatherdale, *The Role of Analogy, Model and Metaphor in Science* (Amsterdam: North-Holland, 1974); Ortony, ed., *Metaphor and Thought* (cit. n. 1); and Roger S. Jones, *Physics as Metaphor* (Minneapolis: University of Minnesota Press, 1982). Warren A. Shibles, *Metaphor: An Annotated Guide and History* (Whitewater, Wis.: Language Press, 1971), gives an extensive introduction and guide to the general problem of metaphor, language, and reality.

8. Thomas S. Kuhn, "Metaphor in Science," in *Metaphor and Thought,* ed. Ortony, pp. 409–19 on p. 414; and Richard Boyd, "Metaphor and Theory Change: What Is 'Metaphor' a Metaphor For?" ibid., pp. 356–408, on p. 360.

9. For a defence of the centrality of analogy to science see N. R. Campbell, "What Is a Theory?" in *Readings in the Philosophy of Science,* ed. Baruch A. Brody (Englewood Cliffs, N.J.: Prentice-Hall, 1970), pp. 252–67. Shibles, in *Metaphor,* p. 3, also argues that each school of science "is based on a number of basic metaphors which are then expanded into various universes of discourse."

10. See Nancy Stepan, *The Idea of Race in Science: Great Britain, 1800–1960* (London: Macmillan, 1982), esp. chap. 1.

11. No systematic history of the race-gender analogy exists. The analogy has been remarked on, and many examples from the anthropometric, medical, and embryological

sciences provided, in Stephen Jay Gould, *The Mismeasure of Man* (New York: W. W. Norton, 1981), and in John S. Haller and Robin S. Haller, *The Physician and Sexuality in Victorian America* (Urbana: University of Illinois Press, 1974).

12. Haller and Haller, *The Physician and Sexuality,* pp. 48–49, 54. Among the several craniometric articles cited by the Hallers, see esp. J. McGrigor Allan, "On the Real Differences in the Minds of Men and Women," *Journal of the Anthropological Society of London,* 1869, 7: cxcv–ccviii, on p. cciv; and John Cleland, "An Inquiry into the Variations of the Human Skull," *Philosophical Transactions, Royal Society,* 1870, 89: 117–74.

13. Havelock Ellis, *Man and Woman: A Study of Secondary Sexual Characters* (1894; 6th ed., London: A. & C. Black, 1926), pp. 106–7.

14. Herbert Spencer, "The Comparative Psychology of Man," *Popular Science Monthly,* 1875–76, 8: 257–69.

15. Ellis, *Man and Woman* (cit. n. 13), p. 491.

16. Carl Vogt, *Lectures on Man: His Place in Creation, and in the History of the Earth* (London: Longman, Green, & Roberts, 1864), p. 81.

17. James Weir, "The Effect of Female Suffrage on Posterity," *American Naturalist,* 1895, 29: 198–215.

18. Charles Darwin, *The Descent of Man, and Selection in Relation to Sex* (London: John Murray, 1871), vol. II, chap. 17–20; Edward C. Cope, "The Developmental Significance of Human Physiognomy," *Amer. Nat.,* 1883, 17: 618–27.

19. Arthur Keith, "Presidential Address: On Certain Factors in the Evolution of Human Races," *Journal of the Royal Anthropological Institute,* 1916, 64: 10–33; Ellis, *Man and Woman* (cit. n. 13), p. xii.

20. See Nancy Stepan, "Biological Degeneration: Races and Proper Places," in *Degeneration: The Dark Side of Progress,* ed. J. Edward Chamberlin and Sander L. Gilman (New York: Columbia University Press, 1985), pp. 97–120, esp. pp. 112–13. for an extended exploration of how various stereotypes of difference intertwined with each other, see Sander L. Gilman, *Difference and Pathology: Stereotypes of Sexuality, Race, and Madness* (Ithaca, N.Y.: Cornell University Press, 1985).

21. Shibles, *Metaphor* (cit. n. 7), p. 15.

22. Stephen Toulmin, "The Construal of Reality: Criticism in Modern and Postmodern Science," *Critical Inquiry,* 1982, 9: 93–111, esp. pp. 100–103.

23. Sander L. Gilman, *Seeing the Insane* (New York: John Wiley, 1982), p. xi.

24. Lakoff and Johnson, *Metaphors We Live By* (cit. n. 2), p. 22. The idea of root metaphors is Stephen Pepper's in *World Hypothesis* (Berkeley/Los Angeles: University of California Press, 1966), p. 91.

25. Winthrop D. Jordan, *White over Black: American Attitudes toward the Negro, 1550–1812* (New York: Norton, 1977), p. 7.

26. Stepan, *The Idea of Race in Science,* pp. 6–10.

27. Francis Galton, "Hereditary Improvement," *Fraser's Magazine,* 1873, 7: 116–30.

28. These instruments and measurements are described in detail in Paul Topinard, *Anthropology* (London: Chapman & Hall, 1878), pt. II, chaps. 1–4.

29. Ibid., p. 311.

30. Black, *Models and Metaphor* (cit. n. 7), esp. chaps. 3 and 13. See also Mary Hesse, *Models and Analogies in Science* (cit. n. 7); Hesse, "The Explanatory Function of Metaphor," in *Logic, Methodology and Philosophy of Science,* ed. Y. Bar-Hillel (Amsterdam: North-Holland, 1965), pp. 249–59; and Boyd, "Metaphor and Theory Change" (cit. n. 8).

31. Black, *Models and Metaphor,* p. 38, quoting I. A. Richards, *Philosophy of Rhetoric* (Oxford: Oxford University Press, 1938), p. 93.

32. Black, *Models and Metaphor,* p. 4.

33. Hesse, *Models and Analogies in Science* (cit. n. 7), pp. 159–60.

34. See Turbayne, *Myth of Metaphor* (cit. n. 6), p. 19, on this point.

35. Black himself believed scientific metaphors belonged to the pretheoretical stage of a discipline. Here I have followed Boyd, who argues in "Metaphor and Theory Change"

(cit. n. 8), p. 357, that metaphors can play a role in the development of theories in relatively mature sciences. Some philosophers would reserve the term *model* for extended, systematic metaphors in science.

36. For an example of the analogous diseases and sexuality of "lower" races and "lower" women, see Eugene S. Talbot, *Degeneracy: Its Causes, Signs, and Results* (London: Walter Cott, 1898), pp. 18, 319–23.

37. Paul Broca, "Sur le volume et la forme du cerveau suivant les individus et suivant les races," *Bulletin de la Société d'Anthropologie Paris,* 1861, 2: 304.

38. Franz Joseph Gall. "The Propensity to Philoprogenitiveness," *Phrenological Journal,* 1824–25, 2: 20–33.

39. Vogt, *Lectures on Man* (cit. n. 16), p. 88. Vogt was quoting Broca's data.

40. Gould, *Mismeasure of Man* (cit. n. 11), p. 103.

41. Broca's work on the cranial capacities of skulls taken from three cemeteries in Paris was the most important source for this conclusion. See his "Sur la capacité des cranes parisiens des divers époques," *Bull. Soc. Anthr. Paris,* 1862, 3: 102–16.

42. Ellis, *Man and Woman* (cit. n. 13), pp. 106–7.

43. Alexander Sutherland, "Woman's Brain," *Nineteenth Century,* 1900, 47: 802–10; and Ellis, *Man and Woman,* p. 98. Ellis was on the whole, however, cautious about the conclusions that could be drawn from skull capacities and brain weights.

44. Stanley Fish, "Working on the Chain Gang: Interpretation in the Law and Liberty Criticism," in *The Politics of Interpretation,* ed. W. J. T. Mitchell (Chicago: University of Chicago Press, 1983), p. 277.

45. Max Black, as cited in Ortony, *Metaphor and Thought* (cit. n. 1), p. 5.

46. Black, *Models and Metaphor* (cit. n. 7), p. 44.

47. Thomas S. Kuhn, *The Structure of Scientific Revolutions* (Chicago: University of Chicago Press, 1962; 2d ed., 1973), esp. chap. 4; and Kuhn, "Metaphor in Science" (cit. n. 8), p. 415.

48. Barry Barnes, *Scientific Knowledge and Sociological Theory* (London: Routledge & Kegan Paul, 1974), p. 49.

49. Gould, *Mismeasure of Man* (cit. n. 11), pp. 73–112. For another example see Stephen Jay Gould, "Morton's Ranking of Race by Cranial Capacity," *Science,* 1978, 200: 503–9.

50. Gould, *Mismeasure of Man,* pp. 85–96.

51. Sutherland, "Woman's Brain" (cit. n. 43), p. 805.

52. Ellis, *Man and Woman* (cit. n. 13), p. 53.

53. Gould, *Mismeasure of Man,* pp. 120–21.

54. Terence Hawkes, *Metaphor* (London: Methuen, 1972), p. 88, suggests that metaphors "will retrench or corroborate as much as they expand our vision," thus stressing the normative, consensus-building aspects of metaphor.

55. Turbayne, *Myth of Metaphor* (cit. n. 6), p. 27.

56. Stepan, *Race in Science* (cit. n. 10), chaps. 6 and 7.

THE BIO-POLITICS OF A MULTICULTURAL FIELD

Donna Haraway

The Mirror and the Mask: The Drama of Japanese Primates

Japanese field study of an indigenous monkey inaugurated post-World War II naturalistic studies of nonhuman primates. The origin of the post-war primate story is within non-Western narrative fields. In the beginning, Japanese primatology was both autonomous and autochthonous—but not innocent, not without history. Human and animal, the actors and authors appeared on an island stage that was not set by the story of Paradise Lost. The Japanese monkeys became part of a complex cultural story of a domestic science and a native scientific identity for an industrial power in the "E/east."

Japanese primate studies originated in 1948 among a group of animal ecologists, including Imanishi Kinji, who had earned a doctor of science degree from Kyoto University in 1940. In the first generation of Japanese to pursue studies of animals in their natural environments, Imanishi led expeditions to several areas outside Japan. The Japanese primatologists were well aware of the Western work, and they cited Yerkes, Carpenter, and others with appreciation and critical evaluation. But the Japanese forged an independent primatology, whose characteristics were part of cultural narratives just as they have been in the West. As tropical primates have been mirrors for Western humans, domestic Japanese monkeys have been mirrors for their skilled indigenous observers.

Before turning to primates, Imanishi studied Japanese wild horses. In 1950 Imanishi and Miyade Denzaburo formed the Primates Research Group. Provisioning began in 1952, about the time of the establishment of the Kyoto University Anthropology Research Group. In Tokyo a medically oriented Experimental Animal Research Committee started up, and in 1956 the Kyoto and Tokyo groups established the Japan Monkey Center, followed in 1967 by the national Primate Research Institute of Kyoto University. By 1961, more than twenty Japanese macaque groups had been provisioned and brought into systematic observation.[1] In 1961 the Japanese began langur monkey studies, with the cooperation of Indian scientists in India, and launched the Kyoto University African Primatological

Expedition. In 1965 they initiated a long-term chimpanzee project in Tanzania's Mahale Mountains.[2] In 1972, Japanese workers started groundwork for their study of pygmy chimpanzees in Zaire.[3]

Westerners were unaware of the Japanese work until after 1956. About 1957, Yale medical primatologist Gertrude van Wagenen found a book with a picture of monkeys in a bookstore in Japan. She wrote Stuart Altmann at the National Institutes of Health and then sent him the book, which was *Japanese Monkeys in Takasakiyama* by Itani Junichiro (1954).[4] The Jesuit John Frisch, Sherwood Washburn's graduate student at the University of Chicago, translated the book and subsequently wrote a description of Japanese primate studies for Western readers. Altmann had several Japanese articles translated and published.[5] Japanese workers were invited to the Primate Year at the Center for Advanced Study in the Behavioral Sciences in 1962–63. The National Institute of Mental Health funded the first English translation of Japanese primate studies, and after that the Rockefeller Foundation sponsored translation from the Japanese journal *Primates,* published in English after the first two issues, reflecting international language politics. From about 1959–60, Japanese and Western workers have been in regular contact, despite on-going difficulties of linguistic, cultural, and scientific communication.

National Primates

It is ideologically and technically relevant that the Japanese studies were initiated on a species, *Macaca fuscata,* native to Japan. Although Japan had been a colonial power since the late nineteenth century, Japanese founding frameworks for watching monkeys and apes did not depend on the structure of colonial discourse—that complex search for primitive, authentic, and lost self, sought in the baroque dialectic between the wildly free and subordinated other. Rather, Japanese monkeys have been a part of the construction of a specifically Japanese scientific cultural identity. Constructing that identity has been a major theme in recent Japanese social, cultural, and intellectual history.[6]

Japanese monkeys might be viewed as actors in a Kabuki drama or a Noh performance. Their stylized social gestures and intricate rule-ordered lives are like dramatic masks that necessarily both conceal and reveal complex cultural meanings about what it means to be simultaneously social, indigenous, and individual for Japanese observers. Seeking the truth of nature underneath the thin, often obscuring layer of culture, the Westerner tends to see in our primate kin a deeper shared animal nature. In contrast, perhaps, Japanese primate observers have seen simian masks expressing the essential double-sidedness of the relations of individual and society and of knower and known.[7] It is not a "truer" nature behind the mask that is sought within Japanese cultural frame; nature is not the bare face behind the mask of culture. Instead, the figure of the Japanese dramatic mask alludes to a powerful abstract stylization of the specific social intricacies and profoundly individual qualities that pattern primate life. The dramatic mask in Japan is a figure of the co-determining relations of inside and outside and of the subtle reversals of position that change inside into outside. Masks cannot be stripped away to reveal the truth; rather the mask is a figure of the two-sidedness of the structure of life, person, and society. I am suggesting that Japanese primatologists constructed simians as masks in these culturally specific senses. Japanese monkeys were crafted as objects of knowledge showing the structure of an interactionist, relational, contextual self in a highly differentiated social world like that inhabited by their skilled observers (Smith 1983: 68–105). "Nature" was made into an object of study in Japanese primatology, but it was nature as a social object, as itself composed of conventional social processes and specifically positioned actors, that intrigued early Japanese monkey watchers.

Let us follow some of the issues raised by this highly modern, richly traditional, indigenous science. Through a gesture appropriate to the Western structures of appropriation of the "other" that this book [*Primate Visions: Gender, Race and Nature in the World of Modern Science*] has not escaped, Japanese primatology can be mined for resources to illuminate questions about gender, feminism, and orientalism. The early ethnographies of Japanese monkeys can be useful distorting mirrors for Euro-American feminists tangled in a culturally given story about nature and organic unity.

The search for the untouched heart of nature seems not to be a dream shared by the Japanese with Western observers. In a dissertation and other writing on different forms of anthropomorphism in Japanese and Western primatology, Pamela Asquith investigates the historical and philosophical roots of Japan's extensive studies of the social lives of nonhuman primates.[8] She argues that the particular related boundaries between human and animal and between mind and body, so crucial to Western Greek and Judeo-Christian mythology and to derivative ideologies of scientific objectivity, are not part of Buddhist or Confucian Japanese cultural heritage. While concern with status, personality, social change and stability, and leadership pervades Japanese primate studies, the split between observer and observed, so crucial to the Western quest for a healing touch across the breach, is missing.

When the human-animal boundary is not culturally crucial, two things change which matter immensely to the themes of this book: First, "nature" cannot be constructed as a health spa for the ills of industrial society; i.e., the tortured negotiation of touch with the representatives of a region from which "man" is banned does not dominate popular consciousness and covertly inform positivist science. A corollary of this first point is that "woman" will not be symbolically and socially required to cross taboo lines in scientific primate studies, in order to allow the field to include certain kinds of practices and theories coded as empathic or intuitive in the West, and so suspect for scientific men. The crucial question of identification with the "object" of study will not have the same gender load. It is hard to know what effect large numbers of Japanese women might have had on Japanese primate studies, which have been more male-dominated than in the United States.[9] The *particular* scientific gender-coding characterizing Western analysis of the relations of women and science are not meaningful in the Japanese context. The second point is that the reliability of scientific knowledge does not depend on enforcing the boundary against the forbidden desire of touch with nature. The dialectic of touch and transcendence in "Teddy Bear Patriarchy" is not a Japanese story. The eros, the politics, and the epistemology of primate science are culturally and historically specific.

Instead, as Asquith (1981) argues in her interpretations of the publications of Japanese primatologists Imanishi Kinji and Kawai Masao, strong Japanese cultural sources posit a "unity" of human beings and animals.[10] But it is hardly a unity that would be comfortable to those who seek in mystifications of the "Oriental" a solution to the forms of alienation built into Western scientific and social practice; it is not a unity innocent of cruelty and power. For example, Kawai explains why children's throwing stones at and bullying animals is not considered unacceptable in Japanese culture. Relations between species are like relations between older and younger siblings or parents and children. What Westerners might consider violence might be seen as acceptable "family" behavior. Kawai argues that the Western (apparently) moral stance rested on a particular notion of superiority to the animals that enjoins human stewardship. The story of Adam's commission in the Garden as planetary park ranger, with the special power to name his charges, is not indigenous to Japan.

In Buddhist traditions, the series of possible transformations among animals, gods, and humans sets up a horizontal system of relationship. Again, lest a Western reader seek in the absence of the kind of hierarchy familiar in the great chain of being a solution to Western problems, Japanese notions of continuum are perfectly consistent with what Westerners would see as quite cruel behavior to animals and to disabled people, based on the available notion of reincarnation in an animal, female, or deformed body as punishment for past imperfections (Asquith 1981: 353). Buddhist approaches can easily insist on the polluting aspects of animals, women, and the body. The ease of interchange among beings can be a source of considerable danger and anxiety. Similarly, within Confucian cultural resources in their Japanese form, the idea of a continuum between animals and humans is not inconsistent with a hierarchy within the unity. What is excluded is the idea of "special creation" or Christian stewardship that has been critical in the Western history of natural history, evolutionary biology, and conservation (Asquith 1981: 352). Buddhist ideals of compassion can ground relationships to animals, women, or other suffering beings in ways similar to masculinist human stewardship in Christian cultures, and certainly Japanese relations with human and nonhuman entities do not exclude, but insist on dominance and subordination within a social and ontological unity.

Stressing the troubling or contradictory dimensions for Westerners of Japanese cultural tendencies in human-animal relations is not to claim that the Japanese are cruel to animals or to categories of humans, but is rather a caution against the cannibalistic Western logic that readily constructs other cultural possibilities as resources for Western needs and action. It is important not to make Japanese primatology "other" in that sense, so that important differences can be appreciated, rather than mystified. In addition to the relevance for primate studies of Japanese reinventions of Buddhism and Confucianism, those early importations from Japan's first "West" (i.e., China and Korea), there is also another relevant "traditional" strand in Japanese cultural reinventions: Shinto and its emphasis on matrilineality and the importance and power of mothers in social life. But it is not simply the obviously "religious" or "cultural" stories that frame the drama of Japanese monkeys' lives. The narratives of modern sciences themselves are equally "traditional" and equally "reinvented" from the point of view of the post-World War II constructions of primate studies.

Asquith emphasizes that Japanese primatology, as it was developed by Imanishi and his co-workers, was neither traditional nor especially congenial to other mid-century Japanese scientists. To make nature an *object* of study is precisely not a Japanese move, and all of Japanese modern science has been in tension with groups crudely lumped as "traditionalists." Neither was Imanishi's science, with its emphasis on identification with the animals and on a disciplined subjectivity, congenial to "Westernizers" or "modernists," who regarded Japanese cultural sources as unproductive for the development of modern science. Imanishi's Japanese scientific contemporaries initially rejected his primatology as excessively subjective or anthropomorphic (Asquith 1981: 350–51).

Asquith argues that Imanishi's approach was an original, "individualistic" synthesis of Western and Japanese strands. Such "individualistic" groups arose in several areas of natural science with the lifting of severe regulations on research (accepting Western technology but rejecting Western philosophies of nature and science) at the end of Meiji Japan in the early twentieth century. And after World War II, the Japanese have forged a nationally specific organization of research and cognitive style in science. Imanishi's and Kawai's version of the synthesis has been part of the framework for a productive, collective Japanese branch of life science in primatology involving several institutions, international study sites, state support, and the training of graduate students in numbers rivaling the largest Western institutions.

What have been the special characteristics of Japanese studies of primates? First, several commentators have remarked on the early introduction of "provisionization" (Imanishi 1963: 70) of the free-ranging animals with food, thereby systematically increasing the observability of the highly mobile animals and altering the relation of observer and observed that compromises the "wild" or "natural" status of the animals from Western points of view. The "wild" status of the primates for the Japanese referred more to their running away from observers than to an essential character that would offer epistemological and symbolic guarantees. In the Japanese view, provisionization expressed an exchange or relationship that *already* existed (Asquith 1981: chap. 6).

A contemporary Western tourist in Japan is impressed by the *visibly* constructed nature which is loved and cultivated. The cultivation or domestication is not only found in the Japanese gardens, which have become such a popular commodity in Western architecture and landscaping. An ancient gnarled tree will be duly marked with a plaque as a national treasure. A famous natural scene, the changing seasons, trees in blossom: all these are deep in literary and other aesthetic practices. Nature is not just beyond the frontier, just beneath the crust of culture, the animal as opposed to the human. Nature is not presented as valuable because it is wild in Teddy Roosevelt's sense.[11] Nature is an aesthetic value and understood to require careful tending, arrangement, and rearrangement. Nature in Japan is a *work* of art. A provisionized monkey troop was seen to be in the process of domestication (Imanishi 1963: 70); that process in no way violated its natural status, which rested not on non-interference but on the particular quality of relationship.

Western observers have experimentally fed animals in the field, prominently in Carpenter's and all following work on Cayo Santiago and in Goodall's chimpanzee studies, but overwhelmingly, Westerners try to maintain—or apologize for violating—a "neutral" relation to the animals, which is believed to minimize the "interference" of the observer with the natural character of the object of knowledge that will be so important to the epistemological status of the resulting report. Deliberate experiment is one thing; "uncontrolled" interaction with the animals quite another. The repeated allegories of violation of this rule in Western primate studies are the stuff of informal culture, popular presentation, admonitory stories of polluted science, or personal idiosyncrasy that should never be allowed to interfere with real science. Studies of provisionized animals do not have quite the same status for Western observers as observations of a previously undescribed species in an area far from human activity. To study monkeys on Cayo Santiago is surely valuable, and much cheaper in a period of declining funding for primate studies, but nothing like the pleasures of the Kibale forest in Uganda or Amboseli National Park in Kenya. The fully controlled laboratory and the fully "natural" field situation ground the most reliable science for Westerners. The intermediate zones have been areas of great nervousness. Pollution of a study is easy if the boundary between human and animal is incautiously crossed (Douglas 1966). Lapses into "anthropomorphisms" are rigorously defended against in the field, and the apparatus of the animal laboratory can be read as an elaborate defense against boundary transgressions.

Western scientific women in particular must negotiate their relation to these taboos. On the one hand, many have deliberately taken advantage of the greater latitude for women in Western culture to acknowledge emotional exchange with the animals and to affirm the importance of identification or empathy in a way that they believe improves the research. On the other hand, these same women, as well as many who allow no greater identification than their male peers, repeatedly report having to guard against incautious admission or cultivation of their feelings, in order to be respected scientifically or to avoid being labeled "naturally" intuitive.

The second marked characteristic of Japanese primatology has been Japanese workers' renown for their individual identifications of large numbers of animals. It has not been atypical for all the Japanese associated with a macaque study site to recognize by face at a glance more than 200 individuals, most of whom are named (and numbered). Western observers also pride themselves on recognizing animals, and many Western scientists name their study animals rather than number them, but the comprehensive, detailed catalogue of the lives of *every* animal in a group is a Japanese trademark. It is instructive to compare the North American Stuart Altmann's tattooing of each rhesus monkey on Cayo Santiago in 1956 and his subsequent system of data collection with the field system of the Japanese. Both recorded detailed information on individual animals, and both pursued long-term research at stable sites. But Altmann's report was severely "objective," while Japanese writing of that period was highly "ethnographic," a kind of interpretation of primate cultures.[12] Altmann's report was at least as laden with cultural values as the Japanese accounts, and in particular I read both literatures of that period to fit comfortably with culturally specific, scientifically coded masculinist concepts and practices.[13]

The skill of recognizing the unmarked animals is associated with a strong sense of the individual animals' "personalities." Practiced Western observers are also renowned for recognition feats, for example, Iain Douglas-Hamilton with elephants and Linda Fedigan with Japanese macaques transplanted to Texas. But the story surrounding Douglas-Hamilton emphasizes the photographs of each elephant and patient memorizing of each nick in the ear or another discrete, tatoo-like natural marker, not the complex "personality" of a physiognomy (I. and O. Douglas-Hamilton 1975). The "technology" of identification is narratively emphasized despite the book's overwhelming story of the hero scientist's and his photographer wife's personal touch with a nature dangerous to ordinary people. The issue of recognition, like each of the "special" characters of Japanese primatology, also is differentiated by gender for Western observers—in a way that puts Western women and Japanese (mostly male) observers in a common symbolic location.

For example, Linda Marie Fedigan notes her "misgivings about female empathy" partly as a response to an annoying experience that warned her about the difficulty of women's being credited with their hard-won scientific accomplishments. After "having put many hours of effort into learning to identify the individual female monkeys of a large group, my ability was dismissed as being inherent in my sex, by a respected and senior male colleague" (Fedigan 1984: 308). Conversely, Irven DeVore reported disappointment that *his* naming and recognition of many animals other than the dominant males went unremarked in the partly gender-determined narrative of his responsibility for masculinist theories of male dominance supposedly based in his failure to see most individuals.[14] The point is not that Western women, Western men, and Japanese scientists have different, mysterious ways of learning the identities of particular animals; all the ways involve quite ordinary hard work and concentration. But the feats or failures of identification carry different cultural meanings according to the powerful markers of national and gender identities. From a structurally Western point of view, to be Japanese is more than a "nationality"; it is to be a representative of the "Orient." White women and the Japanese live in the "East," where Man is not alienated. The *narrative* is more revealing than the method. Similarly, the narrative that leads historians of primatology, including this one, to construct allegories of identification or alienation in discussing the neutral subject of "scientific method" is as important as any technical protocol.

The dialectical relationship of the specific personal character of each animal with the whole social system of relationships has been the basis of a special concept (*specia*), introduced by Imanishi into the primate literature, but never taken very seriously by puzzled Western primate scientists. Asquith related the Japanese arguments that their technique of personal recognition was bound up with a different approach to evolutionary theory and the concept of adaptation. The theory of natural selection was not understood as the center of Darwinism in Western countries until well into the twentieth century, and different national understandings of Darwin and evolution have received considerable attention from historians of biology.

Evolutionary theory in Japan was worked into culturally specific patterns too. The founding Japanese primatologists had no difficulty with the fact of evolution, but their questions and resulting explanatory systems were directed to sociology and social anthropology, and not to questions of fitness and strategies of adaptation. Most Japanese primate writing stressed what Western observers were more likely to see as "proximate" explanation, i.e., the social interactions themselves, their patterns of change and specificity, while neglecting "theory" or the "ultimate" explanation of adaptive strategies and reproductive fitness maximization.

Imanishi explained the concept of *specia* to "denote the aggregation of all individuals belonging to the same species which occupies a definite area on the globe." In addition, he proposed the term *oikia* to refer to the organization of higher vertebrates into particular aggregations denoted usually by terms like family or troop, i.e., by terms stressing social organization.[15] Both terms were constructed within a "culture and personality" framework for studying primates. Japanese workers in this period used definitions of culture suggested by the Boasian culture and personality theorists, and they explicitly compared their observations to issues raised by Margaret Mead.[16] Asquith points out how difficult, or more, superfluous, the concepts of *specia* and *oikia* have seemed to Western primatologists. But Imanishi's suggestions are a window onto Japanese constructions of nature. The social conventions of the monkeys were precisely the natural-technical object of knowledge constructed by the Japanese observers. The gap between natural and conventional is not the crucial issue; but the subtle social surface, the mask, is the essence of the *specia*. The *specia*, specific to an area of the globe, and the *oikia*, specific to a particular troop or monkey kin-organized group, are concepts grounding Japanese concern with the rootedness, i.e., with the native status, of a social entity. Nature as "wild" does not concern the Japanese in the way it does Euro-Americans, but nature as "native" is a matter of great concern. Focus on *specificity* in all its layers of meaning—individual personality, collective culture, habitat, troop identity, kin lineage—is an operation for building primate mirrors for a people preoccupied not with the colonial "other," but with the problem of establishing its uniqueness in the context of a history of extraordinary cultural importations and reinventions, from Buddhism to Darwinism.[17]

The third trait of Japanese primate studies from the beginning was collective, long-term study of several groups of the same species. They did not consider it remarkable for ten observers to study in detail the demographic and social histories of a group of monkeys for ten years and beyond. This orientation persisted in their expansion of primate observations to species outside Japan. While long-term, collective sites have come to characterize Western primate studies as well, initially a person who wanted to make a mark on the field sought an "untouched" species in an "undisturbed" environment. Western stories about the origins of the long-term sites tend to de-emphasize the presence of many people and to stress the role of an individual founder. The popular stories of Jane Goodall and Dian Fossey are perhaps the most extreme version of this common narrative. The tensions among generations of Western workers between those who founded sites, and in some sense see those sites as their personal achievement in making a section of "nature" into an object of knowledge, as well as a personal spiritual resource, and later workers, described by founders as seeking only data and not really caring about the animals, surfaced in my interviews. The quality of Western scientific primatology as travel and quest literature, wherein the individual hero brings back a prize valuable for the whole community, is a covert but important dimension that seems foreign to the social and symbolic organization of Japanese primate studies. Similarly, the story of the isolated Western observer who stays too long and loses his Western rationality—or his life—in a bodily touch with nature which went too far does not seem present in Japan's narratives of natural history.[18]

The final aspect of Japanese method is a philosophic synthesis of the meaning of the practices of provisionization, individual identification, and long-term collective work. Asquith presented in English for the first time Kawai's *Nihonzaru no seitai* (*Life of Japanese Monkeys,* 1969), in which he proposes the concept of *kyokan* ("feel-one") to designate the particular method and attitude resulting from feelings of mutual relations, personal attachment, and shared life with the animals *as the foundation of reliable scientific knowledge. Kyokan* means "becoming fused with the monkeys' lives where, through an intuitive channel, feelings are mutually exchanged" (Asquith 1981: 343). The "sympathetic method," not to be confused with a Western romanticized organicism that excludes power and violence, is crucial to the question of "objectivity." "It is our view, however, that by positively entering the group, by making contact at some level, objectivity can be established. It is on this basis that the experimental method can be introduced into natural behaviour study and which makes scientific analysis possible. . . . It is probably permissible to describe the method of the Primates Research Group as 'the new subjectivity' " (Kawai, in Asquith 1981: 346).

In her interviews with over forty Japanese primatologists, Asquith found that no one but Kawai used the term *kyokan*. The other workers attributed the word to Kawai's eccentricity, and Kawai noted his uniqueness on the point. But perhaps only the word, and not the underlying positions on the subtlety of the connections of subjectivity and objectivity, is at issue. Asquith reported that Itani, professor of the Laboratory of Human Evolution, preferred to call their method "anthropomorphic," stressing their assumption that since monkeys have "minds" of some sort, some kind of empathetic method would be reasonable and likely required to understand simian societies.[19]

Females: A Site of Discourse on Social Order

Both the *kyokan* methodological attitude and the possible cultural tones from Shinto sources sounded in several of the early discoveries of the Japanese primatologists raise interesting questions for a history concerned with the relations of feminism, women, females, and life sciences. Western primatology's "early" notorious focus on males to the exclusion of females and consequent masculinist interpretations of primate life have been noted in many historical accounts of the field. Many of these historical claims are part of a reassurance that the problem is well in hand now, with both women and men properly chastened by the lesson of the bad old days. Heroes who led the way out of biased science differ in the various accounts. Feminist-inclined women tend to emphasize the entry of their conspecifics (congenerics?) into the field in the context of a political women's movement,[20] and others look to ordinary progress in the self-cleansing scientific history of ideas.[21]

The early influential presence of Western women in primatology makes the case complex. It is impossible to separate cleanly their stories from those of their male peers in the same explanatory traditions and moments of primatology. For example, Sherwood Washburn's first two students of primate social life, Irven DeVore and Phyllis Jay, both theorized about male dominance hierarchies as organizers of social cooperation, although differences that could be considered gender related were also prominent. The two principals do not have the same retrospective opinion about their own and each other's work on these issues, and my reading of their early papers adds a third and dissimilar interpretation from either of theirs. Also, current sociobiological male and female theorists emphasize female biology and behavior for excellent reasons, which are *now* seen to be built in neo-Darwinian selection theory. Why now? Is it women who matter? or feminism? or neither? or both? and matter to what?

In the 1950s the Japanese were reporting that the basic structure of Japanese macaque society was "matrilineal," i.e., organized around descent groups of hierarchically related groups of females and their offspring (Kawai 1958). The rank of a male depended more on his mother's rank than on his individual exploits, and the rank of a daughter was stably predicted from her birth order and matrilineage.[22] Upsets could occur, but it did not make sense to see troop structure as the function of dominant males, who nonetheless filled a leadership role-function. Imanishi emphasized that for a male to be accepted into the core group of an *oikia*, so as to be part of the cluster of dominant males and females with their young, he had first to be accepted by the dominant females (Imanishi 1963: 79). He speculated that a psychological process of identification with high-status males was available for the male young of a high-status female. Those males would have the proper confident attitude that would lead to acceptance and high rank later. Males without the crucial maternal history would be permanently peripheralized and possibly leave the troop. Kawamura Syunzo (1958) also reported on a female-led troop, the since famous Minoo-B group, referred to as having a "matriarchal social order." Itani reported on frequent "paternal care" of young by males, especially those of unstable rank who appeared to perform this role as "a sign of interest in the central part of the troop" and to establish their position (Itani 1963: 94). Caring for youngsters and being accepted by important females seemed a better route to success for ambitious young males than fighting their high-status seniors.

Itani (1958) and Kawamura (1963) described the propagation of new food-preparation habits through the social structure of seaside troops fed sweet potatoes and grain, which some animals proceeded to wash and float, respectively. In a famous case, the change in troop habits was observed to be the fruit of the lavatory insight of a juvenile female, who washed her sweet potato free of grit and so spared her teeth. The other youngsters and females got the idea from her in a pattern that flowed through the female-lineage hierarchies. Sub-adult males got the important dental-care idea last because they were most peripheralized from the core group of females and young. However, if a top central male did get a new idea, his practice would spread even more quickly through the society. But social and technical innovation emerged from the practices of youngsters and their mothers.[23] The reports were not about the question of sex in cultural innovation, but about the processes of "tradition" or "protocultural behavior" in a nonhuman species. Read retrospectively in relation to Western debates about gender and science, the description of females stands out in comparison to the early male-authored Western accounts.

That all of these events in the history of a monkey species entered popular and technical literatures in several languages itself speaks to complex interest in the question of female "power." The matrilineal troop structure data were particularly damaging for the male dominance hierarchy explanations of macaques, and these data were cited by some Western (male and female) primatologists as early as they were published in English (Losos 1985). Both Japanese and Western men were interested in reporting what females and youngsters did, and these observers were capable of relating what they saw to explanations of how primate societies worked. Japanese men, not members of a culture famous for its congeniality to women, at least in the last millennium or so, made these points in their original reports in the 1950s. What else must be said about these narratives?

First, they *are* narratives—culturally important stories with plots, heros, obstacles, and achievements.[24] The presence of females, even powerful females, hardly makes a narrative women-centered, much less "feminist." And to be *Woman*-centered and *women*-centered are quite different things. In Japanese (and Western) primatology the bulk of discussion about female-centered organization was directed toward understanding *male* life patterns and to explaining social conservation.

However, there is a strong Japanese cultural preoccupation with mothering and with mother-son relations that has different tones from Western versions. Japanese historians stress the importance of Shinto tradition, with its female shamans and major female deities, especially the sun goddess, Amaterasu. The absence of a monotheistic, patriarchal father god changes men's imagination about women and females. Contemporary Japanese culture is replete with fiction, films, varieties of pornography, and social commentary on the ideology of mother-determined Japanese men's lives (Buruma 1985: 1–63). In complex interplay with Japanese histories of gender domination and conflict, these stories affect how both women and men conceive the social and natural worlds. Neither the stories nor the social and natural worlds split in the same way as in the West.

In addition, Japanese women are traditionally regarded as the source of the most crucial innovation for a modern people concerned about its native roots: Japanese women, from the period of Lady Murasaki's *Tale of Genji* in Heian Japan, originated Japanese written literature, while the men were writing in Chinese. Japanese women, as mothers at the node of kin groups, but also as literary figures, are at the sources of Japanese historical accounts of what it means to be Japanese, to be native, to have one's own language.[25] For the Japanese, the issue, echoing in primate studies as in other cultural practices, seems to be less the *origin* of language, the boundary between animal and human, than the *uniqueness* of one's own language, the boundary between native and stranger, the subtle play between conservation and change. Females and women seem socially and imaginatively to be located at dense intersections of meaning for these issues in Japan. I am not arguing that there was a direct determination between these broad cultural patterns and what Kawai or Kawamura saw Japanese monkeys doing in the 1950s. But the narrative field—the story-laden quality of observation, description, and explanation general to the life sciences, and especially primatology—for any particular Japanese account was structured by different axes of meaning and possibility. The period since Japan's defeat in World War II has been a critical one for Japanese cultural reinvention of identities in extraordinarily complex patterns of "scientific" and "traditional," native and foreign, revolutionary and conservative. In that context, the primatology of a native species may be read for its stories about gender, innovation, and conservation.

For Westerners, it is not remarkable that social stability was reported to rest on female-offspring networks. Nineteenth-century doctrines of the organization of the female around the uterus required that and more. Scientific attention to females has not been lacking. Indeed, the reproductive and nurturing female body has been constructed as a core scientific object of knowledge co-extensive with the history of biology as a discourse on systems of production and reproduction.[26] Women and females appear as scientists and as objects of scientific attention in the wake of twentieth-century global women's political movements; but the kinds of stories, the kinds of narrative fields of meanings, in which those beings appear were profoundly restructured. Feminism, as well as primatology, is a story-telling practice.

The percentage of women among Japanese observers is among the lowest in the world. The 1980 membership lists of the International Primatological Society indicate that about 9 percent of the Japanese members were women. Japanese women primatologists have not had the visibility of their Western counterparts. But from very early there were women; for example, Mori Umeyo's mother was also a primate scientist, resulting in probably the first mother-daughter lineage of primate watchers.[27] Mori Umeyo was a participant in Shirley Strum's 1976 Wenner-Gren baboon conference. Senior Japanese male scientists have commented in publications on the relevance of women observers to the content and accuracy of research.

For example, Pamela Asquith quotes Kawai Masao on his frustration at not being able to remember well enough the identities of females in troops he was observing. Kawai admitted:

> We had always found it more difficult to distinguish among females as we could not see any particular differences among them. However a female researcher who joined our study could recognize individual females easily and understood their behaviour, personality, and emotional life better than that of male monkeys. . . . The reason why the study of female monkeys has lagged behind is that the researchers have all been men. I had never before thought that female monkeys and women could immediately understand each other; but there has been some barrier between female monkeys and male observers. This revelation made me feel I had touched upon the essence of the feel-one method; at the same time I realized the importance of the phenomenon.[28]

Would the unique "female researcher" have seen her results as the fruit of natural affinity, or would she with Fedigan have remembered hours of work, perhaps invisible to the men because most of her life was invisible? Was the barrier between Kawai and the female monkeys a lack of natural affinity or the social history of patriarchy?

Kawai went further, and Asquith, a Western woman writing a history of primatology, noted his usage in a masterpiece of understatement in a modest footnote. Like Yerkes before him, in a different culture which still somehow fostered male researchers' feelings of annoyance at female animals seen to take advantage of their sexual politics to curry undeserved favor, Kawai described an incident in which females chased off a high-ranking male, relying on the implicit support of a still higher ranking male. Kawai perceived the females as "swaggering" and "taking advantage of" their relation to the ascendant male.[29] In *Adam's Rib*, written between 1941 and 1946, and so the first feminist commentary on the history of primatology, Ruth Herschberger (1970 [1948]: 5–15) had the chimpanzee Josie comment on Yerkes's similar perceptions in the 1930s. Herschberger, prescient about the dilemma of male observers isolated from women in the field, titled her first chapter ironically, "How to Tell a Woman from a Man." Between seeing no differences among females and perceiving their actions in terms of his own solidarity with the offended male, Kawai's description of matrilineal rank structure, supposedly crucial to deposing male dominance hierarchy theory as the explanation of the organization of macaque primate society, makes this reader remember that matrilineal organization is eminently compatible with male power and masculinist standpoints in social theory. *The River Ki,* a contemporary popular Japanese fiction written by a major Japanese woman author, makes the same point (Ariyoshi 1980).

My concluding moral is simple: Holism, appreciation of intuitive method, presence of "matriarchal" myth systems and histories of women's cultural innovation, cultivation of emotional and cognitive connection between humans and animals, absence of dualist splits in objects of knowledge, qualitative method subtly integrated with rigorous and long-term quantification, extensive attention to the female social organization as the infrastructure grounding more visible male activities, and lack of culturally reinforced fear of loss of personal boundaries in loving scientific attention to the world are all perfectly compatible with masculinism in epistemology and male dominance in politics. The lessons of Japanese primatology for current analyses in Western feminist philosophical and social studies of science are clear on these points. Western science suggests the same message, but perhaps it is more obvious in the context of sharp cultural difference, the sharpest, in fact—that between the mythic world historical structures called "West" and "East."

Both nineteenth- and twentieth-century Western feminist theorists have argued that the self-contained, autonomous, Western masculinist self, and the knowledge of the world he produces, is somehow truly opposed by women's putatively less rigid selves, issuing messages in another voice. The knowledge of the world imagined to come from this point of view, called women's, is variously described as more holist, less hostile to the body and to nature, promising a healing touch for alienation in industrial societies, and able to circumvent condemnation to the endless chain of substitutions for elusive true knowledge of nature, sometimes called a fully human knowledge. Psychoanalytic theory, history of science, and cognitive psychology are some of the disciplinary tools feminists have used to make these arguments.[30]

In complex sympathy with these claims, the feminist philosopher of science Sandra Harding (1986) noted that contemporary criticism of "Western" science by Afro-American theorist Vernon Dixon aligns him neatly with organicist ideologies of contemporary white women. Elizabeth Fee (1986) systematically showed how oppositional movements in science in the last twenty years have echoed each others' rhetoric and ideologies about science, while each movement claimed to ground its insights in an historically unique, sufficient, and necessary experience of domination, mediated by "dualist" science. In these arguments, there is little or no analysis of the historical and textual forms of power and violence built into "holist," "non-Western" frameworks. It has become clear to critics of anthropology how the observed and described peoples are turned into resources for the solution of other people's dilemmas (Fabian 1983). Those studied are regularly found to have just those properties that the writer's culture lacks and needs or fears and rejects. It is this structure that defines the logical move that constructs what will count as "primitive," "natural," "other."

Feminist theory has repeatedly replicated this "naturalizing" structure of discourse in its own oppositional constructions. It is at least odd that the *kyokan* method described in Japanese primatology (Kawai 1969), a description of the moment of transcendence of gender in a Western white woman's relation to cells she was observing (Keller 1983), a male activist's description of Native Americans' relation to nature before white violation (Means 1980), and an Afro-American man's discussion of organicism (Dixon 1976)—not to mention the sordid history of organicism and rejection of "dualism" in explicitly racist, fascist twentieth-century movements—make similar ideological and analytical moves (Fee 1986). That each of these constructions could be seen as eccentric or exceptional, e.g., not representative of most Japanese workers' views of their method or of women geneticists' approaches to sub-cellular structure, does not weaken their power as privileged allegory about oppositional practice.

What is the generative structure of oppositional discourse that insists on privileging "unity" at the expense of painful self-critical analyses of power and violence in one's own politics? There is at least a century-long tradition of Japanese writing about the difference of its philosophy of science compared to the procedures of Western science, which have played such a crucial role in modern Japanese history. This tradition is an important kind of oppositional literature produced within a culture that both maintained its national independence and adapted the modern sciences to its traditions and institutions, so as to challenge Western scientific hegemony very successfully in critical fields, including particle physics and micro-electronics. But Japan's complex oppositional-assimilationist approach to the sciences has *not* found a natural unity innocent of power and domination.

Japanese monkeys and those who watch them are inserted in the oppositional-assimilationist discourse on science, in a story-telling practice about themselves as industrial peoples who construct nature as an object of knowledge. The eccentric discourse on *kyokan* (and the wider related discourse on "authentic" Japanese approaches to the problem of Western "objectivity") is one product of that practice; it is a discourse on superiority and inferiority couched in a code about unity. Perhaps as a response to marginalization in its myriad forms, the "orientalization" of the self seems built into global systems of oppositional discourse about nationality, race, sex, and class. I read Kawai's text on *kyokan* as an oppositional discourse to the dominant Western ideologies of scientific method. Kawai's text runs parallel for part of its course to the privileging of organicism in Western feminism. Both are oppositional formulations in the face of a dominant scientific ideology and practice, perceived as Western in the one case and as masculinist in the other. And both posit a "new subjectivity" in response to the cultural domination of "objectivity." Both are discourses about a "native" or original unity. Both also have much to say about the charged symbolic and social status of mothers. Both are laced with structurally suppressed internal complexities about power. Perhaps the chief lesson of Japanese primates for feminist theories of science is that living in the "East"—no matter whether that place is found inside a cell, in the right half of the brain, in the Sacred Hills of Dakota, in mothering before or beyond patriarchy, or on Koshima Island in a matrilineal *Macaca fuscata* colony—is no solution for living in the "West."

N O T E S

1. Asquith (1981: 211); Itani (1954, 1975). I have followed the Japanese convention of placing the family name first and personal name second.
2. Nishida (1968, 1979); Hiraiwa-Hasegawa et al. (1983).
3. Kuroda (1980); Kano (1979, 1982); Kano and Mulavwa (1984); Nishida (1972).
4. S.A. Altmann interview, 1 April 1982.
5. Frisch (1959); Kitahara-Frisch resides in Japan. Altmann (1965b).
6. See Traweek (1988) for cultural similarities and differences among United States, European, and Japanese high-energy physicists. She traces the threads of elite international scientific cultures, particular national variants, and gender-specific scientific practices and imaginations woven into the fabric of field theories and built into the hardware of test devices.
7. Doi (1986: 23–33, 76–86).
8. Asquith (1981, 1983, 1984, 1986a, 1986b).
9. Nakane (1982) provides one Japanese woman's account of becoming an anthropologist. I have not found a comparable account by a woman anthropologist studying primates.
10. Just as the Christian ideal of stewardship is complex, historically dynamic, and able to accommodate mutually contradictory forms of social relationship with nature, so too Japanese cultural reworkings of Buddhism, Confucianism, and Western science are multifaceted and historically mobile. For some sense of how modern cultural reinvention works in Japanese popular culture, see Buruma (1985). However, Buruma's "Orientalist" treatment reinscribes for an American audience stereotyped Japanese exoticisms (Kondo 1984). In a structuralist analysis, Ohnuki-Tierney (1987) examines Japanese concepts of self and other by inquiring into the meanings of monkeys and the "special status" people who produce the popular monkey performances. In Japan monkeys have been mediators between deities and people, scapegoats, and clowns linked to social criticism. On "cultural reinvention" and ethnographic narratives of the self, see Clifford (1988).
11. Hern's (1971, orig. 1899) retelling of Japanese ghost stories evokes the regions outside the world of ordinary humans, a kind of naturalistic and demon-filled wilderness, but not one closely resembling the modern Western idea of wilderness (where the deer and the antelope play, etc.). From its origin, this Western wilderness is permeated with nostalgia and a sense of the impending disappearance of nature. That is, this concept of wilderness is implicit in European and Euro-American culture only after the "penetration" and "discovery" of colonized others, including the landscape with its plants and animals, were underway. However, one should not assume that Japanese constructions of nature are necessarily more compatible with conservation or broadly non-exploitative practices necessary for species and habitat survival, nationally or globally, compared to Western constructions. Both inside and outside Japan, the Japanese are enmeshed in terrible environmental problems. My point is that the different ways of loving, knowing, and otherwise constructing "nature" have different strengths or hazards for building non-exploitative conservation and survival practices.
12. Altmann (1962); Itani (1963); Imanishi (1960); Kawamura (1958).
13. Haraway (1981–82); Keller (1985).

14. DeVore (1962, 1963, 1965a), interview, 18 March 1982; Smuts interview, 18 March 1982.

15. Imanishi (1963: 69); Asquith (1981, 1984).

16. Kawamura (1963); Itani (1963).

17. Japan has been a colonial power, and I do not intend to romanticize Japanese treatment of its colonial "others," for example, the Koreans. But Japan's indigenous species have not been enlisted in its cultural symbology marking insider-outsider.

18. Tournier (1972); Akeley (1923); Fossey (1983); Mowat (1987).

19. Asquith, personal communication, 28 Aug. 1985.

20. Hrdy (1986); Hrdy and Williams (1983); Haraway (1978a, 1978b, 1983a); Rowell (1984); Small (1984).

21. Altmann (1967); Losos (1985); Clutton-Brock (1983).

22. A U.C. Berkeley student, Donald Sade, reported the same structure among the rhesus monkeys of Cayo Santiago (Sade 1965, 1967). Sade discounted influence from the women's movement in primatology, and he was not comfortably part of the Washburn network (Losos 1985: 16–19). Losos's citation analysis showed that members of the Washburn network who continued to emphasize the male dominance hierarchy as the organizing axis of society did not often cite Sade on matrilineal rhesus social organization. Losos argued that male dominance hierarchy explanations, never hegemonic, were undermined by socioecology through the late 1960s and early 1970s independently of feminism.

23. For a film stressing that "the young revolutionize the culture" (soundtrack), see National Geographic's Monkeys, Apes, and Man (1971). The remark comes right after the filmic narration of Gray and Eileen Eaton's research with a Macaca fuscata colony at Oregon Regional Primate Research Center. The soundtrack calls the Oregon Japanese monkeys "ambassadors from some foreign nation—the animal kingdom." The rich ambiguities implicit in the words ambassador, colony and nation resonate with the move from human nation to animal species. The next filmic scene is the monkey's "home"—Japan. The first stop, in a snowstorm, shows the adaptation of the monkey citizens in the extreme northern part of their distribution. The viewer learns that this simian is not a tropical creature. The point silently joins the resonances around ambassadors, nations, and colonies. Then we go south, to Koshima Island, to see monkeys swimming happily in the ocean, washing sand out of wheat scattered on the beach, and scrubbing sweet potatoes. "The young revolutionize culture." Commenting on the island culture's similarity to "a small nation," the narration stresses the "primitive inventor" in the "culture of Koshima." On screen, monkeys walk upright, carrying their food to wash it before eating.

From "culture" in Japan, the film goes to West Africa, to narrate the lives of chimpanzees tied to the trees, living in a "carefree style" in the tropics (soundtrack). The codes of race and colonization in the drama of "civilization" in the animal kingdom could hardly be more explicit. Here, the codes override the usual placement of monkeys and apes, in which the apes are ascribed the greater social and behavioral complexity and form the link between animal and human. The film moves out of the rain forest into the open, where progress and civilization can begin, here represented in Adriaan Kortlandt's studies of chimpanzees' understanding of death and of their use of clubs to beat up a threatening stuffed leopard.

24. Landau (1981, 1984).

25. The Konjiki and the Nihongi, the earliest written historical chronicles, from about 720 C.E., were written in Chinese. They are full of accounts of important roles of women and female deities in Japan as a nation, e.g., the story of the Empress Suiko (692–628 B.C.E.). Her title was posthumously bestowed because the writing of history was considered to be an important innovation of her reign. The close association of women with writing at the origin of Japan as a national and linguistic community contrasts markedly with the symbolic function of Eve's eating from the tree of knowledge of good and evil for the Western and Islamic peoples of the Book.

26. Haraway (1979, 1985).

27. S.A. Altmann, speech to the American Society of Primatologists, 3 June 1980.
28. Kawai (1969: 293), in Asquith (1981: 344).
29. Kawai (1965); Asquith (1981: 344n).
30. Chodorow (1978); Irigaray (1985); Gilligan (1982); Keller (1983, 1985); Merchant (1980).

B I B L I O G R A P H Y

Akeley, Carl E. and Mary Jobe Akeley. 1922. *Lions, Gorillas, and their Neighbors*. New York: Dodd & Mead.

Altmann, Stuart A. 1962. A field study of the sociobiology of rhesus monkeys, *Macaca mulatta*. *Annals of the New York Academy of Sciences* 102(2):338–435.

Altmann, Stuart A., ed. 1965b. *Japanese Monkeys: A Collection of Translations*. Selected by Kinji Imanishi. Atlanta: Yerkes Primate Research Center.

Altmann, Stuart A., ed. 1967. *Social Communication among Primates*. Chicago: University of Chicago Press.

Ariyoshi, Sawako. 1980. *The River Ki*. Translated by Mildred Tahata. Tokyo and New York: Kodansha, Ltd.

Asquith, Pamela. 1981. Some aspects of anthropomorphism in the terminology and philosophy underlying Western and Japanese studies of the social behaviour of non-human primates. Ph.D. thesis, Oxford University.

Asquith, Pamela. 1983. The Monkey Memorial Service of Japanese primatologists. *RAIN*, no. 54 (February): 3–4.

Asquith, Pamela. 1984. Bases for difference in Japanese and Western primatology. Paper delivered at the 12th Meeting of CAPA/AAPC, University of Alberta, November 15–18.

Asquith, Pamela. 1986a. Imanishi's impact in Japan. *Nature* 323: 675–76.

Asquith, Pamela. 1986b. Anthropomorphism and the Japanese and Western traditions in primatology. In J. Else and P. Lee, eds. *Primate Ontogeny, Cognition and Behavior: Developments in Field and Laboratory Research*. New York: Academic Press, pp. 61–71.

Bermant, Gordon and Donald Lindberg, eds. 1975. *Primate Utilization and Conservation*. New York: Wiley-Interscience.

Bleier, Ruth, ed. 1986. *Feminist Approaches to Science*. New York: Pergamon.

Buruma, Ian. 1985. *Behind the Mask: On Sexual Demons, Sacred Mothers, Transvestites, Gangsters, Drifters and Other Japanese Cultural Heroes*. New York: Pantheon.

Chodorow, Nancy. 1978. *The Reproduction of Mothering*. Los Angeles: University of California Press.

Clifford, James. 1988. *The Predicament of Culture*. Cambridge, MA: Harvard University Press.

Clutton-Brock, Timothy H. 1983. Behavioural ecology and the female. *Nature* 306:716.

DeVore, Irven. 1962. The social behavior and organization of baboon troops. Ph.D. thesis, University of Chicago.

DeVore, Irven. 1963. Mother-infant relations in free ranging baboons. In Harriet L. Rheingold, ed., *Maternal Behavior in Mammals*. New York: John Wiley & Sons, pp. 305–35.

DeVore, Irven, ed. 1965a. *Primate Behavior: Field Studies of Monkeys and Apes*. New York: Holt, Rinehart & Winston.

Dixon, Vernon. 1976. World views and research methodology. In L. M. King, V. Dixon, and W. W. Nobles, eds. *African Philosophy: Assumptions and Paradigms for Research on Black Persons*. Los Angeles: Fanon Center, Charles R. Drew Postgraduate School.

Doi, Takeo. 1986. *The Anatomy of Self*. Translated by Mark Harbison. Tokyo: Kodansha International, Ltd.

Douglas, Mary. 1966. *Purity and Danger: An Analysis of the Concepts of Pollution and Taboo*. London: Routledge & Kegan Paul.

Douglas-Hamilton, Iain, and Oria Douglas-Hamilton. 1975. *Life among the Elephants*. New York: Viking.

Fabian, Johannes. 1983. *Time and the Other: How Anthropology Makes Its Object*. New York: Columbia University Press.

Fedigan, Linda Marie. 1984. Sex ratios and sex differences in primatology. *American Journal of Primatology* 7:305–8.

Fee, Elizabeth. 1986. Critiques of modern science: The relationship of feminism to other radical epistemologies. In Bleier 1986:42–56.

Fossey, Dian. 1983. *Gorillas in the Mist*. Boston: Houghton Mifflin.

Frisch, Jean (Kitahara). 1959. Research on primate behavior in Japan. *American Anthropologist* 61:584–96.

Gilligan, Carol. 1982. *In a Different Voice*. Cambridge, Mass.: Harvard University Press.

Hamburg, David A., and Elizabeth McCown, eds. 1979. *The Great Apes*. Menlo Park, Calif.: Benjamin/Cummings.

Haraway, Donna J. 1978a. Animal sociology and a natural economy of the body politic. Part I. A political physiology of dominance. *Signs* 4:21–36.

Haraway, Donna J. 1978b. Animal sociology and a natural economy of the body politic. Part II. The past is the contested zone: Human nature and theories of production and reproduction in primate behavior studies. *Signs* 4:37–60.

Haraway, Donna J. 1979. The biological enterprise: Sex, mind, and profit from human engineering to sociobiology. *Radical History Review*, no. 20, pp. 206–37.

Haraway, Donna J. 1981–82. The high cost of information in post World War II evolutionary biology: Ergonomics, semiotics, and the sociobiology of communication systems. *Philosophical Forum* XIII (2–3):244–78.

Haraway, Donna J. 1983a. The contest for primate nature: Daughters of man the hunter in the field, 1960–80. In Mark Kann, ed. *The Future of American Democracy: Views from the Left*. Philadelphia: Temple University Press, pp. 175–207.

Haraway, Donna J. 1985. A manifesto for cyborgs: Science, technology, and socialist feminism in the 1980s. *Socialist Review* 15(2): 65–108.

Harding, Sandra. 1986. *The Science Question in Feminism*. Ithaca: Cornell University Press.

Hern, Lafcadio. 1971 [1899]. *In Ghostly Japan*. Rutland, Vermont, and Tokyo: Charles E. Tuttle & Co.

Herschberger, Ruth. 1970 [1948]. *Adam's Rib*. New York: Harper & Row.

Hiraiwa-Hasegawa, Mariko, Hasegawa Toshisada, and Nishida Toshisada. 1983. Demographic study of a large-sized unit group of chimpanzees in the Mahale Mountains, Tanzania. Mahale Mountains Chimpanzee Research Project, Ecological Report, no. 30.

Hrdy, Sarah Blaffer. 1986. Empathy, polyandry, and the myth of the coy female. In Bleier 1986: 119–46.

Hrdy, Sarah Blaffer, and George C. Williams. 1983. Behavioral biology and the double standard. In Wasser 1983b:3–17.

Imanishi, Kinji. 1960. Social organization of subhuman primates in their natural habitat. *Current Anthropology* 1(5–6):390–405.

Imanishi, Kinji. 1961. The origin of the human family–a primatological approach. *Japanese Journal of Ethnology* 25:119–30.

Imanishi, Kinji. 1963. Social behavior in Japanese monkeys, *Macaca fuscata*. In Southwick 1963:68–81.

Irigaray, Luce. 1985. Is the subject of science sexed? *Cultural Critique* 1:73–88.

Itani, Junichiro. 1954. Japanese monkeys at Takasakiyama. In Imanishi Kinji, ed. *Social Life of Animals in Japan* (in Japanese). Tokyo: Kobunsya.

Itani, Junichiro. 1958. On the acquisition and propagation of new food habits in the troop of Japanese monkeys at Takasakiyama. *Primates* 1:84–98.

Itani, Junichiro. 1963. Paternal care in the wild Japanese monkey, *Macaca fuscata*. In Southwick 1963: 91–97.

Itani, Junichiro. 1975. Twenty years with the Mount Takasaki monkeys. In Bermant and Lindberg 1975:197–249.

Kano, Takayoshi. 1979. A pilot study on the ecology of pygmy chimpanzees. *Pan paniscus*. In Hamburg and McCown 1979:123–35.

Kano, Takayoshi. 1982. The social group of pygmy chimpanzees (*Pan paniscus*) of Wamba. *Primates* 23:171–88.

Kano, Takayoshi, and Mbangi Mulavwa. 1984. Feeding ecology of the pygmy chimpanzees (*Pan paniscus*) of Wamba. In Sussman 1984:233–74.

Kawai, Masao. 1958. On the rank system in a natural group of Japanese monkey, I and II. *Primates* 1 (2):11–48, in Japanese with English summary.

Kawai, Masao. 1965. Newly acquired precultural behaviour of the natural troop of Japanese monkeys on Koshima Islet. *Primates* 6:1–30.

Kawai, Masao. 1969. *Nihonzaru no seitai (Life of Japanese Monkeys)*. Tokyo.

Kawamura, Syunzo. 1958. Matriarchal social ranks in the Minoo-B troop: A study of the rank system of Japanese monkeys. *Primates* 1 (2):149–156 (in Japanese).

Kawamura, Syunzo. 1963. The progress of sub-culture propagation among Japanese monkeys. In Southwick 1963: 82–90.

Keller, Evelyn Fox. 1983. *A Feeling for the Organism*. New York: Freeman.

Keller, Evelyn Fox. 1985. *Reflections on Gender and Science*. New Haven: Yale University Press.

Kondo, Dorinne. 1984. If you want to know who they are . . . *The New York Times Book Review* (September 16):13–14.

Kuroda, Suehisa. 1980. Social behavior of the pygmy chimpanzees. *Primates* 21(2):181–97.

Landau, Misia. 1981. The anthropogenic: Paleoanthropological writing as a genre of literature. Ph.D. thesis, Yale University.

Landau, Misia. 1984. Human evolution as narrative. *American Scientist* 72:362–68.

Losos, Elizabeth. 1985. Monkey see, monkey do: Primatologists' conceptions of primate societies. Senior thesis, Harvard University.

Means, Russell. 1980. Fighting words on the future of the earth. *Mother Jones,* December, pp. 22–38.

Merchant, Carolyn. 1980. *The Death of Nature: Women, Ecology, and the Scientific Revolution*. New York: Harper & Row.

Mowat, Farley. 1987. *Woman in the Mists: The Story of Dian Fossey and the Mountain Gorillas of Africa*. New York: Warner Books.

Nakane, Chie. 1982. Becoming an anthropologist. In Derek Richter, ed. *Women Scientists: The Road to Liberation*. London: Macmillan, pp. 45–60.

Nishida, Toshisada. 1968. The social group of wild chimpanzees in the Mahale Mountains. *Primates* 9:167–224.

Nishida, Toshisada. 1972. Preliminary information on the pygmy chimpanzees (*Pan paniscus*) of the Congo Basin. *Primates* 13:415–25.

Nishida, Toshisada. 1979. The social structure of chimpanzees in the Mahale Mountains. In Hamburg and McCown 1979:73–121.

Ohnuki-Tierney, Emiko 1987. *The Monkey as Mirror: Symbolic Transformations in Japanese History and Ritual*. Princeton: Princeton University Press.

Rowell, Thelma. 1984. Introduction. In Small 1984:13–16.

Sade, Donald S. 1965. Some aspects of parent-offspring and sibling relations in a group of rhesus monkeys, with a discussion of grooming. *American Journal of Physical Anthropology* 23(1):1–17.

Sade, Donald S. 1967. Determinants of dominance in a group of free-ranging rhesus monkeys. In S.A. Altmann 1967:99–114.

Small, Meredith, ed. 1984. *Female Primates: Studies by Women Primatologists*. New York: Allan Liss.

Smith, Robert J. 1983. *Japanese Society: Tradition, Self, and the Social Order*. Cambridge: Cambridge University Press.

Southwick, Charles, ed. 1963. *Primate Social Behavior*. Princeton: Van Nostrand.

Sussman, Randall L., ed. 1984. *The Pygmy Chimpanzee: Evolutionary Biology and Behavior*. New York: Plenum.

Tournier, Michel. 1972. *Vendredi ou les limbes du Pacifique*. Paris: Gallimard.

Traweek, Sharon. 1988. *Beamtimes and Lifetimes: The World of High Energy Physics*. Cambridge, Mass. Harvard University Press.

Wasser, Samuel K., ed. 1983b. *Social Behavior of Female Vertebrates*. New York: Academic Press.

CULTURAL DIFFERENCES IN HIGH-ENERGY PHYSICS
Contrasts between Japan and the United States

Sharon Traweek

The members of the particle physics community are firmly committed to the international, supracultural image of science.[1] Particle physicists from anywhere in the world are fond of remarking that they have more in common with each other than with their next-door neighbors. All of these physicists consider themselves members of an intellectual elite, perhaps *the* intellectual elite, because they believe particle physics works alone at the frontiers of human knowledge. Shared traditions in training and in distinctions serve as stabilizing elements in the international community. It is in the context of this relatively constant structure or "ground state" of predictable smooth behavior that problems in the community can be defined and sometimes resolved.

The overriding issue confronting both Americans and Japanese is how to incorporate new facilities for doing physics, such as PEP, the new collider at SLAC, and KEK,* while maintaining the stable structure of their world. In other words, can these communities reproduce themselves in new contexts? The experimental particle physicists in both countries debate the model of a good laboratory in terms of "the best environment for good physics." In both cases the pivotal issue is the relationship between in-house groups and "users." In the United States, SLAC is considered the American laboratory most strongly controlled by inside, permanent research groups.

• • •

At both KEK and SLAC, new facilities were funded by the respective national governments with the specific injunction that they be open to all qualified users. Both the Japanese and American particle physics communities need to find ways of balancing the interest of insiders and users (usually university-based) in the management and use of important new facilities. The physicists are being forced

*[SLAC is the Stanford Linear Accelerator near San Francisco and KEK is the Japanese National Laboratory for High Energy Physics (Ko-Enerugie butsurigaku Kenkyusho) at Tsukuba, Japan.—Ed.]

to reevaluate what is the best organizational environment for physics. This problem, which confronts the entire particle physics community internationally, is part of a larger issue: the institutionalization of a new and very expensive field of inquiry within a highly conservative university tradition and its impact on the established allocation of research funds.

Their different approaches point to important distinctions between the Japanese and American communities. In the physicists' own opinion their differences are due to their disparate ranking in the international particle physics community: SLAC has been "at the center of the action" and is trying to maintain that position; KEK, although ambitious, is a comparatively modest institution. In my view the differences between Japanese and American practices in laboratory organization and in training new physicists are due not mainly to the relative sophistication of the technology, but to the culture of the physicists. American particle physicists differ in many ways from their Japanese counterparts, and these differences correspond to strong cultural values. They can be grouped under the headings of teaching, group and laboratory organization, leadership styles, inheritance, and historical perspective.

As I present the "Japanese" and "American" styles I remind the reader first that I am describing what Max Weber called "ideal types." These are abstractions, for the sake of analysis: no one person or group would fit the model perfectly. Second, it is crucial to keep in mind that *both* models exist in *each* country. What I will describe as the dominant "Japanese" style also exists in the United States; and the prevailing style in the United States most certainly also exists in Japan.

The Japanese perception of how Japan ought to go about becoming a first-rate particle physics nation places great emphasis on training the next generation. This transfers to the young physicists great responsibility for the future, and also confers upon them great obligation to their teachers. This mutual responsibility and obligation is consistent with the tenets of *amae* (interdependence, particularly in generational ties), a crucial value in Japanese culture.[2]

Americans believe that what is best for the future of physics is for each physicist to provide the best physics possible; what is good for the individual will benefit the community. I discussed earlier how the educational process in physics cultivates this individualistic, competitive drive in each student. This value is consistent with the American cult of *individualism,* a laissez-faire economic model for the growth of knowledge: each contributes as one chooses, and the unfettered marketplace of ideas selects the best. In this model, self-interests are seen as properly and necessarily competing. Not only Japanese but also Europeans find these assumptions alien: one European working at SLAC said that Americans have no understanding of collaborative intellectual exploration, because they see ideas as real estate—that is, private property.[3]

In Japan when I asked group leaders where new ideas for experimental design or data analysis come from, they generally credited the graduate students and *koshi*; they said the group then responds to their ideas, perhaps modifying or amplifying them.[4] In the United States, the senior physicists say that it is the leader who generates ideas, which the group amplifies and executes under his direction. While group leaders each will privately acknowledge that "postdocs often pull me out of the fire," they stress that this must not be conveyed to the postdocs or anyone else in the community. Each speaks as if he were the only one who has experienced this.

Japanese groups see themselves as much more democratic and less hierarchical than the American groups. The Japanese who have worked in the United States indicate that they were quite surprised by the formality and structure they found there, and they wonder if this is really the best environment for physics. In Japan, the groups make their decisions by consensus, even if they sometimes find the process tedious. It is said that the consensus model is closely adhered to in the southwest, especially at Nagoya, and less so as one moves northeast toward Sendai, where a more "traditional" style is said to prevail. In all the Japanese labs I visited, I found everyone actively discussing various matters of laboratory-wide concern before the decisions were made. All seem to feel themselves well informed. Japanese values direct the leaders, even the most feudal, to consult fully with all those in their groups and, in turn, require all members to advise thoughtfully. The leader is to decide on a policy consistent with both good judgment and the health of the group and its members. In accordance with this ethos of *wa*, it is the responsibility of group members to cooperate with the decision *if* they believe this process has been respected.[5] The demonstrations at the site of the Narita airport were a case in which members of a community rebelled—and are now renewing their campaign—because they felt that they had not been properly consulted.

In the United States, although the style is informal, the group structure is hierarchical. Every decision is made by the group leader, who then informs the group of how it is to be implemented. At SLAC when I asked postdocs what they thought of certain issues confronting the lab, almost all said that they did not know what was going on. A few said bitterly that "they only tell us what's happening after they decide." Often they would question me, saying, "You seem to be better informed than we are."

Those at each level of the hierarchy are expected to observe and listen to those above and pattern their behavior accordingly; it is not appropriate to comment negatively on those in positions of greater status, no matter how informal the relationship. Informality is a gift or reward bestowed by those in charge. Competition is a fundamental tenet of American culture; it is very difficult for most Americans to imagine that competition has any negative implications or that there could be any other motivation for performing with excellence. Where competition is unfettered, as it is supposed to be in the American particle physics community, organizational hierarchy is seen as a *natural* ranking of human talents. The leader is the best and most entitled to judge—otherwise, he would not have become the leader. There is occasional discontent among those excluded from the decision process, but there is no self-doubt among the leaders.

In Japan there is no strict division of labor among the physicists in the lab. They feel that this makes for better experimentalists, with a good understanding of the entire experimental process involving their type of detector. Japanese physicists have in general a wider range of responsibilities than their counterparts in the United States: for example, since so much of the research apparatus is constructed by private industry and then assembled at the lab, experimentalists must be able to design what they want, to choose a manufacturing firm, and to communicate with its representatives in fully explicit detail; there is much less room for trial and error in detector design. And because of the difficulties in attracting trained technicians to a lab, experimentalists must train the technicians themselves, even in the most routine tasks, and closely supervise their work.

In Japan one "cultural" model for a work group is the *ie*.[6] Generally speaking, this refers to an entire household, including its privileges and responsibilities in the network of households of which it is a part. It is the obligation of each member of the *ie* to keep the household and its resources intact and pass them on to the next generation. Status in the *ie* is determined by age, not by competition; there is no strict division of labor, and all members contribute their point of view in discussions about decision making and planning. The organization of most particle physics research groups in Japan is consistent with this model of the *ie*.

In the United States a major "cultural" model of a work group is not a large household, but a sports team.[7] That is, the leader is like a coach directing a team of football players, each of whom has specialized, distinctive skills. The coach is the only team member to understand the entire game process and the only one empowered to design the team's strategies and tactics. The membership and organization of the team survives only as long as it is "winning," accumulating a better record in competition with other teams. If the team consistently loses, the owners will disband the team and assemble a new one, perhaps even relocate to a new city. Any particular game may include, for instance, players and coaches who have worn the other team's uniform; people on different teams may have been teammates once. Obviously, this process generates very strong professional loyalties and very weak institutional ties. This team model is congruent with the organization of research groups in American particle physics, as well as of some of the Japanese groups.

At SLAC the problem of technicians does not exist; they are widely recognized in the community as doing excellent work, often on their own initiative, often quite innovative. Some groups have tried to lure technicians away from one group to another but it is a subtle and complicated process. Almost all of the research apparatus, including the accelerator, is constructed at SLAC. Physicists in the groups work closely with the technicians to build and assemble the parts of their group's detector. There is a rather strict division of labor among the physicists; it is said that only newcomers and the group leader have an overview of what is developing. Curiously, at other American laboratories (such as Brookhaven) where there are fewer highly skilled technicians and sections of the research apparatus may be constructed outside the lab, this same strict division of labor seems to prevail within the group.

Another difference concerns the amount of experience the experimentalists have in working with a variety of detectors. In Japan, research groups are very much identified with a specific kind of detector; this is generally a consequence of the patterns of funding from Monbusho and of the *koza* system. Because of the endogamous recruiting system, once students enter graduate school they have effectively delimited the kinds of research they can do for the rest of their careers. Of course, the establishment of KEK is complicating this somewhat, as does the opportunity to study and work abroad for long periods. In Japan, great emphasis is placed on purity (*wabi*), as opposed to contamination. Blends, amalgamations, and mixtures are not valued at all. To be an unmixed product of one school of thought (*iemoto*) is to display self-discipline and commitment; this is the proper context for achievement and creativity.[8]

By contrast, in the United States, postdocs are typically encouraged to vary their experience by working in areas of physics different from their concentration as students. Some groups have worked, as a whole, on different detectors. Many senior experimentalists seem to have deliberately set about working on a variety of machines before they propose the construction of a new detector of their own design. Americans value independence highly, and consider mobility—exposing oneself to many influences—a sign of independence. Intergenerational allegiances come into force only at the end of the postdoc years and then exogamously—a more lasting loyalty is felt to the mentor than to the group leader.

Although the Japanese groups and networks are fixed and recruits to new positions must come from within and the Americans insist upon movement through groups, especially at the early stages of one's career, the Japanese community seems to tolerate much more diversity in leadership styles and group organization than the Americans. This may be the result of the internal recruitment: one need not adapt to another group's style. The Americans move frequently and expect more similarity. Nevertheless, I would argue that there are two main styles of leadership in each country.

In American universities in general taking a position in the department in which one was trained is considered extremely bad judgment by both the student and the department. It is presumed by others that the student could not be placed elsewhere, either because the student's work was inadequate or because the faculty network ties were weak. The only respectable way to take a position in the department of one's training is to go to another school, establish an independent reputation, and then return. As everyone says, "you must go away to come back." Independence is crucial, in this value system, to achievement and creativity of any kind; indeed it is felt to be a condition of self-discipline and intellectual commitment.

Another contrast concerns the opportunity for senior physicists to bequeath to younger physicists their positions, networks, equipment, such as detectors, and access to scarce resources, such as funding, beamtime, and computer time. For the Japanese these are bestowed by the *koza* leader to his successor; in the United States they must be both redistributed and reconstituted in each generation, perhaps even more often.

The most striking distinction of all between the Japanese and American particle physics communities is in their awareness of historical change. In Japan they assume that they are "underdogs," on the periphery of power, internationally, and they are trying to change that.[9] The Americans with whom I talked approach the core-periphery question with complacency. They agree with the Japanese that the United States is "where it's at."

Americans see this as a contest and they are committed to staying on top. Only in winning is one's effort vindicated; to be second is to be a loser. In Japan to be second is not to be a loser, but to be a younger brother, an honorable role and often a preferable one. The Japanese do not seem to regard their movement toward the core as a contest, but as part of a rather predictable historical process of new scientific communities emerging alongside older ones. At the very least they think it is possible to narrow the gap between their community and the Americans. The Americans apparently believe that their own status in the current international ranking is unchallengeable, unless they are crippled by external events like funding cuts. This lack of historical awareness of change among the Americans, and the acute consciousness of it among the Japanese, is also demonstrated in their different explanations of the decline in funding and quality of students in particle physics.

Current conflicts within the Japanese and American particle physics communities expose the latent instabilities in both. In the American case one such conflict is caused by new pressures to incorporate "client groups" (in anthropological terms) as opposed to individuals into a "residential cluster," incorporating user groups rather than individual novice physicists into the day-to-day organization and management of a laboratory. Incorporating user groups into the management of SLAC disturbs the informal but hitherto highly effective balance within the lab, creating a need for extensive political authority to be concentrated formally in the hands of the director, who consequently no longer merely arbitrates or leads by force of personality. The director no longer is first among equals; his role is now that of a chief and all aspects of social relations are in the process of transformation.

For the Japanese the establishment of KEK as a technically advanced national laboratory means that university groups must circulate through KEK in order to maintain their own power. Groups traditionally kept separate could cultivate differences in styles of leadership and organization; but in moving together at KEK they find that their differences are incommensurable and they cannot work together. In response they are relinquishing their diversity and their exclusive loyalty to their chief and beginning to turn to those who are most adept at dealing with another system of organization: those who have worked abroad. The funding environment for each system is changing, leading to instabilities. That is, scientific funding is now expanding in Japan and leveling off in the United States. The research organizations' structures and leadership styles are no longer appropriate in their new funding environments.

One solution would be for each community to adopt the other's organizational structure and leadership styles. As I have said, examples of both exist in each country: the "coach/team" approach can be found at national laboratories in Japan and the "*sensei/iemoto*" (esteemed teachers/home school) approach can be found in the United States at a few universities, such as MIT, and perhaps even at a national laboratory like the Stanford Linear Accelerator Center. It remains to be seen if each country's scientists will shift away from their dominant styles to the less common model. Will "coaches" who have learned to locate players with highly developed skills and to design strategies for winning every encounter with other teams now begin to build long-lived groups and designate successors? Will *sensei* accustomed to maintaining *ie* across generations and defining the boundaries between *iemoto* now begin to form ties with other *sensei* outside their traditional networks and encourage the new recruits to spend time working in various *iemoto*? Will they allow the next generation to name their own leaders and form their own groups?

The cultural differences between the American and Japanese particle physics community and the recent shifts in the nature of their differences can be observed at work in international interactions. Toward the end of my fieldwork, a Japanese group and one of the groups at SLAC began to arrange a long-term collaboration. The motivations of the two groups were clearly distinct. In recent years, the American and European physicists had suffered from funding declines. Negotiations between the Japanese and United States governments during the administrations of President Carter and Prime Minister Fukuda on the subject of trade imbalances led to significant funds being made available by the Japanese for Japanese-American collaborative research on energy, to be conducted in the United States. One of the group leaders at SLAC realized that he could supplement his group's budget with these new funds: the group's membership would be enlarged by Japanese physicists whose salaries would be paid by the Japanese government, and new components for the group's detector could be constructed, although they would remain the property of the Japanese group. The leader was gaining funding on his own while avoiding negotiations with other leaders and networks in the United States, within and outside the lab, and the concessions such negotiations would entail.

The Japanese group was from a university department with firm ties to INS* and its leader was "strong and active." Following traditional patterns, the leader could establish a new international network tie with the collaboration, which would later allow him to send many of his students and *koshi* abroad for advanced training. He was also following a model established by Fermi in the 1920s and 1930s for building a strong group: gain expertise abroad in specific skills, and then use these at home to construct one's own detector. Furthermore, the *koshi* would build personal ties for international leadership in the next generation for their *koza*.

Both group leaders tried to specify their plans and expectations in writing. Such written contracts are unheard of in the United States and, as far as I know, also in Japan; but in this case, the Japanese physicists in particular came to think that a written accord was appropriate. The Japanese group leader spent two

*[INS is the Institute for Nuclear Study at the University of Tokyo. —Ed.]

weeks talking to many people at SLAC and then said bluntly to the SLAC group leader that he would have greater confidence in their agreement if it were written. Collaborations at SLAC, until the conflict over PEP, had been structured on the model of the strong in-house group and weak user group. The Japanese group leader was restructuring that model still further by insisting on a written agreement. The Japanese group's subtle and thorough investigation of the American group's strengths and weaknesses as seen by American physicists displayed both an astute sense of how to gather such information and a confidence in their own bargaining power. The Japanese leader's extensive consultations and his desire for an open agreement, fully explicit and widely known, were consistent with Japanese practices; he was also seen to be in frequent communication with his home base.

The SLAC group leader signed the agreement he and the Japanese leader wrote. He then showed the document to SLAC's director. They were both nervous about the implications of the written agreement. They decided together that the document only meant that the group leader and the lab "had agreed to agree" with one Japanese, and that the legal dangers and uncertainties were compensated for by the large funding that would come to the group. In sharp contrast to the Japanese practice, these two men made the decision for SLAC. The proposals for funding made by each group to its respective governments were rather different, in spite of the written accord. Each group examined the other's funding report carefully. As the SLAC group leader said when showing me the Japanese proposal, "I know how to read between the lines with Americans and Europeans, but this is different. I don't understand." This same group leader had told me early in my fieldwork that culture had no place in the international particle physics community.

As they tried to work out their collaboration, it had become apparent to both group leaders that they could not rely on shared assumptions and expectations. But they did not identify their problem as a cross-cultural misunderstanding. Both saw themselves primarily as members of the particle physics community and consequently expected to have the same views about how to arrange a collaboration. When they found this was not the case, each began to feel distrust for the other. The Japanese group leader dealt with his suspicion by proposing a written contract. The SLAC group leader agreed, but his distrust was expressed in the close readings that he, the lab director, and SLAC's business manager gave the contract. The gap between them widened when their separate funding proposals emerged, and I was asked "to read between the lines" of the Japanese document. The gap between the lines was the gap between Japanese and American culture. What particularly troubled the SLAC physicist was that the participating Japanese physicists were not listed in order of their reputations. He feared that the Japanese group leader planned to use the physicists in the order they were listed, which could only mean that he was not seriously committed to the collaboration. I showed him that the physicists were listed in order of the rank of their institutions, and within that, according to their age. I told him that this order would impress Monbusho and show professional "savvy," just as ordering by reputation would impress SLAC's program advisory committee. Institutional affiliation was implicit in the explicit American ranking of reputations; the ranking by institutions in the Japanese proposal displayed an understanding of traditional forms. It was assumed in the Japanese document that readers would know informally the reputations of the specific individuals. Each document was straightforward and predictable within the set of shared understandings understood by the author: each was trustworthy within its own culture.

Fortunately, the two physicists also share a culture—the culture of the particle physics community. They both realized that the Japanese group leader was dealing with the collaboration as a negotiation between two strong groups to enlarge a detector. They also knew that the SLAC group leader saw it as an arrangement between an in-house group and a user group for the users' temporary access to a detector he controlled. They also knew that the SLAC group leader saw their "top dog" status verified: the Japanese group accepted their "underdog" status, for the time being. They both understood that the detector itself was central.

The immediate issue confronting the Americans and Japanese in changing subsistence ecologies is how to incorporate new facilities for doing physics, such as PEP and TRISTAN, while maintaining the stable structure of their communities. The Japanese and American collaborators were each preparing their own group to be in a better position to compete for effective use of an anticipated facility at their respective laboratories. The SLAC group wanted to build a new detector at PEP and the Japanese group planned to build one at TRISTAN. Each group was garnering from their collaboration different resources to use in their competition with other groups in their own country. Nevertheless, disputes in the collaboration continued to be formulated in terms of the "in-house" and "user" relationship, as understood by each group. This extended even to the decision regarding final possession of the complete set of data (on computer tape) collected in their experiment. The SLAC group wanted to maintain the prerogatives of an "in-house" group at SLAC: the Japanese insisted on their expected rights as users to data they had not only helped generate, but also helped pay for the equipment to collect.

The high-energy physics communities in each country are debating the model of a good laboratory as part of a larger question: how ought the physics community be organized to pursue physics in the future, as well as in the present? Neither of the experimentalist groups in this story expected at the beginning of their collaboration that their long-term goals would require them to continue negotiating after their experiment concluded. When the Americans arrive at KEK they will discover the subtle and significant differences in the Japanese formulation of the debate about the best environment for physics and how this affects the relationship between "in-house" and "user" groups. That is, they will be confronted with a different formulation of how a national high-energy physics community ought to be organized within the context of the larger international community. Leadership in international physics remains the prize; each country's groups would prefer to see their own teams win. Each side acknowledges the general structure of the enterprise, but strategies and tactics will differ significantly and according to each group's cultural repertoire.[10]

N O T E S

1. See Norman W. Storer, "The Internationality of Science," pp. 444, 460, and Sal P. Restivo and Christopher K. Vanderpool, "The Third Culture of Science," pp. 461–72, in *Comparative Studies in Science and Society*, ed. Sal P. Restivo and Christopher K. Vanderpool (Columbus, Ohio: Charles E. Merrill, 1974).

2. See Takeo Doi, *The Anatomy of Dependence*, trans. John Bester (Tokyo and New York: Kodansha International, 1985), and *The Anatomy of Self: The Individual versus Society*, trans. Mark A. Harbison (Tokyo and New York: Kodansha International, 1986), and Thomas P. Rohlen, "The Promise of Adulthood in Japanese Spiritualism," *Daedalus*. Spring 1976. pp. 125–43.

3. On European physicists' views of the entrepreneurial spirit of American particle physicists, see "CERN Courier's Crystal Ball," *CERN Courier*, December 1977, reprinted in *SLAC Beam Line*, March 1978, p. 8.

4. On Japanese decision making, see David Anson Titus, *Palace and Politics in Prewar Japan* (New York: Columbia University Press, 1974); and Ivan P. Hall, "Organizational Paralysis: The Case of Todai," in *Modern Japanese Organization and Decision Making*, ed. E. F. Vogel and S. Vogel (Berkeley: University of California Press, 1975), pp. 304–30.

5. See Thomas P. Rohlen, *For Harmony and Strength: Japanese White-Collar Organization in Anthropological Perspective* (Berkeley: University of California Press, 1974).

6. See Jane M. Bachnik, "Inside and Outside the Japanese Household (*Ie*): A Contextual Approach to Japanese Social Organization," Ph.D. diss., Harvard University, Cambridge, Mass., 1978. See also *Journal of Japanese Studies*, Special Issue on *Ie* Society, Winter 1985.

7. On the transformation of games into organized sport on the model of corporate capitalism in American cultures, see John Dizikes, *Sportsmen and Gamesmen* (Boston: Houghton Mifflin Co., 1981).

8. On the role of the *iemoto* system in the organization of the arts, see Isao Kamakura, "The *Iemoto* System in Japanese Society," *Japan Foundation Newsletter*, October–November 1981, pp. 1–7; on the way an American anthropologist sees contemporary Japanese society as strongly influenced by the *iemoto* system, see Francis L. K. Hsu, *Iemoto: The Heart of Japan* (New York: Schenkman, 1975).

9. On core and periphery, see Storer, "Internationality of Science," and Restivo and Vanderpool, "Third Culture of Science" (n. 1).

10. On cultural models of conflict and change, see Victor Turner, *Drama, Fields, and Metaphors* (Ithaca, N.Y.: Cornell University Press, 1974). On conflict and change in Japan, see *Conflict in Japan*, ed. Ellis S. Krauss, Thomas P. Rohlen, and Patricia G. Steinhoff (Honolulu: University of Hawaii Press, 1984), and Junichi Kyogoku, *The Political Dynamics of Japan*, trans. Nobutaka Ike (Tokyo: University of Tokyo Press, 1987).

THE "RELEVANCE" OF ANTHROPOLOGY TO COLONIALISM AND IMPERIALISM

Jack Stauder

In the aftermath of a large student rebellion at Harvard in the spring of 1969, a graduate student in anthropology raised a criticism of our field which I have often heard:

> Social anthropology—traditionally a field concerned with explaining and un-
> derstanding small-scale cultures and societies, especially in the non-Western
> world—is a field that could make relevant contributions to our understanding
> of major events and problems of the world: wars of liberation, the effects and
> causes of racism, economic exploitation, colonialism, imperialism. . . . [How-
> ever, departments] ensure that anthropology will remain isolated from and ir-
> relevant to social and political problems. . . . (Anon., p.71)

Many students in anthropology want an anthropology that will provide them with an understanding of "major events and problems of the world." Therefore they demand "relevance," meaning an anthropology relevant to their felt needs. I sympathise with this desire and share it. But the basic issues underlying the complaints in the quoted passage cannot be reached by posing the problem in terms of relevance. By and large, anthropology has always been "relevant." The question to ask is, relevant to whom and for what?

Early Development of British Anthropology

The institutional origins and early growth of British anthropology in the nine-teenth century were closely linked to an interest in the possible practical value of anthropology as an applied science. Members of the early anthropological socie-ties in Britain were especially concerned with questions of race and slavery, great issues which agitated British society throughout the first two-thirds of the cen-tury. Anthropological journals of the time were filled with articles making recom-mendations on these questions. Although it was scarcely to be left to scholars to decide a question involving profits and power relations, many early anthropologists nevertheless hoped that their resources might be of some utility to the interests involved in the expansion of European power around the globe.

The slavery issue died down in the 1870s, as slaves in the Americas became poorly paid "free" plantation labour, and as the slave trade was replaced by other, more "legitimate" forms of exploiting Africa. But the last two decades of the nineteenth century witnessed the acceleration and culmination of British imperialist expansion, particularly in the "scramble" for Africa in which Britain succeeded in asserting against other European powers her claims to rule or "protect" diverse territories with large native populations. During the same period, anthropology was attaining academic respectability in Britain (in the form of university chairs), and some of its promoters hoped to ally the new science of man not with controversial popular causes, as had been the case in the pro- and anti-slavery debates earlier in the century, but with the science of good government, specifically the administration of colonial peoples.

A survey of the twenty-seven presidential addresses to the Royal Anthropological Institute from 1893 to 1919 shows that in over half the president raised claims regarding the practical uses to which anthropology could be put in serving the Empire. Frequently the complaint was made that, despite anthropology's potential practical value, neither government nor business seemed interested, and little in the way of funds or official recognition seemed forthcoming. These complaints were largely unheeded in the following years: in 1910 British anthropologists were refused even a grant of £500 from the government to set up an "Imperial Bureau of Anthropology" within the Royal Anthropological Institute (Ridgeway, p. 10).

Thus, around the turn of the century in Britain, anthropology found itself in a peculiar position. The British Empire was at its zenith, rapidly extending its effective rule over millions of new subjects. The period was marked by Victorian confidence in the application of science to achieve progress and profits. British anthropologists were promoting their new science as a potentially valuable tool to be used in the imperial mission, to aid government and commerce and the advance of "civilisation." Anthropologists were desperately courting government for private recognition and especially financial support for anthropology in its potential uses as they saw them. But government and wealthy benefactors were spurning these advances and seemed little interested.

This discrepancy between anthropologists' desire to serve British imperialism and the lack of support for anthropology by the British ruling class is a phenomenon probably explained less by the short-sightedness of the ruling classes than by the shortcomings of anthropology at the time. For despite the assertions of anthropologists, the actual state of British anthropology at the turn of the century was such that in practice it was producing mostly work of little or no possible use to colonial administrators, missionaries and traders. In the years before World War I, anthropology in Britain was dominated by controversies between diffusionists and evolutionists,[1] who held in common, however, an historical and often speculative approach that was primarily concerned with reconstructing the past of mankind. Few professionally trained anthropologists had seen Africa or other colonised areas first-hand, and anthropologists at home were dependent for their data mainly on the reports of untrained observers engaged directly in the colonising process. It is little wonder then that the picture anthropology gave of Africa up to the First World War was very unreal.

It has been argued that it was the very distortions and lack of truth in nineteenth-century anthropology which made it useful during the early periods of imperial enterprise. But if nineteenth-century ethnology[2] was eminently suitable as an intellectual justification for colonial expansion, it was not well suited at all to the succeeding era of colonial consolidation and exploitation. Populations of Africans, once pacified, needed to be administered. Ideas about African culture and society which were grossly unreal or distorted were no help in this second stage of colonialism; in fact, lack of proper understanding of Africans might well stand in the way of achievement of British colonial goals: to rule with a minimum of trouble and cost and with a maximum of stability and profit.

A few astute colonial administrators around the turn of the century realised that they needed better and more systematic information about the people they were ruling. These administrators took the initiative in demanding that anthropology be taught to colonial officers and others working in parts of the Empire, and special anthropology courses were subsequently set up at Oxford and Cambridge for officers on leave and cadets training for the colonial service.

Sometimes administrators who showed an interest in anthropology were assigned to investigations involving the collection of ethnographic materials. Also in a very few cases colonial governments had obtained the services of professional anthropologists to provide the colonial government with knowledge of the social organisation and customs of particular peoples as a background for administration (Forde, pp. 843–46). This handful of persons had begun to write a few relatively systematic and reliable accounts of African cultures by the 1920s.

On at least a descriptive level, some of these early ethnographies achieved their design of providing the kind of information about a subject people's culture and society that could be of some use to administration and missionary work. But while often exhaustively descriptive, their books lacked explanatory power: when necessary they resorted to diffusionist or evolutionary hypotheses to explain particular customs; for although these ethnographers were primarily interested in the present life of the peoples they observed, they lacked a theoretical framework appropriate for their purpose.

By the 1910s and 1920s there was a growing felt need in British colonial Africa for a "newer anthropology" that would be adaptable to the practical requirements of British imperialism. And, as I have indicated, British anthropologists had constantly aspired to serve the Empire and by so doing to serve what they saw as the interests of anthropologists by obtaining funds and recognition. I have suggested that the major obstacle to this mutually beneficial alliance between colonialism and anthropology lay in the current state of anthropological theory and practice, or lack of it. The "older" anthropology, ethnology, diffusionism, and evolutionism stood in the way of progress. The time was ripe for revolution.

The conscious element in the revolution has rightly been identified with the names of Malinowski and Radcliffe-Brown. But it was certainly Radcliffe-Brown who was the more conscious of what he was doing. In the same year (1922) that their pioneering functionalist[3] studies, *Argonauts of the Western Pacific* and *The Andaman Islanders,* were published, Radcliffe-Brown was teaching in South Africa in the new post of professor of social anthropology at the University of Capetown. In vol. 1, no. 3 of the South African journal *Bantu Studies* of that year appeared an article by Radcliffe-Brown entitled "Some Problems of Bantu Sociology." In his opening paragraph the author indicated that to his mind the key problem for "Bantu sociology" was in fact the problem of colonialism:

> In Africa, more perhaps than in any other part of the world, social anthropology is a subject not of merely scientific or academic interest, but of immense practical importance. The one great problem on which the future welfare of South Africa depends is that of finding some social and political system in which the natives and the whites may live together without conflict; and the successful solution of that problem would certainly seem to require thorough knowledge of the native civilisation between which and our own we need to establish some sort of harmonious relation.

Radcliffe-Brown adds that "in the establishment of the department of social anthropology in the University of Capetown this practical importance of the subject has been kept constantly in view, and the teaching and research are being organised on this basis" (p. 38).

In his article Radcliffe-Brown goes on to make several other points: the importance of the study of kinship for understanding African society; the importance of fieldwork; and the superiority of the functionalist approach over an historical or ethnological approach. He explains that

> In dealing with the facts of culture or civilisation amongst primitive peoples who have no historical records there are two methods of explanation that we may adopt. The first may be called the ethnological method; it attempts, by the co-ordinated study of physical characters, language and the various elements of culture, and with the help of such archaeological knowledge as is available, to reconstruct hypothetically the past history of a people in its main outlines. Such problems are very interesting. . . . But interesting as it is, and important as its results may sometimes be, this ethnological method does not often provide, and does not seem likely to provide, results that will be of any assistance to the administrator or the educator in the solution of the practical problems with which he is faced. (P. 39)

An alternative method of dealing with culture Radcliffe-Brown calls the "sociological," i.e., the structural-functionalist:

> The aim of this method is not to reconstruct the history of a people but to interpret their institutions in the light of general laws of sociology and psychology. If, for example, we investigate by this method the custom of [lobola

(bridewealth)], we seek to determine the function of that custom, what essential or important relations it has with other institutions, what part it really plays in the economic, moral and religious life of the tribe, and to what important needs of the social organism it is related. Such an investigation thoroughly carried out would enable the anthropologist to foretell with some degree of certainty what would be the general effects on the life of a tribe of an attempt to abolish the custom in question. (Pp. 39–40)

In "Some Problems of Bantu Sociology" Radcliffe-Brown came to the conclusion that "the study of such problems, the sociological and psychological problems of native life, is certainly far more likely to lead to results of practical value to South Africa than the study of ethnological problems" (p. 40). A year later, in 1923, Radcliffe-Brown returned to this argument in an address entitled "The Methods of Ethnology and Social Anthropology," presented to the South African Association for the Advancement of Science (1923). In this address he opens a full-scale attack on all the different approaches to culture current at the time: the psychological approach, the evolutionist approach, the ethnological or diffusionist approach. To demolish the older kind of anthropology to make way for the newer, sociological and functionalist anthropology he proposes, he raises as a final argument the criterion of which kind of anthropology can best serve the interests of colonialism: "Now while ethnology with its strictly historical method can only tell us that certain things have happened, or have probably or possibly happened, social anthropology with its inductive generalisations can tell us how and why things happen, i.e., according to what laws" (p. 141). Radcliffe-Brown advances his faith that ultimately knowledge of such laws of social behaviour will give men control over social forces and "enable us to attain to practical results of the very greatest importance" (p. 30).

Stability and unity in society were of course the conditions which corresponded to the fundamental theoretical concepts on which Radcliffe-Brownian sociology was to be based: namely the concepts of integration, equilibrium and solidarity. These were more than abstract concepts in the context of South African society, where a subject but increasingly rebellious African population outnumbered the white settlers trying to dominate and exploit them. Radcliffe-Brown continues in relation to the racial confrontation in South Africa:

> Now I think this is where social anthropology can be of immense and almost immediate service. The study of the beliefs and customs of the native peoples, with the aim not of merely reconstructing their history but of discovering their meaning, their function, that is, the place they occupy in the mental, moral and social life, can afford great help to the missionary or the public servant who is engaged in dealing with the practical problems of the adjustment of the native civilisation to the new conditions that have resulted from our occupation of the country. . . . (Pp. 142–43).

In fact much if not most British social anthropology in Africa during the 1930s and 1940s was to be focused on political and legal institutions. Such an emphasis must be seen in the light of the strategy adopted by British colonialism to implement and maintain social control over the millions of people under its government in Africa. This strategy, which came to be known as "Indirect Rule," avoided where possible the use of direct administration and direct coercion—though, of course, military force was always held in reserve. Given a necessity to economise manpower and finances in Africa, British colonial governments preferred to retain and utilise traditional political institutions. These were integrated into the colonial administration, and traditional political authorities were maintained as paid agents of colonial rule. But if African political institutions were to be adapted and used by colonial government, it was imperative to understand what they were and how they worked; to this end, anthropology was often seen as critically necessary. As E. W. Smith noted, "the extension of Indirect Rule has been preceded by, and based upon, anthropological research" (p. xxii).

In the context of Indirect Rule, functionalist social anthropology seemed obviously superior to the older, ethnological approach, for the "newer" social anthropology not only concentrated on identifying and describing the key social and political institutions of a subject people, but it also attempted to analyse how these institutions worked. Those concerned with problems of administration and knowledgeable about anthropology came to accept the validity of Radcliffe-Brown's claims on behalf of the practical superiority of the functionalist method (Hailey, pp. 42–45; Smith, pp. xvii–xxv).

Traditional African societies were usually seen by the functionalists, as well as by the colonial governments, as being "healthy" societies, well-balanced, well-integrated and maintaining an enviable degree of social control over their members. The British strategy of Indirect Rule had aimed to incorporate and preserve these integrated and stable units within an integrated and stable Empire. This intention, however, was progressively being undermined by two other contradictory features of British imperialism: by the racist assumption that European civilisation was culturally superior to African civilisation and destined to replace it; and, more importantly in the long run, by the European drive to exploit Africa economically and the radical socio-economic transformation this entailed in the lives of African people.

Astute colonialists, including foresighted anthropologists like Radcliffe-Brown, regarded the symptoms of social change with alarm. They saw the old tribal systems disintegrating and asked how they could arrest and control the forces which had been unleashed. Radcliffe-Brown definitely considered it the mission of anthropology to provide colonial agencies with the necessary knowledge about the processes of social integration and change. The same concern, both theoretical and practical, can be seen in the work of other British functionalist anthropologists in Africa in the 1920s through the 1950s. Such concern might reflect the hopes, on the part of some anthropologists, that by protecting the social fabric from disruption they could spare the peoples they studied from some of the worst consequences of colonialism. But such conservatism can also be seen as ultimately protective of colonial rule itself, for the social health of native society was linked in the colonial mind with the political health of the British Empire.

For example, Radcliffe-Brown offers a clue as to the ultimate source of anxiety underlying his recommendations: "One can feel quite certain that more knowledge of the nature of Indian culture and proper grasp of the laws of social integration would have prevented our long experiment with India from reaching its present unsatisfactory position" ("Applied Anthropology," p. 279).

In India at that time an organised movement for national independence had emerged as a definite threat to British rule. In Africa less organised rebellions against colonialism had also occurred and would soon develop into movements for national liberation. These anti-colonial struggles were an underlying source of worry to colonialists and anthropologists like Radcliffe-Brown who saw in them the final outcome of the tendencies they regarded as "social disintegration." The ultimate concern of these far-sighted men, it could be suggested, was to arrest the process of disintegration of traditional societies, not for the sake of the people living in them, but in order to arrest the incipient process of disintegration of the British Empire itself.

In retrospect we see of course that Radcliffe-Brown's ambitions for anthropology were unrealistic. Neither social science nor enlightened administration could contain the forces, set in motion by colonialism, which would eventually undermine and overthrow the British Empire. But these developments, and the rapidity with which they would take place, were not clearly foreseen in the 1920s and 1930s, and Radcliffe-Brown's optimism about the potential applicability of a revolutionised sociology and functionalist anthropology carried the opinions of those who counted. For many decades anthropologists had been claiming that they could be of practical service to government and business. But as I have pointed out, before the 1920s these claims were mainly ignored by the interests on whom they were pressed. During the late 1920s and into the 1930s, however, this situation changed fairly rapidly, and the alliance long anticipated by anthropologists was established. British anthropology was suddenly and increasingly successful in gaining recognition and substantial funding from private and governmental sources.

For 1925 the Council of the Royal Anthropological Institute reported a momentous breakthrough. For the first time in the history of the association it had received large donations from outside sources: £1,000 from the Carnegie Trust and $17,500 from the Rockefeller Trust. In 1931 the Rockefeller Foundation made a further grant of $10,500 to the institute. These grants were small in terms of Rockefeller disbursements but they were unprecedentedly large sums in terms of the institute's normal budget, which had always been less than $3,000 a year before 1925, the bulk of this income coming from memberships and subscriptions to the journal (RAI, 1926, 1927, 1930).

But a more important development for the future of anthropology in Africa occurred in 1926 with the foundation in London of the International African Institute. The institute's aims were to bring about "a closer association of scientific knowledge and research with practical affairs" (Lugard, p. 2). The institute was established with contributions and support from all the colonial governments in Africa as well as from the British and French home governments, and from various missionary bodies (Hailey, pp. 51–52). On the governing board of the institute sat a mixture of former colonial administrators, heads of missionary associations, and eminent academics specialising in African studies. The first head of the institute was Lord Lugard, famous not only as a soldier for his role in the "pacification" of many parts of Africa but notable also as an administrator and as the architect of the theory of "Indirect Rule" practised in British Africa. It was Lord Lugard who, in *The Dual Mandate in British Tropical Africa* (1922), had described the "African negro" as follows:

> . . . a happy, thriftless, excitable person, lacking in self-control, discipline, and foresight, naturally courageous, and naturally courteous and polite, full of personal vanity, with little sense of veracity. . . . His thoughts are concentrated on the events and feelings of the moment, and he suffers little from apprehension for the future, or grief for the past. . . .
>
> The African negro is not naturally cruel, though his own insensibility to pain, and his disregard for life—whether his own or another's—cause him to appear callous to suffering. . . .
>
> He lacks power of organisation, and is conspicuously deficient in the management and control alike of men or of business. . . . He is very prone to imitate anything new in dress or custom. . . .
>
> In brief, the virtues and the defects of this race-type are those of attractive children. . . .
>
> It is extremely difficult . . . to find educated African youths who are by character and temperament suited to posts in which they may rise to positions of high administrative responsibility.

The International African Institute was to play a leading role in social science research in British Africa. From the 1930s to the present it has financed the publishing of many of the best ethnographies about African peoples, and its journal *Africa* has carried many of the most important anthropological articles about Africa. Many of these books and articles were closely related to colonial problems and "practical affairs."

That the institute was able to succeed in playing such a vital role in stimulating and shaping anthropological research in Africa was due in no small part to the grant of $250,000 it received in 1931 from the Rockefeller Foundation. Thus the bulk of professional anthropological research in British Africa in the late 1920s and the 1930s was dependent on Rockefeller money in one way or another—money which of course partially derived from the profits of the growing Rockefeller financial and mineral holdings in Africa. Whether or not the trustees of the Rockefeller Foundation had ever heard of Radcliffe-Brown, the "newer" anthropology he was championing, with its emphasis on scientific applicability, stood to thrive on the disbursement of Rockefeller grants.

'Indirect Rule" and the Functions of Functionalism

In any case, it was in the late 1920s and early 1930s that anthropology in the British Empire began receiving in substantial sums the money which allowed the profession to be greatly expanded and which allowed anthropologists to pursue foreign fieldwork as a matter of course. Apparently anthropology had finally convinced colonial governments and capitalist benefactors of its potential practical uses to them. The struggle for acceptance which British anthropology had waged for more than half a century was successful.

However, the kind of anthropology which had succeeded was functionalist social anthropology. Ethnology, the historical approach, inquiries into the origins of culture: this kind of anthropology did not succeed; in fact it hardly survived in Britain. Research and writing was increasingly, and finally overwhelmingly, social anthropological and functionalist in character. Other anthropological approaches were less and less funded, published or practised. A new orthodoxy had been established and was to dominate British anthropology until at least the end of the British Empire in the 1950s and 1960s.

Whatever the theoretical advantages of the new functionalist approach, and whatever the methodological abuses of the historical approaches at the time, one must still ask why functionalism triumphed so rapidly and completely in Britain and her colonies whereas it made slower and only partial inroads into the anthropological currents of other nations such as the United States, France, Belgium, the Netherlands, etc., and no inroads into the anthropology of Germany and Eastern Europe. No doubt many factors can be adduced, but I would argue that this situation may be at least partly explained in terms of the differing colonial commitments and colonial systems of the various powers—or the absence of colonies in the case of Germany (after World War I) and Eastern European countries. To verify this hypothesis would of course require an analysis of the anthropology in other countries, a task which cannot be attempted here. But a crude correlation apparently exists between the successful spread of functionalist social anthropology in several countries and the degree of colonial commitment of each of these countries. In this respect, the British Empire was exceptional. It was far larger than other colonial empires both in terms of the absolute population of non-whites being ruled as well as in terms of the ratio of non-white subjects to the population of the mother country.

In sub-Saharan Africa, British colonies included a larger population than the French, Belgian and Portuguese colonies combined. It was in these African colonies that manpower shortages and the costs involved in administration were especially serious. Lord Lugard and other British colonial officials of the time were explicit about this problem as well as about its importance in arguing for a system of "Indirect Rule." The British attempted a system of adapting and utilising indigenous institutions which made it especially important for administrators and others in the African colonies to understand native institutions—hence the supreme usefulness to them of a social science which attempted to describe and explain the systematic functioning of these institutions.

What I am suggesting, tentatively, is that the critical factor in the British adoption of a thorough-going system of Indirect Rule in Africa is to be found in the magnitude of the British imperialist mission there and elsewhere. And I am also suggesting, again very tentatively, that the critical factor in the thorough adoption in Britain of the functionalist approach in anthropology was related to the same colonial situation: the need to preserve, understand and utilise native institutions in controlling subject populations in Africa. At the very least I think it is possible to demonstrate that the demands for a "practical" anthropology—an anthropology useful to British imperialism—did play an important role in the determination of the theoretical direction British anthropology was to follow.

While recognising that more research is needed in these areas, I believe my interpretation is oriented in the right direction: towards an interpretation of the development of anthropology in terms of the material situation in which it was practised. Accounts by Evans-Pritchard and others of the development of anthropological thought in Britain have tended to be exclusively idealist in their approach: that is, they try to explain ideas in terms only of ideas. In these accounts the synchronic functionalist approach triumphed simply because it was theoretically superior to other approaches. Such interpretations avoid the question: superior for what purpose? or, superior in what situation? In terms of the colonial situation an alternative explanation is possible to account for the success of the synchronic functionalist approach in the anthropology of the British Empire. In this explanation functionalist social anthropology can be seen as itself functionally adaptive to the requirements of British imperialism. Therefore this approach was recognised and supported by the dominant institutions participating in the imperialist enterprise and was thereby greatly aided in becoming the dominant theoretical ideology of British anthropology.

What I have also indicated is the necessity for reassessing the view of British functionalism current among many anthropologists and anthropology students. This view, simply put, seems to be that because a narrowly synchronic functionalist approach was inadequate to explain social change, therefore functionalism is and was irrelevant to social problems or problems of the "real" world such as imperialism. In fact, I am suggesting, functionalism was very relevant to colonialism and the social problems of its day. Such relevance is seen in the attention almost all the noted British functionalists paid to questions of applied anthropology; almost all wrote more than one article on the subject (for references see Forde, pp. 862–65; Mair). And of course the sources of support for British anthropologists, their choice of problems and their activities in the field and elsewhere in co-operation with colonial governments were all politically relevant at the time, whether or not the anthropologists wished to recognise this.

Let us take an example, the origins of a modern anthropological classic: E. E. Evans-Pritchard's research among the Nuer. This research, conducted almost forty years ago, resulted in *The Nuer,* a pioneering study employing structural-functional analysis and an equilibrium model to analyse the Nuer lineage system, their ecology and political behaviour. Students who read *The Nuer* usually find it an interesting or even a fascinating study but generally do not find that it contributes to their "understanding of major events and problems of the world." In this sense *The Nuer* appears to be irrelevant anthropology.

In fact, in its historical context, Evans-Pritchard's research did have a relevance and remains revealing today if we look at its genesis. In the first line of his preface to *The Nuer*, Evans-Pritchard states: "My study of the Nuer was undertaken at the request of, and mainly financed by, the Government of the Anglo-Egyptian Sudan, which also contributed generously towards the publication of its result." The Nuer were clearly not selected for study out of pure scientific curiosity. What was the urgency, the necessity, of a study of the Nuer?

Later in the book Evans-Pritchard supplies us with the information needed:

> The truculence and aloofness displayed by the Nuer is conformable to their culture, their social organisation and their character. The self-sufficiency and simplicity of their culture and the fixation of their interests on their herds explain why they neither wanted nor were willing to accept European innovations and why they rejected peace from which they had everything to lose. . . . Had more been known about them a different policy might have been instituted earlier and with less prejudice.
>
> In 1920 large-scale military operations, including bombing and machine-gunning of camps, were conducted against the Eastern Jikany and caused much loss of life and destruction of property. There were further patrols from time to time, but the Nuer remained unsubdued. In 1927 the Nuong tribe killed their District Commissioner while at the same time the Lou openly defied the Government and the Gaawar attacked Duk Faiyuil Police Post. From 1928 to 1930 prolonged operations were conducted against the whole of the disturbed area and marked the end of serious fighting between the Nuer and the Government. (Pp. 134ff.)

Evans-Pritchard recounts these personal hardships in his introduction to apologise for his work being only a "contribution to the ethnology of a particular area rather than a detailed sociological study" (p. 15). Other than to explain his misfortune in his book, he is not interested in how the Nuer were reacting to colonial aggression, and to himself as a perceived agent of colonialism. And except for the incidental passage quoted above, he does not describe the British war against the Nuer, much less the nature of British colonial policy and administration in the Sudan. Studying the colonial government was not a government anthropologist's job.

The Nuer is therefore mostly irrelevant to our understanding of colonialism, or of how a people might resist it or how they fail and are conquered. But was Evans-Pritchard's work irrelevant to colonialism? That the colonial government should support his work and direct his enquiries indicates that they thought it was not irrelevant for their purposes. Exactly how the intelligence Evans-Pritchard gathered was applied by administrators we do not know since this was not a fit subject for study; but the understanding which had been acquired of the Nuer political system, their values, their ecology, etc., would have a definite usefulness. Bombs, machine-guns and mercenaries were wasted trouble and expense if the Nuer could be dominated and administered "peacefully" (with force in reserve). "Peaceful" domination must rely on manipulation; and manipulation rests on knowledge. Evans-Pritchard's work was therefore *not* 'isolated from and irrelevant to social and political problems'—in fact it originated in the need of British imperialism for information to deal with its problems.

Of course most anthropologists in the colonial era were not directly employed by governments, nor did most arrive to do research in the immediate wake of war or rebellion. Nevertheless the position of most anthropologists in colonial territories was essentially the same. They were expected to gather information and provide insights which would aid colonial governments in administering colonial peoples; most ethnographers of the period prefaced their books with the wish that their work might prove helpful to the administrator.

The funding of anthropology in the 1920s and 1930s has already been described. After World War II funding was increasingly channelled through the various colonial governments and the various regional social science institutes in Africa. That Africa's first social science institute should be established in Northern Rhodesia, in the general vicinity of the largest Western investments in Africa (South Africa, the Rhodesias, Katanga), is probably not coincidental. A full account of the development of the Rhodes-Livingstone Institute, and of the extent to which the intentions of its founders and patrons influenced its research, is a study that remains to be done. But recently some of the most notable theoretical and practical work that has come out of the Institute has come under the sharp attack of an African anthropologist for its pro-colonialist, pro-employer bias (Magubane).

Many colonial anthropologists probably thought of themselves doing work that was primarily "scholarly" rather than "practical," but the distinction was not cut-and-dried in terms of "relevance" to colonial administrators. As Lucy Mair says,

> We should not put an account of the social structure of an African people in a separate category as a "theoretical" study because it was not focused on some problem of special concern to the government of the day, although of course we should agree that many of the generalisations which such accounts make possible are of more interest to the theorist of society than to the practitioner of government. We recognise, too, that some studies bear more closely on problems of policy than others, and priority lists were drawn up with these in mind. Studies concerned with the changes currently taking place in African society have a prominent place among these. (P. 98)

Anthropology in British colonial Africa—and, I would submit, in other areas under colonial domination as well—was basically very "relevant" to the colonial governments and to the imperialist systems of which they were part. Anthropologists helped gather the intelligence about native people which allowed these people to be efficiently ruled and exploited in the colonial interest—that is, in the interests of the white settlers, the colonial administrators, the government in the metropolitan country, and the Western capitalist enterprises in Africa. Most anthropologists accepted as given this imperialist framework and its concomitant myths. Then, as always, the reality of violent domination and exploitation was cloaked by rhetoric and myth assuming a harmony of interest between ruler and ruled, exploiter and exploited.

Naturally many anthropologists developed sympathies for the people they lived with and studied. Some of them, as Kathleen Gough Aberle has noted, took the role of "white liberal reformers" and tried to intercede to protect the people they studied "against the worst forms of the imperialist exploitation" (p. 13). Such attempts, however, did not basically challenge the imperialist system. As this system was predicated on domination and exploitation, it was basically impossible for anthropology and anthropologists to serve the interests of the people they studied by suggesting reforms. What anthropologists may have come to think and say about colonial policies and practices was of little moment compared to the services they rendered colonial interests by providing them with intelligence relevant to these interests' continuing domination and exploitation of the peoples studied. In short, anthropologists were part of the colonial system; few if any of them really opposed this system with the perspective of overthrowing it. In fact, probably most anthropologists, consciously or unconsciously, accepted unquestioned their roles and concomitant privileges in the colonial system, and their work was generally confined and directed by it (see Maquet; also Harris, pp. 514–67).

The Relevance of Contemporary Anthropology: The American Experience

But what of anthropology today? What of its relevance to "major events and problems of the world"? Direct colonial administration of most tropical countries has been abandoned after several wars and numerous rebellions and threats of mass unrest: the colonial powers were forced to accept a policy of strategic retreat. Did this mean the end of imperialism and of anthropologists' service to it? I would argue the contrary, that imperialism as a force in the world is stronger than ever, that neo-colonialism has replaced the older forms of colonialism, and that the "relevance" of anthropology remains essentially the same as I have described it under the old colonialism. The main change has been that the United States has now become the leading imperialist power in the world.

What relevance does anthropology have to U.S. imperialism—specifically to U.S. government and business operations abroad and at home? It is no secret that private and government agencies employ, either regularly or on a contract basis, a not inconsiderable number of anthropologists to do work directly related to furthering the interests of U.S. government and business. The Agency for International Development (AID), the Central Intelligence Agency (CIA), the Defence Department's Advance Research Projects Agency (ARPA), the Centre for Research in Social Systems (CRESS)—formerly the Special Operations Research Organisation (SORO)—the Human Relations Research Office (HumRRO) and their various projects all maintain stables of social scientists including anthropologists. So do other government agencies and numerous private research corporations like the Atlantic Research Corporation, A. D. Little, Human Science Research, Simulmatics Inc., etc., which specialise in classified contract work for the government. Large industrial corporations also occasionally employ anthropologists.

What work do these anthropologists do? We may assume that they are employed to do work "relevant" to the needs of their employers. Much of this work is kept classified: only portions which do not compromise the interests of the sponsor may be allowed to be published for scholarly audiences. What we learn about this work is usually accidental or indirect. For example, titles of classified projects sometimes appear in the *Congressional Record,* e.g., for ARPA; "Rural Value Systems, Republic of Vietnam," by Human Sciences Research; "Thai-Malay Village Study (Project Agile)," by M. L. Thomas, Northern Illinois University, etc. Or, more vaguely, we note a great increase of research interest in poverty-stricken and minority group areas of Thailand since the beginning of guerrilla activity there.

However, here I am not interested in the issue of classified research per se. Rather, I am trying to make the point that anthropology clearly does have a relevance to "major events and problems of the world" we live in. For I assume that the U.S. government and U.S. corporations are paying for, and sequestering, knowledge that is relevant to their interests. [For a select listing of behavioral science contracts from the mid-1960s, see the accompanying table.]

This situation was probably brought home for the first time to most anthropologists by the revelations concerning Project Camelot (see I. L. Horowitz). For this project many social scientists including anthropologists were approached to undertake studies to make

> it possible to predict and influence politically significant aspects of social change in the developing nations of the world. . . . The US Army has an important mission in the positive and constructive aspects of nation-building in less developed countries as well as a responsibility to assist friendly governments dealing with active insurgency problems. (From the recruiting letter for Project Camelot, in I. L. Horowitz, pp. 47–49)

In the words of two commentators:

> The Camelot project is but one of the more blatant large scale counterinsurgency research efforts that the behavioural sciences have shown little hesitancy to undertake, especially if the money is plentiful and if "basic research" can somehow be integrated into the design.

Select Behavioral Science Contracts Related to Foreign Areas and Foreign Populations

Title	Location	Description
1963 American Mount Everest Expedition	Berkeley Institute of Psychological Research	Psychological aspects of stress behavior.
Changing values in Japanese, Americans, and Japanese-Americans	Institute of Advanced Projects, University of Hawaii	Analysis of how Japanese change their values as they come in contact with American culture.
International conflict (Israel and Egypt)	Stanford University	Analysis of relationship of opinions and writings of decision makers and the actual decisions rendered.
Foreign research symposia	Social Sciences Research Council	Meetings of American and foreign scholars in Europe on social psychology.
Persuasive communications in the international field	University of Wisconsin	How foreign nationalities react to various kinds of American communications.
Sociopolitical precursors to insurgency	Pennsylvania State College	Study of insurgency and causes related to it to determine role Navy plays.
Nationalism and the perception of international crises	University of Texas	Perceptions that people have of international crises and relating this to the psychology of the persons involved.
Group factors influencing creativity	University of Illinois	Discovering how a heterogenous group can establish a common communication system in order to be effective; some of these groups composed of individuals of different languages and cultural backgrounds.
Group equilibrium	Rutgers University	Studies made in U.S.A. on small group effectiveness have been replicated in Japan.
Role theory	University of Missouri	Theory of role structure. Work being done with collaborators in Australia and England.
Cross-cultural investigation of some factors in persuasion and attitude change	University of Maryland	Structure and mechanics of attitude change methods; research replicated with Japanese subjects to determine generality of findings.

Source: *Behavioral Sciences and the National Security,* Report No. 4 (Washington, D.C.: U.S. Government Printing Office, 1965).

Camelot was still-born, but counterinsurgency is alive and healthy in the social sciences. (Kaufman and Park, pp. 12–13)

The American Anthropological Association reported to its members that "The Fellows should recognise that although Camelot is dead under that name, in a sense it has only gone underground. Similar types of projects have been conducted and are being planned under different names and through other kinds of agencies" (AAA, p. 9).

Most anthropologists, however, have no direct connections with the Department of Defence or the other agencies I have mentioned. Most anthropologists receive their funds for research from non-defence agencies like the National Institute for Mental Health (NIMH), the National Science Foundation (NSF), the Smithsonian Institution and the Ford Foundation. They apparently choose their own subjects of research, and their research is not classified. What is the relevance of this kind of research to imperialist interests?

Most anthropologists have regarded the NIMH and the NSF as operating in an autonomous manner, as a sort of left hand of the government, oblivious to the requirements of the right hand, the Departments of Defence and State and the CIA. Credence is given this appearance by the fact that anthropologists rather than government officials have been sitting on the panels deciding grants and fellowships. The government, particularly under the Kennedy administration, has not failed to recognise that "basic research" in the social sciences is not at all irrelevant to government requirements, especially in the long run. Thus work not immediately relevant to "defence" purposes has been funded, and anthropologists have been allowed to decide who among them and their students should receive support. Of course such independence is only allowed by a government confident that the profession will police itself: that it will not approve projects likely to conflict with the "national" interests and that it will approve projects that on the whole are supportive of the government's long-range requirements. In general this means useful knowledge about the peoples and problems the U.S. government and U.S. corporations may have to deal with.

The lead in shaping social science research to the needs of the U.S. government and large corporations has been taken less by government agencies than by the major private foundations: Ford, Carnegie and Rockefeller. The top officers and trustees of these foundations come of course from the ruling circles of business and government. And the wealth of these foundations is of course invested in capitalist enterprises, many of them with foreign holdings of the sort that U.S. foreign policy is designed above all to protect and advance. Since their inception, these private foundations have been instrumental in serving the interests they represent by shaping U.S. education in general, and the social sciences in particular. (For an extensive discussion of these activities, see David Horowitz in *Ramparts*.)

An example of the foundations' influence on anthropology is the leading role played by the Ford Foundation in establishing and shaping "area studies" programmes. Ford has sponsored massive research programmes in every strategically important area of the world, and Ford has funded most U.S. centres of foreign affairs research. In African studies alone, Ford has exercised a dominant influence. It has provided hundreds of fellowships for research in Africa and it has helped set up and fund most of the major African studies institutes. What has been Ford's purpose? In 1958 Ford set up a special study committee to report on the needs which African studies had to meet. "Without any reluctance," they wrote,

> the Committee has been able to agree on the unwisdom of academic aloofness from the needs of national policy, or of Africa itself. It seems to us most appropriate and desirable to encourage Africanists individually and in their associations, to provide assistance in professional consultation, in training for specific needs, in designing research so as to be useful to government and business. (Cowan *et al.,* p. 12)

Anthropology and U.S. Imperialism

It is my contention, then, that the two major sources of funds for American anthropological research—the U.S. government and the large foundations—use their money and influence in ways both direct and indirect to ensure that research is done "relevant" to (i.e., serving) their interests in managing "major events and problems of the world" today. Of course some research is more immediately relevant than other research: the more relevant research is a more likely candidate for support, but "basic" research has not been ignored. The most prosaic study of the social structure or religion or psychology of an obscure ethnic group may prove useful for controlling this group. If not critical information at the moment, it may be tomorrow in an unstable world.

What I have been arguing is simply that anthropology, as an institutional activity, is not autonomous and not unrelated to other institutions of our social system. As an activity dependent for its support on the dominant institutions of our society—the federal government, the large corporations and the large private foundations—anthropology is expected to serve the interests that control these institutions and the universities. As these interests extend to foreign countries, anthropological research on foreign peoples can provide "relevant" knowledge to aid the U.S. government and U.S. corporations in achieving their goals. Urban and rural anthropological research within America can aid the same interests to achieve similar goals.

The system of political and economic domination of hundreds of millions of people—U.S. imperialism—is a system which, far from offering hope to the world's people, blocks their aspirations and oppresses them. Neither does U.S. imperialism benefit most people in the United States: in fact it helps the same small class of corporate capitalists and their politicians maintain a system of domination and exploitation at home. (Kaufman and Park, pp. 9–11, 19–23, summarise this argument.) Yet the people anthropologists study are not members of this ruling class or allied elites abroad. Anthropologists study the people who are oppressed by imperialism. We live among them, make friends with them, and most of us come to sympathise with their aspirations. We would like to think that we are responsible to them, that we would serve their interests if we could, that we would side with them against oppression. Do we?

This is the real contradiction in anthropology today—not the question of "relevance." For as I have tried to show, anthropology is in fact relevant, but its relevance is one which presently and potentially serves interests which are contrary to the interests of the people we study. Our science *is* usable, and is often used in the service of imperialism, in the interest of domination and exploitation.

The problem I have posed is not primarily one of individual morality, of doing "dirty" work or "clean" work. Rather, the problem posed is an institutional one: it is that, together with other social scientific research, anthropological research *in general* is systematically shaped and utilised by the dominant interests in our society for ends which many, hopefully most, anthropologists would oppose. In a manner not unprecedented in human society, we as individuals are usually not fully aware of all of the institutional pressures that constrain and shape our work, or of the potential uses that our work may have in the hands of others. We do not see selective funding in operation, nor do we usually investigate why particular programmes are set up rather than others, why particular individuals have access to, or power over, funds which others do not. We accept jobs and grants as they are available, angling for them in ways we think might be successful. We are genuinely interested in phenomena such as social change, social structure, values and motivations, etc., which are also phenomena in which others elsewhere are interested—including agencies that have the power to use such information for purposes we would oppose. Working in a narrow academic context, we tend to see our work in terms of particular theoretical problems and of academic advancement. We are often ignorant of the possible "relevance" our work may have in others' hands—and in any case, after we publish our findings we have no control over their use.

But we delude ourselves if we imagine that most anthropological research has no use and will never be used. Basic run-of-the-mill anthropological research is regarded as "relevant" by those who have the desire and resources and need to render it so. We can only hope that our particular work might not be relevant, or comfort ourselves with notions about the unreliability and uselessness of social science in its present state. Meanwhile millions of dollars in computer technology and in hired minds will be working continuously to make our data relevant, reliable and useful to imperialism.

But how could our data *not* be relevant to imperialism? Anthropological research is research on the people of the world subject to imperialism, but these are people who have always fought back in their ways, off and on, now passively and now fiercely, in one area at one time, in another area at another time, rebelling against forces which oppress them. Such rebellions, mostly futile in the nineteenth century, are becoming more and more successful in this century as people learn how to fight their oppressors. Imperialism, to survive, must counterattack with ever more sophisticated weapons, hard and "soft." It must understand the people it dominates, so as to understand how to prevent them from overthrowing that domination. Social science is necessary to that end; and anthropologists, as social scientists who work most directly in contact with the people oppressed by imperialism, are meant to be the scouts of the imperialist forces in what will be a bitter and protracted war during this century against the forces of resistance, liberation and socialist revolution rising among the world's peoples.

But many anthropologists and anthropology students would not choose this role of serving imperialism. They would want to serve the people they study. To the degree that they come to see this contradiction, the question arises of how they can best resolve it.

It is my opinion that, in the absence of revolutionary changes in the wider society, anthropology as a whole and as an institutional activity cannot be radically changed or reformed so as not to serve imperialism. As long as we live within an imperialist system the same forces which now shape and utilise anthropology will continue to operate and will continue their institutional domination over the practice of anthropology. Are we to try to serve ourselves by serving imperialism? Like Evans-Pritchard, we can go as an agent of the enemy into the camp of the people we study. But we can also choose another road, which I believe holds the future: we can ally with the people abroad and at home—in their struggles to create a new world where science can truly serve the people and not be a tool for their oppression.

N O T E S

This is a shortened version, by Kath Levine, of two articles by Jack Stauder. "The Relevance of Anthropology under Imperialism" was written for the Wenner-Gren Symposium on "Relevance" in Anthropology, held in March 1970. "The Functions of Functionalism" was presented at a meeting of the American Anthropological Association in New York, November 1971.

1. *Evolutionism and Diffusionism:* Rival theories, developed in the late nineteenth century, to describe and explain the development of cultures. Influenced by evolutionist theories of nature, evolutionist anthropologists, led by the "father of anthropology" E. B. Tylor, claimed a linear and separate development of societies from "savagery" through "barbarism" to "civilisation." Evolutionism implies that Western societies are much further "advanced" than "primitive" cultures and hence may have a "civilising" duty to perform. In the early 1920s the evolutionists were briefly contested by the diffusionists who attempted to trace widely dissimilar societies back to shared cultural origins and connections.

2. *Ethnology:* The "natural" history of the cultural development of non-literate societies, largely from hypothetical reconstruction. For an account of the difference between ethnology and functionalism, see Radcliffe-Brown's discussion.

3. *Functionalism:* In this sense the method of analysing a culture or society as an organisation of means designed to achieve certain ends. Closely related to *structural-*

functionalism, an approach which treats a society as an isolable structure or organism composed of elements, none of which can change without effecting change in the other elements. These approaches are characteristically *synchronic,* i.e., ahistorical.

BIBLIOGRAPHY

Kathleen Gough Aberle, "Anthropology and Imperialism," *Monthly Review,* April 1969, 12–27.

American Anthropological Association, "Background Information on Problems of Anthropological Research and Ethics," prepared by R. L. Beals and the Executive Board of the AAA, *Fellow Newsletter* 8, no. 1 (Jan. 1967).

Anon., *How Harvard Rules,* Africa Research Group (P.O. Box 213, Cambridge, Mass. 02138), 1969.

L. G. Cowan, C. Roseberg, L. Fallers, and C. de Kiewiet, *Report of the Committee on African Studies prepared for the Ford Foundation,* 1958.

E. E. Evans-Pritchard, *The Nuer,* Oxford, Oxford University Press, 1940.

Daryll Forde, "Applied Anthropology in Government: British Africa," in A. L. Kroeber, ed., *Anthropology Today,* University of Chicago Press, 1953. pp. 841–65.

Lord Hailey, *An African Survey,* Oxford, Oxford University Press, 1938.

Marvin Harris, *The Rise of Anthropological Theory,* New York, Thomas Y. Crowell Co., 1968.

David Horowitz, "The Foundations (Charity Begins at Home)," *Ramparts,* April 1969.

David Horowitz, "Billion Dollar Brains," *Ramparts,* May 1969.

David Horowitz, "Sinews of Empire," *Ramparts,* October 1969.

Irving L. Horowitz, *The Rise and Fall of Project Camelot.* MIT Press, 1967.

Judy Kaufman and Bob Park. *The Cambridge Project: Social Science for Social Control* (Bob Park, 1590 Cambridge Street, Cambridge, Mass.), 1969.

F. D. Lugard, "The International Institute of African Languages and Cultures." *Africa* 1, 1–12.

B. Magubane, "Pluralism and Conflict Situations in Africa: A New Look." *African Social Research* 7 (June 1969), 529–53.

Lucy Mair, "The Social Sciences in Africa South of the Sahara: The British Contribution." *Human Organisation* 19, no. 3 (1960), 98–107.

J. J. Maquet, "Objectivity in Anthropology," *Current Anthropology* 5, 47–55.

A. R. Radcliffe-Brown, "Some Problems of Bantu Sociology," *Bantu Studies* 1, no. 3 (1922), 38–46.

A. R. Radcliffe-Brown, "The Methods of Ethnology and Social Anthropology," *South African Journal of Science* 20 (1923), 124–47.

A. R. Radcliffe-Brown, "Applied Anthropology," *Report of the 20th Meeting of the Australian and NZ Association for the Advancement of Science 1930,* pp. 267–80.

William Ridgeway, "Presidential Address: The Influence of the Environmental Man." *JRAI* 40 (1910), 10-22.

Royal Anthropological Institute, *Reports of the Council* (1926, etc.).

Rev. E. W. Smith, "Presidential Address: Anthropology and the Practical Man." *JRAI* 64 (1934), pp. xiii–xxxvii.

PART SIX

The Future:
Toward a Democratic
Strategy for World Sciences

The intellectual challenge is to build the basis of resistance to militarization and organized violence, firstly by providing a better understanding of how modern science or technology is gradually becoming a substitute for politics in many societies, and secondly by defying the middle-class consensus against bringing the estate of science within the scope of public life or politics. This plea for the repoliticization of science—by which I primarily mean the political audit of science by those outside the estate of science and by its victims, not state control or mechanical parliamentary or legislative scrutiny—will not be popular with those who run the one-million-strong Indian estate of science, the world's third-largest mass of scientific manpower, nor with the urban middle classes, increasingly hostile to the idea of politics. But it might be more acceptable to those seeking to survive the loving embrace of an increasingly violent science and an increasingly violent model of scientific development at the lower rungs of Indian society.

> Ashis Nandy, "Science as a Reason of State," in *Science, Hegemony and Violence: A Requiem for Modernity*

If we do know that there exists a science which is imperialist in its uses, its organization, its method and its ideology, there must exist, and in fact there does exist, an anti-imperialist science. It is still in its infancy, and it takes different forms, according to the conditions it is found in. . . . We denounce the conversion of science into a commodity and of our universities into corporate offices. From denunciation we move to active criticism: we look for means to put our scientific knowledge at the service of the people, and therefore as an instrument of revolutionary national liberation movements.

> Ciencia para el Pueblo, "Towards an Anti-Imperialist Science"

It is in the Third World that the new ecologically sound future of the world can be born. In many parts of the Third World there are still large areas of ecologically sound economic and living systems, which have been lost in the developed world. We need to recognize and identify these areas and rediscover the technological and cultural wisdoms of our indigenous systems of agriculture, industry, shelter, water and sanitation, medicine and culture. We do not mean here the unquestioning acceptance of everything traditional in the overromantic belief of a past golden age which has to be returned to in all aspects. For instance exploitative feudal or slave social systems also made life more difficult in the past. But many indigenous technologies, skills and processes which are appropriate for sustainable development and harmonious with nature and the community are still integral to life in the Third World. These indigenous scientific systems have to be accorded their proper recognition, encouraged and upgraded if necessary.

> Khor Kok Peng, "Underdeveloping the Third World,"
> in *The Revenge of Athena: Science, Exploitation*
> *and the Third World.*

Many of the essays in the earlier sections have begun to envision different relations between sciences and contemporary societies, and different sciences for the more democratic world communities that they value. The essays in this final section focus directly on these issues. Several are well-known historical documents; others are newer. There are diverse proposals for strategy here, as well as contrasting visions and interesting disagreements.

Joseph Needham makes a case that "democracy might . . . almost in a sense be termed that practice of which science is the theory" and points to the democratic elements within science. He argues, however, that modern capitalism, which needs and uses science more than ever, infuses science with the increasing irrationality that is characteristic of capitalism itself, and thus turns science against democracy. It is capitalism that is the problem, not anything inherent in the science, he argues. (Since Needham is a scholar of Chinese science, one can wonder what historical evidence he would provide to show that science and democracy have been so tightly linked in China or the Islamic world.) Far fewer people these days maintain Needham's optimism that science and democracy are inherently so closely linked. If Needham is wrong, what *is* the relation between science and democracy?

In a widely read analysis written during the Vietnam War, Bill Zimmerman and his co-authors analyze the difficulty of turning U.S. science away from its service to the military and industry. They propose six ways in which science workers can use their skills to create science for the people. While these proposals are expressed in the idiom of 1960s science radicalism, in the 1990s we must ask, nevertheless, if they go far enough.

The Black Scholar calls for African Americans to increase their participation in the sciences in order to create useful knowledge that will enable African Americans "to intelligently take command of their destiny." Robert C. Johnson reviews the bad effects on black Americans of a number of twentieth-century technologies from the automobile and television through technologies of law enforcement. He argues that technological and scientific issues are interwoven with ones of economic development and civil rights, and that "national Black organizations need to identify and pull together groups of committed, concerned and capable Black scientists, technologists, engineers, policy analysts, social scientists, community workers, and activists" to create long-term scientific and technological plans for African Americans. Which institutions might train such scientists? And where are the ones that could fund and employ scientific workers prepared to develop such a science?

David Dickson, who has been European correspondent for *Science* and is the author of several important books on science and technology, argues that the first and second generations of postwar critics of science created political discussion about the applications of science and the conditions under which science is produced. But now a new task is necessary. Because the applications of science to technology have become steadily privatized, we must integrate the perspectives of the first two critiques in order to create a public debate about the conditions of access to science. Dickson's wide-ranging analysis focuses on strategies for democratizing access to science both nationally and internationally.

"Modern Science in Crisis: A Third World Response" was the outcome of a 1986 conference in Penang, Malaysia, organized by the Third World Network and the Consumers' Association of Penang.[1] The conference participants argued that it is not just that social institutions and inequities have blocked modern science from eliminating major social problems. Rather, modern science's inherent form of rationality leads "to innumerable costs and dangers to civilization and human survival itself." Moreover, they point out that modern science has become one of several crucial resources through which the rich societies continue their domination of the Third World. This declaration is particularly valuable for the concrete proposals it makes for the most effective ways to intervene in this crisis.

Many of the earlier essays also contain proposals for the future development of science—Shiva's and Levins' and Lewontin's different arguments for a reappraisal of low-technology agriculture, Grossman's review of the effectiveness of grass-roots politics in ending environmental racism, Proctor's arguments for the importance of encouraging specifically political discussions of the sciences, the many arguments for diversity in the scientific community, the persistent call for more effective ways for scientists themselves to evaluate the relation between their work and regressive politics. And there have been other suggestions.

Can we transform the sciences into solutions instead of primarily problems for those peoples of the world who are trying to develop more democratic ways of living together?

---

[1] The Third World Network publishes two journals, *Third World Resurgence,* and *Third World Economics: Trends and Analysis,* and many books on economic, scientific and technological issues in the Third World. Subscriptions to the journals in the U.S. can be gotten from Michelle Syverson & Associates, 1442A Walnut Street (Suite 81), Berkeley, CA 94709. For information on the journals and books, contact the Third World Network, 87 Cantonment Road, 10250 Penang, Malaysia (Telex CAPPG MA 40989; Fax 60-4-368106).

SCIENCE AND DEMOCRACY
A Fundamental Correlation

Joseph Needham

Perhaps it is a commonplace to say that science is only possible in a democratic medium. But commonplaces may be quite erroneous when carefully examined, and if this one be true, it cannot be thought of as established in the absence of detailed consideration. I believe, however, that there is a fundamental correlation between science and democracy. . . .

In the first place, it is quite clear, and the fact is not contested by any scholars, Marxist or otherwise, that historically science and democracy grew up in Western Civilization together. I refer here, of course, not to primitive science, nor to medieval empirical technology, but to modern science, with its characteristic combination of the rational and the empirical and its systematization of hypotheses about the external universe which stand the test of controlled experiment. To the English Civil War and Commonwealth period we have already referred, but this was only part of that great movement lasting from the fifteenth, perhaps, till the eighteenth century, in which feudalism was destroyed and capitalism took its place. Other aspects of the same change were the Protestant Reformation, the literary Renaissance, and the rise of modern science.

Exactly why modern science should have been associated with these changes still remains to be fully elucidated. Here it may suffice to say that the early merchant-venturers, extremely farseeing men, and the princes who supported them and based their power on them, were interested in the properties of things because on such properties alone could mercantile and quantitative economics develop. At no time in history has scientific research been possible without financial support. In antiquity the aid of princes had to be obtained; Babylonian astronomy was a department of state; Greek physics and mathematics relied on the support of the sovereign city-states; and Alexandrian biology depended on the Ptolemies. In the first beginnings of capitalism the merchants and embryonic industrialists provided the essential funds for the experiments of a Boyle or a Lavoisier, however indirect might be the channels. In the Restoration Court, after the victories of the Commonwealth, scientific and technical experiments were performed under the very auspices of King Charles II; "the noise of mechanick instruments resounded in Whitehall itself." Business had, in fact, become respectable, and science with it. The younger sons of the aristocracy hastened to apprentice themselves to thriving mercantile, mining, and industrial enterprises. Waning shadows of the former feudal exclusiveness appear in the attractive story of John Graunt, the founder of vital statistics and the first man to apply mathematical methods to the "Bills of Mortality." The Royal Society were uncertain whether to admit him of their number, since he was some kind of small tradesman in the City, and they sought the opinion of the King on the matter, who replied that "they should certainly admit Mr Graunt, and if they found any more such tradesmen, they should be sure to admit them also without delay."

This judgment was what we could call the affirmation of a democratic principle, namely that in matters of science and learning birth or descent is a thing indifferent. And indeed it is obvious that if the rising merchant class encouraged the sciences to develop, their slogan on the political side was precisely democracy in all its forms. Everyone knows, of course, that democracy, *sensu stricto*, took its origin in ancient Greece, but it was always based there on a helot or slave population, and it seems extremely unlikely that it would ever have developed as it did if it had not been for Christian theology, with its emphasis on the importance of the individual soul before God. Those who took the individual soul seriously were bound to end, as authoritarian thinkers had always realized, by taking seriously the opinions of its owner, not only on spiritual matters, but ultimately on temporal ones too.

• • •

There can be no doubt that capitalism, democracy, and modern science grew up together. The question arises whether the two latter are essentially dependent upon the former. Many observers today consider that capitalism has ceased to be the matrix for the other two which once it was. . . .

But let us turn now to the philosophical, rather than the historical, connections between science and democracy.

In the first place, Nature is no respecter of persons. If someone takes the floor before an audience of scientific men and women, wishing to speak of observations made, experiments carried out, hypotheses formed, or calculations finished, the status of this person as to age, sex, colour, creed, or race, is absolutely irrelevant. Only his or her professional competence as observer, experimentalist, or computer is relevant. The community of co-operating observers and experimenters upon whose activity science is based is fundamentally democratic. It surely prefigures that world co-operative commonwealth which we see as the inevitable crown of social evolution. The admission of Mr. Graunt to the Fellowship of the Royal Society symbolizes the absolute equality shared by all competent observers of nature. Just as the theologians of patristic Christianity emphasized the importance of each individual soul, so the leaders of modern science at all its stages have recognized the importance of each individual observer. They may, in practice, have given greater credence in any particular age to those whose merit as scientific workers was widely recognized, but the history of science now contains so many examples of the neglect, or persecution, of individuals who afterwards proved to be profoundly right (such as Galileo in astronomy, Mendel in genetics, Semmelweis in pathology, Willard Gibbs and Wollaston in physical chemistry, and many others), that today no one is likely to fail to obtain a fair hearing. A competent observer is a competent observer, no matter whether his genes have given him the pink and white skin-colour of the Euro-American, the golden-brown of the Chinese, the blue-black of the Negro, the dark brown of the Indian, or even the white of the Albino. . . .

If science is democratic as regards "racial" characteristics, it is also democratic as regards age. In science it is so very easy to be wrong that no scientific worker, no matter how great his age or experience, can afford to despise the contribution of some younger man, even if comparatively inexperienced. It has recently been well argued by Waddington in *The Scientific Attitude* that science solves the old problem of authority and freedom in a remarkable way. Authority is safeguarded because the structure of the scientific world-view is based securely on the results of the co-operative labours of a million investigators and is not therefore easily overthrown. But at the same time freedom is provided for in that it is always open for any individual thinker to insist upon its modification, if he can. In the case of an Einstein, the modifications may be fundamental. Were human society organized in a similarly rational way, were there no governing class with vested interests requiring irrational preservation, a similar solution of the problem at the social level might be found.

One corollary of the indifference of science to age is that those civilizations which have developed an exaggerated veneration of the old, and an exaggerated respect for teachers, will have to modify it in taking their place in the modern world, just as Western civilization overthrew the authority of scholastic Aristotelianism.

We may also ask what is the estimate of man to which three centuries of science have led. It is certainly not the estimate which the totalitarian philosophers of our time have formed. Men are not naturally machine-minding slaves, fit only to carry out the undisputed orders of self-appointed leaders in some kind of hierarchy; they are basically rational beings, each with his right to life, love, labour, and happiness, each with his distinctive contribution to make to the wellbeing of the community, each with a right to an opinion and its expression on the community's form, laws, and actions, each with a duty to guard the community's property and to uphold its just laws. As Jennings has so well put it in *The Biological Basis of Human Nature*, the type of human community to which the facts of biology most clearly point is that of "a democracy which can produce experts." Nazi-Shintoist-fascist racialism which purports to have a biological foundation is the greatest scientific fraud yet perpetrated on a public insufficiently critical to detect it.

But what are the experts to whom Jennings refers in the above passage? They are certainly not armchair, office, or library penholders and bookworms, burrowing among the opinions of antiquity to find something useful for the needs of today. They are men with practical experience in the laboratory and at the engineer's bench, in the dyeing-sheds, the steel mills and the hospital wards. It is here that we come upon yet another hidden connection between science and democracy, namely the bridging of the gulf between the scholar and the artisan.

This antithesis has existed throughout history; one can find traces of it in the earliest civilizations. From the very beginning the philosophers and mathematicians and primitive scientists allied themselves, together with all those who were able to master the arts of reading and writing, with the scribes and civil servants who carried out the orders of the government of kings and nobles. The artisans, such as those who understood chemical and smelting processes in ancient Egypt, or the murex dyers in later Roman times, or the jade-cutters of China or the Aztec makers of feathered robes—all were set apart as belonging to the inferior "mechanic" class with whom gentlemen would not associate. Hence the complete gulf between theoretical scientific thought and technical human practice for thousands of years. Aristotelian and Epicurean speculations such as the atomic theory, went their way without any influence on actual techniques; while the Chinese scholars, masters of the ideographic characters, but remote from their own technical artisans, continued until a late date to harp on the primitive theories of the five elements and the two principles; the *yang* and the *yin*. Indeed the Greek distinction between theory and practice, the former suitable for a gentleman and the latter not, finds its exact counterpart in the Chinese distinction between *hsüeh* and *shu*. Only some of the greatest figures broke through these boundaries, as for example Aristotle when he conversed with fishermen and shepherds before writing his immortal *De Generatione* and *Historia Animalium*, or Hippocrates the practical physician, or Archimedes the practical military engineer; or in China, Shen Kua who in the Sung dynasty abandoned Confucian exclusiveness to record with care all natural wonders, such as for the first time the magnetic compass, or the Taoist outcast scholars, whose alchemy penetrating to the West was the foundation of all modern chemistry.

With the coming of capitalism, however, all was changed. Feudal disinclination to soil one's hands by practical manual operations went out of fashion for ever. Now the merchants set the tone. It was now not only a matter of handling exploitable commodities in their warehouses, of examining the properties of oils and waxes, animal and plant products, minerals and metals. The time had come to investigate all such investigatable things to the bottom, and as part of this enterprise, a new interest awakened in the traditional arts and trades which since time immemorial had been gradually developing through the labours of a million empirically minded artisans. The beautifully illustrated books of the eighteenth century describing all the trades and husbandries came into being as a result, in both the Orient and Occident.

This new impulse was profoundly democratic. Henceforward continuously the scholar and the artisan were to meet and ultimately to mingle, until in our own time they find a perfect fusion in the great experimentalists, a Pavlov or a Langmuir, working indifferently with brain and hand. The scholar, from being the support of the king, becomes the comrade of the artisan. . . .

On the psychological side also there are powerful hidden connections between science and democracy. There is a real kinship between the scientific mind and the democratic mentality. There is in both cases a basic scepticism—the scepticism of the experimentalist is mirrored in the scepticism of the voter. The Royal Society's motto *Nullius in Verba*: take nobody's word for it; see for yourself; is also that of government by and of the people. Though it may be a counsel of perfection, it sets the psychological key. Making one's own mind up on the available evidence, deciding for oneself what goal to aim at, weighing the facts from a dozen different quarters, these are characteristics both of the scientist investigating nature, and the democratic citizen taking part in the governance of the State. They do not let others decide on their aims, they do not leave to others the assessment of evidence, blindly believing in the superior leadership of particular men. There is a quality of openness to conviction, of give and take, a live and let live attitude, characterizing both the scientific worker among other scientific workers, and the democratic citizen among his fellows. Applying the rules, too, when no one else is about, does this not also unite the scientific worker and the citizen? Even in very recondite studies, where it is unlikely that he can be checked in his own lifetime, the scientific worker is on his honour to make no falsification of results; he cannot know what might depend on it. So also (as I once thought when observing a driver threading his way tortuously through traffic round-abouts in the middle of the night, with no other vehicle moving for miles around), the democratic citizen adheres to the rules in the absence of all usually present restraints. He does so because in his inmost self he admits them to be good and rational. The laws of a rational society are written in the hearts of its citizens as well as in its codices.

Then objectivity. Authoritarian theory carries over into all life the mechanical system of military discipline. But Nature is not amenable to that. Objective facts are objective facts, irrespective of the leaders' wills. As we have seen in Nazi Germany, scientific anthropology, for instance, may be broken, it may be exiled, but it will not bend. So also in democratic thought. Subjective valuations may flourish for a time, but before long the hard facts of personal well-being or personal misery will indicate to the citizen with indubitable clarity where his interests lie. The subjective and the irrational are anti-democratic, they are the instruments of tyranny.

Authoritarian, tyrannical thought, again, tends always to divide and to keep separate, yet the fundamental urge of science is to form a unified world-picture, in which all phenomena have their proper place. In Thomson's *Aeschylus and Athens*, a work dealing with the anthropological origins of Greek culture and folklore, and the rise of Greek drama and literature from them, this correlation is clearly made. An examination of Ionian science (especially Anaximander's contribution) and Orphic mystical theology, suggests that "the tendency of aristocratic thought is to divide, to keep things apart," while the "tendency of popular thought is to unite." In Orphism, love implied the reunion of what had been sundered. Divisiveness must have followed naturally from the efforts of the earliest aristocrats to maintain separate from the communal land the special enclosure or *temenos* which they had won by cunning or bravery. Maintenance of differences has been throughout history, even when the differences were quite illusory, the basic aim of all tyrannical, aristocratic, or oligarchic social orders. Conversely union and withness, the *ta thung* of Chinese thought, has been the aim of democracies. And since, as we have seen above, the principle of union, attraction, and aggregation persistently triumphs, not only in the living world, but in the non-living world also, throughout the evolutionary process, over the principle of disunion, repulsion, and disaggregation, it is clear that the democratic trend at the human social level has the future before it while the authoritarian trend is doomed.

Democracy might therefore almost in a sense be termed that practice of which science is the theory.

Thus we may summarize the hidden connections between science and democracy. By no coincidence, modern science and democracy arose together during those stormy centuries during which modern society was born. Science is profoundly democratic in its relation to differences of race, sex, and age. It finally solves the ancient problem, so vexatious for theologians, of authority and freedom. Its estimate of human social order is that of a democracy which can produce experts. And these experts finally bridge the age-old gulf between the scholar and the artisan, uniting in single persons the highest human attainments of hand and brain. Lastly, the psychological attitude in science and democracy is very much the same. Both are on the side of union, attraction, and aggregation, leading to the higher organizational levels.

If, then, there is a connection between science and democracy, the opposition must come between science and all possible forms of irrational arbitrary tyranny, authoritarianism and totalitarianism. And the contradiction today is that capitalism, in its late highly developed monopoly form, needs science more than ever, for without it the hitherto unapproached technically high standard of life cannot be maintained or extended. Yet since capitalism is ceasing to be able to appeal to mankind on rational grounds, it more and more tends to have recourse to the irrationalities of authoritarianism. Hence, though capitalism and democracy grew up together, we approach the time when either one or the other of them must go. And since science is indispensable to all future human civilization, it is capitalism that is doomed, and not democracy. . . .

PEOPLE'S SCIENCE

Bill Zimmerman et al.

In the fifteenth century, Leonardo da Vinci refused to publish plans for a submarine because he anticipated that it would be used as a weapon. In the seventeenth century, for similar reasons, Boyle kept secret a poison he had developed. In 1946, Leo Szilard, who had been one of the key developers of the atom bomb, quit physics in disillusionment over the ways in which the government had used his work. By and large, this kind of resistance on the part of scientists to the misuse of their research has been very sporadic, from isolated individuals, and generally in opposition only to particular, unusually repugnant projects. As such, it has been ineffective. If scientists want to help prevent socially destructive applications of science, they must forgo acting in an ad hoc or purely moralistic fashion and begin to respond collectively from the vantage point of a political and economic analysis of their work. This analysis must be firmly anchored in an understanding of the U.S. corporate state.

We will argue below that science is inevitably political, and in the context of contemporary U.S. corporate capitalism, that it contributes greatly to the exploitation and oppression of most of the people both in this country and abroad. We will call for a reorientation of scientific work and will suggest ways in which scientific workers can redirect their research to further meaningful social change.

Science in Capitalist America

Concurrent with the weakening of Cold War ideology over the past fifteen years has been the growing realization on the part of increasing numbers of Americans that a tiny minority of the population, through its wealth and power, controls the major decision-making institutions of our society. Research such as that of Mills (*The Power Elite*), Domhoff (*Who Rules America*), and Lundgren (*The Rich and the Superrich*) has exposed the existence of this minority to public scrutiny. Although the term *ruling class* may have an anachronistic ring to some, we still find it useful to describe that dominant minority that owns and controls the productive economic resources of our society. The means by which the U.S. ruling class exerts control in our society and over much of the Third World has been described in such works as Baran and Sweezy's *Monopoly Capital*, Horowitz's *Free World Colossus*, and Magdoff's *Age of Imperialism*. These works argue that it is not a conspiracy, but rather the logical outcome of corporate capitalism that a minority with wealth and power, functioning efficiently within the system to maintain its position, inevitably will oversee the oppression and exploitation of the majority of the people in this country, as well as the more extreme impoverishment and degradation of the people in the Third World. It is within the context of this political-economic system—a system that has produced the military-industrial complex as its highest expression and that will use all the resources at its disposal to maintain its control, that is, within the context of the U.S. corporate state—that we must consider the role played by scientific work.

We view the long-term strategy of the U.S. capitalist class as resting on two basic pillars. The first is the maintenance and strengthening of the international domination of U.S. capital. The principal economic aspect of this lies in continually increasing the profitable opportunities for the export of capital in order to absorb the surplus constantly being generated both internally and abroad. With the growing revolt of the oppressed peoples of the world, the traditional political and military mechanisms necessary to sustain this imperialist control are disintegrating. More and more the U.S. ruling class is coming to rely openly on technological and military means of mass terror and repression which approach genocide: anti-personnel bombs, napalm, pacification-assassination programs, herbicides and other attempts to induce famines, etc.

While this use of scientific resources is becoming more clearly evident (witness the crisis of conscience among increasing numbers of young scientists), the importance of scientific and technological resources for the second pillar of capitalist strategy is even more central, although less generally accorded the significance it deserves.

The second fundamental thrust of capitalist political economic strategy is to guarantee a steady and predictable increase in the maintenance of the profitability of domestic industry and its ability to compete on the international market. Without this increase in labour productivity it would be impossible to maintain profits and at the same time sustain the living standard and employment of the working class. This in turn makes it possible to sustain the internal consumer market and to blunt the domestic class struggle in order to preserve social control by the ruling class.

The key to increasing the productivity of labor in the United States is the transformation and reorganization of our major industries through accelerated automation and rationalization of the production process (through economy of scale, the introduction of labor-saving plant and machinery, abolition of the traditional craft prerogatives of the workers, etc., such as is now occurring in the construction industry). This reorganization will depend on *programmed* advances in technology.

There are basically two reasons why these advances and new developments cannot be left to the "natural" progress of scientific-technological knowledge, why they must be foreseen and included in the social-economic planning of the ruling class. First is the mammoth investment in the present-day plant, equipment and organizational apparatus of the major monopolies. The sudden obsolescence of a significant part of their apparatus would be an economic disaster which could very well endanger their market position. (One sees the results of this lack of planning in the airline industry.) Secondly, the transformation of the process of production entails a major reorganization of education, transportation, and communication. This has far-reaching social and political consequences which cause profound strains in traditional class, race, and sex relationships, which have already generated and will continue to generate political and social crises. For the ruling class to deal with these crises it is necessary to be able to plan ahead, to anticipate new developments so that they do not get out of hand.

In our view, because planning and programmed advances in technology are absolutely central to ruling class strategy, an entirely new relationship is required between the ruling and the technical-scientific sectors of society, a relationship which has been emerging since the Second World War, and which, deeply rooted in social-economic developments, cannot be reversed. If one looks at the new sciences which have developed in this period—cybernetics, systems analysis, management science, linear programming, game theory—as well as the direction of development in the social sciences, one sees an enormous development in the techniques of gathering, processing, organizing, and utilizing information, exactly the type of technological advance most needed by the rulers.

It is no accident that two of the most advanced monopolistic formations, advanced both in their utilization and support of science and in the efficiency and sophistication of their internal organization, are Bell Telephone and IBM. They represent to capitalist planners the wave of the future, the integration of scientific knowledge, management technique and capital which guarantees the long-term viability of the capitalist order. They also represent industries which are key to the servicing and rationalizing of the basic industries as well as to the maintenance of the international domination of U.S. capital.

• • •

The ruling class, through government, big corporations, and tax-exempt foundations, funds most of our research. In the case of industrial research, the control and direction of research are obvious. With research supported by government or private foundations, controls are somewhat less obvious, but nonetheless effective. Major areas of research may be preferentially funded by direction of Congress or foundation trustees. For example, billions of dollars are spent on space research while pressing domestic needs are given lower priority. We believe that the implications of space research for the military and the profits of the influential aerospace industries are clearly the decisive factors. Within specific areas of research, ruling-class bias is also evident in selection of priorities. For example, in medicine, money has been poured into research on heart disease, cancer and stroke, major killers of the middle and upper classes, rather than into research on sickle cell anemia, the broad range of effects of malnutrition (higher incidences of most diseases), etc., which affect mainly the lower classes. Large sums of money are provided for study of ghetto populations but nothing is available to support studies of how the powerful operate.

Second, on a lower level, decisions by which an individual gets research money are usually made by scientists themselves, chosen to sit on review panels. The fact that these people are near the tops of their respective scientific hierarchies demonstrates a congruence between their professional goals and the scientific priorities of the ruling class. This kind of internal control is most critical in the social sciences, where questions of ideology are more obviously relevant to what is considered "appropriate" in topic or in approach. This same scientific elite exert control over the socialization of science students through funding of training grants to universities, through their influence over curricula and textbook content, and through their personal involvement in the training of the next generation of elite scientists. Thus, through the high-level control of the funding now essential for most scientific research, and second, through the professional elites acting in a managerial capacity, ruling-class interests and priorities dominate scientific research and training.

• • •

The same government-corporate axis that funds applied research that is narrowly beneficial to ruling-class interests also supports almost all of our basic, or to use the euphemism, "pure," research; it is called pure because it is ostensibly performed not for specific applications but only to seek the truth. Many scientific workers engaged in some form of basic research do not envision any applications of their work and thus believe themselves absolved of any responsibility for applications. Others perform basic research in hopes that it will lead to the betterment of humankind. In either case, these workers have failed to understand the contemporary situation.

Today, basic research is closely followed by those in position to reap the benefits of its application—the government and the corporations. Only rich institutions have the staff to keep abreast of current research and to mount the technology necessary for its application. As the attention paid by government and corporations to scientific research has increased, the amount of time required to apply it has decreased. In the last century, fifty years elapsed between Faraday's demonstration that an electric current could be generated by moving a magnet near a piece of wire and Edison's construction of the first central power station. Only seven years passed between the realization that the atomic bomb was theoretically possible and its detonation over Hiroshima and Nagasaki. The transistor went from invention to sales in a mere three years. More recently, research on lasers was barely completed when engineers began using it to design new weapons for the government and new long-distance transmission systems for the telephone company.

The result is that in many ways discovery and application, scientific research and engineering, can no longer be distinguished from each other. Our technological society has brought them so close together that today they can only be considered part of the same process. Consequently, while most scientific workers are motivated by humane considerations, or a detached pursuit of truth for truth's sake, their discoveries cannot be separated from applications which all too frequently destroy or debase human life.

Theoretical and experimental physicists, working on problems of esoteric intellectual interest, provided the knowledge that eventually was pulled together to make the H-bomb, while mathematicians, geophysicists, and metallurgists, wittingly or unwittingly, made the discoveries necessary to construct intercontinental ballistic missiles. Physicists doing basic work in optics and infrared spectroscopy may have been shocked to find that their research would help government and corporate engineers build detection and surveillance devices for use in Indochina. The basic research of molecular biologists, biochemists, cellular biologists, neuropsychologists, and physicians was necessary for CBW (chemical-biological warfare) agents, defoliants, herbicides, and gaseous crowd-control devices.

Anthropologists studying social systems of mountain tribes in Indochina were surprised when the CIA collected their information for use in counterinsurgency operations. Psychologists explored the parameters of human intelligence-testing instruments which, once developed, passed out of their hands and now help the draft boards conscript men for Vietnam and the U.S. Army allocate manpower more effectively. Further, these same intelligence-testing instruments are now an integral part of the public school tracking systems that, beginning at an early age, reduce opportunities of working-class children for higher education and social mobility.

Unfortunately, the problem of evaluating basic research does not end with such obscene misapplications as these. One must also examine the economic consequences of basic research, consequences which flow from the structure of corporate capitalism under which we live. Scientific knowledge and products, like any other products and services in our society, are marketed for profit—that is, they are not equally distributed to, equally available to, or equally usable by all of the people. While they often contribute to the material standard of living of many people, they are channeled through an organization and distribution of scarcity in such a way as to rationalize the overall system of economic exploitation and social control. Furthermore, they frequently become the prerogative of the middle and upper classes and often result in increasing the disadvantages of those sectors of the population that are already most oppressed.

For example, research in comparative and developmental psychology has shown that enriching the experience of infants and young children by increasing the variety and complexity of shapes, colors, and patterns in their environment might increase their intelligence as it is conventionally defined. As these techniques become more standardized, manufacturers are beginning to market their versions of these aids in the form of toys aimed at and priced for the upper and middle classes, and inaccessible to the poor.

Research in plant genetics and agronomy resulted in the development of super strains of cereal crops which, it was hoped, would alleviate the problems of food production in underdeveloped countries. However, in many areas, only the rich farmers can afford the expensive fertilizers required for growing these crops, and the "green revolution" has ended up by exacerbating class differences. Studies by sociologists and anthropologists of various Third World societies have been used by the U.S. government to help maintain in power ruling elites favorable to U.S. economic interests in those countries. Real-estate developers in California have used the mapping studies of geologists, carried out in the interests of basic research, to lay out tract-housing developments that mean massive profits for the few and ecological catastrophe for the entire state.

On a larger scale, nearly all of the people and most organizations of people lack the financial resources to avail themselves of some of the most advanced technology that arises out of basic research. Computers, satellites, and advertising, to name only a few, all rely on the findings of basic research. These techniques are not owned by, utilized by, or operated for, the mass of the people, but instead function in the interests of the government and the large corporations. The people are not only deprived of the potential benefits of scientific research, but corporate capitalism is given new tools with which to extract profit from them. For example, the telephone company's utilization of the basic research on laser beams will enable it to create superior communication devices which, in turn, will contribute toward binding together and extending the American empire commercially, militarily, and culturally.

The thrust of all these examples, which could easily be elaborated and multiplied, is that the potentially beneficial achievements of scientific technology do not escape the political and economic context. Rather, they emerge as products which are systematically distributed in an inequitable way to become another means of further defining and producing the desired political or economic ends of those in power. New knowledge capable of application in ways which would alleviate the many injustices of capitalism and imperialism is either not created in the first place or is made worthless by the limited resources of the victims.

If we are to take seriously the observation that discovery and application are practically inseparable, it follows that basic researchers have more than a casual responsibility for the application of their work. The possible consequences of research in progress or planned for the future must be subjected to careful scrutiny. This is not always easy, as the following examples might indicate.

Basic research in meteorology and geophysics gives rise to the hope that people might one day be capable of exerting a high level of control over the weather. However, such techniques might be used to steer destructive typhoons or droughts into "enemy" countries like North Vietnam or China. As far back as 1960, the U.S. Navy published a paper on just this possibility and the need to develop the requisite techniques before the Russians did. (One has premonitions of future congressmen and presidential candidates warning us about the weather-control gap.) Rain-making techniques were used in Indochina, according to some reports, to induce cloudbursts over the Ho Chi Minh Trail.

Physicists working in the areas of optics and planetary orbits have provided knowledge which the American miliary was, and might still be, considering for the development of satellites in stationary orbit over Vietnam equipped with gigantic mirrors capable of reflecting the sun and illuminating large parts of the countryside at night. While scientific workers perform experiments on the verbal communication of dolphins, the Navy for years has been investigating the possibility of training them to carry torpedoes and underwater cameras strapped to their backs. Not surprisingly much of the support for basic research on dolphins comes from the Office of Naval Research.

Neurophysiologists are developing a technique called electric brain stimulation, in which microelectrodes capable of receiving radio signals are permanently implanted in areas of the brain known to control certain gross behaviors. Thus radio signals selectively transmitted to electrodes in various parts of the brain are capable of eliciting behaviors such as rage or fear, or of stimulating appetites for food or sex. The possibility of implanting these electrodes in the brains of mental patients or prisoners (or even welfare recipients or professional soldiers) should not be underestimated, especially since such uses might be proposed for the most humane and ennobling reasons. Again, the list of examples could be extended greatly.

Science Is Political

An analysis of scientific research merely begins with a description of how it is misapplied and maldistributed. The next step must be an unequivocal statement that scientific activity in a technological society is not, and cannot be, politically neutral or value free. Some people, particularly after Hiroshima and Nuremberg, have accepted this statement. Others still argue that science should be an unbridled search for truth, not subject to a political or a moral critique. J. Robert Oppenheimer, the man in charge of the Los Alamos project which built and tested the first atomic bombs, said in 1967 that "our work has changed the conditions in which men live, but the use made of these changes is the problem of governments, not of scientists."

The attitude of Oppenheimer and others, justified by the slogan of truth for truth's sake, is fostered in our society and has prevailed. It is tolerated by those who control power in this country because it furthers their aims and does not challenge their uses of science. This attitude was advanced centuries ago by people who assumed that an increase in available knowledge would automatically lead to a better world. But this was at a time when the results of scientific knowledge could not easily be anticipated. Today, in a modern technological society, this analysis becomes a rationalization for the maintenance of repressive or destructive institutions, put forth by people who at best are motivated by a desire for the intellectual pleasure of research, and often are merely after money, status, and soft jobs. We believe it would be lame indeed to continue to argue that the possible unforeseen benefits which may arise from scientific research in our society will inevitably outweigh the clearly forseeable harm. The slogan of "truth for truth's sake" is defunct, simply because science is no longer, and can never again be, the private affair of scientists.

Many scientists, even after considering the above analysis, may still feel that no oppressive or exploitative technology will result from their particular research. Two arguments are relevant here. First, even research without foreseeable practical application serves to advance the field generally, and to provide a more sophisticated background from which technology may be derived. The Department of Defense recognizes this and annually invests millions of dollars in such "impractical" research, knowing that in the long run it pays off. The preferential funding of certain areas of basic research makes it more likely that those areas and not others will advance to the point where the emergence of this technology becomes more probable. Second, while formerly scientific activity consumed only an infinitesimal amount of society's resources, the situation has changed drastically in the last twenty-five years. Scientific activity now commands a significant amount of social resources, resources which are in short supply and are necessary to meet the real needs of the majority of the people. The point here is not that scientific activity should cease, but rather that it should truly be a science for the people.

Some scientists have recognized this situation and are now participating in nationally coordinated attempts to solve pressing social problems within the existing political-economic system. However, because their work is usually funded and ultimately controlled by the same forces that control basic research, it is questionable what they can accomplish. For example, sociologists hoping to alleviate some of the oppression of ghetto life have worked with urban renewal programs only to find the ultimate priorities of such programs are controlled by the city political machines and local real estate and business interests rather than by the needs of the people directly affected by such programs. Psychologists, demographers, economists, etc., worked on a master plan for higher education for New York City that would guarantee higher education for all. In practice open enrollment was restricted to the lowest level, which channeled students into menial jobs set by corporate priorities while the main colleges remained virtually as closed as before.

Behavioral and clinical psychologists have tried to develop procedures for applying conditioning techniques to human psychopathology. Their work is now used in state hospital programs which, under the guise of "therapy," torture homosexual people with negative reinforcement, usually electrical, in order to convert them forcefully to heterosexuality. (There are still thirty-three states in which homosexuals may be "committed" under archaic sexual psychopath laws for *indefinite* sentences.) No one is impugning the motives of Pavlov or Skinner, but this is what it has come to in the United States. Thus the liberal panacea of pouring funds into social science research to create Oak Ridge-type institutions for the social sciences is no more likely to improve the quality of life than the namesake institution has. The social sciences are not performed in a political vacuum any more than the natural sciences are. They all ultimately serve the same masters.

Even medical research is not without negative social impact. The discovery of a specific disease cure or preventive measure invariably depends upon prior basic research which is frequently linked to nonmedical misapplications, often before it is used to produce disease cures. For example, the work of microbiologists who are decoding the DNA molecule gives hope for the genetic control of a wide variety of birth defects. Already this research has been used by government and military technicians to breed strains of virulent microbes for germ warfare. Further, it is not unreasonable to expect that someday this research will lead to genetic engineering capable of producing various human subpopulations for the use of those who are in technological control. These might include especially aggressive soldiers for a professional army, strong drones to perform unpleasant physical labor, or "philosopher kings" to inherit control from those already possessing it.

Applied medical research, as well as the more basic variety typified by DNA work, it no less free of the possibility of misapplication. More than purely humane consequences could emerge from one of the latest dramatic medical advances, organ transplantation. Christian Barnard has publicly urged that people be educated to "donate" their organs. It is not overly visionary to imagine that society's underclass, whose labor is decreasingly in demand, might be nourished as a collective "organ bank." If this occurred, it would most probably be on a de facto rather than de jure basis, as is the case with other forms of class and racial oppression. That is, monetary and other incentives would be instituted to encourage "volunteers" so that direct coercion would be unnecessary. Models for the poor selling parts of their bodies already exist in the form of wet nurses, indigent professional blood donors, and convicts and colonial peoples serving as subjects for experiments. An example of the last was the use of Puerto Rican women to test birth control pills before they were considered safe to market in the United States. (And now evidence that had been suppressed by the drug companies, the government, and the medical profession indicates that they are not safe after all—see J. Coburn in *Ramparts*, June 1970.)

The misapplication of medical or premedical knowledge is, however, only half of the problem. The tragically overcrowded and understaffed city and county hospitals of our large metropolitan areas testify to the inequities and class biases in the distribution of medical knowledge as well. People here and throughout the world needlessly suffer and die because the money to pay for, the education with which to understand, or the physical proximity to, modern medicine has been denied them. By virtue of this, much of medical research has taken place for exclusive or primary use by the affluent.

Some medical discoveries have been equitably and, at least in our society, almost universally distributed. The Salk and Sabin vaccines are one example. Yet one is forced to wonder if this would have occurred had polio been less contagious. If the people who are in charge of our public health services could have protected their own children without totally eradicating polio, would they have moved as fast and as effectively? Witness their *ability* to prevent or reverse effects of malnutrition, while thousands of children within our borders alone suffer from it. In fact, while polio vaccines may have been an exception, the gravest problem we face in terms of disease is discovering ways of equitably distributing the medical knowledge we already possess, and that, ultimately, is a political problem.

What Is to Be Done?

In this society, at this time, it is not possible to escape the political implications of scientific work. The U.S. ruling class has long had a commitment to science, not merely limited to short-range practical applications, but based on the belief that science is good for the long-term welfare of U.S. capitalism, and that what is good for U.S. capitalism is good for humanity. This outlook is shared by the trustees of universities, the official leaders of U.S. science, the administrators of government and private funding agencies. Further, they see this viewpoint as representing a mature social responsibility, morally superior to the "pure search of truth" attitudes of some scientists. But they tolerate the ideology since it furthers their own aims and does not challenge their uses of science.

We find the alternatives of "science for science's sake" and "science for progress of capitalism" equally unacceptable. We can no longer identify the cause of humanity with that of U.S. capitalism. We don't have two governments, one which beneficently funds research and another which represses and kills in the ghettos, in Latin America, and in Indochina. Nor do we have two corporate structures, manipulating for profit on the one hand while desiring social equity and justice on the other. Rather there is a single government-corporate axis which supports research with the intention of acquiring powerful tools, both of the hard- and software varieties, for the pursuit of exploitative and imperial goals.

Recognizing the political implications of their work, some scientists in recent years have sought to organize, as scientists, to oppose the more noxious or potentially catastrophic schemes of the government, such as atmospheric nuclear testing, chemical and biological warfare development, and the anti-ballistic missile system. Others shifted fields to find less "controversial" disciplines: Leo Szilard, who had been wartime co-director of the University of Chicago experiments which led to the first self-sustaining chain reaction, quit physics in disillusionment over the manner in which the government had used his work, and devoted the rest of his life to research in molecular biology and public affairs. In subsequent years other physicists followed Szilard's lead into biology, including Donald Glaser, the 1960 recipient of the Nobel prize in physics. Yet in 1969, James Shapiro, one of the group of microbiologists who first isolated a pure gene, announced that for political reasons he was going to stop doing *any* research. Shapiro's decision points up the inadequacy of Szilard's response but is no less inadequate itself.

Traditional attempts to reform scientific activity, to disentangle it from its more malevolent and vicious applications, have failed. Actions designed to preserve the moral integrity of individuals without addressing themselves to the political and economic system which is at the root of the problem have been ineffective. The ruling class can always replace a Leo Szilard with an Edward Teller. What is needed now is not liberal reform or withdrawal, but a radical attack, a strategy of opposition. Scientific workers must develop ways to put their skills at the service of the people and against the oppressors.

Political Organizing in the Health Fields

How to do this is perhaps best exemplified in the area of health care. It is not by accident that the groups most seriously dealing with the problem of people's health needs are political organizations. A few years ago the Black Panther party initiated a series of free health clinics to provide sorely needed medical services that should be, but are not, available to the poor, and the idea was picked up by other community groups, such as the Young Lords, an organization of revolutionary Latins and Puerto Ricans. Health and scientific workers, organized by political groups like the Medical Committee for Human Rights and the Student Health Organization, have helped provide the necessary professional support, and over the past decade literally hundreds of free people's health centers have sprung up across the country.

Health workers, organized into political groups, can provide more than just diagnosis and treatment. They can begin to redefine some medical problems as social problems, and through medical education begin to loosen the dependence of medical people on the medical profession. They can provide basic biological information, demystify medical sciences, and help give people more control over their own bodies. For example, in New York, health workers provided a simple way of detecting lead poisoning to the Young Lords Organization. This enabled the Young Lords to serve their people directly through a door-to-door testing campaign in the Barrio, and also to organize them against the landlords who refused to cover lead-painted walls, often with the tacit complicity of the city housing officials.

It is this kind of scientific practice that most clearly characterizes Science for the People. It serves the oppressed and impoverished classes and strengthens their ability to struggle. The development of People's Science must be marked by these and other characteristics. For example, any discoveries or new techniques should be such that all people have reasonably easy access to them, both physically and financially. This would also militate against their use as a means of generating individual or corporate profit. Scientific developments, whether in the natural or social sciences, that could conceivably be employed as weapons against the people must be carefully evaluated before the work is carried out. Such decisions will always be difficult. They demand a consideration of factors like the relative accessibility of these developments to each side, the relative ease and certainty of use, which will of course depend on the demand, the extent to which the power balance in a specific situation could be shifted and at what risk, and so forth. Finally, scientific or technological programs which claim to meet the needs of the people, but which in fact strengthen the existing political system and defuse their ability to struggle, are the opposite of People's Science.

There is a wide range of activities that might constitute a Science for the People. This work can be described as falling into six broad areas:

1. *Technical assistance to movement organizations and oppressed people.* The free people's health centers have already been described as an example of this approach. Another example would be designing environmental poisoning detection kits for groups trying to protect themselves from pollution and trying to organize opposition to the capitalist system which hampers effective solutions to pollution problems. The lead poisoning test was such an effort, and other kinds of pollution are equally amenable to this approach. These kits would have to be simple to operate, easy to construct, and made from readily available and cheap materials.

Research to aid student and community struggles for free, decent higher education is being conducted by the New University Conference and other groups. Of interest are answers to questions involving the economy of higher education, such as what classes pay what share of the tax bill, how are educational resources apportioned among the classes, how is higher education differentially defined in different types of schools, how does discrimination operate against women and Third World people in education, what role do corporations play in setting up program priorities, especially in the working-class junior colleges. Research also needs to be done on the possibilities for open enrollment in various school systems and on the test instruments and the tracking system which channel students and distribute educational privilege on the basis of social class.

Research could be performed which would assist rank-and-file groups now attempting to organize politically in the factories. Useful information might include the correlation between industrial accident rates and the class, race, and sex of the work force, the mechanics of the unemployment compensation and accident compensation programs which more often make profits for insurance companies than help workers, the nature of union-management contracts, how they have served to undermine workers' demands and how they might be made more effective, and so on. All of these projects would be examples of Science for the People as technical assistance.

2. *Foreign technical help to revolutionary movements.* American scientific workers can provide material aid to assist struggles in other countries against U.S. or other forms of imperialism, or against domestic fascism. For example, the Popular Liberation Movement of Angola, fighting against Portuguese domination, has requested help in setting up medical training facilities. These are sorely needed in those areas of Angola that have been liberated and are undergoing social and economic reconstruction.

Similarly, Americans can aid revolutionary regimes abroad. The effects of the U.S. blockade of Cuba could be reduced by North American scientific workers going there to do research or to teach, as some have already done. Or, they could do research here on problems of importance for development in Cuba, such as on sugar cane and rice production, tropical pest control, and livestock breeding. As a minimum, U.S. scientists should be encouraged to establish regular contact and exchange reprints and other information with their Cuban counterparts.

Another example of this kind of foreign and technical assistance was a Science for Vietnam project, which involved collaboration between scientists from the U.S. and the Democratic Republic of Vietnam and the Provisional Revolutionary Government of South Vietnam on such problems as locating plastic pellets in human flesh (several years ago the U.S. Air Force increased the terrorizing effect of anti-personnel bombs by switching from metal fragmentation devices to plastic pellets, which do not show up on x-rays), reforestation techniques, how to decontaminate herbicide-saturated soils, and many other problems now facing the Vietnamese as a result of the U.S. intervention there.

This kind of foreign technical assistance has important political significance in addition to its material consequences, for it is the most direct way one can oppose the imperialist policies of the U.S. government, undermine its legitimacy, and go over to the side of the oppressed people of the world. If an important sector of the population, like scientific workers, begins to act in this way, it may encourage similar action by workers in other areas.

3. *People's research.* Unlike the technical assistance projects described above, which are directly tied in with ongoing struggles, there are areas in which scientists should take the initiative and begin developing projects that will aid struggles that are just beginning to develop. For example, workers in the medical and social sciences and in education could help design a program for client-controlled day care centers which would both free women from the necessity of continual child care and provide a thoroughly socialist educational experience for the children. As such, it would be useless to those who are trying to co-opt the day care struggle into an extension of social control or as a means of making profits.

For use in liberation struggles, self-defense techniques could be developed that would be readily available to the people, and useless to their highly technological opposition. Biologists and chemists, for example, could develop an all-purpose gas mask for which the necessary materials are simple, easy to assemble, readily available, and inexpensive.

Physiologists and others could perform definitive research in nutrition and disseminate their findings so that poor and working-class people would have information on how to get the most nourishing diet for the least cost. Furthermore, such research could aid them in avoiding the possibly dangerous food additives and contaminants that are now found in most packaged foods.

As a minimal effort, medical researchers could begin to concentrate their work on the health needs of the poor. The causes of the higher infant mortality rates and lower life expectancy of a large part of the working class, particularly racial minorities, should get much more research attention. Occasionally funds are available for this kind of research but the class background and biases of many researchers often predispose them toward work on other problems. In addition, new ways of distributing and utilizing medical knowledge, especially with respect to prevention, must be designed.

4. *Exposés and power structure research.* Most of the important political, mili-

tary and economic decisions in this country are made behind closed doors, outside the public arena. Questions about how U.S. corporations dominate foreign economic markets and governments, how corporate conglomerates control domestic markets and policymaking, how party machines run city governments, how universities and foundations interlock with military and various social-control strategies, how the class struggle in the United States is blunted and obscured, etc., must be researched and the conclusions published to inform all the people.

Exemplary work of this kind has already been performed by research collectives like the North American Congress on Latin America (NACLA), the National Action Research on the Military Industrial Complex (NARMIC), the Africa Research Group and others. These groups have provided valuable information for community and campus groups in campaigns such as those against university collaboration with the Indochina War and exploitation in various Third World countries, against anti-personnel weapons manufacturers (like Minneapolis Honeywell), and against specific corporations involved in particularly noxious forms of oppression (like Polaroid's large investments in South Africa and its current contract to provide the government there with photo-ID cards for all citizens which will help that government to implement more effectively its racist apartheid policy).

There is growing need for research in the biological and physical sciences to expose how the quest for corporate profits is poisoning and destroying irreplaceable and critical aspects of our environment. This information, in a form anyone can understand, should be made available to action-oriented community ecology groups.

5. *Ideological struggle.* Ruling-class ideology is effectively disseminated by educational institutions and the mass media, resulting in misinformation that clouds people's understanding of their own oppression and limits their ability to resist it. This ruling-class ideology must be exposed as the self-serving manipulation that it is. There are many areas where this needs to be accomplished. Arguments of biological determinism are used to keep blacks and other Third World people in lower educational tracks, and these racist arguments have recently been bolstered by psychologist Arthur Jensen's focusing on supposed racial differences in intelligence. Virtually every school of psychopathology and psychotherapy defines homosexuals as sick or "maladjusted" (to a presumably "sane" society). These definitions are used to excuse this society's discriminatory laws and practices with respect to its large homosexual population, and have only recently been actively opposed by the gay liberation movement. Similarly, many psychotherapists and social scientists use some parts of Freudian doctrine to justify sexist treatment of women.

The elitist biases of most American social scientists oppress students from working-class and poor backgrounds, as well as women and minorities, by failing to adequately portray their history and culture. Instead, bourgeois culture and ruling-class history are emphasized as if they were the only reality. This laying on of culture is particularly heavy-handed in community and working-class colleges (for an elaboration of this point, see J. McDermott, *Nation*, March 10, 1969). To combat this, the social scientist should work to make available to the people their true history and cultural achievements.

This kind of Science for the People as ideological struggle can be engaged in at several levels, from the professional societies and journals to the public arena, but for it to be most effective it should reach the people whose lives it is most relevant to, and who will use it. Those in teaching positions especially have an excellent opportunity to do this. For example, courses in any of the biological sciences should deal with the political reasons why our society is committing ecological murder/suicide. Courses in psychopathology should spend at least as much time on our government officials and our insanely competitive economic system as they do on the tortured victims incarcerated in our mental "hospitals," many of whom would not be there in the first place if they lived in a society where normality and sanity were synonymous. Within these and many other disciplines, individual instructors can prepare reading lists and syllabuses to assist themselves and others who are interested in teaching such courses but lack the background or initiative to do the work themselves.

6. Demystification of science and technology. No one would deny that science and technology have become major influences in the shaping of people's lives. Yet most people lack the information necessary to understand how they are affected by technological manipulation and control. As a result they are physically and intellectually incapable of performing many operations that they are dependent upon, and control over these operations has been relinquished to various experts. Furthermore, these same people undergo an incapacitating emotional change which results in the feeling that everything is too complicated to cope with (whether technological or not), and that only the various experts should participate in decision making which often directly affects their own lives. Clearly, these two factors are mutually enhancing.

In the interests of democracy and people's control, the false mystery surrounding science and technology must be removed and the hold of experts on decision making must be destroyed. Understandable information can be made available to all those for whom it is pertinent. For example, the women's liberation movement has taken the lead in teaching the facts about human reproductive biology to the people who need it the most for control over their own bodies. An example of this is a group of women in the Chicago Women's Liberation Union who have written a series of pamphlets on pregnancy and childbirth, giving complete medical information in language everyone can understand. Free schools and movement publications teach courses and run articles on medical and legal first-aid, self-defense, effective nutrition, building houses, repairing cars and other necessary appliances, and so on. Much more of this kind of work needs to be done. In addition, the relevant scientific information on issues that have important political repercussions, such as radiation poisoning and pesticide tolerance, should be made available to the public.

Part of the job of demystification will have to take place internally, within the scientific community. Scientific workers themselves must expose and counter the elitist, technocratic biases that permeate the scientific and academic establishments. One vehicle for doing this has been the publication *Science for the People*. Attempts to demystify science must take place at many levels. The doctrine that problems of technology can be met with technological rather than political solutions is increasingly being incorporated into the ruling ideology. The counterargument should be made that only political reorganization will be effective in the long run, and this argument will need to be bolstered by more research. On the level of daily practice, elitist tendencies can be undermined in laboratories and classrooms by insisting that *all* workers or students participate in decision making that affects what they do and by creating conditions that ensure them the information necessary to make those decisions. The elitism and hierarchical structuring of most scientific meetings and conventions can be opposed by members forcefully insisting that they be given some control over the selection of speakers and that all scheduled speakers address themselves to the political implications of their work. This is already happening with increasing frequency as radical caucuses begin to form in many of the professional associations.

The practice of Science for the People is long overdue. If scientific workers and students want to overcome the often alienating nature of their own work, their impotence in bringing about meaningful social change, their own oppression and that of most of the other people in the world, they will have to relinquish their uncritical devotion to the pursuit of new knowledge. Scientific workers must reorganize scientific work, not in terms of the traditionally defined disciplines, but according to the real problems they consciously set out to solve. The old breakdown into separate disciplines, which produces "experts" who can barely communicate with each other, must give way to new structures which allow more cooperation and flexibility, and which will undoubtedly demand the acquisition of new skills. Such work can be as intellectually stimulating as the work we do now, with the added satisfaction that it is meeting real needs of people.

If projects like those described above are to constitute a real Science for the People, they must achieve more than their immediate technical goals. They should relate to issues around which people can organize to act in their own self-interest. Research projects should both flow out of the needs and demands of the people, and be relevant to their political struggles. This requires consulting with and relying on the experience of community and movement groups, and taking seriously the criticisms and suggestions that they put forth. Scientists must succeed in redirecting their professional activities away from services to the forces and institutions they oppose and toward a movement they wish to build. Short of this, no matter how much they desire to contribute to the solution, they remain part of the problem.

SCIENCE AND BLACK PEOPLE

Editorial, The Black Scholar

The uses of scientific knowledge cannot be separated from the society in which those uses occur. The myth of "pure" science, of science as a detached, ivory tower pursuit, has been exposed. Science is enmeshed in the prevailing social ideologies. The choice of what subjects to investigate, which experiments to undertake, what methods to employ, which results to emphasize as important, to whom to report results, how to use results, etc., all these and countless other decisions made by scientific investigators are colored by ideology. Ideology is not simply a nebulous cloud hanging in the social atmosphere. It is the assumptions underlying scientific education and training; it is the prod held by the public and private bureaucracies which fund research; it is the personal ambition of scientists who live in a bourgeois materialist society.

Consequently, it comes as no great surprise that black people have been largely excluded from the world of science and technology—both as practitioners and as factors relevant to decision making. Of course, there have been outstanding black scientists and inventors, and their achievements are worthy of emulation, but the reality of racism has excluded most of us from the pursuit of science. Regarded as degraded beings, prisoners of undisciplined emotions and suitable only for manual labor, black people have for generations been barred from white institutions of scientific training.

Moreover, racism has meant that white scientists have regarded us as an undifferentiated part of the environment, a given, rather than a subject active in changing the environment. Our cranial capacity and social institutions may be investigated from time to time, but our brainpower and social needs are seldom considered relevant when important scientific and technological decisions are being made. To the white world of research and development, we are indeed invisible.

Unfortunately, our agrarian heritage and general exclusion from the world of science has generated an anti-science, anti-intellectual attitude among many of us. In colleges today many young black people regard the pursuit of scientific training as "copping out," as individual "tripping" at the expense of the struggle. Certainly it cannot be denied that some black scientists and technicians have dropped out of the struggle, but this must be attributed to their subservience to the individualist and materialist values of this society; it is not a result per se of being a scientist.

It is imperative for us to realize that, despite its abuses in this country, science is key to the material development of society. Industrial advancement and social progress would be impossible without scientific research and development. While it is true that science cannot be separated from ideology, it is also true that ideologies can be changed and hence the uses of science can be redirected. It is no accident that the developing countries of the Third World have given highest priority to building scientific and technological institutes and training young scientists and engineers. Their future survival and independence hinge on developing a culture that encourages science and makes it truly serve the people. (And it is with the intention of undermining their struggle against underdevelopment that the capitalist West has instituted a "brain drain" of scientists and technicians from these Third World nations.)

Scientific training and well-informed inputs into the process of technological decision making can be a progressive addition to the general struggle for black liberation. This is the message that must be taken to black youth today. We are oppressed by our exploiters, but to the extent that we remain ignorant and apathetic we are accomplices in our own oppression. No struggle can be undertaken without knowledge, and it is not enough simply to blame others for our ignorance. Like our brothers and sisters in Africa and the Third World, we must encourage the pursuit of useful knowledge—physical, biological and social—that will enable us to intelligently take command of our own destiny.

SCIENCE, TECHNOLOGY AND BLACK COMMUNITY DEVELOPMENT

Robert C. Johnson

Some may consider it odd to find included on the agenda of Black people a topic such as that being presented in this article. Some may ask what do science and technology have to do with Black survival and progress? What do they have to do with urban areas? It is my purpose today to explore the thesis that scientific breakthroughs and technological developments affect Black Americans in very profound, pervasive and substantial manners. So much so that I would argue that without examining and being aware of these various developments, Black Americans risk being subjugated to the vicissitudes of scientific and technological forces which are as oppressive, demeaning and domineering as are the socioeconomic and political forces of racism and exploitation.

I would further maintain that we should go beyond simply becoming aware of these occurrences and begin to make such concerns a top priority in our agendas and programs. Our political and economic advocacies and strategies should entail concerns of a technological and scientific nature, and these should have as much priority as economic development and civil rights. As a matter of fact, I hope to illustrate how these technological and scientific concerns are intricately interwoven with these other political, economic and social matters. I will, indeed, argue that our very existence, and continued survival, growth, and even prosperity in this society and in the world are very much dependent upon the various developments and emerging political debates occurring within the areas of science and technology.

One reason why many people may express reservations about the role of science and technology in Black community affairs is because of the popular view of these two phenomena. Science is generally viewed as some remote, isolated process that occurs by a handful of people in faraway laboratories, wearing white coats and working with test tubes and animals. Technology is viewed as that wonderful process by which marvelous inventions and gadgets are brought into existence. Furthermore, this vision of people in white coats performing miracles is further complicated by the fact that these persons wearing white coats also wear white faces in the popular image. We may have had occasion to hear some Black people use the expression "W-W-M-S-T," which translates to mean "Wonders of the White Man's Science and Technology." Those five letters summarize quite succinctly the whole idea that science and technology are wonders and miracle processes that are somehow created magically and mysteriously by whites.

Such a view is both erroneous and dangerous. It is erroneous because the history of Black Americans and the history of Africans tells us that people of African descent have been in the forefront of scientific and technological break-throughs and have laid the foundation for much of what we currently know as science and technology. It is further erroneous because it assumes that Blacks have been excluded from the scientific and technological process, that process of discovering, manipulating, and creating from natural phenomena goods, prod-ucts, and devices that can be used for social and human purposes. The very fact that Black people have survived and have built and maintained cultures and civilizations demonstrates that they have made judicious use of scientific and technological principles, and have manipulated natural phenomena for their own collective benefit. This popular view of science and technology is also dangerous because it implies that only whites can do science and technology, that Blacks either cannot or should not be part of this process. Furthermore, in a very insidi-ous, albeit indirect manner, it implies that Black people are not capable of pro-ducing in these domains. It is dangerous because it leaves the scientific and technological fate of Black people to others who may not and probably do not have their interests at heart. Such a view removes us from direct participation in and involvement with two aspects of our lives which are growing more and more important in governing and determining the quality of life that we will face on this planet.

Science is generally thought of, at least by the scientific community, as being the process of discovering, explaining and predicting natural phenomena, usually for the purpose of trying to acquire some type of control over these phenomena. We may simply define science as knowledge. (It is defined in Webster as "the body of truth, information, and principles acquired by mankind.") Technology, on the other hand, is the application of knowledge. It is know-how applied to meet social and human needs and ends. While both of these definitions deal with natural forces of the physical environment it must be realized that both science and technology are the creations of man and that they derive their essence and significance from human and social contexts. Science and technology have their origins in humanity. And their development is linked to the development of hu-manity. If we as Black people define ourselves as part of humanity, then, by definition, we are, in part, scientific and technological beings.

The Need for Black Awareness of Science and Technology

Let us now look briefly at the need and importance of Blacks being involved with and aware of scientific and technological developments in our society. Science and technology in American society in the twentieth century are characterized by rapid occurrences and major breakthroughs. Perhaps one of the best accounts of the rapidity and effects of change of a technological nature on the American society has been presented by Alvin Toffler (1970) in *Future Shock*. In this work, Toffler not only chronicles the major scientific and technological changes that have occurred in our society over the past few decades, but more importantly, describes "future shock," which is the "shattering stress and disorientation that we induce in individuals by subjecting them to too much change in too short a time." We can all identify elements of this change in our own personal lives as well as in the world around us—the new gadgets, the new modes of doing things, the new lifestyles, all brought about by technology and science.

In addition to the psychological changes induced by scientific and technological developments, the cultural, economic, political and social institutions of this society have all been affected by science and technology as well. We will touch upon the topic of technology and culture later in this presentation. I will show how Black people have been disproportionately and more adversely affected by these developments than has been the general society at large. It is this heightened state of vulnerability of Blacks that makes technology and science two forces that should compete for our attention, knowledge and efforts along with some of the major issues facing Black people today.

In becoming aware of the fact that science and technology are powerful forces in our lives, we must also come to the realization that the scientific and technological developments are not separate nor removed from the other activities and processes of the society. We must realize that these scientific and technological forces are governed and influenced by the political processes and economic realities of our society. Public policy has as much to do with scientific and technological developments as do intellectual considerations, if not more so. With this awareness of the relationship between science and technology on the one hand and politics and economics on the other, we will be in a position to understand that we can influence technological and scientific developments as they affect the cultural, social, political and economic realities of our lives. Such an awareness will lead us to realize that scientific and technological decisions often times are made in the public arena through the processes of public policy. Hence, our political and economic clout can be harnessed and directed toward these forces.

Earl Graves points out in *Black Enterprise* (October 1979, p. 9) that "politics and economics cannot be separated." He goes on to say "we have reached a stage where we need to develop structures, mobilizing our economic clout. A people who have an annual income of 101 million dollars and who spend far in excess of that possess the potential for clout." He also notes that we have yet to realize and maximize either our political clout or our economic potential. Clearly then, if we lag behind in areas in which we at least recognize the need for maximizing potential, i.e., economics and politics, then we are sorely behind in the area of science and technology, because, as indicated before, we have failed to realize that we have a stake in and the ability to influence these domains. Thus, our potential is even more greatly untapped in these areas, which renders us more vulnerable to these forces.

Understanding the political and economic aspects and implications of science and technology clarifies the need for Black people to be in the position to thwart undesirable innovations and consequences arising from these forces. Such an understanding shows how imperative it is to have a say in policies governing science and technology. Furthermore, such understanding and awareness show the necessity for devising or creating answers or countermeasures to the real and potential adverse effects of these two areas.

Technology and Culture

I would now like to turn my attention to reviewing in summary form some of the more salient effects of scientific innovations and technological inventions on the American society, and show how these have impacted the Black community. It is generally agreed that several technological inventions have affected our manner of living in major ways this century. Among these are the automobile, the television, the computer, and the telephone.

Observers of the phenomenon known as "automobility" have claimed that the automobile has had such industrial, sociological, economical, and environmental impact that it is responsible for the development of a new consumer goods-oriented society and economy that has persisted from the 1920s into the present; that it is responsible for the expansion of local tax systems; that it set the precedent during the 1920s for the great extension of consumer installment credit; that it was a major force unifying Americans during the period between the two World Wars; that the automobile was destructive of "the beneficial, as well as the repressive aspects of community" (Flink, 1975). And they even claim that automobility was also in large part responsible for the depressed condition of agriculture in the 1920s. It is even pointed out that the automobile affected relationships between individuals and their communities. James Flink, in *The Car Culture,* cites a study which says "the opportunities afforded by the automobile provide a basis for new mobility for whites as well as Negroes based upon personal standards rather than community mores—upon what the individual wants to do rather than what the community does not want him to do" (pp. 156–57). Flink goes further in indicating the effects of the automobile on race relations in this society. He notes that the automobile accelerated the exodus of the middle class and businesses to suburbia, thus creating affluent suburbs and isolated ghettos in the central cities, paving way for the widespread riots during the mid-1960s.

While some of these claims about the pervasive influence of the automobile on American society may be open to question and skepticism, it is crystal clear that the automobile has had a substantial impact on individual mores as well as psychological states of citizens of this country in addition to its profound economic, technological and social impacts. One observer, in noting the central role of automobility concluded "no one has or perhaps can reliably estimate the vast size of capital invested in reshaping society to fit the automobile" (quoted in Flink, p. 141). Flink notes: "that American urban life would conform to the needs of automobility rather than vice versa was obvious by the early 1920s." This phenomenon known as automobility has undoubtedly affected our ways of living, ranging from how and where we shop, where we live and work to the dating and mating habits of teenagers and adults. Among other things cars become indicators of social status and social acceptance. It has become a concrete symbol of the crass materialistic attitude that says "I am somebody because I have something." Unfortunately, in the Black community this attitude appears to be quite rampant as we can tell by the steady stream of long, late-model gas-guzzling "rides" that dot our community.

Beyond the attitudinal and social impacts of the automobile, we are becoming increasingly aware of the technological and environmental problems posed by the automobile. We have to face daily the smog, traffic congestion, parking problems created by the automobile culture. There is noise pollution and the problem of junk and abandoned cars. Motor vehicle safety is another major concern and by-product of the car culture in this society. According to Flink, in the last decade over 4 million Americans a year were injured in automobile accidents. There were 570 fatalities for every 10 billion miles of travel by car, versus only 14 for every 10 billion miles flown, 13 for every 10 billion traveled by bus, and 5 for every 10 billion miles traveled by train (p. 215). Flink has identified other disenchanting consequences of the car culture. He points out that the infrastructure built to support the car culture has had these effects: "the building of urban expressways has destroyed cohesive urban neighborhoods and city parks, further alienated racial minorities and contributed to the declining tax base of the central city" (pp. 214–15).

Television has had just as pervasive an impact on American society as the automobile even though it may not be as dramatically obvious. The rise of television has been meteoric. It was possible in 1945 for a national pollster to ask the country "Do you know what a television is? Have you ever seen a television set in operation?" (quoted in Comstock, et al., 1978, p. 1). Today there are few households in the United States without at least one television set, and many households are multiset homes. In a most comprehensive review of television and its effects on human behavior, Rand researchers have delineated some of the principal characteristics of this technological medium (Comstock et al., 1978). It is estimated that there are about 4.7 million hours of programming shown annually in the United States. On any given evening at the peak hour, television has an audience of more than 95 million Americans. While people complain about certain aspects of television, namely the commercials, sex-related content judged inappropriate for children, and violence, most people in this society consider it as the number one medium for receiving forms of entertainment, knowledge and information. Television is the principal source of news; it is considered to be the provider of the most complete coverage and also the most credible or believable source. Television is known to shape the behavior of those viewing it as well. In addition to consuming large amounts of hours of their time, the television also influences the way people act within their households. It has affected relationships within families and between family members. As the Rand study points out:

> the impact of television on the expenditure of leisure time has been sizable. Television has markedly increased the total amount of time spent with the mass media. Television viewing as a primary activity, excluding very disruptive viewing while doing something else, consumes more of the leisure time of Americans than any other activity. Among almost forty kinds of primary activities, exclusive categories into which the day can be divided, television viewing falls behind only sleep and time spent at work. (P. 10)

This study goes on to say that:

> Television's absorption of leisure time naturally occurs at the expense of other activities. One of television's most marked effects appears to have been time spent sleeping. It also appears to have reduced time spent in social gatherings away from home, in radio listening, in reading books, in miscellaneous leisure, in movie-going, in religious activities and in household tasks. (P. 10)

Television viewing also affects other aspects of life in this society. Commercials entice us to buy products that we ordinarily would not be aware of. Television may very well have influence on matters such as health practices, dietary preferences, or basic values (such as the desire to acquire material goods). Television has been considered an important factor in the political socialization of Americans since it dispenses information and because information is a major ingredient in political socialization.

The relationship between television viewing and aggressive or anti-social behavior is also important to consider. The Rand report states: "The viewing of television violence appears to increase the likelihood of subsequent aggressiveness" (p. 13).

The available evidence on the relationship between Blacks and the television shows that Blacks tend to watch more television, that Black children typically spend more time in front of televisions than do white children, and that Blacks are more likely to look upon television as a source of knowledge and information. Additionally, research shows that Blacks are usually portrayed on television either in a very trite fashion, in lesser roles, or relatively infrequently. The implications of these various findings are profound and should be noted. If Blacks are among the heavy viewers of television and they are similarly treated in a very negative and stereotypic manner, but yet and still they put a great deal of faith in television as a source of information and knowledge, then the media tells them that they are nothing, that they are nobodies and they tend to believe it, and therefore act upon it. In this light, let me add parenthetically that we need to ask the question: given that Blacks are major viewers of television and television violence appears to increase the likelihood of subsequent aggressiveness, is there any relationship between television-viewing and the substantial increases that we have noted in Black-on-Black crime?

We can conclude that the net effect of these various situations with television is that they reinforce the position society imposes on Blacks. Therefore, it can be argued that television is oppressive because it maintains and reinforces the status quo of this society which itself is oppressive to Blacks.

This society and our people within it have been affected by other technological innovations this century. The combined effects of industrialization, cybernation and agricultural mechanization serve to shape the employment patterns, or should I say the unemployment patterns, that the Black community faces today. We can even go so far as to say that they even shaped the very existence of the Black community. At the beginning of this century, the Black community in America was essentially a rural one. As agricultural mechanization was introduced on a large scale, massive rural exodus occurred, including that of Blacks. The industries of the North attracted many southern Black migrants to that region, leading to increased Black urbanization in the North and in the South as well. Some scholars (Frazier, Martin and Martin) have pointed to this process as a key factor in the loss of Black community cohesiveness and family spirit. Life in crowded cities increased the opportunities for crime, alcoholism, marital break-up and many other adverse social consequences that take place in Black communities.

An obvious key to the viability of the Black community is employment, or economic stability. Yet, technology has affected Black economic stability. The sociologist, Sidney Willhelm (1971) captures this point in a most poignant and succinct manner. He writes:

> The Negro becomes a victim of neglect as he becomes useless to an emerging economy of automation. With the onset of automation the Negro moves out of his historical state of oppression into one of uselessness. Increasingly, he is not so much economically exploited as he is irrelevant. The tremendous historical change is taking place in these terms: he is not needed. He is not so much oppressed as unwanted; not so much unwanted as unnecessary; not so much abused as ignored. The dominant whites no longer need to exploit the black minority; as automation proceeds, it will be easier for the former to disregard the latter. In short, White America, by a more perfect application of mechanization and a vigorous reliance upon automation, disposes of the Negro; consequently, the Negro transforms from an exploited labor force into an outcast. The Negro's anguish does not rise only out of brutalities of past oppression; the anxiety stems, more than ever before, out of being discarded as a waste product of technological production. (P. 210)

Thus, agricultural mechanization, one form of technology, drove us off the farms in the South and forced us to the industrialized cities of the South and the North. Industrialization, another form of technology, therefore served as a magnet to draw us to the urban areas.

But what has life been like in the urban areas? Again, we are affected by technological forces in this environment. In recent years, studies of cancer rates over the last twenty-five years show that the cancer incidence rate for Blacks is higher than that for whites. During this period of time the overall cancer incident rate for Blacks rose 8 percent, while for whites it dropped 3 percent. During this twenty-five year period, cancer mortality for Blacks increased 26 percent, while for whites it rose 5 percent. Why are these cancer rates different for Blacks and whites? Those who have studied this situation point out than environmental and social factors are the principal causes more so than natural consequences. In a U.S. government document on the topic of Blacks and cancer, the following has been pointed out concerning the higher incidence of cancer among Black Americans:

> . . . more Blacks have been exposed to environmental pollutants that have been linked to cancer, especially in the years since World War II. Also more Blacks are living in cities and the rates of all forms of cancer in all races are higher in more crowded industrialized areas than in rural areas. The increased risks in cities also may be related to lifestyle. People who live in cities generally smoke and drink more and the use of both tobacco and alcohol is related to certain forms of cancer. (U.S. Department of Health, Education, and Welfare, p. 4: see also Silverberg and Poindexter, 1979)

Thus, the forces of technology, which forced us into the urban areas have seen to it that Blacks run a greater risk of being exposed to industrial carcinogens. This risk, coupled with the principal factor of the lack of adequate medical care and facilities in the Black community, explain in large part our greater mortality and illness due to cancer.

Our increased urbanization makes us vulnerable to other problems which are basically technological in nature as well. We can look at the situation of food, food technology, agricultural science, nutrition and the related issues of Black health and life expectancy. Urban dwellers do not produce food. Farmers do. As we became more and more urbanites and less and less farmers, we produced less of our own food. This means, purely and simply, that we are now dependent upon others for the very substance of life—food. Various developments in food technology and agricultural practices have increased the stock of food and the production of food, but they have also increased the risks of food consumption. Because of a greater variety of additives, preservatives, artificial ingredients, and chemicals, we are beginning to note adverse effects upon the health of people. Americans are overfed but malnourished. We eat a lot, but a lot of the wrong things. It has been estimated that collectively, people in this country are one billion pounds overweight.

We do not eat proper diets nor in a very healthy manner. In fact, our eating habits may cause a deterioration in our health status and abort our longevity. It has been strongly suspected for a long time that our diet plays a role in the incidence of heart disease, cancer, hypertension, strokes, hyperactivity in children, and many other medical and health malfunctions. This year, the surgeon general of the United States issued a benchmark but highly controversial study on the prevention of disease. This report, which confirms many of the admonitions and recommendations of health food advocates, calls for Americans to eat less saturated fat and cholesterol, less salt, less sugar, more whole grains, cereals, fruits and vegetables, and relatively more fish, poultry, legumes (which are peas, beans, peanuts, etc.) and less red meat. On the other hand, the meat, dairy and egg industries are up in arms about this report, and can be expected to issue alternative views on the value of these products in our diet and on our health.

Clearly then, this is another arena in which we need to exercise some scientific astuteness and judgment in order to determine the validity of the various claims, and to be in a position to affect an area of our life which is too critical to our existence—food.

Obviously, the food problem can be considered very important given that the food is generally not grown in the cities, particularly the inner cities. There are several ways to deal with this problem. One is the home gardening program that has been implemented in many cities, where patches of unused land are utilized for agricultural purposes. Thus one grows one's own food and therefore one knows what one is eating. Another possibility is what is known as the Farm to Market Project, a program implemented by a group of Blacks at Cornell University. This program has been described as a "strategy for controlling food costs for urban poor people in conjunction with support mechanisms for small farmer cooperatives in the rural southeast." More specifically,

> The Farm to Market Project is conceived as an approach to solving a series of acute problems confronting limited resource farmers in America, particularly in the South. And secondly, to increase the flow of affordable fresh and nutritious food to America's urban centers, particularly to inner-city areas where many poor people, who are in need of additional quantities of fresh food, live. (Agricultural Teams, Inc., Food to Market Project handout)

There are many current situations which have scientific and technological aspects to them that can be noted. There is the energy crisis which is well known to all of us. Lerone Bennett, in a recent article in *Ebony* magazine (October 1979), comments on how this problem, which is both economic and technological in nature, is threatening to set Black people back to a pre-1960 state. This "energy siege," as Bennett and others call it, has already had deadly effect for the less fortunate of those in our race. So much so, in fact, that in St. Louis a predominantly white church in a wealthy section of this city bought wood-burning stoves to give to needy families, many of them Black. Here we are seeing Black people turning to a technological throw-back of the beginning of the century in order to survive in present day America. Of the many technological and scientific issues facing this country, only on this one situation have Black people voiced some concern and opinion. Unfortunately, this commentary from the Black community has been too little, too late, and too divisive, rendering it at this point almost ineffectual. It is clear that we will have to "get our act together" in order to have some impact on the transition era from non-renewable energy sources to other viable, productive and safe forms of energy. Technical, political, and economic influences will have to come to bear on this matter of vital importance to the continued survival of Black institutions and communities.

Another area where the same combination of influence and interest, i.e., technical, political, and economic, will have to be employed is housing. We are facing a housing shortage in this nation and the solution is in part technological in nature. In fact, the National Aeronautics and Space Administration (NASA) has built what it calls the NASA Technology Utilization House. Its billing claims "(the) house of the future is ready today." This agency predicts that for this type of home, which has as its unique features solar energy use, energy and water conservation, safety, security, and cost, will be available for wide spread dissemination in the very near future. To my knowledge, the extent to which this new development has been assessed for its potential impact on Black communities, with a critical housing shortage facing them, has not occurred. Clearly, such an important development should not occur unscrutinized, especially since it has widespread implications for the building, construction, and materials industry, which in turn have broad implications for Black employment.

As the economic and social position of Blacks declines in this society, many Black leaders are hinting that mass social protest and civil unrest may be in store as a response to our deteriorating status. In light of this, we must be mindful of the advances occurring in law enforcement technology. A vast armory of sophisticated, technological weaponry has been created for controlling "urban unrest" and where it is not already employed, it sits stockpiled, awaiting deployment in the case of "civil disobedience." The widespread use of technological and electronic surveillance of Black leaders and civil rights organizations is well known. As a matter of fact, Andy Young's downfall came in part because of electronic surveillance of his premises as well of those of the foreign governments and agents with whom he was dealing.

The influence of scientific developments and technological innovations is so pervasive that they have even entered the traditional realms of our culture. For good or bad, electronics has transformed Black music and has added various dimensions to it, and miniaturization has allowed for us to have this music available to us in many different forms and many different places, i.e., in our homes, our cars, our offices, at our worksites.

Thus, to date it is no exaggeration to claim that science and technology have dramatically affected and even altered traditional Black life as we have known it up until this point in the twentieth century. So while the advent of television and the automobile, for example, have been major technological forces this far in the twentieth century, we can look to other technologies and scientific breakthroughs to be major influences on our lives in the near and long range future.

The computer is a coming force in the decades of the eighties and the nineties. For the twenty-first century technological spin-offs from the space program and developments in bio-medical fields will surely dominate in that century, as the computer, television, and the automobile have dominated the twentieth cen-

tury. For the sake of brevity, I will only highlight some of the possible consequences and implications of these technological and scientific developments. Let
us begin by looking at the application of the computer in the next two decades of
this century.

The computer will be the basis for many systems important in our lives—
communications, education, medicine, finance, economics, transportation, law,
and politics. The computer, coupled with other technologies, such as communications satellites, microwave relays, cable television, will bring about new systems. We will have telemedicine, where diagnoses and health care are dispensed
remotely via various forms of technology. Tele-education will come into existence, where learning laboratories will be established in the homes, based on
micro-computers, various input and output devices, software programs, and
linked to data bases all over the world. Various institutions such as museums,
universities, businesses, and other settings will be hooked up via the computer
and telecommunications systems into an *educational tele-communication technological network* beamed to the child in his own home or some other environment,
rendering the concepts of schools as we know them today obsolete. We will have
tele-finance, where it will be possible to conduct financial and economic matters
without money. In essence, we will be converting to a cashless society.

Numerous other illustrations of the application of computers, satellites, and
various other combinations of technologies can be cited. While these accounts
may sound fascinating, exciting, promising, and glowing we need to be mindful
that widespread use of the computer and the various other technologies increases
the chances of violation of certain basic civil liberties, especially the invasion of
privacy. Since the computer is expected to be a dominating force for the rest of
this century, we need to be critically aware of its potencies.

Technological spin-offs from the space program have already entered our
daily lives, and we can expect to see other direct and indirect applications of
space age technology to our ways of living. It is not inconceivable that in the
twenty-first century space technology will have advanced and have been applied
in such a way that we will have people living in outer space and in enclaves
known as space colonies. Space shuttles between these extraterrestrial colonies
and the earth will be as much a part of our transportation system as airplanes,
cars and buses are today. We have already seen the beginnings of such operations with moon shots, the building of space platforms, the orbiting of various
planets, and with many of the other feats accomplished in outer space by the
Russians and the Americans. Research and plans are already underway and have
been so for several years now, to put factories, health care facilities, farms and
the like in outer space, on other planets, or on the moon. It doesn't take much
imagination to vision large numbers of people fleeing a polluted, decaying, junk-
filled, overcrowded earth for the roominess and solitude of outer-space cities and
farms, just as in the 1950s and 60s large numbers of people fled the cities for the
suburbs. Nor does it take much imagination to see who will be left behind in this
decayed, cancer-producing environment, with fouled rivers and oceans, depleted
resources, and bankrupt institutions as the endangered species. After outer space

has been colonized, generations later Black people and other people of color may find themselves in a situation of trying to prevent the resettlement of the earth by those who have fled it, just as we are now faced with the situation of others who fled the cities now trying to reclaim them.

Of all the technological developments and scientific breakthroughs that I have noted I find most disturbing and most frightening those that are related to the bio-medical fields. With these developments we see not only the possibility of our life-styles, our culture, our social and political institutions being changed, or our environment being altered, but we face the very real possibility of having ourselves, as a species of people, transformed, or if you will, deformed into something else. Developments in the bio-medical fields are occurring rapidly, but disturbingly, very quietly. Persons familiar with the occurrences in this field, make no bones about the profound effects of biological metamorphosis. Pamela Sargent, in *Bio-Futures,* states: "Lest we deliberately turn out backs on biological innovation, or restrict research, biological advances will change our institutions and our attitudes" (p. xviii). She goes on to note: "Biological changes could in time affect our notions of what a human being *is,* we would become many different and divergent species. Each designed for different tasks" (p. xix).

Let us pause and ask what tasks would Black people be assigned? What variety of species will we be destined to become? The means for such biological changes are already available to us through a variety of techniques. Cloning, the use of artificial wombs, test tube fertilization, and hybridization of animal species and humans are new ways of reproducing human beings other than the traditional way that we have customarily used. Other possible biological innovations include somatic alternation, which involves making changes in a grown person's biological construction, and genetic manipulation. People in research labs are now deep freezing tissues and organs. This work may lead to the preservation of sick people until they can be treated by newly discovered methods. As Sargent notes, "a more speculative possibility is that people now alive might be frozen and revived in a future when immortality is a reality." She goes on to say, "immortality itself or a greatly extended lifespan may be realized in the future" (p. xix).

As noted earlier I found these developments to be very frightening. Others share this view. Howard and Rifkin (1977), in *Who Should Play God?* find genetic engineering more dangerous than nuclear technology. They write:

> For many years social commentators have looked upon nuclear weaponry as the most powerful and dangerous tool at the disposal of humanity. With the development of human genetic engineering, a tool even more awesome is now available. It is true that nuclear weaponry poses the ever present threat of annihilation of human life on this planet. But with genetic engineering there is a threat of a very different kind: that by calculation and planning, not accident or the precipitous passion of the moment, some people will make conscious and deliberate decisions to irreversibly alter the biological structure of millions of other men and women and their descendants for all time. This is a form of annihilation, every bit as deadly as nuclear holocaust, and even more pro-

found—whatever forms of future beings are developed will be forced to live the consequences of the biological designs that were molded for them. (Pp. 9–10)

Bio-genetic manipulations, cloning, test-tube babies and the like bode ill for those of us who have been victims of forced sterilization, brutal castration, psycho-surgery, aversion therapy, biased psychological testing, calculated syphilis experiments, persistent campaigns of birth and population control, and many other insidious and inhumane forms of so-called scientific research and human experimentation.

Blacks have always been the favorite sources of supply for medical and scientific research. Transplants of organs in dead or dying Black bodies provide life for white recipients. We are targets of many too many theories positing our alleged mental, biological, genetic, and cultural inferiority. It is only natural and logical that if this movement of genetic engineering grows, we will be likely targets and victims of it.

Needed Black Action

Earlier in this paper, the need for Black political awareness of and participation in the public debates surrounding these scientific and technological issues was pointed out and stressed. Many of these various developments are still underway. The public and scientific debates on them are just beginning. The Black community, which has so much to suffer from these occurrences, should be participating in these debates and should be trying to influence these developments at both the policy and technical levels. I dare say, however, in terms of policy and technical competence, we are thoroughly unprepared to deal with these complex, but yet vital issues facing us today.

National Black organizations need to identify and pull together groups of committed, concerned and capable Black scientists, technologists, engineers, policy analysts, social scientists, community workers, and activists, to review these situations and to devise plans, strategies, and tactics for coming to terms with them. Long-term planning and in-depth analysis must go into the solutions and proposals needed to address these issues. Simply convening a conference, meeting, or seminar or a series of them is not adequate to muster the type of analysis and action demanded by the gravity of these issues. Instead, support must be provided that allows these scholars, technicians, practitioners, and lay persons to devote a considerable amount of time, thought, and energy to these concerns. I argue that these matters should be ranked with our other priorities, mainly because they are inseparable from our concerns for decent and fair living conditions for Black Americans.

On another level, that of educational preparation, we must begin to address ourselves to becoming prepared to live in an increasingly technological society and being able to master a social environment that depends more and more upon technology and science. In order to have sufficient person-power, capable of fathoming the depth of scope of these issues, capable of proposing countermeasures and of informing policy, we must begin to prepare our young for training in the sciences, mathematics and in the various fields of technology.

Blacks, in order to be competitive in the arenas of scientific accomplishment and technological innovation, will have to be exposed to the sciences at an early age. They will have to be inspired to enter these fields, motivated to achieve and given the confidence that allows all the rest to happen. In short, science and technology should become a part of our collective life-style as much as sports, music, dancing, and religion have become. We should seek to reclaim this part of our cultural heritage and to integrate it into our current living patterns. *Science and technology should be integral parts of our socialization process.* They should permeate our personal and social development as Black people. In some of my other writings I have proposed how this may be done, utilizing various strategies and techniques as well as our cultural heritage. And from my current research I am also attempting to identify factors which inhibit or facilitate our participation in math-related fields as a first step, and hope to move beyond this to develop programs that will enable us to overcome the fears and ignorances that we have about these disciplines.

Without these educational and political strategies and tactics, we are in a very vulnerable position, vis-à-vis scientific developments and technological innovations in this society. If we do not begin to address these issues, our chances for survival, be it in a rural, urban or extraterrestrial environment, are almost nil.

R E F E R E N C E S

Bennett, Lerone Jr. "Black America and 'The Energy Siege,' " *Ebony,* October 1979, pp. 31–32, 34, 36, 38, 42.

Comstock, George, Stephen Chaffee, Natan Katzman, Maxwell McCombs, and Daniel Roberts. *Television and Human Behavior.* New York: Columbia University Press, 1978.

Flink, James J. *The Car Culture.* Cambridge, Mass.: MIT Press, 1975.

Frazier, E. Franklin. *The Negro Family in the United States.* Chicago: University of Chicago Press, 1939.

Howard, Ted, and Jeremy Rifkin. *Who Should Play God?* New York: Dell Publishing Company, Inc., 1977.

Martin, E., and J. Martin. *The Black Extended Family.* Chicago: University of Chicago Press, 1978.

Sargent, Pamela, (ed.). *Bio-Futures.* New York: Random House Inc., 1976.

Silverberg, Edwin, and Syril E. Poindexter. "Cancer Facts and Figures for Black Americans—1979." New York: American Cancer Society, Inc.

Toffler, Alvin. *Future Shock.* New York: Bantam Books, Inc., 1970.

U.S. Health Department of Health, Education and Welfare, Public Health Service, National Institutes of Health. "What Black Americans Should Know about Cancer." DHEW Pub. No. (NIH) 78–1635.

Willhelm, Sidney M. *Who Needs the Negro?* Garden City, N. Y.: Doubleday and Company, Inc., 1971.

TOWARDS A DEMOCRATIC STRATEGY FOR SCIENCE

The New Politics of Science

David Dickson

In the immediate postwar period, the single issue that lay heaviest on the conscience and consciousness of the scientific community was its contribution, whether explicit or implicit, to the most horrendous weapon ever conceived, developed, or used—the atomic bomb. Few challenged the escalating budget for science at the time, particularly since, coming primarily from public sources, the funds could be justified as social expenditures relatively untainted by the search for private profit. Where protest movements did spring up, as around the Atomic Scientists of Chicago, the Federation of American Scientists, and the journal *Bulletin of Atomic Scientists,* these tended to focus on the moral schizophrenia that the bomb had created within the scientific community that was projected onto broader debates about the impact of science and society.[1]

Accepting the responsibility for creating the knowledge that had made the bomb possible, these groups tended to characterize critical political questions about science in terms of the balance between the "uses" (such as nuclear power) and the "abuses" (such as nuclear weapons) to which scientific knowledge could be put. Thus the period in which science saw rapidly increased funding, due partly to its contribution to long-term military technology, was only one in which criticism of the implications of this trend, from both within and outside the scientific community, tended to focus on ways of bringing the military uses of science under civilian control. Many of those closely involved in the Manhattan Project, for example, subsequently devoted almost equal efforts to furthering diplomatic initiatives aimed at placing controls on nuclear energy under the Atoms for Peace banner.[2]

In the late 1960s the focus and style of the critique shifted. The use during the Vietnam War of a wide variety of new chemical and electronic weapons, as well as scientific experts in fields that ranged from agriculture to sociology, meant that the taint of collaboration with the military was no longer restricted to nuclear scientists, but affected virtually all disciplines of science. Furthermore, growing awareness of the environmental and occupational health problems associated with science-based industrial processes made it impossible to maintain a clear distinction between the military (i.e., "bad") and civilian (i.e., "good") applications of science. A new generation of critics, taking their lead from the civil rights and free speech movements in the United States, the student revolts in Paris and elsewhere in Europe, made sharp attacks on the political uses of scientific rationality. Groups such as Science for the People demonstrated how social and political values saturate the scientific laboratory and even, in cases such as sociobiology and the claimed links between genes and social behaviour, the ideas and theories claimed to belong to science itself.[3]

Despite the importance of both the analytical and political work carried out on such topics, however, the agenda of the radical science movement has frequently remained restricted to those issues which gave it its initial impetus in the late 1960s and early 1970s. The result was a critical approach that had much to say about the need for the control of the potential health hazards of recombinant DNA research or chemical carcinogens, but less about the increased private control of scientific knowledge resulting from changes in patent laws, attempts to use controls on the dissemination of scientific knowledge as an instrument of foreign policy and capitalist expansion, the use of scientific arguments to legitimize the molding of the regulation of technology into a form compatible with the political needs of the nation's industrial leaders, or several other key issues in what I have described as the new politics of science.

This is the task that now lies ahead. Building on the work of the two generations of earlier critics, it is now both possible and necessary to move forward to address the key political issues that are likely to be expressed through science and science policy for the remainder of the decade, if not the century. To put it schematically, the first postwar generation of science critics demonstrated the need to develop a political debate around the applications of science; the second generation shifted focus to the other end of the spectrum, namely the conditions under which science is produced. The new task is to integrate these two perspectives into a single critique of the whole spectrum, from the most fundamental science through to its most sophisticated high-technology applications. In particular it is necessary to concentrate on ways of politicizing the discussion of the terms and conditions of access to science, the crucial intermediate position between production and application. For it is here, I suggest, that political action is now the most needed, and where the possibilities of opening science to proper democratic control are most in danger of being foreclosed.

At both the institutional and the cultural levels, the nation's industrial and academic leaders have joined forces to preach the message that the scientific method holds the key to the future international competitiveness of U.S. industry and to the decisions that will make the realization of this competitiveness possible. At the same time, however, they have moved to ensure a tightening of private control over the channels through which research results are transferred from the laboratory to the outside world. The apparent efficiency of the marketplace in achieving this is allowed to obscure the extent to which it is also steadily reinforcing the increased concentration of political power in the hands of private decision makers. Thus, despite the fact that the application of scientific results to social uses through technology is becoming one of the biggest single issues on the contemporary political agenda, it is an issue that is steadily being removed further and further from the domain of democratic decision making.

Beyond "Socially Responsible"

The substance of a truly democratic strategy for science and science policy would be the reintegration of those needs and aspirations that are steadily being excluded from both by current trends. Within the United States this means not merely shifting public research priorities away from destructive ends (such as defense) toward socially constructive goals (such as health and nutrition), long the staple demands of those seeking a "socially responsible" science. Equally important, it means changing the conditions of access to the fruits of publicly funded research so that those social groups that lack the economic or political power currently required to exploit such research are placed in a position to do so. Complementary to this need, on an international level, is the need to explore ways in which those countries most in need of the results of this same research to meet their basic requirements for food and energy can also more readily obtain access to it, without being forced to accept the political terms—namely the integration of their economies into a marketplace dominated by the advanced Western nations—on which this research is increasingly being offered.

The need to democratize the practice and applications of science can be divided into three principal stages. The first concentrates on the procedures and work practices of the scientific community. Bacon's prescription for the scientific method, with its strict fragmentation of tasks and its rigid hierarchical patterns of control, still rules in the majority of scientific laboratories. One of the first goals of an alternative science policy would be to demonstrate how neither is necessary for a creative and effective research laboratory, yet how these patterns of organization and control of research are frequently imposed as a reflection of broader political relationships that maintain the subservience of science to capital. Democratizing the laboratory does not mean the laboratory technicians, or even members of the community, should necessarily be given equal weight to principal investigators in the choice of research directions in fundamental science, or of investigative techniques. But it does mean that the criteria by which priorities and practices are decided should be open to discussion at all levels, that the chances of individual scientists being allowed to build research empires whose top priority becomes economic profitability or institutional survival are minimized, and that scientists accept the many ways in which decisions taken inside the laboratory have important social dimensions that should not be resolved behind closed doors.[4]

Democratizing the laboratory would be a first step toward creating a science based on new social relations and a new ideology. A second would be democratizing the institutions that decide how research funds should be allocated. Already this is being done to a limited extent. At the National Institutes of Health, for example, each grant request is discussed by two committees, one a scientific committee whose role is to judge the scientific quality of the application, another a committee including nonscientists which decides whether a particular research proposal should be supported on the basis of the prior scientific evaluation as well as other criteria, such as the general availability of research funds and the importance of the research being pursued. A considerable degree of selectivity in the use of biomedical research funds is also imposed by Congress, where the desires of individual congressmen to be seen securing additional research funds into a particular highly publicized illness have generated what is widely known as the "disease-of-the-month" syndrome. The approach has several weaknesses (many of which are eagerly pointed out by scientists who would like their research funds to come with fewer strings attached, and thus emphasize how cures to a disease may come from completely unexpected areas of research). The extent to which decisions about which diseases shall receive special research treatment are really the result of democratic choices, rather than a vehicle for raising conscience money from the wealthy to be spent on their terms, is also debatable. Nevertheless, as Representative Henry Waxman argued in the summer of 1983 in suggesting that Congress should play a greater role in determining the detailed research programs of the NIH (a suggestion strongly opposed by virtually the whole biomedical research community), the procedures for more direct input into the selection of research priorities exist in embryo form, with enough examples of successful intervention to justify this approach.[5]

At the other end of the spectrum is the need to develop ways of democratizing technological innovation. To give an example, in the middle of the 1970s, workers at the Lucas Aerospace Company in England showed that it was in principle possible to conceive a plan for applying their technical skills as draftsmen, engineers, and computer operators, not toward the military technologies that were at the time their company's chief products, but toward more socially desirable technologies, such as aids for the disabled or novel forms of community transportation. Ideas for the types of machines that were needed, but were not being provided through the market for one reason or another (such as limited production runs), were gathered from a wide number of community groups. As a result, several prototypes—such as a vehicle with two sets of wheels, able to travel either on roads or on railway tracks—have subsequently been developed (although outside the company).[6]

In other European countries a different way of experimenting with the application of scientific knowledge to social problems is being explored through what are known as "science shops" (or, in France, as *boutiques de science*). These could, again, form part of an alternative science and technology policy aimed at meeting community needs by offering a channel through which members of the community can gain direct access to scientific and technical expertise. The science shops originated in Holland in the mid-1970s as an outgrowth of the Dutch radical science movement, the first being created at the University of Utrecht in

1973. (See "The Amsterdam Science Shop: Doing Science for the People," *SftP*, vol. 11, no. 5). Their three principal goals are to provide technical information on demand to individuals or the representatives of community groups who come to the "shops" requesting it; to promote socially relevant research within Dutch universities; and to explore ways of linking this research directly to those working in the areas where it is needed. An important element in the science shop philosophy is the way access to its services is determined. At the University of Amsterdam, for example, requests for assistance are only accepted from those who have not been able to pay for someone to carry out the research, who promise not to use the results they are given for commercial purposes, and who are able to make productive use of the research results once they are obtained. In this way the science shops are intended to act as a kind of "knowledge broker," mediating between university scientists and members of the outside community, finding ways of connecting university research directly to specific social needs, yet bypassing the conventional commercial channels through which these needs are usually addressed.[7]

So far nothing comparable to the Lucas plan or the science shops has been tried in the United States. There have nevertheless been various attempts to explore ways of making available alternative channels of scientific and technical expertise. In Mountain View, California, the Mid-Peninsula Conversion Project, partly funded by a grant from the Science for Citizens Program of the National Science Foundation, has been exploring ways of making science and technology available to community groups, such as labor unions or disabled veterans, who might not otherwise have access to it.[8] Other groups across the country are exploring ways of applying high-technology products to community-based activities. The New Mexico Solar Energy Association has been exploring how microcomputers can help small, self-sufficient farmers make the best use of local resources;[9] in California a small company has developed a technique for linking a personal computer to a hand loom, making it possible to quickly transfer new fabric patterns designed on the computer screen into products that are competitive with machine-made fabric manufacturing. Similarly the California Agrarian Action Project is looking at ways in which biotechnology might be applied to the needs of small-scale organic farmers, for example by improving the overall protein balance in organically grown foods. Other examples of such "bootstrap community revitalization," exploiting the potential of high technology to help provide an alternative source of livelihood to those displaced by the mainstream economy, are being pursued in groups and collectives across the country.[10]

There is less to report on the third point on the spectrum at which pressure for an alternative science policy needs to be applied, namely the question of maintaining public access to the fruits of publicly funded research. Other countries have shown that it is possible to keep this access open; thus in Britain the National Research Development Corporation, a product of the postwar Labour government, had several major successes to its name in helping to move research results into the community before its rights to patents from government-funded research were removed in 1983 as part of Prime Minister Margaret Thatcher's campaign of privatization. In the United States a few Washington-based lobby groups, in particular Ralph Nader's Health Research Group, have vociferously opposed changes in legislation that have steadily removed the public's right to direct access to the results of the research it has paid for; but these groups have had little impact against the economic and political forces moving, as in Britain, in the opposite direction. On the international front, several developing countries have been pushing for changes in the Paris Convention, the agreement signed initially in 1883, under which countries indicate their willingness to respect a certain common set of rules on patent protection. The developing countries want greater control over the way that outsiders can use patents to manipulate market conditions (for example, by buying up patents merely to keep competitors out, but not using them to produce goods); however, the more the developed countries have realized the economic and political importance of patents, the more opposed they have become to the developing countries' proposals for a change in the rules.

The need and the scope exist for a broad reassessment of the patent system, both domestically and internationally. Would it be possible to grant certain social groups privileged access to patented research results (as currently most scientists are free to use the research results of others, even if they have been patented), on the grounds that they are not put to commercial ends? Could new public institutions be created responsible for creating links between university scientists and outside groups wishing to use their research, but without going through commercial channels? Are alternatives to patents possible that would provide both an incentive and a limited reward to individual scientists without the need to provide this reward by guaranteeing monopoly control of the market? Should certain areas of science, such as research into various tropical diseases, be acknowledged sufficiently important to humanity that they should be considered unpatentable—or, alternatively, should all patents in these areas be granted to an international agency, such as the World Health Organization?[11] None of these questions, simple as they may sound, is straightforward. Nevertheless, they are the types of questions that must be addressed by anyone seeking to challenge the present system, under which patents are almost universally used to tighten the control of private corporations over the use of scientific knowledge, and thus to restrict the access to this knowledge of others exploring alternative ways of applying it to social needs.

Mounting the Challenge

Research, access, application: these, then, are the three fields in which the political values expressed through science lie open to challenge. What about the other dimension in our matrix, those groups in a position to mount such a challenge? The first is the women's movement. Part of the broad critique of the values embedded in science developed in the early 1970s was the demonstration that science was essentially a man's world. The majority of scientists are men, for reasons that range from the way girls are put off the "hard" sciences at school to the competitive pressures that discriminate against a scientist who chooses to put substantial effort into a nonscience activity such as childrearing. It also tends to be men who select the way science is applied, even to women's needs. The liberal response is to argue for more opportunities for women in science, in other words for more women to be given the opportunity to fill the roles currently played by men. The more radical argument is that part of the problem lies in the roles themselves, and that the values expressed through science tend to be male values (illustrated, for example, by the predominance on the White House Science Council—and previously the President's Science Advisory Committee—of members representing the hard sciences such as physics and mathematics over the soft sciences of biology and sociology). "The problem is not one of making women more scientific, but of making science less masculine," says Liz Fee of Johns Hopkins University. "When masculinity is seen as an incomplete and thus distorted form of humanity, the issue of making science and technology less masculine is also the issue of making it more completely human."[12]

The women's movement has already shown how different strategies can be used at different positions on the science-society spectrum. Some, such as Fee, have concentrated on the need to change the conditions within the laboratory, and thus implicitly the form of the knowledge that emerges from laboratory research. Others have focused on the application end, exploring ways that women, either individually or in groups, can control the use of those technologies that most directly affect them, particularly in medicine and childbirth.[13] Women's groups have also been actively engaged in campaigns to protect those in other countries against the side effects of modern medical technologies, such as the contraceptive Depo-Provera. And in Britain women have been among the most militant opponents of the deployment of cruise missiles, symbolized by a year-long, ongoing demonstration outside the Greenham Common Air Force Base. Through such actions the women's movement has already shown that it is likely to remain one of the most consistent and powerful voices demanding changes in the way control over science and its applications is distributed.

A second group is made up of the labor unions. American unions, even less than their European counterparts, do not have a history of deep involvement in political debates about science; it is likely to be a long time before the United States sees anything comparable to recent developments in France, where laboratory technicians, nominated through their unions, now sit on some of the policy committees of the principal research-funding agency, the Centre National de la Recherche Scientifique.[14] Nevertheless, there are signs that this involvement is increasing. In the mid-1970s it was generated largely by struggles around occupational health and safety issues, where it was recognized that there was a need to challenge the judgments of scientific experts on, for example, the carcinogenicity of new chemical compounds. During this period officials working with unions such as the Oil Chemical and Atomic Workers and the United Steelworkers discovered at first hand how scientific research could be manipulated to provide results that appeared neutral, but in fact represented political and economic, as much as scientific choices. They also learned the importance of gaining access to the scientific information on which decisions were made, information that companies tried to protect using the argument that it involved trade secrets, but which the unions argued was essential for an informed dialogue on the impact of production techniques on the health of their members.[15]

Other unions, such as the International Association of Machinists, became involved in broader technological issues, such as the safety of nuclear power. Their interest partly reflected a direct interest: those whose members worked as operators in nuclear power plants favored stringent safety requirements, while those employed in power-plant construction were frequently opposed, for they felt the impact of tougher safety standards through higher production costs, expressed in canceled orders and thus lost jobs. Among the more progressive unions, however, there have been signs of a spreading awareness of the broad political challenge to democratic politics being mounted through the control of science and technology.[16] Several prominent union members agreed to serve on a new commission established by Ralph Nader in 1983 to survey the growing impact of private corporations on university research. Others have become active members of the newly formed Committee for Responsible Genetics. At the grassroots level, union members have organized around demands for a direct input into decisions about the new technologies they are expected to work with; some have begun to explore variations on the ideas of the Lucas work force for directing technical skills toward the production of socially useful products.[17] And the Reagan administration's attack on occupational health regulations has done as much as anything to demonstrate that scientific issues need to be firmly placed on the political agenda of the labor movement.

Putting Science in Its Place

The environmental movement is, like the women's movement, already moving firmly in this direction. Many environmentalist groups, such as Friends of the Earth and the Natural Resources Defense Council, have played key roles in challenging the conventional channels of scientific decision making. In the laboratory such groups frequently spearheaded campaigns for stricter controls on recombinant DNA research and greater community participation at both the local and national levels in decisions about this research. More broadly, the central focus of the environmental movement has been to find ways of mitigating the social and environmental impact of science-based technologies, from the use of chemical pesticides to the threats of global annihilation raised by the spread of nuclear technologies, in whatever form. While some groups have continued to present nuclear power as one area in which it is necessary to separate rational from irrational choices (e.g., "safe" from "unsafe" working conditions), others, such as the Abalone Alliance in California, have begun to show how the whole nuclear debate is embedded in a politically determined rationality that, like Frederick Taylor's scientific management, expresses political goals within the neutral-sounding language of science.[18]

The frustrations experienced by many environmentalist groups during the Carter administration, together with the frontal attack to which they have been subjected under President Reagan, have demonstrated the increasing need for such groups to think in political as much as single-issue terms. This is partly a question of embracing a broader agenda; those concerned about the way science is used should, I have suggested, be equally concerned about the way it is produced, as well as about the restrictions placed on its dissemination. The experience of the Office of Technology Assessment, or the National Institutes of Health's Recombinant DNA Advisory Committee, shows that isolated campaigns that ignore this broader political perspective can quickly lose their effectiveness.

It is also a question of building new alliances around these issues. Already efforts have been made by groups such as Environmentalists for Full Employment to bridge the gaps between environmentalists and the labor movement, showing how apparent conflicts between the two (such as the claim that tougher environmental regulation means fewer jobs) are illusory, and that, as the Reagan administration's attack on regulation in all guises has shown, they have many political needs in common.[19] In the past a major weakness of the alternative technology movement was its failure to address the problems encountered in the lives of the majority of the population, who find themselves locked into a technological system they cannot escape without making a major sacrifice. Many are unprepared to experiment with new technologies if this means giving up the economic security of a full-time job; indeed, for many the fight to retain a job during a period in which modern technology is threatening to create an ever-lengthening unemployment line has inevitably become an issue that takes precedence over any discussion about the conditions under which work is carried out.

The worsening employment situation, however, is making it more important than ever before for political movements to address issues around technology that were already framed by the counterculture movements of the 1970s. At that time new forms of work were proposed as alternatives to the alienation of the assembly line and the destruction of natural resources by science-based technologies; today such work has become an economic necessity for those who find themselves pushed to the margins of the economy. Groups such as the newly formed Intermediate Technology Development Group of North America, based on the "small is beautiful" idea of economist E. F. Schumacher, are now exploring new ways of revitalizing communities through self-help schemes that, while drawing on some of the high technology (such as personal computers) offered by the mainstream economy, place it in a context of self-management and self-reliance.[20] The gap between such initiatives and the more conventional political activities of the labor unions and the environmental movement remains wide; but it is a gap that must be bridged if either is to achieve long-term success.

The final set of groups that offer the hope for an alternative science policy are those pressing the demands of the less-developed nations. The scientific needs of these countries demand little elaboration, nor do the barriers that recent experiences (from the United Nations conference in Vienna in 1979 to recent attempts to establish a Biotechnology Center for the Third World) have shown to be formidable. There are a few groups in the United States, such as the Washington-based Center for Concern, that have begun to address these issues. Nevertheless, it is an area that the Third World countries must themselves develop the technical and political skills to address. Much is already happening on this front. The debates that took place during the Vienna conference itself, as well as those that have taken place within agencies such as the United Nations Conference on Trade and Development (UNCTAD) in Geneva on the economic and political consequences of patent laws, indicate the height of current awareness about how much needs to be done and where. Furthermore, over the past ten years even the once radical ideas of Schumacher have gained broad endorsement through bodies such as the Organization for Economic Cooperation and Development.

The danger here remains that development will be portrayed as a technical problem—even if the technology is "intermediate" or "appropriate"—rather than one that also has deep political roots.[21] It is not up to those from the developed world to prescribe which technological strategies are the most appropriate for these countries; nevertheless, it is up to us to help ensure that important opportunities are not foreclosed. This means confronting the various ways that policies created by the advanced industrialized nations to exploit their leadership in science can undermine the efforts by developing countries to enjoy the benefits of science without at the same time sacrificing their newfound political independence.

It is relatively easy to identify, as I have tried to do above, the miscellaneous groups already engaged at one level or another in the struggle to create a more democratic politics of science. Expressing this strategy as a matrix also indicates the current gaps in this strategy, such as the lack of labor union activity around the democratization of scientific work (made all the more difficult by the relative weakness of labor unions within universities, as well as the highly competitive conditions in most laboratories, which act against any chance of collective action). The more difficult task is to see how these different groups will be able to weld themselves into a single political movement sufficiently powerful to mount a direct challenge to undemocratic policies introduced in the name of national efficiency. Given the common political nature of the issues each group is addressing—the concentration of power over science and its applications in the hands of a relatively small elite—coordinated action is necessary for the highest chance of success.

It would be wrong to pretend that there are any easy solutions. Equally, it would be wrong to adopt a fatalistic stance, accepting the advance of science and technology as inevitable, and the social destruction and authoritarian practices that they bring in their wake as the necessary by-products of progress. Science is one of the greatest cultural and intellectual achievements of the modern age. But its social significance must be placed in its proper perspective; it must not be seen as a key to utopia, a blueprint to a perfect future, or even the ultimate expression of human reason. Rather, science must remain firmly identified as a powerful tool that can help us to understand the natural universe in potentially useful ways, but at the same time carries the seeds of human exploitation. How to tap the one without falling victim to the other is the key challenge of the decades ahead. Creating the individuals and the political institutions through which this can be successfully achieved is the principal task now facing all those engaged in struggles over the new politics of science.

N O T E S

1. For a detailed history of the period, see Alice Kimball Smith, *A Peril and a Hope: The Scientists' Movement in America* (Chicago: University of Chicago Press, 1965). Also Robert Jungk, *Brighter than a Thousand Suns: The Moral and Political History of the Atomic Scientists* (London: Gollancz, 1958).

2. See James R. Newman and Byron S. Miller, *The Control of Atomic Energy* (New York: McGraw-Hill, 1948); Robert Gilpin, *American Scientists and Nuclear Weapons Policy* (Princeton, N.J.: Princeton University Press, 1962).

3. See, for example, Ann Arbor Science for the People Editorial Collective, *Biology as a Social Weapon* (Minneapolis: Burgess, 1977).

4. See Barbara Culliton, "House Battles over NIH Legislation," *Science,* vol. 221 (August 19, 1983).

5. A description of one attempt to put such ideals into practice can be found in the Thimann Laboratory Group, "Toward a Liberatory Research Environment," in R. Arditti et al., eds., *Science and Liberation* (Boston: South End Press, 1980). In the article, "a group of scientists and science students at the University of California, Santa Cruz, describe their efforts to develop a more human, creative, and liberating work environment by restructuring their work life along lines of cooperative support." Other information from: Science for the People, 897 Main Street, Cambridge, Mass. 02139.

6. Hilary Wainwright and David Elliott, *The Lucas Plan: A New Trade Unionism in the Making* (London: Allison & Busby, 1982). The principles on which the Lucas campaign was based are outlined in Mike Cooley, *Architect or Bee?* (Boston: South End Press, 1980).

7. See Dorothy Nelkin and Arie Rip, "Distributing Expertise: A Dutch Experiment in Public Interest Science," *Bulletin of Atomic Scientists* (May 1979); Jon Turney, "What Do Science Shops Offer to Their Customers?" *Times Higher Education Supplement* (December 10, 1982). The Dutch science shops found limitations in a strategy based primarily on answering individual queries, so they have recently developed a system of working through "project centers" (one for women, one for environmental problems, one for labor unions, and one for Third World questions). This approach is similar to the "matrix strategy" described in this chapter. See Peter Groenewegen and Paul Swuste, "Science Shops in the Netherlands" (paper for conference at Nijmegen, Netherlands, May 2, 1983). More information can be obtained from: Wetenschapswinkel, University of Amsterdam, Herengracht 530, Amsterdam, Netherlands.

8. See, for example, Joel S. Yudken et al., "Knowhere: A Community-Based Information Utility for the Disabled Using Microcomputers," available (with other information) from Mid-Peninsula Conversion Project Inc., 86 West Dana Street #203, Mountain View, Calif. 94041. The group's work is described in Robert Howard, "Engineers Take the Knowledge and Run," *In These Times* (September 2–8, 1981).

9. New Mexico Solar Energy Association, P.O. Box 204, Santa Fe, N.M. 87501.

10. See "Bootstrap Community Revitalization in North America: An Account of the First Seminar on Tools for Community Economic Transformation," organized by E. F. Schumacher Society in Great Barrington, Mass. May 18–25, 1982.

11. See, for example, *Draft Report of International Forum on Technological Advances and Development* (Tbilisi, USSR, April 12–16, 1983). It proposed that "a new form of international cooperation be considered with the designation of a limited number of new advanced technologies to meet needs of a clear and urgent character to the human community as 'technologies for humanity.' These technologies should be developed as disseminated in the public domain."

12. Liz Fee, "A Feminist Critique of Scientific Objectivity," *Science for the People* (July–August 1982). Also Women's Group from Science for the People, "Declaration: Equality for Women in Science," in Arditti et al., eds., *Science and Liberation.*

13. See Boston Women's Health Book Collective, *Our Bodies, Ourselves: A Book by and for Women* (New York: Touchstone/Simon & Schuster, 1975).

14. See David Dickson, "France Sets Out to Democratize Science," *Science,* vol. 218 (October 29, 1982).

15. For a full account of the growth of political awareness in labor unions around health and safety issues, see Daniel M. Berman, *Death on the Job: Occupational Health and Safety Struggles in the United States* (New York: Monthly Review Press, 1978).

16. See, for example, William Winpisinger, "A Labor View of Technological Innovation," *Technology Review* (April 1981).

17. Karl Frieden, *Workplace Democracy and Productivity* (Washington, D.C.: National Center for Economic Alternatives, 1980).

18. For a discussion of the "scientization" of the debate over the safety of nuclear energy, see David Rosenfeld, "Don't Just Reduce Risk—Transform It," in *No Clear Reason: Nuclear Power Politics* (London: Free Association Books, 1984). Further information from Abalone Alliance, c/o American Friends Service Committee, 944 Market Street, Room 307, San Francisco, Calif.

19. See "Environmentalists Dig In, Form Coalitions," *Chemical and Engineering News* (November 24, 1980); OSHA/Environmental Network "Connecticut Unionists and Environmentalists Protest Reagan Administration Attacks on OSHA and Clean Air Act," press release (October 5, 1981). Details of the growing cooperation between the labor and environmental movements are given in Richard Kazis and Richard L. Grossman, *Fear at Work: Job Blackmail and the Environment* (New York: Environmentalists for Full Employment, Pilgrim Press, 1982). Further information from Environmentalists for Full Employment, 1536 16th Street NW, Washington, D.C. 20036.

20. Information available from: The Intermediate Technology Development Group of North America, Inc., 777 United Nations Plaza, New York, N.Y. 10017.

21. These issues are discussed in David Dickson, *The Politics of Alternative Technology* (New York: Universe Books, 1975).

MODERN SCIENCE IN CRISIS

A Third World Response

Third World Network

Modern science and technology is in a state of acute crisis. This crisis manifests itself in several forms.[1] The most obvious are in the end products of contemporary science and technology systems such as technologies and products, etc., which are often directed towards destruction, waste and the alienation of people from people and people from nature.

The Bhopal gas leak, the Chernobyl nuclear accident, the ozone layer depletion, the destruction of the earth's forest and natural resources—these are just some of the major environmental disasters that have happened or are happening in the world. Disasters which are caused mainly by science and technology. There are numerous examples to show that science and technology are not improving the material and spiritual conditions of the world's people, especially those living in the Third World. So-called technological advancements such as bio-engineering and computers are making a major portion of the human workforce redundant, leading to unemployment and underemployment. More sophisticated science often means greater problems and fewer solutions, reliance on capital-intensive technologies, dependence on non-indigenous resources and the gross misuse of human and material resources.

It is not just the end product of science which is causing concern. There is a growing awareness that there is something intrinsically wrong with the very nature of contemporary science and technology. Even in the most fundamental of the scientific enterprises, namely mathematics and physics, an era of epistemological uncertainties has reigned for over two decades. In biology, the techniques of recombinant-DNA and the possibility of creating and unleashing new and deadly forms of mutant species and even cloning of human beings, have brought the nightmare of Frankenstein very close to reality.

Reductionism, the dominant method of modern science, is leading, on the one

[1]The Third World Network and the Consumers' Association of Penang organized an international conference on "Crisis in Modern Science" in November 1986, bringing together scientists, academics, journalists, and grassroots activists from many countries. Altogether there were 140 participants from countries such as India, Sri Lanka, Argentina, the United States, Japan, Hong Kong and Thailand. This is the final version of the Declaration of the conference.

hand in physics, towards meaninglessness, and on the other, in biology, towards "Social Darwinism" and eugenics. There is something in the very metaphysics of modern science and technology, the way of knowing and of doing, of this dominant mode of thought and inquiry, that is leading us towards destruction.

The romantic notion of science as the pursuit of pure, unadulterated "objective" truth, with the scientist working in isolation from mundane social reality—like a hermit, trying against impossible odds to understand some sort of objective reality—has now become dangerously untenable. In fact, after a decade of research around the world it is clear that science is mediated through a social process. Indeed, some philosophers and historians of science argue that science *is* social process. Social forces, operating at the level of the global economy and structures, and the national political economy as well as in the scientific communities themselves, shape the character, content and style of modern science and technology.

Scientists are strongly committed to beliefs and certain cultural ethos which compel them to convert diversity and complexity into uniformity. In addition to this belief system and cultural ethos—which manifest themselves in the propositions that scientists embrace—science has its own power structure, reward systems and peer groups. All of these combine to ensure that science is closely correlated with the existing, dominant and unjust, political, economic and social order of the world.

Domination and control are inherent and integral parts of the current scientific and technological enterprise. These concepts are at the very heart of scientific methodology and the present process of creation and generation of science. From the inception of modern science, at the beginning of the European Renaissance, goals of science were articulated in terms of domination and control.

The *philosophes* of the seventeenth century Enlightenment movement, in complete contrast to the intellectual heritage of Islam and other civilizations on which they were constructing a new world, claimed to divorce reason from values. They narrowly redefined reason as an instrumental rationality, which hides its true values of control and domination behind a facade of objective neutrality. Any form of reason that acknowledged its values was thus considered as "unscientific." Reason thus became the dominant mode of knowing to the exclusion of all other alternatives. The notion of the domination and control of nature gradually changed into the domination and control of non-European people by means of the scientific method and the linear rationality incorporated within it. The present modern scientific and technological enterprise has evolved within the imperial experience of Europe and North America and the colonial experience of the Third World.

The crisis of science manifests itself in the Third World as well. Modern science and technology has dislocated Third World societies, destroyed traditional cultures and played havoc with the environment of Third World nations. It has also replaced a way of knowing, which is multi-dimensional and based on synthesis, in Third World societies, with a linear, clinical, inhuman and rationalist mode of thought. Western science and technology has systematically plundered

Third World societies in the name of scientific rationality. This was achieved via the Green Revolution and the massive incorporation of modern medicine as well as through the waste of valuable and scarce resources on research into "fashionable" areas such as nuclear power. No figures or indicators can convey the losses of lives and resources that these social engineering experiments—induced by Western "experts" and "consultants"—have brought to our countries.

In most developing countries the transplant of science and technology has not yet taken root. Neither the science nor the scientists have an organic relationship with local problems, resources and the pressing needs of the society. It is often irrelevant, wasteful, unproductive, imitative and bears the hallmarks of a second-rate and second-hand product.

Moreover, the system of modern science and technology in the Third World has grown at the expense of the pre-European scientific cultures that flourished within this region. Before the domination by the European imperial powers, Third World civilizations had their own elaborate and sophisticated systems of knowledge and craftsmanship.

In North Africa and West Asia, Islamic science was the main problem-solving paradigm. Both in terms of quality and quantity, the output of Islamic science, from the seventh to the fourteenth century, remains unsurpassed. Muslim scientists laid the foundation of algebra and trigonometry, measured the circumference of the earth, studied the properties of light and motion, examined the human body and discovered the circulation of blood, and obtained results with an accuracy at which one can only marvel. Yet they did all this in a framework of thought and inquiry which integrated facts and values in a metaphysical framework. Muslim scientists did not accept the tyranny of method but sought to develop and evolve methods in conformity with the nature of inquiry and within a clearly defined ethical matrix.

In Chinese civilization too, science and technology flourished and achieved tremendous heights. Much of our arithmetic originates from the work of Chang Ts'ang (died 152 BC) and our geometry from the classical treatise of Wang Hsia-t'ung (died 727 BC). Chang Ch'iu-chien's (died 650 BC) work on medicine is still a source of wonder. Here again a system of science and medicine, evolved in a metaphysical framework, emphasizes synthesis and the promotion of certain norms and values.

From ancient times, the Indian subcontinent has been known for its technologies of agriculture, metallurgy, textiles, ship-building, architecture and medicine. These technologies were widely practised in the whole of South Asia and the Southeast Asian region until as late as the eighteenth century, as documented in the various European accounts of the period. These technologies were characterised by their simplicity as well as their sophistication. For example in ancient Hindu thought, there were separate *shastra* which outlined the fundamental scientific principles. These various *shastras* were themselves founded on the philosophical basis provided by the various *darshanas*, the schools of philosophy which define the logical, epistemological and methodological structure of Hindu thought.

The guiding principle of all these sciences and philosophies was that the world in itself was the repository of truth and the purpose of science and technology was merely to enable people to live happily and healthily in this world rather than changing and manipulating the world.

Southeast Asian traditions are also replete with countless examples of indigenous science and technologies. Western science and technology have destroyed these systems of knowledge and problem-solving. This destruction manifests itself in the negation of the history of science and technologies of traditional civilizations and cultures. It also takes the form of the suppression and destruction of indigenous medicine, local architecture and building techniques, and ecologically sound farming and irrigation practices.

Given the destructive nature of contemporary science and technology, and the fact that is controlled and directed by industrialized states and multinational corporations, it is essential for Third World countries to create their own indigenous bases for the generation, utilization, and diffusion of scientific and technological knowledge. Third World countries should cooperate with one another in this endeavour. Moreover, the whole notion of the transfer of technology and the importation of Western science should now be critically evaluated.

Evolving indigenous scientific culture requires Third World scientists, technologists, decision makers and activists to appreciate the true value of traditional science and technologies. Traditional technologies and medical systems should be upgraded, developed and promoted. They should form the basis for the evolution of indigenous, but thoroughly contemporary, alternative technologies and health care systems. Similarly, national problems should be solved within the framework of an indigenous mode of thought and inquiry and with locally available resources.

Only when science and technology evolves from the ethos and cultural milieu of Third World societies will it become meaningful for our needs and requirements, and express our true creativity and genius. Third World science and technology can only evolve through a reliance on indigenous categories, idioms and traditions in all spheres of thought and action.

Science, Technology and Natural Resources

Before their colonial conquest, the natural resources of the Third World were utilized through technologies based on local expertise and knowledge and small-scale exploitation. With colonization came the immense demand for the natural resources of the colonies, be it forests, minerals or agricultural products, to fuel the increasing requirements of the Industrial Revolution. This was the first stage in the destabilization of functioning local technologies; it undermined their resource base and market. This process of direct transfer of natural resources was not possible in the colonial era. However, as the process of "development" set in as a national goal, to be achieved with the aid of international finance, the process of resource transfer continued to pay for the imported inputs required for the process of development. The latter included expertise, technologies and equipment as well as luxury consumer items.

This process of development merely serves the easy marketing of obsolete technologies. It also enables the industrially advanced countries in the North to gain access to the remotest natural resources of the countries in the South. In the late sixties, the process of development touched the agriculture of the Third World by introducing the technologies of the Green Revolution. In the decades that followed, this process manifested itself in more undemocratic control over land use in the Third World as international technologies and finance entered the management of land and water use in a big way—including the area of forestry. On the other hand, industrial growth in the South concentrated on industries that pollute the environment, transferred from the North where environmental consciousness did not allow such industries to function any more. These included textiles, dyeing, tanning, hazardous chemicals and the nuclear industry.

It was thus possible for the industrially advanced countries to have the first Industrial Revolution by transferring the natural resources of the colonies, and then, in the 1970s, the second Industrial Revolution, leading to the clean service society in the North with the transfer of obnoxious industries to the South.

Till about the 1980s, the transfer of obsolete technologies was the practice. Thereafter, with the advent of biotechnologies, for the first time the latest technologies from the North began to directly touch the remotest villages of the South in a decentralized manner, proving that the small need not always be beautiful. It is in this era of rapidly changing relationships between technology and natural resources that we have to locate our role.

Proposals

1) There is a need for the creation of a civilized response from Third World countries for the development of resource-prudent technologies and for enhancing the control of local bodies on the decisions related to natural resource use.

2) The use of land and water must be guided on a sustainable basis so as to satisfy the local needs first, starting with the needs of the most needy.

3) Third World governments, scientists and groups must defend their crop and plant genetic resources from destruction.

4) The Third World must actively oppose the dumping of obsolete or polluting technologies in the name of economic development and actively encourage options for economic development with resource prudent, non-polluting indigenous technologies.

5) Equitable access to resources and information on all technologies to be used in a region, including all possible environmental impacts, must be ensured.

6) There is a need to increase people's participation in the choice of technologies and the management of natural resources with the objective of choosing ecologically sensitive technologies.

Science, Inequality and Inability to Meet Basic Needs

Modern science, with its technological advancement, has the capability of fulfilling the basic needs of every human being if social and production systems were properly utilized. The irony is that, in reality, more than half of the world's population (two-thirds of the Third World's people) live in sub-human conditions—deprived of their most basic human needs such as food, clothing and shelter. This tragedy is rendered even more catastrophic by the fact that the same technological capacity that has facilitated the irrational composition of products is also so powerful that it has also enabled the destruction or depletion of a very high proportion of non-renewable resources in the world. Day by day, this gigantic technological capacity uses up more energy, extracts more minerals, chops down more forests, results in more loss of topsoil, and pollutes more water, more land mass, more air and even the stratosphere. At current rates of production, many critical resources would run out within a few decades.

There is a finite stock of world resources available, and in the process of production, a portion of that stock is used up each year. The gross national product with which all nation states are so obsessed is only an annual *flow* which is very much dependent on the available stock of natural resources. When the stock runs out, the flow will dry up. Most resources are non-renewable. The more they are depleted, the less they are available for use in production *in the future*. In other words, the higher the GNP at present, the lower it will be in the future, when the effects of resource depletion are felt. This most simple and elementary of facts is almost completely omitted in economics textbooks. It is hardly in the consciousness of the planners and politicians who plan our future and rule our lives. It is hardly in the consciousness of the scientists and technologists who have made possible the rapid depletion of resources through the development of technological capacity.

Unequal Distribution and Control of the World's Resources

The rapid extraction and utilization of resources is very unequally carried out in terms of control and benefits. Eighty percent of world resources are used up in the developed world and only 20 percent in the Third World. This unequal distribution also determines the nature of goods to be produced. To produce for the elite market, sophisticated technologies are created to produce high-tech products, such as video recorders, compact discs, computers, motorcars, and services such as high-tech medicine, tours abroad, and even tax-evasion legal programmes. A large portion of the developed world's GNP is spent on such consumer goods and on producing capital goods or technologies to make these consumer goods. Meanwhile, the Third World accounts for only 20 percent of the resources used up each year. Since national incomes are also unequally distributed, a large portion of these resources are also used up in making the same high-tech consumer products as are enjoyed in the developed world, and in importing capital-intensive technologies to produce these elite consumer goods. Thus, only a small portion of the world's resources flow towards the making of basic goods required for the survival of the poor majority in the Third World and the making of simple capital goods used by poor farmers and small industrial craftsmen or enterprises.

Growth of the North at the Expense of the South

In this on-going process of resources depletion and irrational use of resources, the main impetus and dynamics are located in political economy and the socio-economic systems which give rise to competition for growth between companies and between nations. But the role of science and technology is crucial. If the level of technology is low, then we may still have the same inequality, but the degree at which resources are depleted would be less. In reality, however, technological levels are increasing rapidly under the pressure of competition between firms and countries (not only in the economic but also military spheres), and so the depletion of resources also increases rapidly. Moreover the ever increasing technological capacity of the developed world leaves the Third World even further behind, thus in itself widening the inequality gap between nations.

In 1980, nations of the North, with only a quarter of world population, earned 80 percent of the gross global product (GGP). In the South, three-quarters of the world population claimed only 20 percent of global income. Since 1980 the world has become even more unequal. Due to the colonial experience, the Third World remains dependent on the developed world for trade, loans, investments and technology. In the past few years, increasing amounts of funds have flown out from the South to the North. In 1985 alone, U.S. $74 billion left the Third World on its debt account alone: it obtained only U.S. $41 billion in new loans but had to pay U.S. $114 billion in debt servicing. If we include the outflow of profits by transnational companies in the Third World, capital flight from the Third World and the capital deficit of West Asian exporters, the outflow of capital from the Third World in 1985 alone would be U.S. $230–240 billion. If we also include the U.S. $65 billion lost due to the fall in commodity prices (*The Economist* estimate), the Third World's loss would be U.S. $300 billion in one year. In 1986, the situation would be even worse with the collapse of oil prices and the prices of other commodities. Total loss could be U.S. $300–350 billion. Given this gigantic flow from the South to the North, it is quite a joke to say that the North is giving aid to the South. Whatever aid is given is a mere drop in the ocean compared to what flows from South to North, and even this aid is tied to conditions.

The North's grip over modern science and technology has contributed to the exploitation of the Third World's economic weakness. The rich countries use their industrial and agricultural technologies to produce surplus goods which they are unable to use themselves (part of the problem of over-development or "over-accumulation"). So they dump the surplus cereals or other crops or materials on the world market, causing prices of Third World commodities to collapse, and thus reduce the incomes and living standards of the poor. Modern technology and information systems have also enabled transnational banks and companies to expand into developing countries and draw them into the world market further. After being drawn deep into the world market, the Third World finds the entry of their industrial goods blocked by protective tariff barriers put up by the rich countries. They also find that the rich countries have developed new technologies for their own advantage. For instance they have reduced their usage of the Third World's raw materials by finding substitutes and by using less materials per unit of product. As a result, export prices and earnings in the Third World have fallen drastically at a time when they have to fork out more funds to service foreign debts.

Unequal Development within Third World

Within Third World countries, the same structure of inequality exists at the national, regional and local levels. Thus, the national composition of goods also follows the same pattern: luxuries for the upper-income group, middle-class goods for the middle level and basic goods or less than that for the bottom 70 percent.

In the commercialized sector, firms compete with one another for higher market shares so that they can maintain or increase profits. Firms with insufficient profits may have to close down or be taken over by a stronger rival. Expansion and growth is thus built into the system of inter-firm competition. Modern technology plays a vital role in expansion, both in seeking more "productive" ways of producing and in developing new products or new models. Thus, modern science and technology is used in the service of firms' desperate need to expand.

In the socialist countries, there is a strong desire to keep up with the rich capitalist countries, both economically and militarily. There is thus also a strong tendency to develop capital-intensive technology and to aim for maximum growth. Thus, the ethos of industrialism is built into both capitalism and socialism.

In the Third World, the nature of development follows that of the North, except that ours is a dependent form of development. Growth takes the form of depletion of resources for export to the North, and the use of surplus from exports and from foreign loans to build expensive infrastructures and to invest in capital-intensive technology which mainly benefits big firms or big farmers.

The commercialized sectors, with superior financial and physical resources and technology, penetrate, invade and take over the traditional, viable sectors, thus dislocating a large portion of people from their livelihood and homes. For instance, small fishermen using ecologically sound production systems are displaced by big commercialized trawler boats which destroy the marine ecology by overfishing and through the use of destructive gear. Or else food-crop farmers have their lands taken back by landowners or bought over by either government or private companies to be converted into middle-class housing estates, free trade zones for industries, or highways.

In many ways, such as the provision of employment, community or producer control over technology and the production process, equity and ecological sound-ness, the indigenous technologies of the Third World are superior to the types of "modern technology" which have invaded us. Yet these indigenous technologies are being wiped out under the impact of the commercialized sectors and under the threat of the consumer culture which changes tastes away from local to West-ern culture, fashion and products. Thus, being sucked in a dependent fashion into the modern world system has been disastrous for Third World nations whose futures in terms of sustainable development would have demanded the rational use of their resources for the genuine development of their people. It is time therefore for a reorientation of the concepts of science, technology and develop-ment.

Proposals

1) There must be a radical reshaping of the international economic and finan-cial order so that economic power, wealth and income are more equitably distrib-uted and so that the developed world will be forced to cut down on its irrationally high consumption levels. If this is done, the level of industrial technology will also be scaled down. There will be no need for the tremendous wastage of energy, raw materials and resources which now go towards the production of superfluous goods simply to maintain "effective demand" and to keep the monstrous eco-nomic machine going. If appropriate technology is appropriate for the Third World, it is even more essential as a substitute for the environmentally and so-cially obsolete high-technology of the developed world. But it is almost impossi-ble to hope that the developed world will do this voluntarily. It will have to be forced to do so, either by a new unity of the Third World in the spirit of OPEC in the 1970s and early 1980s, or by an economic or physical collapse of the system. It must be realized that even in the First World, there are disadvantaged people and groups who are also exploited under the present economic system. On the other hand, local elites in the Third World benefit enormously from the economic system and have a vested interest in preserving it. It is thus important to forge solidarity and support between progressive people and groups in the First World and Third World, people to challenge and change the present international eco-nomic system.

2) It is in the Third World that the new ecologically sound future of the world can be born. In many parts of the Third World and within each Third World nation there are still large areas of ecologically sound economic and living sys-tems which have been lost in the developed world. We need to recognize and

identify these areas and rediscover the technological and cultural wisdoms of our indigenous systems of agriculture, industry, shelter, water and sanitation, medicine and culture. We do not mean here the unquestioning acceptance of everything traditional in the over-romantic belief of a past golden age which has to be returned to in all aspects. For instance, exploitative feudal or slave social systems also made life more difficult in the past. Many of the indigenous technologies, skills and processes which are still part and parcel of life in the Third World are appropriate for sustainable development and are in harmony with nature and the community. These indigenous scientific systems have to be accorded their proper recognition, encouraged and upgraded if necessary, but they have to be saved from being swallowed up by the "modern system."

3) Third World governments and people, in other words, have to first overcome their obsession with modern technologies which absorb a bigger and bigger share of surplus and investment funds and with projects like giant hydro-electric dams, nuclear plants and heavy industries which serve luxury needs. We must turn away from our obsession with modern gadgets and products which were created from the need of the developed world to mop up their excess capacity and their need to satisfy effective demand.

4) We need to devise and fight for the adoption of appropriate, ecologically sound and socially equitable policies for the fulfillment of needs such as water, health, food, education and information. We need appropriate technologies for agriculture and industry, and even more important, we need to set our priorities straight as to what types of consumer products to produce. We cannot accept "appropriate technology" producing inappropriate products, but we must fight for the adoption of appropriate technologies for appropriate products—technologies and products which are safe to handle and use, which are durable, fulfill basic and human needs, and which do not degrade or deplete the natural environment and resources.

But perhaps the most difficult aspect of the fight is the need to "debrainwash" the people in the Third World from the First World's cultural penetration of our societies, so that lifestyles, personal motivations and status structures can be delinked from the system of industrialism, its advertising industry and the creation of culture.

5) Finally, whilst a new science for the masses cannot succeed unless there is an accompanying or preceding change in social structures, it is also true that a change in the socio-economic structure alone is insufficient for developing a new sustainable order. Control and distribution of resources is a crucial determinant of social order but a change in this aspect alone is insufficient and could also lead to similar problems without an understanding of the limits of resources and the environmental, health, ethical and cultural aspects of science and technology. Therefore there can be no meaningful reform of science without a change in the larger society. There can also be no meaningful reform in social structures unless there is a change in the understanding of science and its proper application to serve the people and to be in harmony with nature.

Linkages between Economics and Modern Science

The linkages and inter-relationships between economic factors and modern science work in both directions, namely economic factors having an impact on the direction and policy of science and technology, and science and technology aiding in fulfilling the economic designs of dominant powers. It is only by conceptualizing this bi-directional loop that the full implications can be spelt out.

To put the discussion in perspective, reference is made to what is seen to be disturbing Western interventions in rice research programmes in Southeast Asia to perpetuate their domination. At critical times, when local researchers were nearing perfecting varieties from indigenous genetic resources which would dramatically increase rice yields without necessarily increasing the requirement for imported seeds and fertilizers, the projects were abruptly aborted through political pressure and the offering of financial inducements through agencies like the World Bank. Leading Third World researchers/scientists were branded as "unscientific" and hounded from their posts when they objected to such abject capitulation. These experiences graphically demonstrate the *daring* and *power* of Western financial and technological establishments on indigenous "science and technology."

This example only illustrates the general point that the economic and political domination of the West has enabled it to infuse a love of Western science and technology into the minds of Third World policymakers and this makes them blind to any other equally viable alternative(s). At the same time, the prohibitive cost of *converting* science into technology only leaves the option of importing technology from the West. Expensive high technology, in particular, normally benefits only a small sector of the population, mostly in the urban areas. Governments, in turn, are cajoled into providing expensive infrastructure to make this technology operational. The country's resources are spent on such projects and additional funds are borrowed to make good the foreign exchange shortfall, thus adding to the already crippling debt burden.

More insidious is the effect on the equitable distribution of wealth resulting from the "anti-democratic" nature of this technology. As was demonstrated by the discussion on issues like the *Green Revolution* and the *White Revolution*, the impact of technology is pronounced in shifting resources from rural areas to urban areas. They greatly reinforce the disastrous process of impoverishment of the rural people. Such projects also require foreign inputs like fertilizers, insecticides, pesticides and irrigation machinery. These, in turn, add to the debt burden year after year, without providing any credible level of import substitution.

The impact of economic domination on science and technology, particularly in the development of military technology, is well documented. Indeed, Western states have been referred to as "military industrial complexes." Now, since more than half of the expenditure in the leading Western countries is devoted to such effort, the implications for Western science and technology and their outposts in our countries are too frightening to contemplate. Further doses of such technology can only increase the Third World's subservience and dependence on the West.

If *survival with dignity* is the major objective, then all these linkages need to be understood and strategies for their unravelling put forward. A major plank of any such strategy should be the *delinking* of the Third World from the inherent dynamic which institutionalizes the hegemony of the West. Also present should be a plan to cultivate confidence in indigenous values so that local creativity can flourish and evolve into a more relevant *way of knowing and utilizing nature*. Such a "way of knowing and utilizing nature" will not have the alienating, dehumanizing and inequitable characteristics of *Western* science and technology.

Proposals

1) Increasing the awareness of the linkages between economic forces and the operation of science and technology. This should encompass:

- The awareness of military research budgets and their intended recipients. The extension of such projects/grants into the Third World can be rejected by mobilising popular opinion.
- The identification of prestigious high-tech projects which have little benefit for the masses, but which entrench Western technology in Third World countries and increase the crippling debt burden at the same time.

2) Identification of major "externalities" in science and technology programmes and projects. Thus, those that require excessive borrowing or result in perpetuating inequity can be made the targets of popular protest.

3) Science and technology policymaking institutions must be infused with credible political scientist(s) to help in working out the *total* impact of such policies.

4) Studies must be initiated to chart out more equitable ways of "knowing and utilizing nature." A critique of Western science and technology is a necessary prerequisite for this task.

5) Ways to graft the critical concept of "sustainable" use of resources on any emerging paradigm for "knowing and utilizing nature."

Science and Hazards in Technology

With the startling rise in the occurrence of major high-tech disasters all over the globe, the credibility of modern science has been seriously brought into question. These disasters, which have taken place in capitalist and communist countries and the so-called advanced and developing nations, are associated in the public mind with modern science and technology. They reflect intensely the crisis in this system of knowledge that first saw its rise in the seventeenth century, and which now seems to manifest grave limitations.

The Bhopal gas disaster in India, the Three Mile Island nuclear accident in the U.S., the Chernobyl nuclear explosion in the Soviet Union, the Challenger tragedy in the U.S., the SMON (subacute myelo optic neuropathy) and Minamata tragedies of Japan, and now, the Sandoz-Ciba Geigy-BASF pollution of the Rhine river, have become the major turning points on the road of popular disenchantment with modern science.

The association of science and violence operates, however, at more conscious levels than may be seen in such industrial disasters. In the Vietnam War, for instance, science collaborated closely in an obscene military programme based on the use of chemical and biological weapons that eventually ended in the destruction of the entire living environment of the Vietnamese people.

Yet, none of these developments, horrendous as they are in their consequences, can match those arising out of the close and active alliance of modern science with the nuclear weapons industry and the nuclear arms race. The intensity of the planned violence inherent in this arsenal is not reduced just because it has not been used yet. This is yet another illustration of how modern science is daily and ever more intensively involved in the continuous refinement of these senseless weapons of overkill or mass kill. With the expansion of modern science and technology into the Third World, this madness has also passed on to Third World governments and the science they support.

Thus it can be seen that modern science has become the major source of active violence against human beings and all other living organisms in our times.

This association of science and violence, as exemplified in what we have stated above, cannot be dismissed as being of an accidental nature—industrial disasters are not accidents. The argument should not be that the barbarities of war are not to be used to condemn scientific activities in peacetime. Third World and other citizens have come to know that there is a fundamental irreconcilability between modern science and the stability and maintenance of all living systems, between modern science and democracy. In our view the very idea that science should be free of democratic control has been responsible for much of the violence associated with the scientific system in the past.

Proposals

1) High-tech and large scale industrial units must henceforth be subject to democratic consensus in all countries. Opposition to undemocratically imposed science should be supported everywhere, across the globe.

2) Governments in developed countries should introduce legislation to forbid the export of hazardous products and industries which are banned in their own countries.

3) Third World countries should collaborate and strengthen their capacity to

monitor, regulate and control the import of existing hazardous industries and products. Legislation should be enacted to ensure:

- occupational health standards equivalent to standards in the industrial countries;
- adequate controls over the various types of pollution and environmental degradation;
- that hazardous products are not allowed entry into the country.

4) Third World governments should provide political support to ideas, processes and institutions that utilize non-Western science and technology.

5) Third World governments should pool resources and action to deal firmly with the perpetrators of all high-tech disasters.

6) A $1 billion fund should be raised by Third World governments to take care of victims of modern science and high-tech disasters. This fund should also be used for the care of victims in the First and Second worlds. Multinational corporations responsible for high-tech disasters must be made to pay and contribute to the fund.

Science and Racism

Racial discrimination involves far more than racial prejudice or even inequalities of opportunity. It is part and parcel of science, supposedly the most objective and "neutral" of human enterprises. The racial connotation of the IQ debate, generated by the work of Eysenck and Jenson, is now famous. The recent work of sociobiologist Edward Wilson is not so well known. Sociobiology seeks to promote a notion of humanity that sees intrinsic inferiority in the genes of certain racial and social groups. Eugenics, a "science" which was abandoned in the early 1930s, is set to make a comeback. Sperm banks containing the sperms of intellectually superior people have been established. Those with the means and the desire to produce offspring of a certain racial and intellectual purity will have access to appropriate sperms in the near future. Recombinant-DNA techniques are on the verge of cloning human beings; science has a habit of turning today's fiction into tomorrow's fact.

Racism in Science Education

In science education, racism starts early during secondary level. The dominant Western model of education, by now adopted in most countries, is geared to classifying students for their future roles in the capitalist labour market. Although all students have the capacity to learn, their ability to learn depends partly upon their different cultural backgrounds. Today's competitive individualist structure of schooling widens the differences that students bring to school; it stratifies them along the lines of culture ("race"), as well as class and gender. In addition, teachers' (often unconscious) prejudices influence students' choices of school subjects and levels.

Thus, classroom practice and formal testing procedures turn out to define many students as "low ability" because they either cannot or will not submit to the criteria that the schools set for "achievement." Expectations of such people are correspondingly lowered. Occupational hierarchies then appear as the natural result of "racial" differences in ability, diligence, etc.

Racism in the Use of Technology

At many workplaces, especially in the West, it is the cultural groups labelled as "lower ability" who are relegated to the worst jobs or unemployment. Modern science and technology, as a servant of capitalist power, has helped to intensify that exploitation.

To take just one example, the micro-electronics industry promises us all the benefits of "labour saving" devices, yet it creates drudgery for some and unemployment for others. In the West it generates a two-tier labour force, in which Third World immigrants and their children are stuck in the bottom tier. In the U.S., the mass production of integrated circuits, on which the entire industry depends, reserves the most low-paid and dangerous jobs for Asian and Hispanic workers.

Western multinationals have also exported that model, along with its chemical processes so hazardous that they would not satisfy Western safeguards for health and safety. At their service, Southeast Asian governments have eagerly competed to offer these multinationals the most attractive terms for exploiting their countries. The Free Trade Zone (FTZ) in Penang, Malaysia, employs not the local unemployed but mainly the rural Malay women, whose cultural traditions are manipulated in deference to the authoritarian figures who enforce the rigid discipline of the factories. The deference is reinforced by legal restrictions on the workers' right to organize. In the absence of any effective requirements for protecting the workers' health and safety, many become unemployable after a few years. Thus, in the name of providing employment, Third World governments squander their countries' resources in collaboration with the multinationals.

Proposals

Schools should oppose racist stereotyping in the following ways:

1) Course Content: Science courses should not repeat the claims by some scientists that there are important "racial differences" based on genetics. Instead they should emphasize the scientific evidence against the existence of distinct "races." History courses should teach "race" as a concept that was devised by imperialist countries to justify exterminating or exploiting "inferior races."

2) Structure of Education. To avoid "ability" labelling, the pedagogy should de-emphasize exercises based on memorization and rapid note-taking, in favour of those based on group discussion and co-operative problem-solving. Assessment of students should de-emphasize competitive timed tests, in favour of group assessment of how well the students have helped each other to learn.

3) Cultural Differences—Schools should maintain a respect for the cultural backgrounds of all students. At the same time, they should make students aware of how cultures have been shaped historically.

Efforts should be made to overcome the employers' power to manipulate cultural differences for dividing workers and for super-exploiting those considered "inferior."

4) Wherever low-status (low paid and/or dangerous) jobs are associated with one cultural group, there should be efforts to upgrade those jobs and remove the stigma.

5) To facilitate solidarity, all restrictions on workers' right to unionize should be lifted, as well as all restrictions on their right to express themselves in print or at public assemblies.

6) Employers should be forced to divulge any information relevant to workers' health and safety.

Science, Women and Sexism

Modern science is based on and continually reproduces unequal relations which give white, Western, middle-class men power. Behind the façade of the male scientific and technological elite there is an invisible support network of women: assembling the equipment, cleaning the offices and the labs (often hazardous in itself), and providing the material and emotional support which facilitates life at the top in science.

Women's relatively disadvantaged position in this sexual division of labour within science and technology means that they have little say in the decisions within those realms. Yet, in the 1980s, science and technology are playing ever more powerful roles in shaping their lives. For rural women, this can involve coping with the latest piece of machinery which may render her labour obsolete, ineffective or more difficult; or with pesticides which endanger her (and her unborn) or her family; or cooking by burning biomass the smoke of which is a serious health hazard.

In many cases, technological innovations either push women off the land or draw them into the factories of the cities. In others, the introduction of new technology has led to environmental pollution and deterioration, and resource depletion. This strikes directly at their subsistence, e.g., pollution of water sources and denudation of forests and topsoil. Although the quality of life of the whole family is affected, it is women who bear the brunt of this suffering.

Gender-biased Designs

In urban settings, as homemakers, women's lives are often even more pre-structured by scientific experts. The designs of their homes and the range of domestic appliances at their disposal emerge from technologists who are largely unaware of, and unconcerned with, women's needs and interests. Nevertheless, in both rural and urban environments it is women who cope with the problems and disasters created by technology: dealing with droughts, shortages and famine, and caring for the victims of illnesses and accidents.

Gender-biased designs, for example in the area of fashion, have reduced women to commodities to be consumed. It is a fact that most designers of women's apparel and footwear are men in the First World who deliberately accentuate the female body for their own "pleasure" and titillation. Thanks to the mass media, these fashions have been imitated and adopted by women in the Third World. Often this has been achieved at the expense of their health and nutrition; for example, factory women in Malaysia have been known to work overtime and forgo their meals in order to earn and save enough money to pay for new clothes, shoes and cosmetics.

Women Used as Guinea Pigs in Science and Technology

But science and technology also invade the intimacies of women's lives. They find themselves guinea pigs of the latest technological fashions in contraception and birth control. For instance, women in Bangladesh and longhouse communities in Sarawak were given the injectable contraceptive Depo Provera without being informed of its ill effects. The irony is that the WHO has endorsed its use in the Third World and the contraceptive is included in the WHO model list of essential drugs, when it is banned in the US and Zimbabwe and severely restricted in the Federal Republic of Germany, Great Britain and Sweden. We therefore urge the WHO to withdraw its approval for Depo Provera as a contraceptive in the Third World in view of the dangers of the drug and the fact that many countries have banned or severely restricted the use of this drug.

Innovations in contraception, as in many other areas, are designed mainly by men, for profit, to be used on women. Their rights to control their own bodies have been usurped by medical expertise and the technocratic power of transnationals. High-technology monitoring of pregnancy and regulation of birth, e.g., ultrasound monitoring, mechanical foetal heart monitoring and amniocentesis, are further features of the medicalization and dehumanization of women. In the case of the ultrasound monitor, it has been used to determine the sex of the foetus and very often has led to the aborting of female foetuses in patriarchal societies. This bias is now further enhanced with the advancement made in biotechnology today.

Apart from this, dangerous drugs, e.g., psychoactive drugs, cigarettes and alcohol, are promoted to women as a panacea for their problems which often arise as a result of their socially defined roles and expectations in modern society. Modern food technology has also led to the decline in breastfeeding and infant nutrition with the introduction of infant formulae and weaning foods, which are both costly and hazardous. This craze for profits has led to thousands of infant deaths and untold suffering for millions of children and their mothers in the Third World.

In the field of mass communications, the advertising and movie industries have advanced the "commoditization" of women which is unparalleled in human history. Women have been reduced to objects of sex and violence in all its insidious forms.

In addition to these immediate dimensions of women's encounter with science and technology, they witness the siphoning of resources for military technology. It must be understood that militarization and the buildup in modern nuclear armaments in the First World have been achieved at the expense of Third World resources. This plunder of resources in the Third World affects women first and foremost. Once again, decision making in military science and technology is mainly controlled by men, while most women would not support the build-up of the arsenal.

Today, many women are protesting against the insidious and growing power of scientific and technological experts. They are challenging their hold over their lives.

Proposals

1) Women workers, such as those in the new micro-electronics industries, are paying the price for this technological revolution. More stringent regulation of their working conditions (including health and safety measures, and requirements of shift work), and rates of pay are required. They should be guaranteed full workers' rights (including the right to join trade unions) and the support of other trade unionists. Elsewhere women should demand for appropriately designed machinery and gadgets to suit their needs, and laws must be enacted to ensure that this is carried out.

2) Governments should enact laws to safeguard the dignity of women. Advertisers and the mass media industry should not be allowed to promote or depict women as sex objects or neurotic patients in drug advertisements for psychotropic drugs.

3) In the era of reproductive rights, women must have more control of their own bodies. This necessitates, in the first instance, the banning of dangerous contraceptives such as Depo Provera (many of which have already been banned in the West). It also means that resources should be devoted to non-chemical and accessible forms of birth control. Women must no longer be subjected to the experiments of manufacturers keen on profit in this sector.

4) Related to this, women should have more freedom about the conditions of pregnancy and childbirth. This requires a firm control of medical and technologi-

cal interventions in these processes and the encouragement of breast, rather than infant formula, feeding. Laws should be enacted to protect women from these dangerous technologies.

5) Governments should ban infant formula and only allow its use in exceptional cases. It should be made available on prescription like pharmaceutical products.

6) The sale and marketing of tobacco and alcohol should be restricted. High taxes should be levied on these products to discourage their consumption.

Science and Militarization

Increasing numbers of scientists and technologists from many countries are using their scientific knowledge for destruction, whereas it is the responsibility of scientists to use their knowledge for the betterment of humankind.

It is clear that the social, economic and political problems of the world cannot be solved by military means. All countries must refrain from using threat of force or force itself to settle disputes including disputes within national boundaries. No country should allow the military forces of another country on its soil, as in Afghanistan, nor should any country use its mercenary forces against another, as in Namibia, Angola, Mozambique and Central America. However, it must be noted that self-defence is a recognized principle in international law. As such, every nation has a right to defend itself against foreign aggression.

World militarization is accelerating at an exponential rate. Global military expenditures in 1985 were U.S. $900 billion.

Both superpowers have acknowledged officially that a nuclear war cannot be won, because civilization as we know it would be destroyed. The most dangerous feature of the arms race is its increasing destructive capacity which, when coupled with regional military confrontations, could lead to total annihilation of the human race. Yet nuclear weapons continue to be built.

We face the threat of not only nuclear, but also biological and chemical devastation. The U.S. Congress has just voted to start production of binary nerve gas weapons. This action is a violation of existing international treaties.

All nations, including the superpowers, should abide by existing treaties such as the Geneva Protocol of 1925 and the Biological Weapons Convention of 1972. These treaties have been signed by almost all nations of the world and ban the use of any such weapons. Despite this ban, Iraq has used a number of these weapons.

The worst use of modern science and technology in the Third World is the utilization by despotic regimes and local ruling elites of weapons developed by modern Western science and technology to pacify their own people and preserve the existing exploitative structures. Rising militarism has increased the number of military regimes in Third World countries.

The biggest scandal in Third World development is that these countries utilize a large share of their nations' resources and current budgets to purchase military weapons. Third World countries have vastly increased their military expenditures; they collectively spend three times more on military needs than on health. In the Third World, for every physician there are 25 soldiers. Since the Second World War, scores of wars have been fought in Third World countries in which millions have died. The world needs peace and an end to militarism.

Proposals

1) The world's political, economic and social problems cannot be solved by military methods. There should be no military intervention by any country into any other country. This includes the placement of military bases.

2) All countries should stop wasting billions of dollars on the military, and use money and genius to fulfill basic needs. This is particularly true of the superpowers, which account for 60 percent of military spending. Developing countries should not fall into the trap of purchasing arms or accepting so-called military aid to suppress their own populations, or to prepare for military conflicts with neighbouring states.

3) The most dangerous aspect of militarization is the development of nuclear weapons. Nuclear weapons remove war as a viable instrument of foreign policy. Therefore, we urge the United States to join with the Soviet Union in the stopping of nuclear weapons testing and to sign a Comprehensive Test Ban Treaty as a step towards the abolition of all nuclear weapons.

4) The militarization of outer space, to which the present Reagan Administration is resolutely committed in the vain hope of attaining absolute military superiority, must be halted. We encourage the scientific community to join the 6,500 scientists and engineers in the U.S. who have signed a pledge refusing to engage in Star Wars research.

5) Scientists in the U.S. and the Philippines should urge the Aquino government to abrogate the U.S. Military Bases Agreement, convert the bases to peaceful uses and ask the U.S. and other countries to halt their military aid to and intervention in the country immediately. Southeast Asian governments must make the region a nuclear free zone and ensure that no military bases will be established in the region.

6) Scientists of the world must stand united in pre-empting any attempt by South Africa and Israel to further their political ends through the superiority of their military technology, including nuclear power.

7) We ask the governments of Third World countries to refrain from devoting their limited scientific, technological and economic resources to their ongoing nuclear programmes. Let South Asia become a nuclear free zone in every sense of the word. We call on the scientific communities of those countries in the Third World (for example India, Pakistan, Brazil, Argentina and China) to work out concrete measures to stop the nuclear arms race from escalating.

8) We look with deep concern on the continuing war between Iran and Iraq.

The war has taken on a new dimension due to the use of chemical weapons by Iraq. The use of chemical weapons must be stopped immediately.

9) We demand an immediate halt to French nuclear weapons testing in the Pacific. We support the stand of the people and government of New Zealand in preventing the harbouring of nuclear-capable warships.

10) We support efforts to establish nuclear free zones around the world.

11) There should be an immediate halt to torture and cruel experiments on human beings and animals for military purposes. There should be an immediate ban on the export of animals to any country for experimentation.

Energy

Energy planning and consumption in the Third World is skewed to meet the needs of the elite minority, while the energy needs of the majority remain unfulfilled. For example, in Sri Lanka less than one percent of the total population accounts for almost 45 percent of the total domestic consumption of electricity in the country.

The energy consumption between the First and Third Worlds is also very unequal. An average Indian, for instance, consumes less than one thousandth of the high quality energy (like petroleum and electricity) consumed by an American.

Modern science and technology, which is based on the unscrupulous exploitation of the earth's limited resources, is also very inefficient. On the other hand, traditional societies, based on agriculture and small-scale industries, are efficient and less destructive.

For traditional agriculture, the energy efficiency is much higher than modern agricultural practices because of the use of freely available solar energy. In many cases, they are 50 to 250 times more efficient and also sustainable than the new technologies.

The Western approach to nutrition which emphasizes animal protein is also highly inefficient in terms of energy. Animals consume 10 times the food energy that they eventually supply.

Modern technology that consumes more energy than it produces makes up the deficit by exploiting Third World countries. This is done by extracting energy and resources from the Third World at very low prices. Third World countries that imitate the Western models of industrialization are aiding the West in their own exploitation.

It must be realized that some 50 percent of the energy from biomass is used in the Third World for cooking purposes. The present scarcity of energy for such purposes is a novel opportunity for new manipulation by Western multinationals.

Dangerous and polluting forms of energy like nuclear power should not be used. The use of "peaceful" nuclear power has now led to a large number of countries having the capacity to build their own atomic bombs. Nuclear power plants are also potential military targets of hostile countries. With these plants spread all over the world, a conventional war can now be easily turned into a nuclear holocaust. The nuclear waste from nuclear plants also creates radioactive contamination which can last for hundreds of years.

Proposals

1) While looking for alternative development paths, the Third World countries must develop a sound energy policy which is efficient and serves the needs of the majority. The first condition is that agriculture must remain an energy producing and not an energy consuming sector. The Third World countries should embark on a project of developing and utilizing the renewable natural resources of energy such as solar, wind, waves, hydro and biomass in such a way that they are not amenable to monopolistic control.

2) The planning and development of energy resources must be based on an understanding and evaluation of the needs of the majority with top priority to the basic need of a life with dignity for all. In the first phase it should be done with low energy intensity growth so that there is sufficient time to develop the benign energy sources.

3) Planning and forecasting of energy requirements for a society should be done by identifying the basic human needs and these needs should be studied explicitly to estimate the energy required for their satisfaction. It is recommended that a Third World network be formed for energy policy, consisting of people who are prepared to work on a needs based approach to energy planning.

4) Countries which have nuclear power plants should gradually phase out the use of nuclear power. In other countries, governments should be urged not to use nuclear power. NGOs and the public should join the protest against the use of nuclear power and armaments.

Agriculture

The conference seriously examined and deliberated at length on the status of agriculture in the Third World. It concluded that the resources, techniques and practices of the Third World in the fields of agriculture, irrigation, forestry, animal husbandry and fisheries are in immediate danger of being wiped out under the impact of policies favouring modern Western practices in all these areas. The new practices that are being introduced are inherently incapable of efficiently utilizing the resources available in Third World countries and sustaining Third World populations. These practices are adversely affecting the productivity of land and are destabilizing the ecological balance. They are increasing the dependence of the Third World on the industrialized countries for knowledge, techniques and inputs in areas where indigenous knowledge and resources are capable of and were, until recently, meeting the needs in a satisfactory fashion.

Moreover, logging and forest degradation have also caused tremendous soil erosion in Third World countries.

Agriculture and connected practices being the major way of life of Third World societies, there is an urgent need to defend the indigenous knowledge, practices and resources in these areas from Western onslaught. Third World nations should therefore make efforts for the restoration of the indigenous way of life in their countries.

Proposals

1) A Third World Agriculture Documentation and Research Centre should be established to document the indigenous science and practice of agriculture and irrigation in the countries of Southeast Asia. The centre should also collect information on the available agricultural and irrigational resources in these countries, and work on finding ways and means of putting these resources to the best possible use through indigenous knowhow and practices.

The centre may have its headquarters in Sri Lanka and a regional office in each of the countries in South and Southeast Asia.

2) A Third World Foundation should be established for the preservation of agricultural genetic resources of the Third World. This foundation should be independent and autonomous and not be subject to manipulation from any quarter. The crucial role of NGOs in this initiative must be given due recognition. The foundation should:

- Persuade and help the governments of South and Southeast Asian countries to take steps for the collection and preservation of the agricultural genetic resources in their countries;
- Provide technical and financial help for the immediate establishment of long term storage facilities for the genetic resources in these countries; and
- Encourage research on the indigenous methods of collection and storage of genetic resources prevalent in these countries. In this regard, Third World farmers must be given a major role to preserve their germplasm *in situ.*

3) Third World governments must be persuaded to use only the tree species that are indigenous to their regions in their reafforestation programme. This reafforestation programme must respond to local demands and needs. To help in this, a tree exchange should be established. The exchange should prepare a directory of the tree species, and help the various governments in obtaining the appropriate species from the region for their reafforestation programme. The tree exchange could be established in Malaysia or Indonesia.

4) A regional livestock organization for the region of South and Southeast Asia should be established. The organization should prepare a data base of the livestock breeds of the region and provide facilities for the exchange of livestock

breeds within the region. The governments of the region should be encouraged to restrict cross-breeding of livestock within the breeds available in the region.

5) The Third World Network (TWN) and the Consumers' Association of Penang (CAP) should be requested to immediately establish a "Commission on the Impact of the Green Revolution in South and Southeast Asia." The commission should study:

- The origins of the policy of introducing Western technologies and exotic seeds in the countries of the region;
- The effects of the new technologies on the self-dependence of the countries in matters of agricultural knowledge and inputs;
- The effects of the new technologies on the productivity of land in these countries;
- The socio-economic impacts of the new agricultural technology and practices; and
- The implications of the new technologies for the genetic pool and environment of the region.

6) CAP and TWN should be requested to immediately establish a "Commission on the Impact of the Introduction of Modern Dairy Practices in South and Southeast Asia." The commission should study:

- The origins of the policy of introducing Western dairy technologies in these countries;
- The effects of the new technologies on the self-dependence of these countries in matters of dairying;
- The expenditure made on dairying infrastructure in these countries;
- The effects of the new practices on the production of milk and meat in these countries;
- The effects on the quality of meat and milk;
- The effects of the new practices on the genetic base of indigenous livestock;
- The socio-economic impacts of the new practices; and
- The impacts of the fluctuations in the European dairy market on dairying in these countries.

7) CAP and TWN should be asked to explore the possibilities of establishing commissions to study:

- The impact of the introduction of modern fishery practices in the region of South and Southeast Asia; and
- The impact of large dams and irrigation practices on soil, water tables, water drainage and health in the countries of the region.

8) CAP and TWN should be requested to explore the possibility of a regional organization for looking after the consumer interests of the region of South and

Southeast Asia in the area of agriculture, food and drugs. Activities of agribusiness in this area must be closely monitored by the regional organization which should also collect and convey information on all new agricultural inputs (chemical, biological and mechanical) and drugs and food products entering the area. For this purpose, it shall be necessary to establish a network of similar organizations in all countries of the region. The regional organization will coordinate information gathered in these countries and convey it to other countries in the region.

9) Rice should be singled out for special mention. Grown in nearly 111 countries, it is the staple food of most of the people in the Third World. The "sharing of genetic resources programme," under which nearly 125,000 rice varieties have been documented and are to be assembled at one centre, is threatening the existence of the entire rice germplasm. Therefore:

- Not a single rice cultivar should be withdrawn from cultivation, as it has descended down through many generations in relation to its environment and has been maintained by rice farmers for its suitability, utility and palatability;
- Any programme which aims at centralizing rice germplasm at an international level should be discouraged. The existence of a rare gene should be maintained as a "resistance gene" to the "grassy stunt virus";
- Rice scientists in the Third World should shoulder the responsibility of producing high yielding varieties from their own indigenous germplasm and preserve this heritage in their respective countries. This is because individual rice cultivars can also be high yielding in their own environment with the application of genetic knowledge and improved agronomic practices in relation to their environment;
- Rice growing countries in the Third World should initiate firm steps to preserve their rice germplasm (rice cultivars) through appropriate farm organizations and establish their own germplasm banks, as integrated units to be funded by voluntary organizations and public contributions; and
- A campaign should be initiated to achieve the objectives enumerated above.

10) All these steps should be undertaken by people in the region and with resources from the region.

Health

Today, the Western medical health system has infiltrated all societies in the world. Its modern success is partly due to the aggressive salesmanship of the equipment manufacturers and pharmaceutical companies. In fact, it has had incredible failures and perpetuated serious crimes, but all these are hidden from the public eye by bribing the governments and medical personnel.

The medical industry is a powerful political force in the modern world. The main concern of the health care system is no longer the health of the people. In the area of pharmaceutical products, it has led to the proliferation of useless and dangerous drugs in Third World countries. For example, in Bangladesh before 1982, some 1,700 worthless medicines were available. Presently in Malaysia, there are over 25,000 preparations in the market.

The modern drug industry preys on the fears of normal healthy people and encourages them to take unnecessary drugs. For example, those who are healthy but thin take tonics to gain weight, a normal process such as pregnancy is treated like an illness and everyone is encouraged to take vitamin pills.

Similarly, health education in the Third World is merely a copy of the Western model. The emphasis is on urban curative health care delivery systems with its unquestioned reliance on medical technologies which are imported at great cost, siphoning considerable amounts of the national budget in these countries.

Presently, health research is being carried out on "exotic diseases" which incur massive amounts of resources and funds. This has diverted attention and resources from more serious diseases which affect the majority of people in the Third World. For example, increasing amounts of money are poured into AIDS research, while research for the production of a safe, cheap and readily available form of immunization for hepatitis B, which is a serious disease afflicting Asian populations, is neglected. Research and development in tropical diseases like malaria and diarrhoea are neglected because they are not lucrative.

The Link between Modern Science and Technology, Poverty and Health

Health for the majority of the peoples of Asia, Africa and Latin America and for the growing number of marginalized people in Western nations has become a serious problem. It is adversely affected by the poverty and insecurity that has been brought into millions of human lives, during the last two centuries of "modern" developments. These developments have destroyed the self-reliance of indigenous cultures all across Asia, Africa and South America. There is sufficient evidence to prove that Western science and technology, wedded as they intrinsically are to the capitalist ethic, have been the main ideological and material instruments that have been used for this destruction.

Suppression of Indigenous Health Systems

During the last 200 years of Western cultural domination over non-Western societies, the latter's indigenous and self-reliant health care systems were suppressed. These were based on the use of locally available plants, animals and minerals. The indigenous systems were highly decentralized. They had developed, over thousands of years, a widespread folk culture that dealt with primary health care problems. The folk health culture all over Asia, Africa and Latin America has survived even to this day. Its most significant feature is its autonomous and self-reliant nature supported by an oral tradition of knowledge. In many Asian societies there also exists a comprehensive indigenous science which has its empirical roots in the folk traditions.

The Challenge in Health

There is an awareness today in non-Western societies about the myths that they had been led to believe by the Western world, about the poverty of their own cultures. There is a new realization about the strength and potential within their own roots.

In the area of health, the biggest challenge before the non-Western world is the revitalization of its own indigenous health care system. This is a long-term project that calls for devoted and steady efforts, because many "current" weaknesses, due to the 200 years of suppression of the indigenous health system, have to be overcome.

Immediately, in the transitory phase, an urgent task is to try and rationalize the Western system of medical care that has so far been so exploitative of the people.

Proposals

1) Third World governments should adopt a rational drug policy based on the WHO policy on essential drugs, which recommends that a total of 200 drugs would be more than sufficient for a country's drug requirement.

2) Related to this policy, Third World governments should ban the use of dangerous and inefficacious drugs.

3) Third World governments should promote the use and manufacture of quality generic drugs.

4) Third World governments should formulate national health policies taking into account each country's special needs. The national health policy should incorporate elements discussed in the proposals listed above.

5) The major thrust of the national health policy should be towards preventive health.

6) Emphasis must be given to the education of people on the home care of illnesses and injuries.

7) Hospitals should be planned and designed to suit local cultural and social mores.

8) The national health policy should also incorporate the use and practice of indigenous medicine.

9) Third World governments should urgently document the existing state of health traditions, the ailments they claim to treat, the medicinal plants, minerals or animal parts that they use, and the social ethos in which they function.

10) They should evaluate the indigenous traditions with the help of indigenous sciences and modern tools of evaluation. The Western system has entirely

different principles, concepts and categories and so it is not competent to interpret the indigenous traditions.

11) Third World governments should establish institutes for the research and study of indigenous medical sciences.

12) They should promote at local levels thousands of herbal gardens and medicinal forests throughout the Third World.

13) Networks amongst NGOs should be created to facilitate scientific exchange on various theoretical and practical aspects of indigenous medical sciences.

14) Patent laws must be enacted to protect Third World indigenous medicine and to prevent the transnational corporations from controlling it.

Telecommunications and Micro-electronics

Micro-electronics, telecommunications and new information technology are seen by many as the most significant scientific developments in the second half of this century. Technological developments in this sphere have led to predictions of an "information revolution" which would have the same effect of increasing the capabilities and the powers of the human brain as the Industrial Revolution did on augmenting the capabilities of the human body.

Some technocratic "futurologists" claim that this new technology could democratize work and society. But all evidence suggests that the nature of the micro-electronics industry is leading to a tremendous concentration of capital, knowledge and power in a small number of countries and transnational corporations.

Rather than eradicating unpleasant work, micro-processors have led to a degradation of skills, dignity and job interest for the majority of those working with the new technology. Only a few people, based in the developed countries, are engaged in the creative aspects of this work, with their results affecting millions of others.

Control of Telecommunications and Micro-electronics by Western Transnationals

Control of micro-electronics research and development, product development manufacture, and the marketing of telecommunications services is perhaps more concentrated in the hands of a small number of powerful transnational corporations than most other major industries.

Research and development of microchips is concentrated in the United States and Japan, based on standards, codes and concepts which are wholly Western in origin. Even European corporations are now finding themselves unable to compete with the U.S. and Japan in the capital-intensive area of micro-electronics research and development.

Most of the companies involved with electronics and telecommunications research and development are highly dependent on military contracts for a large proportion of their work, and thus they collaborate closely with the military establishment at the developmental stage and give priority to military uses of the technology. Many of the civilian applications of micro-electronics result only indirectly from this military work, and take second place to this military work if there were to be a conflict of interests.

Unlike the capital-intensive research and development phase, some parts of micro-electronics *production* are labour-intensive. Thus, although controlled by a small number of transnational corporations, micro-electronics production has been spread around the world to take advantage of cheap, unorganized labour and various financial incentives offered by governments eager to attract foreign investment.

The stages of electronics manufacture located in Third World countries generally offer few opportunities for the transfer of skills to workers or the transfer of technology. These manufacturing plants are highly mobile, and, as conditions change, they can be relocated or closed down without serious loss to the company.

Electronics manufacture has now emerged as one of the least stable forms of foreign investment in Third World nations.

Despite the "clean" image of the industry, workers in electronics factories are exposed to a very large number of hazards from a rapidly expanding range of highly complex chemicals, the health effects of which are only just beginning to be documented. In addition to chemicals which cause cancer, reproductive problems and poisoning, the nature of electronics manufacture can subject workers to eye-strain and stress.

In the application of electronics to telecommunications, the control and domination persists. A very small number of transnational corporations design and deploy satellite and undersea cable systems, while another handful of corporations operate the telecommunications services on these systems.

Implications for the Third World

These companies are almost entirely North American and European. The cultural biases inherent in the design and operation of these international communications systems, in such matters as language, conceptual codes, short-forms, etc., clearly enforce a standardization and conformity on users which ultimately changes not only the form but also the content of communication.

The major telecommunications systems are structured to ensure that information useful to corporations and banks can be extracted from Third World nations and used to gain competitive advantage. The most efficient communications channels run throughout the North, and link the South with the North, but do not link Third World nations to one another. With these, corporations and banks can swiftly transfer financial, economic, political and labour information to enable them to out-manoeuvre competitors, and destroy any labour or political opposition to their plans. With this technology in place, national governments are losing their hold on the regulation of the activities of transnational banks and corporations in their countries.

These new computer, communications and control technologies have made it possible for managements to "synchronize, on a worldwide scale, decentralized production with a strictly centralized control over strategic assets," as Dieter Ernst has said.

The control and structure of the world's telecommunications system also assists the penetration of Western entertainment, news and advertising in the South, adding further to the assertion of Western cultural and political values, and expanding the market for Western goods.

Just as companies use the telecommunications systems to amass business information, national governments are able to abuse this information technology for social control in policing, surveillance, and the creation of highly efficient databases on opposition groups and dissidents. They are thereby violating rights to privacy and laying the groundwork for repression on a massive scale.

As with the production of the telecommunications equipment, the operation of telecommunications services seeks to maximize profits. Thus the organization and management takes inadequate precautions against health hazards, for workers operating the system, such as radiation dangers and eye strain from video display screens and stressful alienating work situations.

Proposals

1) Some nations, such as Brazil, have reserved their micro-electronic production for local companies only and restrict the import of electronic goods, thereby developing an indigenous micro-electronics industry. This greatly reduces dependence on foreign goods and can create products more appropriate to local needs and conditions. Efforts by developed nations, led by the United States, to block such moves by demanding the opening of these markets as part of trade agreements, should be resisted.

2) Third World governments should be urged to accept that the complex and sophisticated chemicals and processes used in the electronics industry present severe health hazards, the full extent of which have yet to be realized. Measures should be taken to identify and control health hazards in high-tech industries.

3) Scientists, engineers and designers in the Third World should be educated on the nature of the microprocessor technology, and the exploitation within them, and strive to expose them, and where possible, eliminate these through imaginative reprogramming and redesigning.

4) The control of the micro-electronics industry by a small number of key transnationals is based on a monopoly of technology and know-how. Third World governments and non-governmental groups should look critically at the present criteria for copyright and patent laws imposed upon them by First World

nations, and see if more balanced alternatives cannot be put in place, particularly in such priority development areas as health, housing, education and food production.

5) Non-governmental organizations must take every effort to ensure that access to the latest telecommunications systems does not remain the exclusive right of the foreign corporations, local corporations and governments, but should also be made open to non-profit, non-governmental organizations and individuals for the free exchange of ideas.

6) At the same time, Third World governments must take measures to ensure that telecommunications systems are not abused by transnational corporations. This is to prevent TNCs from transferring funds rapidly from country to country, thereby causing economic instability, or amassing and transferring information with which they can exert unfair influence or control over local economies, national governments, employees or local companies.

7) Third World nations should implement registration and control of databases which will ensure that neither companies nor governments themselves can amass information about individuals. Such information might subsequently be used to violate people's right to privacy, curtail their civil and political rights or to gain unfair commercial influence over them. At the same time, any such law controlling computerized information should not be phrased so as to allow governments unrestricted access to information held by non-governmental or opposition groups.

8) In order to reduce the gap between the powerful and the unempowered, efforts by grassroots groups to learn about information technology, adapt it, and where possible set up small-scale decentralized and democratic alternatives, should be encouraged. However, when applying this technology all organizations should consider carefully the health and hierarchical effects of any equipment they introduce.

9) Wherever micro-electronics applications serve the purpose of state surveillance and repression, or of eliminating jobs, support should be given to those who sabotage the technology involved.

The Concept of Appropriate Technology and Industrialization

Appropriate technology and industrialization is that which advances development, where development is looked upon as a process which leads to a life with dignity through

- the satisfaction of basic needs, starting with the needs of the most needy;
- self-reliance; and
- non-destruction of, and harmony with, the environment.

There are three aspects of appropriate technology, namely its selection, generation and dissemination. Selection is from the available pool of technologies covering the whole spectrum from the technologies of the industrialized countries (which should be scrutinized with utmost care regarding their tendencies to amplify inequalities, undermine self-reliance, destroy the environment and promote violence) to traditional technologies (either in their pristine form or after transformation).

In all three aspects of selection, generation and dissemination, Third World networking has a crucial role to play. Cooperative selection of appropriate technologies is essential particularly when confronted with the technologies of the industrialized countries. Third World countries would benefit greatly from cooperating in the matter of generation. Indeed, they could cogenerate appropriate technologies. And experiences with dissemination of these technologies need to be shared.

The scope of the appropriate technology should cover small-scale, decentralized and large-scale or centralized technologies. Attention should be focussed on both hardware and software, and on all sectors (not only industry, but also agriculture, health, transport, etc.). However, there should be a specific emphasis on appropriate technologies that satisfy (in a self-reliant, ecologically sound way) the basic needs of food, shelter, clothing, health, education, etc., particularly of the most needy sections of society.

Proposals

1) Developing countries should evolve their own appropriate technologies and their own techniques in various areas as in agriculture, industry, health care, housing, water management, transport, energy and so on. It is recognized that the appropriateness of a particular technology or product would also partly depend on the conditions of a particular country. Such appropriate technologies should as far as possible make use of local resources. They should be relatively simple to operate with skills which can be passed on, based on sound ecological principles and of a small scale, suitable for family or community use.

2) Appropriate technology should be a policy, not only for the Third World but also, and especially, for the industrialized countries. These rich countries should not continue to operate highly capital-intensive technologies, producing relatively luxurious or superfluous products, which use up the world's resources. If the Third World adopts resource-efficient appropriate technologies but the rich countries continue to use resource-wasting industrial technology, then the present unequal distribution of resources and power will be perpetuated. Thus, concerned individuals and groups in the industrialized countries should make efforts to convince their people and governments of the necessity to change their technologies and techniques of production and reorientate their approach to science accordingly.

3) In the area of scientific knowledge (which is another kind of experience) exactness is the supreme aim. We know that exactness can never be absolute. Once we admit this, we need not aspire for this unnecessary exactness, which

involves violence to the object of enquiry. Here, the method should live up definitely to humanist values or criteria. If it involves cruelty, that kind of exactness is absolutely unnecessary and hence should be unconditionally abandoned. In the area of technology, humanist values or criteria should be a must as well. We also know that there is no need to have everything on earth for a happy life—which is possible without undue waste, undue suffering to people and animals, and destruction to vegetation and soil, these values all of which we should adopt.

4) Technological innovations should serve the ordinary people and be in their control. An organizational structure can be devised for this purpose comprising the government, non-governmental organizations and people's representatives.

Science Education

Science education in the Third World is a colonial legacy rooted in the Western system of education and has no relevance to our societies. It was designed to create a cadre of workers whose job was to carry out programmes planned and designed in the West. The result of this unfortunate legacy, which has not been completely abandoned in a majority of the Third World countries, is that the efforts of Third World scientists and technologists are merely extensions of the programmes of their Western mentors.

Increasing Western influence in the Third World even more are those students and researchers who go to the West for further training and studies. They return with reinforced Western ideas, exacerbating the problem of indigenous science rather than alleviating them. Their scientific research is a continuation of their Ph.D. theses carried out under the tutorship of foreign scientists. In other words, foreign-trained scientists are the greatest germ-carriers of the Western virus against which our societies are seeking immunity.

Making it worse is the exodus of a large number of scientists and technologists from Third World countries to the West. This brain drain constitutes another form of depletion of resources for the Third World.

In order to remedy this situation, it is essential that the education of scientists and technologists in the Third World take place in such a way as to ensure that they not only retain their cultural and social moorings but that their scientific interest is maintained in solving problems pertinent to their indigenous environment. Clearly, such a system needs to have as its base an education system which appreciates the value of indigenous scientific and technological culture.

The realization of this goal necessitates the re-shaping of the science syllabus at the school and university level as well as a conceptual change in the framework of science education itself.

The goal of scientific education is to produce an imaginative and dedicated personality and to create an individual who is both resourceful and responsible. The teaching of science, therefore, should never be divorced from the value system of the indigenous civilization. The students should also develop a critical faculty so as to enable them to judge the cultural and ideological bias of Western science and technology.

Proposals

1) Science students should learn social realities—economics, politics, culture—particularly about the domination of the Third World within the world system.

2) Science students should be given a thorough exposure to the relations between science and its effects on society, including its potentially harmful effects. The social responsibility of scientists and the political issues surrounding science should be central to the education of the scientist.

3) Science students should be made aware of indigenous science and its roots—to study the elements of indigenous medicine, shelter, food, industry and transport.

4) Science should not be for the elites but given and applied for the benefit and welfare of farmers, fishermen, workers, women, etc. so that it can be of use to improve the livelihood of the people. Science education should be made available to the masses.

5) The ecological and environmental aspects must be central in science education, especially in their inter-relatedness of various natural elements. Students and researchers should focus attention on the destructive nature of man's activities on the environment and the ways of avoiding these and to rehabilitate nature whenever possible.

6) Science research priorities should be given to the identification of positive indigenous technologies, scientific values and systems, knowledge and processes in various spheres like agriculture, industry, medicine, shelter, etc. These systems should be defended and improved on.

Science Policy and Management

Only a handful of Third World nations have explicit science policies. These science policies are geared towards the creation of a scientific and technological infrastructure in the country. Often, this infrastructure has been developed at the expense of national independence, with the new science and technology institutions in the Third World becoming an extension of the scientific establishment of the industrialized countries. Moreover, countries with explicit science policies have tended to focus on prestige areas of science and high technology projects. Much of the established infrastructure has thus tended to be irrelevant to the needs and requirements of the country.

The majority of Third World countries do not have a declared science policy. However, an implicit science policy is in operation everywhere. The overall emphasis is on the transfer of technology, the establishment of fashionable research centres through technical and financial aid, and the use of foreign consultants in solving local problems.

Within this framework of explicit and implicit science policies, a management structure that relies on hierarchy and a one-directional, top to bottom communication and a suffocating bureaucracy, has been adopted. This management structure has isolated the decision makers from the rank and file scientists and technologists as well as from the local working conditions and work environment.

Proposals

1) Governments and scientists in the Third World should review their present bias towards modern, capital-intensive anti-human technology. A profound understanding of the inappropriateness and destructive nature of these technologies should be fostered in Third World national science policies.

2) Science policies in the Third World should focus on establishing an indigenous base for the generation, utilization and diffusion of science and technology. They should not exclusively focus on the transfer of technology or reliance on scientific research done in the industrialized countries, technical assistance, or on foreign consultants. They should strive to promote and upgrade traditional and modern indigenous sources of knowledge and know-how. Our cultural environment, from the tribal to the civilized level, is suffused with potential technologies, scientific insights and methodologies that could, and should, be used to provide a necessary organic linkage with our own roots. New management structures that take into account the fact that science is a political and social process should be encouraged, initiated and institutionalized.

3) Today's science and technology are closely interlinked and the new technology is almost directly science based. In order that Third World countries break out of their dependent condition, they must seek out and establish cross-linkages with each other. Such cross-linked groups would in partnership generate a science and technology which is self-reliant, basic needs oriented, and ecologically sound.

4) The new search for science and technology should be pursued by encouraging viable groups which are both socially conscious as well as aware of their own disciplines. Mechanisms should also be evolved to generate critical masses around such groups so that a creative and society-oriented science and technology is produced. Mechanisms should also be evolved to insulate such socially aware, creative groups from the pressures of various vested groups, while they are encouraged to develop linkages with the mass of people.

NAME INDEX

Abbey, Charlotte, 219
Aberle, Kathleen Gough, 420, 427
Abram, Ruth, 226
Achebe, Chinua, 303
Ackernecht, E. H., 265–66, 267
Adams, Charles F., Jr., 122, 127
Adams, Numa P. G., 225
Adas, Michael, 8, 21, 81
Agassiz, E. C., 114
Agassiz, Louis, 93–100, 112, 114
Akeley, Carl E., and Mary Jobe, 394
Allan, J. McGrigor, 375
Allen, Garland, 357
Alston, Dana A., 327
Altmann, Stuart, 378, 383, 394
Amin, Samir, 25
Anastasi, Anne, 132
Anderson, Caroline Still Wiley, 214
Anderson, K. J., 188
Anderson, Matthew, 226
Anthony, Carl, 332–33
Appiah, Anthony, 182, 192
Aptheker, Bettina, 225
Archimedes, 43, 437
Arditti, R., 482, 483
Aristotle, 57, 62, 362, 437
Ariyoshi, Sawako, 394
Armelagos, George, 77
Arunachalam, S., 261, 267
Asquith, Pamela, 379, 380, 381, 384, 385–86, 389, 392, 394
Atkinson, E. T., 307, 314
Augusta, Alexander T., 211
Avery, Bylle, 167
Ayer, A. J., 374

Bachman, John, 112
Bachnik, Jane M., 407
Bacon, Francis, 30, 197, 339
Baldwin, James, 197
Bandyopadhyay, J., 261, 267, 310, 314
Barker-Benfield, Graham John, 209
Barnard, Christian, 448
Barnes, A. E., 29
Barnes, Barry, 20, 369, 376
Barnicot, Nigel A., 126
Barrows, Isabel C., 211
Barry, D., 299
Bassett, Mary, 82
Beardsley, E. H., 226

Becker, Raphael, 184–85, 193
Beer, Gillian, 189–90
Bennett, Edward L., 132
Bennett, Lerone, Jr., 466, 471
Bentley, Richard, 54, 61, 62
Benton, Ted, 190
Benzer, S., 141
Berger, Erich, 358
Berlin, I., 62
Berman, Daniel M., 483
Bermant, Gordon, 394
Bernal, J. D., 4, 20, 46
Bernal, Martin, 26–27, 28, 62
Bethel, James A., 309, 314
Beyerchen, Alan D., 357
Binet, Alfred, 143–44, 146, 159
Bingham, Hiram, 64
Birdsell, J. B., 126
Black, Max, 364–65, 368, 369, 374, 375–76
Blackall, E., 62
Blackwell, Elizabeth, 210–11, 219, 226
Blackwell, Emily, 219
Blanco, A. G., 62
Bledstein, Burton J., 208, 209
Bleier, Ruth, 394
Block, E. Wilber, 226
Blome, Kurt, 346
Bloor, David, 20
Blumenbach, J. F., 87, 89, 114, 118
Boch, Gisela, 21
Bodin, Jean, 58
Bolk, Louis, 371
Bonham, Professor, 299
Bordo, Susan, 20
Boring, E. G., 147, 160
Bouchet, Edward, 229–30
Bousfield, M. O., 225
Bowles, S., 159, 160
Boyd, Richard, 360, 374
Boyd, William, 126
Boyle, Robert, 54, 440
Bracken, Harry, 57, 62
Braudel, Fernand, 68, 77
Briggs, L. C., 141
Broca, Paul, 366, 367, 369, 376
Brown, E. Richard, 225
Brown, Lucy Hughes, 214, 217
Brown, Sara W., 225
Brown, W. L., Jr., 141
Brown, Warren, 286